Rethinking the Fur Trade

Rethinking the Fur Trade

Cultures of Exchange in an Atlantic World

EDITED BY SUSAN SLEEPER-SMITH

University of Nebraska Press   Lincoln & London

Acknowledgments for previously published
material appear on pages xi–xiv, which
constitute an extension of the copyright page.

Manufactured in the United States of America

⊗

Publication of this volume was assisted by a grant
from Michigan State University.

Library of Congress Cataloging-in-Publication Data

Rethinking the fur trade : cultures of exchange in
an Atlantic world / edited by Susan Sleeper-Smith.
p. cm.
Includes bibliographical references and index.
ISBN 978-0-8032-4329-3 (pbk. : alk. paper)
1. Fur trade—North America—History. 2. North
America—Economic conditions—History—17th
century. 3. North America—Economic conditions—History—18th century. I. Sleeper-Smith,
Susan.
HD9944.N62R48   2009
382'.45685097—dc22
2009025248

Set in ITC New Baskerville by Bob Reitz.

Contents

List of Illustrations .... *viii*

List of Tables... *ix*

Source Acknowledgments .... *xi*

PART 1. New Perspectives

1. Cultures of Exchange in a North Atlantic World........... *xvii*
   SUSAN SLEEPER-SMITH

PART 2. Indian Voices

   Introduction *3*

2. Of the Mission of Saint François Xavier on the "Bay of
   Stinkards," or Rather "Of Stinking Waters" 7
   FATHER ALLOUEZ

3. On the Hunting of the Gaspesians *10*
   FATHER CHRESTIEN LECLERCQ

4. The Hunting of Moose, of Bears, of Beavers, of Lynxes, and
   other animals according to their seasons................. *17*
   FATHER CHRESTIEN LECLERCQ

5. Tarrentines and the Introduction of European Trade Goods
   in the Gulf of Maine............................... 22
   BRUCE J. BOURQUE AND RUTH HOLMES WHITEHEAD

6. The Anishinabeg Point of View: The History of the Great Lakes
   Region to 1800 in Nineteenth-Century Mississauga, Odawa,
   and Ojibwa Historiography.......................... 45
   D. PETER MACLEOD

7. Fur Trade Literature from a Tribal Point of View:
   A Critique 65
   DONALD F. BIBEAU

PART 3. The Social and Political Significance of Exchange

Introduction *83*

8. Agriculture and the Fur Trade *88*
   D. W. MOODIE

9. "Give Us a Little Milk": The Social and Cultural Significance
   of Gift Giving in the Lake Superior Fur Trade. *114*
   BRUCE M. WHITE

10. "Starving" and Survival in the Subarctic Fur Trade: A Case for
    Contextual Semantics *137*
    MARY BLACK-ROGERS

11. The Growth and Economic Significance of the American
    Fur Trade, 1790–1890. . . . . *160*
    JAMES L. CLAYTON

12. "Red" Labor: Iroquois Participation in the Atlantic
    Economy. *181*
    GAIL D. MACLEITCH

13. The Fur Trade and Eighteenth-Century Imperialism *215*
    W. J. ECCLES

14. The Middle Ground. *246*
    RICHARD WHITE

15. Creative Misunderstandings and New Understandings. *305*
    RICHARD WHITE

PART 4. Cloth Trade

Introduction. *315*

16. Indians as Consumers in the Eighteenth Century. *320*
    ARTHUR J. RAY

17. Dressing for Success on the Mohawk Frontier: Hendrick,
    William Johnson, and the Indian Fashion *344*
    TIMOTHY J. SHANNON

18. The Flow of European Trade Goods into the Western Great
    Lakes Region, 1715–1760. . . . .*385*
    DEAN L. ANDERSON

19. The Matchcoat *411*
    GAIL DeBUSE POTTER

20. Chiefs Coats Supplied by the American Fur Company *414*
    ALLEN CHRONISTER

21. The Myth of the Silk Hat and the End of the Rendezvous . .*420*
    JAMES A. HANSON

PART 5. Gender, Kinship, and Community

    Introduction *439*

22. Women, Kin, and Catholicism: New Perspectives on the
    Fur Trade *443*
    SUSAN SLEEPER-SMITH

23. "The Custom of the Country": An Examination of Fur Trade
    Marriage Practices *481*
    SYLVIA VAN KIRK

24. Woman as Centre and Symbol in the Emergence of Metis
    Communities *519*
    JENNIFER S. H. BROWN

25. Prelude to Red River: A Social Portrait of the Great Lakes
    Métis *529*
    JACQUELINE PETERSON

26. The Glaize in 1792: A Composite Indian Community *561*
    HELEN HORNBECK TANNER

27. Festivities, Fortitude, and Fraternalism: Fur Trade Masculinity
    and the Beaver Club, 1785–1827 . . . .*593*
    CAROLYN PODRUCHNY

    Index. *621*

Illustrations

Images

1. Tshusick, an Ojibway woman *319*
2. "The Brave Old Hendrick". *346*
3. Guerrier Iroquois *353*
4. Grand Chef de Guerriers Iroquoise *354*
5. Tee Yee Neen Ho Ga Row, Emperour of the Six Nations. *359*
6. Sa Ga Yeath Qua Pieth Tow, King of the Maquas *360*
7. Hendrick the Sachem, or Chief of the Mohawks *364*
8. Soi-En-Ga-Rah-ta, or King Hendrick *366*
9. Cherokee chief Stalking Turkey. *412*

Figures

1. Great Lakes Métis *552*

Maps

1. Fur trade regions . . . . *xxxv*
2. Fur trading communities in the Great Lakes . . . .*l*
3. The Gulf of St. Lawrence and the Gulf of Maine *25*
4. French-period outposts in the western Great Lakes region. . . *388*
5. French-period Native sites *395*

Tables

1. Functional categories in ranked order by percentage of
   expenditure .... *xlv*
2. Goods distributed by William Johnson at a treaty conference,
   June 1755 .... *370–71*
3. Clothing distributed by William Johnson as Indian presents,
   December 1746–November 1747 .... *372*
4. Number of outfits for each post, 1715–1760 .... *392*
5. Number of types of goods for each post, 1715–1760 ...... *396*
6. Types of goods by functional category *398*
7. Functional categories in ranked order by percentage of
   expenditure *400–1*
8. Rank positions in which each category occurs *402*
9. Ranked order of functional categories for combined
   inventories *403*
10. Importations of beaver pelts to England *432–33*
11. Michilimackinac marriages, 1698–1818 .... *539*
12. Michilimackinac births *540*
13. Green Bay, 1750–1829 .... *541*
14. Based on the 1830 census of Michigan Territory *542*

Source Acknowledgments

"Of the Mission of Saint François Xavier on the 'Bay of Stinkards,' or Rather 'Of Stinking Waters'" originally appeared in *The Jesuit Relations and Allied Documents: Travels and Explorations of the Jesuit Missionaries in New France, 1610–1791*, vol. 54, *Iroquois, Ottawas, Lower Canada: 1669–1671*, ed. Ruben Gold Thwaites, 197–208 (Cleveland OH: Burrows Brothers, 1899).

"On the Hunting of the Gaspesians" originally appeared in *New Relation of Gaspesia: With the Customs and Religion of the Gaspesian Indians*, trans. and ed. William F. Ganong, 274–80 (Toronto: The Champlain Society, 1910). Reprinted with permission.

"The Hunting of Moose, of Bears, of Beavers, of Lynxes, and other animals according to their seasons" originally appeared in *New Relation of Gaspesia: With the Customs and Religion of the Gaspesian Indians*, trans. and ed. William F. Ganong, 426–34 (Toronto: The Champlain Society, 1910). Reprinted with permission.

"Tarrentines and the Introduction of European Trade Goods in the Gulf of Maine" originally appeared in *Ethnohistory* 32, no. 4 (Autumn 1985): 327–41. © 1985 by the American Society for Ethnohistory. All rights reserved. Used by permission of the publisher.

"The Anishinabeg Point of View: The History of the Great Lakes Region to 1800 in Nineteenth-Century Mississauga, Odawa, and Ojibwa Historiography" originally appeared in *Canadian Historical Review* 73, no. 2 (June 1992): 194–210. Published by University of Toronto Press Incorporated. © University of Toronto Press 1992. Reprinted by permission of University of Toronto Press Incorporated (www.utpjournals.com).

"Fur Trade Literature from a Tribal Point of View: A Critique" originally appeared in *Rendezvous: Selected Papers of the Fourth North American Fur Trade Conference, 1981*, ed. Thomas C. Buckley, 83–91 (St. Paul: Minnesota Historical Society, 1984). Used with permission.

"Agriculture and the Fur Trade" originally appeared in *Old Trails and New Directions: Papers of the Third North American Fur Trade Conference*, ed. Carol M. Judd and Arthur J. Ray, 272–90 (Toronto: University of Toronto Press Inc., 1980). © University of Toronto Press 1980. Reprinted with permission of the publisher.

"'Give Us a Little Milk': The Social and Cultural Significance of Gift Giving in the Lake Superior Fur Trade" originally appeared in *Rendezvous: Selected Papers of the Fourth North American Fur Trade Conference, 1981*, ed. Thomas C. Buckley, 185–97 (St. Paul: Minnesota Historical Society, 1984). Used with permission.

"'Starving' and Survival in the Subarctic Fur Trade: A Case for Contextual Semantics" originally appeared in *Le Castor Fait Tout: Selected Papers of the Fifth North American Fur Trade Conference, 1985*, ed. Bruce G. Trigger, Toby Morantz, and Louise Dechêne, 618–49 (Montreal: Lake St. Louis Historical Society, 1987).

"The Growth and Economic Significance of the American Fur Trade, 1790–1890" originally appeared in *Minnesota History* 40 (Winter 1966): 210–20. © 1966 by the Minnesota Historical Society. Used with permission.

"'Red' Labor: Iroquois Participation in the Atlantic Economy" originally appeared in *Labor: Studies in Working-Class History of the Americas* 1, no. 4 (2004): 69–90. Reprinted with permission.

"The Fur Trade and Eighteenth-Century Imperialism" originally appeared in *William and Mary Quarterly*, 3rd ser., 40, no. 3 (July 1983): 341–62. Reprinted with permission.

"The Middle Ground" originally appeared as chapter 2 in *The Middle Ground: Indians, Empires, and Republics in the Great Lakes Region, 1650–1815* (New York: Cambridge University Press, 1991), 50–93. Reprinted with the permission of Cambridge University Press.

"Creative Misunderstandings and New Understandings" originally appeared in *William and Mary Quarterly*, 3rd ser., 63, no. 1 (January 2006): 9–14. Reprinted with permission.

"Indians as Consumers in the Eighteenth Century" originally appeared in *Old Trails and New Directions: Papers of the Third North American Fur Trade Conference*, ed. Carol M. Judd and Arthur J. Ray, 255–71 (Toronto: University of Toronto Press Inc., 1980). © University of Toronto Press 1980. Reprinted with permission of the publisher.

"Dressing for Success on the Mohawk Frontier: Hendrick, William Johnson, and the Indian Fashion" originally appeared in *William and Mary Quarterly*, 3rd ser., 53, no. 1 (January 1996): 13–42. Reprinted with permission.

"The Flow of European Trade Goods into the Western Great Lakes Region, 1715–1760" originally appeared in *The Fur Trade Revisited: Selected Papers of the Sixth North American Fur Trade Conference, Mackinac Island, Michigan, 1991*, ed. J. S. H. Brown, W. J. Eccles, and D. P. Heldman, 93–115 (East Lansing: Michigan State University Press, 1994). Reprinted with permission.

"The Matchcoat" originally appeared in *Museum of the Fur Trade Quarterly* 33, no. 4 (Winter 1997): 2–3. Reprinted with permission.

"Chiefs Coats Supplied By the American Fur Company" originally appeared in *Museum of the Fur Trade Quarterly* 32, no. 2 (Summer 1996): 1–7. Reprinted with permission.

"The Myth of the Silk Hat and the End of the Rendezvous" originally appeared in *Museum of the Fur Trade Quarterly* 36, no. 1 (Spring 2000): 2–11. Reprinted with permission.

"Women, Kin, and Catholicism: New Perspectives on the Fur Trade" originally appeared in *Ethnohistory* 47, no. 2 (Spring 2000): 423–52. © 2000 by the American Society for Ethnohistory. All rights reserved. Used by permission of the publisher.

"'The Custom of the Country': An Examination of Fur Trade Marriage Practices" originally appeared in *Essays on Western History*, ed.

Lewis H. Thomas, 47–80 (Edmonton: University of Alberta Press, 1976). Reprinted with permission.

"Woman as Centre and Symbol in the Emergence of Metis Communities" originally appeared in *Canadian Journal of Native Studies* 3, no. 1 (1983): 39–46. Reprinted with permission.

"Prelude to Red River: A Social Portrait of the Great Lakes Métis" originally appeared in *Ethnohistory* 25, no. 1 (Winter 1978): 41–67. © 1978 by the American Society for Ethnohistory. All rights reserved. Used by permission of the publisher.

"The Glaize in 1792: A Composite Indian Community" originally appeared in *Ethnohistory* 25, no. 1 (Winter 1978): 15–39. © 1978 by the American Society for Ethnohistory. All rights reserved. Used by permission of the publisher.

"Festivities, Fortitude, and Fraternalism: Fur Trade Masculinity and the Beaver Club, 1785–1827" originally appeared in *New Faces of the Fur Trade: Selected Papers of the Seventh North American Fur Trade Conference, Halifax, Nova Scotia, 1995*, ed. Jo-Anne Fiske, Susan Sleeper-Smith, and William Wicken, 31–52 (East Lansing: Michigan State University Press, 1998). Reprinted with permission.

PART 1

New Perspectives

1. Cultures of Exchange in a North Atlantic World

Susan Sleeper-Smith

The fur trade first emerged in a region where geography limited agricultural self-sufficiency and encouraged indigenous people to engage in a mutually negotiated exchange of furs for trade goods. The trade in peltry served a curiously modern function, evolving as part of a credit economy fueled by supply and demand. Indians exercised a precocious consumerism that was well adapted to the "flexible specialization" that characterized early modern production in Europe, where goods could be refined or invented to serve the needs of the consumer. Because the fur trade developed at a time when no one European market could process the quantity of furs that were harvested, furs had a multiplier effect on the economies of Europe's port cities. For instance, many of the furs that were shipped to La Rochelle in France were reserved for immediate re-export to other ports, such as Amsterdam. The Dutch also reserved and reexported beaver pelts to Narva, where they were processed and then returned to Amsterdam and La Rochelle. Eventually, the pelts were transformed into beaver hats to meet the demands of the growing consumer revolution. The hats were then circulated as finished products to all of Europe, and they were simultaneously shipped to the Caribbean and the Americas. In Europe, well-worn beaver hats were repaired by the French and were then exchanged by both the Spanish and Portuguese for slaves in Africa.

Furs from North America's interior landscape became enmeshed in a spider web of seventeenth- and eighteenth-century exchange processes. Indians continued to control the landscape where the richest peltry was harvested, and their demand for specific goods determined what Europe produced for North American exchange. For two centuries, from the seventeenth to the eighteenth centuries, indigenous demand for specific types of finished goods, especially cloth, influenced the goods that were being produced for shipment to North America.

This research explores the exchange processes that came to characterize the North Atlantic commerce in furs. While historians most frequently associate the Spanish domination of South America as the more financially lucrative colonial domain, it was the economically valuable commodities, which were extracted from the Gulf of St. Lawrence, that dominated early resource extraction: fish, whale oil, and furs. Despite the attention that Columbus brought to the Caribbean, by the end of the sixteenth century North Atlantic commercial activity exceeded, in volume and value, that of the Gulf of Mexico.[1]

Indians recognized that Europeans were anxious to acquire furs, resources that were initially harvested in limited quantity. Indians hunted and processed peltry, a skill that few Europeans would successfully acquire. Indians demanded specific types of trade goods and Europeans began manufacturing the types of goods that met those demands. Too frequently we have failed to appreciate the agency of the indigenous consumer. In the United States Indians have been stereotypically obscured by myths of decline and demise, agency has been masked by dependency, and national histories have denied Indian involvement in world histories, especially that of the Atlantic World. This problem is further complicated by confining the fur trade to the parameters of early national history in both the United States and Canada. In the United States the fur trade remains confined to the colonial period and stereotypical of indigenous demise. In Canada the fur trade plays an extended role, shaping "the interplay of economic forces, technology, and geography," and influencing the outcome of Canadian political history.[2] However, Canadians also view industrial and commercial development as restrained by prolonged involvement in the fur

Cultures of Exchange in a North Atlantic World

trade. The scholarly emphasis on the Hudson's Bay Company obscures the expansionary impact the earlier French colonial trade had on the North Atlantic economy.

In both the United States and Canada stereotypical figures dominate the social arena of the fur trade. Both north and south of the border, the fur trade has been mythologized as a masculine landscape, where only the most hardy men survived the rigors of the wilderness. European traders are primarily envisioned as a negative influence, men who transported trade goods, diseases, and alcohol to Indian Country. Indian cultures are concurrently stereotyped as relatively weak, having cultural values and belief systems that were quickly undermined by the intrusion of western goods and the people who conveyed them. Rarely do we see alternative scenarios that involved extended encounter and sustained interaction between Indians and Europeans. Even more rarely do we see this as an Indian-dominated landscape.

Indians are rarely considered as participants in Europe's market economy, other than being its victims. Depictions of European intrusion have mistakenly removed indigenous people from playing significant roles in the emerging Atlantic economy. While disease devastated many eastern coastal villages, there were other numerous villages that moved into trading ascendancy. It was indigenous demand that shaped what Europeans traded, as well as what they produced. Indians harvested highly desirable, universally transportable commodities that brought good returns in Europe. In North America the market for trade goods was much more tenuous because Indians often refused to trade. When goods were priced too high or were of inferior quality, Indians regularly played traders against each other to obtain a greater quantity of goods. Despite European claims to the contrary, Indians were not overwhelmed by the novelty of western goods. Baubles and beads quickly proved to be insufficient to exchange for furs, and for much of the seventeenth and eighteenth centuries Indians frequently ignored demands to collect specific types and quantities of furs. Europeans found themselves controlled by the demands of their Indian customers and frustrated by the inefficient and limited production of the types of manufactured goods that Indians demanded. The natural resources of North America allowed Indians to compete in the emerging transnational Atlantic marketplace. Studied closely, the fur trade reveals how European rivalries, particularly those of the French, English, and Dutch, produced what today we refer to as a seller's market, which encouraged Indian consumers to get what they wanted by playing one country against the other.

This book explores the fur trade as a competitive process that brought Europeans from the coastal regions to the interior of the continent. Each nation established interior trading sites that attempted to nationalize and monopolize the exchange process with Indians. Europeans attempted to establish an advantage over their rivals by moving the fur trade ports from coastal regions to the inland riverways. Each hoped to interrupt the fur supply at its source, and each nation created a series of trading sites in the coastal interior. France drew Indians to the more convenient market space of Montreal, while the Dutch created a fortified market at Fort Orange, now present-day Albany. This research focuses on:

1. how fur trade exchange evolved as part of an expanding trans-Atlantic economy;
2. why the fur trade evolved into a regionalized economic system;
3. how Indians influenced the exchange process;
4. how gender proved an integrative tool that blended the disparate economic systems and provided for indigenous control of the exchange process in the Great Lakes region until the nineteenth century.

Islands and River Ports in the Early Exchange Process

Three cross-oceanic routes dominated the North Atlantic exchange process from the sixteenth to the eighteenth centuries. The midoceanic route connected Europe to the Caribbean; the South Atlantic passage linked it to West Africa and Brazil; and the North Atlantic water route connected it to Newfoundland, Hudson Bay, and the Great Lakes. This last route emerged as initially the most significant because it was the cod fishery and the fur trade of the North Atlantic that produced the greatest sixteenth-century monetary rewards. Over centuries, the cod fishery would retain its initial importance.[3]

It was the ocean's island ports that became the more important geographical features of this emerging Atlantic world. Exchange occurred at these ports: ships from different nations came into port for supplies and there, trade goods could be secured or exchanged while the shipping news circulated. Frequent wars subjected the merchant fleets to seizure and confiscation because no one European country was sufficiently powerful and able to defend all of its ships from piracy. Small coastal islands became important havens for navigating vast oceanic expanses and for the exchange of goods and supplies, which was often illegal. Islands became so important in this early trans-Atlantic world that Madeira, the Azores, and the Cape Verdes possessed "an importance out of all relation to their size and resources." The second geographically important feature of the trade that emerged was the protected bays and coastal riverways of the North American continent, which extended the reach of the ocean into existing networks of indigenous exchange.[4]

Certain resources, such as gold, magnified national rivalries and helped create the borders of empires while other natural resources, particularly fish, found national rivals working the same waterways, adjacent to each other. This trade was dominated by France, England, Spain, and Portugal. These waters were probably first exploited by the Devon fisherman of England's West Country, long before John Cabot's arrival in the fifteenth century. The widespread dissemination of information about Cabot's voyages, which focused on the rich marine resources of the northeastern Atlantic, encouraged the French, Spanish, and Portuguese to invade these North Atlantic fishing grounds. England's prior claims proved unenforceable.[5] During the 1540s as many as three hundred ships ventured west annually to fish. In 1580 the English pamphleteer Robert Hitchcock estimated that there were five hundred French vessels a year engaged in the trade. This estimate, supported by French archival sources, suggests that the total harvest may have been of the same magnitude as the industry in cod in the early twentieth century. However, from earliest times fisherman returned with furs because this enhanced the personal profitability of these voyages. They traded furs for small European articles such as cloth or ironware. Until the first half of the sixteenth century, furs were an adjunct to fishing.[6]

After 1565 national rivalries dramatically changed the nature of fishing.[7] When Elizabeth I's privateering seadogs attacked Spanish and Portuguese fishing vessels in 1585, Philip of Spain pressured the Basque and Portuguese fishing fleet into joining the Armada in 1588. The defeat of the Spanish Armada signaled the end of Portuguese and Spanish fishermen in the North Atlantic, and England became one of two remaining fishing fleets.[8]

Most frequently colonial historians focus on the process of mainland colony formation and fail to recognize that the multiple islands, protected bays, coastal waterways, and Europe's claims to the offshore islands affected the colonization process. Colonies also became intertwined with indigenous trade networks in complicated ways. The exchange process that took place at Tadoussac, in the protected confines of St. Lawrence Bay, existed long before European arrival. Following the influx of these Europeans as many as twenty thousand Native inhabitants may have seasonally relocated at Tadoussac. The island closest to Tadoussac was Newfoundland, and it was this island that emerged as an important piece of real estate in the oceanic landscape. Once France dominated the trans-Atlantic market for fish, its fleet became almost twice as large as that of the English.[9] The internationally shared waters of the early cod industry were gradually transformed by the size of the French merchant fleet and by French land claims to Newfoundland. France exerted increased control over Newfoundland's interior shoreline, and this allowed the French to dominate Great Banks fishing. It was the French who fished Newfoundland's southern waters and had access to both Tadoussac and the Gulf of St. Lawrence. The natural resource base of Tadoussac was the watershed of the Saguenay River, where hunting was the primary occupation. The Saguenay provided Indians access to the forested areas of the Canadian Shield, where expansive hunting grounds facilitated access to beaver, moose, and deer—items that were important sources of food and clothing. The prime-quality furs came from arctic regions, and it was the preponderance of beaver that transformed the fur trade into a highly valued commodity. Beaver was extinct through much of Europe. Indians used the beaver skin as clothing, piecing together five to eight beaver pelts with moose sinew—with constant wear the long guard hairs dropped out and the pelts became greased, pliable, and the fur became downy.[10]

The Newfoundland coast, especially Acadia, was crucial to the early fur trade, although English officials dismissed Acadia as of limited consequence. In 1680 "An Account of His Majesties Plantations in America" described Acadia as sparsely settled, a place that lacked either "government ecclesiastical or civil" and where a few people "live by catching fish." The English Commissioner of Custom, also dismissed Newfoundland and reasoned that "Newfoundland is not to be taken or accompted a plantation."[11] However, it was Acadia's location that gave the French access to St. Lawrence Bay and its adjacent riverway and provided the pathway to the interior of the continent.

All the coastal lands and islands from Cape Canso to the Bay of Islands were controlled by the French.[12] Although populations were sparse, the French government encouraged the loyalty of the Acadian colonists by developing mercantile policies that favored the Acadians. A royal declaration in 1683 allowed the Company of Acadia to bring its beaver pelts to France without taking them to Quebec and freed them from paying the ¼ duty.[13] By the last years of the century, a decree of July 20, 1694, upheld the Acadian's special rights to beaver and gave them the right to bring in two thousand pounds of beaver if they paid the 1664 duties.[14] The Acadians were allowed to retain any surplus above two thousand pounds, which could then be reexported. By 1700 they were given the right to transport six thousand pounds of beaver, burdened only by paying the equivalent of the 1664 duties. The Acadians retained the right to export the rest.[15]

The sixteenth- and early seventeenth-century Atlantic world was defined by imperial ventures that rested on the control of islands and port cities rather than on land-based empires. An oceanic rivalry among the Spanish, Portuguese, French, English, and Dutch evolved in the sixteenth century and was marked by repeated attacks on islands as political rivals sought greater access to the ports and islands that controlled trade.

The sixteenth century was a period of intermittent warfare for the port cities and islands of the Atlantic world. Virginia sent ships to attack Acadia in 1680. Sir William Phipps forced Port Royal to surrender, carried off the French governor, made the inhabitants swear fealty to William and Mary, and then sailed off leaving a French sergeant in charge. Meanwhile, the English sailed up the St. Lawrence, took Quebec from the French and transported their colonials to England. Subsequently, the French successfully attacked the Scots on Cape Breton while the Spanish overwhelmed Providence Island in the Caribbean.

While Europeans engaged in a continuing contest to control the coastal ports, their success often depended on the specialized knowledge of foreign pilots. Voyages of discovery and the subsequent division of the Americas into imperial domains was guided by a merchant fleet of well-traveled foreigners who attested to the complex of nationalities involved in creating this emerging Atlantic world. An Italian, John Cabot, explored for England while Verrazzano, another Italian, sailed for France, and the Englishman Henry Hudson became a Dutch explorer. Specialized knowledge about uncharted areas in the Americas privileged the pilots and the crews that crossed the Atlantic. It was impossible to navigate these lands without the knowledge of "foreigners" or to travel from one point to another in North America without the assistance of one's rivals. Simultaneously, nation-based prejudices incited continuing attacks against port cities where "foreign" populations were annihilated or shipped back to Europe. Europeans labeled these Atlantic islands and ports as the legitimate colonies of nation states, but it remained unclear who would exercise legitimate authority over that landscape until the end of the sixteenth century.[16]

Furs and Politicized Processes of Exchange

By the mid-sixteenth century ships were being sent to transport trade goods and retrieve furs, independent of fish. While fish and furs remained staples of North Atlantic commerce, furs became the more contested and desired products. Furs were highly transportable, required no capital investment in either people or land, and possessed a global receptivity both as a raw material and a finished good.

In Europe the introduction of North American peltry created an elaborate and specialized market and increased the interconnectedness of European port cities. In the seventeenth century supplies of beaver began to arrive regularly in Breton and Norman fishing ports, and by 1612 beaver was incorporated into the manufacture of Parisian hats.[17]

France dominated much of the initial fur trade because Jean Colbert, France's finance minister under Louis XIV, favored the importation of furs. His revenue policies allowed the French to impose import duties on incoming peltry and export duties on the finished product, beaver hats. Mercantilism linked colony and mother country in terms of raw materials, finished products, and recirculated goods. In France the finest peltry became available at reasonable prices, and the expansive supply of raw materials led to the expansion of hat manufacturing. Increased hat production helped stimulate a revolution in the production of consumer goods, and French hatters became known for producing the best hats in Europe. New sites of production emerged in France's port cities and transformed those spaces into sites of trans-Atlantic commerce. Hats manufactured in La Rochelle circulated throughout Europe; when worn out, they were returned to France for reworking, then recast for export to the Americas and for the Luso-African slave trade.

Colbert's policies created a surplus of furs and led to the reexportation of furs outside France. Furs were often sent to specific countries: white fur went to England where white hats were in demand, while the underside fur of the beaver skins was used in Holland and the backs were sent to Russia. Muscovie beaver that arrived in April and May went directly to Amsterdam or Rotterdam or on commission to Russia. A great flotilla took the furs to Russia.[18] The Dutch quickly monopolized the transporting of beaver pelts to Archangel and Narva, and returned with beaver pelts and beaver wool for distribution to the felters and furriers of western Europe. Amsterdam became the center of a new European trade system, while France remained the primary supply source.[19]

Beaver came in two varieties: coat and parchment. Coat was the more desirable fur, acquired after the pelt had been scraped, greased, and worn as coats by Indians—wear removed the stiff outer guard hairs of the pelt, exposing the softer, velvety undercoat. The *Castor sec*, or parchment beaver, that arrived in the autumn in France was usually sold in the following spring: a portion to the hatmakers of France, a portion to Russia, and a portion, the heavy skins with flat hair, to Germany for the manufacture of sleeves and furs. Felt acquired a variety of uses, even serving as material for armor.[20] Parchment beaver was not worn but was cured by being left in the sun to dry, and then it was traded.[21]

The North American Fur Trade
Sometime between 1600 and 1640, the Dutch, English, Swedes, and French initially struggled to control access to North American

peltry. France and England eventually dominated the exchange process by moving the trade to internal river sites. This simultaneously transferred European rivalries to North America. These rivalries were complicated by a colonizing process in which monarchs depended on their wealthy titled favorites to finance these expansionary adventures.[22] New France, like most of the initial colonies, was organized as a commercial venture and granted as a monopoly to the Sieur de Monts, a powerful Huguenot. Quebec was founded in 1608, and an alliance with the Huron, during the summer of 1609, led Champlain to found Montreal. It was the Huron who became France's major ally and who served as the initial middlemen in the exchange process. They collected furs from the *pays d'en haut* and delivered them to the French. It was the Huron who helped shift the trade from Tadoussac to the newly founded Montreal site.[23] Quebec, Montreal, and Lachine were founded at the narrows of the St. Lawrence River, where the furs were stored, loaded on ships, and transported to France, avoiding the vulnerable Tadoussac location.

The shift to these inland trading sites incited warfare among indigenous people. Indian rivalries were ignited when the French attempted to shift the focus of the trade to the shelter of an interior landscape. The establishment of Lachine and Montreal threatened to lessen both the quantity and quality of furs being shipped to the Dutch at Fort Albany. By 1626 the Dutch had provided their Iroquois allies with firearms, and in 1649 the Iroquois launched a devastating attack on the Huron that destroyed most of their villages and claimed hundreds of lives, consigning the survivors to torture and death, or adoption for the more fortunate. The Iroquois effectively dispersed the Huron, intending to become the middlemen of the trade. The Iroquois coveted the intermediary role of the Huron, but that role was quickly filled by the Odawa, who expanded the territorial limits of the old Huron trading circle westward and drew increased numbers of western Great Lakes communities into the exchange process.[24]

Eventually this series of Iroquois attacks subjected parts of the Great Lakes region to intermittent warfare, with hostilities that lasted almost sixty years. The Fur Trade or Beaver Wars brought almost six decades of demographic chaos to the northern regions of the western Great Lakes and ended when the Great Peace was signed at Montreal in 1701.[25]

Between 1654 and 1656, flotillas of Odawa canoes began transporting furs to Montreal, along the Ottawa River route. The Odawa incorporated the *pays d'en haut* communities that stretched north from Lake Superior to Hudson Bay. The annual canoe flotillas were graphically described by one contemporary observer, De Chesneau:

> The Outawa Indians, who are divided into several tribes, and are nearest to us, are those of the greatest use to us, because through them we obtain Beaver; and although they, for the most part, do not hunt, and have but a small portion of peltry in their country, they go in search of it to the most distant places, and exchange for it our Merchandise which they procure at Montreal. . . . They get their peltries, in the North, from the people of the interior . . . and in the south. . . . Some of these tribes occasionally come down to Montreal, but usually they do not do so in very great numbers, because they are far too distant, are not expert at managing canoes, and because the other Indians intimidate them, in order to be the carriers of their Merchandise and to profit thereby.[26]

Iroquois raiding parties intermittently blocked the Ottawa River, the favored Odawa trading route between Michilimackinac and Montreal.[27] The journey to Montreal proved especially hazardous because numerous river portages left the Odawa open to repeated attack. The Odawa canoe brigades made it apparent that Indians were willing to engage in the trade, but they were reluctant to continue the trade when risk levels dramatically increased, and Indians simply refused to journey to Montreal.

In 1656–57, the Iroquois launched a major offensive against the western Indians of the Great Lakes. This extension of the Fur Trade Wars westward brought unusually high fatality levels to northern Great Lakes villages. In arming the Iroquois, the Dutch introduced firepower into hand-to-hand combat. Repeated attacks led thousands of Algonquian-speaking Indians to seek refuge on the western shore of Lake Michigan and to band together in a vast refugee triangle that stretched along the lake shoreline south to the Illinois and Mississippi rivers.[28] One of the largest communities formed around present-day Green Bay, where Father Gabriel Dreuillettes claimed that the village contained as many as "twenty-four thousand souls."[29] Another large village was formed at Kaskaskia and consisted of Ilini-allied villages.

Ironically, it was the Iroquois' relentless pursuit of and attack on Algonquian-speaking nations that led the French to venture west to trade with Indians. Indians refused to journey to Montreal and consequently the city lost access to its most valuable export, furs. In essence it was French fur traders and not Indians who ultimately assumed the risk of traveling the hazardous Ottawa River route to and from the western Great Lakes. The French ventured west when Médard Chouart, Sieur des Groseilliers, officially visited the Ottawa in 1654. He returned two years later surrounded by a flotilla of thirty canoes, overflowing with furs. Groseilliers's western travels dramatically increased his wealth but also made him more aware of other lucrative sites where furs could be obtained; he learned about prime coat or arctic beaver from the Indians who wintered at Green Bay. He came to believe that the richest harvests were waiting to be retrieved from the land surrounding the North Sea, or what the English would rename Hudson Bay.

Despite Groseilliers's triumphant return to Montreal, he was denied official permission to return to the western Great Lakes. He then set a precedent that would be followed quickly by other equally adventuresome young Frenchmen. He simply disregarded the governor's injunction and left for the west. On his second trip, he was accompanied by his more audacious brother-in-law, Pierre

Radisson.[30] Although Groseilliers and Radisson intended to establish a trading post oriented toward Hudson Bay, they failed to pursue this more northerly direction because their canoes were already overflowing with furs. They returned to Montreal accompanied by an even larger flotilla of canoes than that of Groseilliers's earlier voyage. Word of their success spread through the Montreal community; unfortunately, their return was met with official disapproval. They were fined for leaving Montreal illegally and paid a heavy duty on their fur returns.

Radisson and Groseilliers fueled a westward demographic movement of single young men. The financial success of their western journey created a large pool of men who eagerly risked their lives on the high-stakes outcome associated with furs. Radisson and Groseilliers became emblematic of the coureurs de bois, or runners of the woods, the illegal traders whose success brought numerous young Frenchmen into the western Great Lakes. Most followed the Groseilliers-Radisson pathway west, and as their predecessors, they took up residence in Native villages, living among Indians for two to three years. The coureurs de bois relied on Indians for protection and access to furs.[31] Many married Indian women, in part because marriage "after the manner of the country" provided access to peltry. Increasingly, New France also discovered that many illegal traders remained permanently in the west and never returned to Montreal.[32]

In the 1660s there was a rush of traders into the west from Montreal.[33] Ironically, the western Great Lakes offered opportunities for family formation that were hindered by the small population of women in the St. Lawrence region. In 1665 when the westward journeys began, French Canadian men outnumbered French women by nearly two to one. Fifteen years later there were still 55.5 men to every 44.5 women. Only at century's end did the skewed ratios become balanced.[34] French officials often criticized these men because they preferred to live as Indians. However, there were pressing economic reasons why these young men went west.[35] Those who engaged in the fur trade could earn as much in two years as a *habitant* or resident of Montreal might earn in fifteen years.[36] Large numbers of single young men dramatically changed the nature of the exchange process. Within twenty years, the intendant claimed that five to eight hundred men were trading in the "woods," as illegal traders or coureurs de bois.[37] They left on their own and were not always financed by Montreal merchants. Often, they were just as likely to journey to the English at Albany to sell their furs as they were to return to Montreal.[38] By 1676 attempts to restore the Native trade routes to Montreal had failed, and Frenchmen who lived and traded among Indians dominated the exchange process.

Radisson and Groseilliers had inadvertently changed the nature of the fur trade by shifting the exchange process from Montreal to the western Great Lakes.[39] They successfully demonstrated that sizeable profits could be made through the fur trade by heading west. However, the role that Radisson and Groseilliers played in the New France trade has been overlooked because their names are more commonly associated with the English fur trade. The voyages of Radisson and Groseilliers became part of a tangled story that led the English to lay claim to Hudson Bay and created the rivalry that ultimately led to the Seven Years' War.

The unusual story of Radisson and Groseilliers began when the two adventurers journeyed to Versailles to secure funds to establish an outpost at the North Sea; they also hoped to recover the fines imposed on them by the New France intendant. Radisson and Groseilliers quickly discovered that the minister of finance, Colbert, was committed to Robert La Salle's plan to expand the trade of the western Great Lakes in a southerly direction, from the Mississippi River to the Gulf of Mexico. Unfortunately, neither Radisson nor Groseilliers possessed practical knowledge of the North Sea region; they relied on indigenous knowledge rather than practical experience. La Salle's exploration of the Mississippi was financially backed by Colbert's son, and this placed La Salle in a stronger position at the French court. Although Radisson and Groseilliers proposed what would be ultimately a more profitable route, it was La Salle's Mississippi route that triumphed and led France to perilously extend the fragile boundaries of its North American empire. La Salle believed that furs transported southward to the Louisiana delta would reduce French dependence on Montreal, which was closed for bad weather during a major part of the year.[40] Following the failed Groseilliers-Radisson visit to Versailles, La Salle died at the delta of the Mississippi, and his demise eliminated the Mississippi as a viable alternative to Montreal.

Consequently, Radisson and Groseilliers decided to venture into the North Sea, but they did so without financial backing. Fortunately, the Atlantic world was a multicultural landscape where practical geographical knowledge was available from a variety of sources. Thus, Groseilliers and Radisson turned to a New Salem, Massachusetts, pilot who was familiar with the route to the North Sea. He willingly transported Radisson and Groseilliers across the Atlantic, but their successful crossing was marred by being shipwrecked off Sable Island. There, the two Frenchmen were offered a ride to Boston by a group of English commissioners who had been sent to negotiate the transfer of New Amsterdam to England. Ironically, the English commission ship was then captured by the Dutch and its boat, crew, and passengers were landed on the coast of Spain. In 1666 the English commissioners, along with Groseilliers and Radisson and the crew, finally reached England. Word of their adventures spread quickly through the merchant classes, where they won the support of Sir George Carteret and King Charles, who commissioned the Frenchmen to sail under the sponsorship of English investors. In 1668 Radisson and Groseilliers departed England, but severe storms forced Radisson's ship to return to England. It was Groseilliers who successfully established a trading outpost on the North Sea, guided by the colonial sea captain from Salem, Massachusetts. Groseilliers returned with one of the largest cargoes of prime quality arctic furs ever transported across the Atlantic. The English not only renamed the North Sea but they established the Hudson's Bay Company as a corporate entity, headed by Prince Rupert, the cousin of Prince Charles, and by Sir George Carteret.[41]

The English had a substantial presence in the North Atlantic because of the fishing trade, but at this time they possessed only limited imperial commitments beyond Ireland.[42] Following Groseilliers's return from his trans-Atlantic voyage, the English claimed the lands and riverways that drained into Hudson Bay. English land claims in North America dramatically expanded by over 1.5 million square miles when the HBC laid claim to one of the largest landed empires in the world. Carteret viewed Hudson Bay as integral to a well-rounded empire, one "in which northern lands would counterbalance tropical territories, and the control of trade routes would be all-important."[43]

The Hudson's Bay Company changed the nature of the western fur trade because the bay location eliminated the costs associated with transporting trade goods from Montreal to the interior of the country and carrying furs from the interior to Montreal. At Hudson Bay Indians initially brought their furs directly to the company posts and bargained directly with British traders. The rivers were efficient highways, flowing into the tidewater at Hudson Bay. The English established forts along the coastline and, later, established trading posts along the rivers that emptied into Hudson Bay. Large ships, coming directly from Britain, moored adjacent to the posts in the bay. The HBC was immediately competitive with the French because "goods could be obtained on a large scale, with access by sea, at more favorable exchange rates."[44] Because Hudson's Bay Company had direct access to the best furs, prime quality or winter coat beaver, English peltry then brought Europe's highest prices. From their initial arrival in Hudson Bay to their lengthy tenure in the region, the English company reaped handsome profits from the fur trade.

In the 1670s the French had been reluctant to push into Hudson Bay because the market was already glutted with less valuable parchment beaver. Even more problematic was the threat that manpower would be reduced in the Montreal region if new fur-trade locations were established. If the trade was pushed northward into Hudson Bay, the pool of illegal traders would continue to expand, drawing men away from agricultural activity in the St. Lawrence River valley. Thus, the administrators of New France remained firmly committed to a fur trade with a trading cycle that spanned eighteen to twenty-four months, although it often stretched to thirty-six months. They transported trade goods upriver along the Ottawa to the Great Lakes and the following year returned downriver, with peltry destined for Montreal.

By the end of the seventeenth century, three distinct fur trading regions had evolved in North America. The most northern region was Hudson Bay and it had direct trans-Atlantic access to London. The British Crown awarded the entire watershed to the Hudson's Bay Company. This area was defined by the Canadian Shield, a terrain that formed the hilly north-south border initially shaped by the great continental ice sheets. Hudson Bay was drained by a large number of rivers that flowed directly into it, their direction being determined by the shield. The regional network that evolved at Hudson Bay was organized around the transportation of trade goods directly from London. Furs were initially exchanged at the British forts that rimmed Hudson Bay, the exchange process essentially controlled by a corporate entity, the Hudson's Bay Company, rather than by individual fur traders. The British had eliminated the middlemen from the exchange process, and profits accrued primarily to the company, rather than fur traders.

The second region was defined by the Atlantic–Gulf Coastal Plain and extended west to the rolling hills of the Piedmont, a hilly transitional zone that leads to the Appalachian Mountains. The Appalachian Mountains separated the Atlantic region from the Great Lakes. From Maine to southern New York and the regions around Delaware, there was harvestable beaver peltry; farther south the fur trade was focused on deerskin.

The third region, the Great Lakes, extends more than one

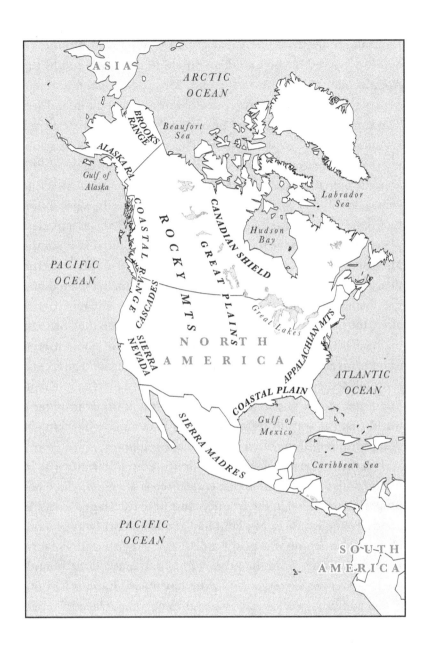

Map 1. Fur trade regions

thousand miles from the Appalachians to the Rocky Mountains and is bordered by the Canadian Shield to the north and by the Appalachian Mountains to the east. This region is the undulating Interior Plain, which was once covered by a great inland sea. The Interior Plain is drained by one of the world's greatest river systems—the Mississippi-Missouri. This riverine landscape is connected to the Great Lakes and to the Gulf of Mexico, providing access to both the Atlantic Ocean and the Caribbean Sea. This fertile central lowland of North America presently forms the agricultural heartland of the United States while the Great Plains is a treeless plateau that rises to the foothills of the Rocky Mountains. It was the Mississippi–Great Lakes region of the Interior Plain that was the heart of the French fur trade. The French eventually traveled into the northern plains; they left from the Great Lakes and moved west along the Grand Portage and Lake of the Woods into the northern plains. These were the French who the Americans encountered when Lewis and Clark explored the Louisiana Purchase. The French routinely settled among Indians, creating a fur trade that relied on interdependence and extended cooperation. It would produce a world that was socially different from the demographic changes that transpired in the other two fur trade regions.

The three regions of the fur trade fostered different types of interactions with Indians. In the eastern, coastal region, which was primarily controlled by the Iroquois, furs were exchanged for trade goods at English forts. England had acquired Fort Orange from Holland, renaming this post Fort Albany. English traders faced increasing rivalry from the French forts that marked the boundary between the two regions. In the Northeast, Indians had the distinct advantage of comparison shopping, often playing French and English traders against each other.

The Hudson's Bay Company and the Iroquois left the colony of New France threatened on both its northern and southern borders. To stem lawlessness and regularize departures, New France began to issue fur trade permits in 1681. While New France never succeeded in completely controlling the trade, it became increasingly regularized. By the end of the seventeenth century many of the coureurs de bois were replaced by voyageurs, who were both experienced traders and good credit risks for Montreal merchants. The westbound contingent of legal traders numbered around one hundred men, but they stayed for two years, and at least two hundred traders a year remained in the western Great Lakes.[45] However, the illegal trade was also considerable. Illegal traders continued to journey into the Great Lakes. This landscape of negotiable riverways and unpatrolled borderlands encouraged illegal exchange processes.

Indians as Consumers

They believe that Lake Superior is a Pond made by the Beavers . . . this God (the great Hare), they add while chasing a Beaver in Lake Superior, crossed with a single stride a bay of eight leagues in width. In view of so mighty an enemy, the Beavers withdrew to another Lake . . . when they afterward, by means of the Rivers flowing from it, arrived at the North Sea with the intention of crossing over to France; but finding the water bitter, they lost heart, and spread throughout the Rivers and Lakes of this entire Country. And this is the reason why there are not Beavers in France, and the French come here to get them.[46]

The numerous ways in which the Indians described the "pull factors" that drew the French to North American shores reveal an indigenous sense of natural superiority. To Indians it was the deficiency in Europe's natural resources that pushed Europeans westward. Even hardy animals like the beaver were dissuaded by the adverse conditions of the European shoreline, dismayed by the salt waters that engulfed Europe. Many of these same furbearing animals were often extinct in Europe because they had been overhunted. Indians actively engaged in the peltry trade, but they rarely traded furs for a handful of glass beads. The fur-trade correspondence, especially the letters from the Hudson's Bay Company archives, suggests that Indians were difficult and demanding customers.

Indians demanded specific types of goods, and they refused to trade when goods were unsatisfactory.

Ironically, many of the goods that were identified with the exchange process emerged from the seventeenth-century experience of Radisson and Groseilliers. Montreal traders would carry the same types of goods when they headed west for the next one hundred years. Radisson chose the goods brought by the English on their first trading expedition into Hudson Bay, selecting the most popular items that had characterized their Great Lakes trading ventures. These were the types of goods that were shipped directly from London to Hudson Bay. Company ships moored offshore and thus, the Hudson Bay trade specialized in heavier goods, such as large iron cooking pots and iron implements. Guns and powder were transported in secure wooden boxes and kegs, and a typical cargo was described as "two hundrewd foweleing pieces & foure hundred powder norms, with a proportionable quantity of Shott fitt thereunto . . . two Hundred Brass Kettles Sizeable of from two to Sixteene gallons a piece, twelve grosse of French knives and two Grosse of Arrow head and about five or Six hundred hatchets." Radisson stressed arms, ammunitions, and metal goods, but he also secured knives made by the French.[47]

In outfitting the HBC ships, Radisson purchased French goods when British manufacturers proved unable to supply those goods. This attempt to match trade goods with "anticipated" Indian demand stimulated the manufacture of particular goods in England and produced cloth that was modeled directly on that produced by the French. The British initially supplied Indians with the goods they wanted by incorporating the goods of their French rivals. Very quickly, British manufacturers began producing the goods themselves. A wide variety of French goods were copied: awls, vermilion, ice chisels, firearms, and gunpowder.[48] For example, within one year of the first Hudson Bay trading expedition, an English ironmonger regularized the supply of knives to the HBC by copying the French knives directly from the patterns with which he was supplied.[49]

Both Britain and France often surreptitiously imported goods from their competitors to meet the demands of their Indian customers. As early as 1682, the governor and board of Hudson's Bay Company obtained French blankets and had suppliers use these as models for the Indian trade. Indians demanded their cloth in specific colors, "un drap bleu, une raye blanche large comme le petit doight del la liziere, et a l'ecarlatine rouge." This familiar French cloth could be produced cheaper in British mills and the quality was improved, an innovation made possible by the migration of Protestant craftsmen from France to England following the reversal of the Edict of Nantes.[50] New France officials believed that the English were able to strengthen their hold over the Indians by providing better rates of exchange for cloth.

The French confronted similar complaints from their Indian customers. A 1707 French report claimed that the Indians preferred English cloth because it more successfully replicated particular color hues. Ironically, each side claimed that the opposition produced the preferred color of cloth. "The cause which makes them go there . . . is that they do not find with us certain 'draps rouge et bleu d'aulne et un cart de large.'"[51] In 1714, the situation seemed so desperate that New France officials recommended that French merchants obtain their cloth directly from England. From Quebec a joint letter sent by Vaudreuil and Begon reflected the urgent appeal caused by Indians who preferred English cloth to that of the French: "You informed us last year that His Majesty had given orders to have goods manufactured in the kingdom to imitate them which is very much desired for country or if they would not suffer the entrance of any foreign goods, since necessity has no law, Srs. De Vaudreuil and Begon believe that if they could not be obtained in France of this quality it is important for sustaining the Colony that His Majesty should permit them to be sent from England to France to be loaded on the armed vessels for this colony."[52]

In 1714 English cloth was sent to French merchants, the next year an imitation manufactured in France was shipped, and the substitute cloth was immediately detected. The Indians refused to trade. The Indians became expert at judging cloth. By the late 1750s the French still encountered problems obtaining the types of cloth that Indians demanded. The need for acceptable goods became increasingly apparent during the Seven Years' War: "Escarlatines from England are an indispensable necessity for the beaver trade in Canada. To get these escarlatines, which they have up to the present tried in vain to imitate in France, the Company is obliged to bring them from England to Holland and from Holland to France on neutral boats."[53]

The Hudson's Bay Company created trade policies that established more effective controls over the types of goods that were shipped to North America. For instance, the company relied on the defective goods returned to London to make changes in the products that were subsequently supplied to the traders. Employees were instructed to "send us home by every return of our Ships all goods as are either defective or not acceptable to the Natives and to inform us wherein they are deficient."[54] This "return" policy attempted to more effectively supply the specific types of goods that Indians demanded. While the London headquarters of the HBC often questioned the demanding nature of Indians, there was often a good reason for Indians to be selective. Products manufactured in a temperate landscape often could not withstand the rigors of an arctic winter. Thus, even barely conspicuous flaws in metal, often referred to as "fire flaws," proved problematic when temperatures plummeted, and iron became brittle. Consequently, Indians refused to accept metal goods with cracks or other apparent flaws. In 1750 James Isham returned guns from the York factory that he identified as Indian "rejects." The HBC governor maintained that it was difficult to locate the purported flaws. Upon "close Inspection we could not find above four of the guns that had any thing like a fault to make them Untradeable." The next year, Isham returned additional guns and further invoked the ire of the HBC, who then expressed thorough surprise that the Indians were suddenly more aware of such flaws, when no such complaints had previously influenced the exchange process. "The guns sent to your Factory are equal in goodness to any we now send or ever did and it is Surprising to us that the Trading Indians that came to York Fort should be more Curious than any of the other Natives."[55]

The quality of guns remained problematic, and Indians continued to reject items that exhibited "fire flaws," but traders also returned other English merchandise with a long list of complaints. In a 1739 letter, James Isham indicated that the Indians detailed a lengthy list of complaints, including dislike of

the colour and size of the large pearl beads; complained that the kettles were too heavy for their size and the wrong shape; and claimed the gunpowder was very weak, foul smelling, and an objectionable ashy colour. Although they liked the shape, quality, and colour of the blankets, the Indians said they were too short. Cloth, on the other hand, was said to be of little service because it was too narrow, weak, and thin. Despite liking their design the Indians also considered the buttons and combs to be too weak. The fire steels were faulty, giving little fire, the gum worms too big for the ramrods, the French flints the wrong shape, the yarn gloves useless, and the knives very displeasing, with bad blades and worse handles. The twine was weak and uneven, as thick as packthread in some places and as thin as sewing thread in others. Powder horns were the wrong shape and rings were too wide for women's fingers.[56]

The HBC "return" policy was reiterated in a continuing stream of letters from London headquarters. The HBC traders supplied the company more precise information, such as the size, shape, or color of the most desirable goods.[57] This policy forced the redesign of manufactured goods so that they were more easily exchanged in Indian country. In the subarctic region, the HBC partially solved the "fire flaws" by allowing forts to manufacture many iron items, especially tools. The HBC shipped iron bars so that the posts were able to produce ice chisels and scrapers.[58] The HBC also became intent on securing the best merchandise in Europe to send to

Indians. They learned, for instance, that Indians preferred Brazil tobacco, treated with molasses, to English or Virginia tobacco. The HBC successfully substituted the preferred alternative, and when London shipments were of inferior quality, they avoided English merchants and purchased tobacco directly from Lisbon.

Judging from the record, Indian dissatisfaction with English merchandise seems to have increased in the mid-eighteenth century. There seems little doubt that much of the complaining was an Indian ploy to lower the costs of their merchandise. In the French correspondence, there are parallel Indian complaints. Indians used similar tactics to deal with the French, and the French traders became convinced that Indians preferred English cloth. By the early eighteenth century, the French imported almost twenty-one thousand yards of English strouds from New York for the Indian trade in the western Great Lakes.[59] The governor of New France wrote to Versailles that, "The English have the better of us in the quality of merchandise in two important articles. The first is kettles—the second is cloth." The Indians successfully pitted the French and English against each other, forcing them to lower prices and getting them to make copies and improvements in each other's merchandise.

Involvement in the fur trade did not radically displace the variety of economic pursuits that structured seasonal patterns of indigenous behavior. In the subarctic and arctic regions, Indians had long hunted furbearing animals in exchange for foodstuffs. In the western Great Lakes and along the eastern seaboard, Indians were accustomed to spending the winter in hunting camps, while most women and families remained in the agricultural villages. In the western Great Lakes hunting camps were proximate to the summer villages, while eastern seaboard Indians journeyed to the interior, especially the lands along the Ohio River valley. The fur trade changed as increased numbers of people became involved in the processing of peltry. Hunting required more intensive labor and drew larger numbers of men and women into the harvesting and processing of furs. Beaver remained the primary quarry in the Great Lakes and in Hudson Bay. However, in other fur-bearing lands, animals like deer, marten, and raccoon were also trapped. Women were the primary processors of fur, and many of these skins, particularly deer, were more difficult to process. Women washed and scraped the skins to remove dirt, tissue, and blood vessels, and then they stretched the skins over wood frames to dry.[60]

From May through the end of July, Indians who resided in the Northeast and those who lived in Rupert's Land, the territory of the Hudson's Bay Company, transported their peltry to the trading posts that lined Hudson Bay. On the East Coast, for most of the seventeenth century, the exchange process was centered at Albany. The English built Fort Oswego, in present-day New York, to counter the French trading post and garrison at Niagara. By the mid-eighteenth century, Fort Oswego displaced Albany as the center of trade. Many Algonquian speaking peoples adjacent to the borderland regions became part of an illegal trade that flourished in the Niagara-Oswego area.

Fort Oswego became a substantial community with approximately seventy log houses behind its walls. Across from the trading community were two rows of buildings where Indians stored their peltry and where visiting traders bargained directly with their Indian clients. Over one hundred traders journeyed annually to Oswego where they encountered Indian customers who expected to receive high-quality goods at reasonable prices. If they disliked a trader or his exchange rates, Indians simply chose a competitor. Indians also helped to shape a new line of products made in the Americas specifically for Indian customers. Items such as wampum, silver brooches and gorgets, and armbands were commissioned by the more successful traders. Even the most organized traders often found themselves scrambling to provide more fashionable seasonal merchandise, and the trade records are replete with last minute special orders such as "calico handkerchiefs."[61] Exchange was more complicated than we normally envision, and Indians were able to profit from the increasingly impersonal exchange process that took place at the eastern forts. It was the proximity of fur-trade posts, competitively operated by the French and British, like those at Oswego and Niagara, that encouraged Indians to identify their best source of bargains. Indians compared exchange rates, noting the numbers of furs each trader expected for his goods. Thus, while Fort Niagara's French traders offered one silver bracelet for ten beavers, the English traders at Fort Oswego offered bracelets that were "as heavy, of a purer silver and more elegant, and did not cost them two beavers."[62] At these centralized fur-trade sites a more depersonalized process of exchange occurred, but Indians remained discerning and demanding consumers.

Imperial rivalry between France and England prevented trade from becoming a wholly commercial phenomenon, but marketplace involvement exposed the eastern tribes to higher levels of consumerism. Over the course of the eighteenth century, eastern Indian communities increasingly substituted manufactured goods for locally produced products. Stone and ceramic cooking and storage vessels were displaced by copper kettles. Metal tools and knives replaced traditional wooden implements, while clothing styles changed radically with the incorporation of European trade cloth. Some items such as cotton shirts, petticoats, and woolen stockings were specifically manufactured for Indian consumers with many personal garments being reinvented as more colorful exterior clothing. Early in the seventeenth century, European trade goods constituted a small percentage of Iroquois housewares, but by the end of that century archaeologists have shown that almost "75 percent or more" of the archaeological evidence consisted of trade goods.[63]

In the western Great Lakes the French fur trade was noticeably different from the eastern exchange process. The lengthy journey west, which took close to two months, coupled with the difficulty of crossing numerous portages, affected the types of goods that were carried west from Montreal. Canoe transport favored lightweight

TABLE 1. Functional categories in ranked order by percentage of expenditure

Detroit		Ouiatenon	
1. Clothing	75.58	1. Clothing	55.04
2. Hunting	11.91	2. Hunting	20.28
3. Alcohol	4.83	3. Cooking and Eating	7.22
4. Cooking and Eating	4.28	4. Alcohol	6.95
5. Adornment	1.73	5. Adornment	5.62
6. Grooming	.54	6. Woodworking	2.25
7. Tobacco Use	.50	7. Grooming	1.24
8. Woodworking	.46	8. Tobacco Use	1.20
9. Cultivation	.09	9. Cultivation	.10
10. Maintenance	.07	10. Amusements	.08
11. Amusements	.02	11. Weapons	.02
12. Weapons	–	12. Fishing	.01
13. Fishing	–	13. Maintenance	–

Michilimackinac		Green Bay	
1. Clothing	72.04	1. Clothing	65.08
2. Hunting	12.40	2. Hunting	18.09
3. Adornment	4.57	3. Cooking and Eating	4.59
4. Cooking and Eating	3.40	4. Alcohol Use	4.37
5. Alcohol Use	3.07	5. Adornment	2.95
6. Tobacco Use	2.05	6. Woodworking	2.39
7. Woodworking	1.32	7. Tobacco Use	1.61
8. Grooming	.95	8. Grooming	.87
9. Cultivation	.16	9. Weapons	.19
10. Weapons	.03	10. Cultivation	.07
11. Amusements	.01	11. Maintenance	.06
12. Fishing	–	12. Fishing	.03
13. Maintenance	–	13. Amusements	.01

Source: Dean L. Anderson, "The Flow of European Trade Goods into the Western Great Lakes Region, 1715–1760," in *The Fur Trade Revisited: Selected Papers of the Sixth North American Fur Trade Conference, Mackinac Island, Michigan, 1991*, ed. Jennifer S. H. Brown, W. J. Eccles, and Donald P. Heldman (East Lansing: Michigan State University Press, 1994), 107.

goods, especially cloth that could be bundled into transportable packages and easily portaged. Iron goods were often too heavy to portage and required protection from the dampness.

Table 1 quantifies several decades of trade goods that were

shipped to four posts in the western Great Lakes by Montreal merchants. There is a high percentage of cloth and there are limited quantities of metal goods, confirming the suggestion that the fur trade might be better labeled the cloth trade. Heavy iron trade goods were more efficiently transported to Hudson Bay where they were deposited for exchange at the forts. It is probable that the British, and formerly the Dutch, followed the same procedure in the East, transporting iron products such as guns directly from New York up the Hudson River to Fort Albany.[64] There are, indeed, interesting questions that arise in considering how these exchange patterns were affected by location. For the French, the lengthy transport by canoe dictated the contents of each cargo and raised the cost of the goods that the French exchanged with Indians. Despite the expenses associated with distance and the number of men required to paddle the transport canoes, it remained the French who frequently appeared more successful and acquired higher grade furs than the British. Even when the British offered superior goods at relatively lower prices, the best furs often went to the Frenchmen.

Indeed, it appears puzzling how the French remained competitive when the French were hemmed in by adjacent English trading ventures at Fort Oswego in the east and in the north by the posts at Hudson Bay. However, it was French ability to establish culturally compatible terms by relying on kinship to bridge cultural differences, assuring Indians that allies and relatives controlled the exchange process, not strangers.[65] Equally important was the reliance on Indians for military assistance. This allowed the French to forego trade profits as a means to secure these alliances, using the gift-giving of trade goods to ensure Indian loyalty to their French allies. "To allow profit alone to govern the fur trade threatened the alliance, and when necessary, French officials subordinated the fur trade to the demands of the alliance.[66]

Fictive Kin Networks and the Fur Trade
In the western Great Lakes fur trade exchange was effectively buffered by kinship. These patterns were established through

either temporary or permanent relationships with Native women. Socially prominent women with extended kin networks became valued partners for French traders because kin networks provided access to peltry. One fur trade *bourgeois* explained the importance of marriage in this way: "Men . . . like to marry into prominent Indian families when they are able to do so; by such a connection they increase their adherents, their patronage is expanded, and they make correspondingly larger profits. Their Indian relatives remain loyal and trade with no other company."[67]

During the French period, this Indian world was dominated by loyalties to kin and community. Indians relied on kinship to structure social relationships. Marriage, whether "after the custom of the country" or sacramentally sanctioned, drew French traders into Native communities and provided both acceptance into a kin network and access to peltry. It assured that the exchange process occurred along a kinship continuum.[68]

Community-based processes rather than individual preference determined decision making. Even the women who legally married Frenchmen did not "marry out"; they remained part of their indigenous communities. This was crucial to the exchange process because furs were secured from the hunting grounds of one's kin network. By cultivating close and familial links with traders, Indian communities were simultaneously guaranteed a continuously stable source of trade goods and interacted with traders as relatives, rather than strangers.

The lands adjoining Lakes Ontario, Superior, and Michigan were ideally suited to the fur trade: it was a physical landscape that offered multiple exchange sites amidst fertile agricultural lands. Most fur-trade communities were situated at riverways and portages. Even at forts like Michilimackinac, the coureurs de bois lived in nearby St. Ignace where they chose "to live with the women in their Cabins."[69]

Across the entire western Great Lakes, relocation by the French among Native people became a common process. For instance, in

Illini Country illegal French traders moved in with Indian women at Peoria. After 1700 traders were drawn to the newly established mission villages of Kaskaskia and Cahokia. In 1715 Governor Ramezay and the intendant of Canada, Begon, reported that one hundred traders had fled to Cahokia where they joined forty-seven others who had previously settled there.[70] The Jesuits initially complained about the traders, whom they considered a lawless lot, but officials and priests could not stop this western demographic movement. Despite the Jesuits repeated pleas for assistance, the religious fathers adapted to a changing world where cohabitation became commonplace. At Cahokia, between 1701 and 1713, the Jesuits recorded twenty-one baptisms, eighteen of the children were born to Indian mothers and French fathers. Within ten years the community had built a large church and the residents had constructed eighty houses, this equated with a base population of four hundred people. In 1714 when an epidemic carried off between two and three hundred people, it became apparent that the village also housed considerable numbers of apostates whose marriages and births left no trace in the official record.[71]

Many of the illegal traders who lived in Illini Country shipped their furs south to the growing port of New Orleans. For the rest of the Great Lakes landscape, it was the newly established post at Detroit that emerged as the early eighteenth-century focus of the fur trade. It was Cadillac, the former Michilimackinac commandant, who established Detroit in 1701. Cadillac brought fifty soldiers, fifty traders, artisans, and several priests to establish the Detroit post.[72] Within a year, he had also relocated almost six thousand Indians to the new post. These included Potawatomi and Miami from St. Joseph, Michigan, and Ottawa, Huron, and Ojibwa from the straits of Michilimackinac. The commandant encouraged comingling and "it was no uncommon thing for a citizen to have left behind him a lawful wife and to have selected another in Detroit."[73]

The French believed that Detroit would serve as a secure gateway into the Great Lakes, but it was also apparent that the trade could not be easily controlled and that even when population gravitated toward Detroit, other sites continued to prosper. The geography of the Great Lakes, with its numerous riverways and portages, made it possible for traders to reach the British as well as the French. Trade increased dramatically at Fort Oswego. By 1714 the French felt threatened by the encroaching English, and they officially reopened the fur trade. They licensed twenty-five traders, established strategic posts (primarily at portages), and extended amnesty to illegal traders if they would return to Montreal. Few traders returned, and the newly licensed traders not only inflated the number of canoes that were brought into the Great Lakes but these canoes began supplying the unlicensed traders.

By 1720 Detroit and Michilimackinac functioned as the hubs of the trade, while the smaller settlements created by both intermarriage and the resettlement of Indians and Frenchmen in the region created a ring of exchange sites. These trading villages included Fort Miami (now Fort Wayne) on the Maumee River in northeast Indiana (1715); Fort St. Joseph at Niles, Michigan (1715); Fort St. Louis at Peoria (1715); Fort St. Francois at Green Bay or La Baye (1717); at Madeline Island (La Pointe) in Chequamegon Bay (1718); at Kaministiquia on the northwest coast of Lake Superior (1717); at Fort Beauharnois between 1727 and 1750 on the western shore of Lake Pepin, near Frontenac, Minnesota; at Sault Ste. Marie; at Quiatanon, Lafayette, and Vincennes, Indiana; at Fort Nipigon on the north shore of the lake of the same name; and at a dozen other forts stretching to Lake Winnipeg and beyond called, jointly, "Posts of the Sea of the West." In 1717 Louisiana was guaranteed status as a separate colony and, while the New Orleans government controlled the Ilini settlements at Kaskaskia and Cahokia, these two towns increasingly served as the southernmost link in the Great Lakes trade network.

The more transient and larger centers of exchange evolved on islands, like Michilimackinac, or at the confluence of lakes and rivers, such as at Detroit. The fur trade was a carrying trade, and many

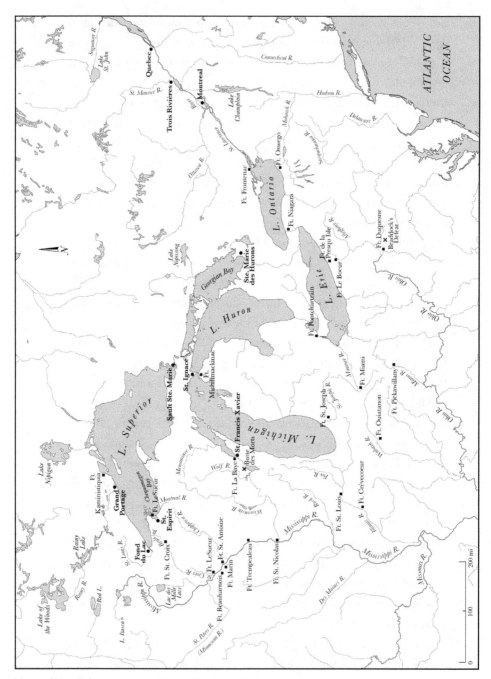

Map 2. Fur trading communities in the Great Lakes

of the smaller posts supplied the goods that could not be carried in the already crowded canoes. It was at these smaller posts, like Fort St. Joseph and Quiatanon, that voyageurs secured fresh food provisions. Many of these smaller communities evolved as the agricultural suppliers of the trade. Indian women became not only the trade's provisioners but also the suppliers of goods manufactured for the trade from canoes to clothing; these women made the moccasins and snowshoes, and did needlework and quillwork.[74] The smaller posts not only replenished dwindling food supplies or lost trade goods, but additional voyageurs could be hired there from among the French population.

The smaller posts became indispensable in the fur trade because they also supplied many of the larger fur trade posts with agricultural produce. Agriculture took root at the smaller sites. At L'Arbe Croche, across the straits from Michilimackinac in northern Michigan, the Odawa became the agricultural supply source for traders who were heading west. The Odawa "raised large supplies of corn and vegetables, produced fish, and later maple sugar, and manufactured canoes, snowshoes, and clothing essential to the Great Lakes fur trade."[75]

Many of the smaller posts in the western Great Lakes had a settled agricultural appearance, with extensive agricultural fields and apple trees. There were the other standard markers of stable agricultural communities: log cabins, framed houses, and barns. Many of the architectural markers that we associate with European societies also characterized Native communities. At Fort St. Joseph, the commandant ordered a French carpenter to build a frame house for a Potawatomi headman. In 1760 the post interpreter, Pierre Deneau dit Detailly, submitted a reimbursement request to receive a thousand livres for building a house for a medal chief. By 1750 there was also a stone jail that measured eight by ten feet, but scattered among the frame houses were older residential buildings that "were constructed of upright timbers, chinked with moss and covered over with bark, both on the sides and roofs. The roofs were apparently weighted with poles laid across the bark."[76] St. Joseph's most prominent house was the commandant's quarters; it alone was surrounded by a stockade. Both Miami and Potawatomi villages were immediately adjacent to the post, and the Jesuit priest lived in the midst of these villages, rather than among the French. From 1720 to 1760, there were French troops stationed at the post, but there were no barracks to house them. Instead, the French lived in the community, many in the homes of traders, while others resided in Indian households.

At many of the posts distinctive housing arrangements signaled the evolution of agriculturally oriented communities. Farms consisted of long, narrow fields that emerged along the riverway, and the traders built their homes in the architectural landscape of an earlier time period. Trader's houses were bark-covered cabins with high peaked roofs, while nearby distinct Indian villages were characterized by both indigenous conical housing and log cabins.

These fur trade communities evolved as social amalgamations of French and Native societies. Both populations resided in village worlds where people defined themselves by those to whom they were related. Individualism was subsumed by the indigenous values that shaped these large extended communities of kin. Large numbers of legal traders as well as coureurs de bois were woven into this cloth of social invisibility. Mixed-ancestry offspring were often raised by their Indian kin, and in the case of a father's disappearance or death, they lived with their mother's brother's family. By the time that the Americans arrived in the 1780s, the interrelationship of Indians and Frenchmen had gone on for nearly "130 years." Travelers recognized the integrative lifestyles of these communities: "Numbers of the inhabitants live as Savages . . . and many people are intermarried with them. . . . These people by a long acquaintance with their Indian neighbors have contracted a friendship and acquaintance which time will never be able to irradicate."[77]

Many of these fur posts became associated with a core of identifiable families, family lineages that sought to monopolize the trade.

Cultures of Exchange in a North Atlantic World

Those who became the most influential emerged from an evolving Catholic kin network at each of the posts. By the outbreak of the Seven Years' War, Catholic kin networks linked all the western Great Lakes posts. Indian women who were Catholic converts used conversion to create "fictive" kin networks under the umbrella of French Catholicism, networks that paralleled and supplemented those of indigenous society. Native women who were married to fur traders served as godmothers to each other's children, and by the mid-eighteenth century these "fictive" kin networks linked dispersed communities and traders throughout the Great Lakes.

How these kin networks functioned became apparent at Fort St. Joseph, an important link in the chain of small supply posts that were located on the St. Joseph River in southwest Michigan. Marie Madeleine Réaume, the daughter of an Ilini woman, Simphorose Ouaouagoukoue, was married "in the eyes of the church" to Augustin L'archeveque. He was a licensed trader in Illinois Country but had relocated to Fort St. Joseph. During the course of their sixteen-year marriage Marie Madeleine gave birth to six children and shortly after the birth of her sixth child she became a widow. It was then that her name began to appear on the reimbursement authorizations signed by the St. Joseph commandant. She supplied goods, especially livestock and grain, to French troops, and she was also reimbursed for large quantities of food required for feasts, such as oxen and pigs. It is apparent from a later census taken in 1679 that her lands included "ten houses, good lands, orchards, gardens, cattle, furniture [and] utensils." Her household produced a marketable surplus and she also manufactured specific fur-trade products, such as bark canoes. After being widowed at age forty, Marie Madeleine remarried and integrated her second fur-trader husband into the community.

Another important trading site was the Long Portage or Carrying Place, a nine-mile strip of land between the Maumee and the Wabash rivers that provided the easiest and shortest river route between the St. Lawrence and the Mississippi river systems. This portage connected the Great Lakes with New Orleans and the Gulf of Mexico. It was traditionally controlled by the Miami and in particular by a Native woman, Taucumwah, who had married the French trader, Joseph Richardville, sometime in the late 1750s or early 1760s. They had four children, baptized by Father Pierre Gibault of Vincennes in 1773. The marriage of Taucumwah and Joseph lasted for about one decade, when she successfully divorced him in a rather nasty and complex public fracas. Richardville had once shared in the resources of the Long Portage, but following the divorce, control was returned to his wife and her brother, Pecan. Subsequently, Taucumwah passed control of the portage to her son, Peshewa or Jean Baptiste Richardville. Born sometime in the 1770s and baptized in 1773, Richardville achieved significant status among the Miami in 1789, when he was left in charge of Kekionga by Pecan. It was the most significant of the Miami villages and remained so until the Treaty of Greenville, in 1795.

Taucumwah and Marie Madeleine were prominent examples of linkages in the southern Great Lakes that evolved at many of the posts. For instance, at Michilimackinac, the Langlade, Bourassa, and Chaboyer women were frequent godmothers to each other's children and grandchildren, as well as the mixed-ancestry children of visiting fur traders. Conversion did not lead to ostracism but allowed Indian women to incorporate their French husbands into communities structured by custom and tradition.[78] Indian wives were important to traders because they facilitated and negotiated the exchange process. Women were the interpreters and intermediaries, and traders often solicited Indian women to teach them the languages of more distant tribes. Bilingualism and multilingualism were passed down from mothers to daughters.[79] It was readily apparent that trading expeditions were doomed to failure if they did not have a female Indian interpreter. For instance, Samuel Hearne decided that his two failed searches for the Coppermine stemmed from his lack of a female translator. Hearne finally succeeded in his third attempt when he brought seven women as interpreters.[80]

French surnames span baptismal registers in the seventeenth and eighteenth centuries and were used by children, grandchildren, and godchildren. Catholicism acquired increased centrality in the fur trade because of its social ramifications. These fur-trade households became so entangled through networks of intermarriage and god parenting that people were difficult to identify as distinct individuals. Social boundaries remained ill-defined, and the children of Native American mothers and fur-trade fathers identified themselves as French or Canadian, but many chose to remain Indian. The lives of people who were involved in the trade were not always ordered by either patrilineal or matrilineal lines of descent. Rather, the social world that grew up around the fur trade left a diversity and multiplicity of names and identities that can never be fully untangled. It led to anonymity but simultaneously determined one's social position in this face-to-face world.

Marriage served as a planned extension of familial kin networks, reinforced by the fictive kinship of Catholic ritual. As children married and frequently moved, mobility became the warp on which the fabric of fur-trade communities was woven. Marie Madeleine L'archeveque's three daughters all married fur traders and moved to other posts: one lived at Cahokia and another at Green Bay. When her son reached adulthood, he remained among the Potawatomi and was considered by the incoming British to be Indian. These families continued to intermarry among Indians. For instance, at Green Bay Domitille Grignon's eight sons all married into the trade: Pierre married a Menomini woman, Charles married the daughter of an Ojibwa band leader, and Augustin married a relative of the Menomini chief Oshkosh. At Michilimackinac, the LaFramboise family relied on intermarriage to establish links with the Potawatomi, Ottawa, and the Dakota.[81] The Chouteau family of St. Louis arranged the marriage of their sons to Osage Indian women, providing that extended family with an advantage in the exchange process. The major residents of the fur-trade posts were related through their Indian or mixed-ancestry wives, and most of the residents were brothers, cousins, fathers, and sons surrounded by their relatives. Kinship distinctly defined these communities that stretched across the Great Lakes and westward into the Great Plains.

It was not unusual for Indian women to use their labor and sexuality to "ensure good relations with outsiders."[82] Pocahontas was the earliest and best known example, but there are other well-known cultural mediators, such as Madame Montour, who spoke on behalf of the Iroquois, and Nancy Ward, who voiced Cherokee grievances and drew attention to increased aggression by the colonial settlers.[83] In the Great Lakes region, women further expanded those roles and promoted intertribal and interracial relationships that were at the center of much of the exchange process. These women created a social system that lasted into the mid-nineteenth century. Their ability to adapt, to mediate disparate cultural and economic systems, was the most prevailing quality about these enigmatic women, given the restricted roles accorded western European women. Unfortunately, the world that these women created turned out to be a dead end in English America, not an avenue to a new social order.[84] The positions that were held by these cultural mediators indicated that a new social order could take place in the United States, but these cooperative relationships did not last, and they failed to create a more egalitarian class system. By the mid-nineteenth century, the racialization of Indians created distinct boundaries between Euro-Americans and Indians.

One can only hypothesize about the demographics of the population following six and seven generations of cohabitation and intermarriage. In 1680 intendant Jacques Duchesneau believed that there were eight hundred traders in the west, and even though traders may have temporarily lived with Native women, most had offspring. Certainly, the phenotypic stereotype of dark-skinned Indians was seriously challenged in the western Great Lakes.[85] This led one Quebec biologist, Jacques Rousseas, to claim that in 1970 40 percent of French Canadians would see at least one Indian when they traced their family trees.[86] Until recently, however, Indian ancestry was often obscured, and the women who helped integrate these disparate societies were barely remembered.

Notes

1. Peter E. Pope, *Fish into Wine: The Newfoundland Plantation in the Seventeenth Century* (Chapel Hill: University of North Carolina Press, 2004), 13.

2. Harold A. Innis, *The Fur Trade in Canada: An Introduction to Canadian Economic History*, rev. ed. (1930; repr., Toronto: University of Toronto Press, 1956), iv.

3. Pope, *Fish into Wine*, 13–14.

4. T. Bentley Duncan, *Atlantic Islands: Madeira, the Azores and the Cape Verdes in Seventeenth-Century Commerce and Navigation* (Chicago: University of Chicago Press, 1972), 1.

5. Pope, *Fish into Wine*, 12–13.

6. Pope, *Fish into Wine*, 20.

7. Pope, *Fish into Wine*, 18.

8. Pope, *Fish into Wine*, 12–13.

9. Pope, *Fish into Wine*, 19.

10. Innis, *Fur Trade*, 14.

11. Pope, *Fish into Wine*, 1–2.

12. Charles Woolsey Cole, *French Mercantilism, 1683–1700* (New York: Columbia University Press), 79.

13. Cole, *French Mercantilism*, 79.

14. Cole, *French Mercantilism*, 79–80.

15. Cole, *French Mercantilism*, 80.

16. "The vision of an archipelagic America was laid to rest only in the nineteenth century, though explorers never gave up on the idea of a polar passage, which was in fact, achieved in the early twentieth century." John Gillis, *Islands of the Mind: How the Human Imagination Created the Atlantic World* (New York: Palgrave Macmillan, 2004), 85.

17. Michael Sonenscher, *Hatters of Eighteenth-Century France* (Berkeley: University of California Press, 1987), 37–38.

18. Innis, *Fur Trade*, 77.

19. E. E. Rich, *The Fur Trade and the Northwest to 1857* (Toronto: McVlelland and Stewart, 1967), 7–8.

20. Innis, *Fur Trade*, 75–77.

21. Sonenscher, *Hatters of France*, 37–38.

22. One of the most glaring failures of colonization by wealthy individuals was Roanoke, which sought to establish an English base for a piracy that

targeted Spanish ships in the Caribbean. The colony repeatedly failed, and its English occupants were abandoned by the founders, their fate unknown. Karen Ordahl Kupperman, *Roanoke: The Abandoned Colony* (Maryland: Rowman and Littlefield, 1984).

23. Innis, *Fur Trade*, 42.

24. Thomas Elliott Norton, *Fur Trade in Colonial New York: 1686–1776* (Madison: University of Wisconsin Press, 1974), 10.

25. Gilles Havard, *The Great Peace of Montreal of 1701: French-Native Diplomacy in the Seventeenth Century*, trans. Phyllis Aronoff and Howard Scott (Montreal: McGill-Queen's University Press, 2001).

26. Innis, *Fur Trade*, 45.

27. Norton, *Fur Trade in Colonial New York*, 11.

28. Richard White, *Middle Ground: Indians, Empires, and Republics in the Great Lakes Region, 1650–1815* (New York: Cambridge University Press, 1991), 10–23.

29. Reuben Gold Thwaites, ed., *The Jesuit Relations and Allied Documents: Travels and Explorations of the Jesuit Missionaries in New France, 1610–1791* (Cleveland OH: Burrows Brothers, 1899), 44:247, 251.

30. Pierre Esprit Radisson, born circa 1636 in southern France, immigrated to New France in 1651. For a detailed biographical sketch of his life, see Martin Fournier, *Pierre-Esprit Radisson, Merchant Adventurer, 1636–1710* (Sillery, Quebec: Septentrion, 2002).

31. Bruce M. White, "The Fear of Pillaging: Economic Folktales of the Great Lakes Fur Trade," in *The Fur Trade Revisited: Selected Papers of the Sixth North American Fur Trade Conference, Mackinac Island, Michigan, 1991*, ed. Jennifer S. H. Brown, W. J. Eccles, and Donald P. Heldman (East Lansing: Michigan State University Press, 1994), 199–216.

32. "Marriage 'after the custom of the country' was an indigenous marriage rite which was evoked to meet the needs of fur-trade society. . . . Although denounced by the Jesuit priests as being immoral, the traders had taken their Indian wives according to traditional native marriage rites and distinct family units had developed." See Sylvia Van Kirk, *Many Tender Ties: Women in Fur Trade Society, 1670–1870* (1980; repr., Norman: University of Oklahoma Press, 1990), 28.

33. Louise Dechêne, *Habitants and Merchants in Seventeenth Century Montreal* (Montreal: McGill-Queen's University Press, 1992), 91.

34. Jacqueline Peterson, "The People in Between: Indian-White Marriage and the Genesis of a Métis Society and Culture in the Great Lakes Region, 1680–1830" (PhD diss., University of Illinois at Chicago Circle, 1981), 26;

W. J. Eccles, *France in America* (New York: Harper Torchbooks, 1972), 76; Jacques Henripen, *La Population Canadienne Au Debut du XVIIIe Siecle, Nuptialite, Fecundite, Moralite infantile*, Travaus et Documents, Cahier no. 22 (Paris: Presses Universitiaires de France, 1954), 19.

35. Eccles, *France in America*, 90.

36. Dechêne, *Habitants and Merchants*, 93–95.

37. Dechêne, *Habitants and Merchants*, 92.

38. Rich, *The Fur Trade*, 78–79.

39. Innis, *Fur Trade*, 57.

40. Robert La Salle was supported by New France's governor, Frontenac, who was financially committed to developing a water route for the trade with the western Great Lakes. Unfortunately, La Salle's death stemmed that southward expansion along the Mississippi toward the warm-water ports.

41. Arthur T. Adams, *The Exploration of Pierre Esprit Radisson* (Minneapolis: Ross and Haines, 1961), xxv.

42. Pope, *Fish into Wine*, 16.

43. Arthur J. Ray and Donald B. Freeman, *"Give Us Good Measure": An Economic Analysis of Relations between the Indians and the Hudson's Bay Company before 1763* (Toronto: University of Toronto Press, 1978), 24.

44. Innis, *Fur Trade*, 47.

45. Dechene, *Habitants and Merchants*, 93–95.

46. Thwaites, *Jesuit Relations*, 54:197.

47. Arthur J. Ray, "Indians as Consumers in the Eighteenth Century," in *Old Trails and New Directions: Papers of the Third North American Fur Trade Conference*, ed. Carol M. Judd and Arthur J. Ray (Toronto: University of Toronto Press, 1980), 256.

48. Ray, "Indians as Consumers," 257.

49. Ray, "Indians as Consumers," 257.

50. Innis, *Fur Trade*, 78.

51. Innis, *Fur Trade*, 78.

52. Innis, *Fur Trade*, 79.

53. Innis, *Fur Trade*, 86.

54. Ray, "Indians as Consumers," 258.

55. Ray, "Indians as Consumers," 262.

56. Ray, "Indians as Consumers," 265.

57. Ray, "Indians as Consumers," 258.

58. Ray, "Indians as Consumers," 262; initially from K. G. Davies, ed., *Letters from Hudson Bay, 1703–40* (London: Hudson's Bay Record Society, 1965), 99–100; HBCA A 6/4, 95–96, Correspondence Outward, 19 May 1725.

59. Ray, "Indians as Consumers," 267; HBCA A 6/6, 66, Correspondence Outward, 1 May 1740.

60. Joseph Francis Lafiteau, *Customs of the American Indians Compared with the Customs of Primitive Times*, ed. and trans. William N. Fenton and Elizabeth L. Moore (1724; repr., Toronto: Champlain Society, 1974, 1977), 2:30–31; Carolyn Gilman, *Where Two Worlds Meet: The Great Lakes Fur Trade* (St. Paul: Minnesota Historical Society, 1982), 40.

61. Ann M. Carlos and Frank D. Lewis, "Trade, Consumption, and the Native Economy: Lessons from York Factory, Hudson Bay," *The Journal of Economic History* 61, no. 4 (December 2001): 1037–63.

62. Daneil K. Richter, *The Ordeal of the Longhouse* (Chapel Hill: University of North Carolina Press, 1992), 247–54; Carlos and Lewis, "Trade, Consumption," 1049–50.

63. James Bradley, *Evolution of the Onondaga Iroquois* (Syracuse NY: Syracuse University Press, 1987). See also Wayne Lenig, "Patterns of Material Culture during the Early Years of New Netherland Trade," *Northeast Anthropology* 53 (Fall 1997): 61–84; Gilbert W. Hagerty, *Wampum, War and Trade Goods West of the Hudson* (New York: Heart of the Lake Publishing, 1985).

64. The Quetico-Superior Underwater Research Project has relied on underwater archaeology to investigate the metal trade objects lost in early fur trade canoe accidents beneath the waters of the old Grand Portage. Much of the region of interconnected lakes and streams is now part of the Superior National Forest in the United States and in Quetico Provincial Park in Canada. The report of their findings reveals an abundant variety of goods, most better preserved than those retrieved from dryland sites. Robert C. Wheeler, Walter A. Kenyo, Alan R. Woolworth, and Douglas A. Birk, *Voices from the Rapids: An Underwater Search for Fur Trade Artifacts, 1960–73* (Minneapolis: Minnesota Historical Society, 1975).

65. Marcel Mauss in *The Gift* contends that socially rather than individually defined values defined the exchange process. From the Mauss perspective these values are defined by kin obligations and reciprocal relations. In what has come to be known as the substantivist approach Marshall Sahlins has further refined this approach by seeing indigenous economies as "a category of culture rather than behavior." Marcel Mauss, *The Gift* (New York: Norton, 1967); Marshall Sahlins, *Stone Age Economics* (Chicago: Aldine-Atherton, 1972), xii.

66. White, *Middle Ground*, 95.

67. Rudolph F. Kurz, "Journal of Rudolph Friederich Kurz: An Account of His Experiences among the Fur Traders and American Indians on the Mississippi and Missouri Rivers during the Years of 1842–1852," ed. J. N. B. Hewitt, Bureau of American Ethnology Bulletin 115 (Washington DC, 1937), 155.

68. Sylvia Van Kirk uses the term "marriage 'after the custom of the country'" as an indigenous marriage rite that evolved to meet the needs of fur-trade society. Jacqueline Peterson indicates that *marriage a la facon du pays* became institutionalized in the Great Lakes and was neither casual nor promiscuous. Van Kirk, *Many Tender Ties*, 28; Jacqueline Peterson, "Prelude to Red River: A Social Portrait of the Great Lakes Metis," *Ethnohistory* 25 (1978): 48, 41–67. See also Jennifer S. H. Brown, *Strangers in Blood: Fur Trade Company Families in Indian Country* (Norman: University of Oklahoma Press, 1980), 62–63.

69. Etienne Carheil to de Callieres, 30 August 1702, in Thwaites, *Jesuit Relations*, 65:239.

70. Natalia Maree Belting, *Kaskaskia under the French Regime* (Urbana: University of Illinois Press, 1948), 12–15.

71. Belting, *Kaskaskia*, 12, 39–40.

72. Note that all the posts were not officially closed, but most closed because trading was not permitted.

73. Clarence M. Burton, *Cadillac's Village or Detroit under Cadillac* (Detroit, 1896), 15.

74. Van Kirk, *Many Tender Ties*, 110–11.

75. James M. McClurken, "Augustin Hamlin, Jr.: Ottawa Identity and the Politics of Persistence," in *Being and Becoming Indian*, ed. James A. Clifton (Chicago: Dorsey Press, 1989), 85.

76. Jane F. Babson, "The Architecture of Early Illinois Forts," *Journal of the Illinois State Historical Society* 51 (Spring 1968): 17–20.

77. Beverley W. Bond, Jr., "Two Westward Journeys of John Filson, 1785," *The Mississippi Valley Historical Review* 9 (March 1923): 328.

78. Sylvia Van Kirk, "Towards a Feminist Perspective in Native History," in *Papers of the Eighteenth Algonquian Conference*, ed. Jose Mailhot (Ottawa: Carleton University, 1987), 386.

79. Devon H. Mihesuah, "Commonality of Difference: American Indian Women in History," *American Indian Quarterly* 20 (1996): 19.

80. Brown, *Strangers in Blood*, 65.

81. Peterson, *The People In-Between*, 159–60.

82. Michael Lansing, "Plains Indian Women and Interracial Marriage in the Upper Missouri Trade, 1804–1868," *The Western Historical Quarterly* 31, no. 4 (Winter 2000): 413–33.

83. Camilla Townsend, *Pocahontas and the Powhatan Dilemma* (New York: Hill and Wang, 2004); Clara Sue Kidwell, "Indian Women as Cultural Mediators," *Ethnohistory* 39, no. 2 (Spring 1992): 103; John Parmenter, "Isabel Montour: Cultural Broker on the Frontiers of New York and Pennsylvania," in

The Human Tradition in Colonial America, ed. Ian K. Steele and Nancy L. Rhoden (Wilmington DE: SR Books, 1999), 142; Nancy Hagedorn, "A Friend to Go Between Them: The Interpreter as Cultural Broker during Anglo-Uroquois Councils, 1740–70," *Ethnohistory* 35, no. 1 (Winter, 1988): 64; James H. Merrell, "The Cast of His Countenance: Reading Andrew Montour," in *Through a Glass Darkly*, ed. Ronald Hoffman, Mechal Sobel, and Fredrika J. Teute (Chapel Hill: University of North Carolina Press, 1997), 25.

84. James Merrell, *Into the American Woods: Negotiators on the Pennsylvania Frontier* (New York: W. W. Norton Press, 1999), 69.

85. Helen Hornbeck Tanner, "The Career of Joseph La France, Coureur de Bois in the Upper Great Lakes," in Brown, Eccles, and Heldman, *Fur Trade Revisited*, 182.

86. Jacqueline Peterson and Jennifer S. H. Brown, eds., *The New Peoples: Being and Becoming Métis in North America* (Manitoba: University of Manitoba Press), 19.

Rethinking the Fur Trade

PART 2

Indian Voices

Introduction

The fur trade was a complex process that has been oversimplified and frequently depicted as a simple extractive resource. The fur trade was a process of human interaction that was symbolic of a broad range of contacts between Indians and Europeans. It led to change across time and space. Both historians and anthropologists discuss the competitive ways in which Indians not only engaged in the trade but also profited from it. Many of these revised interpretations have been gleaned from the reassessment of traditional sources. For instance, historians now are more attentive to hearing an indigenous voice in such traditional European documents as *The Jesuit Relations.* This type of primary source evidence opens this section and, read carefully, describes how the fur trade initiated cultural change without being linked to demise. For example, these documents demonstrate that Indians manipulated the circumstances that shaped exchange and obtained better goods at more reasonable prices. Father LeClercq watched as Indians hid their best furs and waited for specific traders, rather than rush to trade for less desirable goods.[1]

The exchange process was divided into geographically distinct regions, and this book focuses on three of those regions. The first region was located along the coastal Atlantic region, east of the Appalachian Mountains and north of Virginia colony. This trade was initially dominated by the Huron; they were subsequently displaced by the Iroquois. The second region was located north of the Canadian Shield; it was the most lucrative region and encompassed the subarctic and arctic trades. This trade was the province of the

Hudson's Bay Company and was a carrying trade that connected England to Bay Company posts along the Hudson Bay shoreline. The Great Lakes basin was a third region; it functioned as a type of circular hub, an interconnective network of riverways that connected the east and west coasts of the continent, a primary pathway that transported beaver from the Great Lakes south to the Gulf of Mexico or north along the St. Lawrence River to the Atlantic coast. The Great Lakes dominated the trade for most of the seventeenth and eighteenth centuries. Another region, west of the Mississippi, is referred to as the Plains region. It was best known for its buffalo robes, but this region, like the southern Atlantic coastal region, forms only a tangential part of this narrative.

In this section "Indian Voices," we learn that Indians had great disdain for the inferiority of the European landscape. Father Allouez describes how Indians considered France, surrounded by salt water, to be repulsive to fur-bearing animals. Consequently, the French were forced to brave the hazards of trans-Atlantic voyages to acquire beaver, furs that were plentiful on Indian lands.[2] Indians assigned Europeans a supporting role, their most important function was to respond to "the initiatives of the Anishinabeg. They dealt with the French as equals or superiors."[3] Bruce Bourque and Ruth White contend that Indians were the initiators of the Atlantic coastal trade and that it was Indians who first evolved as independent traders.[4] They became the middlemen of the trade, collecting furs from Atlantic coastal villages in barques that they had borrowed, stolen, or copied from European fisherman.

When Europeans established forts or trading posts along the rivers that spanned the interior of the continent, it was indigenous social processes that continued to structure the exchange of trade goods for furs. Kinship structured the exchange process; kin groupings of Native communities determined one's trading partners. One common way that traders established themselves as kin was through intermarriage, when the wife's kin network became the trader's customers. For many traders, marriage to Native women took place in "the manner of the country" and these alliances and friendships were initially confirmed through generosity and gift giving.[5] Exchange was framed by indigenous social interactions rather than being driven by the profit motive.[6]

Nor were Indians overwhelmed by the desire to obtain trade goods. Most Indian communities practiced two modes of production, hunting for furs while simultaneously pursuing agricultural subsistence strategies. As Donald Bibeau so clearly points out, tribal dependency failed to follow contact, and from an indigenous perspective there was neither immediate nor profound cultural change among Indians. Trade goods were not a "trigger factor" that introduced decline in traditional lifeways nor did trade goods elicit the "electrifying touch" of the white man's goods.[7] Rather, Bibeau suggests that the fur trade be understood by first placing it within an indigenous perspective and then situating it within an intercontinental perspective. The fur trade was "only one aspect of an eighteenth- and nineteenth-century colonialism, and it was only one geographic area of a global phenomena. To place it in terms of North America only is mere provincialism."[8] The goal of this book is to place first the telling of the tale within indigenous hands and then to situate it within the global dynamic of encroaching colonialisms.

Notes

1. Father Chrestien LeClercq, *New Relation of Gaspesia: With the Customs and Religion of the Gaspesian Indians*, trans. and ed. William F. Ganong (Toronto: The Champlain Society, 1910), 276–80, 227–28.

2. Reuben Gold Thwaites, ed., *The Jesuit Relations and Allied Documents: Travels and Explorations of the Jesuit Missionaries in New France, 1610–1791* (Cleveland OH: Burrows Brothers, 1899), 54:197.

3. D. Peter MacLeod, "The Anishinabeg Point of View: The History of the Great Lakes Region to 1800 in Nineteenth-Century Mississauga, Odawa, and Ojibwa Historiography," *Canadian Historical Review* 73, no. 2 (June 1992): 204.

4. Bruce Bourque and Ruth Whitehead, "Tarrentines and the Introduction of European Trade Goods in the Gulf of Main," *Ethnohistory* 32, no. 4 (Autumn 1985): 327–41.

5. "Marriage 'after the custom of the country' was an indigenous marriage rite which evolved to meet the demands of fur trade society. . . . Although denounced by the Jesuit priests as immoral, the traders had taken their Indian wives according to traditional native marriage rites and distinct family units had developed." Sylvia Van Kirk, *Many Tender Ties: Women in Fur-Trade Society, 1670–1870* (1980; repr., Norman: Oklahoma University Press, 1983), 28.

6. Marcel Mauss, *The Gift: The Form and Reasons for Exchange in Archaic Societies* (New York: Norton, 1990), 8–46.

7. Donald F. Bibeau, "Fur Trade Literature from a Tribal Point of View: A Critique," in *Rendezvous: Selected Papers of the Fourth North American Fur Trade Conference, 1981*, ed. Thomas C. Buckley (St. Paul: Minnesota Historical Society, 1984), 86.

8. Bibeau, "Fur Trade Literature," 90.

2. Of the Mission of Saint François Xavier on the "Bay of Stinkards," or Rather "Of Stinking Waters"

FATHER ALLOUEZ

Letter from Father Allouez, who has had charge of this Mission, to the Reverend Father Superior. The Jesuit Relations, June 1670.

On the third of November, we departed from the Sault, I and two others. Two Canoe-loads of Prouteouatamis wished to conduct me to their Country; not that they wished to receive instruction there, having no disposition for the Faith, but that I might curb some young Frenchmen, who, being among them for the purpose of trading, were threatening and maltreating them.

We arrived on the first day at the entrance to the Lake of the Hurons, where we slept under the shelter of the Islands. The length of the journey and the difficulty of the way, because of the lateness of the Season, led us to have recourse to saint Francis Xavier, Patron of our Mission; this obliged me to celebrate holy Mass, and my two Companions to receive Communion on the day of the Feast, in his honor, and still further to invoke him, twice every day, by reciting his Orison.

On the fourth, toward noon, we doubled the Cape which forms the detour, and is the beginning of the Strait or the Gulf of Lake Huron, which is well known, and of the Lake of the Ilinois,—which up to the present time is unknown, and is much smaller than Lake Huron. Toward evening the contrary wind, which was about to cast our Canoe upon the shoals of Rocks, obliged us rather to finish our journey.

On the 5th, upon waking, we found ourselves covered with snow, and the surface of the canoe coated with ice. This little beginning of crosses which Our Lord was pleased to allot us invited us to offer ourselves for greater ones. We were compelled to embark with all the baggage and provisions, with great difficulty, our bare feet in the water, in order to keep the Canoe afloat, which otherwise would have broken. After leaving a great number of Islands to the Northward, we slept on a little Island, where we were detained six days by the bad weather. The snow and frosts threatening us with ice, my Companions had recourse to saint Anne, to whom we entrusted our journey, praying her, together with St. Francis Xavier, to take us under her protection.

On the eleventh we embarked, notwithstanding the contrary wind, and crossed to another Island, and thence to the mainland, where we found two Frenchmen with several Savages. From them we learned of the great dangers to which we were about to expose ourselves, by reason of the storms that are frequent on this Lake, and the ice which would soon be afloat. But all that was not sufficient to shake the confidence that we had reposed in our Protectors. After invoking them, we launched the Canoe, and then doubled successfully enough the Cape which makes a detour to the West, having left in our rear a large Island named Michilimakinak, celebrated among the Savages. Their legends about this Island are pleasing.

They say that it is the native Country of one of their Gods, named Michabous—that is to say, "the great Hare," Ouisaketchak, who is the one that created the Earth; and that it was in these Islands that he invented nets for catching fish, after he had attentively considered the spider while she was working at her web in order to catch flies in it. They believe that Lake Superior is a Pond made by Beavers, and that its Dam was double,—the first being at the place called by us the Sault, and the second five leagues below. In ascending the River, they say, this same God found that second Dam first and broke it down completely; and that is why there is no waterfall or whirlpools in that rapid. As to the first Dam, being in haste, he only walked on it to tread it down; and, for that reason, there still remain great falls and whirlpools there.

This God, they add, while chasing a Beaver in Lake Superior, crossed with a single stride a bay of eight leagues in width. In view of so mighty an enemy, the Beavers changed their location, and withdrew to another Lake, Alimibegoung [Nipigon],—whence they afterward, by means of the Rivers flowing from it, arrived at the North Sea, with the intention of crossing over to France; but, finding the water bitter, they lose heart, and spread throughout the Rivers and Lakes of this entire Country. And that is the reason why there are no Beavers in France, and the French come to get them here. The people believe that it is this God who is the master of our lives, and that he grants life only to those to whom he has appeared in sleep. This is a part of the legends with which the Savages very often entertain us.

3. On the Hunting of the Gaspesians

FATHER CHRESTIEN LECLERCQ

(Recollect Missionary to the Gaspé Region, 1676–1688)

Our Indians have, apart from war, no occupation more honourable than hunting; and they acquire no less glory and reputation from the number of Moose and of Beavers which they capture, and which they kill in the chase, than from the number of scalps which they take from the heads of their enemies.

The hunting of the Elk, or Moose,[1] is followed at all times of the year. That in winter is the easiest and most like to succeed, especially when the snow is deep, solid, hard and frozen, for because of this the Indians, having snowshoes on their feet, easily approach the elk, which sinks in and cannot escape the pursuit of the hunters. It is different in summer, because these animals run with such speed that it is almost impossible to overtake them, sometimes not even after ten days of pursuit.

The Moose is tall as a horse; it has grayish hair and a head almost like that of a mule. It carries its antlers branched like the stag, except that they are broad as a board, and two to three feet long; they are provided on both sides with prongs, which fall in autumn and are renewed in the spring with the addition of as many new branches as there are years.[2] It browses on grass, and grazes in the meadows along the margins of the rivers, and in the forests during the summer. In winter it eats the tenderest tips of the branches of trees. Its hoof is cloven, and the left hind foot is a remedy against epilepsy; but it must be secured, say the Indians, at a time when the animal is itself ill from this malady, of which it cures itself by placing this left foot to its ear.[3] In its heart is found a little bone which the Gaspesians call *Oagando hi guidanne*,[4] it is a sovereign remedy for easing the confinements of women, and for relieving the spasms and the sufferings of childbirth, when taken in broth after having been first reduced to powder. This animal weeps like stags and hinds when it is taken and cannot escape death; the tears fall from its eyes as large as peas. It does not fail, however, to defend itself the very best that it can; and an approach to it is somewhat dangerous, because, thanks to a road which it has the cunning to beat out with its feet, it charges at times with such fury upon the hunters and their dogs, that it buries both the one and the other in the snow, with a result that a number of Indians are often crippled by them, while their dogs are killed on the spot. The hunters know the places where the moose have their retreat from certain gnawed or broken tips of branches, which they call Pactagane,[5] that is to say, the depredations of the Elk. They chew this wood, and they recognise from the taste of the branches the time since these animals have passed this place. They capture them sometimes from ambush, and also by use of certain nooses made of large leather thongs set in the usual trail of this animal.

The most ingenious method which our Gaspesians have for taking the Moose is this. The hunters, knowing the place on the river where it is accustomed to resort when in heat, embark at night in a canoe, and, approaching the meadow where it has its retreat, browses, and usually sleeps, one of them imitates the cry of the female, while the other at the same time takes up water in a bark dish, and lets it fall drop by drop, as if it were the female relieving herself of her water. The male approaches, and the Indians who are on the watch kill him with shots from their guns. The same cunning and dexterity they also use with respect to the female, by counterfeiting the cry of the male.[6]

The hunting of the Beaver is as easy in summer as it is laborious in winter, although it is equally pleasing and entertaining in both of these two seasons, because of the pleasure it is to see this animal's natural industry, which transcends the imagination of those who have never seen the surprising evidences thereof. Consequently the

Indians say that the Beavers have sense, and form a separate nation; and they say they would cease to make war upon these animals if these would speak, howsoever little, in order that they might learn whether the Beavers are among their friends or their enemies.

The Beaver is of the bigness of a water-spaniel. Its fur is chestnut, black, and rarely white, but always very soft and suitable for the making of hats. It is the great trade of New France. The Gaspesians say that the Beaver is the beloved of the French and of the other Europeans, who seek it greedily; and I have been unable to keep from laughing on overhearing an Indian, who said to me in banter, *Tahoé messet kogoüar pajo ne daoüi dogoüil mkobit.*[7] "In truth, my brother, the Beaver does everything to perfection. He makes for us kettles, axes, swords, knives, and gives us drink and food without the trouble of cultivating the ground."

This animal has short feet; those in front are formed like paws, and those behind like fins, very much as in the Seals. It walks very slowly. For a time it was considered amphibious, half-flesh half-fish, because it has a tail of appearance very like a sole, furnished with scales which are not removable; but at present it is eaten like fish in Lent, whether it be so in fact, or whether it is in order to obviate abuses which had crept in, some reducing to tail more than half of the body of that animal. It has a large but short head; its jaws are armed with four large cutting teeth, to wit, two above and two below, which are suitable for polishing gold or silver, since they are both hard and soft at one and the same time. With these four teeth the Beaver cuts little poles for building its house, as well as trees as large as the thigh; these it can fell exactly in the very spot where it foresees that they will be most useful and most needed. It cuts these trees into pieces of different lengths, according to the use it wishes to make of them. It rolls them on the ground or pushes them through the water with its forepaws, in order to build its house and to construct a dam which checks the current of a stream and forms a considerable pond, on the shore of which it usually dwells. There is always a master Beaver, which oversees this work, and which even

On the Hunting of the Gaspesians

beats those that do their duty badly. They all cart earth upon their tails, marching upon their hind feet and carrying in their fore-paws the wood which they need to accomplish their work. They mix the earth with the wood, and make a kind of masonry with their tails, very much as do the masons with their trowels. They build causeways and dams of a breadth of two or three feet, a height of twelve or fifteen feet, and a length of twenty or thirty; these are so inconvenient and difficult to break that this is in fact the hardest task in the hunting of the Beaver, which, by means of these dams, makes from a little stream a pond so considerable that they flood very often a large extent of country. They even obstruct the rivers so much that it is often necessary to get into the water in order to lift the canoes over the dams, as has happened several times to myself in going from Nipisiguit to the River of Sainte-Croix,[8] and in other places in Gaspesia.

The Beaver's house is of some seven to eight feet in height, so well built and cemented with earth and wood that neither the rain nor the wind can enter. It is divided into three stories, and in these the large, the mid-sized, and the small beavers live separately and sleep upon straw. And the following circumstance is also worthy of remark, that when the number of these animals, which multiply rapidly, comes to increase, the older yield the house to the younger, which never fail to aid the others in building a house. It is as if these animals wished to give a natural lesson to both fathers and children mutually to aid one another.

The Beaver does not feed in the water, as some have imagined. It takes its food on land, eating certain barks of trees, which it cuts into fragments and transports to its house for use as provision during the winter. Its flesh is delicate, and very much like that of mutton. The kidneys[9] are sought by apothecaries, and are used with effect in easing women in childbirth, and in mitigating hysterics.

Whenever the Beaver is hunted, whether this be in winter or in summer, it is always needful to break and tear down the house, all the approaches to which our Indians note exactly, in order, with greater assurance of success, to besiege and attack this animal which is entrenched in his little fort.

In Spring and Summer they are taken in traps; when one of these is sprung a large piece of wood falls across their backs and kills them. But there is nothing so interesting as the hunting in the winter, which is, nevertheless, very wearisome and laborious. For the following is necessary; one must break the ice in more than forty or fifty places: must cut the dams: must shatter the houses: and must cause the waters to run off, in order to see and more easily discover the Beavers. These animals make sport of the hunter, scorn him, and very often escape his pursuit by slipping from their pond through a secret outlet, which they have the instinct to leave in their dam in communication with another neighbouring pond.[10]

Notes by William F. Ganong

1. *L'élan ou orignac* in the original. The former word is the French name for the European elk which our moose so closely resembles, while the latter, which our author sometimes writes in his book *origniac*, is the Canadian-French name, adopted, as Lescarbot tells us, from the Basque word for deer.

The hunting of the moose in the snow was so important a feature of the winter life of the Indians that it receives mention from practically all of our early writers (Lescarbot, *Histoire*, 804; Champlain, *Voyages*, Laverdière's edition, 191; Denys, *Description*, 2:425; Gyles, *Memoirs*, 19; *Jesuit Relations*, Thwaites' edition, 32:41, 45:61, 49:159). So dependent were they upon this hunting that in winters when snow was scant they were like to starve, while abundant snows meant a winter of good cheer.

2. In this paragraph our author promulgates several errors, which is surprising since he should have known the moose well; but then, as this chapter will show, our good missionary was no naturalist. The colour of the moose is not grayish, except on some under parts and in old age, but is brownish to nearly black; it is not the prongs of the antlers which fall, but the entire horn, and they fall in early winter rather than in autumn; and while the moose does, to a small extent, browse on grass in meadows, it is principally lily-roots and other succulent water plants which it seeks along the margins of streams and lakes.

3. This bit of folk-medicine is also mentioned by Denys (*Description*, 2:320), and doubtless represents a widely repeated belief of the time.

On the Hunting of the Gaspesians

4. The first part of this phrase, *Oagando*, is evidently simply the Micmac word for "bone," which Rand gives as *Wŏkundāoo* (*English-Micmac Dictionary*, 40). The remainder I have not been able to trace in Rand's works, but Father Pacifique suggests that the *hi* is no doubt a misprint for *ni*, making the two words equal to the modern Micmac *nigitami*, which means "for giving birth." This makes the phrase quite clear.

5. Evidently involving the roots of the Micmac *pakadoo*, "to bite" (Rand, *English-Micmac Dictionary*, 37) and the termination *okun*, meaning place of occurrence.

6. This account of the habits and the hunting of the moose accords with other information given in the *Jesuit Relations*, by Denys, and by others, while adding a few new points. The calling of the bull moose by the method here described is also related by Denys (*Description*, 2:424) and is still in extensive use. The killing of cow moose is now prohibited by law; but aside from this, I have never heard of the calling of cow moose by the method of imitating the call of the bull.

7. The modern Micmac equivalents of these words can be traced with considerable certainty through Rand's *English-Micmac Dictionary*, to which the following page numbers refer. *Tahoé* evidently involves the root of *Dā*, meaning "friend," to which the Indian "brother" is equivalent (117); *messet* evidently equals *'Msùt*, meaning "every" (101); *kogoüar pajo* evidently involves the roots of *kokwŏjeā'*, meaning "good," in the sense of "well" (122); *ne daoüi* is the same as *na tŭhŭ*, meaning "it is a fact" (105); *dogoüil* equals *ĕlookwā'*, meaning "to do," the *d* being probably a misprint for *el* (88); while *mkobit* is *kobet* meaning "a beaver," with the *m* perhaps indicating a skin (32). The entire phrase would then read, "My friend, every(thing) well it is a fact does the beaver."

Our author says that an Indian used this expression to him. Yet in the *Relation* of Father le Jeune of 1634 we read: "The Savages [i.e., the Montagnais] say that it [the beaver] is the animal well-beloved by the French, English, and Basques,—in a word by the Europeans. I heard my host say one day, jokingly, *Missi picoutau amiscou*, 'The Beaver does everything perfectly well, it makes kettles, hatchets, swords, knives, bread; and, in short, it makes everything'" (Thwaites' edition, 6:297). I have pointed out in the Introduction . . . the probable meaning of the resemblances between the work of our author and of Father le Jeune.

8. The river here meant, on the old portage route from Nepisiguit to Miramichi, must be Portage River . . . for both the Nepisiguit and the Northwest Miramichi are too large to be dammed by beavers, and Gordon Brook is a very small stream. It interests me to recall that I have myself, within four years past,

seen several fine new Beaver dams on this same Portage River, to which, as to others of their ancient haunts, the Beaver, long nearly extinct in this region, are now returning under the efficient protection they are receiving from the New Brunswick Government.

9. The castor glands are not the kidneys (*roignons*), but special glandular pouches situated in the groin.

10. Except for some exaggeration in certain points, e.g., the height of the dams, the carting of earth on the beavers' tails, and somewhat too confident assertions about their home habits, this account of the beaver is fairly accurate and in accord with other evidence; and the author shows much self-restraint in omitting the marvellous and entertaining tales then current about this animal. His account differs in this, as in many other particulars, from that given by Denys (*Description*, 2:284). Further material on this subject is in the notes to the *Champlain Society's Denys*, 367.

4. The Hunting of Moose, of Bears, of Beavers, of Lynxes, and other animals according to their seasons

Father Chrestien LeClercq

The hunting of the Beaver took place in summer with arrows, when they were taken in the woods, or else in the lakes or ponds, where the Indians placed themselves in canoes at a proper spot to watch until they came to the surface of the water to take air. But the commonest and most certain way was to break their dam, and make them lose the water. Then the Beavers found themselves without water, and did not know any more where to go; their houses showed everywhere. The Indians took them with blows of arrows and of spears; and, having a sufficiency, they left all the rest.

The Beavers, hearing no more noise, reassembled and set about repairing their dam. It is at this we have seen them working, and this makes it well believable that all I have said of their work is true. I do not consider that the work of making their dams entirely anew is so difficult as to repair them when broken in the middle.

In winter the hunting of them was done differently, the dams and the lakes being all frozen. Then the Indians have their Dogs, which are a kind of Mastiff, but more lightly built. They have the head of a Fox, but do not yelp, having only a howl which is not of great sound. As for their teeth, these are longer and sharper than those of Mastiffs. These Dogs serve for hunting the Moose, as I have related, in the spring, summer, and autumn, and in the winter when the snows will bear them. There is no hunter who has not from seven to eight of them. They cherish them greatly. If they have little ones which the mother cannot nourish, the women suckle them; when they are large they are given soup. When they are in condition to be serviceable, they are given nothing but the offal of the beasts which are killed. If eight days pass without any animals being killed, they are just so long without eating. As to the bones, they are not given any, for fear of damaging their teeth, not even those of the Beaver. If they should eat of that, it would keep the Indians from killing any, and the same if one were to burn them. For it is well to remark here that the Indians had many superstitions about such things, of which it has been much trouble to disabuse them. If they had roasted an Eel, they also believed that this would prevent them from catching one another time. They had in old times many beliefs of this kind, which they have no more at the present time, and of which we have disabused them.

Their wealth was in proportion to their Dogs, and as a testimony to a friend of the esteem in which they held him, they give him that Dog to eat which they valued the most; [this was] a mark of friendship. They say that it is very good eating. They still do this, and the French eat it when they are present at their feasts, of which they tell great stories. They like it better than mutton. But that, nevertheless, has never given me any desire to eat it.

When they took their Dogs to hunt the Moose in spring, summer, and autumn, the Dogs would run about for some time, some in one direction and some in another. The one which first met some track followed it without giving tongue. If he overtook the beast, he got in front of it, jumping for the nose. Then he howled. The Moose amused himself, and wished to kick the Dog in front. All the other Dogs which heard it came running up and attacked it from all sides. It defended itself with its feet in front; the Dogs tried to seize its nose or ears. In the meantime the Indian arrives, and tries without being seen to approach within shot below the wind. For if the animal perceives him or his smell, the Moose takes to flight and scorns the Dogs, unless the hunter gives it an arrow-shot. Being injured, it has difficulty in saving itself from the Dogs, which follow it incessantly, as does also the Indian, who overtakes it and shoots again. But sometimes the Dogs, which have seized the ears or the muzzle, drag it to earth before the Indian has come up. They are not inclined to abandon it, for very often they have had nothing to eat for seven to eight days. The Indian arrives, completes the kill, splits open the belly, and gives all the entrails to his Dogs, which have a great junket. It is this which makes the Dogs keen in the chase. As for the winter, when it has rained upon the snow, which [thus] can carry the Dogs, they made use of them as I have already described, because they have not at that time so much trouble to catch the Moose. For these cannot then run so fast; being much heavier than the Dogs, they sink into the snow, and are unable to advance farther except by leaps.

As for that [hunting] of the Beavers, it also was done in winter with Dogs, but they were only used to find the houses in which they smelled the Beavers through the ice. Having found them, the Indians cut through the ice and made a hole large enough to let through a Beaver. Then they made another hole twenty-five or thirty paces away, on the open surface of the lake. In this place an Indian or two took their stand with a bow and an arrow which has a harpoon of bone at the end, made like a barbed rod, like that which was used in fishing the Sturgeon, but smaller. It has also a cord to which it is attached at one end, and the Indian took hold of the other. Everything being ready, another Indian went to the other hole near the house of the Beavers. Lying down on his belly upon the ice, he placed his arm through the hole to find the Beavers' opening, that by which they place their tail in the water. There they are all arranged one against the other, that is to say, all those of one Beaver family. Having found them, the Indian passed his hand very gently along the back of one several times, and, approaching little by little to the tail, tried to seize it.

I have heard it said by the Indians that they have kept the arm so long in the water that the ice froze all around the arm. When they once seized the tail they drew the Beaver all at one swoop out from the water upon the ice, and at the same time gave it the axe upon the head. They killed it for fear lest the Beaver bite them, for wherever these set their teeth they take out the piece. Having thus drawn one out they tried to obtain another, which they did in the same way, rubbing them gently. That does not put them to flight, for they imagine they are touching one another. But nevertheless three or four of them having been removed, the remainder take to flight and throw themselves into the water. Not being able to remain long without breathing, the daylight which shows over the hole out on the surface leads them to go there to get the air. The other Indians who are there in ambush, so soon as they appear, give them an arrow shot; the harpoon, which has teeth, holds in some part of the Beaver from which it cannot be drawn out. The cord is then pulled and the Beaver is drawn out through the hole; then they raise it upon the ice and kill it. Some time after there comes another which is taken in the same way. Few in a house are saved; they would take all. The disposition of the Indians is not to spare the little ones any more than the big ones. They killed all of each kind of animal that there was when they could capture it. It is well to remark here that they were more fond of the young than of the grown of various species of animals, whatever these might be, to such a degree that often when they were chasing two Elks, male and female, they quitted the male if they perceived that the female was pregnant, in order to obtain the young ones, for ordinarily they carry two, and it is for them a great dainty.

As to the Bears, if they killed them in winter, it was necessary that they should happen upon them when hunting. Coming upon some large trees they looked to see whether there came out any breath in the form of vapour from within. If they saw any it was a sign that the Bear was there. They mounted upon the tree and killed the Bear with their spears; then they drew it out. In the spring they met them in the woods, when they followed their track. Or they killed them sometimes upon an Oak where they were eating acorns. Then a shot of an arrow straightway brought it to the ground, and so soon as it was down they gave it another arrow, and then they killed it with blows from axes. If they meet it upon the ground, and they draw upon it, according to whether the Bear is hurt [or not] it [either] flees or comes to the man, who has immediately another arrow ready. If he does not bring it down, the Bear embraces him, and will very soon have torn him to pieces with its claws. But the Indian to escape this throws himself face down upon the ground. The Bear smells him, and if the man does not stir, the Bear turns him over and places its nose upon his mouth to find if he is breathing. If it does not smell the breath, it places its bottom on the [man's] belly, crushes him as much as it can, and at the same time replaces its nose upon the mouth. If it does not then smell the breath, and the man does not move, it leaves him there and goes fifteen or twenty paces away. Then it sits down on its haunches and watches [to see] if the man does not move. If the man remains some time immovable, it goes away. But if it sees him move, it returns to the man, presses him once more upon the belly for a long time, then returns to smell at his mouth. If it perceives that the man breathes it will press him like that until it believes it has suffocated him, if in the meantime its wounds do not bring it down. To guard against this, it is necessary to take good care neither to breathe nor to move until it is far off. They do not do any other harm. When one has Dogs one is guaranteed against all this.

As for the Lynxes, if the Indians meet them and they or their Dogs pursue them, this animal mounts into a tree where it is easily killed, whilst the Dogs are terrifying it with their barkings. All the other animals are not really difficult to kill, and there is not one of them capable of attacking a man, at least unless it be attacked first.

They kill with the arrow only all kinds of game, both water and land, whether flying or upon the ground. As for the Squirrel, the Partridge, and other small game, it is the children who amuse themselves with that.

5. Tarrentines and the Introduction of European Trade Goods in the Gulf of Maine

Bruce J. Bourque and Ruth Holmes Whitehead

Europeans who voyaged to the Gulf of Maine between 1602 and 1610 found that European manufactured goods were abundant among Native people. Many scholars have assumed that these goods came largely from European traders or fishermen who were expanding from their bases in the Gulf of St. Lawrence. On the contrary, before 1610 European visits to the Gulf of Maine were infrequent and intent upon exploration, not trade.

The issue is important to understanding the ethnohistory of this region. Attributing the early fur trade in the Gulf of Maine to European presence there has obscured the fact that the commerce was actually initiated by groups of acculturated Native middlemen from the eastern Gulf and Nova Scotia. Thus, the extent of Native adaptation to, even active exploitation of, European presence has not been recognized. Indeed, these middlemen interacted with and emulated Europeans so extensively that the very cultural dichotomy between Native and European, which is axiomatic to most historical studies of the fur trade, becomes blurred.

Europeans in the Gulf of Maine in the Sixteenth Century

When Bartholomew Gosnold led the first major English expedition to explore the New England coast, in 1602, one member of the company, John Brereton (1906:337), observed that the Natives there possessed "a great store of copper, some very redde, and some of a paler colour." The following year, Martin Pring (1906:347), another Englishman, reported that some of the Natives residing at what is now Saco, Maine had "plates of Brasse a foot long, and half a foote broad before their breasts."

Elsewhere in his narrative, Brereton (1906:330–31) provides a brief but intriguing account of a meeting with Natives off what is now Cape Neddick, Maine. The party included "six Indians in a baske shallop with a mast and saile, an iron grapple, and a kettle of copper [who] came boldly aboard us, one of them apparrelled with a waistcoat and breeches of black serge, made after our seafashion, hose and shoes on his feet." Brereton concluded from their appearance and "from some words and signs they made, that some baske or [other vessel] of St. John de Luz [a French port in the Bay of Biscay] have fished or traded in this place." The "baske" or "Biscay shallop" was a style of boat originally developed during the sixteenth century by the Basques for whaling, but later widely adopted by seafarers of other nationalities for a variety of uses (Baker 1966:12–19).

Brereton suggested early European trading or fishing expeditions to the Gulf of Maine as the source of the trade goods seen in the hands of Natives there, and authors in this century have generally agreed. Frank Siebert (1973:469), for example, claims that "there is adequate documentation demonstrating the presence of large numbers of Basque fishermen in North Atlantic waters from Newfoundland and the Gulf of St. Lawrence southward to Cape Cod during the sixteenth and seventeenth centuries." According to Samuel Eliot Morison (1971:469) "many English and other fishing vessels must have caught codfish on the Maine banks during the last decade of the sixteenth century." Others suggest earlier dates: Dean Snow (1978:32), for instance, writes that "after 1560, when beaver furs were in heavy demand for felting" there arose "compelling reasons for fishermen to seek out contacts with the Indians of New England and elsewhere in the Northeast." David Quinn (1977:387) estimates that in the period 1527–80, "ranging the shores of Nova Scotia and possibly Maine was not unusual for Basque and Breton summer traders and fishermen." Neal Salisbury's observation (1982:53) that by 1524, when Giovanni da Verrazzano visited the Maine coast, "the Abenaki at Casco Bay [were] obviously experienced in dealing with Europeans" is influenced by the Natives' contempt for Verazzano and his crew.

But as Quinn (1977:386–87) has stated, there is little support in the historic record for these assertions. Evidence is firm for only a handful of brief voyages along the Gulf of Maine coast prior to 1600. Few, if any, voyages occurred before the 1520s: the Norse may have visited during the eleventh century (Bourque and Cox 1982:20–25); John Cabot may have come in 1498 (Hoffman 1961:6–15); and Cabot's son Sebastian's claim that he visited the area in 1507 or 1508 has been accepted by some (Hoffman 1961:16–25; Quinn 1977:132–35), but not others (e.g., Morison 1971:195).

The first clearly documented voyage to the region was Verazzano's in 1524, which Morison (1971:195) suspects occurred in the wake of a poorly documented earlier one by the Portuguese João Alvares Fagundes. On the central Maine coast, Verrazzano (1979:140–41) succeeded in trading a few items with some Natives despite a hostility attributable, perhaps, to unfavorable experiences with Europeans, possibly Fagundes or anonymous traders.

One year after Verrazzano's visit, Estévan Gomez explored the coast. One account of his voyage contains a cursory comment on Native settlement patterns in Penobscot Bay but nothing whatsoever about trade (Hoffman 1961:114–16). Two years later, in 1527, the English vessels *Mary of Guilford* and *Sampson* sailed toward Newfoundland looking for the Northwest Passage. One of them—it is uncertain which—seems to have cruised along the New England coast, sending exploration parties ashore, but again there is no mention of trade (Hoffman 1961:117–21; Morison 1971:234–37).

According to Morison (1971:467–69), the next alleged visitor to the Gulf was David Ingram, "an English sailor who, set ashore with two others in October 1567 on the Gulf coast of Florida, managed to walk by Indian trail all the way to the Maine coast. After a couple years' tramping, he hailed a French ship at the mouth of the St. John River, New Brunswick, and returned to Europe." But Ingram's depositions (De Costa 1883, 1890:5–7)

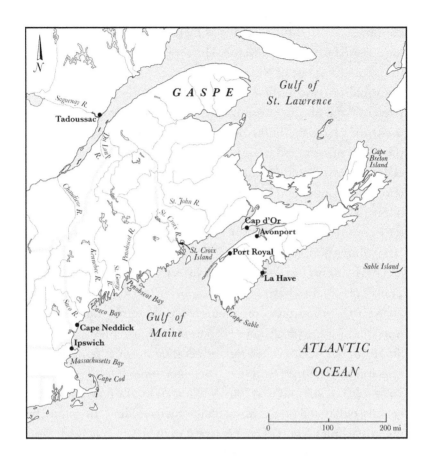

Map 3. The Gulf of St. Lawrence
and the Gulf of Maine

contain at least as much fancy as fact, and he never claimed to have visited the Gulf of Maine. His only reference to the area is to the mythical city of Norumbega on the Penobscot River: "The Canniballs do most inhabite between Nurumbege and Barmiah [west of Cape Breton, possibly on the Miramichi River, New Brunswick] they have teeth like doggs teeth & thereby you may know them" (De Costa 1883:202). Significantly, perhaps, Ingram did claim to have visited Ochala (probably Hochelaga) and Saganas (probably Saguenay), both on the St. Lawrence River, a far more likely place to meet a French ship. Actually, Ingram may never have traveled farther than the coast of the Carolinas (Quinn and Dunbabin 1966:380–81).

There are no further recorded visits to the region until 1580. Thevet claimed to have sailed there prior to 1575, but Hoffman (1961:178–79) argues convincingly that he never did. Between April and June 1580, Simão Fernandez, a Portuguese sailing for Sir Humphrey Gilbert of England, landed at some point in New England and returned with some specimen hides (Quinn 1974:251; 1977:387). Later that year John Walker, an Englishman, landed at Penobscot Bay and took from an unattended building "IIIᶜ [probably 300] drye hides, whereof the most part of them were eighteen foote by the square" (De Costa 1890:7). From their size, these must have been moose hides. Such a large concentration in a single structure meant, we suspect, that they were intended not for the local population, but for export, ultimately to Europeans; but Walker provided no further clues as to their intended destination.

In 1583, Etienne Bellenger cruised the Nova Scotia, New Brunswick, and Maine coasts. On his return voyage, probably somewhere along the southeastern coast of Nova Scotia, he tried to trade with some Natives, but they became hostile, killed two of his crew, and stole his pinnace (Quinn 1962:333).

Thus the historic record examined so far suggests only that Europeans made brief contact with Natives of the Gulf of Maine by 1524. Some, like Verrazzano and possibly Fernandez, did barter a few articles with them, but the purpose of these voyages was exploration, not trade.

It is possible that the anonymous fishermen invoked by Siebert, Morison, Snow and others brought European goods to the Gulf of Maine during the sixteenth century. But it is not probable, because the proposition assumes unrealistically that the Gulf of Maine lay within the range of sixteenth-century Newfoundland fishing fleets. In fact, the distance between the two areas is great: for example, Penobscot Bay is 1300 kilometers from Placentia, Newfoundland (fully one-half the distance from Land's End, England, to Placentia). According to Harold Innis (1940:24–26), "In the first half of the sixteenth century, Europeans discovered and prosecuted the fishery on the southern and eastern coasts of Newfoundland." But not until after Cartier's voyages between 1534 and 1542 did they even reach as far out as the Grand Banks. Between 1520 and 1525, a group of Portuguese, possibly including Fagundes, attempted to establish a settlement on Cape Breton, but it soon failed (Morison 1971:228–33; 248–49; Hoffman 1961:35). The settlers may have visited the Gulf of Maine, but very probably did not, since one account of their venture states that "they had lost their ships" (Biggar 1911:195–97).

During the second half of the sixteenth century, the Portuguese and, later, Spanish components of the fishery actually declined, but the English expanded and began to "force the French to outlying areas, particularly in the Gulf [of St. Lawrence] and on the mainland" (Innis 1940:38). Still, the French did not expand beyond the Gulf until 1598, when they established a short-lived colony composed largely of prisoners on Sable Island (Innis 1940:47; Morison 1971:480–81).

Thus there is little to suggest that the Newfoundland fishery was a staging area for early voyages to the Gulf of Maine. Furthermore, as Churchill (1978:5) states, "Considering the multitude of records of provisioning, voyages, accounts, sales, etc. from the Newfoundland fisheries, it is impossible to believe that numerous vessels could be sent to New England with not one record surviving." He argues further that early seventeenth-century explorers in the Gulf of Maine were genuinely surprised by the abundance of fish there. For example, James Rosier (1912:348), who chronicled Waymouth's voyage to Maine in 1605, described a good day of fishing near the St. Georges River estuary and exclaimed that "In a short voyage [a] few good fishers [could] . . . make a more profitable returne from hence than from Newfoundland: the fish being so much greater, better fed, and abundant with traine [traine-oil]; of which some they desired, and did bring into England to bestow among their friends, and to testify the true report." Significantly, as impressive as this and other early accounts of the New England fishery were, none of their authors were yet aware that the peak fishing season was from January through March (Churchill 1978:25).

A final possible source of sixteenth-century European visitors to the Gulf of Maine were voyages that may have stopped along the coast for reasons incidental to their main purposes. The most likely prospects were French pirates or privateers who preyed upon Spanish shipping off the coasts of Florida and farther north. Quinn (1977:241–42) claims that by 1560, French marauders had been visiting the Atlantic coast as far north as Virginia for many years, and that they traded with Indians. However, their vessels probably would not have ranged as far north as the Gulf of Maine. Indeed, Quinn (1977:533; 1973:189–91) is able to cite only a single 1546 voyage as far north as Chesapeake Bay.

Churchill (1981:26) has pointed out that even the explorers who came after 1600 encountered no other Europeans. During his 1605 visit, Champlain (1922–36, vol. 1:365) learned that George Waymouth had been in the area, but the two did not meet and neither of them saw evidence of previous European visitors. Rosier (1912:342) is explicit on this point: "We diligently observed, that in no place, about either the Ilands, or up in the Maine, or alongst the river, we could not discerne any token or signe, that *ever any Christian had been before*" (emphasis added). Furthermore, Champlain

(1922–36, vol. 1:294) had earlier met a large group of Etchemin from the Penobscot Bay area, including the great sagamore Besabes, who "were much pleased to see us, inasmuch as *it was the first time they had ever beheld Christians*" (emphasis added).

Thus all data indicate that sixteenth- and early seventeenth-century European visitors to the Gulf of Maine were few and far between and certainly insufficient to explain the quantity of trade goods seen by Brereton and Pring among the Natives. In the following paragraphs we suggest two alternative sources for these goods as well as a probable intended destination for the three hundred hides seen by Walker in 1580. Neither alternative depends upon the direct presence of Europeans.

Etchemin in the St. Lawrence Valley

Early French sources (Champlain 1922–36, vol. 2:268–327 passim; Sevigny 1976:46–49) regarded as Etchemin the Native inhabitants between the Kennebec and St. John rivers. But when Samuel de Champlain and Francois Gravé du Pont first visited the St. Lawrence in 1603, they met some Etchemin in the Montagnais village of headman Anadabijou at Tadoussac, an important trading center at the mouth of the Saguenay River on the north shore of the St. Lawrence. On May 27 these Etchemin, in company with some Algonquins and Montagnais, had just returned from a raid on the Iroquois (Champlain 1922:103, 166–67).

Though it was not until 1605—two years after this raid—that the Etchemin at Penobscot first saw a Christian, those involved in warfare on the St. Lawrence may already have met some Europeans in this northern region. Perhaps the late sixteenth-century dislocation of the "St. Lawrence Iroquoians" from the stretch of the St. Lawrence that is across the divide from the St. John and Penobscot Rivers allowed these Etchemin direct access to the St. Lawrence fur trade. The precise date of this dislocation or depopulation is not known, but the available data suggest it took place in the last decade of the sixteenth century (Hoffman 1961:202–3; see also Trigger 1972:72–93).

The Etchemin remained at Tadoussac until at least July 11, and apparently had furs to trade with Native middlemen there (Champlain 1922:166–67). They might have returned to the Gulf of Maine with European trade goods. This was certainly the case by c. 1606–10 when Natives from the area between Pemaquid and the Penobscot River were traveling to the north more than fifty days ". . . to another River where they have a trade with Anadabis or Anadabiion with whom the Frenchmen have had commerce for a long time" (Purchas 1906:400–405). Anadabiion seems clearly to be a mistranscription of Champlain's Montagnais headman, Anadabijou. Natives living west of the Kennebec, whom Champlain (1922–36, vol. 1:312, 325) and his contemporaries (Sevigny 1976:47–48) labeled Armouchiquois, and who include those with European-made metal goods seen by Brereton and Pring, were even more remote from Tadoussac and less likely to have been trading there.

Souriquois in the Gulf of Maine

A second account of Gosnold's encounter in 1602 with Indians sailing a Basque shallop was written by Gabriel Archer, another member of Gosnold's company. It augments Brereton's report and provides important information regarding a source of European goods in the Gulf of Maine prior to 1600: "There came towards us a Biscay shallop, with sail and oars, having eight persons in it. . . . They came boldly aboard us. . . . One that seemed to be their commander wore a waistcoat of black work, a pair of breeches, cloth stocking, shoes, hat and band. . . . These with a piece of chalk described the coast thereabouts, *and could name Placentia of the New found land; they spoke divers Christian words*" (Archer 1843:73; emphasis added).

Here, then, we have Indians encountered on the central Maine coast who were familiar with Placentia and spoke the *lingua franca* that developed in the Gulf of St. Lawrence during the fifteenth and sixteenth centuries (Bailey 1969:19). The prevalence of this St. Lawrence trade language has not been widely recognized. Yet according to Marc Lescarbot (1907–11, vol. 2:24) the Natives along the Gaspé shore spoke "half Baske" during the first decade of the seventeenth century.

Quinn (1977:392) correctly identifies the Native mariners as Micmac (Souriquois). During the next decade, more contacts occurred between Europeans and shallop-sailing Indians and there is little doubt that these, too, were mostly Souriquois, who occupied the area east of the St. John River, though some were Etchemin living from Penobscot Bay eastward.

The first encounter was recorded by Lescarbot (1907–11, vol. 2:309), a passenger aboard Jean Poutrincourt's ship *Jonas* was approached by two "chaloupes," one sailed by fishermen from St. Malo and the other by two Souriquois who had painted a moose on their sail.

A month later two Natives, Messamouet and Secoudon, in their own shallop, accompanied Champlain and Poutrincourt on a voyage from St. Croix Island to Saco on the western Maine coast (Champlain 1822–36, vol. 2:394). We know from other sources, including Lescarbot (1907–11, vol. 2:323), that Messamouet was a Souriquois from La Have, on Nova Scotia's southeastern coast, and that Secoudon was an Etchemin sagamore from Ouigoudi, at the mouth of the St. John River. Champlain implies they visited Saco to improve relations with the Armouchiquois sagamore Onemechin, but Lescarbot's account (p. 324) casts a different light on the visit: "They had much merchandise, gained by barter with the French, *which they had come thither to sell.*" Furthermore, during the negotiations, Messamouet pointed out "how of past time they had often had friendly intercourse together and that they could easily overcome their enemies if they would come to terms, and make use of the friendship of the French . . . in order in future to bring merchandise to them and to aid them with their resources, whereof he knew and could the better tell them, because *he, the orator, had once upon a time been in France and had stayed at the house of M. de Grandmont, mayor of Bayonne*" (emphasis added). Onemechin, however, was unimpressed and his rebuff of Messamouet's offer was one of the factors that led to a major Souriquois and eastern Etchemin raid on Onemechin's village in 1607 (Morrison 1975).

Messamouet's visit to France must have occurred before or shortly after de Grandmont's death in 1580 (Lescarbot 1907–11, vol. 2:324; Harald Prins, personal communication). He may have been one of the first Natives from Acadia to visit France, but he was not the last. A man "from the coast of Acadia" went with Jean Sarcel De Prévert in 1603 (Champlain 1922:188). A Souriquois from southern Nova Scotia named Cacagous (the Micmac word for crow) not only visited France but was baptized in Bayonne prior to 1611 (Thwaites 1896, vol. 1:163; Rand 1972:73). These Natives were probably invited to visit France in order to forge closer French-Indian trade relationships and to increase Native cooperation with French fur traders operating in the Gulf of St. Lawrence.

The third recorded encounter between Europeans and Indians sailing shallops was in 1606 at Port Royal. Panoniac, a Souriquois, had been killed in Penobscot Bay by some Armouchiquois. His body had been delivered by Besabes to another Etchemin, Ouigamont, sagamore of St. Croix. Ouigamont, in turn, carried it in his own shallop to Port Royal (Champlain 1922–36, vol. 2:442–43). The killing of Panoniac was the second and immediate cause of the Souriquois-led raid on Saco. Lescarbot (1907–11, vol. 3:448) tells us that Membertou, the sagamore who organized the multi-ethnic raiding party, traveled with "chaloupes & canots." They had to their advantage some muskets lent by the French (Lescarbot 1907–11, vol. 3:507–8). This is the first mention of firearms in the hands of Natives in the Gulf of Maine.

A fourth encounter occurred off La Have on August 1, 1607, when Englishmen bound for the Kennebec to establish a colony met two shallops sailed by members of Messamouet's band who were "propheringe skins to trook with us. . . ." Furthermore, "ytt seem that the french hath trad w them for they use many french words . . . we take these peopell to be terentyns . . ." (Davies 1906:402–3).

This term, variously spelled, has confused historians of the region, but Siebert (1973) convincingly argues that it applied primarily to the Souriquois, later called Micmac. Our data suggest that it probably includes some eastern Etchemin as well.

A fifth encounter began on July 17, 1609, when Henry Hudson met with Natives at a harbor in Penobscot Bay or just east of it. They told Hudson "that the Frenchmen do trade with them; which is very likely, for one of them *spake some words of French*" (Juet 1906:346; emphasis added). Then, on July 20, "two French Shallops full of the country people come into the Harbour. . . . They brought many Beaver skinnes, and other fine Furres, which they would have changed for redde Gownes. For the French trade with them for red Cassockes, Knives, Hatchets, Copper, Kettles, Trevits, Beades, and other trifles" (p. 347). Hudson was apparently not equipped for trade but he wanted the furs and on July 25 he resorted to force: "In the morning we manned our Scute with foure Muskets, and six men, and Tooke one of their Shallops and brought it aboord. Then we manned our Boat & Scute with twelve men and Muskets, and two stone Pieces or Murderers, and drave the Salvages from their Houses, and took spoyle of them, as they would have done of us" (p. 348). Thus, the shallop-sailing traders were probably local residents (Etchemin) rather than itinerant Souriquois from the east.

That the Montagnais and Souriquois used European vessels during the early seventeenth century has been briefly noted by Bruce Trigger (1976:362), Quinn (1977:392), and Turgeon (1982:11). The encounters cited above indicate, however, that even the Etchemin of Penobscot Bay were employing shallops in the fur trade by 1609.

Native adoption of European shallops meant far more than the mere replacement of one small craft by another. In fact, shallops were generally large. Some ranged up to twelve tons and twelve meters (forty feet) in length and had more than one mast (Baker 1966:20–28). Furthermore, according to a seventeenth-century Jesuit missionary, the Souriquois "handle them as skillfully as our most courageous and active sailors in France" (Thwaites, vol. 47:223–29).

While the primary motivation for coastal trading voyages must have been the barter of European goods for furs, the traders sought other commodities as well. Lescarbot (1907–11, vol. 3:60), for example, said that they imported shell beads from Armouchiquois country and this has been confirmed by the discovery of *Busycon* beads in association with an early historic Native burial at Avonport, Nova Scotia (D. S. Davis, Nova Scotia Museum, personal communication).

Trigger (1976:208) and Salisbury (1982:67–68) suggest that Messamouet and Secoudon traveled to Saco in 1606 to trade for Armouchiquois agricultural surplus. Both argue that because the Souriquois were deeply involved in fur trapping, they tended to run short of food and made up the shortfall through barter with the French and with the agricultural Armouchiquois.

At first glance, this seems a logical hypothesis, but it is at odds with two early accounts detailing the items being offered by traders. The first occurred in 1603, when Champlain (1922:166–67) encountered a party of probable Souriquois on their way to Tadoussac to "barter arrows and moose flesh for . . . beaver and marten" from the Etchemin, Algonquins, and Montagnais in Anadabijou's village. The commodities offered seem particularly well suited for trade to a group recently returned from a war and presumably short of stored food and ammunition. The willingness of the Souriquois to trade moose meat for furs suggests that in this case, at least, they were not worried about their food supply.

The second is the very meeting at Saco to which Trigger and Salisbury refer. Both imply that Messamouet and Secoudon sought agricultural surplus from Onemechin in return for European goods. Although Onemechin did, indeed, provide Messamouet with "corn, tobacco, beans and pumpkins" upon the latter's departure, this gift followed Messamouet's earlier presentation of "kettles, large, medium, and small, hatchets, knives, dresses, capes, red jackets, *peas, beans, biscuits,* and other such things . . . merchandise, which in those parts was worth *more than three hundred crowns*" (Lescarbot 1907–11, vol. 2:323–24; emphasis added). Again, food stuffs, this time of European origin in forms specifically designed for long term storage, were being offered by the traders. Furthermore, Messamouet was clearly not content with Onemechin's insulting response to his largess and vowed revenge upon him because of it (Lescarbot 1907–11, vol. 2:324). Thus, while the shallop-sailing traders may occasionally have sought food, their primary goal was probably the acquisition of furs for resale at a profit to Europeans in the Gulf of St. Lawrence (Bailey 1969:35).

The scope of Souriquois and Etchemin middlemen appears to have been considerable. They probably never rounded Cape Cod to trade in southern New England, but several sources suggest that by the beginning of the seventeenth century they ranged as far west as Massachusetts Bay. Champlain's comment regarding his 1606 visit there is most explicit: "Those who live here have canoes built out of a single piece. . . . This is how they build them. After taking great trouble and spending much time in felling with *hatches of stone (for except a few who get them from the Indians of the Acadian coast, with whom they are bartered for furs, they possess no others)* the thickest and tallest tree they can find, they remove the bark and round off the trunk except on one side where they gradually apply fire through-out its whole length. . . . When it is hollow enough for their fancy, they scrape it all over with *stones, which they use in place of knives.* The stones from which they make their cutting tools are like our musket flints" (Champlain 1922–36, vol. 1:338–39; emphasis added).

This passage clearly identifies Souriquois or Etchemin middle-men as the source of the Massachusett's trade goods, and it also points out a dramatic contrast in the degrees of acculturation at the two opposite ends of the Gulf of Maine, a distance of less than 480 kilometers. One can easily imagine Souriquois traders like Messa-mouet, the former houseguest of the Mayor of Bayonne, profitably exploiting the stone tool-using Natives of Massachusetts Bay.

Native entrepreneurship was probably not new when Champlain and his contemporaries first documented it between 1604 and 1607. Recent archaeological research on the central Maine coast indicates that artifacts made from Nova Scotia chalcedony were common during the late prehistoric period. Also, chert was imported from Ramah Bay, Labrador (Bourque and Cox 1982:13–16). Probably these materials were brought to Maine by exchange patterns that bore little specific resemblance to the early fur trade in New England, but their mere presence demonstrates the existence of long-standing economic ties throughout the northeast.

The ethnohistoric data we have presented also suggest that the pattern we have described had been in place for some time. First, we suspect that the three hundred hides appropriated by Walker in 1580 had been gathered from the Penobscot hinterland for the European market. If Europeans had not yet begun to trade in the Gulf of Maine, as we have argued, Natives themselves must already have begun to transport wholesale fur lots to the Gulf of St. Lawrence. Second, invitations to visit France, like that offered Messamouet, suggest early manipulation of Native entrepreneurs in the fur trade. Third, and perhaps most important, the theft of Bellenger's pinnace in 1583 suggests that the Souriquois of southern Nova Scotia already knew how to handle European vessels. Perhaps they even regarded Bellenger as an interloper on their fur trading territory. In any case, during the next three decades, shallop-sailing traders emerged among Souriquois and eastern Etchemin as far west as the Penobscot.

Finally, there are numerous indications that by 1604, political unrest was widespread in the Gulf of Maine, at least in part because of Tarrentine attempts to control their fur-producing clients there. For example, the sagamores Besabes and Cabahis warmly received Champlain at the Penobscot River in 1604 because they wished to trade directly with the French and obtain protection from "their enemies, the Souriquois and Canadians" (Champlain 1922–36, vol. 1:295). Onemechin's motives in rejecting Souriquois overtures in 1607 were probably similar to those of Besabes and Cabahis in that he, too, perceived a means of bypassing the middlemen to deal directly with the French. However, the French could not save Onemechin, nor could they prevent the Souriquois from later killing Besabes and ravaging his people c. 1615 (Gorges 1890:75–76).

During the first half of the seventeenth century Native middlemen in the lower St. Lawrence lost ground to European traders who bypassed them to establish direct contact with the primary fur producers (Bailey 1969:34–35). In the Gulf of Maine this process seems to have occurred much more rapidly. As early as 1610, aside from trading based at Port Royal, two French ships were trading at the mouth of the St. John and a Frenchman named Platrier had initiated a trading and fishing station at St. Croix that may have persisted until 1613 (Lescarbot 1907–11, vol. 3:55; Thwaites 1896, vol. 3:199–201; Champlain 1922–36, vol. 4:21).

In 1614, Captain John Smith (1910:188, 205) reported that, in addition to his own considerable activity in the fur trade, the French were dominating trade in the eastern Gulf of Maine, that "two French ships . . . had made . . . a great voyage by trade" in the vicinity of Boston, and that Sir Francis Popham's ship was on a routine trading voyage to the Kennebec. It is clear from his remarks that by 1614, Europeans were in direct competition for furs in the Gulf of Maine. This must have led to increased fur prices that would have placed Native middlemen at a disadvantage vis-à-vis their European competition.

Increased European presence in the region brought another, even greater disadvantage for Native middlemen: disease. Smallpox, measles, and other European diseases rapidly reduced Native populations as well as, no doubt, the volume of middleman trade. The impact of the infamous 1617–18 epidemic in the Gulf of Maine was catastrophic (Snow 1978:38). This was not the earliest epidemic, however, as is made clear by the Jesuit Pierre Biard's comment (Thwaites 1896, vol. 3:110) on the Souriquois and Etchemin of 1611–13: "They are astonished and often complain that since the

French mingle with and carry on trade with them, they are dying fast and the population is thinning out . . . one by one the different coasts according as they have begun to traffic with us, have been more reduced by disease."

These early epidemics appear to have resulted from Souriquois contact with European traders in the Gulf of St. Lawrence, for Biard states that west of the Androscoggin "the Armouchiquois do not diminish in population" (ibid.). Probably they were spared because, as Lescarbot (1907–11, vol. 1:195) said, the Armouchiquois "have yet no commerce with us." Among the Souriquois the toll was severe. In 1610 alone, the Souriquois at La Have suffered the loss of sixty persons "which is the greater part of those who lived there" (Thwaites 1896, vol. 1:177). This epidemic may have claimed Messamouet himself, for he is not mentioned after 1607; Secoudon, his trading partner, was dead by 1613 (ibid., 131).

How do we estimate the impact of these diseases? Henry Dobyns (1983) has hypothesized that widespread pandemics affected much of eastern North America during the sixteenth and early seventeenth centuries. One recent reexamination suggests, however, that in northeastern North America, significant outbreaks of disease were probably limited to those mentioned in the literature (Snow and Starna 1984).

When their role as middlemen in the fur trade declined, the Tarrentines resorted increasingly to raiding voyages along the New England coast, probably attempting to maintain control over fur producers or simply to steal what they could no longer obtain by trade. As late as 1632, for example, thirty of them attacked Natives at Agawam (now Ipswich, Massachusetts), killing seven. They also stole some fishnets and supplies from nearby English settlers. Winthrop (1853, vol. 1:72) states in his original manuscript that they arrived in "two fishing shallops" (Harald Prins, personal communication). In 1646, there was "grande guerre" between the Etchemin and Natives of Gaspé (probably Souriquois) (Thwaites 1896, vol. 38:179). Thereafter, this intraregional conflict declined as Natives there began to ally against the common threats, first of Mohawk, then of English expansion.

Conclusions

The earliest detailed ethnographic data from the Gulf of Maine, from the first decade of the seventeenth century, clearly indicates that European trade goods had penetrated the region. By 1602 copper (probably European) and brass were common in western Maine. By 1605 iron axes were common among the Massachusett. Even earlier, in 1580, large numbers of what were probably trade hides were stockpiled at Penobscot Bay. Few European voyages are on record prior to these accounts; the few that were made had minimal contact with Native people in the region.

Many authors have suggested that anonymous European voyages were the source of trade goods in this area. Most often fishermen are implicated, an apparent assumption being that the Gulf of Maine was close enough to the Newfoundland fisheries to be frequently visited. The analysis of the historical record of European activity in the New World during the sixteenth and early seventeenth centuries indicated, however, that while anonymous voyages cannot be ruled out altogether, there is no evidence of them. We have argued here that European fishing and trading activities in the Gulf of Maine remained insignificant until the first decade of the sixteenth century.

Our main concern has been to suggest that the presence of trade goods in the Gulf of Maine prior to 1604 is explained not by direct European trading in the area but by two other more plausible factors. First, by 1603 Maine Natives were directly involved in the St. Lawrence fur trade and even in the warfare that arose over competition for access to European traders. These Natives carried at least some furs and hides up the St. John and Penobscot and down the Rivière du Loup and Chaudière in return for trade goods from those areas.

Second, and more important to the movement of trade goods

west of the Kennebec, were shallop-sailing Native middlemen whose importance in the Gulf of Maine has been overlooked. By the early 1600s Tarrentines—Souriquois middlemen, joined by some eastern Etchemin—had mastered the art of coastal navigation in sailing vessels known as shallops. Apparently they ranged the entire Gulf coast bartering European goods they brought from the St. Lawrence for furs. By the time this pattern was first observed in 1602, it may have been in place for decades.

The Tarrentine entrepreneurs' fortunes declined rapidly after Europeans penetrated the Gulf to trade directly with local fur producers. Almost simultaneously, unfamiliar European diseases decimated their bands. After a major epidemic in the western Gulf in 1617–18, the trade volume probably dropped even further. Despite these setbacks—indeed perhaps because of them—Tarrentines continued some coastal voyages, more often to raid than to trade, until at least 1632.

The Tarrentines were not the only middlemen to arise on the North American fur trade frontier. By 1603 the Montagnais at Tadoussac had also transcended the role of mere fur producers to become middlemen, profitably supplying European traders with furs from the interior in exchange for manufactured goods. Other groups later did the same on the St. Maurice and Ottawa rivers to the west (Trigger 1976:213–17); and Eric Wolf (1982:174) has argued that as the fur trade spread beyond the St. Lawrence, it continued to create short-lived Native middleman groups to service European traders via "natural lines of penetration from the east coast up the rivers, along chains of lakes and over inland areas." After brief prosperity, most were overtaken by disease and warfare or were bypassed when Europeans made direct contact with their fur suppliers.

As Alfred Bailey (1969:34–35) and Trigger (1976:213) have pointed out, the Montagnais at Tadoussac became middlemen primarily because they could control traffic on the Saguenay River, the crucial outlet from a very large and fur-rich hinterland. They and probably later middlemen to the northwest operated by blocking the access of fur producers to European traders, a practice that incidentally triggered much of the warfare that characterized the fur trade frontier. The profitability of such operations was directly linked to the volume of furs funneled through their territories.

The Tarrentine case is somewhat different. Like the Tadoussac Montagnais, local groups in the Gulf of Maine might control the flow of furs from their own hinterlands, but these must have been too small to generate much profit, especially when the distance to market was great. However, by adopting European-style navigation, the Tarrentines were able to amass the yields of several small catchments along the Gulf of Maine coast and efficiently transport the aggregate to markets in the Gulf of St. Lawrence.

The coastal nature of the Gulf of Maine fur supply doomed the Tarrentines to a precipitous decline once European traders arrived there. While middlemen in the St. Lawrence drainage might maintain their market position so long as they could their territories, those in the Gulf of Maine could not hope to stem, even temporarily, direct European penetration to Native fur producers once they entered the region. The Tarrentines survived as middlemen only so long as they could outstrip the Europeans themselves in expanding the fur trade.

Acknowledgments

Earlier versions of this paper were presented at the 1982 meeting of the Canadian Archaeological Association in Halifax, Nova Scotia, and at the Fourteenth Algonquian Conference (1983) in Cambridge, Mass. We wish to thank Edwin Churchill, Bunny McBride, and especially Harald Prins for their many helpful comments.

References

Archer, G. 1843. The Relation of Captain Gosnold's Voyage to the North Part of Virginia, 1602. Collections of the Massachusetts Historical Society (3d ser.) 8:72–82. Boston: Little, Brown.

Bailey, A. G. 1969. The Conflict of European and Eastern Algonkian Cultures 1504–1700: A Study in Canadian Civilization. Toronto: Univ. of Toronto Press.

Baker, W. A. 1966. Sloops and Shallops. Barre, Mass: Barre Publishing Co.

Biggar, H. P. 1911. The Precursors of Jacques Cartier, 1497–1534. Canadian Archives Publications 5. Ottawa.

Bourque, B. J. and S. Cox. 1982. Maine State Museum Investigation of the Goddard Site, 1979. Man in the Northeast 11:21–30.

Brereton, J. 1906. A Brief and True Relation of the Discovery of the North Part of Virginia, 1602. In Early English and French Voyages, H. S. Burrage, ed., 325–29. New York: Scribner's.

Champlain, S. 1922. Des Sauvages, or the Voyage of the Sieur de Champlain Made in the Year 1603. In The Works of Samuel de Champlain 1: H. P. Biggar, ed., 83–189. Toronto: The Champlain Society.

———. 1922–36. The Voyages of the Sieur de Champlain of Saintonge, Captain. In The Works of Samuel de Champlain 1:206–469; vols. 2–6, H. P. Biggar, ed. Toronto: The Champlain Society.

Churchill, E. A. 1978. The Founding of Maine, 1600–1640: A Revisionist Interpretation. Maine Historical Quarterly 18:21–54.

Davies, J. 1906. Relation of a Voyage to Sagadahoc, 1607. H. S. Burrage, ed., 395–419. New York: Scribner's.

De Costa, B. F. 1883. The Relation of David Ingram. Magazine of American History 9:200–208.

———. 1890. Ancient Norumbega, or the Voyages of Simon Ferdinando and John Walker to the Penobscot River, 1579–1580. Albany: Joel Munsell's Sons.

Dobyns, H. P. 1983. Their Number Become Thinned: Native American Population Dynamics in Eastern North America. Knoxville: Univ. of Tennessee Press.

Gorges, F. 1890. A Brief Narration of the Original Undertakings of the Advancement of Plantations into the Parts of America, Shewing the Beginning, Progress and Continuance of that of New England. In Sir Ferdinando Gorges and His Province of Maine, vol. 2, H. P. Biggar, ed., 1–81. Boston: The Prince Society.

Hoffman, B. G. 1961. Cabot to Cartier: Sources for the Historical Ethnography of Northeastern North America, 1497–1550. Toronto: Univ. of Toronto Press.

Innis, H. A. 1940. The Cod Fisheries, the History of an International Economy. New Haven: Yale Univ. Press.

Juet, R. 1906. The Third Voyage of Master Henrie Hudson toward Nova Zambia . . . In Hakluytus Posthumus or Purchas His Pilgrimes, vol. 13, Samuel Purchas, ed., 333–74. Glasgow: James MacLehose and Sons.

Lescarbot, M. 1907–11. The History of New France. 3 vols. Toronto: The Champlain Society.

Morison, S. E. 1971. The European Discovery of America, the Northern Voyages. New York: Oxford Univ. Press.

Morrison, A. 1975. Membertou's Raid on the Chouacoet "Almouchiquois"; the Micmac Sack of Saco in 1607. *In* Proceedings of the 6th Algonkian Conference, 1974, William Cowan, ed., 141–58. Ottawa. Canadian Ethnology Service, Mercury Series 23.

Pring, M. 1906. A Voyage Set Out from the Citie of Bristol, 1603. *In* Early English and French Voyages, H. S. Burrage, ed., 341–52. New York: Scribner's.

Purchas, S. 1906. The Description of the Country of Mawooshen Discovered by the English in the Yeere 1602. *In* Hakluytus Posthumus or Purchas His Pilgrimes, vol. 19, Samuel Purchas, ed., 400–405. Glasgow: James MacLehose and Sons.

Quinn, D. B. 1962. The Voyage of Etienne Bellenger to the Maritimes in 1583: A New Document. The Canadian Historical Review 43:328–43.

———. 1973. England and the Discovery of America, 1481–1620. New York: Alfred A. Knopf.

———. 1977. North America from Earliest Discovery to First Settlements. New York: Harper and Row.

Quinn, D. B. and T. Dunbabin. 1966. Ingram, David, English Mariner, Who Claimed to Have Walked from Mexico to Acadia, 1568–1569. Dictionary of Canadian Bibliography 4:380–81.

Rand, S. T. 1972. Dictionary of the Language of the Micmac Indians, Who Reside in Nove Scotia, New Brunswick, Prince Edward Island, Cape Breton and Newfoundland. New York: Johnson Reprint Co.

Roberts, W. I. 1958. The Fur Trade of New England in the Seventeenth Century. Unpublished PhD Diss., Univ. of Pennsylvania.

Rosier, J. 1912. A True Relation of the Most Prosperous Voyage Made this Present Yeare 1605, by Captaine George Waymouth, in Discovery of the Land of Virginia. *In* Forerunners and Competitors of the Pilgrims and Puritans, Charles H. Levermore, ed., 308–51. Brooklyn: New England Society.

Salisbury, N. 1982. Manitou and Providence: Indians, Europeans, and the Making of New England, 1500–1643. New York: Oxford Univ. Press.

Sevigny, A. P. 1976. Les Abenaquis: Habitat et Migrations (17^e et 18^e siecles). Montreal: Les Editions Bellarmin.

Siebert, F. T., Jr. 1973. The Identity of the Tarrantines, with an Etymology. Studies in Linguistics 23:69–76.

Smith, J. 1910. Description of New England. *In* Travels and Works of John Smith, E. Arber and A. G. Bradley, eds., 117–232. Edinburgh: Grant.

Snow, D. R. 1978. The Archaeology of New England. New York: Academic Press.

Snow, D. R. and W. A. Starna. 1984. Sixteenth-Century Depopulation: A Preliminary View from the Mohawk Valley. Paper presented at the 49th annual meeting of the Society for American Archaeology.

Thwaites, R. G. 1896. The Jesuit Relations and Allied Documents. 78 vols. Cleveland: Burrows Brothers.

Trigger, B. 1972. Hochelaga: History and Ethnohistory. *In* Cartier's Hochelaga and the Dawson Site, James F. Pendergast and Bruce G. Trigger, eds., 3–93. Montreal: McGill-Queen's Univ. Press.

——. 1976. The Children of Aataentsic. Montreal: McGill-Queen's Univ. Press.

Turgeon, L. 1982. Pêcheurs basques et Indiens des côtes du Saint-Laurent au XVIe siècle: Perspectives de Recherches. Etudes Canadiennes: le Canada Atlantique, Acts de Colloque de Nantes 13:7–14.

Verrazzano, G. 1970. The Voyages of Giovani da Verrazzano, 1524–1528. L. C. Wroth, ed. New Haven: Yale Univ. Press.

Winthrop, J. 1853. The History of New England from 1630–1649. J. Savage, ed. Boston: Little, Brown.

Wolf, E. R. 1982. Europe and the People Without History. Berkeley: Univ. of California Press.

6. The Anishinabeg Point of View

The History of the Great Lakes Region to 1800 in Nineteenth-Century Mississauga, Odawa, and Ojibwa Historiography

D. PETER MacLEOD

A prominent feature of the history of seventeenth- and eighteenth-century North America was the presence of several expanding powers that displaced the original inhabitants in region after region and established settlement colonies. Among the best known of these aggressive peoples are the Dutch, English, and French, who landed on the Atlantic littoral and pressed inland. Less familiar are Amerindian groups like the Algonquian bands of the Great Lakes region that referred to themselves as Anishinabeg but were known to whites as the Mississauga, Odawa, and Ojibwa.[1] The Anishinabeg flourished in the geopolitical and economic environment of postcontact North America, and greatly extended the territory under their direct control and economic influence.[2] No less than Europeans, these Amerindians had a keen historical sense, and created and preserved a record of the events of this period. This record, contained in their oral traditions, forms an independent history of the Great Lakes area that both complements and balances history based on contemporary documents, and that cannot be ignored by anyone wanting to produce a comprehensive account of the North American past.

The historiography of seventeenth- and eighteenth-century North America is predominantly Eurocentric. This is perhaps inevitable, given that so much research is based on written records. Notwithstanding the growing propensity of historians to accept and exploit new sources of data, nothing can compete with the power of the written word to convey large quantities of detailed information. In spite of the best efforts of historians, the greater part of the historiography of the Native peoples of North America has remained a chronicle of their interaction with Europeans.

There are, however, both alternative sources and alternative histories. The events of the seventeenth and eighteenth centuries did not pass unremembered by tribal elders, who produced their own version of the history of the Great Lakes region. Transmitted orally for generations, this history was finally preserved in print in the nineteenth century.[3] Although these books enjoyed considerable popular success, they were largely ignored or rejected by mainstream historians during the nineteenth and much of the twentieth centuries, and have only in recent years begun to be used extensively by historians.[4]

These narratives first appeared in print during one of the darkest periods of Anishinabeg history. By the mid-nineteenth century, much of the territory of the Anishinabeg had been occupied by Euramerican settlers, and many bands found themselves in danger of disintegration.[5] Even their past was believed to be on the verge of disappearing forever: "a change is so rapidly taking place, caused by a close contact with the white race, that ten years hence it will be too late to save the traditions of their forefathers from total oblivion. And even now, it is with great difficulty that genuine information can be obtained of them. Their aged men are fast falling into their graves, and they carry with them the records of the past history of their people."[6]

Were this to happen, only Euramerican versions of the past would remain, a prospect that was unsatisfactory to at least one Odawa, who asserted that: "I have seen a number of writings by different men who attempted to give an account of the [Anishinabeg] Indians . . . But I see no very correct account of the Ottawa and Chippewa tribes of Indians, according to our knowledge of ourselves, past and present."[7] With acculturation and the threat of total assimilation, however, came literacy, which became one of the tools employed by individuals who sought to preserve the Anishinabeg heritage by recording their historical narratives. Among these men were

Francis Assikinack, Andrew J. Blackbird, George Copway, Peter Jones, and William W. Warren.

Francis Assikinack, an Ojibwa of Manitoulin Island, was born in 1824. When he enrolled at Upper Canada College at the age of sixteen, he spoke no English, but soon learned not only that language but Greek as well. Although "retiring and generally reticent" at the college, he displayed deep pride in his heritage and was willing to "relate to his friends the history of his people." After graduation, he worked for the Indian Department as an interpreter, clerk, and teacher.[8]

Andrew J. Blackbird, or Mackawdebenessy, the son of a chief of the Odawa of Michilimakinac, was born around 1810 and "brought up in a pure Indian style."[9] But in 1845, after spending several years working as a blacksmith, he was persuaded by a Protestant missionary to attend school in Ohio. Blackbird spent most of his life working for the American government, first as an interpreter for the Mackinac Indian Agency, then as postmaster of Little Traverse, Michigan.[10]

George Copway, or Kahgegagahbowh, was born in 1818 among the Mississauga of Upper Canada. He followed a traditional lifestyle until his family converted to Christianity and he began to attend a Methodist school. Copway himself embarked on a career as a missionary, but left the church after a financial scandal and became a popular lecturer and best-selling author.[11]

Peter Jones, or Kahkewaquonaby, the son of Mississauga and Welsh parents, was born in 1802 and raised by his mother among Amerindians until his father sent him to school, where he first learned English. Jones considered a career as a clerk in the fur trade, but ultimately became both a leading Methodist minister and a Mississauga chief, who forcefully advocated the adoption of Christianity and agriculture in response to the near-disintegration of the Mississauga in the nineteenth century.[12]

William Whipple Warren was born at La Pointe in 1825. The son of an American trader and a woman of mixed French-Ojibwa descent, Warren associated closely with his Amerindian relatives throughout his life. He was employed by the American government as an interpreter until 1850, when he was elected to the Minnesota House of Representatives.[13]

Given that it would have been impossible for an unacculturated Amerindian to write a book in English and find a publisher, it is not surprising that these writers were not conventional Anishinabeg. William Warren was a Euramerican with close family ties to the Ojibwa. The others lived as Amerindians as children, but later in life established and maintained close contacts with white society. All four received a formal education and worked for or were associated with Euramerican institutions. Blackbird, Copway, and Jones were married to Euramericans.

Yet if not typical Anishinabeg, these authors were representative of those individuals who were able to function in both white and Amerindian society, and could attempt to bridge the gap between two very different cultures.[14] As an Ojibwa elder told Warren in 1847: "My Grandson . . . You know how to write like the whites. You understand what we tell you. . . . And we will tell you what we know of former times."[15]

All of these authors, in fact, drew upon their Amerindian background and connections to obtain information regarding Anishinabeg history. Assikinack acquired his material "entirely from what I have learned casually from the Indians themselves in my younger days."[16] Blackbird wrote his history according to "our traditions."[17] The others were more ambitious, and sought out the elders who preserved the traditional narratives of Anishinabeg. Prior to writing his history, Peter Jones consulted "for several years past . . . the aged sachems of the Ojebway."[18] Copway questioned "the chiefs [who] are the repositories of the history of their ancestors."[19] When asked how he became so well informed regarding Ojibwa history, Warren replied that he obtained his information "from the old men of the tribe, and that he would go considerable distances sometimes to see them—that they always liked to talk with him about those matters, and that he would make notes of the principal points."[20]

Although based upon Amerindian narratives, their work was directed at Euramerican readers and shows evidence of their formal education and familiarity with Euramerican authors. Blackbird begins his history by denouncing the writer, probably Francis Parkman, of a history of Pontiac's War.[21] Copway cites European authors and travelers for periods not covered by traditional sources.[22] Assikinack and Jones agree with white authors who suggested that Amerindians were ultimately descended from Asians who came to North America from beyond the Bering strait.[23] Yet these authors carefully distinguish between information obtained from Euramerican printed sources and Anishinabeg narratives, and use the traditional material to produce coherent histories.

Of these histories, the most comprehensive is Warren's *History of the Ojibways* which follows the fortunes of the Anishinabeg from their migration to the north shore of Lake Huron to the mid-nineteenth century. In the works of the other four authors, historical chapters are interspersed with autobiography and descriptions of Amerindian life and customs. Less sweeping than Warren, Assikinack, Blackbird, Copway, and Jones compensate by filling in gaps and by generally confirming the accuracy of his presentation of Anishinabeg oral tradition whenever comparison is possible.

Although Copway and Warren follow continued Anishinabeg warfare against the Dakota southwest of Lake Superior into the nineteenth century, the narratives used by these authors have little to say about one of the most critical periods of Anishinabeg history—the invasion of their homeland by Europeans. Indeed, the traditional history presented by these authors on the whole ends with the eighteenth century, since it is then that one enters the "period in the history of the Ojibways, which is within the remembrance of aged chiefs," and eyewitness accounts together with the personal knowledge of the author, rather than traditional lore, became the primary sources for Anishinabeg historians.[24]

As far as the Anishinabeg were concerned, the history of the Great Lakes region prior to 1800 is the history of their wars and migrations, which were, for the most part, one and the same. Of all the incidents of this period, these were considered by the Anishinabeg to merit inclusion in their narratives.

Three great events dominate the seventeenth and eighteenth centuries in Anishinabeg historiography: their wars with the Mascouten and Winnebago,[25] with the Iroquois in southern Ontario,[26] and with the Dakota and Muskwakiwuk (Fox),[27] which led, respectively, to Anishinabeg expansion into the Michigan peninsula, southern Ontario, and the area south and west of Lake Superior. The Mascouten war is described in fairly general terms, but the battles for southern Ontario are depicted minutely, and the southwestward advance of the Anishinabeg of Lake Superior is traced river by river and lake by lake from Sault Ste. Marie to the headwaters of the Mississippi.

Other matters appear in the narratives, but receive much less attention. Of these, the most important are Anishinabeg expansion northwest of Lake Superior and alliance with the Cree and Assiniboine,[28] contact and trade with the French,[29] Anishinabeg participation in the Seven Years' War[30] and Pontiac's War,[31] the shifting of their alliance from the French to the British empire,[32] the epidemics of the seventeenth century,[33] and the smallpox epidemic of 1757.[34]

If these events are downplayed, others are barely mentioned or are ignored completely. The Anishinabeg enjoyed a longstanding alliance and commercial relationship with the Wendat (Huron) and Khionontateronon (Petun) prior to 1649. Commercial friction between the Anishinabeg and the Wendat, and the destruction of the Wendat confederacy by the Iroquois are mentioned in a confused chapter by Copway.[35] The Khionontateronon do not appear at all. The Anishinabeg relationship with the Dakota is depicted as exclusively adversarial. Only a reference to Anishinabeg living among, and intermarrying with, the Dakota hints at the intervals of peace when the Anishinabeg acted as middlemen between the Dakota and the French.[36] The role of the Anishinabeg as traders is, in fact, passed over almost completely.

Continuous expansion brought the Anishinabeg into conflict with other groups, which produced a history characterized by a strongly military orientation. Peaceful pursuits receive a few paragraphs or, at best, a page or two, but chapter after chapter is devoted to battles with the Dakota, Iroquois, Mascouten, and Muskwakiwuk— or rather to victories over these nations. The Anishinabeg records admit to temporary, swiftly avenged setbacks, but are singularly silent when it comes to defeats.[37] Anishinabeg elders, like many recorders of events, found war a more compelling subject than peace. Histories of war with the Mascouten and the Dakota were evidently considered more worthy of preservation and transmission to the younger generation than recollections of peaceful ties to the Wendat and Khionontateronon.

This focus on military affairs is, however, highly selective. During the seventeenth and eighteenth centuries, the Anishinabeg were the leading power in the upper lakes area. As well as going to war on their own account, they fought consistently for over a century as allies of New France. Serving as French allies demanded a major effort on the part of the Anishinabeg, since it entailed the continuous presence of warriors in a theater of war hundreds of kilometres from their homes for months at a time. But these campaigns do not command a prominent place in Anishinabeg historiography.

Copway and Jones do not mention a single intra-European war of the seventeenth or eighteenth centuries. All five authors, in fact, say nothing about the wars of the League of Augsburg, Spanish Succession, and Austrian Succession—conflicts in which Amerindians fighting alongside the French featured prominently—and devote scarcely more attention to the Seven Years' War. Assikinack cites the Anishinabeg role in the attack on pro-British Miami at Pickawillany in 1752.[38] When describing the smallpox epidemic of 1757 in great detail, Blackbird mentions the Seven Years' War in passing.[39] Warren gives only the name of the war chief who led a contingent to Quebec in 1759.[40]

When the results of Anglo-French conflict directly affected the

Anishinabeg, however, their recollections become much more informative. In 1763 the Anishinabeg went to war against the British, not as before on behalf of the French, but to protect themselves "against what they considered as the usurpation, by the British, of the hunting grounds which the Great Spirit had given their ancestors."[41] The relations in Blackbird and Warren of the careful planning and successful execution of the attack on Fort Michilimakinac are as complete as those of a campaign against the Dakota.[42]

From the limited attention devoted to Anglo-French wars in Anishinabeg narratives, it would appear that the Anishinabeg did not consider their participation and the conflicts themselves to be of great significance, relative to their own preoccupations. French wars waged for French objectives held scant interest for the compilers of the Anishinabeg narratives, who refrained from passing on their memories of these wars to their descendants. Judging from their respective histories, intra-European wars in North America loomed much larger in the consciousness of seventeenth- and eighteenth-century Europeans than in the minds of contemporary Amerindians.

This indifference likely stemmed from the fact that the homelands of the Anishinabeg were not directly threatened by Anglo-French wars in the seventeenth and eighteenth centuries. Located as they were in the Great Lakes region, most Anishinabeg were comfortably distant from the major theaters of intra-European conflict. Only the last campaigns of the Seven Years' War approached the easternmost fringes of their territory.[43] In contrast, Amerindians from outside the Great Lakes region who were directly affected by the Seven Years' War preserved some memories of the military events of that conflict in their own oral traditions. The Abenakis of Odanak (St François), for example, who were attacked by Anglo-American forces in 1759, passed on detailed descriptions of the destruction of that village to their descendants.[44]

Europeans are not ignored in Anishinabeg historiography, but theirs is very much a supporting role. Their most important function is that of commercial associates, who supply the weapons that greatly facilitate Anishinabeg expansion.[45] They are usually portrayed reacting to the initiatives of the Anishinabeg. It is the Anishinabeg who open up trading relations with the French by traveling to Canada, deal with them as equals or superiors, and take the leading role in time of war.[46]

It is possible that the writers predetermined these results by the questions they asked and by their choice of informants. Given, however, that after making inquiries among tribal elders, all of these writers produced similar histories, it would seem that a consensus existed among the elders that war and migration were the important events of the Anishinabeg past.

Few of the occurrences related by these historians, drawn from Anishinabeg oral tradition, are greatly at variance with Western versions of North American history. Their distinctiveness lies in the stress placed on particular events and the situation of the Anishinabeg firmly at the center of the history of the Great Lakes region. Like all recorders of events, the Anishinabeg elders were selective, and attention paid by their narratives to a particular happening can be taken as a rough indication of its significance to contemporary Anishinabeg. When considering the question of whether an event described by Europeans actually took place, Warren asserts that "the Ojibwa . . . are . . . minute in the relation of the particulars of any important event in their history, comprised within the past eight generations."[47] The obvious corollary is that occurrences that were thought to be less important were not transmitted to the younger generation.

The inclusion of a particular event in the oral tradition was determined by the memories of the male elders of the Anishinabeg, who responded to questions about the past with stories of war, very much a male-dominated activity. Had women been consulted, they might, or might not, have given a different version of history.[48] In any event, Anishinabeg narratives recorded in the nineteenth century are oriented exclusively towards male activities. Almost every individual mentioned by name is male. Women appear as wives and victims of Dakota and Muskwakiwuk attacks; men are actors, fulfilling economic and military roles as hunters and warriors in the wars that dominate Anishinabeg historiography.

The prominence of a particular group in this historiography varies not with their importance to the Anishinabeg, but to the nature of the relationship. Those with whom the Anishinabeg established an amicable partnership are taken for granted, and merit only modest attention. Prominence is accorded only to the enemies with whom the Anishinabeg competed for territory and control of economic resources.

Many Anishinabeg bands are neglected. On the whole, the historians of the Anishinabeg directed their attention to the leading edge of Anishinabeg expansion to the west, east, and south. The traditional history of a given region generally ends with the coming of peace. Even Copway and Jones terminate their historical narratives of the Ojibwa in southern Ontario after the expulsion of the Iroquois. The actions of their warriors on the frontier are recalled minutely, while the role of those within Anishinabeg territory is generally confined to providing manpower for major offensives against the Dakota, Iroquois, or Muskwakiwuk.

Those who listened to the narratives of Anishinabeg elders received an education in what the Anishinabeg themselves considered to be the most important events in the history of the Great Lakes region. Just as Euramerican histories pay considerable attention to the establishment of colonies and nation-states in North America, much, but not all, of the Anishinabeg oral tradition is devoted to explaining to future generations how their nation came to possess the territory that it occupied prior to the beginnings of Euramerican settlement. In providing this explanation, the elders bequeathed to posterity the history of the dynamic, enterprising, and successful people who dominated much of the Great Lakes region during the late seventeenth and eighteenth centuries.

This history is valuable both for the insights it provides through comparison with contemporary Euramerican documents and in itself, as an independent record of the past from an Amerindian perspective. It was, of course, possible for the Anishinabeg to be just as ethnocentric as the French or British, yet neither European nor Anishinabeg accounts can be ignored if one wishes to produce a balanced history of the Great Lakes region.

Focused as it is on the concerns of the Anishinabeg themselves, the history preserved in their oral traditions is largely independent of the history of Euramericans in North America. Yet the occasional references to the French in Anishinabeg narratives are of considerable interest, for they make it possible to contrast Amerindian and European depictions of specific incidents, and to bring to light events which were overlooked by contemporary Europeans. The three examples adduced here give some indication of how Amerindian oral traditions can enhance and expand history based upon European documents.

When European traders first traveled to Lake Superior and met with Amerindians, members of both cultures left accounts of their relationship. Pierre-Esprit Radisson gave the impression in his memoir that Franco-Amerindian relations in the upper Great Lakes in the seventeenth century were such that two Frenchmen and their trade goods were able to dominate the nations of Lake Superior: "We weare Caesars, being nobody to contradict us. We went away free from any burden, whilst those poore miserable [Amerindians] thought themselves happy to carry our Equipage, for the hope that they had that we should give them a brasse ring, or an awle, or a needle . . . Wee . . . weare lodged in yᵉ cabban of the chiefest captayne . . . We like not the company of that blind, therefore left him. He wondered at this, but durst not speake, because we were demi-gods."[49]

Yet when the Anishinabeg of Lake Superior described their first experiences with French traders, they portrayed isolated travelers, dependent on the tolerance of the indigenous peoples through whose national territories they traveled: "Early the next morning,

". . . the young men once more noticed the smoke arising from the eastern end of the unfrequented island, and led on by curiosity, they ran thither and found a small log cabin in which they discovered two white men in the last stages of starvation. The young Ojibways filled with compassion, carefully conveyed them to their village, where, being nourished with great kindness, their lives were preserved."[50]

As trade continued, French and Anishinabeg reached a point where it was decided to formalize their relationship with an alliance that was negotiated at a meeting at Sault Ste. Marie in 1671. But the reports that delegates brought home reflected widely varying interpretations of the nature of this relationship. Simon François Daumont de St. Lusson, representing the French crown, produced a description that left nothing to the imagination:

IN THE NAME OF THE MOST HIGH, MOST MIGHTY AND MOST REDOUBT-ABLE MONARCH LOUIS, THE XIVth OF THE CHRISTIAN NAME, KING OF FRANCE AND NAVARRE, we take possession of the said place of S. Mary of the Falls as well as of Lakes Huron and Superior, the Island of Caientolon [Manitoulin] and of all other Countries, rivers, lakes and tributaries, contiguous and adjacent thereunto . . . declaring to the aforesaid Nations that henceforward as from this moment they were dependent on his Majesty, subject to be controlled by his laws and to follow his customs.[51]

St. Lusson was evidently a good deal more circumspect when speaking to Amerindians than when writing reports, for a less baroque but more convincing relation of the same meeting was preserved by the descendants of Ke-che-ne-zuh of the Crane Clan who represented the Ojibwa: "Sieur du Lusson . . . The envoy of the French king, asked, in the name of his nation, for permission to trade in the country, and for free passage to and from their villages all times thereafter. He asked that the fires of the French and Ojibway nations might be made one, and everlasting."[52] Once again, rather than the forceful, dominant newcomers depicted in contemporary Euramerican documents, the French are portrayed by Amerindians as isolated travelers in a foreign land.

The presence of European traders in Lake Superior and the negotiations at Sault Ste. Marie have never been called into question, although acceptance of an Amerindian point of view is relatively recent. In the case of the Ojibwa-Iroquois wars for control of what is now southern Ontario, however, the Anishinabeg version of the past was initially rejected by mainstream historians. Based as they were on what Amerindian elders rather that Euramerican historians considered to be important in history, Anishinabeg accounts of their victories clashed with white preconceptions about the power of the Iroquois.[53] These narratives were thus ignored by generations of scholars, until Leroy V. Eid and Peter S. Schmalz used them to reconstruct the series of successful Anishinabeg campaigns that led to the expulsion of the Iroquois from southern Ontario. In this case, skillful use of Amerindian oral tradition has forced a revision of longstanding opinions regarding the Iroquois and the role of the Ojibwa in the history of Ontario.[54]

European accounts are neither the only, nor necessarily the most reliable record of events in the Great Lakes area during the postcontact period. Amerindians had a particular point of view, and the use of their traditional history allows historians to take account of this perspective. Nonetheless, traditional Anishinabeg history remains a complement to, not a replacement for, history based upon the observations of contemporary European observers. European records, taken down and preserved in print at the time, contain many statements by Amerindians that reveal a much broader range of Amerindian concerns than the oral tradition, especially those involving contact with Europeans. Indeed, a complete history of the Anishinabeg cannot be assembled without recourse to documentary evidence.

Documents, however, contain only those facts observed and deemed relevant by literate Europeans. Relying solely on evidence produced by Europeans leaves events beyond their vision shrouded in darkness, and tells little about how Amerindians viewed the events of their times and the importance they attached to activities that brought them into contact with Europeans relative to other concerns.[55]

To read the works of Assikinack, Blackbird, Copway, Jones, and Warren is to step out of the familiar Eurocentric history of North America into a world where the European presence is off in the distance and Amerindian concerns are at the center. Occurrences that might be of tremendous importance to Europeans are ignored or mentioned only in passing. Those that held significance for the Anishinabeg are recounted at length. For contemporary Amerindians, these were the great events of their time.

Important as the activities of the French and English might be for the future, the Anishinabeg of the seventeenth and eighteenth centuries did not feel compelled to transmit a detailed account of their dealings with Europeans to their descendants. The coming of Europeans was one of the crucial events of North American history, but theirs was not the only story in progress in the post-contact era.

One might be tempted to dismiss this version of history as merely tribal, and thus parochial. The Anishinabeg, however, were the dominant human group from the outlet of Lake Ontario to the headwaters of the Mississippi for much of the seventeenth and eighteenth centuries. The history of the Great Lakes area in this period is *their* history, not that of the European intruders in their scattered outposts.

Then, as now, the history of North America was a history of competing and coexisting human groups interacting with each other and with the environment. In their annals of the past, humans from every group place themselves at the center of events. This would be a harmless enough conceit had not an interpretation of North American history based almost exclusively on documents prevailed, producing a distorted vision of postcontact North America in which Amerindians are fully visible only when they interact with Europeans.

To redress this imbalance, it is not enough to tinker with histo-riography by attempting to tell the "Amerindian side of the story" of those processes and events like the fur trade and Seven Years' War that fall into the categories established by Western historians. Amerindians had their own priorities and their own agenda, which were and are reflected in their historical narratives. Their version of the past deserves to be accepted on its own terms, and fully in-tegrated into the larger history of humans in North America.

"The Ojibways," wrote Warren, "are traditionally well possessed of the most important events which have happened to them as a tribe, and from nine generations back, I am prepared to give, as obtained from their most veracious, reliable, and oldest men, their history, which my be considered as authentic."[56] All things consid-ered, the quickest road[57] to an understanding of the Amerindian past may prove to be by way of the writings of those nineteenth-century Amerindian authors who undertook to preserve the his-torical narratives of the Anishinabeg and "to write their history as they themselves tell it."[58]

Notes

I would like to thank S. Barry Cottam and Professor Cornelius J. Jaenen of University of Ottawa, Professor W. J. Eccles of University of Toronto, and Catherine Desbarats of McGill University, who were kind enough to read and comment upon earlier versions of this paper.

1. Peter S. Schmalz, "The Role of the Ojibwa in the Conquest of Southern Ontario, 1650–1701," *Ontario History* 76, no. 4 (December 1984): 345; Donald B. Smith, *Sacred Feathers: The Reverend Peter Jones (Kahkewaquonaby) and the Mis-sissauga Indians* (Toronto: University of Toronto Press, 1987), 18; Smith, "Who Are the Mississauga?" *Ontario History* 67, no. 4 (December 1975): 211–12.

2. Charles A. Bishop, *The Northern Ojibwa and the Fur Trade: An Historical and Ecological Study* (Toronto: Holt, Rinehart and Winston, 1974), 3–11, 308–35; Peter D. Elias, *The Dakota of the Canadian Northwest: Lessons for Survival* (Win-nipeg: University of Manitoba Press, 1988), 6; Harold Hickerson, *The Chippewa and Their Neighbours: A Study in Ethnohistory* (New York: Holt, Rinehart and Winston, 1970), 13; Tim Holzkamm, "Eastern Dakota Population Movements and the European Fur Trade: One More Time," *Plains Anthropologist* 28, no. 101 (August 1983): 225–33. For a similar assessment of the Cree, see Arthur

J. Ray, *Indians in the Fur Trade: Their Role as Hunters, Trappers and Middlemen in the Lands Southwest of Hudson Bay, 1660–1870* (Toronto: University of Toronto Press, 1974), 1–26.

3. Francis Assikinack, "Legends and Traditions of the Odahwah Indians," *Canadian Journal of Industry, Science, and Art* 3, no. 14 (March 1858): 115–25; Assikinack, "Social and Warlike Customs of the Odahwah Indians," ibid. 3, no. 16 (July 1858): 297–309; Andrew J. Blackbird (Mackawdebenessy), *History of the Ottawa and Chippewa Indians of Michigan: A Grammar of Their Language, and Personal and Family History of the Author* (Ypsilanti MI: Ypsilantian Job Printing House, 1887); George Copway (Kahgegagahbowh), *The Traditional History and Characteristic Sketches of the Ojibway Nation* (London: Charles Gilpin, 1850; reprinted Toronto: Coles Publishing Company, 1972); Peter Jones (Kahkewaquonaby), *History of the Ojebway Indians: With Especial Reference to Their Conversion to Christianity* (London: A. W. Bennett, 1861; reprinted Freeport NY: Books for Libraries, 1970); William Whipple Warren, *History of the Ojibways, Based upon Traditions and Oral Statements* (Minnesota Historical Society, 1885; reprinted as *History of the Ojibway People*, St Paul: Minnesota Historical Society Press, 1984).

4. See, for example, W. J. Eccles, "Sovereignty Association, 1500–1783," *Canadian Historical Review* 65, no. 4 (December 1984): 486; Holzkamm, "Eastern Dakota Population Movements," 226; Francis Jennings, *The Ambiguous Iroquois Empire: The Covenant Chain Confederation of Indian Tribes with English Colonies from its Beginnings to the Lancaster Treaty of 1744* (New York: W. W. Norton, 1984), 21–22; Schmalz, *The Ojibwa of Southern Ontario* (Toronto: University of Toronto Press, 1991), passim; Schmalz, "Role of the Ojibwa," 327–28; Donald B. Smith, "The Life of George Copway or Kah-ge-ga-gah-bowh (1818–1869)—and a Review of His Writings," *Journal of Canadian Studies* 23, no. 3 (Fall 1988): 5, 30n3, 38n128). The oral history of the James Bay Cree has been studied by Toby Morantz in "Oral and Recorded History in James Bay," in William Cowan, ed., *Papers of the Fifteenth Algonquian Conference* (Ottawa: Carleton University, 1984), 171–92. For the place of Amerindians in Canadian historiography, see Bruce G. Trigger, "The Historians' Indian: Native Americans in Canadian Historical Writing from Charlevoix to the Present," *Canadian Historical Review* 67, no. 3 (September 1986): 315–42. In spite of recent developments, the possibility that Amerindians might have their own historical priorities is not yet a prominent feature of the historiography of North America.

5. Bishop, *The Northern Ojibwa and the Fur Trade*, 11–14; Smith, *Sacred Feathers*, 17–33, passim; Schmalz, *Ojibwa of Southern Ontario*, 85–147.

6. Warren, *History of the Ojibways*, 25.

7. Blackbird, *History of the Ottawa and Chippewa Indians*, 7.

8. James C. Hamilton, *Osgoode Hall: Reminiscences of the Bench and Bar* (Toronto: Carswell, 1904), 168–69; Douglas Leighton, "Francis Assikinack," in Francess G. Halpenny, ed., *Dictionary of Canadian Biography*, vol. 9, *1861 to 1870* (Toronto: University of Toronto Press, 1976), 10–11; Schmalz, *The Ojibwa of Southern Ontario*, 237.

9. Blackbird, *History of the Ottawa and Chippewa Indians*, 24.

10. Ibid., i; Bernd Peyer, *The Elders Wrote: An Anthology of Early Prose by North American Indians, 1768–1931* (Berlin: Dietrich Reimer Verlag, 1982), 126.

11. Peyer, *The Elders Wrote*, 75; Schmalz, *The Ojibwa of Southern Ontario*, 152, 156; Smith, "Life of George Copway," 5–38; Smith, "Kahgegagahbowh," *Dictionary of Canadian Biography*, ix, 419–21; Gerald Vizenor, *The People Named the Chippewa: Narrative Histories* (Minneapolis: University of Minnesota Press, 1984), 59–66.

12. Peyer, *The Elders Wrote*, 104; Schmalz, *The Ojibwa of Southern Ontario*, 151–52; Smith, *Sacred Feathers*; Smith, "Peter Jones," in Frances G. Halpenny, ed., *Dictionary of Canadian Biography*, vol. 8, *1851 to 1860* (Toronto: University of Toronto Press, 1985), 439–43; Vizenor, *The People Named the Chippewa*, 66–74.

13. W. Roger Buffalohead, Introduction to Warren, *History of the Ojibway*, ix–xvii; J. Fletcher Williams, "Memoir of William W. Warren," ibid., 9–20; Vizenor, *The People Named the Chippewa*, 56–59.

14. Opportunities in white society for acculturated Anishinabeg were, however, quite limited. Schmalz, *The Ojibwa of Southern Ontario*, 125–26, 151–57, 165.

15. William W. Warren to Jonathan E. Fletcher, 1 May 1850, in "General Correspondence and Related Matters, Henry R. Schoolcraft Papers," cited in Buffalohead, Introduction to Warren, *History of the Ojibway*, xi.

16. Assikinack, "Legends and Traditions of the Odahwah," 117.

17. Blackbird, *History of the Ottawa and Chippewa Indians*, 6.

18. Jones, *History of the Ojebway*, 31.

19. Copway continued: "With these traditions there are rules to follow by which to determine whether they are true or false, By these rules I have been governed in my researches. The first is to inquire particularly into the leading points of every tradition narrated. The second is to notice whether the traditions are approved by the oldest chiefs and wise men. Such are most likely to be true, and if places or persons are mentioned, additional clue is given to their origin and proof obtained of their truth or falsity." Copway, *Traditional History*, 19.

20. Williams, "Memoir of William W. Warren," 15.

21. Blackbird, *History of the Ottawa and Chippewa Indians*, 7–8.

22. Copway, *Traditional History*, 205–52.

23. Assikinack, "Legends and Traditions of the Odahwah," 116–17; Jones, *History of the Ojebway*, 37–38.

24. Warren, *History of the Ojibways*, 298.

25. Assikinack, "Legends and Traditions of the Odahwah," 115; Assikinack, "Social and Warlike Customs of the Odahwah," 307–8; Blackbird, *History of the Ottawa and Chippewa Indians*, 85–95.

26. Blackbird, *History of the Ottawa and Chippewa*, 81–82; Assikinack, "Social and Warlike Customs of the Odahwah," 308–9; Copway, *Traditional History*, 69–94; Jones, *History of the Ojebway*, 111–14; Warren, *History of the Ojibways*, 82–83, 124, 146–88.

27. Warren, *History of the Ojibways*, passim; Copway, *Traditional History*, 55–67; Jones, *History of the Ojebway*, 129.

28. Warren, *History of the Ojibways*, 83–86, 138–40, 179, 189.

29. Assikinack, "Social and Warlike Customs of the Odahwah," 307; Blackbird, *History of the Ottawa and Chippewa Indians*, 92–93; Warren, *History of the Ojibways*, 117, 122, 126, 130–35.

30. Assikinack, "Legends and Traditions of the Odahwah," 118; Blackbird, *History of the Ottawa and Chippewa Indians*, 9–10; Warren, *History of the Ojibways*, 195, 220.

31. Blackbird, *History of the Ottawa and Chippewa Indians*, 7–9; Warren, *History of the Ojibways*, 199–204.

32. Blackbird, *History of the Ottawa and Chippewa Indians*, 7–8; Jones, *History of the Ojebway*, 129; Warren, *History of the Ojibways*, 218–20.

33. Warren, *History of the Ojibways*, 108–12.

34. Blackbird, *History of the Ottawa and Chippewa Indians*, 9–10.

35. Copway, *Traditional History*, 68–76.

36. Warren, *History of the Ojibways*, 158.

37. This reticence was not unique to the Anishinabeg. "The Dakotas," wrote an American missionary in the nineteenth century, "did not like to say much about having been expelled from a portion of their land by . . . the Ojibways; but they often spoke of having driven the Iowas from southern Minnesota." Nonetheless, "The [Dakota] warriors generally made it a point of honour to tell the exact truth [about a military venture] without concealment or exaggeration. If they had been against the Ojibways, we commonly soon heard the Ojibway version of the affair, which seldom differed materially from the account given by the Dakotas." Samuel W. Pond, *The DAKOTA or SIOUX in Minnesota as They*

Were in 1834 (first published in *Minnesota Historical Collections*, vol. 12, 1908; reprinted St Paul: Minnesota Historical Society Press, 1986), 174, 134.

38. Assikinack, "Legends and Traditions of the Odahwah," 118.

39. Blackbird, *History of the Ottawa and Chippewa Indians*, 9–10. For the Anishinabeg of Michilimakinac, the most important event of the 1750s was not the war, but the smallpox epidemic that devastated their community.

40. Warren, *History of the Ojibways*, 195, 220.

41. Ibid., 199.

42. Blackbird, *History of the Ottawa and Chippewa Indians*, 7–9; Warren, *History of the Ojibways*, 199–204.

43. Other Amerindian participants in European wars went to war to protect threatened national interests. During the Seven Years' War, for example, the nations of the Ohio valley were able to fulfill their own goals of defending their homelands from Anglo-American expansion by fighting alongside the French; later, these objectives were fulfilled when the British agreed not to claim lands beyond the Appalachians. See W. J. Eccles, *France in America* (Markham: Fitzhenry & Whiteside, 1990), 207–8; Francis Jennings, *Empire of Fortune: Crowns, Colonies & Tribes in the Seven Years War in America* (New York: W. W. Norton, 1988), 369–414.

44. Gordon M. Day, "'Rogers' Raid in Indian Tradition," *Historical New Hampshire* 17 (June 1962): 3–17.

45. Blackbird and Warren both mention the shattering impact of the first appearance of firearms on the enemies of the Anishinabeg. Warren attributes Anishinabeg success against the Iroquois to the acquisition of adequate supplies of fusils. See Blackbird, *History of the Ottawa and Chippewa Indians*, 94; Warren, *History of the Ojibways*, 120, 124.

46. Assikinack, "Social and Warlike Customs of the Odahwah," 307; Blackbird, *History of the Ottawa and Chippewa Indians*, 92–93; Warren, *History of the Ojibways*, 117–20.

47. Warren, *History of the Ojibways*, 115.

48. For an appraisal of gender bias in Anishinabeg narratives, see Laura L. Peers, "'A Woman's Work Is Never Done': Harold Hickerson, the Male Bias, and Ojibwa Ethnohistory" (Rupertsland Research Centre Conference, Churchill, 1988), 14–16.

49. Pierre-Esprit Radisson, *Voyages of Peter Esprit Radisson, Being an Account of His Travels and Experiences among the North American Indians, from 1652 to 1684*, ed. Gideon D. Scull (Boston: Prince Society Publications, 1885; reprinted New York: Peter Smith, 1943), 198, 200–201.

50. Warren, *History of the Ojibways*, 122. Although the two Frenchmen have

been identified as Médard Chouart des Groseilliers and Pierre-Esprit Radisson, there is no real evidence one way or the other. See Grace Lee Nute, *Caesars of the Wilderness: Médard Chouart, Sieur des Groseilliers and Pierre Esprit Radisson, 1618–1710* (New York: D. Appleton-Century, 1943; reprinted St Paul: Minnesota Historical Society Press, 1978), 62n.

51. "Simon François Daumont Esquire de st. Lusson, Commissioner sub-delegate of my Lord the Intendant of New France, to search for the copper mine in the countries of the Outaouais, Nespercez, Illinois and other Indian Nations discovered and to be discovered near Lake Superior or the French Sea," in E. B. O'Callaghan, ed., *Documents Relative to the Colonial History of the State of New York: Procured in Holland, England, and France, by John Romeym Brodhead, esq., Agent under and by Virtue of an Act of the Legislature Entitled "An Act To Appoint an Agent To Procure and Transcribe Documents in Europe Relative to the Colonial History of the State,"* vol. 9 (Albany, 1855), 803–4. Léopold Lamontagne repeats St Lusson's version of this event in "Simon-François Daumont de Saint-Lusson," in George W. Brown, ed., *Dictionary of Canadian Biography*, vol. 1, *1000 to 1700* (Toronto, 1966), 249.

52. Warren, *History of the Ojibways*, 131. Warren acquired this account from the descendants of Ke-che-ne-zuh.

53. Jennings, *The Ambiguous Iroquois Empire*, 21–22.

54. Leroy V. Eid, "The Ojibwa-Iroquois War: The War the Five Nations Did Not Win," *Ethnohistory* 26, no. 4 (Fall 1979): 297–324; Schmalz, "Role of the Ojibwa in the Conquest of Southern Ontario," 326–52.

55. This is not to say that they cannot be used to illuminate Amerindian opinion regarding specific topics, especially those dealing the Amerindian-European relations. See, for example, C. J. Jaenen, "Amerindian Views of French Culture in the Seventeenth Century," *Canadian Historical Review* 55, no. 3 (September 1974): 261–91.

56. Warren, *History of the Ojibways*, 91.

57. This expression is from G. R. Elton and Robert William Fogel, *Which Road to the Past? Two Views of History* (New Haven: Yale University Press, 1983).

58. Warren, *History of the Ojibways*, 113.

7. Fur Trade Literature from a Tribal Point of View

A Critique

Donald F. Bibeau

The purpose of this paper is to identify and illustrate certain basic assumptions made by fur trade commentators in discussing the North American Indian. One older and six recent studies[1] will be used to illustrate these assumptions. These studies constitute the "literature" referred to in the title.

Nothing exotic or unusual is intended by the "tribal" point of view of this paper. It simply means the author is an enrolled member of a federally recognized tribe (i.e., "Treaty Indian" in Canadian usage) and that his sympathies lie with his tribe. (In an epilogue I will suggest some reasons for which other Indians have refrained from commenting on the fur trade.)

The assumptions developed by this paper grew out of various difficulties I encountered while preparing a course on "Indians in the Fur Trade in Canada and the United States." These problems went beyond the usual ones involving the use of documents, methodology, and theoretical orientation. Problems arose involving assumptions about tribal demography, culture change, tribal material culture and technology, inchoate tribal ethnography (i.e., incomplete descriptions), legal issues, race/racism, the "image" of the Indian, and others that continually confronted me from a number of different sources.

For the purpose of this paper, then, I have reduced these several problems to four. I use them in the form of various assumptions that these authors, and others, make when discussing North American Indians and the fur trade. The four assumptions are:

1. that rapid, if not immediate, aboriginal culture change occurred upon European contact;
2. that rapid tribal dependency on the material culture of the trade followed soon after contact;
3. that, legally, in the absence of reason or authority extant in the rules and principles of international law and conduct, the title to North America somehow belonged to various European nations who periodically claimed all or part of it;
4. that the Western paradigm of civilization versus savagery is a useful if not accurate contrast and depiction of Indian-white relations.

The assumption that aboriginal culture was transformed immediately or quickly after sustained contact with Europeans is widespread, particularly among the older historians like Frederick Jackson Turner and George T. Hunt. Part of the difficulty behind this assumption seems to be a lack of distinction between the concepts of *culture change* and *culture crisis*. This confusion stems in part from the failure of anthropology to define the basic concept "culture." The archaeologist Thomas summarizes the problem this way: "And yet, little general agreement exists among anthropologists about just what culture is . . . In a classic study, A. L. Kroeber and Clyde Kluckhohn (1952) compiled over two hundred discrete definitions of culture, proposed by as many anthropologists and social scientists. Since that time, the number of definitions of culture must have tripled."[2]

The situation with the concept "culture change" is perhaps no better. One can select from a number of theoretical orientations, such as classical evolutionism, diffusionism, neo evolutionism, acculturationism,[3] and so forth. And so the discussion goes on. These efforts by anthropologists do, however, reflect the complexity of basic concepts and the difficulty of deducing theory from seemingly tameless variables that are not easily reduced to predictable patterns or consequences.

Fur trade commentators have made broad generalizations about aboriginal culture and its apparent change. They have also made easy and unexamined assumptions regarding the rapidity and extent of aboriginal culture change and dependency.

The material culture of the fur trade is generally accepted as the *sine qua non* agent of culture changes resulting in rapid (if not immediate) dependency of aborigines on European trade goods. An image of the Indian's susceptibility to the material culture has been created that presents trade goods as possessing some sort of magical power or "electrifying touch" as Hunt claims, such that when exposed to the Indian, VOILA! it instantly catapulted him and his culture into a devastating spiral of change and transformed him into a perpetual state of dependency and need. The Indian, then, is seen as having an incurable and insatiable addiction to the material culture of the trade, particularly guns, traps, kettles, wool, and, of course, alcohol.

The third major assumption I have identified is that in the absence of reason or authority extant in the rules and principles of international law and conduct, the title to North America somehow belonged to various European nations who periodically claimed all or part of it. This notion is one of the most critical issues in all of Indian-white relationships, and yet it is the least commented upon by fur trade scholars. This seems to imply that Indian legal issues are negligible and do not play an important role in fur trade history; yet, there is no other single factor so decisive in the history of Indian-white relations.

The fourth assumption made by fur trade commentators pertains to what might be called the dominant paradigm of Western intellectual thought. It is the civilization versus savagism thesis articulated by Roy Harvey Pearce.[4] It is, perhaps, the single paradigm that is assumed by virtually all Western historical interpretations of Indian-white relations. The paradigm, reflected of the intellectual orientation of Western man, predictably results in pejorative and denigrating images of the Indian.

These four assumptions—rapid culture change and tribal dependency, European presumption of land ownership, and the civilization versus savagery paradigm—are seemingly basic to an understanding of the fur trade. This paper merely suggests that without them we would produce a very different interpretation of the trade and of Indian-white relations in North America.

First Assumption

Of the older historians, George T. Hunt graphically illustrates the assumption of rapid culture change that presumably took place upon European contact with the observation that: "Here the ease of acquisition, the apparently limitless supply, the ready market, and the permanence of the white settlements permitted the constant participation of every Native, expanded the business of trade to unprecedented proportions, and changed, almost overnight, the fundamental conditions of aboriginal economy." And again, noting that: "Old institutions and economies had profoundly altered or disappeared completely at the electrifying touch of the white man's trade, which swept along the inland trails and rivers with bewildering speed and wrought social revolution a thousand miles beyond the white man's habitations, and years before he himself appeared on the scene" (5).

Frederick Jackson Turner in his doctoral dissertation (14) made the same assumption that "the results of the trade upon Indian society became apparent in a short time in the most decisive way," and again (36): "In the course of a few years the Wisconsin savages passed from the use of the implements of the stone age to the use of such an important product of the iron age as firearms," and again (74), "the long-settled economic life of the Indian was revolutionized" since the effect of the trade "upon the savage . . . had worked a transformation" (77).

The effect of the trade upon the Indian was not just an economic one, according to Lewis O. Saum and others: "the Indian was a worse person for his contact with civilization. . . . The trader . . . saw the debasing of the Indian happening directly around him" (77).

More recently the ethnohistorian Charles A. Bishop who, like Saum, adopts a mercantilistic point of view, has modified somewhat the instant or "overnight" transformation of the Indian. Nevertheless, the concept of change is just as profound. According to Bishop, to the Northern Ojibway by 1821: "certain trade items had become essential to survival and trapping, since much of their aboriginal material culture had been replaced gradually by attrition during the previous 200 years" (184). And again, "For the Ojibwe, adaptation involved the replacement of an older mode of subsistence by a new more expedient one under altered conditions. Not only had much of their former subsistence base been destroyed or replaced, but also their means of exploiting it (had been destroyed or replaced)" (298).

Finally, Calvin Martin, in his rather eccentric book, adds lively imagery to the assumption:

> European contact should thus be viewed as a "trigger factor," that is, something which was not present in the Micmac ecosystem before and which initiated a concatentation of reactions leading to the replacement of the aboriginal ecosystem by another. European diseases, Christianity, and the fur trade with its accompanying technology— the three often intermeshed—were responsible for the corruption of the Indian-land relationship in which the native had merged himself sympathetically with his environment. (64–65)

What we have, according to these authors, is an image of rapid, if not "overnight," change of the aboriginal culture at the "electrifying touch" of the white man's trade.

Second Assumption

Beginning with Turner we find that "in Wisconsin the settlers came after the Indian had become thoroughly dependent on the American traders" (78). And Hunt, commenting on the behavior of the Iroquois, states that "any nation with so great an economic need and so strong a military position could hardly have failed to be redoubtable unless it was or became degenerate" (159).

In keeping with this trader's point of view Bishop sees the Northern Ojibway as profoundly dependent on the trading post by the early nineteenth century. (In fact, the dependency assumption is so integral to his text [12, 15, 16, 23, 28–29, 47, 60, 89, 93, 94, 107, 110, 115, 120, 138, 147, 148, 152, 183, 189, 214, 220, 255, 307, 345, 350] that it could be considered something of a "shadow thesis.") He states that "the Ojibwa have become linked to, and ultimately dependent upon, the fur trade" (16) and that, "at least since the early nineteenth century the Osnaburgh Ojibwa have been integrated into and dependent upon the market system of exchange for some of their needs" (23).

Arthur J. Ray notes that as early as 1763 the Cree were taking their own furs in order "to obtain the European goods which they had become dependent upon" (102). For parkland tribes, the "Woodland Assiniboine, Cree, and Ojibwa, participation in the fur trade led to a growing dependence on the trading companies" (147). And that the plains tribes between 1821 and 1970 were ultimately "reduced to the same state of economic dependency as their woodland relatives had begun to experience some fifty years earlier" (213).

Cornelius J. Jaenen in a remarkable study states that "contact with the French brought a dependence on the fur trade, a desperate struggle for the middleman status, and usually an intensification of inter-tribal hostilities" (133). In fact, as early as the mid-1600s, according to Jaenen, "the Amerindians found themselves becoming dependent on their suppliers for ammunition, repairs and replacements" (135).

However, with Saum and Ray a different view of this assumed dependency begins to emerge. Indians do not appear to be as dependent on the material culture of the trade as has been assumed. According to Saum: "if the Indian, whose basic needs were notably small, could be induced to act diligently only when faced with keenly felt needs, then the trader had to create some wants, had to make the Indian feel hard-pressed more often" (167). As for the notion of the plains Indian's dependency on the gun, Saum notes that: "to the plains hunters the white man's cumbersome, muzzle-loading weapon held no great fascination, for the rapid-firing bow and arrows were a more effective buffalo-killer. Consequently, some indians went to no great pains to procure European goods" (168).

In his 1974 text Ray observes that his data from Hudson's Bay Company Archives indicate a "downward trend" in the sale of arms to Indians around the 1750s and that: "there was no major rebound in sales after the French withdrew. In belief, there is little evidence to support a commonly held view that all of the Indians became critically dependent upon firearms very soon after their introduction" (79). Indians, according to Ray, were more than mere passive recipients of the material items of the trade. He states:

> By 1720 a pattern of trade had emerged in which the Assiniboine and Cree middlemen were the central figures. Being in such a position, they were able to dictate the terms of the trade to Europeans and other Indians alike. Furthermore, because of the nature of the system which evolved, they largely regulated the rate of material culture change, and to a considerable extent they also influenced its directions. (69–70)

What emerges from these descriptions is an image of tribal material culture change quite different from the devotees of the Indian's absolute dependence on trade goods.

Third Assumption
The problem presented by the legal assumption is vexing in that it is rarely directly stated; that is, references are oblique and indirect. For example, Turner simply states that, "when St. Lusson, with the *coureur do bois*, Nicholas Perrot, took official possession of the Northwest for France at the Sault Ste. Marie in 1671, the cost of the expedition was defrayed by trade in beaver" (34). Turner does

not appear to be the least aware of or concerned with the legality of these matters.

The assumption is clearly made, however, when he remarks that: "acting under the privileges accorded to them by Jay's treaty, the British traders were in almost as complete possession of Wisconsin until after the war of 1812 as if Great Britain still owned it" (56).

Turner does recognize that whenever it was convenient for them to do so, the British attempted to manipulate Indian legal rights for their own commercial purposes.

Hunt also describes St. Lusson concluding "a ceremony in which he formally took possession of all the country in the name of France" (124). Like Turner, he is not concerned with pursuing the legal issues involved in such a "ceremony."

Bishop refers to several issues having legal implications, such as treaties, treaty payments, treaty rights, government subsidies, Department of Lands and Forests of Ontario, Canadian forms of legal procedure, the Royal Canadian Mounted Police, and land tenure (14, 30, 31–32, 43, 44, 64, 65, 68, 73, 84, 85–88, 206–20). Bishop does not bring these issues into clear focus. His discussion of land tenure is part of his argument dealing with the Northern Ojibway's social organization, not land rights as such.

Professor Jaenen incorporates a brief discussion of aboriginal legal rights into his text. The results are rather revealing. According to Jaenen (159–60): "In contrast to neighboring colonies, the question of Amerindian proprietary rights never gave the French or their native allies much concern. The Spaniards in the fifteenth century had considered it beyond doubt that Spain possessed a legitimate right to conquest and to occupation of the Americas; what was subject to some controversy was the precise basis of that right." Jaenen, however, does not establish what the "precise basis of that right" actually was. He alludes to various papal and religious suppositions but not to legal opinions and arguments, particularly those of Francisco de Vitoria's opinion delivered in 1532.[5]

He continues with the observation that,

like the English, the French did not admit legally that the Amerindians had "sovereign rights" in the land or that they possessed "absolute ownership." Although the French wrote about Amerindian kingdoms and made kings of chiefs and priests of *sachems*, they never accorded them any diplomatic recognition because they did not belong to the accepted "family of nations." (160)

The point here is to illustrate legal assumptions, not to take exception to them. Jaenen, however briefly, at least places the consideration of legal issues within the framework of his study of Indian-white relations, and properly so.

It is my belief that the legal issues inherent in the centuries-long history of the fur trade is the single most crucial and neglected area of fur trade studies. It is, perhaps, the Achilles' heel of fur trade literature.

Fourth Assumption

The fourth and last major assumption made by fur trade commentators is that the Western paradigm of civilization versus savagery informs virtually all fur trade literature dealing with North American Indians. Turner makes the assumption in the first paragraph of his dissertation: "The trading post is an old and influential institution. Established in the midst of an undeveloped society by a more advanced people, it is a center not only of new economic influences, but also of all the transforming forces that accompany the intercourse of a higher with a lower civilization" (3).

Turner sees the trader as "pathfinder for civilization" (19).

Hunt begins the second paragraph of his study with the observation that "in North America . . . a well advanced civilization, in which the mechanism of exploitation was already highly developed, met the Stone Age face to face, in an invasion almost simultaneously continental in extent" (3). And again, "the Stone Age faced the insistent seventeenth century on a fifteen-hundred-mile front which moved swiftly and relentlessly forward" (4).

Jaenen reconstructs early sixteenth-century thinking with his example of the jurist, Juan Gines de Sepulveda, (who) seized on the theory that the imperfect must be subject to the perfect, and that the superior must rule the inferior to justify Spain's title to America. He expanded the argument to assert that the three-fold baseness of the aboriginal tribes—their idolatry, their paganism, and their barbarism—demanded their subjugation by a superior civilization. (15–16)

In fur trade literature and elsewhere the paradigm of civilization versus savagery consistently produces denigrating and pejorative images of Indians, their religion, technology, and culture. The belief emerged among early clerics, as Jaenen points out, that

America is inhabited by marvellously strange and savage people without faith, without laws, without religion, without any civilities, but living like unreasoning beasts as nature has produced them, eating roots, men as well as women remaining ever naked, until perhaps such a time as they will be frequented by Christians, from whom they will little by little learn to put off this brutishness and put on more civil and humane ways. (42)

Another negative image of the Indian emerges from Saum whose "study analyzes the image of the Indian that impressed itself upon the consciousness of the earliest white men among them" (ix), the fur trader. The image Saum garners from the traders is a pathetic one. Although there is recognition of a few virtues, such as "savage generosity," a certain "dignified bearing," "great endurance," "suppression of emotion," and "stoicism" even "under torture," there is not much else found commendable. On the other hand, the Indian's "lack of principles" and "vices" are well drawn. According to Saum and his sources, "the quintessense and dominating force of Indian character . . . was self-interest." He was "a perfect ingrate," "a rank hedonist and materialist," "open to bribes," "dishonest," and a "liar." He had "an amazing penchant for exaggeration," he practiced "deceitfulness," he had "an unenviable reputation for backbiting and slander," he ranged "from caprice and undepend-ability . . . to treachery," he was "indolent," "a loafer, wastrel, and glutton," and a "spoiler," and he even "showed a marked reluctance to answer direct questions" (123, 134, 135, 141, 145, 146, 153, 159, 160, 163, 164, 165, 166, 171, 178, 189, 191, 201).

As bad as this wholesome image is, there's more: "Beyond prefer-ence for certain groups of Indians, the traders almost universally expressed two salient ideas about the appearance of the natives, the women were incomparably more disgusting than the men, and Indian society as a whole was marred by an excessive filthi-ness" (119).

As for the virtues of Indian women, Saum quotes David Thompson that ". . . courage is not accounted an essential to the men, any more than chastity to the women" (83, 198). The fur trader, according to Saum, considered the Indian woman little more than a tough, dusky, woodland whore (83, 85, 120, 175, 176, 208, 212).

Yet another despicable image of the Indian emerges from Mar-tin's maverick study. Martin sets out to debunk the Indian as an early environmentalist. In order to promote this debunking no-tion, Martin employs an arsenal of pejorative images and phrases to illustrate the presumed destruction of Indian-animal relations. According to Martin "the Indian went on the warpath against" the fur-bearing animals. Thus, the Indian is guilty of: "indiscreet slaughter," "overkill," "extermination," "genocide," "unrestrained slaughter," "outrage," "over exploitation," "depletion," "abuse," "perversion," and an "uncompromising callousness toward nature." Martin lifts this supposed "war" against the animals to the meta-phorical level of a religious crusade, that is, "a brief, holy war of extermination," of "exuberant exploitation," which "was nothing short of a 'holy occupation,'" of "ordained killing." "Man and the Beaver . . . were locked in mortal combat, with the Indian the pe-rennial underdog" (8, 18, 19, 27, 39, 61, 62, 63, 65, 74, 106, 107, 109, 113, 116, 185).

Little wonder then the Indian is disqualified from being the "spiritual leader," or "a model, a hero, a guru," or "the great high priest of the Ecology Cult" (157, 159).

It is tempting to get caught up in the huff-and-puff of Martin's steamy rhetoric; however, none of his bombast proves his thesis. His scheme to debunk the Indian's image as a conservationist is pathetically concluded in a footnote at the end of his text. Martin's astounding conclusion is that "we are confronting here an alien ideology of land-use which is antithetical to the central dogmas of Christianity. And I simply cannot imagine how the two views are capable of reconciliation" (188).

For a theologian to hide under the skirts of the Church is one thing; for someone who wants to hatch a serious ethnohistory it is, at best, amusing. In spite of the praise Martin has received in some quarters, the book is overrated and yet another canard on the image of the Indian.

The 450 years of Indian-white relations in North America appears to bear out the fact that Indians will be Indians and perhaps will remain so. And the original dissonance between aborigines and Europeans appears to have survived the centuries to be still very much with us in spite of Euro-Canadian and American catastrophic expectations of being able to re-create Indians in their own image. Belief in this Western paradigm, however, is undiminished and still informs North American attitudes toward Indians today.

Conclusions

In my reading of fur trade literature—from a tribal point of view—I have been struck with the interrelatedness, that is, the consanguinity, of the assumptions presented here. They impress me as being very purposeful and directed toward achieving particular ends. In my opinion, these ends constitute the design of North American history, which is the creation of apology, mythology, and preachment.

Hence, the assumptions discussed in this paper may appear to some to be so basic and so obviously verifiable that without them fur trade studies would be meaningless or would have to proceed along altogether different avenues and toward very different objectives. It is the latter course that I suggest from this attempt to demythologize fur trade literature.

Concepts such as "change" and "dependency" must be placed in their *etiological wholeness*, that is, they must be viewed from their *causal origins* and not from a mere symptomatological perspective. It is an analysis of *causality* that is the missing link in the fur trade studies.

The North American fur trade has yet to be placed in its intercontinental perspective. It was, after all, only one aspect of eighteenth- and nineteenth-century colonialism, and it was only one geographic area of a global phenomenon. To place it in terms of North America only is mere provincialism.

As indicated above, the Western paradigm of civilization versus savagery produces negative images of North American Indians, really without throwing much light on the metaphysics of Western man. It must be said, therefore, that as an interpretive tool or framework for analyzing Indian-white relations, the paradigm is bankrupt.

Finally, after reading Bishop's mercantilistically oriented study of the northern Ojibway and Martin's fugitive interpretation of Indian-animal relations, it appears that the expectation placed on the new discipline of ethnohistory may have reached its limit. The revisionistic task that lies before fur trade studies may well be beyond it. On the other hand, after reading the historian Jaenen's prize-winning study, I am struck with the notion that the task of synthesizing recent studies into a reinterpretation of the Indian and the fur trade ought, perhaps, to be placed back into the portfolio of the historian. This sort of enterprise is well within the range of that ancient discipline's purview.

Epilogue
The following observations are suggested as reasons for which North American Indians are virtually absent from academic discussions about the fur trade.

First, fur trade historians tend to represent the major academic and commercial institutions of Canada and the United States, as well as their respective governments. Canadian and American Indians, even today, remain essentially outside these institutions in spite of the recent advent of Indian studies programs. The academic, commercial, and governmental institutions have produced a general image of history, and particularly fur trade history, as being in the "grand design" of European colonialism and imperialism.

Furthermore, and in spite of recent oral history projects in the United States and Canada, historians tend to disparage the Indian's point of view, even if that point of view is presented through the behavioral sciences such as anthropology and ethnography. George T. Hunt some years ago stated the historian's position on the matter when referring to Lewis Morgan's *League of the Iroquois:* "Notwithstanding Morgan's stature in his own field, his work is valueless as history, for he consulted few or no sources save the Iroquois themselves. As George Hyde has said . . . there is no worse source than unsupported memory or tradition" (187).

Second, for those few Indians who are academically trained, doing any kind of history is something of a luxury neither they nor their tribes can afford. The American Indian intellectual community is very small (though it is currently growing), and those who have virtually any academic training are hard pressed with the immediate and critical concerns of their tribes.

Third, there has been only a slight academic tradition of scholarship and publication among Canadian and American Indians, that is, up to this current generation. There has also been something of a mitigating stigma attached to the so-called academically degreed Indian. It has seemed that the more educated an Indian was, the more acculturated or assimilated he was assumed to be and, consequently, incapable or unfit to do tribal history. It is only recently that this attitude has begun to change.

It must be pointed out, in spite of all this, that the fur trade is a critical part of each surviving tribe's history. The Indians' centuries-long experience is not merely part of Canadian or American history.

The time may have finally arrived when tribes can, indeed *must,* write their own histories, including their experience of the fur trade. Tribal reticence is no longer the virtue it once may have been. Perhaps within this generation, the deep tribal musings may finally be spoken.

Notes

1. See Literature. Parenthetical page numbers throughout paper refer to these works.

2. David Hurst Thomas, *Archaeology* (New York: Holt, Rinehart and Winston, 1979), 103.

3. Clyde M. Woods, *Culture Change* (Dubuque IA: Wm. C. Brown Company Publishers, 1975), 1–9.

4. Roy Harvey Pearce, *Savagism and Civilization: A Study of the Indian and the American Mind* (Baltimore: The Johns Hopkins Press, 1953, 1965).

5. Felix S. Cohen, *Handbook of Federal Indian Law* (Albuquerque: University of New Mexico Press, 1942), 46–47.

Literature

Bishop, Charles A. *A Northern Ojibwa and the Fur Trade: An Historical and Ecological Study.* Toronto: Holt, Rinehart and Winston of Canada, Limited, 1974.

Hunt, George T. *The Wars of the Iroquois: A Study in Intertribal Trade Relations.* Madison: University of Wisconsin Press, 1940.

Jaenen, Cornelius J. *Friend and Foe: Aspects of French-Amerindian Cultural Contact in the Sixteenth and Seventeenth Centuries.* New York: Columbia University Press, 1976.

Martin, Calvin. *Keepers of the Game: Indian-Animal Relationships and the Fur Trade.* Berkeley: University of California Press, 1978.

Ray, Arthur J. *Indians in the Fur Trade: Their Role as Hunters, Trappers and Middlemen in the Lands Southwest of Hudson Bay 1660–1870.* Toronto: University of Toronto Press, 1974.

Saum, Lewis O. *The Fur Trader and the Indian.* Seattle: University of Washington Press, 1965.

Turner, Frederick Jackson. *The Character and Influence of the Indian Trade in Wisconsin: A Study of the Trading Post as an Institution.* PhD diss., Johns Hopkins University, 1891. Miller, David H., and William W. Savage, Jr., eds. Norman: University of Oklahoma Press, 1977.

PART 3

The Social and Political Significance of Exchange

Introduction

As scholars moved beyond the notion that the fur trade was an economic system invented by European merchants and imposed on North American Indians, there was a corresponding shift in understanding motivation. With dependency and the loss of autonomy no longer considered axiomatic concomitants of the trade, scholars increasingly investigated how and why people became involved in the fur trade. With Native people recast as active decision makers, it became apparent that many indigenous communities were able to control both the rate and extent of change.

By the 1970s these changing perspectives created a new social history of the fur trade. Exchange became a process of human interaction in which the economic exchange of raw materials for manufactured goods entailed a broad range of contacts between Indians and Euro-Americans. Researchers like D. W. Moodie demonstrated that as agriculturally oriented communities became involved in the trade, they did not decrease their agrarian activity, but instead, they expanded their range of subsistence activities. Moodie contends that agrarian behaviors were stimulated by trade and that many communities became provisioners of the trade.[1] Meanwhile, Bruce White's article focuses on how that exchange process worked. As White indicates, exchange was defined by an indigenous cultural context, and Indians situated exchange in a symbolic language that was comprehensible to both Europeans and Indians. To twentieth-century readers, an Indian asking for milk may have seemed incongruous but it culturally signaled a request defined by the most basic of human relationships, that of the mother to the child. This image derives from the cultural meanings associated with unbounded generosity. "It is the quintessence of all gifts that a parent gives to a child, because it flows freely from the mother to the infant and is given with absolutely no thought of a return gift." The obvious exchange for mother's milk is the loyalty of child to parent, perhaps one of the strongest manifestations of kinship.[2]

While these types of cultural references described Indian needs, they subsequently led to misinterpretation. Language assumed critical dimensions, and terms like "starving" could possess dire connotations. Among subarctic Algonquian and Athapaskan Indians the literal interpretation of this term meant "to perish with hunger." Among the Ojibwa these same words were intended to remind Europeans to be generous with their resources. The Ojibwa engaged in begging for food because this was routine behavior. As Mary Black-Rogers points out, "The rule [wa]s not to offer food unless it [wa]s requested—a hospitality etiquette the exact reverse of the European: with the Ojibwa. One is supposed to ask, if one is hungry." From a twentieth-century perspective this type of language seems to suggests that Indians were dependent on Europeans for their food supply but as Black-Roger's article indicates, this image of the Indian as "child-like, begging, destitute, starving, and welfare-oriented has been somewhat overdrawn."[3]

It is the language in which these primary-source documents are embedded that has often led to misperceptions about Indians. This type of "begging" language led to misinterpretation in the same way that Indians complained about the depletion of fur-bearing animals. There was no substantial decrease in the availability of beaver but rather the heart of the fur trade moved west of the Mississippi, to more isolated geographic spaces, where furs could be more cheaply harvested. Environmentally, the trade had barely impacted the Great Lakes population of beaver. In "The Growth and Economic Significance of the American Fur Trade, 1790–1890," James Clayton demonstrates that the Great Lakes fur trade remained viable for most of the nineteenth century. However, in the southern Great Lakes Indians became involved in a new type of fur trade. Indians harvested large quantities of black raccoon and most of these furs were sent abroad. From 1820 to 1890, furs were trapped to the north of the Ohio River in Indiana, Ohio, and Illinois, with the finest pelts coming from the Kankakee and White River basins in Indiana. Clayton demonstrates that over four thousand pelts were exported to England during the 1840s with over double that number in the next two decades. Unfortunately, no similar accounts exist to describe the domestic trade, although it produced even larger quantities of peltry.[4]

Involvement in the trade introduced a consumer revolution among Indians. Clothing became increasingly elaborate and highly ornate, as cloth was substituted for skins. Cloth replaced furs, and everyday dress was embroidered with beads, ribbons, and cutwork. Women found ways to participate by manufacturing such salable items as moccasins and leggings, while men exchanged their physical labor and martial skills for money. Gail MacLeitch demonstrates that a nascent understanding of "labor as a commodity" evolved among the eastern Iroquois. The multiplicity of imperial laws encouraged Indians to recognize the market value of their labor and encouraged them to refuse such requests when "payment" disappointed expectations. The Iroquois mediated the economic structural changes by straddling this more modern, commercial world. As MacLeitch points out, they continued to hunt and farm, to Indianize European goods, and to use indigenous forms of currency alongside European coinage.[5]

MacLeitch also points out that profitable involvement in the fur-trade exchange process required a global marketplace. To meet the demands of their Indian customers, products came from a worldwide global market: "from Gloucester stroud used in burial rituals, Chinese vermilion worn as facial decoration by warriors, West Indies rum incorporated into religious rites, to European laced hats, woolen stockings, and ruffled shirts that comprised a new 'Indian fashion,' the Iroquois had integrated foreign goods into all aspects of their cultural life."[6]

The stereotypes that have obscured Indian involvement in the trade have also led to mistaken impressions about how and why Europeans became involved in the fur trade. French involvement was more than an economic process. It was the fur trade that simultaneously promoted French imperial ambitions. Because the Indians and Frenchmen were both trading partners and political allies, a barely discernible line separated economic from social transactions. It was the strength of these indigenous alliances that enabled the French to maintain hegemony over a vast North American landscape. In "The Fur Trade and Eighteenth-Century Imperialism," William Eccles shows how the fur trade became an instrument of foreign policy with the French cause supported by most Indians in the colonial wars. A certain Monsieur Le Maire identified the French position very succinctly, explaining that "one had to have the Indians either as friends or as foes, and whoever desired them as friends had to furnish them with their necessities, on terms they could afford."[7]

In writing *The Middle Ground*, Richard White examined the various ways in which the Indians and the French portrayed themselves as allies, focusing on the complex of cultural perceptions that assumed cross-cultural resonance. Richard White's work has reconceptualized the fur trade, and he has attached new meanings to the fur trade, one suggesting that the Great Lakes was a distinctive region where conditions prevailed that created "a rough balance of power, a mutual need or a desire for what the other possesses, and an inability by either side to commandeer enough force to compel the other to change." For Richard White, the French middle ground did not penetrate much beyond the Mississippi River. In the Great Lakes, Frenchmen "appealed to Indian beliefs and employed the cultural tools that had helped regulate relations" among diverse Indian communities. The French presence created the "infrastructure of empire—from missions, to posts, to a network of alliance chiefs, to a set of mutually comprehensible and oft-repeated rituals," or what scholars now refer to as the middle ground.[8]

Notes

1. D. W. Moodie, "Agriculture and the Fur Trade," in *Old Trails and New Directions: Papers of the Third North American Fur Trade Conference*, ed. Carol M. Judd and Arthur J. Ray, 272–90 (Toronto: University of Toronto Press, 1980).

2. Bruce M. White, "'Give Us a Little Milk': The Social and Cultural Significance of Gift Giving in the Lake Superior Fur Trade," in *Rendezvous: Selected Papers of the Fourth North American Fur Trade Conference, 1981*, ed. Thomas C. Buckley (St. Paul: Minnesota Historical Society, 1984), 192.

3. Mary Black-Rogers, "'Starving' and Survival in the Subartic Fur Trade: A Case for Contextual Semantics," in *Le Castor Fait Tout: Selected Papers of the Fifth North American Fur Trade Conference, 1985*, ed. Bruce G. Trigger, Toby Morantz, and Louise Dechêne (Montreal: Lake St. Louis Historical Society, 1987), 642–45.

4. James L. Clayton, "The Growth and Economic Significance of the American Fur Trade, 1790–1890," *Minnesota History* 40 (Winter 1966): 210–20.

5. Gail D. MacLeitch, "'Red' Labor: Iroquois Participation in the Atlantic Economy," *Labor: Studies in Working-Class History of the Americas* 1, no. 4 (2004): 19–90.

6. MacLeitch, "'Red' Labor," 76.

7. W. J. Eccles, "The Fur Trade and Eighteenth-Century Imperialism," *William and Mary Quarterly*, 3rd ser., 40, no. 3 (July 1983): 362.

8. Richard White, "Creative Misunderstandings and New Understandings," *William and Mary Quarterly*, 3rd ser., 63, no. 1 (January 2006): 10.

8. Agriculture and the Fur Trade

D. W. MOODIE

Agriculture has long served as a key to studies of regional and national development in Canada.[1] It provisioned the staple trades upon which Canadian economic development has been based and, as it expanded, offered incentives for the development of industry, as well as for increased trade and finance.[2] With few exceptions, however, agriculture has been dismissed as an insignificant appendage of the fur trade, the leading export staple of Canada until the early decades of the nineteenth century. Agriculture has received only passing mention in histories of the fur trade; while to the extent that relationships between agriculture and the fur trade have been explored in Canadian history, they have generally been described as competing, if not incompatible, economic enterprises.[3]

Thus, the fur trade has been seen as a negative force in New France that lured men into the wilderness and severely retarded the development of agriculture along the lower St. Lawrence during the seventeenth and eighteenth centuries. Conversely, the establishment of agriculture provided a base and a haven for free traders, thereby disrupting the efficient prosecution of the French fur trade. In a colony where the only opportunity for the rapid accumulation of wealth lay in the fur trade, this was a problem that, despite many edicts against free trading, plagued colonial officials until the end of the French regime. Nowhere, perhaps, have the negative effects of agriculture upon the fur trade been more strongly emphasized than in Galbraith's study of the Hudson's Bay Company's monopoly trade in the nineteenth century.[4] During this period, the company was least successful in defending its trade against the encroachments of agricultural settlers, and against rivals in Rupert's Land who were agriculturally based. Galbraith has argued that the company's trade in the Red River valley, where its competitors were farmers as well as traders, was crippled from within, while in the frontierlands of Oregon, its operations were obliterated when the American settlement frontier leap-frogged the Great Plains to the Pacific Northwest.

These views are consistent with Turner's view of American history wherein the fur trade and agriculture have been depicted as mutually exclusive and successive enterprises in the course of Anglo-American expansion across the continent.[5] In Turner's thesis, agriculture advanced steadily in the form of a settlement frontier, destroying the forest as it progressed and driving the fur trade and the Indians into the uncivilized reaches of the farther west. In Canada, agriculture did not advance steadily westward; and it did not destroy the wilderness resource base of the Indian and the fur trader. If the plough, like a cancerous growth, was devastating for the Indian and the fur trade in America, in Canada it was benign, and the world of the Indian and the trader was destroyed, not by agriculture, but ultimately by the industrial revolution and the market economy of Europe. In the end, the Canadian fur trade was the engine of its own destruction, for the resource base was depleted, the Indian an industrial dependent, and the trade in demise long before agricultural settlers advanced into the southern margins of the fur trade domain.

In Canada agriculture did not destroy the fur trade as it apparently did in America. Canadian historians, however, with the major exceptions of Harold Innis and W. L. Morton, have emphasized the conflicts rather than the complementarities between these two pioneering enterprises. In interpreting Canadian history Innis and Morton looked to agriculture to explain fur trade history at both the regional and national levels. Innis recognized incompatabilities between them, but thought agriculture essential to the expansion of the fur trade to continental proportions. He attributed this dependence to the limited transport technology of the trade and the immense distances over which it was conducted:

> The extension of the trade across the northern half of the continent and the transportation of furs and goods over great distances involved the elaboration of an extensive organization of transport, of personnel, and of food supply . . . The organization of food supplies depended on agricultural development in the more favourable areas to the south and on the abundant fauna of the plains area. Limited transport facilities, such as the canoe afforded, accentuated the organization and production of food supply in these areas. The extension of the fur trade was supported at convenient intervals by agricultural developments as in the lower St. Lawrence basin, in southeastern Ontario, and areas centering about Detroit and in Michilimackinac and Lake Michigan territory, in the west at Red River, though the buffalo were more important in the plains area in the beginning, and eventually in Peace River. On the Pacific coast an agricultural base was established in the Columbia.[6]

Morton examined fur trade agriculture to explain the emergence of a distinct way of life in early Manitoba and the northwest. In his work on the Red River Colony, Morton focused upon the complex interplay between agriculture and the buffalo hunt to elucidate not only the economy of a colony dependent upon the fur trade for its commerce, but also the very nature of Red River society, its institutions, and its ultimate destiny.[7] In exploiting earlier work by Giraud, Morton showed how neither farming nor buffalo hunting could displace one another in the life of the Red River Colony. The river-lot farmer was frequently in need of plains provisions while the colony hunter depended in varying degree upon agricultural produce. Moreover, each depressed the price of the other's produce in the fur trade market, the only external market and a market which neither could be relied upon to fill. Thus, in the fur trade economy of the colony, agriculture played a compromise but nonetheless essential role. It was perhaps for this reason that Morton came to regard agriculture as the indispensable enemy of the fur trade and was the first to emphasize its importance in the trade of the western interior.

In revising Burpee's earlier views about the beginnings of the western trade, Morton demonstrated how provisioning problems complicated and delayed the French penetration of the west as they expanded beyond the Indian agricultural lands of the St. Lawrence-Great Lakes. He has also shown how the fur trade initiated not only the pemmican trade but also the first agriculture in the prairie-parkland west. Although he did not underestimate the value of pemmican as a staple food of the western trade, Morton also wrote that: "It was, however, a last resource rather than the preferred item of the traders' simple menu. They supplemented their diet by hunting, fishing and gardening. These pursuits were often, indeed, the only means of subsistence. The solitary trader who had to buy fish and game for his table found in gardening a considerable aid to survival and a welcome addition to his diet. The great companies also, seeking to check costs mounting with the extension of the trade, encouraged their efforts at horticulture and even more ambitious attempts at agriculture."[8] Thus Morton described how even in the heart of the buffalo country the fur trade called agriculture into being both at the fur posts and at the Red River Colony.

Despite this work by Innis and Morton, it is only recently that studies specifically concerned with fur trade agriculture have begun to emerge. For the most part, this research has focused upon Indian agriculture and that established by the fur companies in western Canada and Alaska. The remainder of this paper draws upon some of this recent work, but its main purpose is to call attention to agriculture as a neglected but worthwhile field for fur trade research.

Three main types of agriculture supported the fur trade: company agriculture, colonial agriculture, and Indian agriculture. That begun by the fur companies and practiced by their personnel developed exclusively in response to the needs of the fur trade. Confined to the trading settlements, company agriculture developed in step with the expansion of the European component of the fur trade. Thus when de Monts and Champlain planted gardens at the first fur trade settlements on the Bay of Fundy and later at Quebec,[9] they began a practice subsequently extended almost everywhere that fur trade posts were built. Although inauspicious at the time, these first plantings also presaged the beginnings of agricultural colonization in Acadia and in the St. Lawrence valley. Colonial agriculture in these areas, and elsewhere, however, emerged subsequent to the fur trade and, unlike company agriculture, was only partially a response to fur trade needs. Colonial agriculture was also highly localized and, throughout the fur trade period, remained confined to four major regions: the Bay of Fundy, the lower St. Lawrence, peninsular Ontario, and the Red River valley.

Indian agriculture antedated the fur trade and provided a pre-existing agricultural base for the development of the European trade in eastern Canada. In penetrating along the axis of the St. Lawrence and the Great Lakes, the French trade expanded along the transition zone between agricultural and hunting Indians in eastern North America. In this zone the complementarity in trade was high, and the exchange of Indian corn and tobacco for hides, furs, and other commodities had long antedated the advent of the French. In this way, the ground was prepared for the European trade which, in its westward advance, followed pre-existing trade routes and used the corn supplies of the south to exploit the richer fur bearing lands of the north. Here Indian agriculture played its most important role in the Canadian fur trade, a role that did not disappear with the collapse of Huronia, but persisted among the Indians of the Great Lakes until the beginning of American and Loyalist settlement in this region in the later eighteenth century.

Commenting upon the neglect of agricultural studies in North American Indian history, Wessel has recently observed that "from the time of the earliest meetings between Europeans and Indians north of the Rio Grande, agriculture played a fundamental role linking Indian and white destinies on the continent."[10] More than any other enterprise, the fur trade forged the first contacts between North American Indians and Europeans and, as it developed throughout most of the United States and much of eastern Canada, the system was largely fueled by Native agriculture. Prior to 1650, the value of Indian agriculture to the French fur trade, and to the Huron middlemen upon whom it depended heavily, can scarcely be exaggerated. As Innis observed:

> The opening of the St. Lawrence route to the Hurons facilitated the spread of European goods to the country tributary to the Ottawa and beyond. But expansion of trade to Georgian Bay and the Interior necessitated the development of a technique by which trade could be carried on over long distances. An important feature of this technique was the existence of a base of supplies in the interior. The semi-agricultural activities of the Indians of the interior, and especially of the Hurons, gave them a decided advantage in the trade. The raising of corn by the Hurons and, to a less extent by the Algonquins, gave them a commodity of high food value, easily cultivated, of heavy yields, and of light weight which could be carried long distances in canoes and which, used with fish and game taken on the journey, gave them sufficient strength to overcome the difficulties of long voyages . . . Moreover, because of the position of the Hurons at the edge of the Canadian shield, they rapidly extended the trade in foodstuffs with the northern hunting Indians . . . These people in turn became traders.[11]

Recent research by Heidenreich[12] and Trigger[13] has so expanded the literature on the Huron that more is now known about their agriculture and its role in the fur trade than about that of any other aboriginal group in North America. Prior to the beginning of the European trade, there existed a widespread commerce centered upon Huronia and involving a variety of sedentary, semi-sedentary, and purely nomadic groups. Included in this commerce was the trade that developed directly between the agricultural Huron and the hunting Algonkin of Lake Nipissing. This trade was centered upon an exchange of Huron corn and tobacco for Nipissing skins and dried fish. The advent of the European trade intensified this commerce, bringing the trade in furs to the fore, and increasing the value of Huron corn, not only for voyaging and subsistence, but also as a commodity for which iron goods, or the furs necessary for their purchase, could readily be acquired. In the middleman trade of the Nipissing, corn figured prominently in both these roles. The Nipissing regularly visited Huronia in winter to acquire corn in exchange for fish and furs. In spring, some of the Nipissing voyaged northward where they traded corn and other commodities with the Cree and the more distant Algonkin bands for their prime northern pelts. The Nipissing then traded these furs, either directly to the French or, as was more frequently the case, to the Huron for ironware and corn, usually at their Lake Nipissing rendezvous. In proceeding to Huronia in autumn, the Nipissing caught and dried fish which they later sold for corn at the Huron villages.

The exchange in corn was therefore scarcely less important than that of furs and European trade goods. The products of their cornfields, together with their strategic location as the northernmost sedentary agriculturalists, permitted the Huron to dominate, if not control, much of the French trade in the interior. Corn eased the subsistence of the different Algonkin bands who wintered over and traded their furs at the Huron villages. It also afforded the Algonkin a valuable, if not unrivaled, commodity with which to victual their canoes on their middleman trading expeditions of summer. Although not to the same extent as ironware, corn was also in demand among the more distant hunting groups from whom traders such as the Nipissing procured furs at a profit. The amount of corn that eventually filtered through to the more distant hunting groups, such as the Cree, was probably very small and its attraction as a trade item to these northern hunters did not lie solely in the amount of food it contributed. It also seems to have had an attraction as an exotic food, one for which there may have been a craving among the purely hunting and gathering populations. In this context, Perrot remarked that: "The kinds of food that the savages like best, and which they make most effort to obtain, are the Indian corn, the kidneybean, and the squash. If they are without these, they think they are fasting, no matter what abundance of meat and fish they may have in their stores, the Indian corn being to them what bread is to Frenchman. The Algonkins, however, and all the northern tribes, who do not cultivate the soil, do not lay up corn; but when it is given to them . . . they regard it as a [special] treat."[14]

Likewise, La Vérendrye, the first European to observe the trade between the hunting Assiniboine and the Mandan agriculturalists of the upper Missouri, witnessed a commerce not unlike that between the Huron and Nipissing. In this case, plains provisions and European wares were traded by the Assiniboine for Mandan corn, tobacco, and other commodities. From La Vérendrye's accounts, Will and Hyde have concluded that the Assiniboine valued the Mandan corn more highly than European goods and that the hunting tribes generally had a craving for the vegetable produce of the upper Missouri agriculturalists.[15] From Father Aulneau, it is known that the Assiniboine regularly traded for Mandan corn prior to European contact,[16] and it is highly likely that this trade intensified following the opening of English trading posts on James Bay in the later seventeenth century. During this period, the Assiniboine, along with the Cree, came to monopolize the middleman trade with the English, and a regular supply of corn in the western interior, like that of the Huron in the east, would have greatly enhanced the position of the Assiniboine in this trade. However, the role of Indian corn in this theater of middleman trading awaits further investigation.

Like the different Indian groups, the French could not break the Huron monopoly upon either the fur trade or the provision supply base around which it revolved. Fully aware that groups such as the Nipissing preferred to trade for merchandise and corn at the Huron villages rather than directly with the French, the latter attempted to cultivate Indian corn and thereby compete with the Huron. Thus, Father Sagard wrote that the French "sow every year Indian corn and pease which they trade with the Indians for furs."[17] Although in his first planting at Quebec, Champlain found that Indian corn grew well, early efforts to develop agriculture at Quebec failed to even render the French agriculturally self-sufficient. As late as 1625, only fifteen acres were under cultivation at Quebec, and it was almost another twenty years before the small French outpost in America was capable of feeding itself, let alone able to generate surplus foodstuffs for the fur trade. Although the Company of New France encouraged agricultural settlement with this objective in mind, Trigger has pointed out that

> the total amount of food available to the French for trade was insufficient to undercut the Huron. Throughout this period the Algonkin, although better located for trade with the French than with the Huron, continued to rely on the latter for supplies of corn. The cost of transporting goods to the New World ensured that French trading in agricultural produce was only with hunting groups, like the Micmac and Montagnais, who lived too far away to make the large scale transport of corn from the horticultural tribes living in the interior a practical proposition. The Huron country remained the granary for the Ottawa Valley Algonkin, as well as for the semi or nonagricultural peoples of the upper Great Lakes and central Quebec.[18]

It would appear, however, that the tentacles of the Huron trading empire even extended at times to the remote Montagnais. On their annual trading expeditions to Three Rivers and Quebec the Huron carried agricultural produce in addition to that required for voyaging, which they were able to trade to advantage with the hunting tribes gathered at the French settlements. According to the Jesuit relation of 1634, this included exchanging corn and tobacco for moose skins from the Montagnais.[19]

Until the 1640s the French colony frequently faced starvation in winter and remained dependent on the annual supply ships from France. Symptomatic of this problem was Champlain's proposal to send some of his men to winter for their subsistence among the far-off agricultural Abenaki on the Atlantic coast; he also endeavored to persuade the Abenaki to transport and sell their corn to the French at Quebec.[20] By this time, however, warfare had so disrupted the Abenaki way of life that they were purchasing extra corn from the Indians of southern New England and, as early as 1625, had begun trading their furs for food from the Plymouth colonists in Massachusetts.[21]

The trade in food for furs that had emerged in New England by this time was perhaps part of the French trade from the beginning, although unlike that of the English, it was more expensive and dependent upon imports from France. In 1626, for example, the ships sent to Quebec contained "all the merchandise which these Gentlemen use in trading to the Savages" which, in addition to iron and cloth goods, included "prunes, raisins, Indian corn, peas, crackers or sea biscuits, and tobacco; and what is necessary for the sustenance of the French in this country besides." Ten years earlier, Father Biard stressed the importance of bread, peas, beans, and prunes, in addition to European manufactures, in the Micmac trade of the Maritimes.[22] Bailey has suggested that the eastern Algonkians in this manner lost a measure of self-reliance and that the new foods promoted disease and higher infant mortality among the Indians involved in the trade.[23] When did this trade begin and how essential was it? Did it intensify among the impoverished Micmac, Montagnais, and Algonkin when the heyday of the middleman trade had passed them by? When did colonial foodstuffs replace those from Europe and did the Indian in this way furnish a significant market for the habitant of Quebec or Acadia? Just as the Home Guard Cree in the English trade of Hudson Bay came to rely on imported foods, so it would seem that agricultural produce, both imported and locally grown, became a conspicuous part of the fur trade as it wore on in Canada and game resources could no longer entirely support the Indian way of life. Unlike the trade in manufactured goods, that in food has virtually been ignored, although it would appear to have been an important part of the trade at the beginning, and vital at its conclusion.

Except for the period of Huron hegemony, very little is known about the role of Indian agriculture in the Canadian fur trade. There is even debate as to whether the Huron increased their corn production, or were incapable of doing so as they rose to dominance in the French trade. In America, where Indian agriculture was ubiquitous to the east of the Great Plains, it has been suggested that Indian farming suffered greatly following European contact. Increased warfare with other Indian groups and with whites, frequent crop destruction, population declines and displacements, an unprecedented focus upon fur hunting, and a growing trade with Europeans for gunpowder, clothing, and food all worked toward a breakdown of traditional agricultural systems.[24] In Canada, the fortunes of war induced by the fur trade led directly to the collapse of Huronia, but there is little evidence that the Huron agricultural system had been seriously weakened prior to the Iroquois onslaught. Wessel has recently postulated that Iroquois warfare was directed against not only the Huron but also agricultural tribes generally because of their ability to dominate the trade at Iroquois expense.[25] At the same time, he has stressed the commercial advantages that accrued to Indian groups such as the Huron living along the continental areas between hunting and agricultural populations, and therefore the exceptional nature of their agriculture in the development of the fur trade.

This transition zone in the Canadian trade lay along the northern frontier of aboriginal agriculture. The northeastern limit of Native agriculture was at the villages of the Malecite Indians in New

Brunswick; the northwestern limit at the villages of the Mandan and Hidatsa in North Dakota. Unlike the Huron, who almost perished as a result of the economic advantages they had won in this zone, the Mandan prospered under similar circumstances until the demise of the fur trade, profiting from both Indian middlemen and the French, British, and American fur traders who followed in their wake. Unfortunately, little or nothing is known of equivalent circumstances in the northeast. Did the Malecite employ their agriculture to commercial advantage in their relations with hunting Indians, or did it languish in the face of turbulent conditions induced by the fur trade? What was the extent and nature of Micmac agriculture in the fur trade of the Maritimes and when and how did it originate?

Following the collapse of Huronia in the center of this zone, neighboring tribes, including refugee Huron, continued to supply the corn needs of the upper lakes trade. Unlike the previous Huron system, agricultural produce at this time was traded both to Indians and to the Europeans now directly involved in the trade. Production also became concentrated at places such as Green Bay, Mackinac Island, and Detroit. It would seem that, in the initial phases at least, the fur trade did not cause the Indians in this region to neglect or abandon their agriculture. Rather, it would appear that agriculture expanded into areas and among people where hitherto it had been unknown.

A major gap in this context is the role of agriculture among the Ottawa who came to dominate the middleman trade of the upper lakes. About the time of contact, Champlain wrote "Most of them plant Indian corn and other crops. They are hunters who go in bands into various regions and districts where they trade with other tribes more than four or five hundred leagues distant."[26] During the period of Huron supremacy, the corn supplies of the Ottawa secured them advantages both in trading and in voyaging among the more remote tribes to the west of Huronia. When the Huron were eliminated, some of the Ottawa, along with other groups, sought refuge from the Iroquois at Chequamegon Bay on the south shore of Lake Superior. The corn produced by the Ottawa and other refugee agriculturalists at Chequamegon quickly assumed a prominent role in the developing trade of Lake Superior. In Huron fashion, it provisioned the Indian canoe brigades that renewed direct trading links with the St. Lawrence, while the corn and European merchandise available at Chequamegon soon attracted the northern hunting Indians. In 1669, for example, Father Dablon reported that the Cree from the north had called at Chequamegon "to the number of two hundred canoes coming to buy merchandise and Corn." In the same year, Dablon further remarked that "more than fifty Villages can be counted, which comprise diverse peoples, either nomadic or stationary . . . they live there by fish and corn and rarely by hunting, and number more than fifteen hundred souls."[27] Thus, with its rich fishery and cornfields, Chequamegon functioned for a brief period as a small scale Huronia in the new French trade of the upper lakes.

Although the history of the Ottawa is known only in sketchy fashion, they continued to profit in the trade from their agriculture long after their middleman role as fur traders had been usurped by tribes to the west. Thus, Alexander Henry the elder, in commenting on the pivotal role of the maize of this region in provisioning the trade of the Ohio, the Mississippi, and the northwest, remarked that "It is the Ottawas, it will be remembered, who grow this grain, for the market of Michilimackinac."[28]

Still less is known about the Ojibwa, who had been solely engaged in hunting and gathering at the time of contact, but commenced to cultivate on the south shore of Lake Superior following the collapse of Huronia and the development of the European trade in this region.[29] Through subsequent migration and conquest, the Ojibwa expanded from the shorelands of Lake Superior and Georgian Bay to occupy an immense territory which, by the middle of the nineteenth century, stretched from southern Ontario in the

Agriculture and the Fur Trade

southeast to the grasslands of Saskatchewan in the northwest. The easternmost of the Ojibwa bands, the Amikwa and Mississauga, were by 1710 cultivating corn on the shores and islands of Georgian Bay and, as the Iroquois threat passed, the Mississauga occupied the old Huron lands of peninsular Ontario and there some of them, like neighboring bands of Huron and Ottawa, raised corn for the French trade at Detroit.

At the height of their territorial extent in the mid-nineteenth century, four main divisions of the Ojibwa can be recognized: the Southeastern, the Northern, the Southwestern, and the Plains Ojibwa. Of the different lands occupied by these people, those of the Southeastern Ojibwa in southern Ontario and in the lower peninsula of Michigan were best suited for corn cultivation. There, living to the south of their rugged homeland in the Canadian Shield, many of the Southeastern Ojibwa continued to cultivate among other agricultural groups and in the milder lands vacated by the Huron and their allies. The Southwestern Ojibwa occupied the south shore of Lake Superior and the northern interior of Wisconsin and Minnesota, including the entire headwater region of the upper Mississippi. They inhabited a country rich in wild rice but not equally suited to maize cultivation. Nevertheless, they introduced corn into areas that lay beyond the prehistoric aboriginal agricultural frontier and, during the first half of the nineteenth century, a small-scale agriculture based largely on this crop became a regular feature of the village way of life that emerged among the Ojibwa of this region.

The most expansive of the Ojibwa territories was that occupied by the Northern Ojibwa, who lived in the agriculturally hostile forest and Shield country to the north and west of Lake Superior. From the Red River valley west to the grasslands of eastern Saskatchewan were the Plains Ojibwa or Bungi. In the early nineteenth century, some of the Plains Ojibwa commenced a desultory agriculture along the northeastern margins of the grasslands. About the same time, agriculture appeared among some of the southernmost of the Northern Ojibwa living in the vicinity of the border lakes of Ontario and Minnesota. The limited and often ephemeral agriculture of the Plains and Northern Ojibwa, in contrast to that of the Southwestern Ojibwa, was not associated with a village way of life. However, it was distinctive in carrying Native agriculture to its northern limit in North America, reaching its outer limits in northwestern Ontario at Eagle Lake and Lac Seul, and achieving its northward extreme on the continent in Manitoba along the Dauphin River at latitude 51°30' north.

The spread of agriculture among the Ojibwa ushered in the final stage in the northward diffusion of Indian domesticated plants (or cultigens) in North America, a process that had begun several millennia before the arrival of Europeans. The antecedents of this diffusion occurred in prehistoric time and are known only indirectly and in limited detail from the surviving archaeological evidence. The poleward thrust of Ojibwa agriculture, in contrast, occurred in historical time and lends itself to the more comprehensive procedures of documentary investigation, thus affording a potentially unique perspective from which to view the general processes of agricultural diffusion in aboriginal North America.

Ojibwa agriculture was also a product of its time and therefore of the fur trade milieu in which it emerged. Their corn and dried squash facilitated fur hunting when the larger food animals were in decline and corn was also sold to the European traders. Henry Schoolcraft, for example, reported in the early 1830s that the Red Lake Ojibwa were supplying corn "to the posts on the Upper Mississippi, and even as far east as Fond du Lac."[30] Ojibwa agriculture profoundly affected their culture as well as their commerce with Europeans and, like Indian agriculture elsewhere, can be highly revealing of the workings of both.

It would seem, for example, that the Ojibwa exchange in corn during the first half of the nineteenth century involved characteristics of both the European and Indian cultures, so that a dual economy was in effect among them at this time. In the Lake of the

Woods, Ojibwa agriculture strongly reflected the impact of the European market system upon their economic behavior. From the outset, corn production in this region was commercial in nature, and traders from both the North West and Hudson's Bay Companies vied with one another for the corn supply to ensure greater mobility in the competition for furs. After union in 1821, Indian agriculture at Lake of the Woods declined, largely because of the drop in price brought on by the cessation of competition. The chief factor at Rainy Lake reported in 1822–23 that during the period of competition the Indians "would never give more than 2 bushels for a three point blanket, which traders, some from competition & some from necessity were obliged to give; as soon as the junction was affected the exorbitant price was reduced to a pint of powder for a bushel. On this, the Indians in great part discontinued their cultivation."[31]

This trade, clearly within a market framework, contrasts with patterns observed among the Ojibwa at both the individual and band levels. The bands, it seems, operated on a reciprocal exchange basis wherein status accrued to those who gave away the most. Thus, it was observed that the Red Lake Ojibwa would live well from their corn and fish, "were it not for the habit of giving it away to any and every one who may have, from laziness or any other cause, failed to secure the necessary store of food for the long winter." Likewise, it was remarked that: "This band would be well supplied with food, if other bands did not pour in upon them during the fall and winter, to live by begging, and thus consume their supplies. Most of the men assist their wives in cultivating their gardens; but some are not only too indolent to assist, but give away very liberally what their wives and daughters raise, and then, as soon as spring opens, leave them to live as best they can while raising another crop."[32]

Like Indian agriculture, the history of European agriculture in the fur trade largely remains to be written and, ultimately, the significance of both will be known only in terms of the overall provision requirements of the fur trade. Morton has observed that the provisioning of the fur trade is a much neglected subject, but described it as a central theme in the history of Manitoba.[33] It is also a central theme in Canadian history and, until further research is conducted, the role of agriculture in the fur trade and in early Canada will not be adequately understood.

Although agricultural foodstuffs were secondary to the products of the hunt and the fishery in provisioning the Canadian fur trade, they were nonetheless indispensable to the trade. From the outset, food was imported from both France and Britain to secure the subsistence of the European personnel against the often extreme vagaries of the hunt and the fishery. As the fur trade expanded inland, agricultural produce, in the same way as pemmican and wild rice, was essential over wide areas to provision the men engaged in the transport of furs and trade goods. Food of this nature relieved the monotonous diets at the trading settlements and was important and at times vital to the health of the Europeans engaged in the trade. Agricultural products were also traded to the Indians for furs, a role that was most conspicuous in the dying days of the trade when the Indian, long accustomed to exchanging his furs for gunpowder and clothing, was reduced to trapping for the food he needed in the company stores. Food was also given to the Indians in lavish trade ceremonies, and frequently without any ceremony at all in times of distress, for the trader, like the Indian, quickly learned to accommodate the needs and expectations of his trading partner in the vital business of provisioning as he did in the exchange of other commodities. When the fishery failed and the hunt was poor, oatmeal from Britain, Indian corn from Michilimackinac, or the potato crop from the traders' gardens was often as vital to the Indian enmeshed in the trade as it was to the European who conducted it.

With the major exception of pemmican, the wild foods that provisioned the fur trade were generally gathered and consumed locally. The demand for agricultural produce, in contrast, generated

Agriculture and the Fur Trade

a widespread commerce that had far-reaching effects in Canada. It afforded a market for the colonial farmer and for the Indian agriculturalist of the Great Lakes, both of whom produced surplus foodstuffs in demand in the fur trade lands to the north. Each of these agricultural systems also sustained a large labor force upon which the fur trade of the north could draw. For both of these reasons, the fur trade spawned agricultural colonization in Canada, first in the east in New France and later in the west at Red River. For the same reasons, company agriculture everywhere preceded the settlement frontier. It was thus an incipient farming frontier beyond the permanent frontier of agricultural colonization in Canada, first in Acadia and the St. Lawrence-Great Lakes lowlands, later in the west in what was to be the agricultural heartland of the new dominion, and finally in the Fraser delta and in the east coast lowland of Vancouver Island. Thus the fur trade carved out not only the political boundaries of Canada but also the agricultural areas of present-day Canada and, as Innis concluded, thereby established the basic geographical framework for subsequent economic growth in Canada: "The economic organization of the fur trade was dependent on the Canadian Shield for a supply of furs and on the development of agriculture at convenient intervals to support the heavy cost of transportation. The economic organization of modern industrial Canada has depended on these agriculturally developed areas and more recently on the Canadian Shield. Agriculture and other lines of economic activity were started in suitable territory south of the Canadian Shield under the direction of the trade."[34]

Much of this story, however, remains to be written. Little is known of the agriculture developed by the French traders living beyond the frontiers of permanent settlement, and still less of the demands of the fur trade for the agricultural produce of New France. The fur trade, however, remained the sole agent of economic growth in New France and, directly or indirectly, provided the only unsubsidized market for surplus agricultural production during the French regime. It thus fostered rather than inhibited the development of agriculture in the colony, a view that conflicts with earlier interpretations. In Eccles' view, for example, French colonial agriculture suffered mainly from chronic labor shortages imposed by the manpower requirements of the fur trade.[35] Innis was of the opinion that the expansion of the fur trade exacerbated this problem because "the population of New France during the open season of navigation was increasingly engaged in carrying on the trade over longer distances to the neglect of agriculture and other phases of economic development."[36]

If the labor demands of the fur trade retarded agricultural development, they did so only in the early years of the colony when the struggle for agricultural self-sufficiency was being waged. Otherwise, the sorry state of French-Canadian agriculture was owing to a surplus rather than to a dearth of labor which, in the face of rapid population increase and limited alternative employment, drifted into a dominantly subsistence agricultural way of life. As for the later labor requirements of the fur trade, Harris has recently concluded that: "The fur trade's requirements for white manpower were small and relatively fixed, and as the colony grew, the trade required a steadily smaller percentage of its men. By the early eighteenth century few men living east of Trois-Rivières had ever participated in it, and in any given season no more than two percent of Canadian men were in the west."[37] Thus, the plight of French-Canadian agriculture did not lie in any inherent conflicts with the fur trade. Rather, it was owing to the lack of external markets and to a population which, for imperial reasons, had expanded beyond both the needs of the fur trade and the agricultural system required to support it.

Similar circumstances lay behind the languishing agriculture of the Red River Colony, where a growing population and lack of economic opportunity led to the freeing of trade which broke the commercial monopoly of the Hudson's Bay Company in the West. Although this damaged the company's trade, it merely accelerated more powerful forces that had long been at work throughout the fur trade lands of the West. Of the many changes in the western interior at this time, Morton has written that "the decline of the fur trade was the most significant. The swarming free traders, whose activities had brought Winnipeg into being and who kept the commerce of the colony thriving, were in fact the scavengers of the trade. They were sweeping up the last remnants of the once great trade of the Winnipeg basin, the westward plains, and the Saskatchewan valley . . . The trade of the great Company suffered from this competition, but its great resources of capital and skill, still fed by the vast preserves of the north and of the Mackenzie basin, little touched by the free traders, were not lightly to be overcome, and sustained it."[38]

Of equal and related significance at this time was the decline in the ability of the land to support the Indian way of life. Just as the free traders fanning out from Red River had heralded the end of the trade in the West, so the steady drift of Indians into the Red River Settlement in search of food, shelter, and employment signaled the beginning of the end of the Indian way of life throughout the region. This was a process that was complete among the Indians of the prairie-parkland and the southern forests by 1876, by which time their old ways could no longer support them and their lands had been ceded to the Canadian government. Thus, the advent of the agricultural frontier to western Canada did not displace the Indian economically nor did it destroy his way of life. Rather, the development of agriculture in this region, as elsewhere in Canada during the fur trade period, served as a buffer between the Indian and starvation, affording him food when his lands would no longer yield and succoring him as his way of life underwent drastic and irreversible change. Finally, as the fur trade retreated into the north, it was increasingly sustained by the products of the expanding agriculture of the south.

As we have seen, Heidenreich and Trigger have elucidated the nature of Huron agriculture and its significance in the changing relations between Europeans and Indians during the first half of the seventeenth century. Elsewhere, I have investigated the agriculture and resource assessments of the Hudson's Bay Company during its confinement to the shores of Hudson Bay (1670–1774).[39] Kaye has described company, colonial, and Indian agriculture and the complex interrelations among them in the northwest between 1774 and 1830.[40] In what is undoubtedly the most important published work on company agriculture, Gibson has elucidated the symbiotic relation that developed between agriculture and the fur trade west of the Rocky Mountains; he has also analyzed the overall provision requirements of the Russian-American trade as well as the commerce in agricultural foodstuffs that ensued between the Hudson's Bay Company and the Russian-American Company.[41]

Although large gaps exist and many themes remain to be explored, from these and related studies it has become increasingly apparent that there were few aspects of the fur trade in which agriculture was not involved, just as there were few areas of Canada in which fur trade agriculture was not the pioneer form of agriculture. Agricultural production for the fur trade involved not only the fur traders themselves but also at different times French, British, and even American agricultural settlers. In the seventeenth and eighteenth centuries, large areas of the fur trade were also dependent upon Indian agriculture so that, as a supporting enterprise of the trade, agriculture spawned a complex set of relations that directly involved Indians, fur traders, and settlers and indirectly soldiers, missionaries, and colonial officials. Thus the agricultural component of the fur trade affords not only another perspective from which the long and varied history of the trade can be studied but also a distinct vantage point from which to view the colonial societies to which it was linked and, more especially, the Indian upon whom the fur trade was entirely dependent.

Notes

I am indebted to Dr. Barry Kaye, Department of Geography, University of Manitoba, for freely given assistance and much valued advice in the course of writing this paper. I would also like to acknowledge the permission of the Hudson's Bay Company to consult and quote from its archives.

1. Easterbrook, "Recent Contributions to Economic History: Canada," 267.

2. Fowke, *Canadian Agricultural Policy, the Historical Patterns*.

3. Jones, in his *History of Agriculture in Ontario, 1663–1880*, has accorded cursory recognition to the role of the fur trade market in initiating commercial agriculture in southern Ontario but, with the major exception of H. A. Innis, Canadian economic historians have either ignored or deemed inconsequential agriculture as a supporting enterprise of the fur trade. See, for example, Easterbrook, "Recent Contributions," 266–67. Most histories of the Canadian fur trade acknowledge that the fur traders planted gardens and kept a few livestock, but this aspect of the trade has not been researched systematically. See Morton, *A History of the Canadian West to 1870–71*; Rich, *The Hudson's Bay Company, 1670–1870*; Rich, *The Fur Trade and the Northwest to 1857*; Phillips, *The Fur Trade*; Davidson, *The North West Company*. It should be noted that the relations between agriculture and the fur trade in other areas have received much closer scrutiny. Gibson, for example, has examined agriculture as part of the general problem of provisioning the Russian fur trade (*Feeding the Russian Fur Trade*), and Wishart has studied agriculture and its role at the American trading posts on the upper Missouri ("Agriculture at the Trading Posts on the Upper Missouri Prior to 1843").

4. Galbraith, *The Hudson's Bay Company as an Imperial Factor, 1821–69*.

5. Turner, *"The Significance of the Frontier in American History."*

6. Innis, *The Fur Trade in Canada, An Introduction to Canadian Economic History*, 389.

7. See Morton's "The Red River Parish: Its Place in the Development of Manitoba"; his "Agriculture in the Red River Colony"; his "Introduction" in E. E. Rich, ed., *London Correspondence Inward from Eden Colvile, 1849*; and his *Manitoba: A History*.

8. Morton, *Manitoba*, 41.

9. For an excellent account of early French attempts at agriculture, see Saunders, "The First Introduction of European Plants and Animals into Canada."

10. Wessel, "Agriculture, Indians, and American History."

11. Innis, *Fur Trade*, 26.

12. Heidenreich, *Huronia: A History and Geography of the Huron Indians 1600–1650*.

13. Trigger, *The Huron, Farmers of the North and the Children of Aataentsic: A History of the Huron People to 1660*.

14. Perrot in E. H. Blair, ed., *The Indian Tribes of the Upper Mississippi Valley and the Region of the Great Lakes*, 1:102.

15. Will and Hyde, *Corn among the Indians of the Upper Missouri*, 172, 180.

16. Aulneau in Thwaites, ed., *The Jesuit Relations and Allied Documents*, 68:293.

17. Sagard in Wrong, ed., *The Long Journey to the Country of the Hurons*, 50.

18. Trigger, *Children*, 1:359.

19. Le Jeune in Thwaites, ed., *Jesuit Relations*, 6:273.

20. Champlain in *The Works of Samuel de Champlain*, ed. Biggar, 5:314, 6:43–44.

21. Snow, "Abenaki Fur Trade in the Sixteenth Century," 7–9.

22. Lalemant in Thwaites, ed., *Jesuit Relations*, 4:207; Biard in ibid., 3:69.

23. Bailey, *The Conflict of European and Eastern Algonkian Cultures 1504–1700*, 56–59.

24. Martin, "Ethnohistory: A Better Way to Write Indian History," 49.

25. Wessel, "Agriculture," 12.

26. Champlain, *Works*, 4:280–81.

27. Dablon in Thwaites, ed., *Jesuit Relations*, 54:195, and 165, 167.

28. Henry, *Travels and Adventures in Canada and the Indian Territories between the Years 1760 and 1776*, 122.

29. The only publication on Ojibwa agriculture is Moodie and Kaye, "The Northern Limit of Indian Agriculture in North America." The discussion that follows is based upon both this paper and more recent unpublished research by the authors.

30. Schoolcraft in Mason, ed., *Expedition to Lake Itasca*, 21.

31. HBCA B 105/e/2, 3, Lac la Pluie report on district.

32. Minnesota Historical Society, St Paul, Division of Archives and Manuscripts: Extracts from Sela G. Wright's Sketch of the Red Lake Mission, 26 Jan. 1852, in Mss Relating to Northwest Missions, Grace Lee Nute, compiler; and J. P. Bardwell to the American Missionary Association [Red Lake], August 1851.

33. Morton, *Manitoba*, 27n.

34. Innis, *Fur Trade*, 398.

35. Eccles, *The Canadian Frontier 1534–1760*, 88.

36. Innis, *Fur Trade*, 390.

37. Harris and Guelke, "Land and Society in Canada and South Africa," 141.

38. Morton, *Manitoba*, 104.

39. Moodie, "An Historical Geography of Agricultural Patterns and Resource Appraisals in Rupert's Land 1670–1774."

40. Kaye, "The Historical Geography of Agriculture and Agricultural Settlement in the Canadian Northwest 1774–ca. 1830."

41. Gibson, "Food for the Fur Traders: The First Farmers in the Pacific Northwest, 1805–1846," 18–30; Gibson, *Imperial Russia in Frontier America.*

Bibliography of Published Works Cited

Bailey, A. G. *The Conflict of European and Eastern Algonkian Cultures, 1504–1700.* 2nd ed. Toronto, 1969.

Bishop, Charles A. *The Northern Ojibwa and the Fur Trade: An Historical and Ecological Study.* Toronto, 1974.

Davidson, Gordon Charles. *The North West Company.* New York, 1918, rpt. 1967.

Davies, K. G., ed. *Letters from Hudson Bay, 1703–40.* London, 1965.

Easterbrook, W. T. "Recent Contributions to Economic History: Canada." In *Approaches to Canadian Economic History,* by W. T. Easterbrook and M. H. Watkins. Toronto, 1967.

Eccles, W. J. *The Canadian Frontier, 1534–1760.* Toronto, 1969.

Fowke, Vernon. *Canadian Agricultural Policy: The Historical Patterns.* Toronto, 1946.

Galbraith, J. S. *The Hudson's Bay Company as an Imperial Factor, 1821–69.* Toronto, 1957.

Gibson, James R. *Feeding the Russian Fur Trade.* Madison, 1969.

———. "Food for the Fur Traders: The First Farmers in the Pacific Northwest, 1805–1946." *Journal of the West* 8 (1968): 18–30.

Harris, R. Cole, and Leonard Guelke. "Land and Society in Canada and South Africa." *Journal of Historical Geography* 3 (1977).

Heidenreich, Conrad. *Huronia: A History and Geography of the Huron Indians, 1650–1660.* Toronto, 1971.

Henry, Alexander. *Travels and Adventures in Canada and the Indian Territories between the Years 1760 and 1776.* Edmonton, 1969.

Innis, Harold A. *The Fur Trade in Canada: An Introduction to Canadian Economic History.* rev. ed. Toronto, 1956.

Jones, R. L. *History of Agriculture in Ontario, 1663–1880.* Toronto, 1946.

Kaye, Barry. "The Historical Geography of Agriculture and Agricultural Settlements in the Canadian Northwest 1774–ca 1830." PhD diss., University of London, 1976.

Lalemant, Father Charles, in R. G. Thwaites, ed. *Jesuit Relations and Allied Documents.* New York, 1959.

Martin, Calvin. "Ethnohistory: A Better Way to Write Indian History." *Western Historical Quarterly* 9 (1978).

Moodie, D. W. "An Historical Geography of Agricultural Patterns and Resource

Appraisals in Rupert's Land, 1670–1774." PhD diss., University of Alberta, 1972.

Morton, A. S. *A History of the Canadian West to 1870–71*. London, 1939.

Morton, W. L. "Agriculture in the Red River Colony." *Canadian Historical Review* 30 (1949): 305–22.

———. In *London Correspondence Inward from Eden Colvile, 1849*, edited by E. E. Rich. London, 1956.

———. *Manitoba: A History*. 2nd ed. Toronto, 1967.

———, ed. *Manitoba Essays*. Toronto, 1937, 89–105.

Norton, T. E. *The Fur Trade in Colonial New York, 1686–1776*. Madison, 1974.

Perrot, Nicholas. In *The Indian Tribes of the Upper Mississippi Valley and the Region of the Great Lakes*, edited by E. H. Blair. Cleveland, 1911.

Phillips, C. P. *The Fur Trade*. 2 vols. Norman, 1961.

Ray, Arthur J., and D. B. Freeman. "'Give Us Good Measure': An Economic Analysis of Relations between the Indians and the Hudson's Bay Company before 1763." Toronto, 1978.

Rich, E. E. *The Fur Trade and the Northwest to 1857*. Toronto, 1967.

———. *History of the Hudson's Bay Company, 1670–1870*. 2 vols. London, 1959.

———, ed. *Hudson's Bay Copy-Book of Letters Outward etc., Begins 29th May, Ends 5 July, 1687*. Toronto, 1948.

———, ed. *James Isham's Observations on Hudson's Bay, 1743*. Toronto, 1949.

———, ed. *Minutes of the Hudson's Bay Company, 1671–1674*. Toronto, 1942.

———, ed. *Minutes of the Hudson's Bay Company, 1679–1684. First Part, 1679–1682*. Toronto, 1945.

———, ed. *Minutes of the Hudson's Bay Company, 1679–1684. Second Part, 1682–1684*. Toronto, 1946.

Sagard, Father Gabriel. In *The Long Journey to the Country of the Hurons*, edited by G. M. Wrong. Toronto, 1939.

Schoolcraft, Henry. In *Expedition to Lake Itasca*, edited by Philip P. Mason. East Lansing, 1958.

Snow, Dean R. "Abenaki Fur Trade in the Sixteenth Century." *Western Canadian Journal of Anthropology* 6 (1976): 7–9.

Thwaites, Reuben Gold, ed. *Early Western Travels, 1748–1846*. Cleveland, 1904.

———, ed. *The Jesuit Relations and Allied Documents*. 72 volumes. Cleveland, 1896–1901.

Triggar, Bruce. *The Children of Aataensic: A History of the Huron People to 1660*. 2 vols. Montreal, 1976.

Turner, Frederick Jackson. "The Significance of the Frontier in American History." In *Frontier American History*, 1–38. New York, 1920.

Wessel, Thomas. "Agriculture, Indians and American History." *Agricultural History* 50 (1976): 9–20.

Will, George, and George Hyde. *Corn among the Indians of the Upper Missouri*. Lincoln, 1917.

Wishart, D. "Agriculture at the Trading Posts on the Upper Missouri Prior to 1843." *Agricultural History* 47 (1973): 56–62.

Wraxall, Peter. *An Abridgement of the Indian Affairs Contained in Four Folio Volumes, Transacted in the Colony of New York from the Year 1678 to the Year 1751*, edited by C. H. McIlwain. Cambridge, 1915.

9. "Give Us a Little Milk"

The Social and Cultural Significance of
Gift Giving in the Lake Superior Fur Trade

BRUCE M. WHITE

Gift giving was an essential custom followed by both Indians and Europeans to pursue trade and diplomatic relations in North America during the eighteenth and nineteenth centuries. Historical studies of this custom, however, have concentrated on European motives and machinations. Historians have equated it with bribery and have suggested that it was introduced by Europeans. But why did fur traders give gifts at all? How did this expensive social act creep into what has usually been portrayed as merely an exercise in capitalism? One plausible explanation for the widespread use of gift giving lies in its social and cultural meanings for American Indians. A promising area in which to seek answers is the Lake Superior region, where the Ojibway Indians were the focus of important and long-lasting relations with the French, British, and Americans.[1]

What was it about the meanings of gifts in Ojibway culture that made their use important in trade and diplomacy? First, a trader going to the Lake Superior country to set himself up in business was one of only a few Europeans living away from home in that foreign land. To his intended producers and customers, the Ojibway, he was a stranger, potentially either an enemy or a friend. In order to do business, the trader had to prove to the Indians that he was trustworthy; he also had to make sure that he could trust these people with whom he wanted to trade. He needed to establish a reciprocal confidence that would minimize the risks on both sides.

The trader could not use European methods to do this. He could not, for example, take the Indians before a notary to sign legal contracts, for there were no written laws and no courts to enforce them. Rather, the trader had to make an agreement with the Ojibway on their own terms, using Indian techniques to establish a binding relationship. The most common way was gift giving.

On the simplest level the Ojibway, like many other cultural groups, believed that tangible objects could be used to signify feelings. The traveler Johann Georg Kohl, who visited Lake Superior in the 1850s, recorded a fur trader's belief that, for the Ojibway, giving gifts was a necessary way of demonstrating one person's esteem for another: "If you say to one of them 'I love thee,'" wrote Kohl, "have a present ready to hand, to prove your love clearly. You will lose in their sight if a present, or some tangible politeness, does not follow on such an assurance. But it is often sufficient to hand them the plate from which you have been eating, and on which you have left a fragment for them."[2]

Gifts also aided in establishing and affirming more elaborate relationships. Depending on the situations in which they were given and on the words and ceremonies that accompanied them, gifts communicated something about what each partner to the relationship wanted from the other.

Among the Ojibway, the family or kin group served as the basic producer and distributor of goods and services. The parents did not exert the same kind of authoritarian power over their children that European parents might have, and in a very real sense family members' roles were defined less by authority than by the ways in which they cared for, or were cared for by, others in the family. Infants were fed at their mothers' breasts. When they were weaned the fathers or elder brothers provided them with meat and clothing by hunting and fishing, and the mothers or elder sisters might also fish and trap, harvest agricultural products, prepare the food, and make the clothing. The parents' role reversed when the grown children took care of old and feeble parents.[3]

The flow of goods and services along family lines was not limited to the nuclear family, although the extent of participation by cousins, uncles, aunts, grandfathers, and grandmothers in the family's material life might vary. Once an individual had grown up and married, many new patterns of exchange would be established, and these also might vary. In any case, marriage would probably broaden a person's economic possibilities and obligations.[4]

Another extension of material relationships was the *dodem* or totem. Every child inherited his father's totem, through which he was related to a wide variety of individuals in his own and other Ojibway communities around Lake Superior. These people, addressed as "brother" and "sister," were important relatives to whom he could appeal when in need and to whom he himself would be obligated should they be without closer kin nearby.[5]

What then did this social pattern have to do with the dealings between Ojibway who were not related, or with the society-wide institutions of trade and diplomacy in which the Ojibway confronted non-Indian societies? Since the exchange of goods and services was basically a function of kinship, it appears that the flow of the goods and services taking place outside the bonds of kinship was structured in kinship terms.

In such nonfamilial circumstances the bond would be invented, not inherited. The power and extent of these new relationships were based on the degree to which they could be made to resemble the social and economic relations that existed among family members. To have relationships with someone in a material sense was to be related in a metaphorical sense. John Tanner, a white man adopted by an Ottawa family, found this to be true when he and his adoptive kin were in need in the early 1800s. An Ojibway family west of Lake Superior took them into its lodge, offering to care for and feed them during the winter. Later on, said Tanner, whenever he or his Ottawa family saw any member of the other family, they called the Ojibway family "brothers" and treated them like relatives.[6]

On the other hand, if one person wished to establish with another a close relationship that encompassed all the rights and obligations found most clearly in the family, he would turn to a tangible definition of such bonds and give gifts. In recent times, anthropologist

"Give Us a Little Milk"

Ruth Landes noted that, among the Ojibway of western Ontario, if a person wanted to adopt someone else, the relationship would be partly affirmed by gift giving. One of Landes's female informants told of being adopted by an older woman:

> She took me for her daughter after her daughter's death, and she called me by her daughter's name. She asked me if she could not have me for a daughter. I said it was alright and I called her "mother." She gave me things and I gave her things as I would to my own mother.

When the woman's husband died, her adopted mother helped provide gifts to her husband's family in a practice known as paying off the mourning.[7]

Gifts resulted in a close relationship, just as a close relationship would result in gifts being given. If you wished to receive or to present goods to someone, you would address the other person as your brother, sister, father, or mother. A mixed-blood named William Johnston, who traded near Leech Lake in 1833, offered an example of this in the hospitality shown him by several Ojibway. "The Indians claimed relationship with me, from some remarks that I made, and that since I had the same totem I should partake of what they had; They gave me a bag of Rice." It was Johnston's mother who was Ojibway; since the totem was usually inherited through the father, the Indians may have invented the relationship with Johnston as an excuse for their kindness to him.[8]

Crucial to certain kinds of gift giving and their meaning in the idiom of kinship was a concept that has been translated as "pity" or "charity." These words occur not only in transcripts of Ojibway meetings with traders and European diplomats but also in more modern ethnographic texts. Landes wrote that "In Ojibwa idiom, to 'pity' another is to adopt him and care for him as a parent or grandparent cares for a child." To give someone a gift with no thought of an immediate return was to "pity" him and thus in a sense to adopt him. This idea was applied not only to relationships between persons but also to those between humans and supernatural beings. A child fasting in search of a vision, for example, sought to evoke the interest of a supernatural spirit. By fasting he made himself "pitiful," hoping to obtain a long-term relationship with a spirit being. Later on, if he were in need, perhaps because of poor luck in hunting, he could call upon his spiritual "grandfather" or "grandmother" for help. One old man described his vision quest to John Tanner:

> When I was yet a little boy, the Great Spirit came to me, after I had been fasting for three days, and told me he had heard me crying, and had come to tell me that he did not wish to hear me cry and complain so often, but that if ever I was reduced to the danger of immediately perishing of hunger, then I should call upon him, and he would hear and give me something.[9]

The Ojibway endowed the animals they hunted with human qualities, frequently addressing them in terms of kinship. The trader Alexander Henry, the elder, who lived with the Ojibway family Wawatam near Michilimackinac in the winter of 1763–64, discovered that the killing of a bear was an occasion for elaborate ceremony and feasting. As soon as Henry had shot the bear, some of the Ojibway took its head "in their hands, stroking and kissing it several times; begging a thousand pardons for taking away her life; calling her their relation and grandmother; and requesting her not to lay the fault upon them, since it was truly an Englishman that had put her to death."[10]

Back at their lodge, the Ojibway took part in ceremonial gift giving designed to allay the bear's anger. Henry wrote:

> As soon as we reached the lodge, the bear's head was adorned with all the trinkets in the possession of the family, such as silver arm-bands and wrist-bands, and belts of wampum; and then laid upon a scaffold. ... Near the nose, was placed a large quantity of tobacco.
>
> The next morning ... preparations were made for a feast to the

"Give Us a Little Milk"

manes [*bear spirits*]. The lodge was cleaned and swept; and the head of the bear lifted up, and a new stroud blanket . . . spread under it. The pipes were now lit; and Wawatam blew tobacco-smoke into the nostrils of the bear, telling me to do the same, and thus appease the anger of the bear, on account of my having killed her.

As this description indicates, one gift given in such exchanges was tobacco. The importance of tobacco as a way of reconciling people and spiritual beings was evident in Ojibway society into the twentieth century. Ethnographer Inez Hilger, after interviewing Ojibway on a variety of reservations in Wisconsin and Minnesota, compared the role of smoking to praying. She quoted an interpreter discussing a Lac Courte Oreille man's spiritual guardian: "Lighting a pipe is the same as praying, for when he lights his pipe he asks his helper to help him." Hilger also cited the words of an Ojibway woman who, taking a root cutting from a plant for medicinal use, placed a small amount of tobacco with the remaining roots, saying, "I'll take just a little for my use, and here is some tobacco for you!"[11] This use of tobacco reflected the fundamental role of smoking in mediation among individuals in Ojibway society. Peezhikee (Buffalo), an early nineteenth-century leader at La Pointe, Wisconsin, described clearly the importance of tobacco at an 1826 treaty meeting with United States government treaty commissioners. He compared his own authority to that of the government agents: "You are strong [enough] to make your young men obey you. But we have no way, *Fathers*, to make our young men listen, but by the pipe."[12]

Gift giving, as shown in these examples, was an important factor in Ojibway life. Linked specifically to the idiom of kinship, it was used in a variety of human, animal, and spiritual relationships. It remains to show how it extended to the Indians' associations with people outside their society.

Many examples can be found in Ojibway dealings with their neighbors, the Dakota. Although warfare between the two groups often occurred, there were also occasions when they made peace.

In a society with no central authority and where chieftainship was the result of winning public support through persuasion, the process of peacemaking often consisted of individual Ojibway making friends with individual Dakota.[13]

When groups of Ojibway hunters traveled into territory occupied by the Dakota, they might turn potential enemies into friends by an exchange of goods as well as by a mutual smoking of tobacco in a calumet. One special kind of exchange involved clothing. A well-known painting of the Ojibway leader Okeemakeequid in Thomas L. McKenney's and James Hall's Indian portrait collection shows the result of such an exchange. He is dressed not in Ojibway costume but in the garb of a Dakota warrior obtained during negotiations at the United States–sponsored treaty of 1825 held at Prairie du Chien. After Okeemakeequid and a Dakota exchanged clothing, the Dakota called him "brother."[14]

Eight years later William Johnston, trading at Leech Lake, reported: "Ten canoes arrived[.] The Principle [*sic*] Chief among the number and two of the young warriors, were drest in Sioux dresses[.] While hunting they met the Sioux, who came up, and extended the hand of friendship; and to ratify it, as is their custom they exchanged all there [*sic*] articles of clothing." The two incidents show that by making this even trade the two individuals established a relationship, however little binding on other members of their societies, in which each renounced his own self-interest. In the process they ceased being enemies and became brothers and friends.[15]

Another, possibly more permanent, kind of exchange by which the Ojibway and Dakota made peace with each other was intermarriage. As anthropologist Claude Lévi-Strauss has clearly shown, intermarriage can be an important way for two societies, by joining their kin groups, to establish a reciprocity of trust and allow many other peaceful exchanges to take place. Describing a period in the early 1700s, historian William Warren noted: "On the St. Croix the two tribes intermingled freely. . . . They encamped together, and intermarriages took place between them." Another example Warren

"Give Us a Little Milk"

used was that of two celebrated Indian leaders, Ma-mong-e-sa-da, an Ojibway, and Wabasha I, a Dakota. They were half-brothers, sons of an Ojibway woman who married twice.[16]

Diplomatic relations between the Ojibway and representatives of European governments had many of the formal characteristics of the Indians' friendly relationships with each other. Tobacco, food, and hospitality were shared, and goods such as clothing, guns, and household equipment were also given. One special item transcended kinship diplomacy. It was wampum, belts or strings of shell beads, and it served as a record of transactions in diplomatic exchanges between tribes as well as with Europeans. Wampum represented in an enduring way the words spoken in an encounter. When two parties had not met face to face, wampum, accompanied by a speech delivered by a messenger, could initiate a transaction. The speech came to be called by the French word *parole*, and the wampum was the tangible, physical manifestation of the message. It was preserved and honored just as were the written treaties that Europeans professed to respect so much. If someone were not interested in making an agreement or did not accept the substance of the *parole*, he would refuse the wampum and any other gifts, just as European governments might refuse to sign treaties or accept diplomatic notes.[17]

Another feature of Ojibway-European diplomacy, however, was somewhat different from the Ojibway-Dakota relations discussed above. While the kinship of brother to brother may have come to typify certain peacemaking efforts of the two Indian groups, it was the relationship of parent to child that often embodied diplomatic relations between European governments and the Ojibway.

It is part of traditional knowledge of Indian-white relations throughout North America that Indians would sometimes refer to a European king, an American president, or a diplomatic agent as "father" and that Europeans similarly called the Indians their "children." Who initially established this metaphor is not known, but the diplomatic idiom fits with what is known about the paternalism of European authority structure just as it coincides with the Ojibway tendency to project the family metaphor onto a multitude of other situations. How did this idiomatic language reflect the aims of the treaty meetings between Europeans and American Indians? How were these purposes reflected in the objects used in accompanying gift exchanges? In the nineteenth century these meetings usually had to do with land purchase. Looking farther back into the seventeenth and eighteenth centuries, however, it is clear that European powers in the area of the Great Lakes vied with each other mainly to win Indian loyalty to their military causes.[18]

Although it has yet to be shown in a quantified way, the Europeans apparently did the bulk of the gift giving in many of these diplomatic transactions, just as in the family group it was initially the father who gave to the child. In effect then, such gifts became an expression of the role Europeans sought to play in relation to the Indians. Indians gave many gifts of furs and ceremonial presents during these exchanges. But they did not necessarily give tangible, equal presents in an economic sense, as in the peace talks between Ojibway and Dakota. Their gift was something more profound—the loyalty that a child feels toward the parent, a long-term tie that was expressed by a defense of the parent against insult and violence and a willingness to avenge an attack. The result was a military alliance cast in kinship terms.

The meaning that this metaphorical kinship had for the Ojibway is evident in the rich and significant speech given by one leader, Minavanana, to Alexander Henry at Michilimackinac shortly after the fall of Quebec in 1761:[19]

> Englishman, you know that the French king is our father. He promised to be such; and we, in return, promised to be his children.— This promise we have kept.
>
> Englishman, it is you that have made war with this our father. You are his enemy; and how, then, could you have the boldness to venture among us, his children?—You know that his enemies are ours. . . .

"Give Us a Little Milk"

Englishman, our father, the king of France, employed our young men to make war upon your nation. In this warfare, many of them have been killed; and it is our custom to retaliate, until such time as the spirits of the slain are satisfied. But, the spirits of the slain are to be satisfied in either of two ways; the first is by the spilling of the blood of the nation by which they fell; the other, by *covering the bodies of the dead,* [*in new clothing and ornaments before burial*], and thus allaying the resentment of their relations. This is done by making presents.

Englishman, your king has never sent us any presents, nor entered into any treaty with us, wherefore he and we are still at war; and, until he does these things, we must consider that we have no other father, nor friend, among the white men, than the king of France; but, for you, we have taken into consideration, that you have ventured your life among us, in the expectation that we should not molest you. You do not come armed, with an intention to make war; you come in peace, to trade with us, and supply us with necessaries, of which we are in much want. We shall regard you, therefore, as a brother; and you may sleep tranquilly, without fear of the Chipeways.—As a token of our friendship we present you with this pipe, to smoke.

For the Ojibway this parent-child idiom was the function of a particular type of diplomatic contact with European governments. The Ojibway might reject the use of the metaphor when whites attempted to impose it on a relationship that it did not fit. In 1832 Eschkebugecoshe (Flat Mouth) of Leech Lake objected when Indian agent Henry R. Schoolcraft called them "children" in a speech to the assembled warriors of his band. "You call us children. We are not children, but men," he insisted. He criticized the American government for failing to enforce the agreement it had brought about between the Ojibway and Dakota at Prairie du Chien in 1825.[20]

Our great father promised us, when we smoked the pipe with the Sioux at Prairie du Chien in 1825, and at Fond du Lac in 1826, that the first party who crossed the line, and broke the treaty, should be punished. This promise has not been fulfilled. . . . I do not think the Great Spirit ever made us to sit still and see our young men, our wives, and our children murdered.

Since we have listened to the Long Knives [American soldiers], we have not prospered. They are not willing we should go ourselves, and flog our enemies, nor do they fulfill their promise and do it for us.

Laying the medals of all the Leech Lake leaders and a string of wampum given to him previously by the Americans at Schoolcraft's feet, Eschkebugecoshe went on:

These and all your letters are stained with blood. I return them all to you to make them bright. None of us wish to receive them back until you have wiped off the blood. . . .

The words of the Long Knives have passed through our forests as a rushing wind, but they have been words merely. They have only shaken the trees, but have not stopped to break them down, nor even to make the rough places smooth.

Eskebugecoshe's objection to the term "children" appeared to have had little to do with resentment at being treated like children. Instead he seemed to resent being called "children" by a representative of the "Great Father," who had not kept the obligations of this metaphorical parenthood defined in the treaty at Prairie du Chien. Eshkebugecoshe rejected not only the term of address, but also the misrepresentations of the government's words, the medals, and the strings of wampum. Were the government to validate its words through actions, perhaps someone like Schoolcraft would again be able to call the Indians "children," for then the words would not be empty or hypocritical.

Sir William Johnson, in charge of the British Indian department in the early 1760s, recognized better than most Europeans the importance of gift giving. The year after the Ojibway-led attack on Michilimackinac in 1763, Johnson sent a messenger to the

"Give Us a Little Milk"

western Great Lakes with a wampum belt and a speech inviting the Indians to a feast at Fort Niagara. The speech also promised them presents that would establish the tangible concern of the British government.[21]

Alexander Henry, who was at Sault Ste. Marie when Johnson's messenger arrived, helped to persuade the Ojibway to accept the spirit of Johnson's words and agreed to accompany a group eastward. Henry described an incident that took place en route, which graphically showed what the Ojibway expected of Johnson and helped to place this act of diplomacy in the context of other types of exchanges that occurred in Ojibway society. One day Henry discovered a rattlesnake not more than two feet from his naked legs. He ran to get his gun. Henry wrote:

> The Indians, on their part, surrounded it, all addressing it by turns, and calling it their *grandfather*; but yet keeping at some distance. During this part of the ceremony, they filled their pipes; and now each blew the smoke toward the snake, who, as it appeared to me, really received it with pleasure. In a word, after remaining coiled, and receiving incense, for the space of half an hour, it stretched itself along the ground, in visible good humour . . . . at last it moved slowly away, the Indians following it, and still addressing it by the title of grand-father, beseeching it to take care of their families during their absence, and to be pleased to open the heart of Sir William Johnson, so that he might *show them charity*, and fill their canoe with rum.

It is significant that these Ojibway should have associated rum with "charity," for in diplomatic dealings between the Ojibway and the Europeans, rum, brandy, whisky, and other forms of alcohol seem to have crystallized the idiom of kinship more than any of the other gifts. The names given alcohol are important. Although it was known in nondiplomatic situations by a term translated as "firewater," when it was given away by European government agents in a ceremonial way, the Ojibway referred to it as "milk," meaning mother's milk.[22]

One could postulate various psychological explanations for this metaphor. For example, under the influence of alcohol, a drinker might revert to childish behavior. What also of the possible associations between sucking from glass bottles—in which rum was sometimes given to the Ojibway—and sucking from a breast?

There are also possible ironies in the use of the term "milk." One can imagine the thoughts of the military officers at Drummond Island in 1816 when a noted leader of the Sandy Lake Ojibway, Katawaubetai (Broken Tooth), stood before them and said: "Father—I come from a great distance and have waited patiently in hopes of getting some of your milk to drink but I find you do not seem inclined to let me draw near your breast." What did Thomas McKenney and his fellow commissioners at the treaty meetings of Fond du Lac ten years later think when Peezhikee said: "*Fathers,*— you have many children. But your breasts drop yet. Give us a little milk, *Fathers,* that we may wet our lips."[23]

There probably was no better way for the Ojibway leaders to insult the Europeans and still get what they wanted. In effect, they could be saying: "You call us your children. We do not think so much of you. You are women. Are you our mothers? Then feed us as a mother should." This rich, suggestive image contains many contradictory facets of relations between Europeans and Indians. But the image probably derives from the cultural meanings of mother's milk.

Milk is the first gift that a child receives when he is born. It is no exaggeration to suggest, as Marshall Sahlins has, that it is a prime example of the pure gift. It is the quintessence of all gifts that a parent gives to a child, because it flows freely from the mother to the infant and is given with absolutely no thought of a return gift. The obvious exchange for mother's milk is the loyalty of child to parents, perhaps one of the strongest manifestations of kinship.[24]

The strength of this image must have been especially powerful for Ojibway society, in which mothers nursed their children as long as four years, so that breast feeding might well be a strong memory for all. The geographer and ethnologist Joseph N. Nicollet, who traveled among the Ojibway of the upper Mississippi River in 1837, remarked that "One often sees a little boy leave the playground with his bow and arrow, find and unveil his mother's breast, suckle a few moments, then return to his game with his little friends." It is also interesting to note that it was only while she was still nursing the child that an Ojibway mother had any authority over her sons, and, in fact, then she had as much authority as the father later had.[25]

Rum, that valuable European liquid, came to represent mother's milk, the gift which more than any other signified the concern of a parent for her child and the loyalty of a child for his mother. Rum, given in diplomatic dealings, symbolized the seriousness with which the Ojibway and other Indian groups treated these diplomatic transactions; it also demonstrated how the Ojibway could give a foreign product unique meanings far from its original European context. The adoption of European material objects did not, therefore, necessarily endanger the Indians' own cultural values.[26]

Because rum held this symbolic meaning in diplomatic exchanges with the Ojibway, it would be inaccurate to think that its full significance resided simply in its intoxicating qualities. Who would say the same of the wine that, in Christian communion, becomes the "blood of Christ"?

What evidence associates the metaphorical meanings of rum and other diplomatic gifts with those same gifts used in the fur trade? Is it valid to suggest that they served the same purposes in trade that they did in diplomacy? There was a similarity between the traders' requests of the Indians and those of governments. On the simplest level, the trader was a stranger seeking material exchange with the Indians. To succeed, he had to make an agreement, to establish relationships that resembled family ties. He also wanted to obtain loyalty that would bind the Indians to him and not to another trader. But in this respect the trader did not want to do all the giving; he did not want to be a "father" or "mother" to the Indians. Rather, he wanted reciprocity—the Indians providing furs equal in value to the trade goods he offered. Like the Dakota who exchanged clothing with his "brother" Ojibway, the trader wanted to give clothing, blankets, and tools and receive in return the Indian's clothing, the beaver robes that he had worn, as well as all the other furs that he did not wear.

In some ways the fur trade relationship could exactly parallel that between the Indian agent and his "children." Sometimes a large fur company took on the characteristics that one would expect only a government to have had. The Ojibway of Lac du Flambeau, Wisconsin, were in the habit of referring to William McGillivray, one of the chief partners of the North West Company, as their "father." When François Victoire Malhiot arrived there in the winter of 1804–05 as North West trader, his men circulated the rumor that he was McGillivray's brother. The Indians thereupon began addressing him as "father."[27]

McGillivray, a distant figure who did not come to visit the Ojibway, performed in effect the function of a king or president. It was in McGillivray's name that presents were given at the beginning of the trading year. The actual exchanges of goods took place with a trader who more nearly represented a brother to them. Perhaps for this reason Malhiot undertook to represent himself not as their "father" but as an equal to the Ojibway, calling them either his comrades or his relatives. In other ways he sought to capitalize on McGillivray's parental position. For example, Malhiot gave some presents to a chief named l'Outarde (Bustard), saying,

My Relation. The coat which I have just placed upon you is sent by the Great Trader [McGillivray]. It is with this clothing that he honors the most eminent of a nation. This flag is [also] a real mark of a leader with which you must feel honored, since we do not give them to just any Indian. You must be what you are to get one, that is to say, you must love the French [the mostly French-Canadian traders who represented the company in the area] the way you do and protect them and help make packs of furs for them. . . . Look

"Give Us a Little Milk"

at me, all of you, see before you the trader sent to you. I am the one you asked for. I received this summer three *paroles* from the chiefs on the prairies to go back to winter in their land. But I refused them in order to live up to what the Great Trader told you. He sent me here to be charitable toward you but not to be scorned. . . . be devoted to our fort, protect its doors, and I will carry good news about you all to your Father in the spring.

The smaller companies and independent traders, who were more typical of the Europeans trading among the Ojibway, had little chance to win their loyalty by giving gifts in the name of a "Great Trader." Often they merely represented themselves. Yet they used many of the same gifts as North West Company traders. The account of John Long, an independent trader among a group of Ojibway northeast of Lake Nipigon in Ontario in the 1760s, demonstrated the process by which inexperienced traders could be initiated into gift giving by the Ojibway themselves.[28]

On arrival at his wintering place, Long was greeted by a large band of people and their leader Kesconeek (Broken Arm), who gave him skins, dried meat, fish, and wild rice. In return Long gave them some gifts, but he did not report what they were. Then the Indians went into Long's house. Kesconeek, "standing upright with great dignity in the centre of the tribe," delivered a speech which the trader recorded in both Ojibway and English: "It is true, Father, I and my young men are happy to see you:—as the great Master of Life has sent a trader to take pity on us Savages [the Ojibway version of this speech gives this word as "Nishinnorbay," or Anishinabe, meaning simply people or Indians], we shall use our best endeavours to hunt and bring you wherewithal to satisfy you in furs, skins, and animal food."

In Long's opinion the speech was an attempt to

induce me to make them further presents; I indulged them in their expectations, by giving them two kegs of rum of eight gallons each, lowered with a small proportion of water, according to the usual custom adopted by all traders, five carrots of tobacco, fifty scalping knives, gunflints, powder, shot, ball, &c. To the women I gave beads, trinkets, &c and to eight chiefs who were in the band, each a North-west gun, a callico [*sic*] shirt, a scalping knife of the best sort, and an additional quantity of ammunition. These were received with a full yo-hah, or demonstration of joy.

In the metaphorical relationship of parent to child, the parent is seen at least initially, as giving the greater quantity of goods. Thus, when an Ojibway wanted to establish a reciprocal, gift-giving relationship with someone, he would, like Kesconeek, address the other as "father" and appeal to his "pity." The Ojibway also sought to evoke the pity of spiritual beings by fasting—a way of showing that he was truly in need of any aid that beings might offer. Long may very well have been correct in assuming that Kesconeek wanted the trader to give more presents. But did it necessarily follow that ceremonial demonstrations were made strictly with immediate material return in mind? If an Indian told a trader or a government agent that he was "destitute" and in great need, did this mean that he was simply acquisitive? Was it not also possible that he was interested in establishing a social and political tie with the trader or government agent?[29]

Such a possibility might put into perspective many accounts of diplomatic and trade meetings between the Ojibway and Europeans in which the latter reported their distinct impressions that the Indians were suffering, starving, and greatly dependent on them— perhaps far more than was actually the case. The Europeans may have been confusing objects and what they represented, ignoring the important contextual factors.[30]

An incident recorded by Alexander Henry, the elder, on his first trading voyage west of Lake Superior in 1775, suggests that occasionally the Ojibway claimed to be in need when they were really well off. His description of a typical transaction at Lake of the Woods contained many of the elements found in other such

"Give Us a Little Milk"

trades, but in this case the trader was just as much in need as the Indians claimed to be. Henry wrote:

> From this village, we received ceremonious presents. The mode with the Indians is, first to collect all the provisions they can spare, and place them in a heap; after which they send for the trader, and address him in a formal speech. They tell him, that the Indians are happy in seeing him return into their country; that they have been long in expectation of his arrival; that their wives have deprived themselves of their provisions, in order to afford him a supply; that they are in great want, being destitute of every thing, and particularly of ammunition and clothing; and that what they most long for, is a taste of his rum, which they uniformly denominate *milk*.
>
> The present, in return, consisted in one keg of gunpowder, of sixty pounds weight; a bag of shot and another of powder, of eighty pounds each; a few smaller articles, and a keg of rum. The last appeared to be the chief treasure, though on the former depended the greater part of their winter's subsistence.
>
> In a short time, the men began to drink, while the women brought a further and very valuable present, of twenty bags of rice. This I returned with goods and rum, and at the same time offered more, for an additional quantity of rice. A trade was opened, the women bartering rice, while the men were drinking. Before morning, I had purchased a hundred bags, of nearly a bushel measure each. Without a large quantity of rice, the voyage could not have been prosecuted to its completion.[31]

Were the Indians in this ceremonial exchange saying that without the European's aid they would not be able to survive? Or were they simply following the etiquette of such encounters as they saw it?

The possible ambiguities in the metaphorical kinship ties that the Ojibway used for establishing friendship with strangers are evident. In terms of gift giving, for instance, a trader might function as a "father" or "mother"; in terms of direct trade, the relationship might be that of a "brother." Certainly such contradictions in the relationship might cause some confusion in regard to what each party expected from the other. But the trader might make another more durable bond, possibly assuring more clarity in his relations with the Ojibway, by changing a metaphorical tie into a "real" one. He might marry an Indian woman.

Frequently, the influence and success that a trader had with Indians corresponded to the strength and renown of his father-in-law. Leading traders often married the daughters of leading Ojibway; in marrying a chief's daughter, the trader gained a powerful ally among his Indian customers. Since the authority of a chief was generally the result of extended kinship ties, the trader may have formed actual ties with a larger number of people. The chief's influence over kin and nonkin alike depended largely upon his persuasive abilities—especially his oratory. Thus, through marriage, the trader gained an alliance with a man of demonstrated ability to influence his fellows. The father-in-law became in a sense a diplomatic agent for the trader, useful in persuading his people to be friends and customers.[32]

For the chief there were comparable advantages. Allying with a trader could bolster his own influence and power with his people, since the chief would often distribute the gifts that his son-in-law brought each year to trade. In so doing, the leader gave material demonstration of concern for the welfare of the other Indians within his family or within the larger group, showing that he was worthy, generous, and unselfish. These attributes might strengthen his ties to nonkin.

In any case, gift giving was of continuing importance to the fur trader. Marrying into an Indian family did not lessen his obligation to give gifts; it simply provided him with a previously defined kinship network in which to carry on his gift giving. Only by continuing this was the trader's position in this kinship system validated.

Far from being bribery, gift giving—whether in personal relationships, trade, or diplomacy—was an important social act among the Ojibway. Without participating in the process a foreigner, whether he be a diplomat or a trader, could not hope to arrive at his political or economic ends. By their participation, fur traders and diplomats

"Give Us a Little Milk"

demonstrated more than a superficial understanding of Ojibway culture.[33]

Notes

The author wrote this article while on sabbatical leave under a grant from the Minnesota Historical Society's Charles E. Flandrau Research Fund to conduct a social-business study of independent traders in the Lake Superior area from 1760 to 1820 as partial fulfillment of a master's degree in history at McGill University in Montreal.

1. This paper also appeared in the Summer 1982 issue of *Minnesota History*. The author thanks Deborah L. Miller, Roger Buffalohead, Donald F. Bibeau, and Trevor Barnes for their valuable advice and criticism. Gift giving in diplomacy is described in Wilbur R. Jacobs, *Wilderness Politics and Indian Gifts: The Northern Colonial Frontier, 1748–1763* (Lincoln NE, 1967). Fur-trade gift giving is mentioned in Wilcomb E. Washburn, "Symbol, Utility, and Aesthetics in the Indian Fur Trade," in Dale L. Morgan, et al., *Aspects of the Fur Trade: Selected Papers of the 1965 North American Fur Trade Conference* (St. Paul, 1967), 50. On the supposed European origins of gift giving, see Ida Amanda Johnson, *The Michigan Fur Trade* (Lansing MI, 1919), 65.

2. Johann George Kohl, *Kitchi-Gami: Wanderings round Lake Superior* (reprint ed., Minneapolis, 1956), 133. To allow someone to eat from your plate is an intimate gesture characteristic of family life. The implications of this are discussed below.

3. This is neither an argument for nor against theories of the "atomistic" social organization of the Ojibway discussed in Harold Hickerson, *The Southwestern Chippewa: An Ethnohistorical Study* (American Anthropological Association, *Memoir 92*, Menasha WI, 1962), 9–11; Victor Barnouw, *Wisconsin Chippewa Myths and Tales and Their Relation to Chippewa Life* (Madison WI, 1977), 5–8. To argue that the family was the basic unit of organization among the Ojibway is not to suggest that there were not other important institutions of society. What is proposed here is that the family provided a metaphor for other more extensive links between individuals in Ojibway life. On parental authority, see Peter Jones, *History of the Ojebway Indians* (London, 1861), 67.

4. Ruth Landes, *Ojibwa Sociology* (New York, 1937), 27.

5. Landes, *Ojibwa Sociology*, 43; Sister M. Inez Hilger, *Chippewa Child Life and Its Cultural Background* (Bureau of American Ethnology, *Bulletin 146*, Washington DC, 1951), 155.

6. Edwin James, ed., *A Narrative of the Captivity and Adventures of John Tanner* (reprint ed., Minneapolis, 1956), 24.

7. Landes, *Ojibwa Sociology*, 16, 17. See also Hilger, *Child Life*, 34.

8. William Johnston, "Letters on the Fur Trade 1833," in *Michigan Pioneer and Historical Collections* (Lansing, 1909, 1910), 37:177.

9. Ruth Landes, *The Ojibwa Woman* (New York, 1938), 6. See also Johnston, in *Michigan Pioneer and Historical Collections*, 37:182; James, ed., *John Tanner*, 143. Here and throughout this article, English translations of Ojibway words and speeches are used; unfortunately there are no Indian versions of most of these documents. In using these translations, the author assumes that there is a fair accuracy on the part of the translator and that the consistency found in many of these translations is not simply accidental but a reflection of real consistency in the original Ojibway terminology and the ideas in back of them. Work with modern Ojibway informants by researchers skilled in the Ojibway language may be the only way to deal linguistically with the issues presented here.

10. Here and two paragraphs below, see Alexander Henry, *Travels and Adventures in Canada and the Indian Territories* (reprint ed., New York, 1976), 73, 143, 144. See also Landes, *Ojibwa Woman*, 15. Wawatam was an Ojibway whom Henry had first met at Michilimackinac and who adopted the trader as a brother soon after.

11. Hilger, *Child Life*, 47, 92.

12. Thomas L. McKenney, *Sketches of a Tour to the Lakes* (reprint ed., Minneapolis, 1959), 462. The spelling of Ojibway names throughout this article follows that in the cited source; variations may be found in Newton H. Winchell, *The Aborigines of Minnesota: A Report* (St. Paul, 1911), 707–31.

13. For a discussion of the roots of traditional Ojibway authority, see James G. E. Smith, *Leadership among the Southwestern Ojibwa* (National Museums of Canada, National Museum of Man, *Publications in Ethnology*, no. 7, Ottawa, 1973), 17. The words "chief" and "leader" are used interchangeably here to mean a person of influence rather than an individual with coercive power.

14. Thomas L. McKenney and James Hall, *The Indian Tribes of North America* (Edinburgh, 1933), 256.

15. Johnston, in *Michigan Pioneer Collections*, 37:186. See also William W. Warren, "History of the Ojibways, Based Upon Traditions and Oral Statements," in Minnesota Historical Society (MHS), *Collections* (St. Paul, 1885), 5:268; Marshall Sahlins, *Stone Age Economics* (Hawthorne NY, 1976), 220. Sahlins' work, especially his essay "On the Sociology of Primitive Exchange" (185–275), is a very useful guide to understanding the cultural meanings of gift giving.

16. Claude Lévi-Strauss, *The Elementary Structures of Kinship* (Boston, 1969), 45–47; Sahlins, *Stone Age Economics*, 222; Warren, in MHS, *Collections*, 5:164, 219.

17. J[ohn] Long, *Voyages and Travels of an Indian Interpreter and Trader* (reprint ed., Toronto, 1974), 47.

18. See Jacobs, *Wilderness Politics*, 11. Michael Paul Rogin examines the diplomatic parent-child metaphor and its role in United States Indian policy in his work *Fathers and Children: Andrew Jackson and Subjugation of the American Indian* (New York, 1976). His discussion of the paternalism of European and American authority is useful (19–26), but his statement that the family metaphor "was not an Indian conceit but a white one" (209) is based on little evidence.

19. Here and three paragraphs below, see Henry, *Travels and Adventures*, 43–45.

20. Here and four paragraphs below, see Edward D. Neill, "History of the Ojibways and Their Connection with Fur Traders," in MHS, *Collections*, 5:480.

21. Here and two paragraphs below, see Arthur Pound, *Johnson of the Mohawks, A Biography* (New York, 1930), 404–9; Henry, *Travels and Adventures*, 176.

22. Friedrich Baraga, *A Dictionary of the Otchipwe Language* (reprint ed., Minneapolis, 1969), 1:216, 2:158; Alexander Henry, *New Light on the Early History of the Greater Northwest* (reprint ed., Minneapolis, 1965), 203.

23. Minutes of Councils (bound volume), July 22, 1816, in William McKay Papers, McCord Museum, Montreal, 16; McKenney, *Tour to the Lakes*, 462.

24. Sahlins, *Stone Age Economics*, 194. For some, the material exchange between mother and child symbolized the relations between all people in a "primitive tribal community." Karl Marx for example, sees the primitive individual as "man . . . who has not yet severed the umbilical cord that unites him with his fellowmen." Marx, *Capital* (New York, 1977), 1:79.

25. Martha Coleman Bray, ed., *The Journals of Joseph N. Nicollet: A Scientist on the Mississippi Headwaters, with Notes on Indian Life* (St. Paul, 1970), 188.

26. The variety of works that suggest this last possibility are discussed in Donald F. Bibeau's valuable paper "The Fur Trade from a Tribal Point of View: A Critique," also given at the 1981 North American Fur Trade Conference.

27. Here and below, see author's translation from François Victoire Malhiot, Journal, 1804–05, 3 Sept. 1804, p. 13, in Rare Books and Special Collections, McGill University Libraries, Montreal.

28. Here and two paragraphs below, see Long, *Voyages and Travels*, 55.

29. Among the Australian Bushmen, for example, to ask someone for something was to show your love for him; Sahlins, *Stone Age Economics*, 232.

30. See McKenney, *Tour to the Lakes*, 460.

31. Here and three paragraphs below, see Henry, *Travels and Adventures*, 243.

32. The behavior of the Ojibway chief Keeshkemun (La Pierre à Affiler) toward his son-in-law, XY trader Simon Chaurette, suggests, however, that ambiguities might still be present in the relationship of father and son-in-law. Keeshkemun seemed to be Chaurette's ally as long as Chaurette was present. When he was gone, Keeshkemun dealt with Chaurette's rival, Malhiot. See Malhiot, Journal, 5 Aug. 1804, p. 6, 4 Feb. 1805, p. 27. Even more distant Indian-trader kinship was useful; trader Michel Cadot, at Lac du Flambeau in the 1780s, derived benefits from the intercession of his wife's uncle; Warren, in MHS, *Collections*, 5:302.

33. For more about cultural communication and understanding as important by-products of the fur-trade process, see Bruce M. White, "Parisian Women's Dogs: A Bibliographical Essay on Cross-Cultural Communication and Trade," in Carolyn Gilman, *Where Two Worlds Meet: The Great Lakes Fur Trade* (St. Paul, 1982), 120–26. There are of course many unanswered questions having to do with the economic impact of gift giving on fur trade rates of exchange and traders' profits. At what point did metaphorical and real kinship become an impossible economic burden? The author is engaged in a study of these problems in relation to the Lake Superior fur trade.

10. "Starving" and Survival in the Subarctic Fur Trade

A Case for Contextual Semantics

MARY BLACK-ROGERS

Fur traders' journals, although written in "the English language," are laced with terminology that may confound or mislead today's English-speaking readers. One such term, "STARVING," when examined in context over a large number of occurrences, leads to the discovery of related trade terms forming a semantic complex peculiar to the trader-Indian contact situation. This study focuses on subarctic Algonquian and Athapaskan Indians as they interacted with the eighteenth- and nineteenth-century traders who invaded their territory for commercial purposes and who kept diaries in which was recorded their view of the daily events that affected their business.

In the subarctic environment, survival assumes critical proportions and accounts for some central and productive parts of the lexicon—in both traders' and Indian languages. The stem-word /STARV-/ in all its syntactic forms is a key that opens a Pandora's Box of variable usages, as found in trading post journals. It comes in measures of quantity and quality (STARVing much and STARVing hard), of duration (still STARVing, STARVed half the winter), of approximation (almost STARVed, half STARVed), and of extent (a family STARVing, we are all STARVing together). There is also a scale of credibility (the usual yarn, STARVation) and of fatality (perished of STARVing).

A notable data example comes from the caustic pen of Willard Ferdinand Wentzel written at Fort Simpson in March 1824:

> [He] brings us the lamentable news that Many of the Indians are starving and have eaten their Furs, and that it is firmly believed that one family have actually starved of Starvation.[1]

Taking Wentzel's inference about multiple meanings of /STARV-/ out from between the lines and looking at it systematically and cross-culturally, one can seek to identify the kinds of messages that passed between Indians and traders with the use of this term. Of particular note should be the meanings to the Indians who were, after all, the principal starvees and oft-reported utterers of the word. (The "word" as translated by the trader, in these cases.) Readers of fur trade documents are likely to get a rather lopsided idea about the trader's Indian customers if they rely solely on his business records—for in these writings he seldom stops to elucidate either the fur trade jargon used or his knowledge of Indian culture beyond what is of "interest to the Concern."

To try to discern the variety of meanings intended, fur trade documents were sampled that were written at trading posts from James Bay to the Mackenzie Valley. Over the past ten years E. S. Rogers and I have read well over seven hundred such post records of traders' grassroots encounters with Indians. Occurrences in our notes of any form of the stem /STARV-/ were extracted along with the context. There were such exuberant numbers of /STARV-/s that only a fraction, less than five hundred, have been entered and coded to date. These are judged to be representative, however. Although contexts were coded for such factors as sickness, weather, and location, statistical correlation with known epidemics or climatic records was ruled out for the present, due to uneven geographical and temporal coverage, non-literal usages, and the use of synonyms. Historical lexicon changes and dialect differences could also be charted, as well as comparison with non–fur trade usage. The present study simply focuses on varieties of meanings as used by fur traders. An incipient glossary of related fur trade terms appears in Appendix A.

Three major varieties of /STARV-/ were found in the data. These will be called LITERAL USAGES, TECHNICAL USAGES, and MANIPULA-TIVE USAGES. Proceeding from first to third, one finds the messages increasing in complexity and in cultural disparities—between Indian and European, trader and layman. There is accordingly a progressive likelihood of communicative failure.

Literal Usage

Webster defines starve: "to perish with hunger; also to suffer from extreme hunger."[2] Literal fur trade usage could be expected to deal with lack of food and going without eating. It was found to extend to a set of related factors, including nutrition, clothing, equipment, and mobility. On what evidence is a data case classified as literal? Context may help: "this was his fourth day since he tasted anything except water" or "in a miserable condition . . . mere skeletons & barely able to walk." Malnutrition is indicated when /STARV-/ is accompanied by "having nothing but Rabbits to subsist on." Then there is the drastic evidence: "they having been obliged to kill six of their children for food," and finally: "Seven of their number was Starved to Death in the early part of February."[3]

It is necessary to consider what literal "starving to death" consisted of. Death, when it came to that, appears to have been the end results of a sequence of interdependent events and conditions; the final cause of death more than likely was freezing, in subarctic winters. The sequence toward death could be slow and halting, frequently interrupted and sometimes arrested by a turnaround in the availability of food. A firsthand view can be found in diaries kept by Lt. John Franklin and his officers during the days and weeks of 1821 (16 Aug. to 1 Dec.) when their overland arctic party was gradually decimated by starvation (nine of the twenty survived to reach Great Slave Lake). Their words fill in the flesh of the bald /STARV-/ statements of traders, as they described felt symptoms and fallen comrades day by day: periods of no game relieved by temporary respite, weakness replacing hunger as the greatest enemy, resistance to cold undermined by malnutrition, the nutritional value computed of singed furs and fried bones, "debilitated frames" too weak to lift a gun while reindeer were "sporting on the river," erosion of the will to keep going contrasted with energy renewal kindled by new hope of relief.[4]

Usage of the term /STARV-/ appears to begin with food deprivation sufficient to initiate the start of such a sequence, including states of malnutrition where food is not totally absent but is of the kind that fails to provide resistance to cold, illness, and debilitating weakness. Such weakness meant inability to keep moving after game, or to find shelter, or to hunt even when game was present— bringing further deprivation not only of food but also of materials for essential clothing and cover, since dependence on game animals for all three basic needs and on the mobility to secure them was supreme. This sequence might more aptly be termed a Starvation Syndrome.[5] Usage of the related fur trade term, /NAKED-/, to refer to lack of appropriate clothing for hunting, shows the place of this factor in the syndrome—particularly leather for lightweight "action" garments and for proper snowshoe lacings, pointing in turn to the importance of the mobility factor.

The Starvation Syndrome is found explicitly expressed by traders: "[they arrived] in a most miserable Condition, Lame, Sick, and Starved . . . part of their Familys a days Journey of crawling after them . . ."; "Starving all winter having no other snowshoes than Pieces of Boards . . . not Being able to Subsist long in one Place"; "all most perishing to death with Starvation . . . being so Reduced . . . not able to make a hole in the Ice . . . to Hook."[6] Literal starving means food-hunt failure, but the causes are embedded in a matrix of factors that are variously conceived and planned for. They form the basis for subsistence strategies, contingency plans, and decisions made by the hunter at given points in the sequence. Factors beyond his control, such as climatic conditions, game cycles, epidemics, and sometimes fur traders, must be dealt with each season within a flexible plan that calls for a delicate balancing of calculated risks.[7]

The concept, of "being in control" may be significant, here. The Indian's perception of his relationship to the natural and social environment probably involved notions alien to the European. (The description that follows is based on personal ethnographic work with Ojibwa Indians, and on others' field data gathered among the Cree and other Algonquians. It does not refer to Athapaskan work, but may apply in part).[8] In Ojibwa belief systems, events and conditions beyond one's control had special rules for handling, manifested in behavior referred to as 'respect.' The Indian perception did not separate the natural and social environment; all of nature's things were living and humans interacted with them. There was no accidental or nonpurposeful event; all were caused by 'persons,' whether human or other-than-human. The natural elements and the animal, botanical, and mineral species had their own modes of 'power.' Power resided in everything, but not with equal strength; the measure of every interaction was an assessment of relative power—which could change from day to day, although a general continuum existed from the most powerful spirits to the lowest of insects, with humans scattered throughout the middle of the spectrum. There was no break between "natural" and "supernatural" in this continuum. Humans, however, were dependent upon 'gifts' of power in the form of 'blessings' from their individual spirit helpers, with whom a private 'respect/bless' relationship obtained. It was not good policy to speak of one's own powers (boasting and competitive motivations were frowned upon), and it was bad policy to try to control others against their will (coercive powers were recognized but considered 'bad medicine'). Individual autonomy and self-sufficiency were revered, but the facts of dependence and interdependence were not overlooked. One had the most 'respect' for those upon whom one was most dependent.

It is not surprising, then, that center stage was generally occupied by the relationship of men to the major game animals. This is probably the deepest and oldest level of the religion of Ojibwa and Cree people—the core aspects of which are still too sensitive and important to be spoken of except ritually. Perhaps this was part of the reason they do not frequently surface in trading-post documents.[9]

At the transition from literal to technical usage are the cases where trappers were reported to have "singed and eaten their furs." An ironic situation. From an outpost at Duck Lake (east of Lake Winnipeg), here is part of a 1799 journal entry:

> . . . on approaching ny ye house [he] called out starving . . . he informed me that his Children has Singed and eaten above 20 Br in furs . . . [10]

This is a double-barreled kind of communication: a literal message, in that furs would not be eaten except in the absence of other food, and a technical message in that if furs have been singed and eaten then they are lost to the trader—sometimes a few hours prior to when they might have been delivered to his door. Literally and miserably, the Indian had eaten up the profits.

Technical Usage

The technical definition of the term /STARV-/ that is proposed here will not be found in a standard English dictionary. It belongs in a specialized glossary of fur trade language. There it might read, "A condition in which primary attention must be directed to the food quest, allowing little leeway for other activities." In fur trade language it would read HUNTING FOR THE BELLY AND NOT FOR FURS. A goodly number of data cases can be analyzed as technical and many others partly technical. The fur trade meaning of /STARV-/ in the pure cases does not necessarily involve hunger. On the other hand, it is seldom divorced from food: "Most of them has not payd their Debts upon the Account of Starvation in the winter"; "a poor hunt indeed . . . they have been looking for Deers which prevented them hunting fur animals . . . now going to a rabbit ground where they can hunt nothing except them"; or simply "they Say we must Strive to live not to hunt."[11] The trapper who reported that he had to subsist on his fur catch was giving the technical message that he had not brought pelts sufficient to pay his debt because eating had become a first priority. It was a statement based on a business transaction. The Indian was recognizing the trader's priority, which was to obtain furs. Sometimes he added the message: "send some food to my brother's tent (where they are singeing their furs) and you may yet save his catch for yourself."

The basic technical case—"[they] complain of starving hard which prevents them from hunting furs"—did not generally refer to present hunger. Some, in fact, brought food rather than furs, due to technical starving.[12] In short, technical /STARV-/ referred to having escaped starvation at the expense of obtaining furs. It may be argued, that an Indian who is literally starving is likely also to be short of furs. Yes, but just as logically, he may be literally starving because his decision had been to hunt furs.[13] He often enough ended up with furs for dinner. And the trader's report nearly always calculated the eaten revenue among his losses—here is 1799 at Duck Lake again, more fully:

> . . . on approaching ny ye House [he] called out starving . . . he informed me that his Children has Singed and eaten above 20 Br in furs which I am very sory being a good Indn and had about 60 Br in Debt from me last fall . . . [14]

Traders of course endeavored to "save" Indians from this kind of starving, first, by giving advances in the fall to allow the necessary leeway for hunting furs in the coming season. (These were "necessaries," along with some "gratuities," in fur trade terms; they did not include food items; see glossary.) Also traders are found specifically trying to prevent Indians from resorting to fishing places rather than trapping areas or from carrying out their threats to go off to distant caribou grounds and be independent of the post.[15]

Survival formulas are embedded in these issues and the Starvation Syndrome expands to take in the technical aspect. As has been pointed out, for hunting peoples of the Subarctic, "starving to death" is somewhat of a misnomer, a kind of shorthand phrase standing for a sequence or syndrome of events initiated by going without food and eventuating in death. Technical usage can be seen to rest upon this literal, slow process of succumbing. It is an expression of the attempt to interrupt or arrest the process, a decision to escape from the syndrome. The need to maintain strength sufficient to secure food and cover had taken precedence at the point in the sequence which that party decided was the danger point. From an 1828 Trout Lake Journal:

> [he] says that there is very few martens . . . he seed a few Tracks on the Borders of the Wennisk But . . . was Starving at that time and could find nothing where-with to Subsist he was fain to Leave that Place and to try for a Livelihood But he is to go Back thither and Trap During the Spring.[16]

The survival formula was typically flexible enough to accommodate the technical fur trade factors—some of which put new hazards into the Starvation Syndrome: European-introduced epidemics, for example, or defective technology ("the occasion of his starving is oweing to ye badness of his hatchets and Gun"). Some were caught in traveling to the post beyond their usual known track and thereby starved. Others were wary of such an outcome; in 1780 it was noted that Tinnewabeno refused to go on to Albany when Gloucester had no goods to trade for his furs, because "they have no provision to bring them back."[17]

The trader's survival formula was simpler (once his own "necessaries" were secured).[18] His formula was to keep the Indians just above the level of technical starvation—strong enough and motivated to continue pointing their exertions in the direction of the fur bearers—even when first signs of the syndrome might hint at other decisions.

Although humanitarian feeding of literally starving Indians took place, traders also were capable of enticing Indians into risking falling into that state by rewarding the most productive fur hunters with coats, "presents," and titles—as if to instill a spirit of competition for these prizes. Again, there are cultural differences. The Indian ethic (at least among Ojibwa) tended to control the disruptive effect of competition within the group by teaching that such a motive was to be suppressed and that a man does not try to be greater than others. It is likely that Indians viewed trader-endowed chieftainships rather skeptically, once removed from the trading post context. Gifts, however, could be accepted as symbols of valued relationships (see under manipulative usage)—even passed on to other Indians with that objective[19]—and being "cloathed" had its practical as well as its ceremonial aspects, whether or not the Indian went along with the curious white-man ethic that intended it as a reward for his being "industrious" rather than "indolent" or "lazy."

The related term /LAZY-/ appears to have been used almost exclusively in a technical sense. In the fur trade it meant not hunting for furs. It did not signify Indians sitting around doing nothing. A report written during hard times in 1830 at Lac Seul notes

> . . . that these starving Indians . . . should pay their debts . . . is expecting impossibilities . . . altho some of them have Slept in idleness . . . the procuring of the means of existance keeps the very best Indian constant employment every day of the year . . . merely to exist.[20]

In 1978, an old free trader of the 1920s defined /LAZY-/ for us: "There were no lazy Indians then . . . even the lazy ones worked hard." He explained that "lazy" was not used "for the fact that he didn't work, but for the fact that the work he was doing was useless." For this trader (who was translating from a Cree-speaking event), /LAZY-/ meant incompetence, not inactivity; it meant nonproductive activity.[21]

A fur trader of a century earlier appears to have applied the same definition. An Indian who was busy doing something other than trapping was lazy, indolent, indifferent, idle,—and of course failed to pay his debt. The Albany 1824 report names five different individuals not paying due to "indolence," while another "always exerts himself—when he fails paying his debt it cannot be attributed to Indolence." Two of the lazy ones are remarked: "can hunt well when he pleases," exemplifying the finding that indolence is an attribute of those who show independence of the fur trade.[22] (On the other hand, /STARV-/ and /POOR-/, used technically, usually denote dependence but nonpayment.[23]) Where the trader called it indolence, and the Indian called it starve, there may be room for a difference of opinion . . . or: it may signal a third usage: Manipulative.[24]

Manipulative Usage

Chief Trader Robert McVicar was asking for a raise when he wrote to George Simpson in 1829:

> I am now about to retire from the service (with a shattered constitution, worn down by a series of years of hard toil and starvation of which it is now useless to complain).[25]

This can be analyzed as a mixed case, partly metaphor, partly malnutrition, with an openly manipulative purpose. Manipulative usage includes metaphorical, deliberately ambiguous, or untruthful statements.

This kind of usage by Indians is harder to judge, for what is customary for one group may fall into the unethical category of another. Ambiguous Indian messages appear to be numerous[26] but whether deliberate—and with what motive—may not be certain. Lying was sometimes charged, but the concept of lying appears to differ among cultures (see glossary) as well as gambits for playing on words, the latter an activity much practiced and enjoyed by Ojibwa people. As for humor: it is known to be culturally variable and generally mysterious to the outsider.

Recall now the simple technical message "we have had to hunt for food" and the literal one "have tasted nothing but water." If either of these should be judged an untruth, it would point to suspicion of "pretence." The Albany factor warned his trader at Martin Falls, "you are to be very strict and particular in demanding the Debts of any who come to you under pretence of being in distress." A Moose

Factory trader wrote, "[they] told us their father & mother were dead, being starv'd . . . this is a Lye of their own inventing, several others have preach'd ye same Story, which we have detected."[27]

Trading-post personnel had frequently to make such judgments of credibility, for which their cues are only partly recoverable. Context often reveals whether the source was their own observing, a firsthand eye-witness report, or a rumor. They sometimes made errors. Consider trappers' reports that other Indians were "starving" when last seen. Technically, this would be a message that the absent party may not arrive, having no furs. The Albany Report for 1816–17 stated that several absent parties of northern Indians "starved all the winter and had no furs to come in with." Yet in the succeeding three years this trader reported these same Indians as "wanderers between Albany and Severn . . . [who] lead an unsettled and vagabond life"—and more to the point, "Are all missing and I have great reason to believe they are all gone to Severn with their Furs." By 1820 he was accusing the Fort Severn trader of enticing his Indians and stealing his trade.[28]

Whether these Indian reports of starving were "lies" or the trader only pretended this was so in order to build up his case to his superiors, this is an example of manipulative use of the term /STARV-/. On the part of the Indian, such a "lie" could be a case of manipulating the traders' competitive spirit—a threat that the other post was more attractive, that they could have starved from the treatment received, or that they will likely starve unless treated better.[29] It should be noted that an Indian threat would indicate a position of perceived power vis-à-vis the traders, contrasting with the more usual 'powerless' stance.[30] Traders' openly competitive tactics helped reveal their ultimate dependence on Indians for furs, allowing such threats and show of power. The latter no doubt considered the white people's lack of self-control to be rather primitive behavior, from a society that apparently had not learned the merits of curbing or concealing these savage passions. (An ethnographic report on Ojibwa concepts of competition is in preparation by the author, analyzing their denial and rejection of competitiveness per se as part of a moral value against surviving at the expense of others.)

The related term /PITY-/ is now pertinent. Traders found certain local behavior patterns and ceremonial conventions useful to their business. They entered into gift-exchange systems and established real or fictive kin relationships in the Indian way. Bruce White, in his perceptive treatment of the subject of Indian-trader gift exchange, noted the use of "pity" in connection with the Indian's expectation of receiving aid from someone more powerful—not necessarily right away, but more typically at some future time when he might be in need, for example, should he ever be in danger of "perishing from hunger."[31] Traders who understood the Indian concept that is usually translated into English as "pity" would probably be better able to identify manipulative messages.

It may be asked, how was the /PITY-/ transaction expressed in the Indians' language? There are a few clues, though no fullscale study as yet, for Algonquian languages. A form /-šaweni-/ occurs in certain ritual encounters between persons of differing power status. An Ojibwa elder in 1965 gave the way to ask for 'blessings' in his language. The request ended, ´gašawenimid adiso.ka.n/ 'take pity on me and bless me, Spirit.'[32] The part /-šaweni-/ here stands for both 'pity' and 'bestow blessing.' To be 'pitied,' then, is the desire of a person who wishes to receive a gift of power—a promise of help in getting through life. This refers to an action (or transaction). To GIVE THE BLESSING and to PITY is all one act. To BE PITIED and to RECEIVE A GIFT of this kind is the same thing. Such gifts consisted of specific powers, abilities to perform life's jobs both great and small—in short the requisite "necessaries" in order for the Indian to survive. He did not "pay" for them, except by properly using them—and this might be delayed for years. His indebtedness to the bestower was not exactly measured in Made Beaver, nor was a time-limit put upon it. It was seen, rather, as a continuing relationship with reciprocal, though not equal, obligations and benefits.

This important relationship between individual human beings and the inherent power holders of the Ojibwa world is fairly elusive for the European to grasp. Ojibwa preoccupation with relative power mixes human persons in with all others. Europeans were placed rather high on the scale of power holders when they first made their appearance. They were at times referred to in Ojibwa by a form of the 'power' term /manido./ Quite reasonably, the white trader, with his goods, his technology, and his "gratuities" ranked with the bestowers of blessings.

The English word "pity" occurs frequently in translations of Indian speeches, always implying the receipt of needed articles or benefits. The word also occurs in traders' accounts of dealings with Indian customers: "[he] Hopes that I will Pitty Him & He will Strive to do better next Year." Was this a request for trapping advances? Another: "on his beging Me to take pitty on Him I gave Him the usual Presents." This trader got the message, whether or not he was aware of the Indian religious context—although he may have missed a more subtle point: that it could have been more a move to establish or reinforce a relationship than a request for immediate gifts.[33]

The trader used "pity" when rendering the above statements into English. What had the Indian actually said? The /-ša weni-/ form is likely, but there is a second, grammatical, form by which to render 'pitiful' in Ojibwa—a suffix creating a "verb of compassion," reported by linguist John Nichols to have occurred most frequently in the first person. He considered that it could have functioned as a "self-humbling device" and associated it with a "poor pitiful me" theme. The form is closely related to both the diminutive and pejorative; José Mailhot, finding it in Montagnais data on a third-person verb, called it an "affectionate diminutive form" used when talking "about someone affectionately or when you pity someone." Her third-person verb happens to have been /Kwa:kutew/ 'he died of starvation,' rendered as /kwa:kutešt/ '. . . pitifully.'[34] Further semantic analyses by linguists of these Indian language forms would be most welcome.

The concept 'pity' relates to manipulative usage of /STARV-/ because of its role in asking for food. It is often interpreted by modern readers as an abject and beggarly request for a "handout," even as a forerunner of "welfare society" mentality.[35] There is evidence that some traders too tended to view with contempt individuals who pointed to themselves as pitiful and expected generosity on that score. To announce or advertise a position of powerlessness was not noble behavior in the eyes of the English. This could be a serious kind of misunderstanding.

The position of powerlessness as a factor in manipulative usage of /STARV-/ should be further examined. For Ojibwa Indians, presenting oneself as powerless was not only accepted but recommended; the ignoble (and imprudent) thing would be to boast of a powerful position. Measures to avoid being (or appearing) coercive were much adhered to. This may help toward solving the final riddle—the trader's strangely frequent type of observation: "on approaching ny ye house he called out starving . . ." now repeated more fully yet, from the Duck Lake journal:

> on approaching ny ye House [he] called out starving—this being the common word when they have greatest plenty I took no notice of it . . . he informed me that his Children has Singed and eaten above 20 Br in furs which I am very sory . . . etc.[36]

Starvation—as the "common word," "the old song,"—and especially as the first word "called out" on arrival at the trading post—is all too frequent to be ignored. Most such entries imply a suspicion of manipulation. These range from the paranoia of James Duffield at Moose Factory in 1744 who suspected all Indians of manipulating him by feigning hunger, to the Osnaburgh complaint more than a century later: "[he] reports Annung to be starving, a comprehensive phrase with Indians."[37]

Upon closer examination, this "comprehensive phrase with Indians" becomes truly mysterious. Traders did not always "take no notice of it," as we have seen. How did they detect cases they termed "the old song," "the usual yarn"? Since these cases are those where "the word" was uttered by Indians, it is unfortunate that no case has been found that provides the words as spoken in the Indian language. Both Nichols and Mailhot have noted two 'starve' verbs; one simply 'hungry' but used over a range of meanings including dying of hunger, the other restricted to death or final collapse from lack of food. It would be interesting to know which was spoken by Indians approaching the post. Even more interesting to the present question is use of a /STARV-/ verb with the "compassion" form affixed—as Mailhot finds in her data. A self-humbling device attached to /STARV-/ . . . is this what the Indians "called out"? Was this the comprehensive phrase? Was it always a request for food? /STARV-with-pity-attached/ may even have come to function metaphorically as a ritual affirmation of relationship—almost as a greeting.

A curious description of Indian scenes in northern Minnesota in the later 1800s may give illumination. Missionary Joseph A. Gilfillan wrote that when a white man approached a camp of Ojibwa, the people would "often call out from a long distance, as far as they can see him, 'we are very hungry, we are starving to death; we have not eaten a morsel for three days.' At the same time they laugh heartily and slap their thighs, as if it was the best joke in the world." Gilfillan also described Ojibwa families as fond of telling their visitors about "their extreme poverty, and the hunger they suffer. They seem to think there is a special merit in it, in fact seem proud of it . . . Often two families will chaff each other, in a good-natured way, about it."[38] These scenes suggest, again, a metaphorical (or satirical?) usage of /STARV-/. Were they making a joke or game out of their own self-humbling etiquette, a kind of competition to see who can be humbler?

The trader at Rainy Lake in 1825 recorded another curious observation: "Nothing pleases an Indian more than in giving him something to eat immediately on his arrival. It is the Grand Etiquette of Politeness amongst themselves." He doesn't mention that "amongst themselves" the rule is not to offer food unless it is requested—a hospitality etiquette the exact reverse of the European: with the Ojibwa, one is supposed to ask, if one is hungry.[39] Indeed, the Indian word for such requesting is more like 'begging for,' according to Nichols' translation of a term used by Maude Kegg, an Ojibwa woman who told a story of her childhood, in which she was being taught the way they did things long ago. As a little girl, in urgent need of some beads, she was told to go around to different wigwams and 'beg' for them, repeating 'I'm poor, I'm poor in beads.' Her grandmother explained, "Long ago, the Indians used to do that when they were short of anything . . . zaagido . . . they['d] go around begging for what they are short of." Maude added, "The old lady said that when anyone was hungry, he goes around to the wiigiwaaman and begs, and so is given lots of food."[40] Did the traders' "old song" go: 'I'm Poor, I'm Poor in Food—I'm starving?' If so, it was simply the approved way of behaving as visitor—the host having avoided being coercive by politely allowing the guest to decide whether he wished to receive food.[41] Recall also that "poor" was something to be proud of, in Reverend Gilfillan's observation.

Maude added further that when she returned with the gifts of beads from the wigwams, the old ladies were "laughing just hard at me." The final mystery is to penetrate the humor—or rather, the laughs. Occasions for Ojibwa laughter are not always humorous ones, though usually highly charged. The sound of Indians "laughing just hard" could mean, for example: that everything has gone all wrong,—that a particularly gruesome scene in a cannibal story has been told, or—that elders are reacting to children's trial-and-error education (they teach by laughing at the errors).[42] As a brighter end to what started as a very sad topic, can we propose that sometimes the comprehensive phrase 'I'm starving'—called out on arrival at the white man's trading post—was not literally or technically true, or even manipulative, but was a greeting, or joke: a typical mysterious way to make fun out of the most serious crises in life? Something to act proud of? Whether or not this was the true message of some of the data cases of this study, one of the findings surely is that reports of "starvation" in trading-post documents are by themselves an unreliable index to historical events. Another finding might be that fur trade archives will yield a rather selective but at the same time illuminating view of Indian cultures. (Hopefully, this paper has done the same.)

In conclusion, it appears that contextual/cultural analysis of fur trade terminology will reveal that the image of Indians as dependent, child-like, begging, destitute, starving, and welfare-oriented has been somewhat overdrawn. The power relationships between traders and Indians were complex, fluid, and interchangeable—a situation that was familiar to the Indian whose cultural wisdom taught him long ago to appear powerless in order to wield power.

Appendix A: Incipient Glossary of Technical Fur Trade Terms Surrounding the Concept of Technical STARving

STARVING: a condition in which primary attention must be directed to the food quest, allowing little leeway for other activities; hunting for the belly and not for furs.

NAKED: insufficient or inappropriate clothing for successful fur hunt, e.g., "walking on pieces of boards," or clothed in beaver and marten furs (which are likely too warm for heavy activity, but appropriate for jigging for fish).

LAZY: not hunting furs. More generally: engaged in nonproductive or incompetent activity [synonyms: INDOLENT, INDIFFERENT, INDISPOSED TO HUNT, IDLE].

INDUSTRIOUS: disposed to hunt furs; opposite of "lazy" [synonyms: PROVIDENT, INTERESTED (in the "interest of the Concern")].

EXERTION: energy directed toward procuring furs for trade; exhibiting nonlaziness.

HUNT: to hunt or trap for furs [synonym TRAP used less frequently; "hunt" becomes ambiguous, used also for hunting game].

DEBT: preseason advancing of trade goods, to be paid in furs or provisions at current Made Beaver rate [synonyms (noun or verb): CREDIT, ADVANCE, TRUST].

MADE BEAVER: the unit of value for furs traded [synonyms: MB, MBr, BEAVER].

TRADED: brought furs in excess of debt, "traded" the rest; PAID: brought furs to pay off advances.

NECESSARIES: articles of trade necessary for pursuing fur hunt, including items to expedite hunting for belly in order not to STARVE.

GRATUITIES: trade goods given gratis "for nothing" at discretion of trader (overlaps with PRESENTS, the latter typically involving gift exchange and contributions to rituals, see FROLIC).

CLOATHE: to present personal items of clothing (e.g., Captain's coat) to worthy fur hunters or leaders at end of fur hunt.

FROLIC: ritual Indian gathering, at or near trading post, usually at end of season's hunt; involves distribution and consumption of alcohol and/or other dainties provided by trader.

TO PITY: to be the donor of gifts, the more powerful person in the given encounter. PITIFUL deserving of pity.

POOR: lacking or in need of items for trade (poor in pelts); lacking necessaries for fur hunt; dependent on traditional or pretrade mode of life; POOR IN x: lacking or in need of x.

TO BEG: to request something one is short of, expressed in terms of being POOR and PITIFUL.

BY INDIAN REPORT: rumors or news received from Indians (typically by moccasin telegraph, i.e., not from eyewitnesses) [synonym: AS THEY SAY].

LYING: (from traders' view): a false report or rumor; information deliberately falsified; (from Indian view): an incorrect prognosis or foretelling; not keeping one's word about promises of future acts.

NEIGHBOUR: competing trader at same location (for same group of Indians): [synonym: OPPOSITION].

THE PEOPLE: Company servants, engagés.

Notes

Acknowledgments. First, to my husband E. S. Rogers for sharing data, field experience, and his splendid library. We acknowledge our dependence on aid and blessings from Hudson's Bay Company, Public Archives of Canada, and McGill University Archives, and on teachings of Indian hosts and friends at Weagamow Lake (Ontario), Lake Mistassini (Quebec), and Ponemah (Minnesota). I especially appreciate mutual gift exchange with Bruce White, whose 1981 Fur Trade Conference paper revealed our mutual interests and whose draft chapters from his McGill University thesis "'Give Us a Little Milk': Economics and Ceremony in the Ojibway Fur Trade" (1985) led to the Gilfillan, Kegg, and Rainy Lake 1825 citations. Linguistic tidbits from José Mailhot and John Nichols are much appreciated, although I STARV- for more. Reactions and data supplements from other colleagues are also gratefully received.

1. HBCA (Hudson's Bay Company Archives), B. 200/a/4, fo 1.

2. Oxford and Canadian dictionaries concur. An interesting "now rare" (Oxford) or "now dialectal" (Webster) meaning occurs: "to perish or suffer with cold, to freeze to death;" three bilingual dictionaries (French, Cree, Ojibwa) give "freeze" as an additional English translation; and thesaurus lists "starve" as one synonym for "cold, being cold, etc." Readers of an earlier version of this paper provided etymological sources locating this usage in the north of England and in Scotland, where it was still heard in their childhood (thanks to Jane Fredeman and Tim Ball).

3. HBCA, B. 155/a/38, fo 13; B. 198/a/66, fo 26; C. M. Gates, Five Fur Traders of the Northwest (St. Paul, 1965), 130; HBCA, B. 3/a/57, fo 19; B. 155/a/37, fo 23. Cases involving cannibalism are assumed to represent a serious degree of literal starving; one in which an entire family fell victim was reported by the trader as due to starvation (B. 155/a/37, fo 20). Descendants of the seven who "Starved to Death in the early part of February" (1826) now live at Weagamow Lake, Ontario. Their oral history version of the event carries most of the same particulars, but /STARV-/ does not occur in it; instead, after failing in the food quest, 'they all froze in their tents . . . they all died frozen' (field notes, MBR, 8/12/74).

4. John Franklin, Narrative of a Journey to the Shores of the Polar Sea in the Years 1819, 1820, 1821 and 1822 (Edmonton, 1969); C. Stuart Houston, ed., Arctic Ordeal: The Journal of John Richardson, Surgeon Naturalist with Franklin, 1820–22 (Kingston and Montreal, 1984). The only use of /STARV-/ during this period occurs early in their syndrome on 10 Sept. when a musk ox had been shot after six days without a good meal: "This success infused spirit into our starving party" (Houston, 129; Franklin, 406). The graphic details, put down with scientific precision, offer a rich variety of synonyms for /STARV-/, eloquent in their simplicity: "The privation of food . . . absorbed every other terror (Franklin, 393; Houston, 116). George Back's journal has not yet been examined; his chapter in Franklin contains no /STARV-/. It is not certain whether their nonuse of the word was due to their very closeness to it or to their not being traders.

5. Alternatively, the sequence could start with illness or accident, the condition of the hunter having a direct effect on the food supply and any member's loss of mobility endangering the chase. The disastrous effect of illness is well represented in the /STARV-/ data. See also S. Krech III, "Disease, Starvation, and Northern Athapaskan Social Organization," American Ethnologist 5 (1978): 717, for relationship of epidemics to incidence of reported starvation. The prominence of illness in Ojibwa belief systems has been labeled hypochondria

by R. Landes, The Ojibwa Woman (New York, 1938), 178, and A. I. Hallowell, Culture and Experience (Philadelphia, 1955), 173, but seems reasonable in terms of beliefs about power-loss as described by M. B. Black, "Ojibwa Power Belief System," in The Anthropology of Power, R. D. Fogelson and R. N. Adams, eds. (New York, 1977), 148. In light of these beliefs, G. Morris sums it up for the Ojibwa in the time when they were dependent upon the hunt: "A Concern with illness could not in these circumstances be characterized as 'obsessive.' It was a concern with life itself" ("Will They Have the Last Laugh? Traditional Health Care among the Ojibwa," unpub. ms., University of Minnesota, 1985, 32).

6. HBCA, B. 3/a/57, fo 18d; B. 220/a/5, fo 22; B. 220/a/12, fo 25.

7. E. S. Rogers and M. B. Black, "Cultural Ecology in the Subarctic," Review article of R. K. Nelson, Hunters of the Northern Forest: Designs for Survival among the Alaskan Kutchin, Reviews in Anthropology 1 (1974): 343–48; E. S. Rogers and M. B. Black, "Subsistence Strategy in the Fish and Hare Period, Northern Ontario," Journal of Anthropological Research 32 (1976): 1–43. For economy of planning, see also A. Tanner, Bringing Home Animals (New York, 1979), 133.

8. For listing of ethnographic field data sources through 1969, see Handbook of North American Indians, vol. 6, Subarctic (Washington DC, 1981), 22; this includes Athapaskan sources. Single quotation marks beginning in the following section enclose English glosses of words uttered in another language.

9. See, however, HBCA, B. 198/a/71, fo 10d and J. Long, Voyages and Travels of an Indian Interpreter and Trader (London, 1791), 113. For talk taboo, see M. Black-Rogers, "Ojibwa Power Interactions: Creating Contexts for 'Respectful Talk,'" in Native North American Interaction Patterns, R. Darnell, ed. (Hull, Quebec: Canadian Museum of Civilization, National Museums of Canada, 1988). For Algonquian man-animal relations, see A. Tanner, Bringing Home Animals, ch. 6 and 7; H. Feit, "The Ethno-Ecology of the Waswanipi Cree, or How Hunters Can Manage their Resources," in Cultural Ecology, B. Cox, ed. (Toronto, 1973), 116–20; E. S. Rogers, The Quest for Food and Furs: The Mistassini Cree, 1953–1954 (Ottawa, 1973), 10–15; J. Rousseau, "Les Indiens de la forêt Québeçoise," La Patrie (Montreal, 1951), issues of 21 Jan., 18 Feb., and 6 May through 24 June. For illness beliefs in relation to animals, see sources cited in S. Krech III, ed., Indians, Animals and the Fur Trade: a Critique of Keepers of the Game (Athens, 1981), Krech's own paper giving sources on Athapaskan ethnography, and C. A. Bishop and W. Sturtevant papers on Algonquian; this volume took issue with historian C. Martin's Keepers of the Game: Indian-Animal Relations and the Fur Trade (Berkeley, 1978).

10. HBCA, B. 54/a/1, fos 12–12d, Duck Lake post, 1799.

11. HBCA, B. 198/a/70, fo lld; B. 155/a/38, fo 14d; B. 155/e/11, fo 3. Note technical use of "hunt" in the last.

12. HBCA, B. 220/a/16, fo 29d; B. 220/a/5, fo 3d.

13. This accounts for the cases where furs were offered for provisions (HBCA, B. 200/a/4, fo 12) or debts were paid in furs though "starving" (HBCA, B. 123/a/13, fo 13).

14. HBCA, B. 54/a/1, fo 12–12d.

15. McGill University Rare Book Department, Masson Collection (McGill, Masson) CH176.S158, 8/16/1807; HBCA, B. 181/a/4, fo 4; McGill, Masson CH25.S61, 8/27/1802. The question of Indian dependence on the fur trade was as sensitive an issue then, among dedicated traders, as it is now among some scholars (see T. Morantz, "The Fur Trade and the Cree of James Bay," in Papers of the Third North American Fur Trade Conference, C. Judd and A. J. Ray, eds. [Toronto, 1980]; C. A. Bishop, "The First Century: Adaptive Changes among the Western James Bay Cree between the Early Seventeenth and Early Eighteenth Centuries," in The Subarctic Fur Trade: Native Social and Economic Adaptations, S. Krech III, ed. [Vancouver, 1984], 46–47; and S. Krech III, "The Trade of the Slavey and Dogrib at Fort Simpson in the Early Nineteenth Century," in The Subarctic Fur Trade, S. Krech III, ed.). Traders also voiced the issue explicitly and their nightmares showed them visions of independent Indian renegades clothed regally in furs, eating well while lolling at a fishing spot, surrounded by envious fellow tribesmen who still did an "honest day's work" for a living (see this lovely 1825 flight of fancy by Fort Severn's James Sutherland in its entirety, HBCA, B. 3/e/10, fos 4–4d). Indian protest by deliberately not bringing furs to trade was especially noted when debt was cut off in the 1820s; see HBCA, B. 155/a/36, fos 6d–7d, 2od, 22; B. 155/e/11, fos 3, 5; and B. 3/e/10, fos 11d–12.

16. HBCA, B. 220/a/5, fo 20.

17. HBCA, B. 54/a/1, fo 12; B. 93/a/6, fo 9–9d; B. 78/a/5, fo 24d.

18. Starving by fur trade personnel accounts for a number of data cases, in all three categories; LITERAL: 16 HBC men die on Peace River 1816 (PAC, Selk. Papers 61, 16357; HBCA, B. 39/z/1, fos 71–72); TECHNICAL: John Mac-Donell uses "starvation" to refer to going "on short allowance" of European provisions: "we shall have to live like Indians upon fish or flesh: as providence supplies us" (McGill, Masson CH179.S161: 6, 16, 21 Sept. 1793); MANIPULA-TIVE: outpost men communicate desire to abandon wintering site by use of /STARV-/ (HBCA, B. 123/a/15, fo 5).

19. A much decorated Moose Factory Indian named Sakie was reprimanded by the donor for giving away his Captain's coat (HBCA, B. 135/a/11, fo 62d).

20. HBCA, B. 107/e/4, fo 2d.

21. Field notes, MBR/ESR, July 1978.

22. HBCA, B. 3/e/9, fo 4–4d.

23. /POOR-/ has an interesting technical usage. While the Severn trader's nightmare of fur-clad independent Indians pictured their "mode of life so congenial to their natural indolence" (HBCA, B. 3/e/10, fo 4d), a Martin Falls trader, finding Indians dressed in beaver furs but trying to pay their debts, chose to put it differently: "the poereast Indians that ever I saw . . . most of their clothen bevar Skins and ther shows and metens of the Sam Kind" (HBCA, B. 123/a/23, fo 10). Modern Indian usage may enlighten us here: northern Ojibwa bilinguals in 1969 used "poor" in English to refer to lack of store goods and dependence on traditional home-made things, explaining that "poor" meant to them the "hard life" of the past—indicating pride in that hard life. (For which compare Rev. Gilfillan's observation that poverty was something to be proud of, and Maude Kegg's learning the dignity of 'begging' when 'poor' in some needed article—see manipulative usage.) To these should be added (as Jennifer Brown has reminded me) the reputed use of bungi "a little bit" by Ojibwa when, as Peter Fidler put it, "their supplies was not adequate to their wants" (HBCA, B. 51/e/1, fo 15d).

24. It is hard to resist citing the famous first sentence of Simpson's Character Book. Number one on his list of traders to evaluate is Colin Robertson (not his favorite person), of whom he wrote: "No. 1. A frothy trifling conceited man, who would starve in any other Country and is perfectly useless here" (G. Williams, ed., Hudson's Bay Miscellany 1670–1870 [Winnipeg, 1975], 169). This sentence is "metaphorical" if /STARV-/ stands for not being able to make a living. In that case it is the fur trade technical term extended to nonhunting occupations, so that it is clear Simpson was making effective use of his acquaintance with the business language of his empire.

25. HBCA, D. 5/3, fo 181.

26. And ambiguous messages could be expected from Ojibwa; see M. B. Black, "Ojibwa Questioning Etiquette and Use of Ambiguity," Studies in Linguistics 23 (1973).

27. HBCA, B. 123/a/13, fo 3; B. 135/a/14, fo 33.

28. HBCA, B. 3/e/3, fo 4; B. 3/e/4, fo 3; B. 3/e/5, fo 3; B. 3/e/6, fo 6–6d.

29. See HBCA, B. 155/a/36, fos 6d—7d for a case of the last, when Crane Indians at Osnaburgh House predicted their own starvation—accurately, it turned out.

30. B. Black, "Ojibwa Power Belief System," 148; M. Black-Rogers, "Ojibwa Power Interactions."

31. B. White, "'Give us a Little Milk': The Social and Cultural Significance of Gift Giving in the Lake Superior Fur Trade," in Rendezvous: Selected Papers of the Fourth North American Fur Trade Conference, T. C. Buckley, ed. (St. Paul, 1984).

32. Field notes, MBR, 8/19/65. Single quotation marks enclose English glosses of words uttered in another language.

33. HBCA, B. 3/a/59, fo 42; B. 3/a/60, fo 31; as in White's example, "'Give Us a Little Milk,'" 193–94.

34. John Nichols, "The Ojibwe Verb of Compassion," Unpub. ms., 1973, Algonquian Conference, Green Bay; José Mailhot, pers. comm.

35. A. J. Ray, "Periodic Shortages, Native Welfare, and the Hudson's Bay Company 1670–1930," in The Subarctic Fur Trade, S. Krech III, ed., 2, 11.

36. HBCA, B. 54/a/1, fo 12–12d.

37. HBCA, B. 220/a/16, fo 29d; C. Judd, "Sakie, Esquawenoe, and the Foundation of a Dual-Native Tradition at Moose Factory," in The Subarctic Fur Trade, S. Krech III, ed., 87; HBCA, B. 155/a/84, fo 22d.

38. J. A. Gilfillan, "The Ojibways in Minnesota," Collections of Minnesota Historical Society 9 (1897): 113. Two passages from George Nelson Papers (courtesy J. S. H. Brown) regarding his Cree and Saulteaux associates are highly supporting: "so light hearted that in their greatest distresses and Starvation they cannot . . . refrain from 'cracking their jokes' on each other" (Reminiscences 1825ff), and "[they] arrived here bag & baggage, starving like lusty fellows & bawling out Eat Eat" (Tête au Brochet journal 11/23/1818).

39. HBCA, B. 105/e/6, fo 4; field notes, MBR.

40. M. Kegg, Gabekanaansing/At the End of the Trail: Memories of Chippewa, a Childhood in Minnesota with Texts in Ojibwe and English, J. Nichols, ed. and trans. (Greeley, 1978), 47–49.

41. M. Black, Ojibwa Questioning Etiquette, 19, 22.

42. Field notes, ESR, MBR.

11. The Growth and Economic Significance of the American Fur Trade, 1790–1890

James L. Clayton

Although there are excellent works on almost every aspect of the American fur trade, an over-all statistical study has never been compiled. Consequently, while most of the virile adventures of fur trade history have been told in vivid detail, several fundamental questions of considerable significance have been left unanswered. Foremost among these questions are: To what extent, if any, was the fur trade related economically to the westward movement? Did the fur trade ever have real economic importance, either nationally or by region? Was the center of its operations always in the Far West? Was the beaver actually the leading fur, or did it only appear to be? Finally, were the famous trading companies we know so much about more important than the thousands of independent traders who left few if any records? The answers to these and similar questions can be approached only through statistical methods.[1]

The use of the word "fur" in such a study needs careful definition at the outset. As employed here the term includes all animal peltries of commercial significance used as material in lining or trimming articles of wearing apparel, or for constructing entire garments. Heretofore, certain somewhat exotic species of fur bearers, such as the fur seal, and some very common but not exotic furs, such as the raccoon, have been excluded from many fur trade studies for reasons that are not entirely clear.

American fur traders usually divided their pelts into four categories: furs, skins, robes, and hides. Under "furs" were grouped all of the fur-bearing rodents (including the fiber-producing beaver), felines, canines, weasels, and marsupials. "Skins" almost always meant those of deer, bear, or raccoon, but might include a few elk, moose, and, later, antelope. A "robe" always referred to one side of a winter-killed buffalo cow or of a young bull dressed with the fur on, and a "hide" was the full pelt of a summer-killed buffalo cow, dressed without the hair, or of a short-haired bull. These definitions will be followed throughout this paper. When the term "furs" alone is used, it is meant to include skins also, where appropriate.

To acquire reliable data on the growth of the American fur trade for the period 1790 to 1890, when the buffalo herds were gone, the frontier was settled, and urbanism was well advanced, it would normally be necessary to determine the number, kind, and value of all pelts gathered throughout the United States for every year in question. This is impossible. Such data exists neither for the country as a whole nor for any given region within it. There are accurate production records for a few of the larger companies during a limited number of years, but such data alone is too scanty to show production flows by region.[2]

Fortunately there are other ways of measuring the growth of the fur trade. All available data indicates that before the Civil War the bulk of American furs were exported rather than consumed at home. Records of the leading fur companies clearly testify to this. They are substantiated by the census returns of 1840, the only year in which the trade was surveyed, and by a statement of the leading fur merchant in London. For the decades following the Civil War, supporting data is less voluminous but no contrary evidence is apparent, and the pattern of exports remained unchanged. Export figures, therefore, are the most reliable indicators of the growth of the American fur trade during the nineteenth century.[3]

During the whole of this period the majority of furs shipped abroad went to Great Britain. Figures compiled before 1822 are not always reliable, but from that date until 1890 Great Britain received 74 percent by value of all United States fur exports. A record was also kept of both the number and kind of furs shipped from the United States to Great Britain; consequently, the trends of the trade for that period can be determined with reasonable accuracy. Henry Poland compiled a list of fur importations into Great Britain by species and origin for every year from 1763 to 1891. This record is the best starting point for any extended analysis of the fur trade of North America.[4]

Historians have been reluctant to use Poland's data, possibly because the sources cannot be verified. When corroborated by available records of the major American fur companies and by data from government sources, however, Poland's figures can be most valuable for showing trends over a fairly long period. For example, his general accuracy can be checked by valuing each species of fur bearer according to the prices offered by the American Fur Company for number 1 prime skins, less 20 percent for nonprime skins. The writer did this for all years from 1820 to 1850, except six for which price data is unavailable. Poland's figures were found to be within 10 percent of the value of fur exports to Great Britain as listed in the annual reports of the secretary of the treasury. Again, one may also check Poland's tabulations for the major fur bearers during the years 1831–43 against those given in John MacGregor's *Commercial Statistics* (1850). Although the data often differs widely for any given year, the trends are invariably the same.[5]

Prior to 1822, Poland's data is not very useful. His figures are rounded and appear to be estimates rather than tabulations, and before the 1820s many British companies were gathering furs within the United States and their returns cannot be separated from Poland's figures. For this period, therefore, one must rely on United States export tabulations alone.

Judging from the annual reports of the secretary of the treasury, the American fur trade grew rapidly during the latter part of the 1790s, fell off somewhat at the turn of the century, and then almost doubled its production until it was cut short by the embargo of 1808. Thereafter it languished until the close of the Napoleonic Wars in 1815, only to rise again with renewed vigor as Europeans, long deprived of luxuries, began buying furs in large quantities.

Unfortunately, there seems to be no way of breaking down the trade on a fur-by-fur basis for these early years. All authorities agree, however, that the beaver was of commanding importance.

Beginning in the 1820s the American fur trade entered a period of sustained growth which was not to abate until the Great Depression of the 1930s. According to Poland, the total number of furs and skins exported from the United States to Great Britain increased substantially in every decade from 1820 to 1890. His data is substantiated by the annual reports of the secretary of the treasury, which show that the value of fur exports to Great Britain increased in every decade. Together, these figures indicate that the American fur trade underwent considerable growth from 1820 to 1860 instead of declining, as many have supposed. More important, they show that a further fivefold increase in exports occurred between 1860 and 1890. Paradoxically, this later period of greatest expansion has received the least attention from historians.

Not all of the furs exported increased in quantity during this period, and some actually declined. According to Poland, of the twelve varieties shipped to Great Britain prior to the Civil War, there was a substantial and steady increase in muskrat, raccoon, fox, and mink, and a moderate increase in deer, otter, and wolf. The number of fisher and bear pelts rose in the 1830s but diminished thereafter. Only two furs decreased consistently: beaver and marten. Poland's figures clearly indicate a general pattern of growth during the years 1820–60, not simply a large increase in one or two furs.

These trends are substantiated by the available records of the major companies engaged in the trade before the Civil War. The American Fur Company—by far the largest and most important trading concern in the United States at that time—kept accurate lists of all furs received from its outfits. These are available in summary form for the years 1829–31 and in complete detail for 1834–45. The Chouteau companies of St. Louis kept a partial record of the furs and skins marketed, and this information is also available for the years 1831, 1835–39, and 1860–61. This data represents a sizable percentage of the United States fur returns from the late 1820s to the early 1860s.[6]

To illustrate, from 1829 to 1831 the American Fur Company harvested annually an average of 708,000 furs, mostly muskrat, raccoon, deer, and beaver. These figures include the harvest from both the Far West and the Great Lakes region. A decade later, from 1835 to 1842, the American Fur Company, having yielded its territory west of the Missouri River to the Chouteaus, averaged 589,000 robes, furs, and skins annually. These returns, however, were for the Great Lakes region alone. Add to this approximately 214,000 furs that were marketed yearly by the American Fur Company for the various Chouteau companies. These furs were included in the earlier figure, and if they are taken into account the total is 803,000 compared with 708,000 for the 1829–31 period. This is an impressive increase in light of the fact that by 1835–42 the fur trading area had been considerably reduced by settlement.

The growth of the American fur trade from 1820 to 1860 can also be shown by the value of furs harvested. This method of measurement affords a number of insights not apparent if the trade is gauged by numbers only. Figures for the average annual value of furs and skins exported from this country are available in the United States Treasury reports for all but four years since 1790. Although they are probably not absolutely accurate for any single year prior to the 1820s, they show conclusively that except for the period of the embargo and the War of 1812 the value of exports was steadily growing from 1796 to 1890. It is apparent that the rate of growth from the 1820s to the 1890s, measured by value of exports, is somewhat less than when measured by the numbers of furs and skins shipped to Great Britain. This difference is easily explained. The furs which constituted the bulk of the export trade depreciated in value; if an increase in price occurred, it lagged considerably behind the proportionate increase in numbers. The average annual price of muskrat skins in the 1850s, for example, was only nine cents; hence, although the number of muskrats exported to England increased by 8,930,000 during the decade, the value added was only $80,280.[7] Also, those furs that increased most rapidly in numbers were generally the least valuable.

Thus far we have said nothing about the growth of the trade in relation to the domestic market. What evidence we have—and it is admittedly scanty—suggests that no single pelt was of greater importance during the second (and possibly the third) quarter of the nineteenth century in the domestic market than the buffalo robe.[8] In every year for which we have reliable records of peltries sold by the Chouteaus, robes were from two to three times more valuable in the aggregate than any other pelt. By the early 1860s, robes represented almost 90 percent by value of all pelts marketed by that company. Buffalo robes were second in aggregate value in the returns of the American Fur Company from 1835 to 1842.

Beyond a crude estimate, the number of robes marketed in the United States during any decade is undeterminable. For the 1820s, receipts at New Orleans are probably the best indicator of robes harvested. From 1822 to 1830 an annual average of 8,689 packs or approximately 104,000 robes was deposited for reshipment to New York City. During the 1830s this figure fell to 3,140 packs or about 37,600 robes per year, but by that time many western robes were beginning to be shipped via more northerly routes to eastern and midwestern markets. Available data for St. Louis receipts during the 1830s indicates that about 90,000 robes per year were sent down the Missouri River, and this increased to 100,000 per year during the 1850s and 1860s.[9] Beyond this, one cannot be specific. The domestic trade in furs was probably never as important, however, as the export trade.

As to the nature of the American fur trade, it is abundantly clear that it may be divided economically into three major eras characterized by the dominant fur of the time. From 1790 to the 1820s this was, of course, the beaver. Through the 1860s the raccoon was most important, and from the 1870s to the 1890s the fur seal predominated.

The era of the beaver is the best understood and on it there is little new information to offer. The trade in beaver reached its apogee during the first decade of the nineteenth century. These ten years saw pelts estimated at $160,000 sent to Great Britain annually. Following the War of 1812, production fell markedly. According to Poland the number of beaver skins imported into Great Britain from the United States plummeted from about 56,000 annually between 1818 and 1822 to less than 7,000 yearly from 1823 to 1827. Because before 1822 beaver exports had represented more value than all other furs combined, the removal of this bulwark brought a decline in the trade as a whole. In 1825, however, the price of beaver began to rise rapidly and by 1830 it had almost doubled. This increase naturally led to more vigorous and extensive trapping, particularly in the Far West, and in 1828 exports were rising again. Receipts of furs at New Orleans, for example, show a steady increase from 24,000 pelts in 1827 to over 96,000 pelts in 1833.[10]

From 1828 to 1833 the fur trade grew vigorously and during this period almost all of the companies expanded operations. Exports rose steadily from $442,000 in 1827 to $842,000 in 1833, the latter figure the highest for any year since the War of 1812. The price of beaver averaged $5.99 per pound in Philadelphia during these years and was higher than for any comparable time between 1784 and 1861.[11] This five-year period is sometimes considered the heyday of the American fur trade. If one compares it only with the years immediately preceding and considers beaver alone, such an interpretation is partially justified. It is more correct, however, to view the late 1820s and early 1830s as the last vigorous gasp of a dying era, whose glory was perched perilously on high prices and romantic exploits rather than upon solid production.

In 1834 the substantial control of the trade by the American Fur Company was broken when John Jacob Astor sold out to his partners, Ramsay Crooks, Pierre Chouteau Jr., and others. Before that year the firm had probably controlled about three fourths of the export market, but thereafter the company, together with its exclusive agents, was to be content with about half the market. By the late 1830s new concerns had moved into areas previously controlled by the American Fur Company, and unusually bitter competition was the result. This was notably the case in the Ohio Valley—a prolific fur-producing region—where the firms of George and William Ewing pressed the older company especially hard. As a direct consequence of this renewed competition, the quantity and value of fur exports doubled after 1838, and in 1840 they were larger than for any previous year in the century.[12]

Contrary to some accounts, figures indicate that the depression of 1837–39 had little effect on the American fur trade. The value of exports remained stable from 1836 to 1838; thereafter it rose sharply until 1841. Prices were set by the London auctions, and European demand held steady until May, 1841, when the market collapsed, as it did periodically. By 1843 exports had experienced the severest decline since the 1820s. Beaver dropped to $2.62 per pound, the lowest price since 1809, and muskrat fell to the lowest figure since the American Revolution, except for a short period in 1838–39. Even with this disastrous situation, however, the average annual value of exported furs from 1840 through 1845 was higher than for any peak year since the War of 1812.[13]

The key to this incongruous situation is not hard to find. During the mid-1830s the ubiquitous and unpretentious raccoon quietly replaced the august beaver as the dominant fur in the American trade. Raccoon exports to England during the 1830s more than doubled over the previous decade, rising to above 2,500,000, with a value estimated at $1,431,000.[14] Moreover, unlike beaver, substantial numbers of raccoon pelts were retained in the United States for use as hats, coats, and trim. Unfortunately there is no way of measuring the extent of this domestic trade, although it was undoubtedly large.

This shift not only marked the end of an epoch but also the end of a process as old as the trade itself. From the very beginning of the North American fur trade, the beaver had been the most sought-after fur bearer. Strangely enough, it was popular not for its pelt but for its fiber, the short, downy gray felt at the base of the guard hairs. This fiber was pounded, mashed, stiffened, and rolled into hats by experts in Europe. In the 1830s wool, silk, and other materials came into use for hats. Strictly speaking, therefore, the period before the 1830s should be called the fiber trade and not the fur trade, because the "fine fur" bearers played only a minor role in comparison with the beaver.

The place of the raccoon as a fur bearer is not generally recognized. It was trapped in significant numbers only to the north of the Ohio River, and that area received little attention from writers on the fur trade after the raccoon became important. Outside the Great Lakes region the raccoon was of no significance. Only a few were found in Canada and the Far West. Within the Ohio Valley, the raccoon was trapped primarily in Indiana, Ohio, and Illinois, but it was found in considerable numbers throughout the region. The finest pelts came from the Kankakee and White River basins in Indiana and were darker in color than those taken elsewhere, some being almost completely black. Those taken to the east of this region were nearly as good, but raccoons from south of the Ohio had short, thin pelts and were not marketable.[15]

Several factors were responsible for the increased significance of the raccoon trade. In 1837 the Russians lowered their fur tariff, and raccoon skins were particularly sought after by Russian Jews and Poles, who demanded coonskin caps à la Davy Crockett. The czar interdicted their use in 1846, but in the meantime demand for the heavy, long-haired, densely furred pelts had risen in Germany, where they were used not only for hats but for trimming coats and were preferred to the lighter, less bulky furs in use today. During these years almost all raccoon pelts were sent first to London, where C. M. Lampson and Company controlled (and stabilized) the market, re-exporting in turn to eastern Europe.[16]

At the same time a uniquely favorable situation in America aided the expansion of raccoon production. In 1825, at the request of the Osage Indians, the federal government began to pay individual Indian debts to fur traders out of tribal funds. The philosophy behind this practice was simple: The government was vitally interested in Indian land cessions to meet the needs of an expanding population. Since the good will of a trader was often crucial to the successful conclusion of a treaty, United States authorities saw no evil in speeding the negotiations by providing for the satisfaction of traders' claims. This practice—perhaps innocuous at first—grew gradually but steadily until by the late 1830s about $200,000 was secured annually by traders from Indian treaties, and in 1842 such claims amounted to over $2,000,000. The bulk of this money was paid to individuals in the Great Lakes region—the heartland of raccoon production.[17]

This powerful government subsidy, most of which was doled out during the depression years of 1837–42, gave several companies and many individual traders a new lease on life and invigorated the region's fur industry. A small operator with a capital investment of only $1,000 might receive more than that amount in claims paid, while large corporations fared even better. From 1835 to 1838, for example, the American Fur Company received over two thirds the value of its stock in government money and paid dividends totaling 50 percent. Although payments to other firms are not so well documented, it is known that the Ewings of Indiana continued their fur trading operations long after these had ceased to be profitable, solely as an excuse for submitting further claims.[18] Thus, when the demand for raccoon increased, conditions for meeting it were unusually propitious.

The price of raccoon varied widely after the late 1830s. Before that a pelt was worth about fifty cents; thereafter sometimes as much as $1.25. About two thirds of the raccoon crop of the American Fur Company was graded number 1 prime, and about a third of this was labeled "Indian Handled."[19] Such pelts were more carefully cured, usually softened by chewing, and were consequently worth more.

Every effort was made to expedite handling because the raccoon pelt deteriorated faster than most other furs.

Despite the Russian interdiction of 1846, the raccoon continued to dominate the American fur trade until after the Civil War. According to Henry Poland, over 4,000,000 pelts were exported to England during the 1840s, almost double the number sent in the 1830s, and the two decades which followed accounted for over 9,000,000. Other furs such as muskrat were produced in greater quantities, but their total value was still considerably less than that of raccoon. Although we do not have reliable price data on all the furs in the trade, it is incontestable that until the 1870s the raccoon continued to be America's most important fur export.[20]

If Poland's figures are reliable for showing trends before the Civil War, we may fairly assume that they continued to be, and we may use them for the same purpose in the years that followed the conflict. Exports to Great Britain indicate that three furs showed remarkable growth after the Civil War: mink, skunk, and fur seal. During the 1860s approximately 32,000 mink were exported annually to Great Britain; by the end of the eighties this figure had risen almost tenfold. Behind this increase in mink exports was a rise in price from about $2.50 per pelt in 1860 to $4.00 in 1873.[21] This increase—dictated by fashion—led to the domestication of mink and the establishment of mink ranches in the United States during the mid-1870s. Beginning in 1876, however, the price of mink declined rapidly and did not rise again until the twentieth century.

The growth of the skunk fur industry was about half as fast as that of mink. During the 1860s annual exports of skunk to Great Britain amounted to about 100,000 pelts; by the eighties this figure had tripled. Worth not more than 25 cents in 1860, the value of a skunk pelt rose to $1.00 by 1870 and remained about there until the 1890s.[22]

It was the fur seal, however, which clearly dominated the American trade from the 1870s to the 1890s. No other fur was even half so important in aggregate value.[23] Indeed, the seal was by all odds the most important pelt economically in the American fur trade until the twentieth century.

During the early part of the nineteenth century, hundreds of thousands of seal pelts were taken from the South Pacific. These were usually marketed in China and Russia, but owing to indiscriminate slaughter the seal rookeries in that area were soon depleted. During the early and mid-nineteenth century, agents of the Russian government had also been harvesting about 20,000 fur seals annually from the Bering Sea, but because the pelts were poorly cured, demand for them was insignificant.[24]

With the purchase of Alaska by the United States in 1867, however, the number of fur seals exported from American jurisdictions increased almost immediately to over 100,000 a year. We have accurate and reasonably complete data on the fur seal industry after that date. The United States government in 1870 awarded a twenty-year lease of the seal fisheries on the Pribilof Islands to the Alaska Commercial Company, which was allowed to harvest 100,000 mature bachelor seals annually, paying in return a yearly rent of $55,000, and $2.62 in taxes on each pelt taken. From 1870 to 1890 the company harvested over 1,800,000 fur seals at an estimated profit of $18,754,000.[25]

During this period the industry was developed under careful management and in co-operation with C. M. Lampson and Company of London, consignee for nearly all Alaska sealskins. Improvements in dyeing, constancy of supply, and considerable advertising encouraged expansion in the market and a consequent rise in price from $5.26 per pelt in 1870 to a high of $35.47 for superior lots in 1890. The skins were shipped first to the west coast of the United States and thence to London. After being sold there they were dyed and dressed, and then about 75 percent of the total crop was re-exported to the United States. When they entered, an import tax of 20 percent ad valorem was levied. Thereafter the pelts were dressed again, cut, and finally sold for trimming on coats, sleigh robes, and other popular items. What had begun on the misty rookeries as a fatty fur worth a few dollars was finally sold for about $70.[26]

In 1890 a new twenty-year lease was granted to another concern, but the era of the fur seal was virtually over. Although between 1890 and 1910 only 343,356 seals were harvested on the islands, and in 1893 a treaty was signed limiting the wasteful practice of pelagic sealing, by 1910 a mere 133,000 fur seals remained.[27]

The aggregate value of pelts taken from 1870 to 1891 was $29,788,582. In addition to this, the United States government had received $4,894,323 in taxes and $1,100,000 in rent under the lease with the Alaska Commercial Company. Not to be neglected is more than $3,000,000 in tariff revenue from the dressed skins shipped back from London for final processing and sale in the United States.[28] All told, almost $40,000,000 was added to the United States economy by the fur seal industry during these two decades, or about eight times the total returns for beaver before the Civil War.

Looking back to 1790, one is particularly struck by two major organizational changes in the American fur trade during its first century which correspond closely with the growth pattern just discussed. From the 1790s to the War of 1812 there were no powerful fur trading monopolies in the United States.[29] The sea otter trade was handled by a number of small merchants in Boston, seals were sought by an entirely different group, and beavers were taken by literally hundreds of individuals. Competition was fairly open and exports were heavy, amounting to well over $800,000 annually during the peak years 1804–07. During the 1820s and 1830s, however, when large and powerful concerns such as the American Fur Company, the Rocky Mountain Fur Company, and the Chouteau companies sent hundreds of men great distances into the wilderness in search of pelts, exports fell. Indeed, only in one year (1833) did fur exports exceed $800,000 during the two decades. These figures give the impression that large companies and monopolistic practices tended to retard rather than expand production.

The Growth of the American Fur Trade

This impression is strengthened by the history of subsequent decades. By the early 1840s most of the large and famous companies either were leaving the scene or were restricting their activities and taking proportionately fewer furs than before. Replacing them was a host of farmers, lumbermen, and other permanent settlers who began trapping in their spare time. Again exports increased markedly, rising to over $1,000,000 annually in 1840, 1845, 1846, and from 1857 to 1861. This change is made graphic by comparing the number of furs sent down the Missouri River to St. Louis by the "mountain men" (most of whom worked for some concern) with those sent by farmers and other part-time trappers of a later day. During the era of the mountain men, seldom were more than 3,000 packs of furs sent via the Missouri to St. Louis. From 1879–88 an average of 19,000 packs arrived. There may have been some difference in the size of the packs for these two periods, but it is unlikely that a sixfold difference existed. It seems certain therefore that the ubiquitous part-time trapper—the unheralded "egg-money man"—was of considerably more economic importance than the famous mountain man.[30]

The second major organizational change in the trade relates to the pattern of marketing. In 1870 there were less than two hundred furriers in the United States. They employed 2,900 people and had a gross product of $8,900,000. By the end of the century, however, the number of furriers had grown fivefold. They then employed over 27,000 workers and had a capital investment of $30,000,000 and a gross product of over $55,000,000. The basic reason for this spurt in activity was a rapid increase in the number of persons in the United States able to buy luxuries. This enhanced demand was stimulated by increased advertising.

During those thirty years the United States had begun importing more furs than it exported, thus meeting to a large extent the needs of the wealthier group within its rising population and at the same time beginning to challenge the traditional European fur processing centers of London and Leipzig. By 1900 over $12,000,000 in duty-free and dutiable skins were entering the United States market—three times the quantity exported. Most of these came partly processed from Great Britain and Germany. By the end of World War I this shift was completed and the United States was the world's leading marketer of furs.[31]

As one might expect, New York State had almost as many furriers as all other states combined. Three other Middle Atlantic states—Connecticut, New Jersey, and Pennsylvania—together almost equaled New York, an indication that the fur industry of the United States was a highly concentrated one. In the Midwest, Chicago, St. Paul, and Detroit were the most important fur-processing centers, and in the Far West only San Francisco had a fur industry worth talking about.[32]

The above data on the growth of the fur trade, its three distinct eras of production, and its shifting organizational patterns suggest a number of conclusions:

First, the American fur trade was never very important economically, even in its palmiest days. This is true for the colonial period and for the present century as well. Regardless of continued growth, the fur trade as a business simply did not amount to much, anytime, anywhere. Despite the romanticism in which it has been wrapped for many years, despite the number of books about it which continue to appear, it was actually of no importance to the economy of the United States as a whole, and nearly the same is true of its regional significance.

Second, it is incorrect to speak, as some have done, of the "decline of the American fur trade" for any extended period during the nineteenth century. Except for the 1820s and 1880s, fur exports increased, often substantially, in every decade. As one type of pelt fell off in importance, it was simply replaced by another. Nor did the American fur trade decline in relative economic significance, for all during the century it represented approximately 1 percent of total exports.

The Growth of the American Fur Trade

Third, the popular idea that the coming of civilization automatically caused the fur trade to decline must be discarded. It not only grew with increased settlement, but on at least one occasion its principal base of operations actually shifted toward the center of population and away from the frontier. The beaver, bear, fur seal, and buffalo declined with the westward movement, but the smaller animals such as the raccoon, mink, and muskrat seemed to thrive as settlement increased. In short, the inevitable thrust of civilization actually stimulated the vigor of the fur trade and enhanced its relative importance.

Fourth, it is clear that the American fur business was not primarily a far-western phenomenon. From 1790 to the War of 1812 the center of the trade lay east of the Mississippi River and north of the Ohio. Not until after the War of 1812 did it shift to the Missouri River basin and the Rocky Mountains. In the years between 1815 and 1830 most of the beavers trapped in the United States were taken in the Far West, but as beavers began to decline during the 1830s and 1840s, the brief heyday of the western fur trade drew to a close.[33]

No other fur took the place of the beaver in that region, although the harvest of buffalo robes increased modestly until after the Civil War. This conclusion is substantiated by the returns received at New Orleans and St. Louis, by available company records, and, more important, by John E. Sunder in the only thorough account of the fur trade of the Far West for this period.[34] The Great Lakes region was, in fact, economically more important in the American fur trade than any other. By 1840 the United States Census Bureau estimated the value of fur returns for that year from the Great Lakes region at $515,000. The Far West, on the other hand, yielded only $373,000 in furs and skins. In 1841 the Detroit Department of the American Fur Company alone produced $377,200 in furs and skins.[35] This represented about 40 percent of the total United States fur exports of that year, and the company was but one of several outfits trading in the Great Lakes region. An important reason, of course, is the fact that the habitat of the raccoon was confined to that area.

As the Great Lakes region eclipsed the Far West, it was in turn overshadowed by the Bering Sea and its islands. The value of raccoon exports almost doubled from the 1860s to the 1880s and domestic consumption may also have doubled, but during the 1870s the raccoon was overwhelmed in importance by the fur seal, whose aggregate value in that decade was almost five times greater than raccoon exports. For the whole period under discussion it is quite possible that the fur seal added twice as much value to the United States economy as any other wild animal sought for its skin.

Fifth, and finally, the above evidence lends support to the contention that the fur trade as such did not play a very important role in our dynamic westward expansion. It is true that some trappers eventually became guides for government and emigrant expeditions, but their contributions were minor. There is no correlation between the health of the fur trade and population shifts. Nor, as we have seen, is there consistency in direction of movement. The number of persons involved was insignificant and the value of the trade, even locally, not very impressive. This is not to say that the American fur trade had no importance as a vehicle of westward expansion, but that its importance must be sought in areas other than economics.

Notes

1. This study is arbitrarily limited to the United States during the century 1790–1890 because substantial fur trade data of a statistical nature already exists for the Colonial period—see Murry G. Lawson, *Fur: A Study in English Mercantlism, 1700–1775* (Toronto, 1943)—and because the frontier had virtually disappeared by 1890. By "United States" is meant not only the territory within its jurisdiction but also the territorial waters and furs taken on the high seas by hunters flying the Stars and Stripes. The writer has chosen the path of conformity rather than accuracy in using "United States" and "America" synonymously—a practice for which he owes an apology to Canadian and Mexican readers. Finally, a note of gratitude to several persons who have made helpful comments on this paper: Dale L. Morgan, Oscar O. Winther, Douglass C. North, Paul W. Gates, David M. Ellis, John E. Sunder, and some whose names are not known to the writer.

2. Among a dozen depositories, the most complete American Fur Company production statistics seen by the writer are in the company records at the New-York Historical Society. All Americans Fur Company papers cited in this article are in this collection.

3. See especially "Furs and Skins," American Fur Company Papers; "Packing Book, 1830–33," and "Fur Sales at New York City, 1859–64," Chouteau Collection in the Missouri Historical Society, St. Louis. Returns of the 1840 census show that furs and skins worth $1,065,896 were gathered in the United States that year; the secretary of the treasury reported that furs and skins exported for the year beginning October 1, 1839, were valued at $1,237,789. In 1842 *Niles Weekly Register* said the value of furs and skins gathered in that year was $760,214. Exports for the year beginning October 1, 1841, amounted to $598,000. These figures, although not absolutely reliable, tend to substantiate available company records. *United States Census*, 1840, *Statistics of the United States*, 408; 26th Congress, 2nd session, *House Executive Documents*, no. 122, p. 252 (serial 386); 27th Congress, 3rd session, *House Documents*, no. 220, p. 10, 46 (serial 425); *Niles Weekly Register* (1842), 63:27. C. M. Lampson, London's leading fur merchant of the time, maintained that the whole of the American fur crop eventually found its way to the London market. Lampson to Ramsay Crooks, December 1, 1845, American Fur Company Papers. For a thorough bibliography on the economics of the post–Civil War fur trade, see Ernest Thomas Seten, *Life-Histories of Northern Animals: An Account of the Mammals of Manitoba* (New York, 1909), 2:1203–20.

4. Poland, *Fur-Bearing Animals in Nature and Commerce* (London, 1892), xxvii–xxx. Figures on fur exports may be found in the annual treasury reports, published as *House Executive Documents* and also bound separately after 1817 as *Annual Reports of the Secretary of the Treasury*. These figures have been compiled for the years prior to 1884 in 48th Congress, 1st session, *House Miscellaneous Documents*, no. 49, part 2, p. 32, 130 (serial 2236). They are lacking for the years 1792–95. Herein they are cited as Secretary of the Treasury, *Annual Reports*, except where a specific report is quoted.

5. Poland's figures may have come from Hudson's Bay Company records, from trade information available when he compiled his work or from His Majesty's Custom and Excise. Alice M. Johnson of the Hudson's Bay Record Society, London, to the author, June 26, 1962; R. W. Hyman of the British Museum, London, to the author, June 25, 1962.

6. See 22nd Congress, 1st session, *Senate Documents*, vol. 2, no. 90, p. 78 (serial 213); "Furs and Skins, 1834–42," and "Receiving Books," vol. 3–6, American Fur Company Papers; "Packing Book, 1830–33," Chouteau Collection.

7. Figures on muskrat skins are calculated from a table in Anne Bezanson, Robert D. Gray, and Miriam Hussey, *Wholesale Prices in Philadelphia, 1784–1861* (Philadelphia, 1936), 2:150. Bezanson's price data is based on the average monthly price of number 1 prime muskrat at Philadelphia, second only to New York City as a fur marketing center in the United States. World prices were set at London and Leipzig.

8. The most useful studies of the economic aspects of the buffalo robe trade are Frank Gilbert Roe, *The North American Buffalo* (Toronto, 1951); William T. Hornaday, "The Extermination of the American Bison," in Smithsonian Institution, *Annual Report*, part 2 (Washington, 1889), 367; Seton, *Life-Histories of Northern Animals*, 1:247–303; Martin S. Garretson, *The American Bison* (New York, 1938).

9. See Roe, *The North American Buffalo*, 489–520; Hornaday, in Smithsonian Institution, *Annual Report*, part 2, 502; Merrill Burlingame, "The Buffalo in Trade and Commerce," *North Dakota Historical Quarterly* 3 (July 1929): 262–91.

10. Poland, *Fur-Bearing Animals*, xxvii–xxx; Bezanson, Gray, and Hussey, *Wholesale Prices in Philadelphia, 1784–1861*, 2:7; Isaac Lippincott, "A Century and a Half of Fur Trade at St. Louis," *Washington University Studies* 3 (April 1916): 233–39.

11. Calculated from a table in Bezanson, Gray, and Hussey, *Wholesale Prices in Philadelphia, 1784–1861*, 2:7.

12. 22nd Congress, 1st session, *Senate Documents*, vol. 2, no. 90, p. 78; Secretary of the Treasury, *Annual Reports*. The Detroit Department of the American Fur Company harvested 132,000 furs in 1838, and increased competition raised this figure to 727,000 by 1840; see "Furs and Skins," in American Fur Company Papers.

13. Bezanson, Gray, and Hussey, *Wholesale Prices in Philadelphia, 1784–1861*, 2:7, 150; Secretary of the Treasury, *Annual Reports*; Anne Bezanson et al., *Wholesale Prices in Philadelphia, 1852–1896* (Philadelphia, 1954), 269; Poland, *Fur-Bearing Animals*, xxx–xxxii.

14. Seton believed that not more than half of the raccoons killed were marketed in London. *Life-Histories of Northern Animals*, 2:1017.

15. Of the 561,000 raccoons gathered by the American Fur Company in 1835–42, almost 500,000 came from the Ohio Valley. On the natural habitat of the raccoon, see Seton, *Life-Histories of Northern Animals*, 2:1013; John James Audubon, *Quadrupeds of North America*, vol. 2 (New York, 1849), under "raccoon." On the raccoon trade, see Bert Anson, "The Fur Traders in Northern Indiana: 1796–1850," PhD thesis, University of Indiana, 1943; Anne Ratterman, "The Struggle for Monopoly of the Fur Trade," master's thesis, University of

Minnesota, 1927. References to the basins of the Kankakee and White rivers in Indiana are numerous in the American Fur Company Papers.

16. See especially the correspondence between Ramsay Crooks and C. M. Lampson in the American Fur Company Papers, and the Crooks-Ewing correspondence in the George W. and William G. Ewing Papers, Indiana State Library, Indianapolis.

17. See Charles Kappler, *Indian Affairs: Laws and Treaties* (Washington DC, 1904), 2:220; 23rd Congress, 1st session, *House Reports*, no. 474, vol. 4, p. 95–128 (serial 263); 31st Congress, 1st session, *House Reports of Committees*, vol. 3, no 489 (serial 585). Debt claims are provided for in many of the treaties in Kappler, *Indian Affairs*, vol. 2. Claims payments to traders and companies may be found in the index to the "Special Files," a series of unclassified folders in the Records of the Bureau of Indian Affairs, National Archives.

18. See Ramsay Crooks to Wildes and Company, July 30, 1836; John Whetten to William Brewster, February 20, 1837; Crooks to Brewster, May 18, 1839; all in American Fur Company Papers; 23rd Congress, 1st session, *House Reports*, no. 474, p. 95–128.

19. "Furs and Skins," in American Fur Company Papers.

20. Poland, *Fur-Bearing Animals*, xxx–xxxii; Bezanson, Gray, and Hussey, *Wholesale Prices in Philadelphia, 1784–1861*, 2:150. See also Bezanson et al., *Wholesale Prices in Philadelphia, 1852–1896*, 17, 101, 203, 206, 269, 302.

21. Poland, *Fur-Bearing Animals*, xxx–xxxii; Bezanson et al., *Wholesale Prices in Philadelphia, 1852–1896*, 302.

22. Poland, *Fur-Bearing Animals*, xxx–xxxii; Bezanson et al., *Wholesale Prices in Philadelphia, 1852–1896*, 302.

23. This is based on Poland's returns and Bezanson's prices for beaver, muskrat, mink, skunk, raccoon, and deerskins. For other furs, estimates for scattered years were used.

24. For the most complete study of the fur seal industry, see United States State Department, *Fur Seal Arbitration: Proceedings* (Washington, 1895). Volumes 2, 3, and 9 are especially valuable, specifically, 2:264–67, 9:529–34. The best authority on the subject is Henry W. Elliott. See especially his "The Fur Seal Industry of the Pribylov Islands, Alaska," in George Goode, *The Fisheries and Fishery Industries of the United States* (Washington, 1887), 2:321; and his report in 54th Congress, 1st session, *House Documents*, vol. 54, no. 175 (serial 3421).

25. *Appendix to the Case of the United States before the Tribunal of Arbitration* (Washington, 1892), 1:104. This is bound with *Fur Seal Arbitration*, vol. 2. See also 63rd Congress, 2nd session, *House Reports (Public)*, vol. 2, no. 500, part 1, p. 1.

26. For a summary of this subject, see *Fur Seal Arbitration*, 2:187–218.

27. 63rd Congress, 2nd session, *House Reports (Public)*, vol. 2, no. 500, part 1, p. 2.

28. *Fur Seal Arbitration*, 3:540–47.

29. See Paul C. Phillips, *The Fur Trade* (Norman OK, 1961), 2:54, 57, 99, 100, 137, 152.

30. Lippincott, in *Washington University Studies*, 3:233–39; 51st Congress, 1st session, *House Executive Documents*, no. 6, part 2, p. 391 (serial 2738).

31. *United States Census*, 1870 Compendium, 802; 1900, *Manufactures*, part 1, p. 8, 218–23, 537; Secretary of the Treasury, *Annual Reports*. See also Harold A. Innis, *The Fur Trade in Canada* (Toronto, 1956), 386–92.

32. *United States Census*, 1890, *Manufactures*, part 1, p. 334–639.

33. Hiram M. Chittenden states that a "fair" estimate of the value of beavers trapped in the Far West from 1815 to 1830 at $4 per pelt would be about $1,500,000. *The American Fur Trade of the Far West* (New York, 1902), 1:7. During these years the value of beaver exports to England, if computed at the same price, would have been about $2,000,000 according to Poland's figures. Since most pelts went to England, it would appear that the Far West was the major source of beaver during these years.

34. See William F. Switzler, "Report on the Internal Commerce of the United States," part 2, in Bureau of Statistics, *Treasury Documents*, no. 1039b, p. 191 (Washington DC, 1888); "Packing Book, 1830–1833," and "Fur Sales, 1859–1864," in Chouteau Collection; "Furs and Skins, 1859–1864," in American Fur Company Papers; John E. Sunder, *The Fur Trade on the Upper Missouri, 1840–1865* (Norman OK, 1965), 16, 79, 104, 159, 201, 216–20. From 1844–53, fur arrivals at St. Louis varied from 1,000 to 3,000, the average being about the same for the end of the period as for the beginning. See Lippincott, in *Washington University Studies*, 3:233–39.

35. *United States Census*, 1840, *Statistics*, 408; "Detroit Department," in Miscellaneous File, American Fur Company Papers.

12. "Red" Labor

Iroquois Participation in the Atlantic Economy

GAIL D. MACLEITCH

In 1756 the Oneida sachem Canaghquayeson protested heartily to Sir William Johnson, British superintendent for Indian affairs, that Iroquois warriors should receive cash wages for martial labor rendered during the Seven Years' War (1754–63). General William Shirley had instigated this policy during the 1755 Niagara campaign when he paid warriors four shillings per day, and Colonel John Bradstreet recently offered natives ten shillings daily for escorting supplies to the beleaguered Fort Oswego. Johnson objected, arguing that as allies of the British, the Iroquois were obligated to lend military support. Moreover, since the British already provided Indian warriors with guns, ammunition, and provisions for their families, they had little right to expect remuneration. Canaghquayeson disagreed. The economic dislocation created by war necessitated cash payments. "As we are now debarred from going to Canada where our wants used to be supplied and our hunting hindered by your dayly orders to hold ourselves in readiness to join the army," he contended, "we think it not unreasonable that those who go on such fatiguing and dangerous service should be well paid." If wages ceased, warriors would no longer work for the empire. A few months later, Mohawk men proved equally resolute not to forgo their income. A ranger company's lieutenant had offered them four shillings per day, plus a ten-dollar bounty, to scout the French-Canadian border. Johnson admonished the Mohawks about the impropriety of such a practice, but the Mohawks refused to yield, telling him that "they thought they deserved as much, if not more than the Rangers, as they were better acquainted with such service than any others."[1]

These interactions reveal a fascinating if unfamiliar image of Indian laborers haggling about wages with their imperial employer. Yet, by the mid-eighteenth century, instances of Indian paid labor in British North America were commonplace. Throughout the colonies, officials hired Indians as messengers, guides, and escorts and employed them in colonial wars as soldiers, scouts, and spies. Impoverished Indians on the eastern shores of Maryland and Virginia earned cash supplying settlers with meat and hunting wolves that threatened livestock. In New England, dispossessed Indians found employment in the whaling industry and as domestic servants. Native Americans who lived near waterways or forts acquired money by transporting the canoes and packs of traders and by supplying garrisons with food. Some earned money capturing army deserters or runaway slaves.[2] Indian labor assumed various forms. Principally, it involved the straightforward exchange of physical and mental toil for goods or cash. However, in addition to selling their labor, Indians also sold the fruits of their labor by manufacturing salable goods, including moccasins, baskets, brooms, and pottery. Petty commodity production allowed Native women, in particular, to participate in market-oriented activities.[3]

While the phrase "forest proletariat" exaggerates the situation of Native Americans in the colonial era, a shift occurred for many Natives in their relationship to the means of production, as indigenous subsistence economies became reoriented toward new commercial concerns.[4] This study of Indian labor is important for what it reveals about the impact of a burgeoning Atlantic economy on Native modes of subsistence. Far from existing as isolated frontier communities, eighteenth-century Native Americans inhabited a larger imperial Atlantic world in which the forces of global economic transformation directly impinged on their lives. The widespread existence of Indian paid labor reflects the partial integration of Native Americans into an external marketplace.

Unfortunately, notable gaps exist in the historical literature on the topic of Indian labor specifically, and Indian involvement in the Atlantic economy more generally.[5] Scholars of the Atlantic world have greatly enriched our understanding of the complex economic ties and processes that bound the British colonies to Europe, Africa, and South America, but they have had relatively little to say about the role of Native peoples. The Atlantic economy evolved in an era of tremendous economic growth, as the forces of "primitive accumulation" restructured the economies of northern Europe along capitalist lines. A new set of market relations gained ascendancy, typified by the drive to produce surplus for profit. The expansive nature of the emergent capitalist economies meant that primitive accumulation quickly spread across the Atlantic Ocean. Three main features defined the Atlantic economy: an international trade in colonial natural resources and agricultural staples; the commodification and accumulation of land; and the creation of a new class of wage laborers.[6] All three trends directly affected Native Americans, pulling them into a commercial marketplace as both producers and consumers, creating greater demands for their land, and precipitating their involvement in new forms of paid labor. Yet, in the growing literature of the Atlantic economy, Indians frequently are absent, treated as if they lived unconnected with and therefore were unaffected by the material forces reshaping the early modern world.[7]

Indian economic history has received greater attention from anthropologists, social scientists, and practitioners of the New Indian History.[8] In the 1970s, scholars, influenced by world-systems theory, examined how a global capitalist order (the core) absorbed Native societies (the periphery), documenting the indigenous economic and political dependency that resulted.[9] While this literature has rightly drawn criticism for stressing all-powerful capitalism and denying Indian agency, it should be commended for considering Native peoples within the broader context of global capitalism. Recently, New Indian historians have produced more nuanced readings of Native participation in regional, national, and transatlantic economies. Their studies examined the inventive ways Indians responded to and resisted the intrusion of market forces.[10] Nonetheless, most of these scholars generally shied away from employing class analysis, preferring instead to adopt political or cultural themes and frameworks. If economic issues are considered, they usually are inadequately theorized; topics like the fur trade or land accumulation are often discussed in a political context of diplomatic relations with European powers or issues of Indian sovereignty. Desiring to empower their subjects and influenced by the persuasive "middle ground" paradigm, New Indian scholars emphasized Indian agency while downplaying material constraints.[11]

Employing class analysis to study Native Americans not only achieves a more comprehensive account of their historical experience but also bridges the divide between Indian and non-Indian histories. The rise of Atlantic capitalism transformed the lives of *all* early Americans, whether they were bound, free, white, black, or Indian. Like European settlers, Native Americans confronted the advancing forces of a protocapitalist economy. Still, any attempt to draw parallels between Native peoples and other segments of an "Atlantic working class" needs to proceed with caution. The development of capitalism was far from a benign process. Conquest, coercion, violence, and theft underpinned primitive accumulation. A transatlantic trading empire depended in large part on the labor and exploitation of indigenous peoples, many of whom were enslaved. Accumulation also involved the forced expropriation of indigenous land and resources.[12] Thus Native peoples encountered and responded to commercial economic forces in discrete ways and with differing consequences, but they were exposed nonetheless.

The eighteenth-century experiences of the Mohawks and Oneidas—the two easternmost nations of the Six Nations of the Iroquois—demonstrate the value of applying class analysis to Native American history.[13] For the eastern Iroquois, the underlying cause of change in the colonial era was economic, not political.[14] As they came into increased contact with a European profit-driven economic order, oriented around commercial agriculture, manufacture, and mercantile trade and surmounted on a system of hierarchical class relations, the eastern Iroquois underwent significant change. First, involvement in the transatlantic fur exchange irrevocably wed them to a new set of commercial trading relations. Second, the commodification and expropriation of their land by colonists slowly undermined their economic autonomy. Third, a growing propensity to sell their labor for cash led to the partial monetization of their economy. Yet Iroquois men and women were never simply victims of early capitalism. Many derived tangible material benefits from engaging in new forms of commercial behavior. Most devised strategies that enabled them to resist and mediate the forces of change. Nonetheless, there were limits to their power. However much they tempered the encroachment of a market economy, they could not wholly evade it. By examining the interplay between material realities and cultural responses, a more realistic picture of Native peoples emerges. The eastern Iroquois were neither helpless fatalities of a waxing Atlantic economy nor complete masters of their destiny.[15]

The Mohawks and Oneidas inhabited a series of villages stretching from the Schoharie Valley in the east to Lake Oneida in central New York. Their precontact economy was largely subsistence-oriented, based on a mixture of horticulture and hunting. The cultivation of maize, beans, and squash formed the bulk of their diet, supplemented by wild game and fish. Although the Iroquois produced articles of everyday life—housing, utensils, tools, and clothing—from local resources, they still engaged in small-scale trade with other Native groups to procure spiritually valued articles, such as precious stones and minerals, which they used in burial rites. Besides practical considerations, trade also served a vital cultural function as a way to maintain alliances and promote ties of social and political obligations between groups and individuals. Through "gift giving," Indians signified friendship and alliance, as well as social deference. Within the village community, all members labored to serve the needs of their household, but gender, age, and rank determined who did what. Generally, men hunted and women farmed, while children and the elderly performed age-appropriate tasks. Ties of mutuality united the sexes, as each contributed valuable skills and resources to the village economy.[16] Other lines of hierarchy, however, existed. Precontact Iroquoia was a ranked society in which certain lineages held hereditary titles and formed an elite. The men who assumed these titles, the elder women who elected them, and their closest relations who acted as advisers constituted the nobility, or *agoïander*. Differences in wealth paralleled social demarcations, as these families tended to reside in the largest longhouses and enjoyed access to prestige goods.[17] Nonetheless, cultural practices centered on gift giving and communal ownership prevented extremes of wealth from developing.

The erosion of Mohawk and Oneida economic autonomy and the trend toward new forms of paid labor were set in motion in the seventeenth century when the Iroquois intensified long-standing hunting practices to become central players in a transatlantic fur trade.[18] For over a century the eastern Iroquois enjoyed genuine advantages from this trade, as they accessed an array of English-manufactured goods, including cloth, guns, household wares, alcohol, and jewelry. They valued these items for their religious and aesthetic attributes, as well as the greater convenience and comfort they offered. Rarely unwitting participants, Indian peoples found ways to ensure that the traffic in furs conformed to their own cultural preferences. They "Indianized" foreign goods, thereby making their integration into Native life less disruptive. They asserted their weight as discerning consumers, forcing traders to cater to their specific tastes. They forged close and often familial relations with traders, thus encouraging exchange to take place within kinship networks and along customary modes of gift giving and reciprocity.[19] They also took advantage of their geopolitical position between two rival empires to certify that market forces did not dominate the nature of exchange. In competition to secure Iroquois allegiance, France and England found it necessary to observe Indian etiquette and consequently provided the Iroquois with diplomatic gifts, subsidized trade, and blacksmiths.[20]

However much hunters and their families were able to shape their daily and immediate contact with the fur trade, they remained largely ineffectual in halting the economic transformation taking place. Examples of Indian agency need to be moderated with a consideration of the broader material constraints under which they lived. The fur trade inextricably drew Indians into a market economy. As energetic partakers in a transatlantic "consumer revolution," the Iroquois by the mid-eighteenth century had become extremely reliant on foreign trade. From Gloucester stroud used in burial rituals, Chinese vermilion worn as facial decoration by warriors, West Indies rum incorporated into religious rites, to European laced hats, woolen stockings, and ruffled shirts that comprised a new "Indian fashion," the Iroquois had integrated foreign goods into all aspects of their cultural life. In 1768 the missionary Eleazor Wheelock was hard-pressed to find a single article of Indian manufacture among the Iroquois not "without the least Mixture of foreign Merchandize." Most notably, the Iroquois had ceased to create their own tools of production. Women farmed with European ironware and warriors hunted with guns and powder, tools that required regular maintenance and periodic replacement. However much Indians may have "Indianized" foreign goods, their well-being largely depended on maintaining access to such goods. The need for European goods wedded the Iroquois to transatlantic commercial networks.[21]

As participants in an Atlantic economy, the Iroquois became subject to its rules. Despite their insistence that ideals of alliance should determine exchange, the eastern Iroquois quickly discovered that they were unable to control the price of trade goods relative to furs. Indeed, from the founding of the trade, external factors such as changing tastes in Europe, fluctuating rates of shipping insurance, and colonial wars created a fickle marketplace. Economic reliance on European wares rendered the Iroquois vulnerable. King George's War (1744–48), which hampered the efforts of hunters and inflated the price of trade goods, generated impoverishment among the Mohawks. Some left their children as pawns with traders until they could pay their debts. Others, in their poverty, chose to relocate to Canada.[22] The Seven Years' War created similar conditions. By 1761, as some Iroquois complained, "we are now (by the dearness of goods sold to us in our Country, and at the different posts,) obliged to pay such exorbitant prices, that our hunting is not sufficient to purchase us as much cloathing as is necessary to cover us, & our families."[23]

Playing the French and British against each other had afforded the Iroquois some protection from the marketplace, but this ended with the fall of French Canada in 1761. With New France no longer offering an alternative source of trade and gifts, Iroquois dependency on the British deepened. William Johnson used the shifting balance of power to the empire's advantage. Even before the war's end, he wielded trade as an imperial weapon to pressure the Iroquois to lend military support. "My orders from the King your father are, to take care of and supply with necessaries such good & faithful Indians as will go out and fight for him," he informed them. When headmen complained about the high cost of trade goods, Johnson dismissed their claims as "ill-founded." Abandoning his usual rhetoric of reciprocity, he instead blamed the market economy: "You do not or at least are unwilling to consider that a Scarcity of any Commodity makes it dear."[24] Although the Anglo-Indian War (1763–65), erroneously called Pontiac's Rebellion, forced the British to reconsider their Indian policy, a strapped treasury meant that the postwar practice of gift giving became a watered-down version of its former self. Furthermore, following the war, a new breed of trader saturated the fur market: men who had little experience in Indian protocol, but who instead relied extensively on rum to facilitate the traffic in furs. In the contest over whose customs would dictate the nature of exchange, the Iroquois had been considerably edged out.[25]

At the same time the Iroquois confronted the commercialization of exchange, shifting material conditions added to their difficulties.

"Red" Labor

By the early 1700s, decades of overhunting had exhausted local beaver supplies. The growing presence of colonial settlements placed further pressure on local game, forcing Iroquois hunters to venture farther afield. Even if they maintained access to animal skins, the fur trade itself was in transition. As the eighteenth century progressed, fur and skin exports became an ever-shrinking percentage of the New York economy. Superseded by the commercial production of grains and timber, fur dropped to less than 25 percent of total exports to London in the 1740s. By midcentury, the center of the trade relocated west, first to the Ohio Valley and then, following the Seven Years' War, to the Great Lakes. In growing numbers, New York merchants and traders bypassed key trading posts in Iroquois country at Oswego and Niagara, as they headed to the western posts of Detroit and Michilimackinac.[26] Increasingly sidelined in the fur trade, yet still desirous for foreign goods, the eastern Iroquois began to develop alternative means to participate in commercial exchange.

Access to land and its resources provided the Iroquois with a crucial buffer against the market economy. As long as they possessed enough land to engage in subsistence farming, hunting, and fishing, involvement in an external marketplace could be casual and limited. However, a defining theme of the Mohawk's and Oneida's eighteenth-century experience was the commodification and expropriation of their lands by a steady stream of Dutch, German, and English settlers.[27] In the early decades of contact, the eastern Iroquois exercised some control over this process: they loaned land from a position of strength and as a way to forge alliances. In the 1690s the Mohawks "lent" a plot of land to the Dutch community of Schenectady "for a Range for their Cattle," accepting in return a small gift of cash. They still maintained ownership of this land, but as Schenectady was a prosperous community, with whom the Iroquois traded, offering grazing land was a way to strengthen socioeconomic ties.[28] The arrival of impoverished Palatine Germans to the region in the 1710s provided other useful allies. The Mohawk chief

Hendrick noted that they had loaned "Poor Germans" land "because we always pity the poor, and they are our Neighbours."[29]

Becoming sensitive to commercial values, the Mohawks and Oneidas gradually developed a new understanding of land as a commodity from which they could extract revenue. Assuming the role of property owner, they began to require Euro-American tenants to pay rent in corn or cash.[30] Additionally, they sold land for money, such as when the Mohawks received "155 pieces of eight" for a plot of land purchased by Jacob Glen in 1735.[31] Selling and renting land fulfilled a social function by enabling the Mohawks to cultivate alliances with handpicked neighbors, but this practice was also economic. Money made from land provided access to the marketplace to procure other goods.

Yet the rising number of colonial settlers, insatiable in their desire for land and unscrupulous in their efforts to secure it, slowly undermined Iroquois ability to control the nature and degree of land transfers. The Mohawks faced mounting pressure to cede land by colonists who fraudulently took up more land than the Mohawks had agreed to sell and who claimed ownership of land the Mohawks had only loaned. Grievances mounted until Hendrick, incensed by the New York governor's inability to redress their complaints, formally broke off the Covenant Chain of Friendship with the English in 1753.[32] The Seven Years' War brought temporary respite to the accumulation of Iroquois lands, but following the war, new confidence in the safety of the frontier along with a swelling colonial population intensified the drive for western lands. During the 1760s settlers invaded northern Mohawk hunting grounds around Lake George and southern Oneida hunting grounds on the upper Susquehanna, cutting down trees to build homes and farms and dispersing wild game.[33] Closer to home, subsistence activities were also impeded. Hostile neighbors purposely let cattle graze on Mohawk cornfields.[34] Soldiers garrisoned at posts near Lake Oneida confiscated the fish and furs of returning Oneida warriors. After these soldiers moved out, settlers moved in, attracted by the abandoned fort and outhouses.[35] The Fort Stanwix Treaty of 1768, which established a boundary between Indian country and lands belonging to the British Crown, formalized Iroquois encirclement by British colonists. By the terms of this treaty, Mohawk and Oneida lands fell on the east side of the boundary, and during the next years speculators raced to survey and patent this area.[36]

Colonial expropriation of Indian lands was a major factor hastening Iroquois entanglement into an Atlantic economy and new forms of paid labor. Intrusions onto Mohawk and Oneida hunting grounds incapacitated their ability to hunt. As one warrior complained, "We know not where to go for subsistence tomorrow. . . . good hunting is no more known amongst us, since the encroachments of the white people."[37] Women, too, were painfully aware that loss of land would leave them "being Reduced to make Brooms."[38] Although hunting and farming persisted into the next century, external pressures encouraged the eastern Iroquois to develop additional economic pursuits.

As Iroquois village economies became slowly enmeshed within a larger Atlantic world, Iroquois men and women formulated creative responses to meet the exigencies of a new economic order. Reliance on European trade goods, the unpredictability of the fur market, depletion of fur-bearing animals, and the growth of colonial settlements all propelled the eastern Iroquois to sell their labor and the products of their labor for goods and cash. Participation in new forms of paid labor was casual and limited, but it grew more commonplace by midcentury. Natives served as guides and interpreters, offered safe passage across rivers and lakes, supplied forts with food, and hunted wolves as forms of paid employment.[39] Colonists often provided trade goods in compensation for services, but over time, Indians increasingly expected and received cash. This new penchant for money reveals the extent to which Natives had become involved in a market economy. More and more, in their daily encounters with settlers and traders, cash rather than ties of friendship was required to obtain food and clothing.

Oneidas acquired cash as carriers at the Great Carrying Place. This was a valuable passageway between the Mohawk River and Wood Creek used by traders on their way to the Oswego trading post on the southeast shore of Lake Ontario. In addition to expecting a "gift" of rum or a blanket for the privilege of using the portage, the Oneidas charged a specific price for each transported item. When German settlers attempted to carve out a niche in the carrying business in the 1730s, the Oneidas aggressively sought to have them removed. By the 1750s traders remonstrated against the intimidating behavior of the Oneidas who "force our goods from us . . . and not content with making us pay a most exorbitant price, for each freight, but rob us of our Rum, stores and other goods." In addition, "they force away the High Germans . . . that we may be under a necessity of employing them, and paying whatsoever they please to demand."[40] The Oneidas were not profit-maximizing entrepreneurs, but merely men and women who sought to maintain control over a necessary form of employment. The eastern Iroquois also accessed a cash economy through participation in the booming ginseng trade of the early 1750s. Valued for its medicinal properties, the ginseng root fetched a high price in the China market. Albany merchants, keen to capitalize on this commercial enterprise, paid Indians and colonial settlers alike to gather this naturally grown vegetable. When a Moravian minister, J. Martin Mack, traveled through Iroquoia in 1752, he noticed villages virtually abandoned as men, women, and children scoured the woods for the root. "The Indians sell them to the people hereabouts, or exchange them for goods with the traders," he reported.[41]

Mohawk and Oneida men found significant opportunities to sell labor for cash during wartime. By providing martial manpower in imperial conflicts, the Iroquois helped defend and enlarge the resources essential to the British Empire.[42]

During King George's War, warriors received regular payments for carrying supplies to Fort Oswego and bounties for captives and scalps. During the Seven Years' War, bounties, special commissions, and daily wages were issued.[43] Colonial officials regarded Indians as an inexpensive labor source. William Shirley, who served briefly as commander in chief of the British forces in North America, observed, "I should think if the Indians were kept in constant Pay, they might be made as cheap soldiers." However, it was the insistence of Native Americans themselves that ensured that cash payments became common practice.[44] By lending their martial support to the British, Iroquois men neglected many traditional economic pursuits, which warfare disrupted in any case.[45] Imperial wars accelerated the commodification of Indian labor. War not only expanded opportunities to exchange labor for cash, but, more important, it also created a greater necessity to do so. Men required wages to purchase the goods they previously procured through trade. Throughout the 1750s and 1760s, Indians frequently purchased European wares and food with money.[46]

Although a uniform wage system never materialized, cash payments to Iroquois warriors became widespread during the Seven Years' War. Johnson, who eventually warmed to the idea of wages as a cost-effective way to employ Indian labor, established himself as key paymaster, recruiting warriors and disseminating funds.[47] Indians received payments for diverse services: delivering messages, escorting interpreters, transporting goods, capturing army deserters, and driving cattle to military posts. Johnson expended sizable payments on soldiering. Obtaining prisoners, scalps, and intelligence was a guaranteed way to earn steady cash. In 1759 Johnson paid a party of warriors £45 for securing three prisoners. For another group who returned from Canada with "a deal of Intelligence," he paid £15 each. Indians who participated in major campaigns earned special commissions. Warriors in the 1759 Niagara campaign made money by destroying blockhouses surrounding the fort and escorting the captured French general to Fort Stanwix.[48] The exchange of labor for cash never became wholly commercialized. British need for Iroquois military support obliged them to acquiesce to Native protocol. Johnson engaged in a full range of Indian rituals to induce warriors to fight and maintained a generous distribution of gifts alongside cash payments.[49] Nonetheless, the war increased the occurrence of Indian paid labor and expedited the infusion of cash into Iroquois village economies.

Men continued to find opportunities to exchange labor for cash in the postwar decade. Economic upheaval generated by war and the intrusion of settlers onto hunting grounds rendered paid labor necessary. The Anglo-Indian War encouraged warriors once again to sell their martial labor.[50] Outside the arena of warfare, Mohawk and Oneida men earned wages transporting traders and their goods over rivers and portages. In the early 1760s Mohawk men charged £4 a trip to carry goods and people by boat from Schenectady to Fort Stanwix.[51] Local settlers hired Indian men to shepherd their flocks, to perform manual labor on their estates, and to track down runaway slaves. Cash was also acquired by supplying forts and settlers with venison and fish, as well as serving as guides.[52] A handful of men earned a livelihood through their services to the church, as catechists, schoolteachers, and missionaries. Oneida Deacon Thomas, for example, received £20 a year for his work as a catechist and schoolmaster from the New England Company for the propagation of the Gospel.[53] Throughout the 1760s and 1770s Johnson continued to pay Indians for carrying correspondence, providing intelligence, and escorting Army officers, as well as for laboring on his estate.[54]

Native women also found ways to participate in a market economy, chiefly through the manufacture of salable goods. Women had long produced baskets, moccasins, and leggings, which they exchanged with colonial neighbors for food and, increasingly, cash. During the Seven Years' War, Johnson became a principal customer, purchasing "Indn. Shoes" for his scouting parties. He also bought prepared animal skins, wampum belts, and rum.[55] Following the war, women continued to engage in petty commodity production. The increased rarity and thus exoticism of Indian handicrafts enhanced their market value. In 1769 an ex-army officer, Richard Smith, noted the production of moccasins, garments, and wampum belts among the Iroquois and observed that the manufacturers "demand high Prices for their Labor." Another army officer stationed in the valley in 1776, Joseph Bloomfield, encountered the presence of "Squaa's" at his military encampment. He observed, "They are here almost as much [as] at home" producing "Mockinsons & such other Things" to sell to soldiers.[56] Gender differentiated the nature of Indian involvement in a market economy. Men generally exchanged their physical labor and martial skills for cash, while women produced salable goods. Because both found a means to access a cash economy, they maintained a significant degree of gender parity.[57]

The exchange of labor for money marked an important development in Iroquois economic and cultural behavior. The eastern Iroquois developed a nascent understanding of labor as a *commodity*, exchangeable for a specific monetary value. The high demand placed on their services during imperial wars encouraged them to recognize the market value of their labor and led them to refuse to work if conditions of pay were unsatisfactory. Johnson censored this new commercial spirit, reminding them how "in former times when we went to war together . . . your ancestors never even thought of Pay." The Indian agent Thomas Butler commented on the changing economic behavior of warriors who seemed more concerned with obtaining sufficient pay than fulfilling reciprocal bonds: "When I talkt or Mententioned to the Indians of Going a Scouting they askt for pay in C. [commission?] for the Same besides their dayley wages which I was obliged To do To some." He went on to complain, "There Seems no Such thing as Sattisfieing the Indians."[58] By the 1770s the Mohawks and Oneidas had established practices for price setting. Richard Smith, after paying his Indian guide "James the Mohawk" a half dollar per day, noted, "The Indian Custom, probably derived from the Dutch, is to be paid for the time of returning as well as going." He further observed, "The Oneidas and most other Indians are said to be extortionate and very apt to ask high Prices especially when they perceive a Necessity for their Assistance." Familiar with the standard rates of pay, Indians complained if they believed their employer cheated them out of fair wages.[59]

Iroquois labor was never fully commodified. While some Indians were exacting in their demand for a specific payment, others continued to provide labor for a more casual exchange of goods. Furthermore, despite disruptions caused to subsistence activities by the growing presence of Euro-American settlers, the Mohawks and Oneidas never became entirely dependent on paid employment. As they continued to hunt, fish, and farm, they avoided total encapsulation in an emerging capitalist economy. Nonetheless, involvement in new commercial behaviors left an indelible mark on their material and cultural reality. The Iroquois resourcefully adapted to suit the demands of an increasingly commercial world, but the very act of adaptation further precipitated their entanglement.

The commodification of their land, labor, and resources led the Iroquois to experience a growing dependence on money. Indians had always had their own multipurpose forms of currency—such as furs, corn, and wampum—and for a long time resisted European coins as the principal medium of exchange.[60] Yet extended contact with colonists increased Iroquois exposure to and reliance on foreign currency. Access to pounds, shillings, and dollars was fast becoming a necessity if Indians wished to acquire the goods on which they had long depended. During the Seven Years' War, the Iroquois, in their impoverishment, relied on money to purchase provisions. Johnson's accounts are replete with entries of regular cash payments to Indians "to buy them Provisions" or "to purchase Indn. Corn" from colonists.[61] Following the war, the Mohawks could no longer depend on the once-taken-for-granted hospitality of German neighbors for provisions. After meetings with the Mohawks at his frontier estate, Johnson was obliged to supply them with cash so that they could purchase food on their way home. In 1769, when crops failed, Smith observed that many Indians survived the winter and spring by living on the money they had received from the Fort Stanwix Treaty. He noted, "They were continually passing up to the Settlements to buy Provisions and sometimes shewed us the money in their Bosoms." Account books of valley traders also reveal that by the late 1760s Indians used cash as frequently as furs to purchase goods.[62]

European money did not yet govern their economic lives. Indians continued to use alternative and preferred forms of currency. During his travels, Smith encountered a group of Oneida women who adorned themselves with silver brooches, "each of which passes for a Shilling and are as current among the Indians as Money." Alternatively, Bloomfield noted that wampum was "the current money" among the Iroquois. Yet both of these articles were of European manufacture. Therefore, to trade in the currency of their preference, the Iroquois still needed to enter the market to sell goods or labor in order to purchase brooches and wampum.[63] The Iroquois experienced only partial integration into a cash economy, but it was enough to undermine their economic autonomy. Iroquois engagement in commercial exchange enhanced their dependence on cash, which drew them further into the marketplace.

An even more significant consequence of growing involvement in an Atlantic economy was the emergence of class stratification, particularly among the Mohawks. The war loss claims filed by the Mohawks following the American Revolution demonstrate that private ownership was not only widespread but also significantly unequal.[64] In regard to total wealth encompassing land, standing property (houses and barns), farming implements, and livestock, the smallest claim was for £25, the largest for over £1,200, pointing to sharp divisions between the haves and have-nots. Archaeological findings, and the fact that the value of standing property ranged from £15 to £250, demonstrate the existence of an elite pattern of residential housing. Although the Mohawks still held the majority of land in common, the war loss claims reveal that by the 1770s some individuals had acquired private lots. Individual landholdings were a logical outcome of adopting European legal definitions of private property. Ownership of land, like everything else, was unequal. Approximately 80 percent of the Mohawks who filed claims owned just 36 percent of all private lands. Individual landholdings ranged from three to almost six hundred acres.[65]

Similar discrepancies of wealth are also evident among the Oneidas. In 1794 the U.S. Government agent Timothy Pickering carried out a detailed report of the losses sustained by the Oneidas during the Revolution. Unlike the Mohawks, they experienced less extremes of wealth and did not privately own land.[66] Nonetheless, private property was still common and unequal. In regard to total wealth, Oneida claims ranged from £1 to £287. Most claims were for £65 or less, with the exception of seven families that claimed £65 or more. Also evident in Pickering's report are differences in housing structures, which ranged from small "Indian" or "bark" houses valued between £2 and £8 to large framed houses complete with cellars, windows, and chimneys, worth as much as £48.[67]

Divisions of wealth and status were not without precedent in Iroquois society, given the existence of the *agoïander*. However, enmeshment within a market economy changed the nature of hierarchy. By the 1770s the older ranked society had given way to a new system of class stratification. The system of hereditary sachemship still functioned, but political power and status increasingly rested with those who enjoyed access to material wealth. Membership in a particular lineage no longer carried so much weight in determining an individual's status; instead, economic success became more important. Involvement in a frontier exchange economy provided opportunities to acquire wealth, and some individuals and families were more successful than others in this endeavor. The Mohawks and Oneidas who claimed the greatest wealth were head warriors and their female relations.[68] Warriors enjoyed ample access to the market economy from the 1740s through the 1760s by exchanging their martial skills for monetary rewards. This wealthy elite owned a disproportionate number of barns, plows, hoes, and livestock. Such fixtures of Euro-American agriculture were not purely an indication of wealth but also an important source of wealth. By the late eighteenth century, the eastern Iroquois had intensified agricultural pursuits, producing surplus crops and livestock for trade and sale.[69]

To some extent, the British, through their agent William Johnson, further aggravated the trend of economic inequality. Throughout his career, Johnson engaged in the unequal distribution of gifts to Indians who demonstrated loyalty, thus facilitating the creation of an economic elite composed of pro-British families.[70] A notable example of this new economic elite was Joseph Brant, who emerged as an important leader during the American Revolution. When Richard Smith met Brant in 1769, he noted that the latter was "dressed in a suit of blue Broad Cloth as his Wife was in a Callicoe or Chintz Gown." Impressed by Brant's personal wealth, Smith commented, "This Mohawk it seems is a considerable Farmer possessing Horses and Cattle and 100 acres of rich land at Canejoharie." He also observed how Brant's wife wore "several tier[s]" of brooches on her dress "to the amount perhaps of 10 or £15." Brant's close ties with the British—his sister, Molly Brant, was William Johnson's common-law wife—no doubt assisted his personal fortunes.[71]

Both facilitating and resulting from this material shift was important cultural change. Extended exposure to market forces chipped away at older values of reciprocity and communalism as Indians engaged in new forms of behavior centered on accruing wealth. Indian agents familiar with the Iroquois observed how individual families began to accumulate private property. Guy Johnson remarked, "They have no Property in Common, the Product of the Labour & Hunting of each Individual, being at his own Disposal." George Croghan agreed, noting that "every family have thire Distinct property." Even the custom of hospitality, which had meant "the Community Can Never Suffer fer Want," was in decline, "Sense they become more acquainted with Europians."[72] The presence of an impoverished class of Mohawks who relied on the British Crown for their support partially substantiates this observation. In the

1770s Johnson buried a number of indigent Mohawks "destitute of friends." He provided aid to "a sick Mohawk unable for these 2 Years past to help himself." He also supported "the Oldest Sachem of the Mohawks" and his family, they "being very Poor."[73] That Johnson took charge of what would have once been a communal responsibility to look after one's own says something about changing preoccupations of the Mohawks on the eve of the Revolution.

The development of class identities accompanied these discrepancies in prosperity. Iroquois men and women expressed a new class status by their visual displays of wealth. By embellishing their clothes with silver brooches, purchasing horses and cattle, or choosing to drink tea out of porcelain teacups, this Mohawk elite cultivated a new cultural identity for themselves that set them apart from less wealthy Indians. Clothing and personal adornments, in particular, were important for establishing social standing. Smith observed variations between "the Dress of the common sort," which included "a Shirt or Shift with a Blanket or Coat, a Half-Gown and Petticoat," and that of leading sachems and their families, who wore more expensive fabrics and who "imitate the English Mode." Bloomfield was struck by the very visible distinction between "the almost naked Savages" who attended a conference, "the Men having a Clout only round them & the Women a skirt & Blanket," in contrast to "the Heads & Chiefs & their squaas who were elegantly dressed with mockinsens Leggings &c."[74]

Although decades of exposure to market forces left their mark on the cultural world of the Iroquois, it is important not to overstate the degree or pace of change. The eastern Iroquois were in transition, increasingly tied to an emerging capitalist order, yet remaining decidedly apart from it. They exhibited new commercially tinged attitudes at the same time that they clung onto distinctly noncommercial practices. Bloomfield may have encountered Mohawk women busily engrossed in petty commodity production, but he also experienced affecting examples of Iroquois hospitality. When visiting the Oneida village at Kanestio, he noted how he and his companions, although strangers, were "Hospitably given" a meal and warm resting place. While Smith may have observed Iroquois men keen to secure decent pay, he also noted the persistence of strong communal practices. At the Oneida community of Aughguaga on the Susquehanna River, he visited a shad fishery where "all persons present including strangers, such is their laudable Hospitality have an equal Division of Fish." He further noted how "Debts and Thefts seem to be almost unknown among them, Property being in some Degree common to all." Iroquois women may have worn brooches as a demonstration of their wealth and status, but they continued to value the jewelry's spiritual qualities, choosing to be buried with their garments "set off with rows of silver brooches, one row joining another."[75] The capitalist market economy and its attendant value system may have made inroads into Mohawk and Oneida society by the late eighteenth century, but it did not yet dominate the Iroquois' existence.

While it is crucial that scholars remain sensitive to the particularities of the Amerindian experience, it is equally important that they do not lose sight of the larger historical forces—Atlantic mercantile capitalism—that shaped Native people's material and cultural reality. The story of Iroquois entanglement in a new economic order shares parallels with other segments of the Atlantic working class. Broader economic forces also dislodged the traditional "moral economy" of subsistence agriculture and noncommercial exchange among Anglo-American settlers of the New York hinterland.[76] In the Mohawk Valley, both frontier settlers and Iroquois Indians relied on subsistence activities—picking wild fruit, hunting game, fishing, and growing crops—yet both increasingly tapped into a local and transatlantic marketplace by selling crops, furs, and their labor for cash. For both groups, contact with a dynamic Atlantic economy in the late eighteenth century resulted in the partial monetization of their economies and gradual commodification of their labor. They both, to differing extents, straddled a divide between a traditional/subsistence and a modern/commercial world. The Iroquois never became proletarianized. They creatively responded to encroaching commercial forces in a way that lessened their transforming effect. By continuing to hunt and farm throughout the eighteenth century, by Indianizing European goods, and by using Native forms of currency alongside European coins, the Iroquois mediated structural changes through their own cultural practices. Yet, through the very act of accommodating to the forces of Atlantic capitalism, the Iroquois became inextricably absorbed into the Atlantic world.

Notes

Earlier versions of this article were presented at the International Seminar on the History of the Atlantic World, 1500–1800, Harvard University, 1999; at the McNeil Center for Early American Studies, 2003; and at the "Class and Class Struggles in North America and the Atlantic World, 1500–1820" conference, Montana State University, 2003. I am grateful to the participants at all of these conferences for their valuable commentary. I especially thank Billy Smith, Daniel Richter, Jenny Pulsipher, and Peter Way. I also thank the School of Humanities, King's College, London, for providing financial support that enabled me to complete research at the New York State Library in Albany, the New York Historical Society, and the New York Public Library in New York City.

1. Journal of Sir William Johnson's Proceedings with the Indians, August 13, 1756, in *Documents Relative to the Colonial History of the State of New York*, 15 vols., ed. E. B. O'Callaghan and Berthow Fernow (Albany NY: Weed, Parsons, 1853–87), 7:184–85 (hereafter cited as DRCHNY); Johnson to Lord Loudoun, March 17, 1757, in *The Papers of Sir William Johnson*, 14 vols., ed. James Sullivan et al. (Albany: University of the State of New York, 1921–65), 9:641 (hereafter cited as WJP).

2. John A. Sainsbury, "Indian Labor in Early Rhode Island," *New England Quarterly* 48 (1975): 378–93 (hereafter cited as NEQ); Daniel Vickers, "The First Whalemen of Nantucket," *William and Mary Quarterly*, 3rd ser., 40, no. 4 (1983): 560–83 (hereafter cited as WMQ); Daniel H. Usner, Jr., *Indians, Settlers, and Slaves in a Frontier Exchange Economy: The Lower Mississippi Valley before 1783* (Chapel Hill: University of North Carolina Press, 1992), 232; Kathryn E. Holland Braund, *Deerskins and Duffels: The Creek Indian Trade with Anglo-America, 1685–1815* (Lincoln: University of Nebraska Press, 1993), 73–74; Daniel R. Mandall, *Behind the Frontier: Indians in Eighteenth-Century Eastern Massachusetts* (Lincoln: University of Nebraska Press, 1996), 197–98; Helen C. Rountree

and Thomas E. Davidson, *Eastern Shore Indians of Virginia and Maryland* (Charlottesville: University Press of Virginia, 1997), 76.

3. On petty commodity production, see James H. Merrell, *The Indians' New World: Catawbas and Their Neighbors from European Contact through the Era of Removal* (New York: Norton, 1989), 210–11; Rountree and Davidson, *Eastern Shore Indians*, 75–76. Other forms of Indian labor beyond the scope of this article are slave labor and indentured servitude. See Almon W. Lauber, *Indian Slavery in Colonial Times within the Present Limits of the United States* (New York: Columbia University Press, 1913); Alan Gallay, *The Indian Slave Trade: The Rise of the English Empire in the American South, 1670–1717* (New Haven CT: Yale University Press, 2002); Rountree and Davidson, *Eastern Shore Indians*, 76–78; David Silverman, "The Impact of Indentured Servitude on the Society and Culture of Southern New England Indians, 1680–1810," *NEQ* 74 (2001): 622–66.

4. Discussing the Creek involvement in the fur and hide trade, the anthropologist Harold Hickerson referred to them as "a kind of vast forest proletariat" ("Fur Trade Colonialism and the North American Indians," *Journal of Ethnic Studies* 1 [1973]: 39).

5. Research on Indian paid labor is minimal and consists largely of scattered references; see note 2. On this phenomenon in the nineteenth century, see Rolf Knight, *Indians at Work: An Informal History of Native American Labor in British Columbia, 1858–1938* (Vancouver BC: New Star Books, 1978); Alice Littlefield and Martha C. Knack, eds., *Native Americans and Wage Labor: Ethnohistorical Perspectives* (Norman: University of Oklahoma Press, 1996).

6. For recent work that deals with these themes, see Paul E. Lovejoy and Nicholas Rogers, eds., *Unfree Labour in the Development of the Atlantic World* (Portland OR: Cass, 1994); David Hancock, *Citizens of the World: London Merchants and the Integration of the British Atlantic Community, 1735–1785* (New York: Cambridge University Press, 1995); Robin Blackburn, *The Making of New World Slavery: From the Baroque to the Modern, 1492–1800* (London: Verso, 1997); Allan Kulikoff, *From British Peasants to Colonial American Farmers* (Chapel Hill: University of North Carolina Press, 2000); Peter Linebaugh and Marcus Rediker, *The Many-Headed Hydra: The Hidden History of the Revolutionary Atlantic* (London: Verso, 2000).

7. On the neglect of Native Americans in broader historical narratives and suggestions for inclusion, see Daniel H. Usner, Jr., "New Directions in the Economic History of American Indians," *Overcoming Economic Dependency: Occasional Papers in Curriculum Series, no. 9* (Chicago: Newberry Library, D'Arcy McNickle Center for the History of the American Indian, 1988), 229–33;

Daniel K. Richter, "Whose Indian History?" *WMQ* 50 (1993): 390–91; Ian K. Steele, "Exploding Colonial American History: Amerindian, Atlantic, and Global Perspectives," *Reviews in American History* 26 (1998): 70–95; Linda Barrington, ed., introduction to *The Other Side of the Frontier: Economic Exploration into Native American History* (Boulder CO: Westview, 1999).

8. For an overview of the literature, see Patricia Albers, "Labor and Exchange in American Indian History," in *The Blackwell Companion to Native American History*, ed. Neal Salisbury and Phil Deloria (Oxford: Blackwell, 2002), 269–86.

9. Immanuel Wallerstein, *The Modern World System: Capitalist Agriculture and the Origins of the European World Economy in the Sixteenth Century* (New York: Academic, 1974); and Wallerstein, *The Modern World System II: Mercantilism and the Consolidation of the European World Economy, 1600–1750* (New York: Academic, 1980); Eric R. Wolf, *Europe and the People without History* (Berkeley: University of California Press, 1982); Richard White, *The Roots of Dependency: Subsistence, Environment, and Social Change among the Choctaws, Pawnees, and Navajos* (Lincoln: University of Nebraska Press, 1983); Denys Delage, *Bitter Feast: Amerindians and Europeans in Northeastern North America, 1600–1664*, trans. Jane Brierley (1985; repr., Vancouver: University of British Columbia Press, 1993).

10. Notable examples include Usner, *Indians, Settlers, and Slaves*; Braund, *Deerskins and Duffels*; John H. Moore, ed., *The Political Economy of North American Indians* (Norman: University of Oklahoma Press, 1993); James T. Carson, "Horses and the Economy and Culture of the Choctaw Indians, 1690–1840," *Ethnohistory* 42 (1995): 495–513; Carson, "Native Americans, the Market Revolution, and Cultural Change: The Choctaw Cattle Economy, 1690–1830," *Agricultural History* 71 (1997): 1–18; Claudio Saunt, *A New Order of Things: Property, Power, and the Transformation of the Creek Indians, 1733–1816* (Cambridge: Cambridge University Press, 1999). After the colonial period, see Frank Tough, *As the Natural Resources Fail: Native Peoples and the Economic History of the Northern Manitoba, 1870–1930* (Vancouver: University of British Columbia Press, 1996); Brian C. Hosmer, *American Indians in the Marketplace: Persistence and Innovation among the Menominees and Metlakatlans, 1870–1928* (Lawrence: University Press of Kansas, 1999).

11. The "middle ground" paradigm is a product of Richard White's classic study of Indian-colonial relations in the Great Lakes region. White argued that because neither Indians nor Europeans could initially conquer or control the other, relations were marked by a high degree of interdependence, mutual accommodation, and cultural synthesis (*The Middle Ground: Indians, Empires, and Republics in the Great Lakes Region, 1650–1815* [New York: Cambridge University Press, 1991]).

12. For a study that explores the relationship between violence and capitalist development, see Kenneth Pomeranz and Steven Topik, *The World That Trade Created: Society, Culture, and the World Economy, 1400 to the Present* (New York: Sharpe, 1999), chap. 5.

13. The Six Nations included the Mohawks, Oneidas, Tuscaroras, Cayugas, Onondagas, and Senecas. The Tuscaroras did not become the sixth tribe until 1722, when the Iroquois Confederacy formally adopted them.

14. Iroquois historiography is dominated by political themes and perspectives. The standard monographs are Barbara Graymont, *The Iroquois in the American Revolution* (Syracuse NY: Syracuse University Press, 1972); Richard Aquila, *The Iroquois Restoration: Iroquois Diplomacy on the Colonial Frontier, 1701–1754* (Detroit: Wayne State University Press, 1983); Francis Jennings, *Ambiguous Empire: The Covenant Chain Confederation of Indian Tribes with English Colonies* (New York: Norton, 1984); Daniel K. Richter, *The Ordeal of the Longhouse: The Peoples of the Iroquois League in the Era of European Colonization* (Chapel Hill: University of North Carolina Press, 1992); José Antonió Brandão, *"Your Fyre Shall Burn No More": Iroquois Policy toward New France and Its Native Allies to 1701* (Lincoln: University of Nebraska Press, 1997); William N. Fenton, *The Great Law of the Longhouse: A Political History of the Iroquois Confederacy* (Norman: University of Oklahoma Press, 1998).

15. On the merits of this conceptual framework, see Patricia C. Abler, "Marxism and Historical Materialism in American Indian History," in *Clearing a Path: Theoretical Approaches to the Past in Native American Studies*, ed. Nancy Shoemaker (New York: Routledge, 2000), 107–36.

16. Sara H. Stites, *Economics of the Iroquois* (Lancaster PA: New Era, 1905); William N. Fenton, "Northern Iroquois Culture Patterns," in *Handbook of North American Indians*, ed. William C. Sturtevant, vol. 15, *Northeast*, ed. Bruce Trigger (Washington DC: Smithsonian Institution, 1978), 296–321; Elizabeth Tooker, "Women in Iroquois Society," in *Extending the Rafters: Interdisciplinary Approaches to Iroquoian Studies*, ed. Michael K. Foster et al. (Albany: State University of New York Press, 1984), 115–16; Richter, *Ordeal of the Longhouse*, 13–14, 28–29, 42–43; Michael Recht, "The Role of Fishing in the Iroquois Economy, 1600–1792," *New York History* 76 (1995): 5–30 (hereafter cited as *NYH*).

17. Reuben G. Thwaites, ed., *The Jesuit Relations and Allied Documents: Travels and Explorations of the Jesuit Missionaries in New France, 1610–1791*, 73 vols. (Cleveland OH: Burrows Bros., 1896–1901), 26:305, 54:93–95, 218, 58:183, 63:183, 185, 64:77, 79, 81, 105; Daniel Richter, "Stratification in Eastern Native America" (paper presented at "Class and Class Struggles in North America and the Atlantic World, 1500–1820" conference, Montana State University,

2003). I am indebted to Daniel K. Richter for encouraging me to rethink my understanding of socioeconomic hierarchy in precontact Iroquois society.

18. Iroquois involvement in the fur trade is well documented: George T. Hunt, *The Wars of the Iroquois: A Study in Intertribal Trade Relations* (Madison: University of Wisconsin Press, 1940); Thomas E. Norton, *The Fur Trade in Colonial New York, 1686–1776* (Madison: University of Wisconsin Press, 1974), chap. 3; Aquila, *Iroquois Restoration*, pt. 1; Richter, *Ordeal of the Longhouse*, chap. 4.

19. On the "Indianization" of foreign goods, see Christopher L. Miller and George R. Hamell, "A New Perspective on Indian-White Contact: Cultural Symbols and Colonial Trade," *Journal of American History* 72 (1986): 311–28. On Indians as active consumers, see Arthur J. Ray, "Indians as Consumers in the Eighteenth Century," in *Old Trails, New Directions: Papers of the Third North American Fur Trade Conference*, ed. Carol M. Judd and Arthur J. Ray (Toronto: University of Toronto Press, 1980), 255–71; and Dean L. Anderson, "The Flow of European Trade Goods into the Western Great Lakes Region, 1715–1760," in *The Fur Trade Revisited: Selected Papers on the Sixth North American Fur Trade Conference, Mackinac Island, Michigan, 1991*, ed. Jennifer S. H. Brown et al. (East Lansing: Michigan State University Press, 1994), 93–115. On the use of intermarriage to facilitate noncommercial trade, see Susan Sleeper-Smith, *Indian Women and French Men: Rethinking Cultural Encounters in the Western Great Lakes* (Amherst: University of Massachusetts Press, 2001).

20. Aquila explores the economic advantages the Iroquois enjoyed because they were positioned between two imperial powers, in *Iroquois Restoration* (112–28). On the centrality of gift giving to Indian diplomacy, see Wilbur R. Jacobs, *Wilderness Politics and Indian Gifts: The Northern Colonial Frontier, 1748–1763* (Lincoln: University of Nebraska Press, 1950), chap. 4; Peter Cook, "Symbolic and Material Exchange in Intercultural Diplomacy: The French and the Hodenosaunee in the Early Eighteenth Century," in *New Faces of the Fur Trade: Selected Papers on the Seventh North American Fur Trade Conference, Halifax, Nova Scotia, 1995*, ed. Jo-Anne Fiske et al. (East Lansing: Michigan State University Press, 1998), 75–100.

21. On the eighteenth-century consumer revolution, see T. H. Breen, "An Empire of Goods: The Anglicization of Colonial America, 1690–1776," *Journal of British Studies* 25 (1986): 467–99; and Breen, "'Baubles of Britain': The American and Consumer Revolutions of the Eighteenth Century," *Past and Present* 119 (1988): 73–104. For an Indian perspective of this revolution, see James Axtell, "The First Consumer Revolution," in *Beyond 1492: Encounters in Colonial America* (New York: Oxford University Press, 1992), 125–51; Timothy J. Shannon, "Dressing for Success on the Mohawk Frontier: Hendrick, William

Johnson and the Indian Fashion," *WMQ* 53 (1996): 13–42. Wheelock is quoted in *New Worlds for All: Indians, Europeans, and the Remaking of Early America*, by Colin G. Calloway (Baltimore MD: Johns Hopkins University Press, 1997), 46.

22. Journal of William Johnson's Mission to the Iroquois, April 24–26, 1748, George Clinton Papers, vol. 7, William L. Clements Library, Ann Arbor MI (hereafter cited as WLCL); Clinton to Johnson, January 6, 1749, *WJP*, 1:207; Johnson to Clinton, January 22, 1749, *WJP*, 9:36; Robert Sanders to Johnson, May 8, 1751, *WJP*, 1:330; Johnson to Clinton, July 30, 1753, *WJP*, 9:109.

23. Minutes of Sir William Johnson, March 8, 1761, p. 20, part 1, vol. 6, Indian Records, Canadian Public Archives, taken from photocopies deposited at the Manuscript Division, Library of Congress, Washington DC (hereafter cited as Indian Records volume/part/page). For similar complaints regarding trade, see Indian Records 6/1/48, 6/1/60, 6/4/416. On general economic distress caused by the Seven Years' War, see Gail D. Danvers, "Contact, Conflict, and Cultural Dislocation along the Anglo-Iroquois Frontier, 1740s–1770s" (PhD diss., University of Sussex, 2002), 85–100.

24. Journal of Indian Affairs, December 10–12, 1758, *WJP*, 10:71; Journal of Sir William Johnson's Proceedings, June 16, 1757, *DRCHNY*, 7:261. For other examples of Johnson's use of trade as a political weapon, see *WJP*, 9:911, 928–29, 10:72–73.

25. On Indian complaints against trade, see *WJP*, 7:86, 348–49, 717, 1139–40, 12:170, 209–10, 287, 860; *DRCHNY*, 8:475, 476; Johnson to Frederick Haldimand, June 30, 1773, Additional Manuscripts, 21670, fol. 62, British Library, London. Johnson and other officials also complained about traders; see Johnson to Earl of Hillsborough, August 14, 1770, pp. 93–96, vol. 71, ser. 5, Colonial Office Papers (hereafter cited as CO series/volume/page), Public Records Office, Kew, London (hereafter cited as PRO); James Stevenson to Johnson, December 18, 1770, and January 8, 1772, *WJP*, 7:1041, 8:363.

26. Murray G. Lawson calculated that "in the first half of the century" fur exports "loomed quite large in the New York economy, comprising more than a quarter of the total value of her exports to England. In the third quarter, however, it underwent a rapid eclipse declining from 16 percent in 1750 to slightly more than 2 percent in 1775" (*Fur: A Study in English Mercantilism, 1700–1775* [Toronto: University of Toronto Press, 1943], 71–72). See also Norton, *Fur Trade in Colonial New York*, 100–103, 149, 221–23; Stephen H. Cunliffe, "Colonial Indian Policy as a Measure of Rising Imperialism: New York and Pennsylvania, 1700–1755," *Western Pennsylvania Historical Magazine* 64 (1981): 240–44; Richter, *Ordeal of the Longhouse*, 270–71; Cathy Matson, *Merchants and Empire: Trading in Colonial New York* (Baltimore MD: Johns Hopkins University

Press, 1998), 222–26; Walter S. Dunn, *Frontier Profit and Loss: The British Army and the Fur Traders* (Westport CT: Greenwood, 1998), chap. 4, esp. 70, 74.

27. Older studies emphasized Iroquois victimhood at the hands of land-hungry colonists; see Georgiana C. Nammack, *Fraud, Politics, and the Dispossession of the Indians: The Iroquois Land Frontier in the Colonial Period* (Norman: University of Oklahoma Press, 1969). More recent work has emphasized Iroquois agency; see Wyllys Terry, "Negotiating the Frontier: Land Patenting in Colonial New York" (PhD diss., Boston University, 1997); and David L. Preston, "The Texture of Contact: European and Indian Settler Communities on the Iroquoian Borderlands, 1720–1780s" (PhD diss., College of William and Mary, 2002), chap. 1.

28. Meeting Relating to Indian Lands, March 23, 1763, *WJP*, 4:65. On Iroquois relations with this community, see Thomas E. Burke, Jr., *Mohawk Frontier: The Dutch Community of Schenectady, New York, 1610–1710* (Ithaca NY: Cornell University Press, 1991), chap. 4.

29. Council Held in the City of Albany, July 2, 1754, CO 5/1199/16; Indian Proceedings, September 15, 1757, *WJP*, 9:832. On German migration to the region, see Robert K. McGregor, "Cultural Adaptation in Colonial New York: The Palatine Germans of the Mohawk Valley," *NYH* 69 (1988): 4–34. On German-Iroquois relations, see Terry, "Negotiating the Frontier," chap. 3, and Preston, "Texture of Contact," chap. 4.

30. In 1762 Johnson noted the presence of tenants "living on said Lands abt. 20 years and paying Rent to the Indians" (*WJP*, 10:487). See also Johnson to Cadwallader Colden, March 19, 1761, *New York Historical Society Collections* 65 (1932): 18 (hereafter cited as *NYHSC*); *WJP*, 3:356, 10:216, 367.

31. Indian Deed, 1735, New York, Ayer, N.A. MSS 404, no. 17, Newberry Library, Chicago.

32. Mohawk land grievances are summarized in Nammack, *Fraud, Politics, and the Dispossession of the Indians*, chap. 2. For a firsthand account, see Conference between Governor Clinton and the Indians, June 1753, *DRCHNY*, 6:783–88.

33. Mohawk reports of settlers encroaching onto their hunting grounds are documented in Johnson's Minutes of Indian Affairs. See entries for August 10, 1763, Indian Records 6/5/484; September 20, 1764, Indian Records 7/2/177; January 31 and February 25, 1765, Indian Records 7/3/258, 262; June 21, 1766, Indian Records 7/4/381. The Mohawks eventually ceded a significant portion of these hunting grounds by a compromise brokered in 1768. See An Indian Congress, August 2–4, 1768, *WJP*, 12:572–78; Henry Moore to the Earl of Hillsborough, August 17, 1768, *DRCHNY*, 8:92. Terry estimates that the Mohawks relinquished 600,000 acres of land ("Negotiating the Frontier,"

223). On colonial settlement in the upper Susquehanna Valley, see Indian Proceedings, April 24–28, 1762, *WJP*, 3:705, 714; Johnson's Minutes, May 12, 1763, Indian Records 6/4/407–10; At a Conference . . . in the Colony of Connecticut, May 28, 1763, Indian Records 6/4/419–25; Peter C. Mancall, *Valley of Opportunity: Economic Culture along the Upper Susquehanna, 1700–1800* (Ithaca NY: Cornell University Press, 1991), chaps. 4–5.

34. Johnson to Colden, September 1764, *NYHSC* 65 (1932): 346–47; Journal of Indian Affairs, June 21 and December 25, 1765, *WJP*, 11:817, 985.

35. For the disruptive behavior of soldiers, see Johnson's Minutes, July 21 and April 25, 1761, Indian Records 6/1/61, 221; September 9, 1762, Indian Records 6/3/301–2; May 28, 1763, Indian Records 6/4/418. Johnson to Board of Trade, November 13, 1763, *DRCHNY*, 7:577. On the growing presence of settlers in the region, see Johnson's Minutes, June 18, 1766, Indian Records 7/4/379–80; Johnson to Gage, June 27, 1766, Thomas Gage Papers: American Series, vol. 53 (hereafter cited as GP), WLCL; Gage to Johnson, July 12, 1767, GP, vol. 67; John Galland to Johnson, August 11, 1767, *WJP*, 5:613–14; Johnson to Gage, August 6, 1767, GP, vol. 68; Gage to Johnson, September 7, 1767, GP, vol. 69; Galland to Johnson, September 9, 1769, *WJP*, 5:663; Johnson to Gage, September 22, 1767, GP, vol. 70.

36. The Fort Stanwix Treaty minutes are reprinted in *DRCHNY*, 8:111–34. The standard works on this treaty are Ray A. Billington, "The Fort Stanwix Treaty of 1768," *NYH* 25 (1944): 182–94; Jack M. Sosin, *Whitehall and the Wilderness: The Middle West in British Colonial Policy, 1760–1775* (Lincoln: University of Nebraska Press, 1961), chap. 7; Peter Marshall, "Sir William Johnson and the Treaty of Fort Stanwix, 1768," *Journal of American Studies* 1 (1967): 149–79; Dorothy V. Jones, *License for Empire: Colonialism by Treaty in Early America* (Chicago: University of Chicago Press, 1982), chap. 5. On land patenting in New York, see Bernard Bailyn, *Voyagers to the West: A Passage in the Peopling of America on the Eve of the American Revolution* (New York: Knopf, 1986), 576–82.

37. Walter Pilkington, ed., *The Journals of Samuel Kirkland: Eighteenth Century Missionary to the Iroquois, Government Agent, Father of Hamilton College* (Clinton NY: Hamilton College, 1980), 71.

38. A Meeting with Canajoharies, March 10, 1763, *WJP*, 4:58.

39. Whitfield J. Bell, ed., *A Journey from Pennsylvania to Onondaga in 1743 by John Bartram, Lewis Evans, Conrad Weiser* (Barre MA: Imprint Society, 1973), 61, 62; Samuel Hazard, ed., *Minutes of the Provincial Council of Pennsylvania*, 16 vols. (Harrisburg PA: Theophilius Fenn, 1838–53), 4:583; William M. Beauchamp, ed., *Moravian Journals Relating to Central New York, 1745–66* (New York: AMS, 1976), 64, 65, 85; "Item 863: Receipt for Wolves Heads," in *The Old Stone*

Church and Fortress: Catalogue and Historical Notes, ed. Chauncey Rickard (New York: Schoharie Historical Society, 1933), 67.

40. Proceedings of the Colonial Congress held at Albany, June 1754, DRCH-NY, 6:857–58; Reports of the Council of Commissioners of Indian Affairs of Albany, June 18, 1754, 37, Native American History Collection, WLCL; David Armour, *The Merchants of Albany, New York, 1686–1760* (New York: Garland, 1986), 195–96.

41. *Moravian Journals*, 113; see also 120, 122, 123. See also *WJP*, 1:347, 371; "A Letter from Rev. Gideon Hawley of Marshpee, Containing an Account of His Services among the Indians of Massachusetts and New-York, and a Narrative of his Journey to Onohoghgwage," *Massachusetts Historical Society, Collections* 4 (1795): 53; A. H. Young, ed., "Letters from and concerning the Reverend John Ogilvie . . . Written to the Society for the Propagation of the Gospel in Foreign Parts," *Ontario Historical Society* 22 (1925): 314.

42. On other non-European groups who provided labor during the war, see Patrick Frazier, *The Mohicans of Stockbridge* (Lincoln: University of Nebraska Press, 1992), 107–43; Peter MacLeod, *The Canadian Iroquois in the Seven Years' War* (Toronto: Dundurn, 1996), 14–16; Peter Way, "The Cutting Edge of Culture: British Soldiers Encounter Native Americans in the French and Indian War," in *Empire and Others: British Encounters with Indigenous Peoples, 1600–1850*, ed. Martin Daunton and Rick Halpern (Philadelphia: University of Pennsylvania Press, 1998), 136–38; Scott A. Padeni, "The Role of Blacks in New York's Northern Campaigns of the Seven Years' War," *Bulletin of the Fort Ticonderoga Museum* 16 (1999): 153–69.

43. Clinton to Johnson, August 28, 1746, *WJP*, 1:60–61n1; A Receipt, July 2, 1747, *WJP*, 9:8; Johnson to Clinton, August 13, 1747, *WJP*, 1:108. In early 1756 warriors received a steady wage of four shillings a day for scouting activities; see *WJP*, 9:446; DRCHNY, 7:184. By August 1755 the commander in chief had granted Hendrick a "Commission of a Captain of Indians" and "advanc'd him 20 Dollars in part of his Pay"; see "Documents: The Papers of Sir William Johnson: Addenda," ed. Milton W. Hamilton, *NYH* 60 (1979): 86. See also *WJP*, 2:626.

44. Shirley to Johnson, April 10, 1756, *WJP* 9:427. See also Shirley to Johnson, March 23, 1755, *WJP*, 1:462; Measures Proposed by William Shirley . . . [December 1755], in *Correspondence of William Shirley, Governor of Massachusetts and Military Commander in America, 1731–1760*, ed. Charles H. Lincoln (New York: Macmillan, 1912), 2:366. The Mohawks suggested the formation of a salaried Indian regiment (Expense of an Indian Regiment, March 15, 1757, *WJP*, 9:639; Johnson to Lord Loudoun, March 17, 1757, *WJP*, 9:641).

45. Danvers, "Contact, Conflict, and Cultural Dislocation," 87–89.

46. Unidentified Account Book, Schenectady, April 7, 1756–July 23, 1764, fols. 40, 52, 221, box 18, Campbell Family Papers, New York State Library, New York; Account Book of an Unidentified Mohawk Valley Indian Trader, 1762–1776, Fonda Family Papers, New-York Historical Society, New York.

47. Johnson to Board of Trade, September 10, 1756, DRCHNY, 7:129. Army officers appealed directly to Johnson for Indian labor; see WJP, 9:401–2, 423–24.

48. Evidence of payments to Indians is well documented to Johnson's Accounts, WJP, 2:566–645, 3:149–81, 9:644–58. For examples cited, see WJP, 3:173, 165, 174.

49. Danvers, "Contact, Conflict, and Cultural Dislocation," 94, 111, 114, 115–16.

50. Daniel, a Mohawk Indian, received £62 for 155 days of military service; Gage Warrants, box 8, fol. 47 (hereafter cited as Gage Warrants, box:fol.), WLCL; Johnson to Gage, December 30, 1763, GP, vol. 11; Johnson to Henry Montour, February 21, 1764, WJP, 4:336–37; Minutes, January 30, 1764, Indian Records 7/1/63; Mohawk Indians under Henry Gladwin, Certificate of Services, May 13, 1764, 49, Ferdinard J. Dreer Autograph Collection, vol. 1, Officers in America before the Revolution, Historical Society of Pennsylvania, Philadelphia.

51. Proceedings of the Fort Stanwix Treaty, DRCHNY, 8:124–25; Account of David Schuyler Jun'r, February 9, 1762, WJP, 3:631–33; Debtor Account, July 1769, WJP 7:32; Journal of Wade and Keiuser's Trading Expedition, May–June 1770, WJP, 7:724–25; Benjamin Davis's Affidavit, August 8, 1775, box 13, Philip Schuyler Papers, New York Public Library, New York (hereafter cited as NYPL).

52. Johnson's Minutes, December 21, 1764, Indian Records, 7/3/254; Francis W. Halsey, ed., *A Tour of the Hudson, the Mohawk, the Susquehanna, and the Delaware in 1769: Being the Journal of Richard Smith* (New York: Purple Mountain, 1989), 114, 115, 139; Account Book of an Unidentified Mohawk Valley Indian Trader, fols. 49, 88, 98, 111, 117, 118; WJP, 5:331, 339, 681, 6:566, 12:693–94, 13:517.

53. Pilkington, *Journals of Samuel Kirkland*, 70, 85–86, 88n13; William B. Hart, "'For the Good of Our Souls': Mohawk Authority, Accommodation, and Resistance to Protestant Evangelicalism, 1700–1780" (PhD diss., Brown University, 1998), 216, 231, 244, 299–300.

54. Gage Warrants, 15:32, 23:129, 24:116, 27:20; WJP, 7:70–71, 12:665–67. For Johnson's private hire of Indian labor, see WJP, 7:867, 918–19, 974, 979.

55. Johnson's Account, *WJP*, 2:579, 636, 3:157, 158, 160, 161, 162, 164, 167, 997. See also Aileen B. Agnew, "Silent Partners: The Economic Life of Women on the Frontier of Colonial New York" (PhD diss., University of New Hampshire, 1998), chap. 4.

56. Anne Grant, *Memoirs of an American Lady: With Sketches of Manners and Scenery in America* (London: Longman, Hurst, Rees, 1808), 121–23, 132; Halsey, *Journal of Richard Smith*, 152, 137; Joseph Bloomfield, *Citizen Soldier: The Revolutionary Journal of Joseph Bloomfield*, ed. Mark E. Lender and James Kirby Martin (Newark: New Jersey Historical Society, 1982), 77. See also "Journal of Warren Johnson, 1760–1761," in *In Mohawk Country: Early Narratives about a Native People*, ed. Dean R. Snow, Charles T. Gehring, and William Starna (Syracuse NY: Syracuse University Press, 1996), 255. On the rarity and thus increased value of Indian handicrafts, see Wanda Burch, "Sir William Johnson's Cabinet of Curiosities," *NYH* 71 (July 1990): 261–82.

57. A number of studies have explored how integration into a market economy affected native gender relations. Older studies stressed female subordination. See Carol Devens, *Countering Colonization: Native American Women and the Great Lakes Missions, 1630–1900* (Berkeley: University of California Press, 1992). Recent studies provide a more nuanced reading. See Saunt, *New Order of Things*, chap. 6; Carson, "Native Americans, the Market Revolution, and Cultural Change."

58. Journal of Sir William, August 13, 1756, *DRCHNY*, 7:184; Butler to Johnson, August 29, 1756, *WJP*, 2:553. See also Johnson to Board of Trade, September 28, 1757, *DRCHNY*, 7:278.

59. Halsey, *Journal of Richard Smith*, 139, 137; Johnson to Gage, November 23, 1769, *WJP*, 7:264; Gage to Johnson, December 11, 1769, *WJP*, 7:298–99.

60. James W. Bradley discusses the use and development of wampum as a currency in *Evolution of the Onondaga Iroquois: Accommodating Change, 1500–1655* (Syracuse NY: Syracuse University Press, 1987), 177–80. On the use of corn as a currency, see Beauchamp, *Moravian Journals*, 208, 209, 211.

61. Johnson's Accounts, *WJP*, 3:149, 150ff. See also Johnson to John Stanwix, December 16, 1758, pp. 68–69, vol. 39, ser. 34, War Office Papers: Jeffrey Amherst Collection, PRO; Butler to Johnson, January 30, 1759, *WJP*, 10:93; Journal of Indian Affairs, February 3, 1759, *WJP*, 10:97.

62. Johnson's Minutes, March 4, 1767, Indian Records, 7/4/436; Johnson's Account against the Crown, *WJP*, 7:1092, 1094; Gage Warrants, 17:91, 27:20; Halsey, *Journal of Richard Smith*, 150. References to Indians paying "cash in full" are noted throughout the Account Book of an Unidentified Mohawk Valley Indian Trader. See, for example, fols. 1, 2, 5, 23, 24, 40, 42, 43, 47, 90, 117.

63. Halsey, *Journal of Richard Smith*, 134–35; Bloomfield noted "our people make & sell [wampum beads] . . . or exchange them for Beaver-skins &c. and many, at Albany particularly, make a handsome living by that Trade" (*Journal of Joseph Bloomfield*, 82). On Indian purchases of wampum, see Account Book of an Unidentified Mohawk Valley Indian Trader, fols. 23, 80, 84b. On the increased popularity of broaches, see William M. Beauchamp, "Metallic Ornaments of the New York Indians," *New York State Museum, Bulletin 73* (Albany: University of the State of New York, 1903), 76.

64. The Mohawk war loss claims are documented in two attachments sent in a letter by Frederick Haldimand to Secretary of State, Lord Sydney, June 21, 1785; see CO 42/47/238–52. David Guldenzopf has transcribed these documents in the appendix of "The Colonial Transformation of Mohawk Iroquois Society" (PhD diss., State University of New York at Albany, 1987). Class stratification developed among other Indian communities by the late eighteenth and early nineteenth centuries. See, for example, Braud, *Deerskins and Duffels*, 130; Saunt, "Taking Account of Property," 733–60.

65. CO 42/47/238–52; Guldenzopf, "Colonial Transformation," 83–130.

66. "Losses Sustained by the Oneida and Tuscaroras in Consequence of Their Attachment to the United States," Timothy Pickering Papers, pp. 157–65, reel 62, Massachusetts Historical Society, Boston. Anthony Wonderley analyzed this document in "An Oneida Community in the 1780s: Study of an Inventory of Iroquois Property Losses during the Revolutionary War," *Northeast Anthropology* 56 (1998): 19–42. He found the average Mohawk claim to be £108 or £180, depending on whether they resided in the upper or lower castle. For the Oneidas, the average claim was for £30.

67. "Losses Sustained by the Oneida and Tuscaroras," 157–65; Wonderley, "Oneida Community in the 1780s," 23, 26.

68. Guldenzopf, "Colonial Transformation," chap. 6; Wonderley, "Oneida Community in the 1780s," 26–27.

69. On innovations in Mohawk and Oneida agriculture including the sale of livestock, see Charles Inglis, "A Memorial Concerning the Iroquois, 1771," in *Documentary History of the State of New York*, ed. E. B. O'Callaghan (Albany NY: Weed, Parsons, 1849–51), 4:665; WJP, 7:39, 12:666, 667; Peter Gansevoort to John Sullivan, October 8, 1779, General Peter Gansevoort, Jr., Military Papers, 1778–1779, vol. 5, NYPL; Pilkington, *Journals of Samuel Kirkland*, 70, 83; Bloomfield, *Journal of Joseph Bloomfield*, 66, 84–85; Halsey, *Journal of Richard Smith*, 90, 132–33. See also David Levinson, "An Explanation for the Oneida-Colonist Alliance in the American Revolution," *Ethnohistory* 23, no. 3 (1976):

280–81; Thomas R. Wessel, "Agriculture and Iroquois Hegemony in New York, 1610–1779," *Maryland Historian* 1 (1970): 93–104. For evidence of Indians selling and exchanging crops, see Account Book of an Unidentified Mohawk Valley Indian Trader.

70. Johnson's "private presents" to loyal chiefs and warriors are well documented in the Gage Warrants, 8:47, 15:32, 17:19, 20:74, 23:129, 24:116, 27:20.

71. Halsey, *Journal of Richard Smith*, 150, 126, 135. For a historical account of Joseph Brant, see Isabel T. Kelsay, *Joseph Brant, 1743–1807: Man of Two Worlds* (Syracuse NY: Syracuse University Press, 1984). Brant's wealth is detailed in CO 42/47/240.

72. "The Opinions of George Croghan on the American Indians," *Pennsylvania Magazine of History and Biography* 71 (1746): 156; "Guy Johnson's Opinions on the American Indians," *Pennsylvania Magazine of History and Biography* 77 (1953): 321.

73. Gage Warrants, 23:129, 24:116; Account against the Crown, WJP, 12:1019, 897, 898.

74. Halsey, *Journal of Richard Smith*, 149–50; Bloomfield, *Journal of Joseph Bloomfield*, 90–91. See also comments of John Heckewelder as quoted in Beauchamp, "Metallic Ornaments of the New York Indians," 76.

75. Bloomfield, *Journal of Joseph Bloomfield*, 65; Halsey, *Journal of Richard Smith*, 134, 150; Heckewelder as quoted in Beauchamp, "Metallic Ornaments of the New York Indians," 74–75.

76. Thomas S. Wermuth notes that inhabitants of the Hudson Valley of colonial New York "alternated their economic strategies, employing the complementary strategies of production for consumption, local exchange with neighbors, and commercial export." Neither fully capitalistic nor entirely premodern, "their goals were to subsist, acquire consumer goods, increase landholdings, and transmit legacies to their heirs" (*Rip Van Winkle's Neighbors: The Transformation of Rural Society in the Hudson River Valley, 1720–1850* (Albany: State University of New York, 2001), 6. This description is equally applicable to Mohawk Valley inhabitants.

13. The Fur Trade and Eighteenth-Century Imperialism

W. J. Eccles

The North American fur trade of the seventeenth and eighteenth centuries has usually been viewed, until recently, as merely another commercial enterprise governed by the premise "buy cheap, sell dear" in order to reap the maximum profit. Of late, the Canadian end of the trade has come to be regarded as having been more a means to a noncommercial end than a pursuit conducted solely for economic gain. As European penetration and dominance of the continent progressed, the trade, which had begun as an adjunct of the Atlantic shore fishery, became a commercial pursuit in its own right. After 1600, when the first Roman Catholic missionaries were sent to New France, it became a means to finance and further that tragic drive to convert the Indian nations to Christianity. This attempt continued until mid-century, when the Jesuit mission in Huronia was destroyed, along with the Hurons as a nation, by the Iroquois Confederacy.[1] For the rest of the century the fur trade of New France went through vexed and troubled times.[2]

Stability was temporarily restored to the trade in 1663, when the crown took over the colony from the Company of One Hundred Associates. Near the end of the century a huge glut of beaver fur completely disrupted the market in Europe and caused Louis Phélypeaux de Pontchartrain, the minister of marine responsible for the colonies, to try to force the Canadian fur traders to withdraw from the west completely. For political reasons this could not be done. Despite its economic unviability, the French, in order to maintain good relations with the Indian nations, were forced to continue the trade in furs. Then, in 1700, on the eve of a new war in Europe, Louis XIV embarked on an expansionist policy in North America to hem in the English colonies on the Atlantic seaboard. From that point forward, the fur trade was used mainly as a political instrument to further the imperial aims of France.

In the 1650s, after the Iroquois had virtually destroyed the Huron nation and scattered the Algonkian nations allied with it far to the west, French traders began to push into the interior of the continent, where they established direct trade relations with the hunting nations that had previously supplied furs to the Huron middlemen. These traders, a mere handful at first, voyaged through the Great Lakes and beyond, then down into the Mississippi Valley. This French thrust into the west occurred just as the Five Nations Iroquois Confederacy, having subdued the tribes surrounding them and being well supplied with firearms by the Dutch and English merchants of Albany, embarked on an imperialistic drive to conquer and control the Ohio Valley, a region almost as vast as the kingdom of France.[3] Their first incursion into the region in 1678 was repelled by the Illinois nation. The following year Robert Cavelier de La Salle began establishing fur trade posts on the Illinois River and thereby claimed suzerainty for the French crown over the lands of both the Illinois and the Miami nations.[4]

In 1680 the inevitable clash came between these rival imperial powers. La Salle's lieutenant, Henri de Tonty, attempted to mediate when an Iroquois army invaded the Illinois country. He received a nasty wound for his pains but managed to escape to Michilimackinac with his men.[5] The French presence in the west was now seriously threatened. An attempt to cow the Iroquois by military force failed miserably. Instead, the Iroquois dictated humiliating peace terms to the governor general of New France, Le Febvre de La Barre, and stated their determination to destroy the Illinois, whom the French claimed to be under the protection of Louis XIV. When La Barre protested this arrogant Iroquois declaration, the great Onondaga chief and orator, Hotreouati, brusquely retorted, "They deserve to die, they have shed our blood."[6] To that La Barre could make no response. He was, when Louis XIV was informed of what had transpired, summarily dismissed from his post and recalled to France in disgrace.[7]

The long-range aim of the Confederacy appears to have been to bring under subjection all the Indian nations south of the Great Lakes as far as the Mississippi, and at the same time to divert the western fur trade from Montreal to Albany with the Confederacy controlling it. Because the Iroquois failed to provide a written record of their aims, their motives cannot be determined with certainty, yet their actions and the policies they pursued during the ensuing decades indicate clearly enough that what they sought was power—dominance over this vast region—rather than mere commercial advantage.

A few years after this Franco-Iroquois struggle in the interior of North America was joined, events occurred in Europe that were to affect it profoundly. The Revolution of 1689 ousted James II and brought William of Orange, bitter enemy of Louis XIV, to the throne of England. This ushered in hostilities between England and France that were to occupy nineteen of the ensuing twenty-four years. The Iroquois, now confident of English military aid, pressed their attacks against the French in the west and at their settlements in the St. Lawrence Valley, inflicting heavy casualties. The settlers, aided by some 1,500 *Troupes de la Marine*, regular troops sent from France, managed to beat back these attacks and in the process became, of necessity, highly skilled at guerrilla warfare. The alliance with the Indian nations who had long feared the Iroquois was strengthened, and the war carried to the enemy. Iroquois casualties mounted, and the frontier settlements of their ineffectual English allies were ravaged by Canadian war parties. Both the Iroquois and the English colonials were relieved when, in 1697, the war ended in Europe. The Iroquois, now bereft of English logistical support, their fighting strength reduced by casualties and disease to half what it had been, were forced to sue for peace.[8]

This proud people had, however, not been brought so low that they would accept any terms that the French cared to impose. Consequently, the negotiations dragged on for four years. Moreover, the twenty-eight tribes allied with the French had to be party to the peace treaty that was eventually drawn up at Montreal in 1701. The principal factor that now made possible an enduring peace between the French and the Iroquois, thereby ending a war that had lasted for nearly a century, was that the French negotiators recognized the Iroquois presence to be an essential buffer between their Indian allies in the northwest and the English colonies. Moreover, the Iroquois had learned to their cost that they could not rely on the English for military support. Rather, they perceived that the English had always sought to make use of them merely to serve English ends. There was no longer any question of the French seeking to destroy the Iroquois; in fact, just the reverse had become the case. The Iroquois had now to abandon all hope of ever driving the French out of Canada or from the posts in the west. The French presence had become essential to them to balance that of the English and to allow them to play one off against the other. Thus the French negotiators were able to insert a clause into the peace treaty declaring that in any future war between England and France the Iroquois would remain neutral. At one stroke the greatest military threat to New France and the main defense of New York had been eliminated; and this occurred just as England and France were preparing for a renewal of hostilities that were to last for more than a decade.[9]

On the French side, the preceding wars had been fought for a specific Canadian aim, control of the western fur trade, and France had provided the military aid needed to achieve that end. The ensuing wars were to be fought solely for French imperial aims. In 1701, with the War of the Spanish Succession about to erupt, Louis XIV declared that the English colonies must be hemmed in between the Atlantic and the Appalachians. On no account were the English to be allowed to flood over that mountain range to occupy the region between it and the Mississippi. Were they to do so, Louis feared, their numbers would swell immeasurably and England's wealth and power would increase proportionately. In all likelihood they would then push southwest to conquer Mexico with its silver mines. With Louis XIV's grandson now on the throne of Spain, France had to defend the Spanish colonies as though they were her own.[10] Louis XIV feared that English domination of North America would upset the balance of power in Europe. The French in America, with their Indian allies, were to be the means of containing the English colonies.[11] In the implementation of this imperial policy the fur trade had a vital role to play, of an importance far in excess of its economic value.

In 1701 Louis XIV gave orders for the creation of the new colony of Louisiana, in the Mississippi Valley, to forestall the English, who, it was reported, planned to establish a settlement at the mouth of that great river.[12] Another French settlement was ordered to be placed at the narrows between Lake Erie and Lake Huron. This new colony, to be named Detroit, was intended to bar English access to the northwest and maintain French control of the western Great Lakes.[13] It is not without significance that the Canadian merchants and the royal officials at Quebec were bitterly opposed to both these settlements, declaring that they would be the ruin of Canada—Detroit, because it would bring the Indian nations allied with the French into close proximity to the Iroquois, who might grant them access to the Albany traders; Louisiana, because the fur traders who obtained their trade goods on credit from the Montreal merchants would be tempted to defraud their creditors by shipping their furs to France from the port to be established on the Gulf of Mexico.[14]

French imperial policy now required that the Indian nations of the west and of Acadia be welded into a close commercial alliance and that all contact between them and the English colonists be prevented by one means or another. The main instruments of this policy, it was envisaged, would be missionaries and fur traders. The great age of French proselytization that had produced the Jesuit martyrs was, however, a thing of the past. The clergy were eager enough to serve, but some of them were ill suited for the task and too often their efforts were hampered by squabbling among rival groups, secular priests with Jesuits, Capuchins with both. For several years the bishop of New France was an absentee, unable to restore order and discipline from his residence in Paris.[15] Thus the implementation of this new policy was left to two groups, the Canadian fur traders and the officers and men of the colonial regulars, the *Troupes de la Marine*, who garrisoned the reestablished posts.

The fur trade was now definitely subordinated to a political end. It was required to pay a large share of the costs of maintaining a French presence in the interior to bar the English from it. The west was divided into regions, each with a central post commanded by an officer of the colonial regulars. For some years these officers were not permitted to engage in the trade, the sole right to which in each region was auctioned off to merchants on a three-year lease.[16] When it was found that this led to exploitation of the Indians by merchants whose only aim was to make as great a profit as possible during their lease, the trade was turned over to the commandants, who could, it was thought, be kept under tighter control by the senior officials at Quebec.[17] Complaints against them by the Indians could bring instant recall and might jeopardize promotion or the granting of commissions to sons.

The post commandants usually formed companies in partnership with Montreal merchants who provided the trade goods, hired the voyageurs, and marketed the furs, and professional traders who took charge of the actual trading with the Indians. The modus operandi was thus very simple; the companies usually comprised three men for a three-year term, at the end of which the merchant who had supplied the goods withdrew their cost, and whatever profit or loss remained was shared by the partners.[18] At the main bases of Michilimackinac and Detroit the trade was open to all who obtained a permit from the governor general and paid the base commandant his 500-livre fee. From these fees the commandants had to pay the costs of maintaining the posts, thereby sparing the crown the expense.[19]

Louis XIV, in order to end the war that was reducing his government to bankruptcy, agreed to make sweeping concessions on the Atlantic frontier of New France to avoid having to make them in Europe. He therefore agreed to cede Newfoundland and Acadia, the latter "within its ancient limits," to England. A joint commission was appointed to determine those limits, but, predictably, no agreement could be reached and France retained Cape Breton, where it proceeded to construct the fortress of Louisbourg as a naval base for the protection of French maritime interests in the North Atlantic. The British continued to claim title to all the land up to the St. Lawrence River, and it was upon the Indian nations of the region—the Abenakis, Micmacs, and Malecites—that the French relied to hold the English back from the vital St. Lawrence waterway.[20] The governor general at Quebec made sure that those nations were well supplied with all the European goods they needed and that a continual state of hostility existed between them and the expanding population of New England.[21]

In the implementation of this policy the French received unwitting aid from the New England settlers. What the latter coveted most was land for settlement, the very lands that the Indians required to maintain their hunting economy and that they believed had been granted them by God for that very purpose. The Indians denied that they were or ever had been subjects of either the French or the English crown. They asserted vehemently that the French could not have ceded their land by treaty as the Massachusetts authorities claimed, since no one could cede what had never been his.[22] Although the French, with their meager population, did not covet any of that land, they were determined to deny it to the English. In 1727 the king stated in a *memoire* to the governor general and intendant at Quebec that he had learned with pleasure that the Abenakis of Saint-François and Bécancourt intended to continue the war against the English and not to entertain any proposals for peace until the

English had razed the forts they had built on Abenaki lands. "This is so important for Canada," the *memoire* went on, "that the Sieur de Beauharnois could not take measures more just than such as would foment that war and prevent any accommodation."[23]

To the north, where France had relinquished its claims to Hudson Bay, dispute arose over the interpretation of the covering clause in the Treaty of Utrecht. The British claimed that they had thereby gained title to all the lands whose waters drained into Hudson Bay—almost a quarter of the continent. They themselves, however, negated their claim by insisting that the operative clause in the treaty state that France *restored* rather than *ceded* to Great Britain the lands claimed by the latter—this in order to establish that Britain had always had the prior claim. France agreed but riposted by declaring that only the lands that Britain had formerly occupied could be restored to her: by definition, restoration could not be made of lands that had never been conquered, purchased, or occupied.[24] In fact, merely an infinitesimal fraction of that vast territory had ever even been seen by a British subject. The argument was really an academic one since the Hudson's Bay Company made no attempt to challenge French control of the interior. As long as enough furs reached its posts to produce a dividend for its shareholders, the company's servants were content to remain in a "sleep by the frozen sea."[25]

The French now established fur trade posts on the rivers that ran down to the bay and thereby controlled the flow of furs to the English. They kept the choicest furs for themselves and allowed the Indians to trade only their poorer quality pelts at the Bay Company's posts.[26] Had it not been that the Indians were astute enough to maintain trade relations with both the English and the Canadians in order to reap the advantages of competition, Britain's hold on Hudson Bay would early have been severed.[27]

From the signing of the Treaty of Utrecht in 1713 to the conquest of New France, the French maintained their presence among the nations of the west, penetrating steadily farther into the interior until

The Fur Trade

they eventually reached the barrier of the Rocky Mountains.[28] Only at Detroit, Kaskaskia, and Cahokia in the Illinois country, and on the lower Mississippi, were they able to establish small agricultural settlements.[29] Elsewhere they merely maintained fur trade posts consisting of three or four log buildings surrounded by a palisade. Always these posts were placed in an area that no Indian nation claimed as its own—Detroit, for example—or were established with the express permission of the dominant nation of the region. Some of the posts had been maintained during the Iroquois war, ostensibly as bases and places of refuge for the nations allied with the French against the Iroquois Confederacy. Experience had proven that posts on the fringe of Iroquois-controlled territory were more prisons than forts. Their garrisons did not dare venture beyond musket range of the palisades, and too many of the men, deprived of fresh meat or fish, reduced to hard rations of stale salt pork and sea biscuit, succumbed to scurvy.[30]

After the Iroquois wars of the seventeenth century, and with the proclamation of Louis XIV's containment policy in North America, fur trade posts had to be sustained among all the nations that could conceivably have contact, direct or indirect, with the English colonials or the Hudson's Bay Company. With the exception of the Sioux nation, who always kept the French at arm's length, most of the nations were glad to have these posts on their territory. Although the French maintained that the posts gave them title to the land, their claims were made to exclude the English, not to deny the Indians' title, something they did not dare do. The French were certainly not sovereign in the west, for sovereignty implies the right to impose and collect taxes, and to enforce laws—and they were never able to do either. The Indians never considered themselves to be French subjects, and the French were never able to treat them as such.[31] Moreover, the Canadian voyageurs who transported trade goods and supplies to the western posts and took the furs back to Montreal always had to travel in convoy for protection against the Indians through whose lands they passed. One or two canoes alone were an invitation to extortionate demands or outright pillage.[32] The Indians allowed the French only the right of passage to the posts, since this assured them a ready supply of European goods close at hand. The land on which the trading posts stood they considered still to be theirs, the French occupants being mere tenants during the Indians' pleasure.

Another significant factor in this imperial rivalry was the superiority of most French trade goods. In only one item, woolen cloth, did the English have an advantage, and even this is open to question. The factors at the Hudson's Bay Company's posts were continually pleading with their superiors in London to provide them with goods of the same quality as those traded by the French.[33] In one of the more important trade items, liquor, the French had a distinct advantage. Showing commendable good taste, the Indians greatly preferred French brandy to the rot-gut rum and gin supplied by the British and Americans. The Hudson's Bay Company produced imitation brandy made from cheap gin with alarming additives to give it the color and something resembling the taste of cognac, but it never replaced the real thing in the Indians' opinion.[34] Alcohol was crucial in the fur trade for two reasons. First, the Indians craved it more than anything else; even though they knew that it could destroy them, they could not resist it, and they would go to any lengths to obtain all that was available.[35] Second, from the purely economic aspect of the trade, alcohol was the ideal exchange item. Of other goods—cloth, wearing apparel, pots, knives, axes, muskets—the Indians had a limited need. It is now coming to be recognized that they were by no means as dependent on European goods as has been claimed.[36] A musket would last many years, as would other metal goods. A few items of clothing each year per family did not result in large entries in the Montreal merchants' ledgers. An Indian hunter could garner enough pelts in a couple of months' good hunting to provide for his family's needs, but the appetite for *eau de vie* was virtually insatiable, driving the Indians to produce furs in ever larger quantities. In the 1790s a Nor'wester,

Duncan McGillivray, remarked, "When a nation becomes addicted to drinking it affords a strong presumption that they will soon become excellent hunters."[37]

The French traders who lived among the Indians were only too well aware of the terrible effects that liquor had on their customers. Frequently they paid for it with their lives when Indians, in their cups, went berserk and set about them with knife or *casse tête*.[38] Some of the senior French officials who were involved in the fur trade for personal gain tried to make light of these dread effects. Gov. Gen. Louis de Buade, comte de Frontenac, for example, contended vociferously that the Indians did not get any more drunk, or behave any worse when in their cups, than did the average Englishman or Netherlander.[39] The French missionaries, in particular the Jesuits who resided in the Indian villages, knew better. They fought to have liquor barred completely from the trade and threatened excommunication for any traders who persisted in its use.[40] Gov. Gen. Philippe de Rigaud de Vaudreuil and his successor, Charles de la Boische, marquis de Beauharnois, both recognized the horrors caused by the liquor trade, but for political reasons they had to condone it, while at the same time striving to restrict its use to prevent the worst abuses. As they and others pointed out to Jean-Fréderic Phélypeaux, comte de Maurepas, appointed minister of marine in 1723, were they to refuse to trade alcohol the Indians would go to the Anglo-American traders, who had no scruples whatsoever, despite frequent pleas from tribal chieftains to keep the rum pedlars out of their villages.[41] Thus in the imperial contest liquor was a powerful but pernicious weapon.

Throughout the eighteenth century the Montreal fur traders took the lion's share of the North American fur trade. The customs figures for fur imports at London, La Rochelle, and Rouen make this plain.[42] Moreover, the Albany merchants who dominated the Anglo-American fur trade admitted that they obtained the bulk of their furs clandestinely from the Canadians.[43] It could hardly have been otherwise since they did not have access to the northwest, which produced the fine quality furs. The minister of marine, Maurepas, and after 1749 his successor, Antoine-Louis Rouillé, comte de Jouy, continually demanded that the smuggling of Canadian furs to Albany be stopped, but to no avail.[44] They simplemindedly believed that if the English desired something, then France must strive to deny it them. The senior officials at Quebec well understood the complexity of the situation. They declared vociferously that they were doing everything possible to curb this clandestine trade, but the evidence indicates that their unenthusiastic efforts were less than efficacious. They tolerated the existence of an agent of the Albany traders at Montreal and frequent visits of the merchants themselves. Similarly, Montreal traders called at Albany from time to time, and credit arrangements between the merchants of the two centers were extensive.[45] One suspects that the governor general and the intendant despaired of bringing first Maurepas, then Rouillé, ministers of marine, to grasp how closely intertwined were the economics and politics of the situation. Certainly, they did not make a determined attempt to explain the subtleties of the issue.

The main agents of this clandestine trade were the Christian Indians of Sault St. Louis and Lake of Two Mountains missions, both close by Montreal.[46] The Canadian officials claimed that they dared not forbid these Indians to trade at Albany whenever they pleased lest they become disaffected and remove from New France. Since their services were vital in time of war, and in peacetime as intelligence agents, they had to be indulged. Thus they quite openly transported Canadian furs to Albany, along with fine French cloth, wines, and spirits, for the accounts of Canadian merchants.[47] In fact, Governor General Beauharnois declared that the Mission Iroquois of Sault St. Louis constituted virtually an independent republic over which he had no authority.[48]

Although the Canadian fur traders undoubtedly reaped considerable benefits from this clandestine trade, a far more significant consequence was that it removed any incentive the Albany merchants might have had to contest the hold of the French over the western nations.[49] This issue was of great concern to the crown officials of New York, who took an imperial view of the situation, but the Albany merchants were interested only in preserving their well-established Canadian trade. When furs were shipped to their doors by the Canadians at prices that afforded them a good profit, they saw no reason to incur the great risks, capital outlay, and trouble that would be involved in trying to compete with the Canadians on their ground, the Indian country of the northwest. Moreover, they lacked the birchbark canoes, the voyageurs to man them, and the prime requisite, the willingness to accept the Indians on their own terms—in short, all the special skills needed for this particular trade.[50] In November 1765 Sir William Johnson commented sadly on this phenomenon to the Lords of Trade:

> I have frequently observed to Your Lordships, that His Majesty's subjects in this Country seem very ill calculated to Cultivate a good understanding with the Indians; and this is a notorious proof of it, for notwithstanding the Expence of transporting Goods from New Orleans to the Illinois is greater than by the Lakes and Consequently French goods are in general Dearer than Ours, yet such is the Conduct of all persons under the Crown of France, whether Officers, Agents, Traders, that the Indians will go much farther to buy their Goods, and pay a much higher price for them. This all persons acquainted with the nature of the Commerce to the Westward can fully evidence.[51]

Nor was the trade all one way. The Iroquois made annual trips to Canada to confer with the French authorities. The crown officials of New York were deeply worried by the influence that the French gained over the Iroquois during these visits. The French entertained the Iroquois delegates lavishly, after a fashion that the British officials could not or would not match.[52] In October 1715 the Albany Indian commissioners stated: "Trade between Albany & Canada is of fatal Consequence to the Indian Interest of this Colony, that of our Indians who are employed in it many stay at Canada &

others return so Attached to the French Interest & so Debauched from ours that it puzzels them how to preserve amongst them that Respect & Regard to this Gov't so necessary to the Public Good and Tranquillity."[53]

By 1720 the French had gained a secure hold on the Great Lakes basin by ringing it with garrisoned fur trade posts. Although the mercantile interests of New York were not perturbed by this development, the crown officials were, and they sought to counter it. In 1719 the governor general of New France, Vaudreuil, heard reports that New York intended to establish a fort at Niagara, which would have given the English access to the west, including the Mississippi Valley. Vaudreuil very adroitly forestalled them by obtaining the permission of the Senecas to establish a post on their land at the mouth of the Niagara River. Ostensibly, the post was to serve their needs; in reality, it barred the west to the English.[54] The following year another post was established at the Toronto portage, barring that route from Lake Ontario to Lake Huron.[55]

Although the Iroquois had given the French permission to establish the post at Niagara and bluntly told the protesting Albany authorities that they had "given the French liberty of free Passage thru Lake Ontario,"[56] they had no desire to see the French become overpowerful in the region. To balance their position they therefore granted New York permission to build a trading post at Oswego on the south shore of Lake Ontario across from Fort Frontenac. At the same time, deputies from the Iroquois Confederacy met with the Albany Indian commissioners, who reported that the Indians "exhort us to live in Peace and Quiet with the French and carry on our Trade without Molesting each other."[57] The Quebec authorities responded by claiming that the south shore of the Great Lakes belonged to France by right of prior discovery and conquest.[58] Governor General Beauharnois began making preparations for a campaign to take and destroy Oswego, but he was restrained by the government in France, which at the time enjoyed good relations with Great Britain, this being the era of the *entente cordiale* established by

Cardinal André-Hercule de Fleury and Robert Walpole.[59] Nevertheless, the Canadian authorities replaced the trading post at Niagara with a solid stone edifice that would have required heavy cannon to demolish, greatly to the dismay of the Albany authorities.[60]

Events were to demonstrate that Oswego posed no serious threat to French control of the Great Lakes. The fear was that it would seduce the western nations out of the French alliance by undercutting the French prices for furs and, more particularly, by the unrestricted sale of liquor. But here again, as at Albany, the New York traders were their own worst enemies. They did indeed supply all the cheap liquor the Indians desired, but the latter, when under its influence, were unmercifully cheated and their womenfolk debauched.[61] This bred bitter resentment.

Oswego posed an additional problem for the authorities at Quebec. Some of the less scrupulous Canadian traders found it convenient to obtain large supplies of cheap rum there, as well as English woolens, which they traded at the distant Indian villages.[62] In an attempt to keep both the allied Indians and the renegade Canadians away from the English post, the French government retained the trade at forts Frontenac, Niagara, and Toronto as crown monopolies so that prices could be kept competitive with those at Oswego by selling at a reduced profit or even a loss if necessary. The commandants at these posts had to see to it that nothing transpired that could upset the Indians and endanger their alliance with the French.[63]

The French thus managed to maintain a tenuous hold over the interior of North America west of the Appalachians and in the vast region north and west of the Great Lakes as far as the Rocky Mountains. This tremendous feat was, moreover, accomplished at very little cost to the French crown and by a mere handful of men. In 1754, when this military fur trade empire was nearing its greatest extent, the cost to the crown for maintaining the garrisoned posts was but 183,427 livres.[64] The number of officers and enlisted men in these garrisons in 1750 was only 261,[65] but in addition there were the men engaged directly in the trade with the Indians—the voyageurs, traders, clerks, and merchants—whose number cannot be calculated with any great degree of accuracy. All that can be offered here is an educated guess that the number directly employed in the western fur trade for the period 1719–1750 would range from about 200 for the earlier years to some 600 at most by mid-century.[66] This means that with fewer than 1,000 men France maintained its claim to more than half the continent.

Had the French been content to confine their activities to the fur trade they might well have retained their control, in alliance with the Indian nations, over the northern half of the continent, that is, over the area that today forms the Dominion of Canada. However, the interests of the Canadian fur traders and French imperial policy began to diverge at mid-century, immediately after the War of the Austrian Succession. Fur traders from Pennsylvania and Virginia, serving as advance agents of land speculation companies, had begun to penetrate the Ohio Valley by way of the Cumberland Gap with pack-horse trains.[67] To win the allegiance of the Indian nations they flooded the region with cheap trade goods, liquor, and expensive presents for the chiefs. A Canadian officer later declared, "The presents that they receive are so considerable that one sees nothing but the most magnificent gold, silver, and scarlet braid."[68] The Canadian fur traders had no interest in the furs of that region, which were of poor quality.[69] They preferred to confine their activities to the northwest, where the furs were the best obtainable, river communications far easier than they were south of the Great Lakes, and the Cree tongue a lingua franca in the entire region.

Marquis Roland-Michel Barrin de la Gallissonière, governor general of New France, in opposition to the prevailing and strongly held Canadian sentiment, advocated that the Ohio Valley be occupied by the French and that forts be built and garrisoned, merely to deny the region to the English. He freely admitted that it would be of no economic benefit to France in the foreseeable future, but he

The Fur Trade

feared that were the English to succeed in occupying and settling the valley they would become extremely powerful and dangerous. They would eventually sever communications along the Mississippi between Canada and Louisiana and then go on to conquer Mexico with its silver mines.[70]

The minister of marine, Rouillé, newly appointed to the post and without previous experience in colonial affairs, accepted this policy. Despite the strong opposition of the senior Canadian officials in the colonial administration,[71] and at immense cost in funds and Canadian lives,[72] the French drove the Anglo-American traders out of the region. They established a chain of forts and supply depots from Lake Erie to the fork of the Ohio, thereby overawing the local tribes, who quickly abandoned their commercial alliance with the Anglo-Americans and pledged their support to the French.[73] This was accomplished by force majeure pure and simple, and the Indian nations remained in this uneasy alliance only as long as it appeared to them to suit their interests and, as events were to show, not a day longer.

Previously when the French had extended their fur trade empire into new territory, they had always done so at the invitation, or at least with the tacit consent, of the Indians. In the Ohio Valley, however, Gallissonière's successor, Ange de Menneville, marquis Duquesne, made it plain to the Iroquois, who claimed sovereignty over the region, that he would brook no interference, that he regarded the valley as belonging to the French crown, and that if they chose to oppose him he would crush them.[74] Some of his Canadian officers, long accustomed to dealing with the Iroquois, were more diplomatic. They pointed out that the French did not covet the land but merely wished to prevent the English from seizing it, and that the Indians could hunt right up to the walls of the French forts, whereas wherever the English went the forest was destroyed and the animals driven out, the Indians with them.[75]

Here also the Anglo-Americans were the agents of their own defeat. They had treated two nations on the frontiers of Pennsylvania and Virginia, the Shawnee and the Delaware, so ruthlessly, seizing their land by dint of fraudulent title deeds, debauching them with liquor, murdering them with impunity, that it did not require a great deal of persuasion by the French to bring these Indians into a close military alliance once hostilities broke out.[76] This rejection of the Anglo-Americans was immeasurably strengthened by the initial French victories, first over Maj. George Washington's motley provincial force at Fort Necessity, where Washington accepted humiliating terms and fled back over the mountains; then, a year later when Maj. Gen. Edward Braddock's army of 2,200 British regulars and American provincials was destroyed near Fort Duquesne by 250-odd Canadian regulars and militia and some 600 Indians.[77]

The French were now able to arm and send out Indian war parties, accompanied by a few Canadian regulars or militia, to ravage the frontiers of the English colonies from New York to Georgia, thereby retaining the initiative and tying down large British and provincial forces. Successful though it was, this strategy posed massive problems in logistics that the minister of marine, Jean-Baptiste de Machault d'Arnouville, and his staff at Versailles were never able to comprehend. Appalled by the Canadian accounts for 1753, he warned Governor General Duquesne that unless the excessive costs of the western posts were reduced, the king would abandon the colony.[78] He thereby blandly overlooked the fact that the expenditures had been incurred in consequence of his ministry's policy and direct orders. To implement this policy all the needs of the Indian allies had to be supplied.[79] This required the transport of vast amounts of goods from Montreal to forts Niagara and Duquesne by canoe, barque, horse, and pirogue. The wastage at the Niagara portage alone was appalling. In 1753 Duquesne complained to Capt. Paul Marin de la Malgue, commander of the Ohio expedition, that he had learned that forty-eight canoe loads of supplies had been stolen or spoiled by being left uncovered in the rain. He voiced the suspicion that the Canadians, who were bitterly opposed to the Ohio adventure, were destroying the supplies deliberately to force its abandonment.[80]

For many years the western Iroquois had demanded and received the right to carry all fur trade and military supplies over the portage, which they regarded as their territory. This was a cost that the crown officials at Quebec had been quite willing to see imposed on the fur traders in order to maintain good relations with the Iroquois Confederacy. Governor General Duquesne, however, considered excessive the 40,000 livres a year that it was now costing the crown to have military supplies transported around Niagara Falls by the Senecas. At the grave risk of alienating them and the other Iroquois nations, he had horses shipped from Montreal and dispensed with the Senecas' services. Many of the horses then mysteriously vanished.[81]

For the Canadian officers charged with the implementation of these orders, the task at times seemed insuperable. A lack of rain meant low water in the shallow rivers that linked Lake Erie, with a fifteen-mile portage, to the Ohio. The supply boats and pirogues then had to be manhandled along the river beds, driving both officers and men to despair.[82] To make matters worse, the Indian allies were extremely demanding and wasteful. Their loyalty could be counted on only as long as their demands for goods and services were met, and frequently not even then. In 1756 Vaudreuil ruefully explained to the minister of marine:

> I am not in the least surprised that expenses have risen so high, the Indians are the cause of immense expenditures, forming the largest part of those charged to the crown in the colony. One has to see to believe what they consume and how troublesome they are. I deny and reduce their demands as much as I can at Montreal, but despite it they succeed in having themselves equipped several times in the same campaign. They continually come and go between the army or the posts and Montreal, and one is forced to supply them with food for every trip which they justify by claiming that they have been refused things by the army, or that having been on a raid they must now return home, or they dreamt that they ought to do so. Every

time that one wants to send them to support the army one cannot avoid supplying them. When they go on a war party they are given 10, 12, or 15 days rations . . . at the end of two days they return without food or equipment and say they have lost it all, so they have to be provided afresh. They consume an astonishing quantity of brandy and a Commandant would be in grave difficulties were he to refuse them, and so it is with all their requests.[83]

One important factor, all too often overlooked, was that these Indian nations fought alongside the French purely to serve their own ends. They were allies, not mercenaries. In fact, they regarded the French as little more than an auxiliary force aiding them in their struggle to preserve their hunting grounds from further encroachment by the Anglo-Americans and to oblige the latter to treat them with respect.[84] This was compellingly illustrated when, in May 1757, the American colonial authorities entered into negotiations with Iroquois, Shawnee, and Delaware tribes to end the fighting that had destroyed their frontier settlements to a depth of over a hundred miles. For once, the Indian negotiators refused to be put off with vague promises; in the past, they had been hoodwinked all too often. Eventually a Moravian missionary, Frederick Post, who sympathized deeply with the Indians, went to the villages of the Shawnee and Delaware. There, within sight of Fort Duquesne, with frustrated French officers in attendance the proposed terms of the Easton Treaty were promulgated.[85]

The Indian nations south of the Great Lakes then ceased to support the French. When Brig. Gen. John Forbes, marching on Fort Duquesne with an army of some 7,000 British regulars and American provincial troops, suffered heavy and humiliating losses at the hands of the Canadians and Indians in one brisk battle, he deliberately slowed his advance until he received word that the Indians had signed a separate peace, the Easton Treaty. That defection left the French no choice but to abandon Fort Duquesne and, with it, control of the Ohio Valley. Col. Henry Bouquet commented: "After

God the success of this Expedition is intirely due to the General, who by bringing about the Treaty of Easton, has struck the blow which has knocked the French in the head . . . in securing all his posts, and giving nothing to chance."[86]

The following year, 1759, Quebec and Niagara fell. Despite a valiant last attempt by the French and Canadians under François de Lévis to retake Quebec in the spring of 1760, six months later they were compelled to surrender to the armies of Maj. Gen. Jeffery Amherst at Montreal. This spelled the end of French power on the mainland of North America.

The fate of that empire had been decided by the incompetence of its government at home and that of the headquarters staff—with the exception of the Chevalier de Lévis—of the army sent to defend Canada. During the course of the war there had been four controllers general of finance, four of foreign affairs, four of war, and five of the marine.[87] In the fateful year, 1759, the minister of marine was Nicolas-René Berryer. Before his appointment to that post in November 1758 he had been *lieutenant de police* for Paris.[88] As for the army sent to Canada, its morale and efficiency steadily deteriorated under the command of the incompetent, defeatist Louis-Joseph, marquis de Montcalm. It was not a shortage of supplies or overwhelming enemy superiority or corruption that brought on the British conquest of Canada. The west was lost when the Indian allies defected. Louisbourg fell because it lacked a fleet to protect it. Canada fell after the loss of Quebec in a battle that should have been won crushingly by the French but was lost owing to the stupidity and panic of Montcalm.[89] Even then Quebec might well have been retaken by Lévis had the minister of marine dispatched in time the reinforcements that Lévis had requested.[90] Etienne-François, duc de Choiseul, who was given charge of the ministries of war, foreign affairs, and marine, then decided that it would serve the interests of France better were England to acquire Canada, since, with the menace of French power removed from mainland America, England's colonies could be counted on to strike for independence in the not-too-distant future. France's loss of Canada, Choiseul decided, would be as nothing compared to England's loss of her American colonies.[91]

If the Canadians had had control of French policy in North America, neither the decisive battle at Quebec nor, for that matter, the war itself would likely have taken place, for the Canadians had no real quarrel with the English colonies. In war the Anglo-Americans had demonstrated time and again that they were no match for the Canadians and their Indian allies. Their record in the Seven Years' War indicated clearly enough their lack of enthusiasm for the conflict.[92] The Canadians knew that they had little to fear from that quarter, nor did they have any illusions that they could conquer the English colonies. In commerce there was no real conflict between them. The fur trade was of vital economic importance to the Canadians but certainly not to France, and of little, and that declining, importance to the Anglo-Americans. Among the latter, a group of well-placed, rapacious land speculators and a barbarian horde of would-be settlers coveted the lands of the Indian nations on their frontier, a region that the Canadians had made plain was of no interest to them. The Albany merchants who dominated the Anglo-American fur trade chose not to compete with the Canadians; instead they entered into a cozy commercial partnership. They had not exhibited any eagerness to dispute the French hold on the west. As for the Hudson's Bay Company, its steadily declining returns indicated its inability to compete with the Canadians; moreover, it no longer had the same influence that it once had wielded in government circles. It was a monopoly, and all trade monopolies were then being looked at askance in Britain.[93] Only the shareholders would have wept had the Hudson's Bay Company been driven to the wall by the Canadians.

For over half a century the fur trade was used by France as an instrument of its foreign policy and, owing to the peculiar skills of the Canadians, with considerable success. By means of it, most of the Indian nations supported the French cause in the colonial

The Fur Trade

wars, but they did so only as long as it appeared to them to serve their immediate interests. The French were acutely aware of the Indians' true feeling toward them. Governor General Beauharnois remarked that they had their policies just as had the French. "In general," he stated, "they greatly fear us, they have no affection for us whatsoever, and the attitudes they manifest are never sincere."[94] A certain Monsieur Le Maire put the French position very succinctly, explaining that there was no middle course: one had to have the Indians either as friends or as foes, and whoever desired them as friends had to furnish them with their necessities, on terms they could afford.[95] The policy of the Indian nations was always to play the French off against the English, using the fur trade as an instrument of their own foreign policy.[96] Their tragedy was not to have foreseen the consequences were the French to be eliminated from the equation.

Notes

1. On the Huron-Iroquois conflict, see Bruce G. Trigger, *The Children of Aataentsic: A History of the Huron People to 1660*, 2 vols. (Montreal, 1976), and John A. Dickinson, "Annaotaha et Dollard vus de l'autre côté de la palissade," *Revue d'histoire de l'Amérique française* 35 (1981): 163–78.

2. The best study of this early period is Marcel Trudel, *The Beginnings of New France, 1524–1663*, trans. Patricia Claxton (Toronto, 1973). The period 1663–1701 is covered in W. J. Eccles, *Canada under Louis XIV, 1663–1701* (Toronto, 1964). The latter work is now somewhat dated.

3. In order of conquest or dispersal these tribes were the Mahicans, 1628; Hurons, 1649; Neutrals, 1651; Eries, 1653–1657; and Susquehannocs, 1676.

4. Mémoire de Henri Tonty, Nouvelles Acquisitions, vol. 7485, fol. 103, Bibliothèque Nationale, Paris; Duchesneau au ministre, Nov. 13, 1680, c11A, vol. 5, fols. 39–40, Archives Nationales, Colonies, Paris.

5. W. J. Eccles, *Frontenac: The Courtier Governor* (Toronto, 1959), 82–84, 107–10; François Vachon Belmont, *Histoire du Canada, D'après un manuscrit à la Bibliothèque du Roi à Paris* (Quebec, 1840), 14.

6. Belmont, *Histoire du Canada*, 15–16; Eccles, *Frontenac*, 167–71; Presens des Onontaguez à Onontio à la Famine le Cinq Septembre 1684, Le febvre de la barre, c11A, vol. 6, fols. 299–300.

7. Le roy au Sr. de Meules, Mr. 10, 1685, B, vol. 11, fol. 96, Archs. Nationales.

8. Eccles, *Frontenac*, 157–97, 244–72.

9. Ibid., 328–33.

10. Ibid., 334–37; Marcel Giraud, *Histoire de la Louisiane française*, vol. 1, *Le règne de Louis XIV (1698–1715)* (Paris, 1953), 13–23.

11. M. Tremblay à M. Glandelet, May 28, 1701, Lettres, Carton O, no. 34, Archives du Séminaire de Québec, Quebec, Canada.

12. Giraud, *Histoire de la Louisiane*, 1:39–43.

13. Yves F. Zoltvany, *Philippe de Rigaud de Vaudreuil: Governor of New France, 1703–1725* (Toronto, 1974), 39–41.

14. Ibid., 40, 86–87; Champigny au ministre, Aug. 8, 1688, C11A, vol. 10, fols. 123–24; Callières et Champigny au ministre, Oct. 5, 1701, ibid., vol. 19, fols. 6–7. That this fear was soon to be realized is made clear in d'Iberville's journal for 1702 where he mentions his accepting furs from Canadian coureurs de bois for shipment to France. See Richebourg Gaillard McWilliams, trans. and ed., *Iberville's Gulf Journals* (University AL, 1981), 165, 178.

15. Charles Edwards O'Neill, *Church and State in French Colonial Louisiana: Policy and Politics to 1732* (New Haven CT, 1966), passim.

16. Archives nationales du Québec, *Rapport de l'Archiviste de la Province de Québec* (Québec, 1921–), 1938–1939, 69, hereafter cited as *Rapport de l'Archiviste*.

17. Beauharnois et d'Aigremont au ministre, Oct. 1, 1728, C11A, vol. 50, fols. 31–33; minister to La Jonquière and Bigot, May 4, 1749, State Historical Society of Wisconsin, *Collections*, vol. 18 (1908), 25–26; Beauharnois to the minister, Oct. 18, 1737, Michigan Pioneer and Historical Society, *Historical Collections*, vol. 34 (1905), 146–47.

18. For a revealing commentary on the working of a typical fur trade company of the period, see Meuvret au Lt. Joseph Marin de la Malgue [Commandant, la Baie des Puants], May 15, 1752, Fonds Verreau, Boite 5, no. 38 ½, Archs. Sém. Québec. See also Acte de Société, May 23, 1726, Jean Le Mire Marsolet, de Lignery, Guillaume Cartier, Greffe J-B, Adhemar, no. 1854, Archives Nationales du Québec à Montréal.

19. Pierre-Jacques Chavoy de Noyan to the minister, Oct. 18, 1738, Mich. Pioneer Hist. Soc., *Hist. Colls.*, vol. 34 (1905), 158–59; Le Conseil de Marine à MM de Vaudreuil et Bégon, Oct. 20, 1717, C11A, vol. 37, fols. 378–79; Beauharnois et Hocquart au ministre, Oct. 5, 1736, ibid., vol. 65, fols. 57–58; Greffe J., David, Apr. 28, 1723, Archs. Québec (Mtl.), is but one of hundreds of permits that specify the obligations to the crown of those allowed to trade in the west. See also ibid., Greffe J-B, Adhemar, no. 1257, May 23, 1724, and no. 1211, May 8, 1724; Beauharnois et d'Aigremont au ministre, Oct. 1,

1728, C11A, vol. 50, fols. 31–33; Wilbur R. Jacobs, *Dispossessing the American Indian: Indians and Whites on the Colonial Frontier* (New York, 1972), 194n38; and Zoltvany, *Vaudreuil*, 174–75.

20. Zoltvany, *Vaudreuil*, 166–68, 196–209.

21. Canada. Conseil. MM de Vaudreuil et Bégon, Oct. 26, 1720, C11A, vol. 41, fols. 390–91.

22. Parole de toute la Nation Abenaquise et de toutes les autres nations sauvages ses alliés au gouverneur de Baston au sujet de la Terre des Abenaquise dont les Anglois s'Emparent depuis la Paix . . . fait à KenasK8K au bas de la Rivière de Kenibeki Le 28 Juillet 1721, F3 Moreau de St. Méry, vol 2, fols. 413–16, Archs. Nationales.

23. Mémoire du Roy à MM de Beauharnois et Dupuy, Apr. 29, 1727, *Nouvelle-France. Documents historiques. Correspondance échangée entre les autorités française et les gouverneurs et intendants*, vol. 1 (Québec, 1893), 64.

24. E. E. Rich, *The History of the Hudson's Bay Company, 1670–1870*, vol. 1, *1670–1763* (London, 1958), 423–25, 482–86; "Memorial of the Governor and Company of Adventurers of England Trading into Hudson's Bay to the Council of Trade and Plantations," in W. Noel Sainsbury et al., eds., *Calendar of State Papers, Colonial Series, America and the West Indies* 31, no. 360 (London, 1860–); Mr. Delafaye to the Council of Trade and Plantations, Nov. 4, 1719, ibid., no. 443; Observations et réflexions servant de réponses aux propositions de Messieurs les Commissaires anglais au sujet des limites a régler pour la Baie d'Hudson, *Rapport de l'Archiviste*, 1922–1923, 95–96.

25. Rich, *Hudson's Bay Company*, 1:554, 434, 556, 575, and *The Fur Trade and the Northwest to 1857* (Toronto, 1967), 118.

26. Lawrence J. Burpee, ed., "The Journal of Anthony Hendry, 1754–55," Royal Society of Canada, *Proceedings and Transactions*, 2d ser., 13, pt. 2 (1907), 352–53.

27. Rich, *Hudson's Bay Company*, 1:482, 526, 529; Arthur J. Ray, "Indians as Consumers in the Eighteenth Century," in Carol M. Judd and Arthur J. Ray, eds., *Old Trails and New Directions: Papers of the Third North American Fur Trade Conference* (Toronto, 1980), 255–71; W. J. Eccles, "A Belated Review of Harold Adams Innis, *The Fur Trade in Canada*," *Canadian Historical Review* 60 (1979): 427–34.

28. Memoire ou Extrait du Journal Sommaire du Voyage de Jacques Legardeur Ecuyer Sr de St. Pierre . . . chargé de la Descouverte de la Mer de l'Ouest, Fonds Verreau, Boite 5, no. 54, Archs. Sém. Québec.

29. The population figures for these settlements are revealing: Detroit in 1750, 483; Illinois in 1752, 1,536; lower Louisiana in 1746, 4,100.

30. Denonville et Champigny au ministre, Nov. 6, 1688, C11A, vol. 10, fol. 8, and le ministre à Denonville, Jan. 8, 1688, B, vol. 15, fol. 20, Archs. Nationales.

31. Similarly the Iroquois specifically rejected British claims that they were subjects of the British crown. See Acte authentique des six nations iroquoises sur leur indépendance (Nov. 2, 1748), *Rapport de l'Archiviste*, 1921–1922, unnum. plate following p. 108.

32. d'Iberville au ministre, Feb. 26, 1700, C13A, vol. 1, fol. 236, Archs. Nationales; Pièces détachées judiciares 1720, Archs. Québec (Mtl.); Vaudreuil à Beauharnois, Nov. 9, 1745, Loudon Collection, Henry E. Huntington Library, San Marino CA; Ordonnance de Beauharnois, June 8, 1743, Fonds Verreau, Boite 8, no. 96, Archs. Sém. Québec; Duquesne à Contrecoeur, June 12, 1753, ibid., Boite 1, no. 19; Duquesne à Contrecoeur, June 24, 1754, Fernand Grenier, ed., *Papiers Contrecoeur et autres documents concernant le conflit anglo-français sur l'Ohio de 1745 à 1756* (Québec, 1952), 193.

33. On this controversial issue, see Ray, "Indians as Consumers," in Judd and Ray, eds., *Old Trails and New Directions*, 255–71, and Eccles, "Belated Review of Innis," *Canadian Hist. Rev.* 60 (1979): 419–41.

34. Rich, *Hudson's Bay Company*, 1:545.

35. Calvin Martin, *Keepers of the Game: Indian-Animal Relationships and the Fur Trade* (Berkeley CA, 1978), 63–64; André Vachon, "L'eau de vie dans la société indienne," Canadian Historical Association, *Report* (1960), 22–32.

36. Ray, "Indians as Consumers," in Judd and Ray, eds., *Old Trails and New Directions*, 255–71.

37. Arthur S. Morton, ed., *The Journal of Duncan M'Gillivray of the North West Company at Fort George on the Saskatchewan, 1794–5* (Toronto, 1929), 47.

38. Beauharnois et Hocquart au ministre, Oct. 12, 1736, C11A, vol. 65, fols. 49–51; Observation de la Conseil de la Marine, June 1, 1718, ibid., vol. 39, fols. 242–46. See also Reuben Gold Thwaites, ed., *The Jesuit Relations and Allied Documents: Travels and Explorations of the Jesuit Missionaries in New France, 1610–1791* (Cleveland OH, 1896–1901), passim.

39. Eccles, *Frontenac*, 66.

40. For a brief overview of this contentious issue, see ibid., 61–68.

41. Peter Schuyler to Gov. Dongan, Sept. 2, 1687, E. B. O'Callaghan et al., eds., *Documents Relative to the Colonial History of the State of New-York . . .* (Albany NY, 1856–1887), 3:479, hereafter cited as *N.-Y. Col. Docs.*; Propositions made by four of the Chief Sachems of the 5 Nations to his Excell. Benjamin Fletcher . . . in Albany, Feb. 26, 1692/3, ibid., 4:24; Dec. 27, 1698, Peter Wraxall, *An Abridgement of the Indian Affairs . . . Transacted in the Colony of New York, from*

the Year 1678 to the Year 1751, ed. Charles Howard McIlwain (Cambridge MA, 1915), 31; Relation de ce qui s'est passé de plus remarquable en Canada . . . 1695, F3 Moreau de St. Méry, vol. 7, fols. 370–72, Archs. Nationales; Vaudreuil au ministre, Oct. 25, 1710, *Rapport de l'Archiviste*, 1946–1947, 385; Vaudreuil et Bégon au ministre, Sept. 20, 1714, ibid., 1947–1948, 275–76; Beauharnois et Hocquart au ministre, Oct. 12, 1736, C11A, vol. 65, fols. 44–46.

42. Eccles, "Belated Review of Innis," *Canadian Hist. Rev.* 60 (1979): 434.

43. Thomas Elliot Norton, *The Fur Trade in Colonial New York, 1686–1776* (Madison WI, 1974), 100–103, 122, 124.

44. Jean Lunn, "The Illegal Fur Trade out of New France, 1713–1760," Canadian Hist. Assn., *Report* (1939), 61–76; Wraxall, *New York Indian Records*, ed. McIlwain, passim.

45. Le Ch^er Dailleboust à Madame d'Argenteuil, Jan. 5, 1715, Collection Baby, g 1/12, Université de Montréal, Montréal, Que.; Ordonnance de Gilles Hocquart, Apr. 25, 1738, C11A, vol. 69, fols. 180–83; Pierre-Georges Roy, ed., *Inventaire des Ordonnances des Intendants de la Nouvelle-France, conservées aux Archives provinciales de Québec*, vol. 1 (Beauceville, Que., 1919), 160–61, 222; J. W. De Peyster à Jean Lidius, Sept. 23, 1729, NF 13–17, Procédures Judiciares, vol. 3, fols. 389–93, Archs. Québec (Mtl.); Myndert Schuyler à Jean Lidius, Oct. 15, 1729, ibid.; Extrait des Registres du Conseil Supérieur de Québec, Sept. 28, 1730, ibid., fols. 385–88.

46. Lunn, "Illegal Fur Trade," Canadian Hist. Assn., *Report* (1939), 61–76.

47. Vaudreuil et Bégon au ministre, Nov. 12, 1712, *Rapport de l'Archiviste*, 1947–1948, 183–84; Mémoire du Roy pour servir d'instructions au Sieur marquis de Beauharnois, gouverneur et lieutenant-général de la Nouvelle-France, May 7, 1726, *Nouvelle-France. Documents historiques*, 1:57; Reports of Messrs. Schuyler and Dellius' Negotiations in Canada, July 2, 1698, *N.-Y. Col. Docs.*, 4:347; Bellomont to Council of Trade and Plantations, Aug. 24, 1699, Sainsbury et al., eds., *Calendar of State Papers*, 17:406.

48. Beauharnois to Maurepas, Sept. 21, 1741, *N.-Y. Col. Docs.*, 9:1071.

49. Arthur H. Buffinton, "The Policy of Albany and English Westward Expansion," *Mississippi Valley Historical Review* 8 (1922): 327–66.

50. For contemporary British comment on the superior skills of the Canadian traders, see *American Gazetteer* . . . (London, 1762), 2, s.v. "Montreal": "The French have found some secret of conciliating the affections of the savages, which our traders seem stranger to, or at least take no care to put it in practice." See also Burpee, ed., "Journal of Anthony Hendry," Royal Soc. Canada, *Procs. and Trans.*, 2d ser., 13, pt. 2 (1907), 307.

51. Johnson to the Lords of Trade, Nov. 16, 1765, C.O. 5/66, fol. 296, Public Record Office. I am indebted to Dr. Francis P. Jennings for providing me with this piece of evidence.

52. For a specific instance of this, see the entry for Teganissorens in David M. Hayne, ed., *Dictionary of Canadian Biography*, vol. 2 (Toronto, 1969), 619–23.

53. Wraxall, *New York Indian Records*, ed. McIlwain, 111.

54. Zoltvany, *Vaudreuil*, 168–69; Wraxall, *New York Indian Records*, ed. McIlwain, 132–35.

55. Percy J. Robinson, *Toronto during the French Régime: A History of the Toronto Region from Brulé to Simcoe, 1615–1793*, 2d ed. (Toronto, 1965), 66.

56. Wraxall, *New York Indian Records*, ed. McIlwain, 161.

57. Ibid.

58. Memoire touchant le droit françois sur les Nations Iroquoises, Nov. 12, 1712, C11A, vol. 33, fol. 284. The Iroquois admitted to the Albany commissioners that the French had five posts on the south side of Lake Ontario, from Niagara to Cayouhage, east of Oswego. See Sept. 10, 1720, Wraxall, *New York Indian Records*, ed. McIlwain, 130–31.

59. On Anglo-French relations at this time, see Paul Vaucher, *Robert Walpole et la politique de Fleury (1713–1742)* (Paris, 1924).

60. Zoltvany, *Vaudreuil*, 199.

61. Wraxall, *New York Indian Records*, ed. McIlwain, 111, 113; Charles Thomson, *An Enquiry into the Causes of the Alienation of the Delaware and Shawanese Indians from the British Interest* . . . (London, 1759), 56, 76, 114, 118–22; Wilbur R. Jacobs, ed., *The Appalachian Indian Frontier: The Edmond Atkin Report and Plan of 1755* (Columbia SC, 1954), passim.

62. Duquesne à Contrecoeur, Apr. 30, 1753, Fonds Verreau, Boite 1, no. 13, Archs. Sém. Québec.

63. Mar. 14, 1721, Apr. 25, 1726, Roy, ed., *Inventaire des Ordonnances des Intendants*, 1:196, 282; Hocquart au ministre, Oct. 25, 1729, C11A, vol. 51, fol. 264; Vaudreuil, Beauharnois, et Raudot au ministre, Oct. 19, 1705, *Rapport de l'Archiviste*, 1938–1939, 87–88.

64. Mémoire sur les postes de Canada . . . en 1754 . . . , *Rapport de l'Archiviste*, 1927–1928, 353.

65. Extrait Général des Reveues des Compagnies Entretenues en la Nouvelle-France . . . 1750, D2C, vol. 48, fol. 130, Archs. Nationales.

66. Many of the voyageurs hired to serve in the west had notarized contracts, a copy of which had to be preserved in an official register by the notary. Unfortunately, many voyageurs were instead hired *sous seing privé*, that is, with a

written contract not drawn up by a notary. A few of the latter type of contract have survived by accident or because they were submitted as evidence in legal proceedings. Many men may well have been hired with a mere verbal understanding of the terms of service. Statistical studies based on the notarized contracts alone therefore cannot help but be misleading since there is no way of knowing what proportion of the total number of voyageurs employed in any given year the contracts represent. See Gratien Allaire, "Les engagements pour la traite des fourrures, évaluation de la documentation," *Revue d'histoire de l'Amérique française* 34 (1980): 3–26.

67. W. J. Eccles, *France in America* (New York, 1972), 178–79.

68. La Chauvignery à [Contrecoeur], Feb. 10, 1754, Fonds Verreau, Boite 1, no. 77, Archs. Sém. Québec.

69. As early as 1708 François Clairambault d'Aigremont, sent to investigate conditions in the west, stated in a momentous report to the minister that the French could not take enough precautions to conserve the trade north of Lake Superior, since the furs at Detroit and those of the region to the south were not worth much. The reluctance of the Canadian fur traders to engage in trade in the Ohio country is made plain in Gov. Gen. Duquesne's correspondence with Claude-Pierre Pécaudy de Contrecoeur, commandant at Fort Duquesne. Le Sr Daigremont au Ministre Pontchartrain, Nov. 14, 1708, C11A, vol. 29, fol. 175; Grenier, ed., *Papiers Contrecoeur*, 126, 128, 209, 224, 248–49, 253.

70. Galissonière au ministre, Sept. 1, 1748, C11A, vol. 91, fols. 116–22.

71. Donald H. Kent, *The French Invasion of Western Pennsylvania, 1753* (Harrisburg PA, 1954), 12; Sylvester K. Stevens and Donald H. Kent, eds., *Wilderness Chronicles of Northwestern Pennsylvania* . . . (Harrisburg PA, 1941), 56; Duquesne à Contrecoeur, Sept. 8, 1754, Grenier, ed., *Papiers Contrecoeur*, 250; Duquesne à Rouillé, Nov. 31 [*sic*], 1753, C11A, vol. 99, fols. 139–43; Duquesne à Rouillé, Sept. 29, 1754, ibid., fols. 242–43; Duquesne à Rouillé, Nov. 7, 1754, ibid., fol. 259.

72. By Oct. 1753, of over 2,000 men who had left Montreal the previous spring and summer only 880 were fit for service. Duquesne à Marin, Nov. 16, 1753, Grenier, ed., *Papiers Contrecoeur*, 81; Ministre à Duquesne, May 31, 1754, B, vol. 99, fol. 199, Archs. Nationales; Kent, *French Invasion*, 64.

73. Duquesne à Contrecoeur, July 1, 1754, Grenier, ed., *Papiers Contrecoeur*, 207–8.

74. In Apr. 1754 Capitaine de Contrecoeur warned the Indians who were trading with the English at their post on the Ohio that he intended to drive the English out. If the Indians chose to support the enemy, they too would be crushed; it was up to them to decide whether or not they wished to be destroyed.

Paroles de Contrecoeur aux Sauvages, Grenier, ed., *Papiers Contrecoeur*, 116–17. See also Duquesne à Contrecoeur, Apr. 15, 1754, ibid., 113–16.

75. Duquesne à Contrecoeur, Aug. 14, 1754, ibid., 248; Duquesne to the minister, Oct. 31, 1754, *N.-Y. Col. Docs.*, 10:269; Thomas Pownall, cited in Louis De Vorsey, Jr., *The Indian Boundary in the Southern Colonies, 1763–1775* (Chapel Hill NC, 1961), 56–57.

76. Thomson, *Enquiry into the Causes*, passim; Journal de Chaussegros de Léry, *Rapport de l'Archiviste*, 1927–1928, 409–10.

77. For French and British casualties, see Grenier, ed., *Papiers Contrecoeur*, 390–91.

78. Ministre à Duquesne, May 31, 1754, B, vol. 99, fol. 199, Archs. Nationales.

79. Vaudreuil au ministre, Oct. 13, 1756, C11A, vol. 101, fols. 117–19.

80. Duquesne à Marin, June 20, July 10, 1753, Fonds Verreau, Boite 5, nos. 62, 66:6, Archs. Sém. Québec; Duquesne à Contrecoeur, July 22, Aug. 6, 1753, ibid., Boite 1, nos. 27, 28; Varin à Contrecoeur, Aug. 18, 1753, ibid., Boite 5, no. 311.

81. Memoire sur les sauvages du Canada jusqu'à la Rivière de mississippi . . . Donné par M. de Sabrevois en 1718, C11A, vol. 39, fol. 354; Varin à Contrecoeur, May 17, June 1, July 26, 1753, Fonds Verreau, Boite 4, nos. 501, 502, 307, Archs. Sém. Québec; Varin à de la Perrière, Oct. 21, 1754, ibid., Boite 8, no. 78; Contrecoeur à Douville, Apr. 14, 1755, Grenier, ed., *Papiers Contrecoeur*, 310–11.

82. Duplessis Faber à Lavalterie, Apr. 16, 1756, BABY, no. 137; Péan à Contrecoeur, June 15, 1754, Fonds Verreau, Boite 1, no. 80, Archs. Sém. Québec; Varin à Contrecoeur, Feb. 4, 1753, ibid., no. 294; Varin à (?), May 10, 1753, ibid., no. 300; Contrecoeur à Douville, Apr. 14, 1755, Grenier, ed., *Papiers Contrecoeur*, 310; La Perrière à Contrecoeur, Apr. 20, 1755, ibid., 321; Benoist à Contrecoeur, June 30, 1755, ibid., 370–73; Saint-Blin à Contrecoeur, au for [*sic*] de la riviere au beouf [*sic*] le 3 juilietts [*sic*] 1755, ibid., 374–75; Journal de Joseph-Gaspard Chaussegros de Léry, 1754–1755, *Rapport de l'Archiviste*, *1927–1928*, 385.

83. Vaudreuil au ministre, Oct. 13, 1756, C11A, vol. 101, fols. 117–19.

84. Thomson, *Enquiry into the Causes*, 108–14.

85. Ibid., 138–60.

86. Niles Anderson, "The General Chooses a Road," *Western Pennsylvania Historical Magazine* 43 (1959): 138, 249, quotation on p. 396.

87. Lee Kennett, *The French Armies in the Seven Years' War: A Study in Military Organization and Administration* (Durham NC, 1967), 3–13.

88. H. Carré acidly remarked, in describing the chaos that reigned in the Ministry of Marine, "enfin le lieutenant de police Berryer, sous l'administration duquel s'effondra la marine. A la fin, il suspendit les travaux des ports et vendit à des particuliers le matériel des arsenaux. Choiseul, son successeur, relèvera la marine, mais trop tard pour le succés de la guerre engagée" (*La Règne de Louis XV (1715–1774)*, in Ernest Lavisse, ed., *Histoire de France . . .* , vol. 8, pt. 2 [Paris, 1909], 272).

89. W. J. Eccles, "The Battle of Quebec: A Reappraisal," French Colonial Historical Society, *Proceedings of the Third Annual Meeting* (Athens GA, 1978), 70–81.

90. Dec. 28, 1758, C11A, vol. 103, fols. 453–55; Guy Frégault, *La guerre de la conquête* (Montréal, 1955), 365–72.

91. Memoire du duc de Choiseul, Dec. 1759, Manuscrits français, Nouvelles Acquisitions, vol. 1041, fols. 44–63, Bib. Nationale.

92. One interesting aspect of this attitude, as manifested in New England, is discussed by F. W. Anderson, "Why Did Colonial New Englanders Make Bad Soldiers? Contractual Principles and Military Conduct during the Seven Years' War," *William and Mary Quarterly*, 3d ser., 38 (1981): 395–417.

93. Rich, *Fur Trade and the Northwest*, 115, and *Hudson's Bay Company*, 1:554, 572, 575–86.

94. Beauharnois au ministre, Oct. 17, 1736, C11A, vol. 65, fol. 143.

95. MG7, I, A-Z, Fonds français, MS 12105, Memoire de Le Maire 1717, fol. 83, Public Archives of Canada.

96. Conférence avec les Onondagués et Onneiouts, July 28, 1756, and Conférence, Dec. 21, 1756, C11A, vol. 101, fols. 55–61, 263.

14. The Middle Ground

RICHARD WHITE

> For every time we make others part of a "reality" that we alone invent,
> denying their creativity by usurping the right to create, we use those
> people and their way of life and make them subservient to ourselves.
> —Roy Wagner, *The Invention of Culture*

> In action, people put their concepts and categories into ostensive rela-
> tions to the world. Such referential uses bring into play other deter-
> minations of the signs, besides their received sense, namely the actual
> world and the people concerned.
> —Marshall Sahlins, *Islands of History*

I

Because the French and Algonquians were trading partners and allies,
the boundaries of the Algonquian and French worlds melted at the
edges and merged. Although identifiable Frenchmen and identifiable
Indians obviously continued to exist, whether a particular practice
or way of doing things was French or Indian was, after a time, not so
clear. This was not because individual Indians became "Frenchified"
or because individual Frenchmen went native, although both might
occur. Rather, it was because Algonquians who were perfectly comfortable with their status and practices as Indians and Frenchmen,
confident in the rightness of French ways, nonetheless had to deal
with people who shared neither their values nor their assumptions
about the appropriate way of accomplishing tasks. They had to arrive
at some common conception of suitable ways of acting; they had to
create what I have already referred to as a middle ground.[1]

The creation of the middle ground involved a process of mutual invention by both the French and the Algonquians. This process passed through various stages, of which the earliest is at once the most noticed and the least interesting. It was in this initial stage that the French, for example, simply assimilated Indians into their own conceptual order. Indians became *sauvages*, and the French reduced Indian religion to devil worship and witchcraft. Algonquians, for their part, thought of the first Europeans as manitous. On both sides, new people were crammed into existing categories in a mechanical way.[2]

Literacy gave this initial stage a potency and a durability for Europeans it might otherwise have lacked. Because the French were literate, knowledge of Indians was diffused far from the site of actual contact. Such knowledge, unchallenged by actual experience with Indians, survived as a potent cultural relict. Long after it ceased to govern the actions of those who actually lived among Indians, the idea of Indians as literally *sauvages*, or wild men embodying either natural virtue or ferocity, persisted among intellectuals and statesmen in France. Assimilated into European controversies, these imaginary Indians became the Indians of Chateaubriand and Rousseau. They took on importance, but it was one detached from the continuing processes of contact between real Algonquians and real Europeans. In the *pays d'en haut*, actual Indians and whites of widely different social class and status had, for a variety of reasons, to rely on each other in order to achieve quite specific ends. It was these Frenchmen (for Frenchwomen would not appear until much later) and Algonquian men and women who created a common ground—the middle ground—on which to proceed.[3]

This process of creation resulted quite naturally from attempts to follow normal conventions of behavior in a new situation. Each side sought different goals in a different manner. French officials and merchants sought to rationalize and order what they saw as the unpredictable world of the *sauvage*; Algonquians sought, in a sense, the opposite. They wanted to change or readjust the given order by appeals for personal favor or exemption. In much the same way that they sought special power to readjust the order of the world of plants, animals, and spirits by appealing to the manitous, so they sought beneficial changes in the social world by appeals to the French. Often, in the examples that follow, when the French sought the imposition of hard-and-fast rules, the Algonquians sought the "power" that comes from knocking the order off balance, from asserting the personal, the human exception. The result of each side's attempts to apply its own cultural expectations in a new context was often change in culture itself. In trying to maintain the conventional order of its world, each group applied rules that gradually shifted to meet the exigencies of particular situations. The result of these efforts was a new set of common conventions, but these conventions served as a basis for further struggles to order or influence the world of action.[4]

The middle ground depended on the inability of both sides to gain their ends through force. The middle ground grew according to the need of people to find a means, other than force, to gain the cooperation or consent of foreigners. To succeed, those who operated on the middle ground had, of necessity, to attempt to understand the world and the reasoning of others and to assimilate enough of that reasoning to put it to their own purposes. Particularly in diplomatic councils, the middle ground was a realm of constant invention, which was just as constantly presented as convention. Under the new conventions, new purposes arose, and so the cycle continued.[5]

Perhaps the central and defining aspect of the middle ground was the willingness of those who created it to justify their own actions in terms of what they perceived to be their partner's cultural premises. Those operating in the middle ground acted for interests derived from their own culture, but they had to convince people of another culture that some mutual action was fair and legitimate. In attempting such persuasion people quite naturally sought out congruences, either perceived or actual, between the two cultures. The congruences arrived at often seemed—and, indeed, were—results of misunderstandings or accidents. Indeed, to later observers the interpretations offered by members of one society for the practices of another can appear ludicrous. This, however, does not matter. Any congruence, no matter how tenuous, can be put to work and can take on a life of its own if it is accepted by both sides. Cultural conventions do not have to be true to be effective any more than legal precedents do. They have only to be accepted.

The middle ground of the *pays d'en haut* existed on two distinct levels. It was both a product of everyday life and a product of formal diplomatic relations between distinct peoples. For historians, however, the middle ground is initially easiest to perceive as it was articulated in formal settings.[6]

In June 1695 the alliance of the Huron-Petuns, Ottawas, and French was in one of its recurrent crises. The Ottawas and Huron-Petuns, fearing that the French would make a separate peace with the Iroquois, had undertaken secret negotiations of their own with the Five Nations. These negotiations had received added impetus from English promises of trade at rates considerably below those of the French. The French commander at Michilimackinac, Antoine Laumet de La Mothe, Sieur de Cadillac, suspecting the existence of such talks but not knowing the details of them, attempted to halt the negotiations by soliciting war parties led by French partisans among the Ottawas. Though relatively few, the war parties threatened the Iroquois and thus disrupted plans for peace. The leaders of those who favored peace, particularly a Huron chief known as the Baron, sought to stop the war parties without mentioning the Huron-Petuns' negotiations with the Iroquois. To succeed, the Baron had to accomplish one of two things. He had to provide reasons acceptable both to the French and to their partisans as to why the war parties should not depart. Or, failing this, he had to alienate the pro-French Ottawas from Cadillac and the Jesuits. To achieve these ends, he convened a "grand and numerous" council of the nations of Michilimackinac to meet with one another as well as with Cadillac, the Jesuits, and "the most respectable Frenchmen of the post."[7]

The council convened to do little more than hear a story from the Baron. He told his listeners that recently there had been discovered in the country around Saginaw Bay an old man and his wife, each about a hundred years old. They had resided there ever since the expulsion of the Hurons from their own country. The old man knew and had related all that had passed in the western wars since the destruction of the Hurons and had paid particular attention to the embassies of the Iroquois to Onontio. He knew all these things because of his communications with the Master of Life who spoke directly to the old man and who sent him animals and made his fields abound with corn and pumpkins. The old man, too, knew of the present de facto truce with the Iroquois and insinuated that the first side to break it would inevitably be destroyed.[8]

The old man exhorted the Indians to be attentive to the Black Gowns and to apply themselves to prayer because, if the Master of Life "who is one in three persons, who form but one Spirit and one Will" was not obeyed, he would kill the corn as he had last year. Finally the old man had told them the eighth day should be observed by abstinence from work and should be sanctified by prayer. The dead, he said, should be given scaffold burials instead of being buried in the ground, so that they could more easily take the road to Heaven. Finally, the old man had urged that they all hearken to the voice of Onontio and follow his will. On concluding his recitation of the old man's message, the Baron offered Cadillac a present of beaver from the old man himself. Cadillac, who thought that of the whole story only the beaver was not imaginary, refused the present, "this voice being unknown to him."[9]

The Baron's story was an attempt to use and expand the middle ground so that his own interest—peace with the Iroquois—could be secured. Peace could not be protected through normal Huron cultural forms. If the matter had depended only on non-Christian Ottawas and Huron-Petuns, the Baron would not have had to resort

The Middle Ground

to the story of the old man, with all its Christian and prophetic elements. If he had been addressing Indians only, the council could have been convened to consider a dream that contained the same message. Dreams, however, as the Baron realized quite well, had no legitimacy for the French who were urging their partisans to action. What did have legitimacy for them was divine revelation, and so the Baron gave them one. Baron's attempt failed because, as the chronicler of his speech huffily observed, the French only attached "belief to certain revelations and visions . . . because they are authorized." The old man was unauthorized and so proved an unsuccessful device for conveying a message in a manner that had legitimacy for Europeans.[10]

Nonetheless, the Baron's tactics were both clever and revealing. He had consciously tried to buttress the legitimacy of the old man's message by filling it with fragments of Christian doctrine (the Trinity, exhortations to prayer, attentiveness to the missionaries) and with the commands to follow the will of Onontio, the French governor. These were all items the French could hardly quarrel with. Yet the Baron also gave the message a definite Huron tinge. The prophet was an Indian who changed the Sabbath from the seventh day to the eighth. It is unlikely this was accidental. As early as 1679, the Jesuits had praised the Huron-Petuns for their particularly scrupulous observance of Sundays and feast days. The Huron-Petuns even had a special officer of the faith who gave notice of the meeting days. It would be surprising if the Baron had forgotten all this. It seems more likely that the Baron's movement of the Sabbath was intentional and that he meant it, along with the command for scaffold burials, to set the old man apart as an Indian prophet with an Indian message from the Christian God. It is unclear if the Baron seriously believed the French would accept the legitimacy of an Indian prophet, but by framing the story as he did, he created a situation in which even their rejection of the old man might serve his purposes. When Cadillac and the Jesuits rejected the old man, they rejected, too, exhortation to prayer and obedience to missionaries and Onontio. More than that, by rejecting the story, the French seemed to insinuate that God spoke directly only to whites, and not to Indians.[11]

Cadillac denounced the story as ridiculous, mocked the Baron's apparent confusion about the Sabbath, and demanded that the Indians strike the Iroquois. He left behind a troubled council. To the gathered Ottawa and Huron-Petun elders it now seemed that "the French were unwilling to listen to the voice of their pretended man of God, alleging that the Black Gowns were very desirous of being heard when they recounted stories about Paul and the anchorites of olden times; wherefore then, they asked, shall not our old man possess the same light?"[12]

The council was merely a skirmish within the larger diplomatic battle being waged over participation by the Michilimackinac Indians in the Iroquois war, but it reveals the process that formed the middle ground and made the boundaries between French and Algonquian societies so porous. To further its interests, each side had to attain cultural legitimacy in terms of the other. The Baron and Cadillac, as much as each might mangle the subtleties of the other's cultural view, had created a forum in which they could speak and understand each other. They did so by using, for their own purposes and according to their own understanding, the cultural forms of the other. The Baron appealed to a Christian tradition of prophecy and put it to Indian purposes. He sought to validate it, in Indian terms, by a gift of beaver. Cadillac, appearing in an Indian council, followed Algonquian forms and, knowing what acceptance of the gift signified, refused it. To accept the gift was to acknowledge the old man, whom the Baron would then make "talk on every occasion that he would judge favorable for his pernicious designs." He rejected an Indian adaptation of a Christian device through his own use of Algonquian-Iroquoian diplomatic forms. Both used the cultural forms of the other cleverly, if crudely. The crudeness of the Baron's Christianity or Cadillac's mastery of Indian diplomacy mattered less than the need for each to employ these foreign elements at all. They merged them into something quite different from the Algonquian, Iroquoian, and French cultures that gave them birth.

The Baron's encounter with Cadillac took place in a diplomatic forum where representatives of each culture dealt with a well-formulated body of ideas and practices. This was one aspect of the middle ground and the one in which its methods are best documented and exhibited. The middle ground itself, however, did not originate in councils and official encounters; instead, it resulted from the daily encounters of individual Indians and Frenchmen with problems and controversies that needed immediate solution. Many of these problems revolved around basic issues of sex, violence, and material exchange. The need to resolve these problems, perhaps even more than the problems of alliance, forced the middle ground into existence. But even this misstates the issue, for the distinction between official dealings and personal dealings was a hazy and confusing one in Algonquian society, where coercive mechanisms and hierarchical structures were notoriously weak.

Although French officials spoke of their relationship with the Algonquians in economic, political, and, less often, religious terms, paradoxically economic and political institutions could not control the context of contact. In the day-to-day relations of the western country, the relationships of Algonquians and Frenchmen as trading partners and allies were abstractions, pertinent, perhaps, to Indians and French as aggregates, but having little to do with actual people in face-to-face relationships. In another society, with more coercive mechanisms at an elite's disposal, personal relations between intruders such as the French and the members of the host society might be kept to a minimum and mattered little. Traders might be isolated in special quarters and granted special privileges; they might be governed by separate rules and taxed at stated rates. Isolation, however, was impossible among the Algonquians, who lacked a state with coercive institutions and in whose society obedience to authority was usually neither a social fact nor a social virtue.[13]

This weakness of political authority and lack of subordination in Algonquian society struck both the Algonquians and the French as a major difference between the two peoples. For the French this lack of subordination, not the Algonquians' state of material or technological development, was at the heart of Algonquian "savagery." The northern Indians, according to the Sieur d'Aigremont, "possess no subordination among themselves . . . being opposed to all constraint. Moreover, these peoples [have] no idea of Royal grandeur nor Majesty, nor of the powers of Superiors over inferiors."[14]

Father Membre, traveling south along the Mississippi with La Salle in 1682, clearly regarded authority as being at the heart of not only society but humanity. The Natchez and the hierarchical societies of the Mississippi were technologically like the Algonquians. They were a Stone Age people, but they were "all different from our Canada Indians in their houses, dress, manners, inclinations and customs. . . . Their chiefs possess all the authority. . . . They have their valets and officers who follow them and serve them everywhere. They distribute their favors and presents at will. In a word we generally found men there."[15]

The French did not err in noting the absence of class divisions and state and religious institutions among northern Algonquians, but they were mistaken when they took this for an absence of social order. Tradition was the storehouse of a tribal people's knowledge of themselves as a people and a guide to how they should act. As war and disease reduced populations and forced the amalgamation of previously distinct peoples, the survivors seemed to cling to their traditions. But they were like infants sucking the breasts of their dead mothers; tradition could no longer sustain them.[16]

The weakness of coercive authority among the Algonquians would have mattered less if French authority had officially reached the West. With the decline of the trade fairs, however, official French supervision of exchange became a mirage. Indians no longer traveled long distances to fortified European towns or outposts to exchange furs. Some limited exchanges of this type took place at Fort Saint

Louis, in the Illinois country, and at Michilimackinac and the posts Perrot erected among the Sioux, but most trade was the work of small groups of Frenchmen traveling to Indian villages and hunting camps. Once these traders had lost their status as manitous, they were strangers without social standing in Algonquian villages. They were also wealthy strangers, with goods far in excess of their own immediate needs, who stood virtually defenseless. If they were to succeed as traders, they had to find means to protect themselves either through force or by establishing personal ties within the communities in which they traded.[17]

The French elite feared the consequences of such contact. French authorities thought that Frenchmen moving within Algonquian society would slip the net unless kept under tight control. What horrified French officials quite as much as the economic damage they believed the coureurs de bois did was the social threat they represented. According to officials, the coureurs de bois were metamorphosing into *sauvages,* that is, men beyond the control of legitimate authority. What was particularly horrifying about the "savagery" of the coureurs de bois was that they seemed to glory in it. They used their freedom to mock the men who never doubted that they were their betters. On his return to the Illinois in 1680, La Salle found that his men had not only deserted but had also demolished his fort, stolen his goods, and, in the hand of a man La Salle recognized as Le Parisien, had left scrawled on a board a parting epithet: *Nous sommes touts Sauvages* ("We are all savages").[18]

Le Parisien, of course, was no more a *sauvage* than La Salle. He merely shared with his superiors a common misunderstanding of Algonquian society as a place of license without order. It was this misperception that gave the word *sauvage* its power as a metaphor for what officials regarded as a danger and men like Le Parisien saw as an opportunity—the escape from subordination. That most coureurs de bois could fully escape the restraining hands of the state and the church was an exaggeration. Yet, in another sense, the fear of the authorities and the hope of Le Parisien were not fully misplaced. Frenchmen in the West could to a remarkable degree act independently, if only temporarily, in reaching accommodations with the Algonquians among whom they traveled and lived. They made contact a complex social process only partially under the control of church and state. In the West, this process centered on Frenchmen whom the authorities did not regard as legitimate representatives of their own society and who were actually seen as a danger to it. There was always a tension between these men and those other Frenchmen who possessed legitimate standing: men who like La Salle, came with grants from the Crown; or missionaries, like the Jesuits; or military commanders; or licensed traders. Frenchmen in the West often cooperated, but such cooperation could never be presumed. Indians thus had to establish appropriate social ties with a diverse and often quarreling group of Frenchmen.[19]

Certain of these diverse Frenchmen, in turn, posed dangers to Algonquian social order because they struck at the heart of Algonquian identity by arguing that traditional practices were not innate, but transferable from one people to another. Missionaries and Christianity, in this sense, represented a potentially subversive force that, if not assimilated into Algonquian traditions, could destroy the very identity of those who accepted it. Only in the Illinois country was this threat soon realized, and there, where the dangers of Christianity were most fully faced, the arguments of the opponents of the missionaries are revealing. The adversaries of the church based their attack partially on the argument that prayer was ineffective and baptism brought death, but they also worked from the assumption that Christianity displaced traditions central to the identity of various Illinois groups and appropriate to them. In a style of argument that foreshadowed later appeals to an "Indian way," Illinois elders contended that since identity was innate, Christianity was proper for the French; Illinois beliefs were proper for the Illinois. As a leading Peoria chief, an opponent of Christianity's, phrased it:

The Middle Ground

I shall hold a feast . . . and I shall invite all the old men and all the chiefs of bands. . . . After speaking of our medicines and of what our grandfathers and ancestors have taught us, has this man who has come from afar better medicines than we have, to make us adopt his customs? His fables are good only in his own country; we have ours, which do not make us die as his do.

Or, in the words of a Kaskaskia elder, "full of zeal for the ancient customs of the country and apprehending that his credit and that of his class [*son semblable*] would be diminished if their people embraced the faith":

All ye who have hitherto hearkened to what the black gown has said to you come into my cabin. I shall likewise teach you what I learned from my grandfather, and what we should believe. Leave their myths to the people who come from afar, and let us cling to our own traditions.[20]

The operation of the middle ground must be understood within a dual context. First, there was the weakness of hierarchical controls within Algonquian villages and the frailty of any authority French officials exerted over Frenchmen in the West. Second, there was the cultural threat each society seemed to pose to the elite of the other. What this meant in practice was that both the extent and meaning of social relations between Frenchmen and Algonquians were often negotiated largely on a face-to-face level within the villages themselves, and that these relations were not what either French authorities or Algonquian elders might have preferred them to be. This does not mean that there was no official element involved, but rather that official decisions could not determine the course of actual relations.

II

The array of relations negotiated in the middle ground was quite large, but leaving aside for now the liquor trade, problems in two arenas of contact—sex and violence—seem to have been particularly acute. Sexual relations between Frenchmen and Indian women and violence between French and Indians, both men and women, accompanied trade throughout the West. One facilitated trade, and the other threatened to destroy it; both presented problems of cultural interaction that had to be negotiated. Sex and violence are thus important not only in their own right but also as avenues for understanding how cultural accommodation on the middle ground, in fact, worked.

What made sexual relations between Frenchmen and Indian women so central to contact in the West was that until the 1730s relatively few Frenchwomen ever came west. Frenchwomen were a curiosity in the upper country. The appearance of Madame Le Sueur at Fort Saint Louis in the 1690s created such an uproar that she, like Indians visiting Europe, had to consent to a public display so that the curious could see her. The absence of Frenchwomen meant that French males actively sought out Indian women as sexual partners. Not all French males did so, of course. The Jesuits and often their donnés were celibate. This was a condition which, if not unknown among the Algonquians, was regarded by them with the same combination of curiosity and revulsion with which the French regarded the berdaches of the Illinois and the acceptance of homosexual relations among many Algonquian peoples.[21]

Algonquians eventually accepted Jesuit celibacy, but the Jesuits never accepted Algonquian sexual mores, particularly when other Frenchmen proved so enthusiastic about them. Sex was hardly a personal affair; it was governed and regulated by the appropriate authorities. The supreme arbiters of sex among the French were precisely those who, theoretically, had the least practical experience, the priests. The Jesuits took a vocal and active interest in the sexual activities of both the French and the Indians.[22]

It was the interest of the Jesuits in other people's sexual conduct, along with the more immediate experience and observations of men like Perrot, Lahontan, and Deliette, that makes possible reconstruction of their contemporaries' sexual relations, but the very nature of these sources requires that they be used carefully. To understand sexual relations between Algonquians and Europeans, we must remove the combination of sexual fantasy, social criticism, and Jansenism with which the French often veiled their descriptions. A few relatively straightforward descriptions of sexual relations exist, but sources are often openly polemical. The Jesuits were interested in denouncing and restraining what they regarded as Algonquian and French sexual immorality—polygamy, adultery, and prostitution—whereas, at the other extreme, the Baron de Lahontan sometimes delighted in using Indians as weapons in assaulting European law, custom, and hypocrisy.[23]

Despite their differing purposes, nearly all French accounts were united, first, by their inability to understand the status of women vis-à-vis men except in terms of conjugal relations and, second, by their tendency to group actual sexual relations in terms of two opposite poles of conduct, with marriage at one extreme and prostitution and adultery at the other. In attempting to impose their own cultural categories on the actions of Algonquian women, the French tended to select material that made the women seem merely a disorderly and lewd set of Europeans, not people following an entirely different social logic. The immediate result was to define a woman in terms of a person—her actual or potential husband—who may not have been anywhere near being the most significant figure in the woman's life. Depending on her tribal identity, an Algonquian woman often had a more durable and significant relationship with her mother, father, brothers, sisters, or grandparents, or with other, unrelated women than with her husband or husbands. Nor was an Algonquian woman's status dependent solely on her husband. Her own membership in ritual organizations or, among some tribes such as the Shawnees, Huron-Petuns, and Miamis, her own political status in offices confined to women had more influence on her social position than the status of her husband did.[24]

Even when the most careful and sensitive of the European observers talked about the status of women and sexual relations, therefore, they eliminated much of the actual social world that gave those relations their full meaning. Perrot and Father Lafitau, for example, wrote dispassionate accounts of Algonquian marriage customs. They recognized marriage as a social contract between families, as it was in Europe, even if gifts were given to the bride's family, in exchange for, as Perrot said, the bride's body, instead of to the groom as in Europe. In marriage coercive authority, elsewhere so weak in Algonquian society, stiffened. Once married, a woman was clearly subordinate to her husband. The French viewed the harsh punishments inflicted on women for adultery among the Illinois and the Miamis as the most graphic evidence of subordination. Deliette said that he had seen evidence that more than a hundred women had been executed for adultery during the seven years he had spent among the Illinois. Others emphasized the mutilation of adulterous women by husbands, who cut off a nose or an ear, and the gang rapes inflicted on unfaithful wives by men solicited for the purpose by the husband. There were no equivalent penalties for adultery by men. For Frenchmen, these property exchanges, the subordination of women, and the double sexual standard made this a harsh but recognizable and comprehensible world.[25]

The problem was that this portrait, as the French sources themselves make clear, was incomplete. A woman's subordination to her husband was not necessarily permanent. She could call on male relatives to protect and vindicate her. She could leave her husband and return to her own family whenever she chose. Among many groups adultery was not harshly punished. According to Cadillac, the sexual freedom of married Ottawa and Huron-Petun women was so great that it made adultery a meaningless category. And, indeed, it was the categories themselves that were the problem. European conceptions of marriage, adultery, and prostitution just could not encompass the actual variety of sexual relations in the *pays d'en haut.*[26]

Jesuits and other Europeans did not impose these cultural categories as an ethnographic exercise; they did so in an attempt

The Middle Ground

to understand and regulate sexual activity. This was a task that missionaries saw as an essential part of their purpose in the West. Adultery, prostitution, and marriage obviously existed, but most sexual contact took place between Frenchmen and single Indian women, who enjoyed considerable sexual freedom but were not prostitutes. There was no appropriate French category for such free, unmarried Algonquian women.

Because of this lack of readily available parallels from French society, and because of differences between the hierarchical Miamis and Illinois, on the one hand, and the remaining Algonquians, on the other, French accounts of the sexual standards expected of unmarried young women among the Algonquians vary widely and are often internally contradictory. Deliette, for example, says the Illinois valued chastity highly, but he then goes on to say that virtually all women, even married women, took lovers.[27]

Lahontan credited unmarried Algonquian women with virtually complete sexual freedom.

> A Young Woman is allow'd to do what she pleases; let her Conduct be what it will, neither Father nor Mother, Brother nor Sister can pretend to controul her. A Young Woman, say they, is Master of her own Body, and by her Natural Right of Liberty is free to do what she pleases.

The only social barrier to premarital intercourse was fear of pregnancy, which would make it impossible to obtain a high-ranking husband, but Lahontan said women knew how to abort unwanted pregnancies. Among most groups such sexual freedom apparently ended with marriage. But some women never did marry. There was, according to Lahontan, a class of women called Ickoue ne Kioussa, or Hunting Women—"for they commonly accompany the Huntsmen in their Diversions." Such women argued that they could not endure "the conjugal yoak," that they were incapable of bringing up children and were "too impatient to spend winters in the village." Lahontan regarded all this as a "disguise for lewdness," but he noted that these women were not censured by their parents or other relatives, who asserted, for instance, "that their daughters have the command of their own Bodies and may dispose of their persons as they think fit." The children these women bore were raised by their families and "accounted a Lawful issue"; they were entitled to all privileges except that they could not marry into families of noted warriors or councillors.[28]

Such quotations from Lahontan must be read with caution, since Indians often served him as mere vehicles for his own critique of French society, and his analysis often differed from those of more experienced observers of the Algonquian nations. Lahontan, for example, made divorce among the Algonquians a far more trivial event than did Perrot, who spent much of his life among the western Indians. And certainly among the Illinois, women were not totally free before marriage; brothers greatly influenced their sisters' sexual lives. Nevertheless, despite Lahontan's tendency to overgeneralize and his notorious inventions, his assertions cannot be dismissed as simply romantic fabrication. Other accounts corroborate his descriptions of young Algonquian women. Joutel's memoir about the Illinois, although it confuses cohabitation with hunting women and marriage, substantiates Lahontan's description. According to Joutel, the marriages of the Illinois lasted no longer than the parties desired to remain together, for they "freely part after a hunting bout, each going which way they please without any ceremony," and he notes, "There are women who make no secret of having had to do with Frenchmen." Cadillac, too, noted that girls "are allowed to enjoy themselves and to experiment with marriage as long as they like and with as many boys as they wish without reproach."[29]

Younger women and hunting women thus enjoyed substantial freedom in engaging in sexual relations with Frenchmen and played a major part in establishing the customary terms of sexual relationships between the Algonquians and the French. Initially, many Frenchmen, like the Jesuits, may have viewed this sort of relationship as simple prostitution or, like Joutel, as a loose, easily

The Middle Ground

dissolved marriage, but by the 1690s they recognized it as a separate, customary form for sexual relationships in the fur trade. Basically, women adapted the relationship of hunting women to hunters to the new conditions of the fur trade. Such women not only had sexual intercourse with their French companions, they also cooked and washed for them, made their clothes, and cut their wood. In denouncing these women, the Jesuit Father Carheil described them in terms similar to Lahontan's:

> The traders have become so accustomed to have women for their use in the trading-places, and these have become so necessary to them, that they cannot do without them even on their journeys. . . . I refer to single women, women without husbands, women who are mistresses of their own Bodies, women who can dispose of them to these men, and whom the latter know to be willing to do so—in a word, They are all the prostitutes of Montreal who are alternately brought here and taken back; and They are all the prostitutes of this place, who are carried in the same way from here to Montreal, and from Montreal to here. . . . The pretext that they usually allege for taking women in preference to men on these journeys is, that women cost them less than men, and are satisfied with lower wages. They speak the truth; but the very Fact of their being Satisfied with less wages is a Manifest proof of their dissoluteness. . . . The women, Being depraved, want them as men; and they, on their part, want them as women, on all their journeys—after which . . . they quit one another. They separate from these only to Seek others.[30]

What Father Carheil misunderstood and denounced as *prostitution* had little to do with that term as commonly understood. These women did not solicit customers, and they did not sell discrete sexual acts. Sex accompanied a general agreement to do the work commonly expected of women in Algonquian society. Nor was the relationship a temporary marriage. In marriage a wife received no payment from her husband, nor was she as free as a hunting woman to dissolve one relationship and begin another. Finally,

---

these relationships were not contracts between families. They were, instead, a bridge to the middle ground, an adjustment to inter-racial sex in the fur trade where the initial conceptions of sexual conduct held by each side were reconciled in a new customary relation. The appeal of unions that offered both temporary labor and sexual companionship to the coureurs de bois is obvious, but these relationships also may have flourished because of the badly skewed sex ratios within Algonquian societies, apparently the result of warfare.

Many late seventeenth-century accounts of western Algonquian population stress both sexual imbalance and the presence of soral polygamy—the practice of a husband marrying two or more sisters. Sexual relations with the coureur de bois offered an alternative to polygamy. Polygamy was also a particular target of Jesuit mission-aries, who were not reluctant to assert a connection among the famines, the epidemics sweeping the villages, and plural marriages. Jesuit denunciations of polygamy appear to have achieved at least some temporary success in the Michilimackinac region. In 1670, in response to an epidemic, the men at Sault Sainte Marie took back their first wives and put away those wives they had taken since their first marriage. Subsequently, the Kiskakon Ottawas, the most Christianized of the Ottawas, were also the Ottawa group with the fewest polygamists, and, supposedly, the Kaskaskias abandoned polygamy entirely by the early eighteenth century. Elsewhere the Jesuits never succeeded in completely eradicating polygamy, but even partial success yielded ironic results. Given the population imbalance between men and women, any increase in the class of single women yielded more women who might be willing to attach themselves to the French.[31]

That Jesuit battles against polygamy may have increased the number of women who consorted with Frenchmen was only one of the ironies created by French and Algonquian attempts to arrive at mutually intelligible patterns of sexual conduct. Hunting women, as a group, carried and modified one Algonquian pattern of sexual relations into the fur trade in their liaisons with the coureurs de bois, but a smaller group of Christian Indian women were also influential in creating other patterns of sexual conduct through their own relationships with both Algonquian men and Frenchmen. The influence of these women was not felt everywhere; necessarily, it was confined to groups in which the Jesuits had succeeded in making a significant number of converts: the Huron-Petuns, the Kiskakon Ottawas, and above all the Kaskaskias of the Illinois confederation.[32]

The influence of Christian women emerged most clearly among the Illinois. In the late seventeenth and early eighteenth centuries, there were signs of sexual crisis among the Illinois. They had a badly skewed sex ratio, which Deliette, probably exaggerating, estimated at four women to each man. The Illinois themselves thought that their traditional marriage pattern was in decay, and in French accounts, they combined draconian punishments for adultery with widespread sexual liaisons between Frenchman and Indian women. By 1692 the Illinois had largely abandoned Starved Rock and had built villages at the southern end of Lake Peoria, thus creating a new collection of villages at Pimitoui. The French who accompanied the Illinois had built the second Fort Saint Louis near these villages. Pimitoui also served as the headquarters for Jesuit mission activity among the Illinois and surrounding nations. Father Gravier, missionary to the Illinois since 1688 or 1689, established a permanent mission there in 1693. By 1696 the priest estimated that over the preceding six years he had baptized some two thousand persons. Even allowing for large numbers of deathbed baptisms and baptisms of infants who did not grow up to be practicing Catholics, this is a substantial figure. Much of Gravier's lasting success took place among the Illinois, particularly among the young women, who, according to Deliette, "often profit by their teaching and mock at the superstitions of their nation. This often greatly incenses the old men."[33]

By the 1690s the differential sexual appeal of Catholic teaching began to have significant repercussions among the Illinois. This, in turn, influenced the way the French and Illinois societies were linked. Jesuit teaching among the Illinois in the 1690s stressed the cult of the Virgin Mary, and with it came a heavy emphasis on chastity and virginity. This stress on a powerful female religious figure, whose power, like that of the Jesuits, was connected with sexual abstinence, attracted a congregation composed largely of women, particularly young women and older girls. How these young women understood Christianity and the cult of the Virgin is not entirely clear. They may have identified it in terms of women's ritual organizations, but given their tendency to mock Illinois traditions, they also clearly saw it in opposition to existing religious practices. During a period of warfare, direct cultural challenge by the Jesuits, population decline, and, if French accounts are correct, widespread violence of men against women, the actions of these women had direct social and cultural implications. Women took the common Algonquian dictum that unmarried women were "masters of their own body" and justified not sexual experimentation but sexual abstinence. They then assayed the religious powers they derived from prayer and Catholic doctrine against the powers the elders derived from visions and tradition. Their actions outraged both the young men, who found their own sexual opportunities diminished, and the elders and shamans who were directly challenged.[34]

In this dispute, Christianity and the Algonquians' social and cultural world were becoming part of a single field of action, and the outcome influenced not just Algonquian but also French society. Frenchmen in the West were no more enthusiastic about the new Christian influence among Illinois women than were Illinois men. Frenchmen, too, resented the new ability of Jesuits, through their influence over women, to control the sexual lives of the coureurs de bois and the voyageurs. Their resentment went beyond this.

Jesuit influence threatened not only sexual activity but also the ability of traders and coureurs de bois to create the ties to Algonquian society on which their trade, and perhaps their lives, depended.

The critical issue here was not casual liaisons, but marriage. Formal marriages between Indian women and Frenchmen were quite rare during the seventeenth century. Marriage *à la façon du pays*, that is, according to local Algonquian custom, may have occurred, but there are few references to interracial marriage of any kind until the 1690s. In 1698 Father St. Cosme mentioned voyageurs with Illinois wives, and about the same time Father Carheil mentioned other voyageurs at Michilimackinac who had married among the Indians. In theory, the Jesuits and the colonial elite in general might have been expected to approve marriage between Frenchmen and Indian women as an alternative to the unregulated sexual relationships of the *pays d'en haut*. Along the same line, the French voyageurs, operating in a world of abundant sexual opportunities, might have been expected to be indifferent to formal conjugal ties. In fact, however, their positions were nearly the opposite during the 1690s. The seemingly sudden rise of interracial marriages in the 1690s may be connected with the increasingly serious attempts of the French to force the coureurs de bois out of the *pays d'en haut*. These culminated in the French abandonment of most western posts in the late 1690s. Through marriage, the coureurs de bois may have been attempting to establish the necessary kin connections with Indians that would be vital to the ability of any Frenchman to remain safely in the West.[35]

Such attempts met with considerable sympathy from French commanders, usually with trading interests of their own, who were responsible not for larger policies but for day-to-day relations with the Indians. Both Henry de Tonti and the Sieur de la Forest at Fort Saint Louis supported attempts to fortify ties with the Illinois through intermarriage. Cadillac's plan for Detroit in the early eighteenth century included the promotion of marriages between soldiers and Indian women. He explained: "Marriages of this kind will strengthen the friendship of these tribes, as the alliances of the Romans perpetuated peace with the Sabines through the intervention of the women whom the former had taken from the others."[36]

Indians, like the commanders, saw marriage as an integral part of their alliance with the French. Male heads of families, at least, greeted marriages enthusiastically. Marriage, far more than the prevailing French liaisons with hunting women, put sex firmly in the political arena. As both sides recognized, marriage was an alliance between families that concerned many more people than the marital partners. Not only did property move into the hands of the bride's family, but kinship relations were established that enabled both families to call on their relatives for aid and protection. Because of the wider social implications of marriage, as compared to relations with hunting women, a woman found her family much more interested in her choice of a permanent French partner than in her casual liaisons.[37]

Jesuits and higher French officials, however, were unenthusiastic about marriage both because it gave voyageurs and coureurs de bois an independent hold in the *pays d'en haut* and also for racist reasons. The Jesuits did not favor interracial marriage in the seventeenth century. Their preferred solution to the problems of sexual morality was to banish most Frenchmen from the upper country and to place those who remained under strict Jesuit supervision. Gradually, however, the Jesuits and other priests in upper Louisiana came to condone interracial marriage if the wife was Catholic. Of twenty-one baptisms recorded at the French village of Kaskaskia between 1704 and 1713, the mother was Indian and the father was French in eighteen cases. In 1714, the Sieur de la Vente, the curé for Louisiana, praised intermarriage as a way to people the colony. He contended that the women of the Illinois and neighboring tribes were "whiter, more laborious, more adroit, better housekeepers, and more docile" than Indian women found elsewhere in the West and the South.[38]

Leading colonial officials were much more consistent in their opposition to intermarriage than the priests were. In Canada they preferred that Frenchmen marry and settle around Quebec or Montreal. As long as official policy involved the suppression of the

The Middle Ground

coureurs de bois and their removal from the West, officials could not be openly enthusiastic about marriages there. They coupled such policy considerations with racist disgust at the results of French-Indian intermarriage. As Governor de Vaudreuil explained in opposing interracial marriage at Detroit in 1709: "Bad should never be mixed with good. Our experience of them in this country ought to prevent us from permitting marriages of this kind, for all the Frenchmen who have married savages have been licentious, lazy and intolerably independent; and their children have been characterized by as great a slothfulness as the savages themselves." By the time he was governor of Louisiana, Cadillac, who had once advocated intermarriage, and his intendant, Duclos, opposed intermarriage in the same terms. Indian women were, they said, licentious and would leave men who did not please them, and even if the marriage lasted, the result would be a population of "mulattos [*mulâtres*], idlers, libertines, and even more knaves than [there] are in the Spanish colonies."[39]

Given this range of social and cultural concerns, the divisions within each society, and the inevitability of members of both societies being integral figures in deciding outcomes, it is not surprising that the prospect of a marriage between a Christian Illinois woman and a Frenchman precipitated a crisis that was ultimately decided on the middle ground. In 1694 Michel Accault's attempt to wed Aramepinchieue brought to light both the full complexity of the relations between the two societies and the processes by which the middle ground was emerging.

The controversy over the marriage of Accault and Aramepinchieue did not pit the Illinois against the French. Rather, it divided each group in a way that can only be grasped by looking at the social positions of the bride and the groom. Aramepinchieue was the daughter of Rouensa, a leading Kaskaskia chief. She was a fervent Christian and the pride of the Illinois mission. Michel Accault was a Frenchman who had first come west with La Salle. He had later accompanied Father Hennepin on his voyage to the Sioux.

Afterward, he had traded widely in the West and had established a reputation among the Jesuits as a libertine and an enemy of the faith. Aramepinchieue thus had links both with the Kaskaskia elite and Father Gravier. Accault was leagued with Henry de Tonti and the Frenchmen around him at Fort Saint Louis and was an enemy of Gravier's. His marriage with Aramepinchieue would strengthen the connections of a prominent Kaskaskia family with the French to the benefit of both. Rouensa announced the marriage in precisely those terms. He was strengthening his alliance with the French.[40]

The problem was that this proposed union, while it might link French and Algonquians, also emphasized the internal divisions within each group. Aramepinchieue refused to marry Accault. Father Gravier supported her decision. His immediate target was Accault. He would not sanction the influence within Indian society of a Frenchman he regarded as dissolute. He might grudgingly permit the marriage of Catholic Frenchmen with Christian Indian women, but he would do so only in circumstances that would advance the cause of the true faith. He told Aramepinchieue's parents and her suitor that "God did not command her not to marry, but also that she could not be forced to do so; that she alone was mistress to do the one or the other." Gravier's statement demonstrates that no matter how repressive Catholic morality may appear in retrospect, it could be used to buttress women's influence over their lives and their families. Women like Aramepinchieue had always had some control over their choice of marriage partners, but Christianity presented them with a new mechanism of control. What made this unique was not the woman's ability to reject unwanted suitors but, rather, the allies who could be mustered to maintain her decision against family pressures.[41]

In one sense, Aramepinchieue's decision represents a clear rejection of Algonquian norms and an appeal to an alien set of standards, but in another sense Aramepinchieue was appealing to such standards only to strengthen a very Algonquian sense of a woman's autonomy. Gravier's assertion that she was "mistress to

The Middle Ground

do either the one or the other" did, after all, echo the Algonquian tenet that unmarried women were "masters" of their own bodies. Gravier, who sought to subvert traditional Illinois sexual practices because they contradicted Catholicism, and Aramepinchieue, who used Catholicism to maintain the values that supported those same practices, thus found themselves allies. By definition, then—the involvement of both French and Indians, the need for members of each group to get assistance from members of the other to fulfill desires arising within their own society, and the inability of either French or Indian norms to govern the situation—this was a conflict of the middle ground.

The initial result of the bride's refusal was a standoff, which both Rouensa and the French commander tried to break with the limited coercive means available to them. Rouensa drove Aramepinchieue from his house, but she was protected by Father Gravier, who secured her shelter with a neophyte family. Her rejection of her parents' wishes pained her deeply, but she justified her actions by appeals to Catholic doctrine. The chiefs in council retaliated by attempting to halt Catholic services at the chapel. At least fifty persons, virtually all of them women and girls, persisted in going to church. The council then (although they denied it) appears to have dispatched a warrior armed with a club to disrupt the services. The women defied him. Among the Illinois, the opposing sides had clearly formed along gender lines. Not all of the women abandoned the chiefs, but Christianity was, for the moment, a women's religious society acting in defiance of a male council. Among the French, the division was necessarily among males. The French commander, far from stopping this interference with the mission, gloated over it and denounced Gravier publicly before both the French and the Indians. When these tactics failed to sway the priest, neither the commander nor Rouensa felt confident enough to escalate the level of violence, although the Kaskaskias left the option of further coercion open.[42]

Such a face-off did not serve the interests of either side. Aramepinchieue was in turmoil over her alienation from her parents, to whom she was closely attached. Gravier found further missionary activities virtually impossible in the face of council opposition, which threatened to confine his promising mission to a besieged group of young women and girls. On the other hand, Gravier and the bride together blocked a marriage that both the Kaskaskias and the French deeply wanted.

The situation, in the end, was solved by a series of trade-offs. Aramepinchieue, in effect, negotiated a compromise with her father. She told Gravier, "I think that if I consent to the marriage, he will listen to you in earnest, and will induce all to do so," and she consented to the marriage on the terms that her parents, in turn, "grant me what I ask." They agreed. Rouensa disavowed his opposition to Christianity in full council and urged those present to "obey now the black gown." His agreement was sincere, and he and his wife began instruction for baptism. Accault, too, became a practicing Catholic once more and an ally of the Jesuits. In return, the Kaskaskia chief, as he informed the other headmen of the confederation with considerable presents, was "about to be allied to a Frenchman."[43]

The marriage, therefore, was a great coup for Gravier. It brought into the church the most prominent Kaskaskia civil leader and his brother, an equally prominent war leader, and opened the way for making the Kaskaskias the most Catholic of the western Algonquians. The main agent in these events was a seventeen-year-old woman who appealed to alien standards both to control her condition and, eventually, to alter the condition of her nation. By 1711 the Kaskaskias were supposedly virtually all Catholic, and missionaries had made significant inroads among other Illinois groups. Aramepinchieue had maintained and strengthened the relationships that mattered most to her—those with her parents and the Christian congregation of women. The price was marriage to Accault, but this may very well have remained for her a subsidiary social arrangement. Christianity did not immediately transform marriage. French officials would later claim that Christian Illinois women less devout than Aramepinchieue still felt free to leave their French husbands whenever they chose.[44]

Women like Aramepinchieue are rarely visible in the documents, but their traces appear everywhere. Diplomatic negotiations and warfare, the large trading expeditions, these were the work of men, but the Frenchmen who appeared in Algonquian villages either traveled with Algonquian women or had liaisons with them there. Much of their petty trading was probably with women. The labor they purchased was usually that of women. On a day-to-day basis, women did more than men to weave the French into the fabric of a common Algonquian-French life. Both in and out of marriage, these women bore children with the French, some of whom in time would come to form a separate people, the *métis*, who themselves mediated between French and Algonquians and became of critical importance to the area.

Gravier himself would continue to make his greatest gains among the women of the Illinois, but in other tribes of the confederation he would not acquire allies of the status of Aramepinchieue. In 1706 Gravier returned to Pimitoui. The Kaskaskias had by now left to resettle on the Mississippi, the French had abandoned Fort Saint Louis, and the Peorias who remained at the site resented Gravier's aggressive tactics enough to attack him physically. They wounded him and, revealingly, left him in the care of "some praying women" until Kaskaskias sent by Rouensa rescued the priest. Father Gravier never fully recovered from his wounds, and eventually he died of complications. His death, a reminder of how tentative and tenuous the middle ground could be, also serves as a transition to the second issue demanding French-Algonquian cooperation—violence and interracial murder.[45]

III

Although not all murders, as the killing of Father Gravier demonstrates, grew out of the trade, violence and interracial murder as a whole were inextricably bound up with commerce. In 1684 alone, the only year for which a summary is given, thirty-nine Frenchmen trading in the West died at the hands of their Algonquian allies. Indians murdered Frenchmen during robberies, killed them in disputes over debt or gift exchanges, attacked them in attempts to stop weapons from going to their enemies, killed them to avenge killings by the French, and, as the liquor trade expanded, killed them in drunken quarrels. The French, in turn, used force against thieves, which did not prevent theft from becoming as established a part of the exchange as gifts or bargaining.[46]

Commerce, in short, was not a peaceful process; violence was an option both for acquiring goods and for protecting them. In part, violence was so prevalent in the early trade because common agreement on the nature of the exchange itself developed only gradually. Frenchmen did not always meet Indian demands for gifts; they did not act as generously as friends and allies should; they, as the Indians soon discovered, asked more for their goods than the English asked; and finally, Frenchmen supplied arms to their allies' enemies. The Indians, in turn, stole. French traders readily classified Algonquian nations by their propensity to steal. The Fox were thieving; the Illinois carried off everything they could lay their hands on; the Chippewas on the north shore of Lake Superior would pillage any French canoe they caught alone. The Sauks were also thieves, but they did not have the skill of the neighboring Fox. When the French were supplying the Sioux, small-scale theft gave way to organized plunder, so that Father Nouvel thought no Frenchman's life was safe journeying to or from the Sioux country. Eventually theft itself became institutionalized, as French traders learned to leave out small items to be pilfered, but a certain level of violence remained endemic to the trade.[47]

Perhaps the most perplexing intercultural concern of the French and the Algonquians was how to settle and limit the number of murders arising from the trade, when there was no authority in the West capable of creating a monopoly on violence and establishing order. Violence became one of the central concerns of the middle ground. When murders occurred between Algonquians and Frenchmen, each side brought quite different cultural formulas to bear on the situation. For northeastern Indians, both Algonquians and Iroquoians, those people killed by allies could be compensated for with gifts or by slaves or, failing these, by the killing of another member of the offending group. The decision about how to proceed was made by the dead person's kin, but extensive social pressure was usually exerted to accept compensation short of blood revenge, since killing a person of the offending group often only invited future retaliation. Among the French the matter was simpler. Society at large took the responsibility for punishing murder. Punishment was not left to the kin of the victim but rather to the state. The expected compensation for murder was the death of the murderer.[48]

Of the obvious differences here, two were particularly important. In the French scheme of things, exactly who committed the murder was of supreme importance, since the individual killer was held responsible for the crime. Only when a group refused to surrender a known murderer did collective responsibility arise. For the Indians, identifying the murderer was not as important as establishing the identity of the group to which the murderer belonged, for it was the group—family, kin, village, or nation—that was held responsible for the act. Both sides established cultural measures of equivalence in compensating for the dead, but the French equivalence was invariably another death. As the French emphasized again and again in the cases that follow, death could only be compensated for by more death. Indians would, if necessary, also invoke a similar doctrine of revenge, but their preference was always either, in their words, "to raise up the dead," that is, to restore the dead person to life by providing a slave in the victim's place, or "to cover the dead," that is, present the relatives with goods that served as an equivalent.[49]

Most murders in the West left no trace in the documents, but an examination of those that are recorded can be rewarding. Three incidents in particular offer enough documentation for cultural analysis. The first occurred in 1682 or 1683, when two Frenchmen were waylaid on the Keweenaw Peninsula in Lake Superior and murdered by a Menominee and several Chippewas. These murders took place when the *pays d'en haut* was in a state of near chaos. Iroquois attacks, which had devastated the Illinois, had so far gone unavenged. Iroquois parties had recently struck the Illinois and the Mascoutens and were edging closer to Green Bay itself. Not only did the French seem unable to protect their allies, but an epidemic that the Potawatomis blamed on Jesuit witchcraft had recently ravaged the villages around the bay. The Potawatomis had murdered two French donnés in retaliation and had begun efforts to create a larger anti-French alliance. A recent alliance between the Saulteurs and the Sioux, which Daniel Greysolon Dulhut had helped orchestrate, had further inflamed the peoples of Green Bay against the French. They attempted to block French trade with the Sioux. The Fox had already fought and defeated a large Sioux-Chippewa force at a considerable loss to themselves, and a full-scale Chippewa-Fox war seemed imminent. But apparently not all the Chippewas relished the new alignment. Achiganaga, an important headman at Keweenaw, had attacked the Sioux and planned further attacks. His war parties, as well as those of the peoples at Green Bay, threatened the lives of French voyageurs.[50]

In the midst of this turmoil a party led by Achiganaga's sons and including at least one Menominee, a member of a Green Bay tribe, murdered two Frenchmen. Their motive may have been robbery. Or Achiganaga may have sought to disrupt the Sioux trade, break the new alliance of other proto-Ojibwa bands with the Sioux, and join with the peoples of the bay in a large anti-French movement. In any case, his sons murdered two Frenchmen and stole their goods. Dulhut, despite the powerful kin connections of the accused murderers, seized the Menominee at Sault Sainte Marie and sent out a party that successfully captured Achiganaga and all his children at Keweenaw. The local Algonquian peoples reacted to Dulhut's acts by resorting to customary procedures. The Saulteurs offered the French the calumet—the standard ceremony for establishing peace and amity—and then they offered slaves to resurrect the dead Frenchmen and end the matter. Dulhut's emissary refused all such offers and denied the legitimacy of such cultural equivalence, telling them "that a hundred slaves and a hundred packages of beaver could not make him traffic in the blood of his brothers."[51]

Up to this point, all seems to be merely another example of something that appears in the literature many times: an ethnocentric European imposing by force proper cultural forms on a people he regards as savages. Savagism as a way of looking at Indians was, however, of limited utility in the woods. Dulhut was hardly in a position to act as if Indians were without culture. The French state did not command a monopoly of violence in the West and its authority was feeble. Dulhut did not have an established judicial system to appeal to, unless he wished to try to convey his prisoners to Quebec or Montreal. When the murderers had been disposed of, he and his men would remain to travel among the surrounding Indians who were not likely to forget whatever action he took. Their thoughts on the matter could not be safely ignored, and Dulhut, having rejected Indian norms, relaxed his own considerably.

What followed at Michilimackinac was a series of rather extraordinary improvisations as Dulhut and various Ottawa, Huron-Petun, and Chippewa headmen and elders struggled to create a middle ground where the matter could be resolved. Dulhut's primary appeal throughout was to French law and custom, but he tried repeatedly, if necessarily somewhat ignorantly, to justify his recourse to law and custom by equating them with Indian practices. Having rejected the preferred means of settling killings among allies—the covering or raising up of the dead—he insisted on the penalty exacted from enemies: blood revenge. The Indians, for their part, paid little attention to what mattered most to the French, the proper way of establishing guilt and punishing the perpetrator. They only sought to offer suitable compensation to the living and reestablish social peace.[52]

Richard White

The result was a series of bizarre cultural hybrids. The various Ottawa, Chippewa, and Huron-Petun bands convened in council with Dulhut only to find themselves transformed into a jury by the French for the trial of the Menominee, Achiganaga, and two of his sons. Kinsmen of the accused were drafted as lawyers, testimony was given and written down, and the murderers, with the exception of Achiganaga, freely admitted the crime. The elders cooperated with this French ritual, apparently believing that after it was performed the French would accept appropriate compensation. Instead, Dulhut demanded that the Indians themselves execute the murderers. To the Indians, Achiganaga's failure to confess constituted acquittal, and he was no longer part of the proceedings, but execution of the remaining three men, after compensation had been refused, would have been the equivalent of a declaration of war on the Saulteurs and Menominees by the executioners. The elders were so shocked and confused by this demand that they did not even make an answer.[53]

Dulhut, at this point, decided unilaterally to execute the Menominee and the two sons of Achiganaga as the admittedly guilty parties. This decision not only upset the Indians at Michilimackinac, it also appalled the French wintering at Keweenaw, who sent Dulhut a message warning that if he executed the murderers, the Indians' relatives would take revenge on the French. They begged him to act with restraint. French standards simply could not be imposed with impunity. Dulhut, after consulting with the Sieur de La Tour, the man longest among the lake tribes and most familiar with their customs, sought once more to appeal to Indian custom and return the matter to the middle ground. He again tried to find some connection between French law and what he regarded as Indian custom. Since two Frenchmen had died, Dulhut would execute only two Indians—the Menominee and the eldest of the two sons of Achiganaga—for "by killing man for man, the savages would have nothing to say, since that is their own practice." He announced this decision in the cabin of an Ottawa headman the French called Le

Brochet, adding that although French law and custom demanded the execution of all the men involved in the robbery, he would be content with a life for a life.[54]

By his decision, Dulhut established a tenuous connection between Algonquian and French customs—a life for a life—but he also revealed the very different meanings such a dictum had in each culture. Only now, according to Dulhut, did the Ottawas believe that the French would actually execute two of the men. The headmen of the Sable Ottawas and the Sinago Ottawas, themselves uninvolved in the murder, begged Dulhut to spare the murderers. They, too, sought a middle ground and appealed to French precedent. At the request of Onontio, the Ottawas had spared an Iroquois prisoner. The French should now do the same for them. Dulhut denied the situations were equivalent. The Iroquois was a prisoner of war; these men were murderers. Here the glaring differences between Ottawa and French cultural categories emerged in action.[55]

Blood revenge was appropriate in each society but for different categories of killing. For the Algonquians there were two kinds of killings—deaths at the hands of enemies and deaths at the hands of allies. The appropriate response depended on the identity of the group to whom the killer belonged. If the killer belonged to an allied group, then the dead were raised or covered. If the murderers refused to do this, then the group became enemies and the price appropriate to enemies, blood revenge, was exacted. For the French also there were two kinds of killings—killings in war and murders. Killing enemies in war theoretically brought no retribution once the battle ended. For them, the battlefield was a cultural arena separate from the rest of life. Releasing the Iroquois was thus only appropriate; he was a soldier, not a murderer. Algonquians in practice recognized no such cultural arena as a battlefield; they killed their enemies when and where they found them unless they were ritually protected. For the French it was murder that demanded blood revenge; for the Algonquians, it was killings by enemies, killings which the French saw as warfare. The French insistence on blood revenge in an inappropriate category, therefore, created great confusion. To the Ottawas the logic of such a response—that enemies should be spared but that allies should be killed—was incomprehensible.[56]

The way out of this deadlock was created by a man named Oumamens, a headman of the Amikwas (a proto-Ojibwa group). He spoke for the Saulteurs in council and resorted to the kind of cultural fiction that often disguises the beginnings of cultural change. He got up and praised, of all things, Dulhut's mercy, because he had released Achiganaga and all but one of his children. In effect, Oumamens chose to emphasize those of Dulhut's actions which conformed to Algonquian custom. He announced that the Saulteurs were satisfied. Dulhut, for his part, stressed not mercy but deterrence. If the elders "had from the beginning made known to the young men that in case they committed any evil deed the tribe would abandon them, they would have been better advised, and the Frenchmen would still be alive." Both sides thus tended to stress the aspect of the affair that made cultural sense to them. An hour later, at the head of forty-eight Frenchmen with four hundred warriors watching, Dulhut had the two Indians executed.[57]

The executions did not establish the legitimacy of French justice. Indeed, in the days that followed the executions, the Indians treated them as two more murders to be resolved, and Dulhut consented to their proceedings. Because Achiganaga's son and the Menominee had been executed in the territory of the Huron-Petuns and the Ottawas, these groups were implicated, and they took steps to settle the whole affair.[58]

Three Ottawa tribes—the Sables, Sinagos, and Kiskakons—gave two wampum belts to the French to cover their dead and two other belts to Achiganaga and to the Menominee's relatives. The next day the Huron-Petuns did the same. Dulhut, for his part, held a feast for Le Brochet, the Sable headman, to "take away the pain that I had caused him by pronouncing the death sentence of the two savages in his cabin, without speaking to him of it." Dulhut

The Middle Ground

then loaded Achiganaga with presents, and the Saulteurs gave the French at Keweenaw additional belts "to take good care that no trouble be made over the death of their brother; and in order, should any have evil designs, to restrain them by these collars, of which they are bearers."[59]

The incident is revealing precisely because it was so indecisive, so improvised, precisely because neither French nor Algonquian cultural rules fully governed the situation. Both French and Algonquian customs were challenged, consciously explained, and modified in practice. Dulhut did not establish the primacy of French law, and he did not prevent further killings. What he did do was to shake, but not eliminate, the ability of Algonquian norms to govern murders of Frenchmen by Indians. Both sides now had to justify their own rules in terms of what they perceived to be the practices of the other. What happened in 1683 was, in the end, fully in accordance with neither French nor Indian conceptions of crime and punishment. Instead, it involved considerable improvisation and the creation of a middle ground at a point where the cultures seemed to intersect, so that the expectations of each side could find at least some satisfaction. At Green Bay the next spring, Father Nouvel thought that Dulhut's executions had produced a good effect, but at the same time he attributed the Potawatomi and Sauk desire for reconciliation with the French to their growing fear of the Iroquois, not their fear of French reprisals. Nouvel, for his part, demanded no further executions; he was willing to accept the Potawatomi and Sauk offer to cover the deaths of the two French donnés they had murdered.[60]

At Michilimackinac in 1683, Dulhut had operated without specific authority from the French government for his actions. He had improvised his solutions. The killings at Detroit, some twenty years later, in 1706, led to negotiations with the highest colonial officials, at a time when the French-Algonquian alliance had created a considerably more elaborate middle ground on which Indians and Frenchmen might work. Indeed, it was the alliance itself that both created the conditions that caused the murders and provided the ceremonial forms that compensated for them.

IV

In 1706, as Ottawa warriors departed to attack the Sioux, a Potawatomi warned them that in their absence the Huron-Petuns and the Miamis would fall on the Ottawa village and kill those who remained. The Ottawa war leaders consulted with the civil leaders and, although some wavered, the old and powerful Sable chief whom the French called Le Pesant convinced them to strike first. The Ottawas ambushed a party of Miami chiefs, killing five of them, and then attacked the Miami village, driving the inhabitants into the French fort. The French fired on the attacking Ottawas and killed a young Ottawa who had just been recognized as a war leader. Although the Ottawa leaders tried to prevent any attacks on the French, angry warriors killed a French Recollect priest outside the fort and a soldier who came out to rescue him.[61]

The Ottawas tried all the ceremonial means at their disposal to effect a reconciliation with the French, but they were rebuffed by the man commanding in Cadillac's absence. In subsequent fighting, the French sided with the Miamis, as did the Huron-Petuns (the nation the Ottawas claimed had actually organized the plot against them). Before the Ottawas withdrew to Michilimackinac, three Frenchmen, about thirty Ottawas, fifty Miamis, and an unknown number of Huron-Petuns were dead. The critical issue between the French and Ottawas, however, was the men killed during the first exchange: the young Ottawa leader, another Ottawa man with powerful kin connections at Michilimackinac, the Recollect, and the first French soldier killed.[62]

The fighting at Detroit in 1706 sprang from some basic breaches in the alliance the French had constructed and threatened to dissolve the alliance completely. In his zeal to promote Detroit, a post he had founded in 1701, Cadillac had recruited French allies to settle there without much thought for the outstanding disputes among them. In 1706, the residents included, among others, members of three Ottawa tribes—Sinagos, Kiskakons, and Sables—Huron-Petuns, and Miamis. Basic to the alliance and critical to such multitribal settlements was mediation. The French had to make sure that killings between the tribes were settled and the dead covered. Cadillac had promised to do this, but uncovered and unrevenged dead continued to poison the relations between the Miamis and the Huron-Petuns, on the one hand, and the Ottawas on the other. Le Pesant himself had presented a list of the dead left uncovered and unavenged before the departure of the fateful war party. The result of the French refusal to act was the fighting of 1706 and a threat to the entire alliance.[63]

The killings at Detroit produced a situation neither the French nor the Ottawa leaders desired. As Vaudreuil lamented in his report of the affair to Count de Pontchartrain, the fiasco at Detroit threatened to "begin a war which can cause us only considerable expense, the loss of a nation that has served us faithfully, and, in addition to that, a considerable trade, every year." For the Ottawas the outcome looked no more favorable. Cut off from trade goods, impoverished, and driven from their fields, they found that "all the land was stupefied, and want had taken possession of our bones." Settling such a conflict was, however, far from simple. The prominence of the dead on both sides intensified the difficulties of settling the killings. The dead Ottawas had powerful kinspeople; the French stressed the particular horror of killing a priest; and Cadillac promised the Miamis and Huron-Petuns the destruction of the Ottawas as revenge for their own dead. The negotiations to resolve these killings would be, according to Governor de Vaudreuil, one of the most important affairs in the history of the upper country.[64]

The ceremonial forms of the Ottawa-French alliance shaped the negotiations from the beginning. The alliance was centered on Quebec, the home of Onontio, and it was formulated in the language of kinship to which both the French and the Algonquians attached great significance. Leaders of both the French and the

Algonquians negotiated according to ritual forms which placed the French governor, Onontio, in the position of father to the Indians, of whom the Ottawas were his eldest sons. The French were quite at home with such patriarchal formulations and attached quite specific meanings to them. For them all authority was patriarchal, from God the Father, to the king (the father of his people), to the father in his home. Fathers commanded; sons obeyed. The Ottawas understood the relationship somewhat differently. A father was kind, generous, and protecting. A child owed a father respect, but a father could not compel obedience. In establishing a middle ground, one took such congruences as one could find and sorted out their meanings later.[65]

Within the alliance, these ritual forms for father and son thus had a built-in ambiguity that would influence the course of the negotiations that followed the fighting at Detroit. Negotiations in the West (at Sault Sainte Marie and Michilimackinac) covered the Ottawa dead to that nation's satisfaction, but covering the French dead proved more difficult. Many of the matters at issue here revolved around questions of the proper way for a father to act toward his errant sons. At Quebec, Vaudreuil, in his negotiations with the Ottawas in the fall of 1706 and the spring of 1707, insisted on phrasing the alliance and Ottawa obligations in terms of Christian patriarchy. The governor demanded that the Ottawas appear before him as penitent sinners appear before the Christian God. The customary Ottawa compensation for the dead was inadequate and inappropriate.

> I am a good father and as long as my children listen to my voice, no evil ever befalls them. . . . It is not belts that I require, Miscouaky, nor presents when my children have disobeyed me and committed such a fault as yours; the blood of Frenchmen is not to be paid for by beaverskins. It is a great trust in my kindness that I demand; a real repentance for the fault that has been committed, and complete resignation to my will. When your people entertain those feelings, I will arrange everything.[66]

The Ottawa response to these demands, in the usual manner of the middle ground, was to seek cultural congruence. They, too, focused on patriarchy, but of a different kind. Otontagan (or Jean le Blanc), the Sable chief second in influence to Le Pesant, spoke for the Ottawas when they came to Quebec the next summer. He admitted his guilt (even though he had, in fact, tried to save the Recollect) but attempted to place the primary responsibility for the affair with Le Pesant. Otontagan's major concern, however, was to get Vaudreuil to act like an Ottawa, not a French, father. He stressed Vaudreuil's beneficence. Vaudreuil certainly had the power to kill him, but "I have nothing to fear because I have a good father." Since Vaudreuil had specifically rejected covering the dead, Otontagan concluded that he must want the dead raised up. The delegation accordingly brought two adopted captives to give to Vaudreuil "to bring the gray coat again to life." Vaudreuil held out for a stricter patriarchy. He demanded vengeance; he demanded the head of Le Pesant because "the blood of French is usually repaid among us only by blood." But such a demand, Otontagan told Vaudreuil, was impossible. Le Pesant was allied to all the nations of the Great Lakes. They would prevent his delivery and execution.[67]

On the surface, the negotiations at Quebec appear to be another example of a stubborn French refusal to compromise. The situation was, in fact, much more complex. Vaudreuil knew that no Ottawa leader possessed sufficient authority to hand over anyone, let alone someone of Le Pesant's stature. His intention was not to secure Le Pesant's death, rather it was to cut him off from the French alliance, destroy his influence, and demonstrate that any chief held responsible for the death of a Frenchman would suffer the same fate. Since Vaudreuil did not expect Le Pesant to be surrendered, the actual restoration of the Ottawas to the alliance would involve a compromise of some sort. Since patriarchs do not compromise, he sent the Ottawas back to Detroit, telling them to negotiate a peace with Cadillac. He would approve such a peace as long as Le Pesant was not included in any pardon Cadillac granted. By this maneuver Vaudreuil could make an impossible demand, while leaving the responsibility of negotiating what might be an embarrassing compromise to his rival and subordinate, Cadillac.[68]

At Detroit the larger issue remained—how the alliance could be restored within the cultural parameters of the parties involved. Le Pesant was called "that great bear, that malicious bear," and Vaudreuil's demand for his execution loomed over the proceedings. The people struggling with this problem were themselves political actors who were not necessarily wedded to the welfare of either Le Pesant or Vaudreuil. The chief Ottawa negotiators, Otontagan and Onaske from Michilimackinac, were Le Pesant's political rivals. They protected him not out of love but because they had no means at their disposal to deliver him, and they feared the repercussions if they tried. Cadillac, for his part, was a long-standing opponent of Vaudreuil and only too glad to use the affair to benefit himself and embarrass the governor. Both Cadillac and the Ottawa chiefs could conceivably use the cultural demands of outsiders to advance their interests within their own society while simultaneously renewing the alliance.[69]

The willingness of both Cadillac and the Ottawa negotiators to move from their initial positions reflects this sense of their own political advantage. They could also violate the usual norms of their own cultures because the alliance, itself the middle ground, created cultural demands of its own. Cadillac shifted his position first. He indicated that the surrender of Le Pesant was more important than his death. "I wish him to be in my power, either to grant him his life or put him to death," he told Otontagan. Cadillac was, in effect, putting Le Pesant in the place of the slaves or captives usually given to raise the dead. Such cultural logic was more comprehensible to the Ottawas than a demand for execution, even if the surrender of a chief was without precedent. These were unusual conditions; the alliance itself was at stake. Otontagan agreed to deliver Le Pesant: "He is my brother, my own brother, but what can we do?" Since Otontagan and Kinouge, another headman, were, like Le Pesant,

Sable Ottawas, they agreed to take responsibility for his surrender, thus making the matter an internal Sable matter and limiting the repercussions. In effect, a cultural fiction was agreed on. Cadillac and the Ottawas agreed to act as if Le Pesant were a slave being offered to the French in compensation for their dead. Cadillac would then determine if he lived or died. This made cultural sense in a way that Le Pesant's execution did not; it preserved the alliance, and it served the personal interests of both French and Ottawa negotiators.[70]

There were two formidable obstacles to this solution. The first was the Miamis and the Huron-Petuns, whom Cadillac had made simple observers of the whole affair. For their benefit, Cadillac treated the Ottawa delegation imperiously. He gave the Huron-Petuns—and tried to give the Miamis—the Ottawa captives intended for Vaudreuil in order "to revive your dead a little—I do not say altogether." He even, in council, made the Huron-Petuns the elder brothers of the French alliance in place of the Ottawas. But he denied them revenge. He warned both nations that with the delivery of Le Pesant, he would consider the matter closed. "There shall be no blood left to be seen."[71]

The second obstacle was a practical one: Who exactly would persuade or force Le Pesant to consent to serve as a slave to the French? Who provided the solution to this problem is not known, but how it was solved is clear enough. A proceeding that had been half theater and half negotiation now became fully theater. After considerable negotiations at Michilimackinac, Le Pesant agreed to come to Detroit and surrender himself as a slave to the French. According to Vaudreuil, all that followed was prearranged between Le Pesant and an emissary of Cadillac. How much the other Ottawas or other Frenchmen knew of these arrangements is not clear.[72]

Cadillac compared the astonishment provoked by the appearance of Le Pesant at Detroit to that produced by the arrival of the Doge of Genoa in France. To evoke such a response, to make the Indians marvel at the culturally unimaginable things Cadillac and the French could achieve, was, in fact, the sole point of the drama now enacted at Detroit. Cadillac's production of "The Surrender of Le Pesant," however, had to play to a suspicious and critical audience of Miamis, Huron-Petuns, and those French officials who watched from afar. All of them were concerned not so much with the plots as with the culturally symbolic details that gave the drama its meaning. Vaudreuil delivered the most extended review of the performance, although, as shall be seen, the Miamis were the most critical.[73]

Le Pesant, until now the Godot of this drama, put in his appearance at Detroit on September 24, 1707. He delivered his only recorded lines while looking to shore from the canoe that brought him. He trembled, either from malaria or fear, and said, "I see I am a dead man." Yet what Vaudreuil noted was his escort. He came with ten warriors who were not Kiskakon or Sinago Ottawas, but Sable Ottawas from his own village. They were sent, Vaudreuil said, not to deliver him but to protect him from angry Huron-Petuns and Miamis. Cadillac verbally abused Le Pesant, referring to him as his slave, but Cadillac spoke to Le Pesant on a wampum belt. One did not speak to slaves on wampum. One spoke to representatives of nations in that manner. The Ottawas then asked for Le Pesant's life and, offering a young slave, asked that they be allowed to return to Detroit.[74]

With Le Pesant's ritual submission, the first act ended. Le Pesant, Vaudreuil pointed out, had served his purpose. His continued presence now became a problem for Cadillac. Vaudreuil had ordered his death and Cadillac had earlier promised the Miamis and Huron-Petuns that he would kill him. But if Cadillac actually killed Le Pesant, he risked conflict with the Sable Ottawas and their allies on the Great Lakes. Le Pesant's surrender was useful; his continued presence was not.[75]

Cadillac and the Ottawas solved the problem by writing Le Pesant out of the script. That night, leaving behind his shoes, his knife, and his shabby hat, Le Pesant escaped from the fort at Detroit. Cadillac, in retaliation, locked up his escorts for a day and then released them, contending that Le Pesant would perish in the woods, and, in any case, his influence was now gone. Vaudreuil was skeptical. Le Pesant—whose name translates from the French as the heavy one, or the fat one—was notoriously obese and nearly seventy years old. That a seventy-year-old fat man whose surrender had been the object of French policy in the upper country for more than a year could escape past sentinels from a French fort on the first night of his captivity strained credibility. Cadillac's only explanation was that Le Pesant had lost a lot of weight lately. With Le Pesant gone, Cadillac assured the Ottawas that he had intended to pardon him anyway, thus freeing himself from complicity in his death if the Huron-Petuns or Miamis should catch him.[76]

Vaudreuil, skeptical and critical as he was, appreciated good acting and clever staging, even as he deciphered the drama and explained away the illusions it sought to create. With both the Ottawas and the French acting according to script, the cultural demands of each had been met by creating an artificial and controlled stage, a special kind of middle ground. Vaudreuil appreciated this.[77]

The Miamis and Huron-Petuns were less enthusiastic. Their response to the drama was so harsh that Cadillac did not choose to fully report it. Instead, he reported only the closing part of the council that followed Le Pesant's escape and was attended by the Miamis, the Huron-Petuns, the French, and the Ottawas. In council, following the usual ritual forms, he calmed the waters, removed the fallen trees, smoothed the land, and opened the way for peace and the return of the Ottawas to Detroit.[78]

Unfortunately for Cadillac, the audience in historical dramas of this sort must consent to the script, for they always have the option of adding a final act. Le Pesant returned to Michilimackinac in the same canoe and with the same warriors who had escorted him down to Detroit, but this did not close the play. Cadillac had gained the Ottawas but lost the Miamis, who soon killed not only Ottawas but also Frenchmen, and so began yet another round of negotiations.

The resolution of the killings at Detroit was thus only partially successful, but the negotiations are, nevertheless, illuminating. They reveal the substantial and expanding middle ground the French-Algonquian alliance had created. Here common problems could be worked out and mutually comprehensible solutions arrived at. The negotiations also reveal the extent to which solutions could be elaborately scripted cultural fictions, political theater. Such fictions deeply influenced events in both societies.[79]

V

Once established, the middle ground was extended in surprising directions. Killings the French once considered solely their own concern became issues to be settled on the middle ground. On April 25, 1723, a French soldier spoke "impertinently" to a warehouse keeper, a man named Perillaut, who responded by running his sword through the soldier's body. The French tried Perillaut and condemned him to death, but Perillaut, as warehouse keeper (or *maître de la marchandise*, as the Indians called him), had had many dealings with the Illinois, and his death sentence disturbed them deeply. On April 29 three chiefs of the Kaskaskias, accompanied by thirty warriors, appeared to plead for his life. They were followed in early May by a Cahokia delegation that included Marie Rompiechoue (or Rokipiekoue). This woman, who was "greatly respected in her village and among the French," was the wife of a Cahokia, Joseph Ouissakatchakoue. In all likelihood, Marie Rompiechoue was Aramepinchieue, the daughter of Rouensa who had married Michel Accault thirty years earlier. The actions and speeches of these delegations, particularly those of the Kaskaskia chiefs Kiraoueria and Michel, present a clear picture of eighteenth-century Algonquian views on murder and revenge, and of how such views could influence French actions.[80]

Kiraoueria, a Kaskaskia chief who was "of the Prayer" (a Christian), held a particularly advantageous position for articulating Indian logic and extending it to French affairs. The Kaskaskias opened matters by presenting the calumet, a symbol of friendship and alliance.

The Middle Ground

The French knew from a half century of experience that to accept the calumet was to grant the giver's request. Kiraoueria then tried to bring the French to their senses. "Would you," he asked, "spill the blood of a Frenchman to blot out the blood of another and would you add to the loss of one man the loss of another?" This was folly. If the French insisted on killing someone to cover the body of the soldier, then they should strike the Fox and Chickasaws, their enemies. These people would be full of joy when they heard that the French had, in effect, avenged the Chickasaw and Fox dead by killing one another.[81]

Kiraoueria then went on to explain the Algonquian view of murder. Murderers were madmen, and no nation could glory in being free of them. But they were not permanently mad. They could be redeemed, and rather than their being killed, the relatives of their victims should be compensated and the blood of the victim covered. More blood should not be spilled on top of it. But Kiraoueria did not expect the French simply to accept Algonquian logic. In the usual manner of creating the middle ground, he connected what he was saying with French culture. He joined it with Christianity:

> I know that the Great Spirit, the Spirit Creator, God, forbids us, my father, to kill our children. . . . But does not God, who is Master of all, raise his eyes above our follies when we ask him to be no longer angry? He forgives; pardon as He does, my fathers, and for the love of Him.[82]

Finally, Kiraoueria and Michel, a war chief, appealed to the underlying basis of the middle ground, the alliance, and the symbol of peace and alliance, the calumet. Kiraoueria begged the French not to humiliate him and his chiefs by refusing their request. Michel cited times when Kaskaskias had lost their lives to avenge the French and how those warriors remained unavenged at the request of the French. Those men, warriors for whom revenge should be taken, lay uncovered, and now the Kaskaskias were being asked to watch the French take inappropriate vengeance on one another.[83]

The affair, so phrased, was, as the French commander Boisbriant realized, "a delicate matter." To send the Illinois away without a concession was dangerous, particularly when Michel had obliquely raised the matter of the uncovered Kaskaskia dead. Boisbriant, in delivering his response, insisted that the affair set no precedent, but he agreed to petition the king for Perillaut's pardon and release. Those Kaskaskias who "have died to avenge the Frenchman, cover the body of the one who has now been killed." So ended the first recorded criminal case tried by the French in Illinois. Perillaut was free that May. He owed his freedom, just as fifty years before the son of Achiganaga owed his death, to an evolving cultural logic that sprang from the convergences, some accidental, some quite close, of two different cultural systems faced with a common set of problems.[84]

Separately, the stories of Dulhut and Achiganaga's sons, of Le Pesant and Cadillac, and of Perillaut and Kiraoueria are incidents widely scattered over time and space, but together they form an evolving ritual of surrender and redemption that would be central to the French-Algonquian alliance. This ritual of the middle ground clearly drew elements from both cultures but fully corresponded to neither. The ritual operated by analogy. The murderer was to the governor as a sinner was to God. The governor was to the murderer as a stern but forgiving father was to an erring son. Such analogies were hooks, both attaching the new ritual to the purely Algonquian or French way of settling murders and pulling elements of the older process into the middle ground. As under the French system, Indian murderers would be imprisoned while their crimes were investigated; as under the Algonquian system, Indian and French dead would be covered or raised up.

Once formulated, this ritual of surrender and redemption became a centerpiece of the middle ground. Orders from Governor Duquesne to the Sieur de Pean in 1754 expressed its basic elements well: "He must manage to see that he obtains the murderers, to whom he will grant pardon in the customary manner." The ritual,

The Middle Ground

however, was under constant pressure from Frenchmen who, having seen to it that murderers were surrendered, wished to see these murderers executed, and from Algonquians who hesitated to surrender kinspeople for even temporary imprisonment before their pardon "in the customary manner." Each murder, each surrender, and each pardon thus became a test of the health of the alliance. Onontio's failure to pardon and his children's failure to surrender signaled crises that only a renewal of the ritual could resolve. Like all structural elements of culture, the ritual remained meaningful only insofar as it was constantly replicated in action.[85]

What was being created in social action was a world very different from the one historians would expect to find if they relied on the older ethnographies. Nor does the evolution of this world conform to much acculturation literature with the gradual adoption by Indians of certain European values. Instead, members of two cultures established an alliance that they both thought furthered interests generated within their own societies. They maintained this alliance through rituals and ceremonials based on cultural parallels and congruences, inexact and artificial as they originally may have been. These rituals and ceremonials were not the decorative covering of the alliance; they were its sinews. They helped bind together a common world to solve problems, even killings, that threatened the alliance itself. These solutions might have been, as at Detroit, elaborate cultural fictions, but through them change occurred. Such changes, worked out on the middle ground, could be remarkably influential, bringing important modifications in each society and blurring the boundaries between them.

Notes

1. The impossibility of considering any society in isolation is one of the major themes of Eric Wolf in *Europe and the People Without History* (Berkeley: University of California Press, 1982), 3–23, 385. It is also a position taken by Anthony Giddens, *A Contemporary Critique of Historical Materialism* (Berkeley: University of California Press, 1981), 23–24.

2. For concentration on European images, see Bernard Sheehan, *Savagism*

and Civility: Indians and Englishmen in Colonial America (Cambridge: Cambridge University Press, 1980); Olive P. Dickason, *The Myth of the Savage and the Beginnings of French Colonialism in the Americas* (Edmonton: University of Alberta Press, 1984); Cornelius Jaenen is correct when he points out that the French lacked the power to force American Indians to acculturate. Cornelius Jaenen, *Friend and Foe: Aspects of French-Amerindian Cultural Contact in the Sixteenth and Seventeenth Centuries* (New York: Columbia University Press, 1976), 195. James Axtell's work is an exception to the usual tendency to impose static categories on Indians and whites, and Karen Kupperman disputes the extent to which cultural concepts derived from early accounts actually governed relations. Karen Ordahl Kupperman, *Settling with the Indians: The Meeting of English and Indian Cultures in America, 1580–1640* (Totowa NJ: Rowman & Littlefield, 1980).

3. Cornelius J. Jaenen, "Les Sauvages Ameriquians: Persistence into the Eighteenth Century of Traditional French Concepts and Constructs for Comprehending AmerIndians," *Ethnohistory* 29 (1982): 43–56.

4. A useful discussion of these processes is found in Roy Wagner, *The Invention of Culture* (Chicago: University of Chicago Press, 1981), 1–70, particularly 46–52, 87–88. Many Frenchmen of peasant backgrounds were probably closer to what Wagner calls the differentiating mode of tribal peoples than to the systematizing mode of French officials.

Attempts to get around the confining model of a basically static structure which is combined with an ephemeral history has been most thoroughly developed by Anthony Giddens, *Central Problems in Social Theory: Action, Structure and Contradiction in Social Analysis* (Berkeley: University of California Press, 1979); *Critique of Historical Materialism*; and *The Constitution of Society* (Berkeley: University of California Press, 1984). It has simultaneously emerged in anthropology; see Marshall Sahlins, *Islands of History* (Chicago: University of Chicago Press, 1985).

5. For this, see Wagner, *Invention of Culture*, 52–55.

6. The creation of the middle ground might serve as an example of what Anthony Giddens calls structuration. Giddens, *Central Problems in Social Theory*, 2–7, 69–73, 82.

7. Callières au Ministre, 20 oct. 1696, AN, C11A, v. 14, ff. 216–17. Narrative of . . . Occurrences . . . 1694, 1695, NYCD, 9:604–9.

8. Narrative of . . . Occurrences . . . 1694, 1695, NYCD, 9:607.

9. Ibid.; it is interesting to note here that some Ottawas eventually did adopt scaffold burials, HBNI, 15:777.

10. Narrative of . . . Occurrences . . . 1694, 1695, NYCD, 9:607.

11. For Huron-Petuns and Sabbath, see JR, 61:105.

12. Narrative of . . . Occurrences . . . 1694, 1695, *NYCD*, 9:608. For a similar instance, see *JR*, 59:223.

13. Narrative of . . . Occurrences . . . 1694, 1695, *NYCD*, 9:608. For the development of trading enclaves, see Philip D. Curtin, *Cross-Cultural Trade in World History* (Cambridge: Cambridge University Press, 1984), 11–12, 38, 46–49, 111–15.

14. For Sieur d'Aigremont, see D'Aigremont to Pontchartrain, Nov. 14, 1708, *WHC*, 16:250.

15. Chrétien Le Clercq, *The First Establishment of the Faith in New France*, 2 vols. (New York: J. G. Shea, 1881), 192.

16. See Giddens, *Critique of Historical Materialism*, 93–94, 160, for a general discussion of these issues.

17. *JR*, 65:239. W. J. Eccles, *The Canadian Frontier* (Albuquerque: University of New Mexico Press, 1974), 110; Champigny au Ministre, 4 nov. 1693, AN, C11A, v. 12; Memoire . . . Denonville, aoust 1688, AN, C11A, v. 10 (765–66); Callières au Ministre, 15 oct. 1694, AN, C11A, v. 15; Memoire sur le ferme . . . 10 fev. 1696, AN, C11A, v. 16; Commerce du castor . . . 1696, AN, C11A, v. 14; Milo Quaife, ed., *The Western Country in the Seventeenth Century: The Memoirs of Lanothe Cadillac and Pierre Liette* (Chicago: Lakeside Press, 1917), 16–18. Untitled mémoire (Par tout ce qui . . .), AN, C11A, v. 17, f. 193.

18. Duchesneau to M. de Seignelay, 10 Nov. 1679, *NYCD*, 9:133–34; Denonville à Seignelay, 13 Nov. 1685, AN, C11A, v. 7; Champigny Memoir, 10 mai 1691, AN, C11A, v. 11; Denonville to Seignelay, Jan. 1690, *NYCD*, 9:442–43. For quotation, see Relation du voyage de Cavelier de La Salle, du 22 Aout 1680 a l'automne de 1681, Margry, *Découvertes*, 2:133. On coureurs de bois, see Jaenen, *Friend and Foe*, 115; Eccles, *Canadian Frontier*, 90.

19. Louise Dechene, in examining records of those going west between 1708 and 1717, found that of a total of 373 different individuals, 179 made just one trip and 112 made three or more. These 112 formed "l'armature du commerce interieur." The others made such voyages "une activité temporaire ou occasionnelle"; Dechene, *Habitants et Marchands de Montréal au XVII siècle* (Paris: Libraire Plon, 1974), 219–20.

20. *JR*, 64:173, 183.

21. For Madame Le Sueur, see De Gannes (Deliette) Memoir, *IHC*, 23:338. For berdaches and homosexuality, see De Gannes (Deliette) Memoir, *IHC*, 23:329–30; Le Clercq, *First Establishment*, 135; Relations des découvertes, in Pierre Margry, *Découvertes et établissements des Français . . . de l'Amerique Septentrionale, 1614–1698*, 6 vols. (Paris: Maisonneuve et Cie, 1879, repr. New York: AMS, 1974), 1:488.

22. *JR*, 54:179–83; *JR*, 65:235–45; Cadillac, Account of Detroit, Sept. 25, 1702, *MPHC*, 33:143. Ordonnance du M. le Comte de Frontenac pour la traite et commerce du outaouacs . . . 8 avril 1690 (avec remarques faites par l'intendant), AN, F3, v. 6, f. 366.

23. *JR*, 65:193–99, 229–43; Reuben Gold Thwaites, ed., *New Voyage to North America by the Baron de Lahontan*, 2 vols. (Chicago: A. C. McClury, 1905), 2:455–56, 460–61, 605–18.

24. For general difficulties with European observations on Indian women, see Katherine Weist, "Beasts of Burden and Menial Slaves: Nineteenth-Century Observations of Northern Plains Indian Women," and Alice Kehoe, "The Shackles of Tradition," both in Patricia Albers and Beatrice Medicine, *The Hidden Half: Studies of Plains Indian Women* (Washington DC: University Press of America, 1983), 29–52, 53–73. Women among the Illinois gained power from visions and could become shamans. The culturally very similar Miami had female chiefs whose duties paralleled the male chiefs'. They inherited their status from their fathers and did not obtain it through their husbands. See *HBNI*, 15:675, 677, 684–85.

25. For Perrot and Lafitau on marriage, see Nicolas Perrot, *Memoir on the Manners, Customs, and Religion of the Savages of North America*, in Emma Helen Blair, ed., *The Indian Tribes of the Upper Mississippi Valley and Region of the Great Lakes*, 2 vols. (Cleveland: Arthur H. Clark, 1912), 1:64–65; Joseph-François Lafitau, *Customs of the American Indians Compared with the Customs of Primitive Times* (Toronto: Champlain Society, 1924–77), 1:336–37, 339. For adultery among the Illinois, see De Gannes (Deliette) Memoir, *IHC*, 23:327, 335–37; Reuben Gold Thwaites, ed., *Father Louis Hennepin's A New Discovery of a Vast Country in America* (facsimile ed., Toronto: Coles, 1974, repr. ed. of 1903 ed.), 167–68; Jolliet and Marquette, in Louise P. Kellogg, ed., *Early Narratives of the Northwest, 1634–1699* (New York: Charles Scribner's Sons, 1917), 243.

26. For Cadillac, see Quaife, ed., *The Western Country*, 63. For references to prostitution, see *JR*, 65:241; Memoire touchant l'yvrognerie des sauvages, 1693, AN. C11A, v. 12, f. 384.

27. De Gannes (Deliette) Memoir, *IHC*, 23:328–37; Thwaites, ed., *Lahontan's Voyages*, 2:453. Joutel gives a contradictory account similar to Deliette's; see Joutel's Memoir, in Isaac J. Cox, *The Journeys of Robert Cavelier de La Salle*, 2 vols. (New York: A. S. Barnes, 1905), 2:222.

28. For quotation, see Thwaites, ed., *Lahontan's Voyages*, 2:453; ibid., 454, 463. For pregnancy, see ibid., 454, 463; for hunting women, see ibid., 463–64.

29. On divorce, compare Lahontan to Perrot and Cadillac; Thwaites, ed., *Lahontan's Voyage*, 2:453; Perrot, *Memoir*, 64–65; Quaife, ed., *The Western Country*,

38–39. For brothers' control over sisters, see De Gannes (Deliette) Memoir, *IHC*, 23:332, 337, and Raudot, "Memoir," in W. Vernon Kinietz, *The Indians of the Western Great Lakes* (Ann Arbor: University of Michigan Press, 1965), 389. For Joutel, see Joutel Memoir, in Cox, ed., *Journeys of La Salle*, 2:222. For Cadillac quotation, see Quaife, ed., *The Western Country*, 45.

30. For customary relation, see *JR*, 65:233. For quotation, see ibid., 241.

31. For references to sexual imbalance and soral polygamy, see Relation du voyage de Cavelier de la Salle, du 11 aout 1680 à l'automne de 1681. Margry, *Découvertes*, 2:157; *JR*, 54:219, 229; La Salle on the Illinois Country, 1680, *IHC*, 23:10. De Gannes (Deliette) Memoir, *IHC*, 23:329. *JR*, 54:219. For Jesuit attacks on polygamy and connections between polygamy and disease, etc., see v, 57:215–19; v, 57:231; *JR*, 56:113. For renunciation of wives, see *JR*, 55:129–31. For decline of polygamy, see *JR*, 61:1312; *JR*, 57:231, 81. Emily J. Blasingham, "The Depopulation of the Illinois Indians," *Ethnohistory* 3 (Summer 1986): 386–87.

32. *JR*, 65:67, 79; De Gannes (Deliette) Memoir, *IHC*, 23:361. For emphasis Jesuits placed on sexual conduct among Kiskakon Ottawas and Kaskaskias, see *JR*, 54:179–83, and *JR*, 65:67–69.

33. De Gannes (Deliette) Memoir, *IHC*, 23:329–30, 335–37; Joutel Memoir, in Cox, ed., *Journeys of La Salle*, 2:222. Emily Blasingham estimates the ratio of adult warriors to the rest of the population at 1:3.17 which obviously would not allow for Deliette's estimate, but her estimate is perhaps even more of a guess than his. Blasingham, "Depopulation of the Illinois," 364. For village sites, see J. Joe Bauxar, "The Historic Period," in Elaine Bluhm, ed., *Illinois Archaeology Bulletin No. 1*, Illinois Archaeological Survey, Urbana (Carbondale: Southern Illinois University Press, 1959), 49. For Gravier's mission, see Mary Borgian Palm, "The Jesuit Missions of the Illinois Country (1673–1763)," PhD diss., St. Louis University, 1931 (Cleveland: privately printed, Sisters of Notre Dame, 1931), 22, 24–25. For Father Gravier's claim of baptism, see *JR*, 65:33. For conflict, see *JR*, 65:67, and Fr. Rale quoted in Mary Elizabeth Good, "The Guebert Site: An Eighteenth-Century Historic Kaskaskia Indian Village in Randolph County, Illinois," *Central States Archaeological Societies Memoir*, vol. 2 (n.p., 1972), 14.

34. For Virgin Mary, see *JR*, 59:187; 193, 201, 207; *JR*, 63:217–19. For opposition of young men, see *JR*, 65:67.

35. For marriages, see *JR*, 65:241; *JR*, 65:69; St. Cosme, in Kellogg, ed., *Narratives*, 251. The best work on intermarriage on the Great Lakes is by Jacqueline Peterson, "Prelude to Red River: A Social Portrait of the Great Lakes Metis," *Ethnohistory* 25 (1978): 41–68. For intermarriage in the Northwest,

see Olive Dickason, "From One Nation in the Northeast to New Nation in the Northwest: A Look at the Emergence of the Metis," in Jacqueline Peterson and Jennifer S. H. Brown, *The New Peoples: Being and Becoming Metis in North America* (Lincoln: University of Nebraska Press, 1985). Interracial marriage within the later fur trade has been the subject of two recent books, but both studies look at situations significantly different from those of the late seventeenth-century West, where many of the earliest Catholic marriages were solemnized by priests. See Sylvia Van Kirk, *Many Tender Ties: Women in Fur-Trade Society, 1670–1870* (Norman: University of Oklahoma Press, 1980), and Jennifer S. Brown, *Strangers in the Blood: Fur Trade Company Families in Indian Country* (Vancouver: University of British Columbia Press, 1980).

36. *JR*, 64:201–3; Cadillac to Minister, 18 Oct. 1700, *MPHC*, 33:189. For Cadillac's later opposition, see Mariage des francais avec les sauvagesses, 1 sept. 1716, AN, C13A, v. 4, f. 255.

Who was commanding at Fort. St. Louis in the Illinois at the time is unclear. Tonti was there in April 1694, Declaration de Henri de Tonti, 11 avril 1694, AN, C13A, Louisiana, v. 1, f. 27, but in the fall of 1693 he was in Montreal. Engagement of Viau to La Forest and Tonti, Sept. 11, 1693, *IHC*, 23:273–75. Given the absence of Tonti and La Forest, Deliette may have been in command.

37. *JR*, 64:195, 197, 207, 211. Quaife, ed., *The Western Country*, 39, 45; Perrot, *Memoir*, 64–69; Lafitau, *Customs*, 1:336–37.

38. For official attitudes toward marriage, see Jaenen, *Friend and Foe*, 164. For Father de la Vente, see Mariage des francais avec les sauvagesses, 1 sept. 1716, AN, C13A, v. 4. For banishment and supervision, see *JR*, 65:233–45. For baptism, see Palm, "Jesuit Missions," 43–45.

39. For governor's opposition, see Vaudreuil and Raudot to Minister, Nov. 14, 1709, *MPHC*, 33:454. For Duclos and Cadillac, see Mariage des francais avec les sauvagesses, 1 sept. 1716, AN, C13A, v. 4, f. 255. For renewed concern in 1730, see Bienville et Salmon au Ministre, 16 mai 1735, AN, C13A, v. 20, f. 85. Memoire concernant les Illinois, 1732 AN, F3, v. 24.

40. For Accault, see *JR*, 64:213, 180. For Aramepinchieue and Rouensa, see *JR*, 64:179–81, 193–237. Aramepinchieue took the Christian name Mary or Marie; see Palm, "Jesuit Missions," 38.

41. *JR*, 64:205–7, 213, 280. *JR*, 64:211, 195. For Aramepinchieue, see *JR*, 64:193–95, 205–7, 213–29.

42. *JR*, 64:195–205.

43. For Aramepinchieue quotations, see *JR*, 64:207–9; otherwise, *JR*, 64:179, 213, 211.

44. *JR*, 64:79–81, 231–35; Palm, "Jesuit Missions," 38; André Penicault, *Fleur*

de Lys and Calumet: Being the Penicault Narrative of French Adventure in Louisiana, ed. Richebourg Gaillard McWilliams (Baton Rouge: Louisiana State University Press, 1953), 139–40. For claims of success among other Illinois nations, see Callières et de Champigny au Ministre, 18 oct. 1700, AN, C11A, v. 18.

45. *JR*, 65:101–3; Palm, "Jesuit Missions," 36, 47; Blasingham, "Depopulation of the Illinois," 201; Bauxar, "Historic Period," 49. For Gravier, see *JR*, 66:51–63.

46. Some historians continue to divide Indian-white relations between peaceful commerce and violent conflict. For such a position, see Francis Jennings, *The Ambiguous Iroquois Empire* (New York: W. W. Norton, 1984), 83. In fact, violence cannot be separated from the trade. The larger question of the role of violence in commerce has recently been raised by Curtin, *Cross-Cultural Trade*, 41–45. It is a question still illuminated by the work of Frederic Lane, *Venice and History* (Baltimore: Johns Hopkins University Press, 1966), 412–28; see, particularly, the "Economic Consequences of Organized Violence." For the number of murders, see Raisons qu'on a proposee a la Cour, 1687a, AN, C11A, v. 15, f. 271.

47. For Fox, see *JR*, 54:225; Illinois, see Joutel Memoir, in Cox, ed., *Journeys of La Salle*, 2:212; Chippewas, see Raudot and De Gannes (Deliette) Memoir, *IHC*, 23:328, Memoir in Kinietz, *Indians of the Western Great Lakes*, 374; Sauks, see ibid., 381–82. For dangers of Sioux trade, see Pere Nouvel à M. de La Barre, 23 avril 1684, AN, C11A, v. 6, f. 523. For institutionalization of theft, see Gary C. Anderson, *Kinsmen of Another Kind: Dakota-White Relations in the Upper Mississippi Valley, 1680–1862* (Lincoln: University of Nebraska Press, 1984), 63.

48. In the cases that follow, both sides try to make these positions clear. See, e.g., extract from a letter by Dulhut, April 12, 1684, WHC, 16:120, hereafter cited as Dulhut's letter. For Algonquian custom, see Jaenen, *Friend and Foe*, 123. For a discussion of murder, revenge, and compensation that stresses revenge rather than compensation among the Cherokee, see John Phillip Reid, *A Law of Blood: The Primitive Law of the Cherokee Nation* (New York: New York University Press, 1970), 73–112. Reid says that a retaliatory killing does not bring revenge (78). This does not appear to have been true among the Algonquians. Note how in the Dulhut case below Achiganaga is given presents to compensate for his son's death.

49. Report of Boisbriant Diron Desursins Legardeur De L'isle Ste. Therese Langloisere, June 17, 1723, in J. H. Schlarman, *From Quebec to New Orleans: Fort De Chartres* (Belleville IL: Beuchler, 1929), 226–31. See also Jaenen, *Friend and Foe*, 97. Jaenen makes the distinction between the French emphasis on punishment and the Indian emphasis on compensation.

50. For conditions at Green Bay, see Enjalran à Lefevre de La Barre, 16 aoust 1683, Margry, *Découvertes*, 5:4–5. For Saulteur-Fox conflict, see ibid., 5; Claude Charles Le Roy, Sieur de Bacqueville de la Potherie, *History of the Savage Peoples Who Are the Allies of New France*, in Emma Helen Blair, ed., *The Indian Tribes of the Upper Mississippi Valley and Region of the Great Lakes*, 2 vols. (Cleveland: Arthur H. Clark, 1912), 1:358–63; Dulhut letter, *WHC*, 16:114. Durantaye à A. de la Barre, 11 avril 1684, AN, C11A, v. 6, 1.521–22. For activities of French traders and danger they were in, see Denonville au Ministre, aoust 1688, AN, C11A, v. 10, f. 66; Nouvel à M. de la Barre, 23 avril 1684, AN, C11A, v. 6.

51. The only detailed account of this murder is Dulhut's own, but since he was in a position to justify his actions, he provided considerable detail. See Dulhut letter, April 12, 1684, *WHC*, 16:114–15, 123.

52. Dulhut letter, April 12, 1684, *WHC*, 16:119.

53. Ibid., 118–20.

54. Ibid., 119–21.

55. Ibid., 120–21.

56. Ibid. See also Jaenen, *Friend and Foe*, 132–34. It should be noted that by 1690 the French had begun imitating the Iroquois and were torturing and killing prisoners of war. Narrative of . . . Occurrences 1690, 1691, *NYCD*, 9:518.

57. Ibid., 120–21.

58. Ibid., 124.

59. Ibid., 124–25.

60. Fr. Nouvel à M. de la Barre, 23 avril 1684, AN, C11A, v. 6, f. 523. Reconciliation was also forwarded by Governor de la Barre who approved of Dulhut's actions, but the French court, which often had only a shaky grasp of what was going on in the upper country, confused Dulhut's executions with the killing of an Iroquois at Michilimackinac and denounced Dulhut and his presence in the backcountry, De la Barre au Ministre, 5 juin 1684, AN, C11A, v. 6. Louis XIV to De La Barre, July 21, 1684, *DHNY*, 1:108–9.

61. For the Ottawa version of these events, see Speech of Miscouaky, Sept. 26, 1706, *MPHC*, 33:288–92. For the French investigation, see Report of D'Aigremont, *MPHC*, 33:435. For Cadillac's account, see Cadillac to de Vaudreuil, Aug. 27, 1706; E. M. Sheldon, *The Early History of Michigan from the First Settlement to 1815* (New York: A. S. Barnes, 1956), 219. For mention of a second French soldier killed later, see Instructions to D'Aigremont, June 30, 1707, *WHC*, 16:243.

62. For Ottawa attempts to negotiate, see Speech of Miscouaky, 26 Sept. 1706, *MPHC*, 133:290–92; Report of D'Aigremont, *MPHC*, 33:435–36. For various casualty figures in the fight, see "Council with Ottawas, June 18, 1707," in

Sheldon, *Early History of Michigan*, 228, where Jean le Blanc puts the Ottawa dead at thirty; Speech of Miscouaky, Sept. 26, 1706, *MPHC*, 33:294, where the figure is twenty-six for the Ottawas and fifty dead and wounded for the Miamis. For the significant Ottawa dead, see Speech of Miscouaky, Sept. 26, 1706, *MPHC*, 33:290, and Fr. Marest to Vaudreuil, Aug. 14, 1706, *MPHC*, 33:262–69. For the French emphasis on the priest and the first soldier killed, see Council with the Ottawas, June 20, 1707, Speech of Vaudreuil, Sheldon, *Early History of Michigan*, 242; Speech of Vaudreuil, June 21, 1707, ibid., 245.

63. "Account of Detroit," Sept. 25, 1702, *MPHC*, 33:137–38, 147; Cadillac to Pontchartrain, Aug. 31, 1703, in Sheldon, *Early History of Michigan*, 105–6. For mention of quarrels and unsettled killings, see Cadillac to Vaudreuil, Aug. 27, 1706, in Sheldon, *Early History of Michigan*, 218–19. For earlier attack, see Memorandum of . . . Cadillac, 19 Nov. 1704, *MPHC*, 33:234; Report of D'Aigremont, Nov. 14, 1708, *MPHC*, 33:432–37. For a Miami-Huron-Peton rapprochement as early as 1703, see Speeches of Ottawas . . . 24 Sept. 1703, *MPHC*, 33:223–25. For Vaudreuil's orders to keep the peace, see Vaudreuil au Cadillac, 10 juin 1706, *AN*, Moreau St. Mery, F3, v. 7, f. 308. For Huron-Petun resentment, see Vaudreuil to Minister, May 5, 1705, *MPHC*, 33:242.

64. For Vaudreuil quote, see Vaudreuil to de Pontchartrain, Nov. 4, 1706, *WHC*, 16:242. For Ottawas, see Words of Ottawas to Cadillac, Sept. 24, 1707, *MPHC*, 33:349. For difficulties, see Father Marest to Vaudreuil, Aug. 14, 1706, *MPHC*, 33:262–69; Council with the Ottawas, Speech of Vaudreuil, June 20, 1707, Sheldon, *Early History of Michigan*, 242. Cadillac to Vaudreuil, Aug. 27, 1706, ibid., 228–29. For importance of negotiations, see Vaudreuil to Father Marest, n.d. (1707), Sheldon, *Early History of Michigan*, 273.

65. Many examples of the French councils survive. For examples for the period under consideration here, see Parolles des sauvages . . . , Archives Nationales, Archives Coloniales, F3, v. 8, ff. 136–41; Talk between Marquis de Vaudreuil and Onaskin . . . , Aug. 1, 1707, *MPHC*, 33:258–62; Speech of Miscouaky . . . to Marquis de Vaudreuil, Sept. 26, 1706, *MPHC*, 33:288–96; Conference with Ottawas, June 18, 1707, in Sheldon, *Early History of Michigan*, 232–50. For the differences in how the Great Lakes Indians and the French perceived the relationship between parents and children, see Father Gabriel Sagard, *The Long Journey to the Country of the Hurons* (Toronto: Champlain Society, 1939, facsimile ed., Greenwood Press), 130–31; Pierre de Charlevoix, *Journal of a Voyage to North America* (London: R. & J. Dodsley, 1761, Readex microprint facsimile ed., 1966), 2:55, 89–90, 109, 114–15; Lafitau, *Customs of the American Indian*, 1:362; Perrot, *Memoir*, 1:67; Thwaites, ed., *Lahontan's Voyages*, 2:458. See also Jaenen, *Friend and Foe*, 94–97.

66. Kischkouch, the young Sinago chief killed at Detroit, had a brother, Merasilla, who had actually gone among the Saulteurs and Amikwas to raise a party to avenge his brother "and restore the name of Kischkouch." In the end, Merasilla excused himself from the war party, despite reproaches that he showed "no love for his brother," and helped negotiate a peace. The war party went to Detroit, accompanied by other Ottawas, but did not attack. Another Ottawa killed at Detroit had as relatives two of the principal women at Michilimackinac, and they went from cabin to cabin, weeping and demanding the deaths of Frenchmen there until negotiations covered their loss. Marest to Vaudreuil, Aug. 14, 1706, *WHC*, 16:232–34; Marest to Vaudreuil, Aug. 16, 1706, and Aug. 27, 1706, *MPHC*, 33:262–71; Cadillac to Vaudreuil, Aug. 27, 1706, Sheldon, *Early History of Michigan*, 226–27. For quote, see Reply of Vaudreuil to Miscouaky, Nov. 4, 1706, *MPHC*, 33:295.

67. For Otontagan, see Vaudreuil to Minster, July 24, 1707; *MPHC*, 33:328–29, Council with Ottawas, June 18, 1707, Speech of Jean le Blanc, Sheldon, *Early History of Michigan*, 233–39. For Vaudreuil's position, see Council with Ottawas, June 20, 1707, Reply of Vaudreuil, Sheldon, *Early History of Michigan*, 242; Reply of Jean le Blanc, June 21, 1707, ibid., 243–44.

68. See the speech of Vaudreuil to Jean le Blanc, June 22, 1707, Sheldon, *Early History of Michigan*, 245–47; Vaudreuil to Minster, July 24, 1707, *MPHC*, 33:328–30. For the rivalry of Vaudreuil and Cadillac, see Vaudreuil to Minister, Nov. 12, 1707, *MPHC*, 33:371–72.

69. Otontagan (Jean le Blanc), Kinouge, Meatinan, and Menukoueak were joined partway through the proceedings by Kataolauibois (Koutaouileone) and Onaske, who was headman of the Kiskakon Ottawas at Michilimackinac. Council held at Detroit, Aug. 6, 1707, Aug. 8, 1707, *MPHC*, 33:331, 334; Speeches of Three Indians from Michilimakina [*sic*], Oct. 7, 1707, *MPHC*, 33:362–64.

From the beginning of these negotiations, Otontagan and his brother, Miscouaky, had tried to lay the blame for the incident on Le Pesant. Speech of Miscouaky, Sept. 26, 1706, *MPHC*, 33:288–89; Council with Ottawas, Speech of Jean le Blanc, June 18, 1707, Sheldon, *Early History of Michigan*, 234–35. Onaske and Le Pesant were engaged in a rivalry over whether the Ottawas should concentrate their settlements at Michilimackinac or Detroit. Onaske accused Le Pesant of giving the Iroquois gifts to come and attack the Ottawas of Michilimackinac. Father Marest to Vaudreuil, Aug. 14, 1706, *WHC*, 16:238. Cadillac had earlier accused the Michilimackinac Ottawas of soliciting other nations to attack Detroit to force the Ottawas there to withdraw to Michilimackinac, Sheldon, *Early History of Michigan*, 196–97. Koutaouileone was also involved in the attempt to reunite the Ottawas at Michilimackinac. Marest to Vaudreuil, Aug. 27, 1706, *MPHC*, 33:271. Cadillac's maneuverings will be discussed below. The French, of course, tried to use Ottawa divisions to their advantage, see Vaudreuil's comments on Cadillac's letter of Aug. 27, 1706, *MPHC*, 33:282.

70. Council Held at Detroit, Aug. 6, 1707, Speech of Cadillac, *MPHC*, 33:332. Council Held at Detroit, Replies of Otontagan, Aug. 6, 1707, Seventh Council, Speech of Onaske, *MPHC*, 33:332–33, 335–36. Speeches of Three Indians from Michilimakina [*sic*], Oct. 7, 1707,*MPHC*, 33:363–64.

71. The Huron-Petuns and Miamis wondered out loud why Cadillac should bother to demand Le Pesant when there were so many Ottawa chiefs in Detroit upon whom they could take revenge. Council Held at Detroit, Aug. 7, 1707, Aug. 9, 1707, *MPHC*, 33:333–35; Speeches of Three Indians from Michilimakina [*sic*], Oct. 7, 1707, *MPHC*, 33:363–64.

72. How Le Pesant was persuaded, or forced, to come was not clear. Kataolauibois told Vaudreuil that it was Onaske, Sakima, Meyavila, and himself, all of them Kiskakons and Sinago Ottawas from Michilimackinac, who compelled Le Pesant to embark. He minimized the role of Otontagan, even though Onaske had stressed at Detroit that the surrender of Le Pesant was Otontagan's responsibility. Kataolauibois's account of negotiations is, however, sketchy and he told Vaudreuil that he would leave it to the Sieur de St. Pierre, who had been present, to give a full account. It appears clear, however, that Le Pesant in reaching his decision to come had to deal with strong pressure from leading men that he go. The pressure was strong enough so that Kataloauibois feared Le Pesant's revenge if Cadillac did not execute him. Speeches of Three Indians from Michilimakina [*sic*], Oct. 7, 1707, *MPHC*, 33:365. Vaudreuil, deriving his account from the Sieur de St. Pierre, says that Le Pesant made private arrangements with the Sieur d'Argenteuil, Cadillac's emissary, to come to Detroit. Vaudreuil to Minister, Oct. 1, 1707, *MPHC*, 33:354.

73. Cadillac to Vaudreuil (copy made), Oct. 1, 1707, *MPHC*, 33:352–52. Words of the Ottawas to Cadillac, Sept. 24, 1707, *MPHC*, 33:346–50. Vaudreuil to Minister, Oct. 1, 1707, *MPHC*, 33:350–53.

74. Cadillac to Vaudreuil (copy made), Oct. 1, 1707, *MPHC*, 33:351–52; Words of the Ottawas to Cadillac, Sept. 24, 1707, *MPHC*, 33:346–48; Vaudreuil to Minister, Oct. 1, 1707, *MPHC*, 33:354–57.

75. Vaudreuil to Minister, Oct. 1, 1707, *MPHC*, 33:355–58.

76. Cadillac to Vaudreuil (copy made), Oct. 1, 1707, *MPHC*, 33:351; Vaudreuil to Minister, Oct. 1, 1707, *MPHC*, 33:355; Words of Ottawas to Cadillac, Sept. 25, 1707, *MPHC*, 33:348–50.

77. Vaudreuil to Minister, Oct. 1, 1707, *MPHC*, 33:355.

78. Words of Ottawas to Cadillac, Sept. 25, 1707, *MPHC*, 33:348–50.

79. For the retaliation of the Miamis and the events which followed, see Vaudreuil and Raudot to Minister, Nov. 14, 1708, *MPHC*, 33:403–5, 408; Father Marest to De Vaudreuil, June 4, 1708, *MPHC*, 33:383–87; De Vaudreuil to Minister, Nov. 5, 1708, *MPHC*, 33:395–99; Report of D'Aigremont, Nov. 14, 1708, *MPHC*, 33:937–40. For the reaction of the Ottawas to Le Pesant's surrender, see Speeches of Three Indians from Michilimakina [*sic*], Oct. 7, 1707, *MPHC*, 33:365.

80. This account is partially drawn from the report of Boisbriant Diron Desurins Legardeur De L'isle Ste. Therese Langloisere of June 17, 1723, in Schlarman, *From Quebec to New Orleans*, 225–31. For original, see Chefs du villages . . . , 17 juin 1793, AN, F3, v. 24, f. 157 Moreau St. Mery. The account of the Cahokia delegation and Marie Rompiechoue is from a document of May 11, 1723, entitled Remis par M. Diron, AN, C13A, v. 7, f. 322. That Marie Rompiechoue was Aramepinchieue is made likely by (1) the similarity of their names, (2) the fact that Aramepinchieue's baptismal name was Marie (see Palm, "Jesuit Missions," 38), and (3) the high standing of both women among the Illinois and the French. Aramepinchieue was still alive in 1723 because four years later the French ransomed "the Illinois woman who passed as the wife of michelako" from the Fox who were about to burn her. Accault was by now presumably dead. Deliette to Lignery, Oct. 15, 1726, *WHC*, 17:18. For an additional, briefer account of the murder, see "Journal of Diron D'Artaguiette . . . ," in Newton D. Mereness, *Trends in the American Colonies* (New York: Macmillan Company, 1916), 75–77.

81. Ibid., 226–27. Kiraoueria's position was not unusual; Joachim, a Michigame chief, was also of the prayer. He had married three of his daughters to Frenchmen. St. Ange au Ministre, n.d., (1733) AN, C13A, v. 17, f. 248. For an Illinois interpretation of patriarchal relations, see Parolles de Chachagouesse . . . chez Illinois du 20 aoust 1712, AN, C11A, v. 33.

82. Ibid., 227.

83. Ibid., 227–30.

84. Ibid., 228–31.

85. Instruction de Duquesne à Pean, 9 may 1754, in Fernand Grenier, ed., *Papiers Contrecoeur, et autres documents concernant le conflit anglo-français sur l'Ohio de 1745 à 1756* (Quebec: Les presses universitaires, Laval, 1952), 122.

15. Creative Misunderstandings
and New Understandings

RICHARD WHITE

Since I wrote *The Middle Ground*, it has taken on something of a life of its own. I really do believe that once a book is published, it stands in relation to intelligent readers the way an exam stands in relation to a professor. The refrain professors tell students—"I have no way of judging you on what you *intended to say*, I can only grade what you wrote"—can come back to haunt professorial authors. What I intended to say in *The Middle Ground* may be of some interest to you, yet what matters is the text: what I wrote. I am also enfeebled as an authority about *The Middle Ground* because of the thesis of the book. This book is, among other things, about mutual misunderstandings and the ways that new meanings are derived from them. It is about the virtues of misreading, which puts an author who accuses his readers of misreading in something of an awkward position. I think that there have been misreadings of the book, but one of my points is that such misreadings can be fruitful in their own right.

The phrase "middle ground," I realize now in ways that I did not really fully comprehend when writing the book, had twinned meanings. First, I was trying to describe a process that arose from the "willingness of those who . . . [sought] to justify their own actions in terms of what they perceived to be their partner's cultural premises." These actors sought out cultural "congruences, either perceived or actual," that "often seemed—and, indeed, were—results of misunderstandings or accidents." Such interpretations could be ludicrous, but it did not matter. "Any congruence, no matter how tenuous, can be put to work and can take on a life of its own if it is accepted by both sides." The middle ground is thus a process of mutual and creative misunderstanding.[1]

Second, I was trying to describe—and this attempt took up the bulk of the book—a quite particular historical space that was the outcome of this process. This place was the *pays d'en haut*. Because the middle ground is itself a spatial metaphor, the phrase has allowed a conflation between the process of expedient and creative misunderstanding and the actual space that I was discussing: the *pays d'en haut*, or the Upper Country of French Canada.

So, do I think that the middle ground as a process is replicable in other places and other times? Yes, I do. Is every instance where academics find this process at work the equivalent of the Upper Country? No, but sometimes other academics might think so. I was fairly specific about the elements that were necessary for the construction of such a space: a rough balance of power, mutual need or a desire for what the other possesses, and an inability by either side to commandeer enough force to compel the other to change. Force and violence are hardly foreign to the process of creating and maintaining a middle ground, but the critical element is mediation.

Other scholars have identified the process at work in places about which I know relatively little. I have absolutely no desire to become chief judge in the court of the middle ground. I think that the process is, if not a universal aspect of human communication and interaction, a common one. I am thus more than willing to think such scholarly sightings are correct.

The middle ground as process is quite common, yet the construction of a historical space in which the process becomes the basis of relations between distinct peoples is probably less common. This construction of space occurred in other places in North America, the region I know best, but it did not occur everywhere. There are instances where the process can be evident, but the space may fail to emerge. The space depended on the creation of an infrastructure that could support and expand the process, and this infrastructure was, I argue, possible only when there was a rough balance of power and a mutual need between the parties involved.

The middle ground that the French created in Canada, for example, did not penetrate much beyond the Mississippi, though the French themselves did. These Frenchmen were, in effect, graduates of the school of the middle ground. They appealed to Indian beliefs and employed the cultural tools that had helped regulate relations in the *pays d'en haut*. What they failed to create was the infrastructure of empire—from missions, to posts, to a network of alliance chiefs, to a set of mutually comprehensible and oft-repeated rituals—that is the imperial middle ground as a historical space.

The story of Etienne de Véniard Bourgmont can carry my point. Bourgmont had been commander in Detroit in 1706, when the numerous nations Antoine Laumet de Lamothe Cadillac had gathered there exploded into the internecine violence that Bourgmont and the French alliance were supposed to prevent. Cadillac had established the post with his usual grand ambition and inattention to practical detail. He had left Bourgmont in charge, and Bourgmont had failed miserably. The resulting bloodbath threatened to wreck the Indian alliance that New France depended on. Fearing disgrace, demotion, or worse, and in love with the wife of another man, he deserted and pursued his lover into the forests near Lake Erie.[2]

Disorder in the French empire was always unregulated life in the woods. Some Frenchmen, the coureurs de bois, excelled at it; other Frenchmen, such as officials in Montreal or Quebec, feared it. Bourgmont, reported to be "living in the woods like a savage," had not only failed in his duty but also become a danger to imperial order. Bourgmont was living in the woods with Madame Tichenet (also known as Elizabeth Couc, or La Chenette, but best known as Madame Montour). She was what would later be called *métis*, the daughter of a European father and an Indian mother. She would build her own reputation as a dangerous woman with a voracious sexual appetite that consumed and discarded men. Cadillac claimed she had had one hundred men, Indian and European, and left them all. She threatened not only the men she loved and left but also the careful patriarchal model of empire that the French and their allies crafted. She would, when her liaison with Bourgmont was over, travel to Albany, and become a power broker along the borders where the French and English competed for influence, trading partners, and allies. She became a person much more widely known and influential than Bourgmont.[3]

Bourgmont made his way west, supposedly in ardent pursuit of a Missouri Indian woman, and married among that tribe and had a son, whom neighboring peoples called Little Missouri. Bourgmont's domestic arrangements helped rehabilitate his imperial standing. He became a man who, with the aid of his relations, had traveled up the Missouri and knew more about the Missouri River country and its peoples than any other Frenchman. Having an outlaw with considerable influence among neighboring peoples created significant unease among the French authorities in the Illinois country, yet the French did not seem to have tried very hard to capture him. In time Bourgmont's service in imperial wars and knowledge of the Missouri country made him an asset to France.

Bourgmont was reintegrated as an agent of the French empire, and in 1723 he was trying to extend a common set of largely Indian forms—calumets, councils, the ordering of peoples as kin with the French as fathers and the Indians as children—on which the French alliance depended west of the Missouri River. Where Bourgmont was going, however, the infrastructure of this common world did not exist. There were neither French Jesuits nor French garrisons; there were no licensed traders. There were none of the common meanings of the alliance and none of its history of success against common enemies such as the Iroquois and the English. And arrayed against Bourgmont were years of hostility along the prairie-plains margins and the ambitions of other Frenchmen and other Indians. Bourgmont could achieve a temporary success—mediating peace, ending slaving in which the French were involved, and weaning the plains Apache away from the Spanish—but it did not outlast

Creative Misunderstandings

Bourgmont, who returned to France with a French title and a French wife awaiting him. With him gone, and no Frenchmen with gifts and mediation to sustain it, the peace Bourgmont negotiated on the Great Plains fell apart. The French abandoned Fort Orleans, which was his post on the Missouri near the Little Osages and the Missouri.[4] The Apache suffered the most. They resumed their long, slow, stubborn retreat from the plains. The middle ground as a process existed, but not the middle ground as a space.

There is, finally, a scholarly aspect of the middle ground that I have come to appreciate in the last dozen years. Historians know of the distant pasts of many colonized people largely through their interactions with colonizers. If the colonizers could not find common ground or meaningfully communicate with the people they lived among, traded with, fought with, and had sexual relations with, then on what grounds can historians make such a claim? If scholars assert that colonizers didn't get it, is it the assumption that modern historians somehow know the *it* that their own sources got wrong? If the colonizers had no valid knowledge of the other and never produced a common world, then how can modern historians, who, in effect, look into the colonizers' eyes and see the Indians reflected there, claim to know much better? Scholars might know more about seventeenth- and eighteenth-century Indians than the Europeans of the period because of alternative paths to knowledge: scholars can talk to modern descendants of the people in question who somehow embody unchanged aspects of the worlds the French and other colonizers encountered centuries ago. But there are several problems. First, this method assumes aspects of an unchanged tradition among descendants of seventeenth- and eighteenth-century peoples who were either preliterate or only becoming literate and whose own oral traditions have been disrupted by epidemics, war, dispossession, and massive population loss. Second, asserting such a claim means indulging in what I consider the main fault of so much Indian history: marking Indian peoples a people of tradition, outside the realm of the modern, as if they had no role in forging modernity and as if their history had no part in it. And, finally, embedded in this claim is the notion that historians can understand these supposedly unchanged portions of Indian cultures though Europeans who lived among Indian peoples, often quite intimately, centuries ago, could not.

I do not suggest that these colonizers were modern ethnologists or that they had sophisticated understandings of Indian cultures, though sometimes they did. I argue that they had the ability to establish avenues of communication and creativity through the unlikely path of misunderstanding. They created with Indian peoples mutually comprehensible worlds. I do not contend that middle grounds occur everywhere, but I do demonstrate that such worlds arose. Biased and incomplete information and creative misunderstanding may be the most common basis of human actions.

There is, I think, a culturalist disease of the late twentieth and early twenty-first centuries that amounts to a fascination with purity and otherness to which I intended *The Middle Ground* to be a partial antidote. The book assumes that people are not necessarily stupid, simple, or parochial; contact situations created not only violence, xenophobia, and, as the warden in *Cool Hand Luke* put it, a "failure to communicate," but also new cultural formations and new understandings. The warden's famous phrase sprang from the fact that Luke's ostensible misunderstandings communicated his disdain and intentions all too well. The larger problem that inspired *The Middle Ground*, and which continues to fascinate me, is how, when historically and in modern society people get so much wrong, does the world still manage after a fashion to work?

Notes

1. Richard White, *The Middle Ground: Indians, Empires, and Republics in the Great Lakes Region, 1650–1815* (Cambridge, 1991), 52–53.

2. Frank Norall, *Bourgmont, Explorer of the Missouri, 1698–1725* (Lincoln NE, 1988), 3–17.

3. Ibid., 16–17 (quotation, 16).

4. French missionary activity took place among people who hunted to the

west, such as the Quapaws, but the missions proper remained close to the Mississippi (see Kathleen DuVal, "'A Good Relationship, and Commerce': The Native Political Economy of the Arkansas River Valley," *Early American Studies* 1, no. 1 [Spring 2003]: 75–77). Extrait des Instructions données à M. Périer, Sept. 30, 1726, in Pierre Margry, *Découvertes et Établissements des Français dans l'ouest et dans le sud de L'Amérique Septentrionale (1614–1754)*..., vol. 5, *Première formation d'une chaine de postes entre le fleuve Saint-Laurent et le Golfe du Mexique (1683–1724)* (Paris, 1883), 452; Willard H. Rollings, *The Osage: An Ethnohistorical Study of Hegemony on the Prairie-Plains* (Columbia MO, 1992), 91, 117.

PART 4

Cloth Trade

Introduction

During the first decades of operation the Hudson's Bay Company sought a suitable supply of trade goods that could be routinely supplied to Indians. That task proved far more difficult than the company had anticipated. The Indians let the English traders know that they expected "favorable rates of exchange, good quality merchandise, items stylistically pleasing and well suited to their nomadic life-style in the harsh subarctic environment" but traders often became dismayed at the difficulty of fulfilling those demands. As Arthur Ray's article so clearly demonstrates, the HBC quickly learned to purchase what Indians demanded, rather than risk the specter of shipping goods that had no market among Indians. For example, while it was logical to obtain tobacco from their own English colonies, London merchants quickly discovered that Indians refused to trade for the inferior colonial Virginia product and the company was forced to turn to Lisbon merchants to supply the Indian demand for Brazilian tobacco. London repeatedly turned to foreign suppliers to meet Indian demand, but even then, there was no guarantee that Indians would be satisfied. The company received continual complaints about the quality of the merchandise from their traders, who reiterated Indian complaints. By the 1740s, Indians still complained about the quality of the merchandise and frequently refused to trade. One trader, James Isham, complained that "the Indians disliked the colour and size of the large pearl beads; complained that the kettles were too heavy for their size and the wrong shape; and claimed the gunpowder was very weak, foul smelling, and an objectionable ashy color. Although they liked the shape, quality, and color of the blankets, the Indians said they were too short. Cloth, on the other hand, was said to be of little service because it was too narrow, weak, and thin." Not only was the list lengthy but the trader sent samples of the products that Indians preferred—which the company relied on as models for their future purchases.[1]

There was a logical pattern to Indian demand: they wanted favorable rates of exchange, and they sought products that were durable in the harsh arctic conditions. They demanded goods that were both utilitarian and fulfilled their aesthetic orientation. For instance, cloth was highly valued both for its durable quality but also for its color. Indian aesthetics were often difficult to decipher, for both the English and French. As Timothy Shannon's article so clearly indicates, Indians "engaged wholeheartedly in the consumer revolution, but on their own terms and in ways shaped by their cultural values and practices."[2]

Dean Anderson conducted an all-encompassing survey of the Montreal Merchants' Records; these included all goods transported from Montreal to the Great Lakes from 1715 to 1763. His results demonstrate that cloth constituted the majority of trade goods at all Great Lakes posts. Both clothing and the materials with which to make clothing dominated exchange, even at remote posts. Anderson's analysis also suggests that women had considerable input into the types of trading decisions that would be made, since it is women whose time and labor was invested in the production of clothing.[3]

This section also includes articles on the type of cloth and clothing available to a wide range of Indian participants, one that dramatically transformed the Indian appearance. Gail Potter describes the matchcoat, made from the cloth in which Cherokee burdeners were paid. Indian fashions influenced Euro-American dress and George Washington wore a matchcoat into the 1754 expedition against the French.[4] By the early nineteenth century matchcoats had evolved into Chiefs Coats. Allen Chronister describes the Chiefs Coats that were fashioned at tailor shops at fur trade posts; they were either traded or given as gifts to plains Indians. Although few Chiefs Coats remain, they were as elaborate and striking as the matchcoats and were also manufactured from either red or blue cloth.[5]

One of the most common of all fur trade products was the beaver hat. It was beaver that led the French to settle the St. Lawrence River valley and led to their movement into the continent's interior. It was the French beaver trade that led to British involvement in the Seven Years' War. Much has been said about the beaver trade but no myth has been more widespread and accepted than was the general assumption that the beaver trade collapsed when silk replaced beaver in the manufacture of hats. It is clear from James Hanson's article that silk hats were fashionable well before the end of the eighteenth century, and the fur trade did not collapse until almost fifty years later, in 1840, when the last western rendezvous was held. Although the trapping of furs began in the 1670s the quantity of furs did not seem to impact the landscape until the 1830s, when only the most determined of traders ventured into the Northern Rockies to trap. They found themselves competing with the Canadian trappers who controlled the Snake and Columbia River basins, and their furs traveled to market by ships bound for England and China, rather than the New York market of the American Fur Company.[6]

The beaver trade stimulated a consumer revolution in Europe in the seventeenth century, and it did the same thing among North American Indians. Too often, we spend so much time associating consumer revolutions with European fashion that we neglect to understand the extent to which a consumer revolution also impacted Indians. One can only imagine the extent to which the first easterners that crossed the Appalachians encountered Indians that did not fit the prevailing stereotypes. They wore manufactured cloth, rather than furs. Often, Indians were better dressed than their incoming American counterparts. Perhaps, shocked not simply by the eclectic dress of Indians but by the incredible richness of their clothing, we might better appreciate the extent to which fashion had been put to new uses and refracted through the lens of indigenous fashion. For those readers who have the time, a visit to the Tippecanoe Archives in West Lafayette, Indiana, contains the unpublished sketches of dozens of portraits left by George Winter. He captured striking portraits of the Potawatomi and Miami, who lived in the river valley communities south of Lake Michigan and who were engaged in the black raccoon trade. They are on a par with this portrait of a fashionable Indian woman who traveled to Washington; her image was captured in the portraits assembled by Thomas L. McKenney. This portrait speaks both to the aesthetic of Indian sensibilities: the quality and beauty of her garments are striking but so is her sense of how she incorporated and displayed the luxury trade cloth of European manufacture. Tshusick's portrait is a wonderful introduction to one of the last sections of this book, as we explore the extent to which women's positionality was changed by involvement in the fur trade.

Notes

1. Arthur J. Ray, "Indians as Consumers in the Eighteenth Century," in *Old Trails and New Directions: Papers of the Third North American Fur Trade Conference*, ed. Carol M. Judd and Arthur J. Ray, 255–71 (Toronto: University of Toronto Press, 1980).

2. Timothy J. Shannon, "Dressing for Success on the Mohawk Frontier: Hendrick, William Johnson, and the Indian Fashion," *William and Mary Quarterly*, 3rd ser., 53, no. 1 (January 1996): 13–42.

3. Dean Anderson, "The Flow of European Trade Goods into the Western Great Lakes Region, 1715–1760," *The Fur Trade Revisited: Selected Papers of the Sixth North American Fur Trade Conference, Mackinac Island, Michigan, 1991*, ed. J. S. H. Brown, W. J. Eccles, and D. P. Heldman, 93–115 (East Lansing: Michigan State University Press, 1994).

4. Gail DeBuse Potter, "The Matchcoat," *Museum of the Fur Trade Quarterly* 33, no. 4 (Winter 1997): 2–3.

5. Allen Chronister, "Chiefs Coats Supplied By the American Fur Company," *Museum of the Fur Trade Quarterly* 32, no. 2 (Summer 1996): 1–7.

6. James A. Hanson, "The Myth of the Silk Hat and the End of the Rendezvous," *Museum of the Fur Trade Quarterly* 36, no. 1 (Spring 2000): 2–11.

1. Tshusick, an Ojibway woman. Hand-colored lithograph, Plate 42.
Thomas L. Mckenney and James Hall, *History of the Indian Tribes of North
America*. Philadelphia: F. W. Greenough, 1838–44. Photo courtesy of
the Edward E. Ayer Collection, Newberry Library, Chicago.

16. Indians as Consumers in the Eighteenth Century

Arthur J. Ray

You told me Last year to bring many Indians, you See I have not Lyd. here is a great many young men come with me, use them Kindly! use them Kindly I say! give them good goods, give them good Goods I say!—we Livd. hard Last winter and in want, the powder being short measure and bad, I say!—tell your Servants to fill the measure and not to put their finger's within the Brim, take pity of us, take pity of us, I say!—we come a Long way to See you, the french sends for us but we will not here, we Love the English, give us good black tobacco (brazl. tobacco) moist & hard twisted, Let us see itt before op'n'd,—take pity of us, take pity of us I say!— the Guns are bad, Let us trade Light guns small in the hand, and well shap'd, with Locks that will not freeze in the winter, and Red gun cases . . . Let the young men have Roll tobacco cheap, Ketles thick high for the shape and size, strong Ears, and the Baile to Lap Just upon the side,—Give us Good measure, in cloth,—Let us see the old measures, Do you mind me!, the young men Loves you by comming to see you, take pity, take pity I say! . . . they Love to Dress and be fine, do you understand me!—.

According to James Isham, a Hudson's Bay Company trader, the foregoing address was typical of those given by Indian trading leaders during the smoking of the calumet that preceded trade at the bayside posts in the early eighteenth century.[1] Isham's account of the Indian trading speech gives us a rare, fleeting picture of what the Indian was like as a consumer. While politely couching their demands in the form of a plea "take pity of us," and professing that they "love the English," the Indian leaders let the English traders know they expected favorable rates of exchange, good quality merchandise, items stylistically pleasing and well suited to their nomadic life-style in the harsh subarctic environment.

To what extent were the Indians able to press these demands? Did the Hudson's Bay Company make a concerted effort to meet them? By seeking answers to these basic questions we should be able to fill out our sketchy image of the Indian as a consumer, and obtain a clearer picture of his English counterpart and of the nature of Indian-European exchange. This paper will consider the Indians' concern with the quality of merchandise offered by Europeans and its suitability for their needs[2] and the efforts of the Hudson's Bay Company during its first century of operations to develop an inventory of goods acceptable to the Indians.

When the Hudson's Bay Company was chartered in 1670, the founders addressed a number of difficult problems in their efforts to establish trade. In Europe, contacts had to be developed with reliable suppliers of suitable merchandise. In North America, the company faced the difficult task of luring the Indians away from the French. The Indians of the James Bay area and the shield uplands to the south toward the Great Lakes had been receiving French trade goods for a considerable period of time prior to 1668 when the first English trading expedition was sent into the Bay.[3] Therefore, in the beginning the company was at a considerable disadvantage: the French had considerably more experience dealing with the Indians of central Canada, and the Indians had grown accustomed to their merchandise.

The English handicap was offset somewhat by the fact that the two famous French traders and explorers, Medard Chouart, Sieur des Groseillers, and Pierre Esprit Raddison, played active roles in the early history of the Hudson's Bay Company. Both helped the company establish its policies for dealing with the Indians and helped set the first standards of trade for the exchange of goods and furs. Besides assisting the company in its early contact with the Indians, they helped the governor and committee in London select trade goods. Radisson appears to have played the more important role.

At its meeting of 4 March 1671, the governor and committee ordered: "Mr. Bailey with the Advise of Mr. Radisson & Mr. Groseleyer treate with such persons as they think fitt for Such goods as may bee needfull for Supplyeing a Cargo for the next years expedition for Hudson's Bay, that is to Say, two hundred fowleing pieces & foure hundred powder hornes with a proportionable quantity of Shott fitt thereunto, first bringing patterns of the gunns to bee bought unto the next Committee & . . . two Hundred Brass Kettles Sizeable of from two to Sixteene gallons a piece, twelve grosse of French knives & two Grosse of Arrow head & about five or Six hundred hatchets."[4] The order consisted of arms, ammunition, and metal goods, and at least the knives were said to be French. The hatchets were perhaps of French origin judging from instructions that Radisson received from the London committee the following year. On 21 May 1672 they ordered: "that Mr. Raddison attende Mr. Millington forthwith with a pattern of biscay hatchetts to be provided for this Company, such as are usually sent from thence to France to Serve the Indians in & about Canada, & that Mr. Millington bee desired to give order for two thousand hatchetts to be brought from Biscay by the first opportunity." Since the Biscay hatchet was an important trade item, the company's directors hoped to get them manufactured in England. On 4 December 1673 they instructed a Mr Rastell to: "make enquiry among the mchants if hee can finde any Biscay hatchets to bee bought to the ende that by the Samples of them Such hatchets may be provided here as may be most agreeable to the minde of the Indians and that Mr. Millington gett patternes forthwith from Biscay of three . . . Seizes, Vizt of 1 ¼, 1 ½, & 2 lb a piece."[5]

This sequence of events with the Biscay hatchets highlights a pattern developed very early. The company attempted to obtain goods the Indians were already accustomed to in type, style, or pattern. They drew on the considerable experience of Radisson, who advised the company what to buy and assessed the quality of the merchandise obtained for shipment to the bay. Although several key items in the early inventories were of French origin, the company quickly turned to British manufacturers to produce copies. By 1679 an English ironmonger, Robert Carnor, was supplying most of the hatchets. In 1683, the company placed an order for knives with Samuel Bannor. Between that date and 1715, Bannor supplied the company with the bulk of its knives, hatchets, awls, and fire steels. As late as 1697, Bannor was still using French patterns to make some of the company's knives.[6]

English manufacturers also copied other French trade goods. For example, on 25 January 1682, the governor and committee ordered two of their suppliers to contact agents in France to buy samples of blankets so that the company could have similar ones made in England. Six French blankets were eventually bought at a cost of £4 13s. A wide variety of French goods were copied at various times, including awls, vermillion, ice chisels, firearms, and gunpower.[7]

While the company was thus obtaining patterns for goods and developing contacts with suppliers in England, its men in the bay were gaining experience in the conduct of trade with the Indians. Increasingly these men were able to offer advice to augment that of Radisson and they were able to assess the degree to which the company was meeting Indian consumer demand. Indeed, at an early date the men in the bay were required to provide the governor and committee with this information. For example, in their letter to Governor John Nixon dated 29 May 1680 they informed him that he was supposed to: "send us home by every return of our Ships all such goods as are either defective or not acceptable to the Natives and to inform us wherein they are deficient And also to direct us exactly as you can of what form, quality & conditions [of] every sort of goods wch is demanded there for the best satisfaction of the Indians, And wee will do our utmost that you shall be supplied with every species of Commodity in perfection."[8] This order became standing policy and it was often repeated in later letters with only slight revisions. The revisions were designed to give the governor and committee more precise information. For instance, the traders were ordered to give an exact accounting of the quantity of each good sold (including sizes, shapes, colors, etc., wherever appropriate); samples of goods the Indians disliked were to be sent back to London; and examples of items highly prized were also to be returned.[9]

In spite of its concerted effort, the company still fell short of achieving its objective of supplying the Indians with the variety and quality of goods demanded. In 1682, Governor Nixon filed a report to the governor and committee recommending a series of policies be implemented to improve trade. Many of the goods manufactured in England were of such poor quality that he believed the company should consider sending raw materials and tradesmen to the posts and manufacturing many trade goods in Hudson Bay. "It is a great vexation to me," Nixon wrote,

> to see a poore Indiane with his coat all seem-rent, in less than 6 weeks tyme, and when they are torne, the poore rogues can not mend them, but must suffer could in winter, and just occasione have they to say we have stole their beaver, to my great shame and your loss, I humbly conceave that if yow had taylers in the country they would benefit yow . . . The lyk of your smiths. It is a wonder to me that for all our wryting since the country hath been settled, that England can not furnish us with good edge toules, you have verry bad fortoun that you can find non, I have seen good edge tweles made in England, but I feare it is your fate to be cheated.
>
> Wherefore it be a great deall better that they were to be made by the smithes in the country. I am sure that 5d worth of stuff will mak a hatchet . . . as for the smith we must have hime (whither he make your iron worke or not) for the use of the factories . . . so that I conclud the smiths will pay their wages by their worke, and the ware too the Indian's minds, the ice chissels nor indeed no other

Indians as Consumers

iron worke that yow send over is to their mindes, and that is the great cause that a great deall of beaver goeth to the frens which otherways would come to us.

Nixon considered the company's goods to be of such poor quality that he lowered the standard of trade without obtaining the prior approval of the governor and committee.[10]

The London directors were so upset by Nixon's actions that they met three times in June 1684 to discuss the matter. Soon after they wrote to Governor Henry Sergeant, Nixon's successor, and informed him:

> We are heartily troubled that Governor Nixon has altered the Standard of Trade . . . we have strickly examined him and finde that he gives us a very slender account of that alteration, take all those arguments he musters up in his Councell booke as he calls it & you will finde them but weake. Likewise we have examined Geo. Geyer (upon the premisses who was Chiefe at Rupert River, who assures us that the Indians he Traded with . . . (who Lye nerer the French then any factorey) were all pleased with the Goods they bought & the Quantety and no murmering amongst them or craving more goods then at other times . . . we have at this time sent you very good goods, choise goods as can be bought for money especially the Guns, Kettles, hatchets & knives in which we thinke we doe very much outvey the French . . .
>
> The Goods we have now sent you are very good cost us much more then formerly as we have mentioned in the former parte of our letter. Therefore, we wold have you indeavor what leyes in your power to bring our goods to the old Standard.[11]

For the time being, then, the governor and committee decided not to try to improve the quality of their merchandise by having some articles manufactured in the bay. Rather, they decided the best way to upgrade their trade goods was to offer higher prices to English suppliers. It was for this reason that the committee members took exception to Nixon's action of lowering the standard of trade. In fact, one committee member believed that Nixon's action was so prejudicial to the company's interest that he opposed the committee's decision to pay Nixon the £305 salary they owed him.[12]

Despite selling imitations of many French goods and paying higher prices for its commodities in England, the committee received an unabated stream of complaints from the bayside. Even George Geyer, who in 1682 had said the Indians were pleased with company goods, reported widespread dissatisfaction eight years later. This prompted the governor and committee to order that: "all persons against whome Complaints has been Made by Governr Geyer in his Generall Letter [of 1690], shall not furnish the Compa with any goods, untill the Committee are satisfied in that Matter & have otherwise determined it."[13]

Judging from Indian complaints, of all of the goods sold in the early years of the company's operations, those manufactured from metal were the least satisfactory. Most of the Indians' basic tools had traditionally been fashioned from stone, bone, or wood, and if they broke, the hunter could easily repair or replace them. However, the situation was quite different when the Indian was using firearms, metal hatchets, knives, awls, firesteels, and kettles. If a blacksmith or gunsmith were not available, metal tools could not be repaired. Since few Indians lived near the posts in the seventeenth and early eighteenth centuries, tools could only be repaired or replaced once a year. The record clearly shows that the Indians for these reasons became very critical of the firearms, metal tools, and utensils the English and French offered them in trade. There is also reason to believe that European manufacturers did not have the technological capability to make metal goods that met exacting Indian requirements and local environmental conditions.

In the case of firearms, Indian complaints were most frequent in the 1670s and 1680s, but declined thereafter. Between 1700 and 1745 comparatively few criticisms were made. Thereafter, until the close of the period, they were more common. Complaints generally

Indians as Consumers

centered around apparent defects in the metal which the Indians believed caused gun barrels to burst. For example, on 22 August 1748 George Spence wrote from Fort Albany: "Our armourer hath over hauld the Guns & can find no fault with them, but our Indians complain last Year that the Barrels are not so good as usual, they are full of flaws and apt to burst." The governor and committee considered the matter and concluded that the fault did not lie with the guns, but with the Indians. Accordingly, on 16 May 1749 they responded: "Upon examining Strictly into the Complaints made of the Guns We find it is chiefly the Indians Own faults by not puting Dry and Proper Wads in when they charge them or by firing them when the Muzzel is Slopt with Snow which will burst the best Gun that can be made, but as to the flaws, We have given such Strict Orders that We hope you will hear no farther complaints in that Head."[14] The attitude of the London committee is understandable given that all of the guns were viewed by a gunsmith in London before they were packed. In addition, the gunsmiths at the posts were supposed to open the gun cases as soon as they arrived in the bay, examine the guns, immediately return those that were defective, and oil and repack the others.[15] Therefore, any guns the Indians received should have been inspected at least twice.

Most probably some of the problems the Indians experienced with firearms stemmed from harsh usage, given their life-style and their early stage in acquiring an iron-age technology. The Indians may not have fully appreciated that care and prescribed procedures had to be followed when they used their guns. However, the problems the Indians experienced with their firearms were more complicated than the governor and committee suspected. On 10 August 1749 Spence responded to the committee: "We Agree with Your Hons in Opinion that the Guns proving bad is in a Great measure owing to the Carelessness of the Indians, we had Several Gun Barrels brought to us to mend this Summer that were Traded last Year and our Armourer thinks that it is owing to the Stuff [metals used in manufacture] and Likewise being filed too thin." In their final comment to Spence on this subject the governor and committee replied on 21 May 1750: "We are still not withstanding your Armourers Sentiments of Opinion that the Bursting of some of the Guns is entirely owing to the Indians Mismanagement either by Over charging, Improperly Wading, or Suffering Snow to get into them, and not to the Badness of the Shaft which is the same it allways was. And as to the Barrels being filed too thin it has been done by express desire of the Natives themselves to make them more portable if you are of the same opinion as your Armourer, you shall in future have the Barrels thick if you think it needfull, but then we are Convinced you will not be able to Trade them on account of their being To heavy, besides We have no Such Complaints from the Northward and your Guns are equall in strength and goodness to theirs."[16]

This episode underscores the problems the company faced when trying to cater to Indian demands regarding metal goods. The Indians wanted goods as lightweight as possible, that could withstand hard usage and the severe climate. English manufacturers had had little prior experience designing for such conditions. Indeed, the patterns for some goods, such as firearms, were simply copied from those used by other exporting companies which often traded into temperate or tropical areas. For instance, the early firearms were patterned after those of the East India Company. However, goods well suited to those areas were often inadequate for the Canadian environment.

Experience had taught the Indians that even the most minute flaws in metal were potential sources of trouble during the winter when temperatures plummeted and made the iron very brittle. Accordingly, they would not accept any goods with cracks or other apparent defects no matter how minor they appeared to the traders. For instance, in 1750 James Isham returned a considerable number of guns from York Factory saying that they were untradeable. The governor and committee examined them and wrote back to Isham the following year: "We were much concerned on reading your

Indians as Consumers

General Letter to find you had returned so many guns so defective as not fit for Trade . . . but how great was our Surprize when on Strict Examination and the most close Inspection we could not find above four of the guns that had any thing like a fault to make them Untradeable the rest being altogether marked wherever there was a fire flaw / a Scratch as tho made with the Point of a Pin / which no Gun Barrel ever was or can be made without." The following year Isham returned four more firearms saying that they were substandard because of "fire flaws" in the barrels. Isham's action provoked the ire of the committee. In their 1752 letter to Isham, the governor and committee said they thought it extraordinary that he should have sent the guns back in view of their letter of the previous year and added: "the Defects that you Condem them for are only Fire flaws as we said before which / were we to give ever so much for our Guns / it is impossible to get them without, therefore we cannot still help imputing it to the Ignorance of your Armourer, more especially as the Guns sent to your Factory are equal in goodness to any we now send or ever did and it is Surprizing to us that the Trading Indians that came to York Fort should be more Curious than any of the other Natives, and more so within these two years then ever they were before."[17]

The problem of "fire flaws" was not limited to guns. Other metal goods were said to have the same defect. As with firearms, the governor and committee insisted these blemishes were not serious. In 1753 the traders at Fort Churchill returned some knives and firesteels as unacceptable to the Indians. The London committee considered the matter and the following year wrote Ferdinand Jacobs and the council at Fort Churchill telling them: "the flaws you mention in the Knives and Steels we apprehend to be Fire Flaws which are not any real defect but a Mark of their Hardness."[18] It is unclear what the "fire flaws" were. Presumably they were small holes resulting from the casting processes used. It is uncertain whether they seriously affected the durability of arms and metal goods. Perhaps such minor defects were not a problem in England but were sources of difficulty in the subarctic. In any event, the company clearly had problems obtaining metal goods without them and the Indians tended to reject items with these flaws.

As early as 1682, Governor Nixon had suggested one solution would be to have some articles manufactured at company posts. Although the governor and committee did not accept Nixon's suggestion, they eventually decided to pursue this course after other traders made similar suggestions. For example, in his letter of 16 August 1724 from York Factory, Thomas McCliesh informed the governor and committee: "We desire that no more ice chisels nor scrapers be sent out of England, our smiths' making here being preferable and more taken with [*sic*] the Indians." The Governor and committee complied with McCliesh's request and sent bar iron in place of the chisels and scrapers.[19]

The company also confronted similar problems in its efforts to obtain other staple goods acceptable to the Indians. Only one other item, Brazil tobacco, will be considered here. Brazil tobacco ranked high on the Indians' list of priorities; therefore, it indicates the demanding consumer taste the Indian had, even for items not affecting his livelihood. The governor and committee devoted more attention to securing a suitable supply of this commodity than they did for any other item.

Initially the company shipped English tobacco (probably Virginia) to its posts. Its first order for Brazil tobacco, a twisted tobacco treated with molasses, was placed on 7 January 1684.[20] The shipment was received in February and placed on board the company's ships in May 1685. In their 22 May 1685 letter to Governor Sergeant, the governor and committee wrote: "We are sorry the Tobacco last sent you proves so bad, we have made many yeares tryall of Engleish Tobacco, by several persons & whiles we have Traded, we have had yearly complaints thereof. We have made search, [of] what Tobacco the French vends to the Indians, which you doe so much extoll, and have this yeare bought the like (vizt) Brazeele Tobacco, of which we have sent for each Factorey a good Quantity, that if approved of we are resolved in the future to supply [you] with the like, as you have occation."[21] The Indians heartily approved of this innovation and the company was soon engaged in a continuing search for the best Brazil tobacco that could be purchased in European markets. Initially the company ordered its tobacco from London merchants. Typical of these early orders was one that was placed with the firm of Brooke and Gulston on 27 February 1712. On that date the company's secretary, John Perry, indicated: "The Hudsons Bay Compn will have ocasion for about one thousand weight of the Choicest Brazill Tobacco of the Sweetest Smell, but of A Small Role, about the Size of a Mans Little finger."[22]

After receiving an unsatisfactory shipment of Brazil tobacco from their London supplier in 1722, the governor and committee decided to deal directly with Lisbon tobacco merchants. Since Lisbon was one of the leading Brazil tobacco importing cities, they believed they would have a better chance of getting the best tobacco available. The record suggested this was a wise decision. In 1735 the Lisbon firm of John and James Wats informed the company that 8335 rolls of Brazil tobacco had been landed in November and they intended to select twenty of the best for the company. Thereafter, the company had with its Lisbon suppliers a standing order for the twenty best rolls of tobacco as soon as the Bahia fleet arrived in port.[23]

Dealing directly with Lisbon merchants helped the company obtain better tobacco, but the governor and committee still had to check its tobacco cargoes closely to prevent abuses and maintain quality. For instance, Mawman and Company of Lisbon was a major supplier between 1735 and 1743. On 29 March 1743 the governor and committee wrote: "the Tobacco is received, but find on looking into some of the Rolls, they are the worst they have had for some Years past, as being of a very bad Staple much of it wilted and to a great fault Loaded with Melosses which they are informed is done since it came from the Brazils together with a bad scent and too Large a twist for their Trade."[24] The next year the company turned to a different merchant and apparently had no further dealings with Mawman and Company. Suppliers who failed to meet the company's rigid specifications lost its business.

The company closely watched Indian reactions to its goods, kept a watchful eye on the quality and variety of articles their French competitors were selling, and secured the best merchandise available in Europe; but the Indians were still not satisfied. In fact, judging from the record, Indian discontent was increasing toward the middle of the eighteenth century. For instance, on 8 August 1728 Thomas McCliesh wrote the governor and committee from York Factory informing them:

> I have sent home two bath rings as samples, for of late most of the rings sent are too small, having now upon 216 that none of the Indians will Trade. I have likewise sent home 59 ivory combs that will not be traded, they having no great teeth, and 3900 large musket flints and small pistol flints, likewise one hatchet, finding at least 150 such in three casks that we opened this summer which causes great grumbling amongst the natives. We have likewise sent home 18 barrels of powder that came over in 1727, for badness I never saw the like, for it will not kill fowl nor beast at thirty yards distance: and as for kettles in general they are not fit to put into a Indian's hand being all of them thin, and eared with tender old brass that will not bear their weight full of liquid, and soldered in several places. Never was any man so upbraided with our powder, kettles and hatchets, than we have been this summer by all the natives, especially by those that borders near the French. Our cloth likewise is so stretched with the tenter-hooks, so as the selvedge is almost tore from one end of the pieces to the other. I hope that such care will be taken so as will prevent the like for the future, for the natives are grown so politic in their way of trade, so as they are not to be dealt by as formerly . . . and I affirm that man is not fit to be entrusted Company's interest here or in any of their factories that does not make more profit to the Company in dealing in a good

commodity than in a bad. For now is the time to oblige the natives before the French draws them to their settlement.[25]

In their response, the governor and committee indicated that steps had been taken to rectify the problems detailed.[26]

Writing from the same post eleven years later, James Isham sent a long list of Indian complaints. In a letter of 1739, Isham indicated that the Indians disliked the colour and size of the large pearl beads; complained that the kettles were too heavy for their size and the wrong shape; and claimed the gunpowder was very weak, foul smelling, and an objectionable ashy colour. Although they liked the shape, quality, and colour of the blankets, the Indians said they were too short. Cloth, on the other hand, was said to be of little service because it was too narrow, weak, and thin. Despite liking their design, the Indians also considered the buttons and combs to be too weak. The fire steels were faulty, giving little fire, the gun worms too big for the ramrods, the French flints the wrong shape, the yarn gloves useless, and the knives very displeasing, with bad blades and worse handles. The twine was weak and uneven, as thick as packthread in some places and as thin as sewing thread in others. Powder horns were the wrong shape and rings were too wide for the womens' fingers. Isham concluded his list of Indian criticisms by remarking: "Those are the only things of dislike of trading goods to the best of my knowledge, and according to your honours' desire, [I] have sent home samples of most part which is pleasing to the Indians, and most conducive to your honours' interest." Isham must have sent home few examples of articles that pleased the Indians! Only the hatchets were said to be extraordinarily good.[27]

Indian dissatisfaction with many goods continued. Owing to the quantity and variety of goods imported, the governor and committee could not maintain complete control over all of their suppliers in any given year. Some defective merchandise probably slipped their notice every year. English manufacturers had probably still not come to grips with the problem of making light-weight durable goods. McCliesh said the Indians found the kettles thin and weak. Eleven years later Isham reported they thought them too heavy for their size. There was apparently some difficulty making articles stylistically pleasing and sturdy. Isham said the Indians found the combs and buttons pleasing in design but too weak; the governor and committee wrote: "Buttons and Combs are made Neat but if made to Strong will look Clumsy and heavy."[28]

Another aspect of Indian complaints cannot be overlooked. These criticisms were part of the bargaining ploys the Indians used to pressure the traders to lower the prices of goods. Since this strategy was most effective when European trading rivalries were strong, there should perhaps be some correlation between the frequency of Indian complaints and the intensity of English-French competition. This was probably the case.

French opposition was strongest between 1730 and 1755 when the company was forced to relax the standards of trade at all posts except Fort Churchill.[29] During this period Indian criticisms of company trade goods were most prevalent. McCliesh noted in his 1728 letter that it was particularly the Indians living near the French who "upbraided" him for the poor quality of company merchandise; also, the Indians were becoming increasingly "politic" in their way of trade as the French drew near.[30]

Besides holding McCliesh and other company traders up to ridicule for the "substandard" trade goods offered for exchange, these "Frenchified" Indians, as they were called, claimed that the French traded superior merchandise.[31] The governor and committee were puzzled as to why the Indians seemed to prefer French articles to those of the company—many company goods had been copied from French patterns and subsequently improved. Accordingly, on 18 May 1738 they wrote to Thomas Bird at Fort Albany: "Wee Shall Expect by the return of the Ship this Year Samples of Such Sorts of Commodities which the French furnish the Indians . . . that you not only say are better than ours but also more acceptable to the Natives,

Indians as Consumers

And also your remarks thereon." Bird sent to London a variety of French goods obtained from the Indians. After inspecting these articles, the governor and committee wrote back in 1739: "We have received the two pieces of Cloth and the Samples of other knives you sent us which you say are French, the worst piece is very coarse and loose and Narrow and not near so good or broad as what we have formerly & do now send, and therefore we do Expect you will write us the reasons why the Indians like the French better then ours which you have omitted to do, the Finest piece is also narrow. As to the knives the Difference is only in the Handles. Wherefore we have sent you Six hundred large Long Knives with box handles over and above ye Quantity you Indented for."[32]

The governor and committee clearly believed the cloth they were shipping to the bay superior to that of the French; nonetheless they took steps to improve the quality. On 1 May 1740 they wrote to Rowland Waggoner at Moose Factory: "we have taken very great care about the cloth for it is thick and Strong of good Wool and Spinning full Breadth & well dyed, much better then the french cloth, so do not Doubt but it will be very pleasing to the Indians . . . The flannell now sent is thicker and better then what was sent heretofore, therefore let us know how it is approved of."[33] Similar letters were sent to the factors at Fort Albany and York Factory. Thus the Indians not only successfully pressured the company to relax the standards of trade, but also brought about an improvement in the quality of goods offered to them. They effected change in this and many other instances even though company officials were convinced the merchandise they offered was the best available locally.

The Indians apparently used the same tactics in their dealings with the French. For example, the French were convinced that English woolens were better and cheaper than French and were preferred by the Indians. In the early eighteenth century over twenty-one thousand yards of English strouds were imported into New France annually from New York for the Indian trade.[34] At mid-century, the governor and intendant of New France wrote to the French government: "The English have the better of us in the quality of merchandise in two important articles. The first is kettles—the second is cloth. They [the traders] believe that up to the present the Indians wish only English cloth and they become so well accustomed to it that it would be difficult to introduce others."[35] The governor's remarks are interesting given that French manufacturers had been producing imitations of English cloth for the Indian trade since the 1720s.[36] His comments were made during the very period when the Indians were telling company traders English woolens were not equal to French. Ironically, the cloth the Indians brought to the bay from the French posts may well have been made in England or copies of yard goods formerly sold by the company. The Indians were clearly successful in pitting the two European groups against each other, forcing them to lower prices, and getting them to make copies and improvements of each other's merchandise.

In conclusion, an examination of the early Hudson's Bay Company fur trade reveals the Indians as shrewd consumers who knew how to take full advantage of the economic opportunities offered to them. In this respect the Indians were clearly equal to their European counterparts. The old stereotype of the Indians being a people easily tricked by crafty Europeans and made to part with valuable furs for worthless trinkets obviously does not apply to the central subarctic before 1763.

In casting away the old stereotype and searching the rich historical record we find a consistent and logical pattern to Indian consumer demand. They wanted to barter their furs at the most favorable rates of exchange that competitive conditions permitted. They wanted light-weight durable goods well suited to the harsh subarctic environment. Given the widely scattered posts, Indians were usually unable to have their European manufactured tools repaired or replaced more than once a year. Therefore, they expected more from these tools than from those they traditionally made from local materials. Indeed, the Indians needed more reliable metal tools than did the European traders, who had access to blacksmiths and gunsmiths or to warehouses for replacements when the smiths could not effect needed repairs.

Perhaps we have dwelt too long on the sorry tale of the European abuse of Indians in the fur trade after 1763—a well-known tale which usually casts the Indians as passive figures pushed around by different trading companies. By looking at an earlier period, when a more equal partnership existed between the Indian and the trader, the active role of the Indian is more readily apparent. In this instance, by recognizing that the Indians had well-defined demands and a critical eye to assess trade goods, we find that the Indian was probably an agent of technological change even though his culture was not as advanced technologically as that of his European partners. The latter were forced to make a number of changes in the manufacture of firearms and metal goods. The tempering and casting of metal had to be improved to produce knives, hatchets, kettles, ice chisels, and guns that were less prone to breaking in the severe cold. The record indicates that some of the craftsmen working the trading posts were able to make certain tools that were more to the Indians' liking than those manufactured in Europe. The nature and importance of technological innovations resulting from attempts to meet the consumer demands of the Indian is a story that has yet to be told.

Notes

1. Rich, ed., *James Isham's Observations and Notes, 1743–1749*, 83–87.

2. See also Ray and Freeman, *"Give Us Good Measure,"* 163–97.

3. For discussions of early trade into this region, see Bishop, *The Northern Ojibway and the Fur Trade*; Heidenrech and Ray, *The Early Fur Trades: A Study in Cultural Interaction*; Ray, *Indians in the Fur Trade*, 3–26.

4. Rich, ed., *Copy-Booke of Letters Outward*, 147.

5. Rich, ed., *Minutes of the Hudson's Bay Company, 1671–74*, 26–27, 58–59, 61.

6. On 3 Feb. 1679, the company ordered three hundred hatchets from Robert Carnor at a price of ten pennies per hatchet (ibid., 32).

The first order with Bannor appears to have been placed on 7 Dec. 1683 (Rich, ed., *Minutes of the Hudson's Bay Company, 1679–84*, 2nd part, 171–72).

In a letter of 24 Feb. 1697 the company secretary informed Bannor that the company wanted him to make 1,200 Jack Knives "imitating the French," (HBCA A 6/3, 37, Letters Outward).

7. Rich, ed., *Minutes 1679–84*, 1st part, 177, 2nd part, 9. The common practice was to have the men buy French goods from the Indians. These goods would then be sent to London and used as samples. For evidence that the French patterns were being followed, see the various minutes of the company edited by E. E. Rich. Other examples can be found in the unpublished minutes and outward correspondence books of the company.

8. Rich, ed., *Letters Outward*, 8.

9. The first order was sent to John Bridgar on 27 April 1683 and became standing policy (ibid., 86–89). The second policy was implemented in 1680 (ibid., 8). The governor and committee initiated the third policy to prevent confusion in the indents (HBCA A 6/3, 31, Letters Outward, 31 May 1697 to York Factory).

10. Rich, *Minutes 1679–84*, 1st part, 251–52. The governor and committee questioned Nixon's right to take such actions (Rich, ed., *Minutes 1679–84*, 2nd part, 251).

11. Rich, ed., *Letters Outward*, 120–21. For the three meetings, see Rich, ed., *Minutes*, 2nd part, 251–52 and 256.

12. Rich, ed., *Minutes 1679–84*, 2nd part, 256. Sir Edward Dering was in opposition.

13. Meeting of 3 Dec. 1690 (HBCA A 1/13, 4, Minutes).

14. HBCA A 11/2, 136, Letters Inward; A 6/8, 9, Letters Outward.

15. The company had been doing these inspections since the early 1670s. On 24 March 1674 an attempt was made to enlist the services of the East India Company's gun surveyor (Rich, ed., *Minutes 1671–74*, 91).

In their general letter of 3 May 1745, the governor and committee wrote: "We do direct you that you take all the Guns out of the Chests immediately [upon receipt] and that they be overlooked by the Armourer and then Oiled and repacked and in case of any Defect to give the Committee the number on the Case and the Name of the Maker of the Gun and . . . what the defects are that we may get them rectified" (HBCA A 6/7, 71, Letters Outward). This became a standing policy thereafter.

16. HBCA A 11/2, 140, Correspondence Inward, Fort Albany, 10 August 1749; A 6/8, 36, Correspondence Outward, 21 May 1750.

17. HBCA A 6/8, 67, Correspondence Outward, 16 May 1751; A 6/8, 95, Correspondence Outward, 12 May 1752. When he sent the guns in question, Isham sent a covering letter in which he informed the committee, "the reason of our sending no others home have My self/ as I did those/ examined them very carefully & find several [4] that has flaws in the Barrells, which no Indian will trade" (A 11/114, 146–50, Correspondence Inward, York Factory, 8 August 1751).

18. HBCA A 6/8, 120, Correspondence Outward, 24 May 1753.

19. Davies, ed., *Letters from Hudson Bay, 1703–40*, 99–100; HBCA A 6/4, 95–96, Correspondence Outward, 19 May 1725.

20. Meeting of 7 Jan. 1684, HBCA A 1/8, 9.

21. Rich, ed., *Letters Outward*, 140–42.

22. HBCA A 6/3, 120, Correspondence Outward, 27 Feb. 1712.

23. The company had ordered the tobacco from a London merchant named Edward Bridgon. On 22 Nov. 1723 the company's secretary wrote Bridgon informing him: "Complaint having been made to the Comitte that the Brazil Tobacco Imported last yeare by Mess Gutson Simens & Co of Lisbone for ye Comp account was not soe good as formerly I am ordered by them to acquaint you therewith, desiring you would Informe those Gent. of it" (HBCA A 6/4, 82, Correspondence Outward). On 14 July 1724 the company began dealing with the firm of Lewsen, Gibbs and Potter of Lisbon (A 6/4, 82, Correspondence Outward, 14 July 1724).

The merchants, Lewsen, Gibbs and Potter, had suggested to the governor and committee that tobacco be specially ordered in Brazil to meet their requirements. However, the committee believed that this arrangement would not be as satisfactory as selecting from the best that was available in Lisbon (HBCA A 6/4, 94, Correspondence Outward, 27 Oct. 1724).

For John and James Wats, see HBCA A 6/5, 103, Correspondence Outward, 25 Nov. 1735.

In their yearly letters to their tobacco suppliers, the governor and committee repeatedly stressed that the Brazil tobacco had to be the newest and freshest available or their Indian customers would refuse to buy it.

24. HBCA A 6/7, 13, Correspondence Outward, 29 March 1743. The London correspondence indicates that the company began dealing with Chase and Company of Lisbon (A 6/7, 32, Correspondence Outward, 22 Dec. 1743).

25. Davies, *Letters*, 136.

26. The governor and committee responded to McCliesh saying: "We take notice of the complaints mady by the Indians of ye unsizeableness and badness of some of our trading goods and have given such orders and directions

to the persons that serve us with those goods that we hope will prevent the like complaints for the future" (HBCA A 6/5, Correspondence Outward, 21 May 1729, 26–28).

27. Davies, *Letters*, 278–80.

28. HBCA A 6/6, 74–75, Correspondence Outward, 1 May 1740. The governor and committee added in their letter that they would again contact their suppliers to correct the defects in the other merchandise.

29. Ray and Freeman, *"Give Us Good Measure,"* 163–97.

30. Pierre Gaultier de Varennes de La Vérendrye had been placed in command of the northern posts of the French in 1728. Under his direction the French began pushing into the hinterland of York Factory in the late 1720s and the 1730s. Heidenreich and Ray, *Early Fur Trades*, 41–43. As noted earlier in the paper, guns were an exception to the escalation of complaints.

31. This term was used as early as 1703 to describe Indians who also traded with the French. In a letter from Fort Albany dated 2 August 1703, John Fullartine wrote "there came an abundance of Indians down who used the French and were so much Frenchified that they asked for the goods which they traded in French" (Davies, *Letters*, 8).

32. HBCA A 6/6, 9–15, Correspondence Outward, 18 May 1738; A 6/6, 31–35, Correspondence Outward, 17 May 1739.

33. HBCA A 6/6, 66, Correspondence Outward, 1 May 1740. A letter to Richard Staunton at Moose Factory indicated that he had sent a French coat along with the French cloth the previous year. Many of the company goods were made in the bay and there is no indication that the Governor and Committee attempted to copy the coat Staunton sent (HBCA A 6/6, 71, Correspondence Outward, 1 May 1740).

34. Wraxall, *An Abridgement of the Indian Affairs Contained in Four Folio Volumes, Transacted in the Colony of New York from the Year 1678 to the Year 1751*, ed. McIlwain, lxvii. According to Thomas E. Norton, Montreal-based traders had a preference for many English goods and French smugglers made their largest profits bringing strouds into Canada from New York (Norton, *The Fur Trade in Colonial New York 1686–1776*, 126).

35. Quoted in Innis, *The Fur Trade in Canada*, 85. According to Innis, English manufactured trade goods were generally cheaper and superior to those made in France in the early eighteenth century. For this reason a considerable trade developed between merchants in Montreal and the colony of New York (ibid., 84–85).

36. Wraxall, *Indian Affairs*, lxxii.

Bibliography of Published Works Cited

Bailey, A. G. *The Conflict of European and Eastern Algonkian Cultures, 1504–1700.* 2nd ed. Toronto, 1969.

Bishop, Charles A. *The Northern Ojibwa and the Fur Trade: An Historical and Ecological Study.* Toronto, 1974.

Davidson, Gordon Charles. *The North West Company.* New York, 1918, rpt. 1967.

Davies, K. G., ed. *Letters from Hudson Bay, 1703–40.* London, 1965.

Easterbrook, W. T. "Recent Contributions to Economic History: Canada." In *Approaches to Canadian Economic History,* by W. T. Easterbrook and M. H. Watkins. Toronto, 1967.

Eccles, W. J. *The Canadian Frontier, 1534–1760.* Toronto, 1969.

Fowke, Vernon. *Canadian Agricultural Policy: The Historical Patterns.* Toronto, 1946.

Galbraith, J. S. *The Hudson's Bay Company as an Imperial Factor, 1821–69.* Toronto, 1957.

Gibson, James R. *Feeding the Russian Fur Trade.* Madison, 1969.

———. "Food for the Fur Traders: The First Farmers in the Pacific Northwest, 1805–1946." *Journal of the West* 8 (1968): 18–30.

Harris, R. Cole, and Leonard Guelke. "Land and Society in Canada and South Africa." *Journal of Historical Geography* 3 (1977).

Heidenreich, Conrad. *Huronia: A History and Geography of the Huron Indians, 1650–1660.* Toronto, 1971.

Henry, Alexander. *Travels and Adventures in Canada and the Indian Territories between the Years 1760 and 1776.* Edmonton, 1969.

Innis, Harold A. *The Fur Trade in Canada: An Introduction to Canadian Economic History.* Rev. ed. Toronto, 1956.

Jones, R. L. *History of Agriculture in Ontario, 1663–1880.* Toronto, 1946.

Kaye, Barry. "The Historical Geography of Agriculture and Agricultural Settlements in the Canadian Northwest 1774 ca 1830." PhD diss., University of London, 1976.

Lalemant, Father Charles, in R. G. Thwaites, ed. *Jesuit Relations and Allied Documents.* New York, 1959.

Martin, Calvin. "Ethnohistory: A Better Way to Write Indian History." *Western Historical Quarterly* 9 (1978).

Moodie, D. W. "An Historical Geography of Agricultural Patterns and Resource Appraisals in Rupert's Land, 1670–1774." PhD diss., University of Alberta, 1972.

Morton, A. S. *A History of the Canadian West to 1870–71.* London, 1939.

Morton, W. L. "Agriculture in the Red River Colony." *Canadian Historical Review* 30 (1949): 305–22.

———. In *London Correspondence Inward from Eden Colvile, 1849*, edited by E. E. Rich. London, 1956.

———. *Manitoba: A History.* 2nd ed. Toronto, 1967.

———, ed., *Manitoba Essays.* Toronto, 1937, 89–105.

Norton, T. E. *The Fur Trade in Colonial New York, 1686–1776.* Madison, 1974.

Perrot, Nicholas. In *The Indian Tribes of the Upper Mississippi Valley and the Region of the Great Lakes,* edited by E. H. Blair. Cleveland, 1911.

Phillips, C. P. *The Fur Trade.* 2 vols. Norman, 1961.

Ray, Arthur J., and D. B. Freeman. "'Give Us Good Measure': An Economic Analysis of Relations between the Indians and the Hudson's Bay Company Before 1763." Toronto, 1978.

Rich, E. E. *The Fur Trade and the Northwest to 1857.* Toronto, 1967.

———. *History of the Hudson's Bay Company, 1670–1870.* 2 vols. London, 1959.

———, ed. *Hudson's Bay Copy-Book of Letters Outward etc., Begins 29th May, Ends 5 July, 1687.* Toronto, 1948.

———, ed. *James Isham's Observations on Hudson's Bay, 1743–1749.* Toronto, 1949.

———, ed. *Minutes of the Hudson's Bay Company, 1671–1674.* Toronto, 1942.

———, ed. *Minutes of the Hudson's Bay Company, 1679–1684. First Part, 1679–1682.* Toronto, 1945.

———, ed. *Minutes of the Hudson's Bay Company, 1679–1684. Second Part, 1682–1684.* Toronto, 1946.

Sagard, Father Gabriel. In *The Long Journey to the Country of the Hurons,* edited by G. M. Wrong. Toronto, 1939.

Schoolcraft, Henry. In *Expedition to Lake Itasca,* edited by Philip P. Mason. East Lansing, 1958.

Snow, Dean R. "Abenaki Fur Trade in the Sixteenth Century," *Western Canadian Journal of Anthropology* 6 (1976): 7–9.

Thwaites, Reuben Gold, ed. *Early Western Travels, 1748–1846.* Cleveland, 1904.

———, ed. *The Jesuit Relations and Allied Documents.* 72 volumes. Cleveland, 1896–1901.

Triggar, Bruce. *The Children of Aataensic: A History of the Huron People to 1660.* 2 vols. Montreal, 1976.

Turner, Frederick Jackson. "The Significance of the Frontier in American History." In *Frontier American History.* New York, 1920, 1–38.

Wessel, Thomas. "Agriculture, Indians and American History." *Agricultural History* 50 (1976): 9–20.

Will, George, and George Hyde. *Corn among the Indians of the Upper Missouri.* Lincoln, 1917.

Wishart, D. "Agriculture at the Trading Posts on the Upper Missouri Prior to 1843." *Agricultural History* 47 (1973): 56–62.

Wraxall, Peter. *An Abridgement of the Indian Affairs Contained in Four Folio Volumes, Transacted in the Colony of New York from the Year 1678 to the Year 1751*, edited by C. H. McIlwain. Cambridge, 1915.

17. Dressing for Success on the Mohawk Frontier

Hendrick, William Johnson, and the Indian Fashion

Timothy J. Shannon

In the mid-eighteenth century, colonist William Johnson and Mohawk leader Hendrick forged a partnership that dominated European-Indian relations in the Mohawk Valley of New York. Johnson, an Irish fur trader and merchant who settled in the region in 1738, served as New York's Indian agent from 1746 to 1751 and in 1755 became the British crown's first Superintendent of Indian Affairs. Hendrick, a Mohawk from the village of Canajoharie, had been active in European-Indian diplomacy since the late 1690s; by the 1740s he was the most widely recognized Indian leader in the northern colonies. Together, Johnson and Hendrick exerted a tremendous influence on the Covenant Chain, an alliance governing economic and diplomatic relations between the Iroquois confederacy and Great Britain's North American colonies.[1]

Visual images of Johnson and Hendrick provide insight into the roles they played within the Covenant Chain. In an early portrait, Johnson appears in a fine scarlet coat, green vest, and cravat—dress that declared his status as a colonial merchant and militia officer.[2] This portrait contrasts with another recorded by Cadwallader Colden, a New York councilor and contemporary of Johnson's. Colden attended a Covenant Chain treaty conference in Albany in August 1746, where he saw Johnson enter the city gates, "riding at the head of the *Mohawks*, dressed and painted after the manner of an *Indian* War Captain," followed by Indians "likewise dressed and painted, as is usual when they set out in War."[3] Such a dramatic scene offers a striking juxtaposition to the portrait of a staid, well-dressed colonial gentleman.

An impressive portrait of Hendrick dates to a visit he made to London in 1740, when he was about sixty years old (image 2). Hendrick appears in costume appropriate for the royal court: blue suit and cocked hat trimmed in lace, a ruffled shirt with long cuffs, and cravat. Tradition has it that King George II presented this outfit to him.[4] Hendrick holds a tomahawk in one hand and a string of wampum in the other, combining the attire of eighteenth-century English gentry with symbolic props of North American Indian diplomacy. Four years later, Dr. Alexander Hamilton, an Annapolis physician touring the northern colonies, provided a verbal description of Hendrick to complement this visual one. In Boston, Hamilton observed a procession of Indians attending a treaty conference. He noted that Hendrick and the other Indian leaders "had all laced hats, and some of them laced matchcoats and ruffled shirts."[5]

Scholars of material culture have long noted the importance of clothing in self-presentation. Costume and fashion provide what one cultural anthropologist has called "an expressive medium" through which individuals communicate with others.[6] Such factors as the color, fabric, and fit of the clothing, along with posture and manners, tell us about the wearer's social position, occupation, and elements of personal identity from religious beliefs to sexual preferences. In addition to keeping the body warm and dry, clothing may denote status, signify a rite of passage, or even convey spiritual powers. The importance of clothing to material culture therefore extends far beyond its utility to include a variety of expressive properties that may be manipulated by its wearer.[7]

Historians of the British-Atlantic world have applied these insights in studying the eighteenth-century consumer revolution. In England, the expansion of markets and consumer choices profoundly affected clothing fashion and the public's buying habits.[8] In North America, consumption of British manufactures increased dramatically after 1740, altering colonists' everyday activities and reshaping their notions of taste and refinement. Through goods

The brave old *Hendrick* the great *SACHEM* or *Chief* of the *Mohawk Indians*, one of the *Six Nations* now in *Alliance with & Subject to the King of Great Britain*.
Sold by *Eliz Bakewell opposite Birchin Lane in Cornhill*.

2. "The Brave Old Hendrick."
Anonymous engraving, 1755.
The John Carter Brown Library
at Brown University.

and styles imported from England, provincial Americans imitated British consumers and cultivated new standards of gentility based on self-presentation.[9]

For the Indians of northeastern America, this consumer revolution had been underway since European contact. They too encountered expanding markets and new choices as they became increasingly dependent on European weapons, tools, and clothing. Indians adopted these goods when they found them technologically advantageous but valued them also for aesthetic properties, such as color and shape, and for ceremonial uses, such as mourning the dead, that Europeans were slow to comprehend. Indian consumers were selective and demanding, often haggling over prices and refusing inferior goods. In short, they engaged wholeheartedly in the consumer revolution, but on their own terms and in ways shaped by their cultural values and practices.[10]

Within this consumer revolution, both Europeans and Indians found uses for the expressive properties of clothing. As the portraits of Johnson and Hendrick indicate, costume played an important role in intercultural contact and exchange. The Mohawk Valley in which Johnson and Hendrick lived was a jumble of differing ethnicities and languages. Clothing helped the Valley's inhabitants communicate in ways other than the written or spoken word. Apparel had been a popular trade good in the Mohawk Valley since the early seventeenth century. Under the Covenant Chain alliance, it acquired considerable importance as a tool of diplomacy. Indians and colonists gathered periodically in Albany to make speeches and renew the alliance that preserved peace and trade between them. Treaty participants exchanged presents, usually bundles of furs from the Indians and manufactured items from the colonists. Over the course of the eighteenth century, the Indians' presents remained small and symbolic, but the colonists' grew into substantial donations of material goods. Clothing included in such grants ranged from cheap woolens to fine linens, from such necessaries as shirts and blankets to ornamental ribbons, earrings, and beads.

Europeans also presented Indians with weapons, liquor, tools, food, and even cash, but none of these items had the universal appeal and diversity of choice that clothing offered to Indian men, women, and children.[11]

Clothing helped the Mohawk Valley's inhabitants establish what Richard White calls a "middle ground" of cultural mediation. In White's study, middle ground both refers to a geographic region between the Mississippi River and the Appalachian Mountains and describes a culturally constructed space shaped by the rituals and customs that governed the fur trade and European-Indian diplomacy.[12] Clothing helped establish such a space in the Mohawk Valley. Through their participation in the consumer revolution, Indians and colonists there did more than simply imitate the fashions of English gentlefolk. They used trade goods to invent new appearances, new ceremonies, and a new, visual language by which they communicated in a diverse and contentious world.

Clothing provided an important means of cultural mediation in the Mohawk Valley because it endowed its possessor with a capacity for self-fashioning. Other assets, such as multilingual fluency and political connections, certainly helped overcome cultural differences, but the careers of Johnson and Hendrick prove the importance of looking the part as well. Costume, when used correctly, increased the cultural mobility of its wearer. Clothing was acquired more easily than a foreign language and changed more readily than a Native accent. It provided people with constant opportunity to re-invent themselves from one audience to the next, to create new appearances, and to gain influence through participation in trade.[13] In the Mohawk Valley, no one manipulated these opportunities more skillfully than Hendrick and Johnson.

From the perspective of London or Paris in the mid-eighteenth century, the Mohawk Valley divided North America into three distinct units: British to the east, Indian to the west, French to the north. In actuality, colonial and Native populations did not neatly arrange themselves *in partes tres*. Albany, its population still predominantly Dutch, served as an eastern gateway to the region from the Hudson River. It was also a trading center for Indians who carried furs and goods between Canada and New York by way of Lake Champlain. The Mohawks inhabited two villages west of Albany: Tiononderoge, which Europeans called the "lower castle," and Canajoharie, the "upper castle." German, Irish, and Scots-Irish colonists lived near Tiononderoge, where the Schoharie River met the Mohawk; many of them were tenants of William Johnson and his uncle Peter Warren. Mount Johnson, Johnson's diplomatic and mercantile headquarters, stood north of the Mohawk between the two Indian villages. Moving farther upstream, a traveler entered German Flats, settled by German Palatines in the 1720s. More Germans and Scots-Irish lived south of this region in Cherry Valley, near the headwaters of the Susquehanna River. Farther west, on the southeastern shore of Lake Ontario, a handful of British soldiers garrisoned Oswego, a post that attracted Indian and colonial traders throughout the Great Lakes region to its summer markets.[14]

Although far inland from major seaports, the Mohawk Valley's inhabitants actively engaged in the British-Atlantic economy. Indians and colonists ferried goods along the Mohawk River between Albany and Oswego.[15] Johnson lived in the middle of this trade. To agents in New York City and London, he sent furs, along with wheat and peas grown by local farmers and ginseng gathered by Indians. He imported clothing, tools, weapons, and liquor for his storehouse, which he located to intercept Indians and colonists headed downstream to Albany.[16]

The goods that flowed into the Mohawk Valley had a pervasive effect on cultural identities there, allowing inhabitants to engage in behaviors and habits not normally associated with colonial frontier life. Johnson himself is an excellent example. By 1749, he had amassed a fortune large enough to live in the style of an English gentleman. On the Mohawk River, forty miles removed from the nearest colonial population center, he built a home "60 foot long, by 32 Wide two Story High, all Stone."[17] He purchased household slaves and servants and imported the luxuries that defined colonial gentility: books and newspapers, the *Gentleman's Magazine* from London, fine writing paper and sealing wax, musical instruments, and prints.[18] In 1763, Johnson built his own Georgian-style mansion, Johnson Hall, to complement the baronetcy the crown awarded him during the Seven Years' War.[19]

Johnson was not the only Mohawk Valley inhabitant to indulge in imported goods. Traveling in the region in 1748–49, Swedish naturalist Peter Kalm encountered a world shaped by consumerism. While he found Albany overwhelmingly Dutch in character—its citizens spoke Dutch, had Dutch manners, and practiced Dutch religion—he qualified this observation with one telling remark: "Their dress is however like that of the English."[20] English clothing had managed to penetrate the insular world of Dutch Albany well in advance of English language or politics. Even more noteworthy are Kalm's observations on tea drinking, a practice he found almost universal among colonists. In the Mohawk Valley, he saw Indian women enjoying this new luxury as well. Johnson, recorded Kalm, said that "several of the Indians who lived close to the European settlements had learned to drink tea." Kalm, who criticized colonial women for drinking tea as hot as possible, added that "Indian women in imitation of them, swallowed the tea in the same manner." Johnson included tea, sugar, and teapots for "Chief Familys" among his Indian presents.[21] Tea drinking, a consumer activity by which colonial Americans commonly expressed their gentility, became an agent of cultural assimilation between Europeans and Indians in the Mohawk Valley.[22]

Clothing exchanged in the Mohawk Valley trade also challenged traditional cultural differences. Indians wore European clothing, but they did so in a distinctive way that contemporaries recognized as the "Indian Fashion."[23] Indian consumers rarely adopted European costume from head to foot, and they expressed strong distaste for tight-fitting clothing such as breeches and shoes. Instead, they traded for European cloth cut from the bolt, which they put to any number of uses. The coarse woolen blankets, strouds, duffels, and half-thicks that made up the bulk of this trade they arranged around their bodies as shirts, skirts, robes, and coats. Indian men also favored long linen hunting shirts, which they wore draped over the waist. On the lower body, Indians used European cloth as loincloths, leggings, and moccasins that left more skin exposed than Europeans considered proper. The Indian fashion favored certain colors and fabrics, and European traders adjusted their stock accordingly.[24] Johnson provided woolens in shades of blue, red, and black as well as flowered serge and striped calicoes in "lively Colours."[25]

The Indian fashion also adopted European goods for bodily decoration. Indians painted and tattooed their bodies with such traditional materials as bear's grease and natural dyes; they added to this mix with imported verdigris, which has a green pigment, and vermillion, which has a red. Objects of European origin became jewelry for the hair, nose, ears, and arms. Johnson listed glass beads, silver armbands, brass wire, and medals embossed with the British arms among his trade goods as well as buttons, buckles, lace, and brightly colored ribbons. Indians could incorporate these items into their dress with cloth-working tools provided by European traders: scissors, needles, thread, pen knives, and awl blades. Items for personal grooming included buckling combs and looking glasses.[26]

Indians of both sexes valued these European goods, but contemporaries noted gender differences in their tastes and habits. Kalm observed that women were not as quick to "clothe themselves according to the new styles," although he occasionally saw some wearing caps of homespun or "coarse blue broad-cloth" in imitation of colonial women.[27] Men frequently examined their decorations in mirrors and "upon the whole, [were] more fond of dressing than the women." Another indication of male immersion in fashion is Johnson's inclusion of ribbons, combs, razors, and looking glasses among the presents he made to warriors.[28] Johnson gave women and children blankets, shirts, and stockings earmarked in special sizes for them, and women adopted European items as jewelry. Richard Smith, a land speculator visiting the Mohawk Valley in 1769, recalled that some women wore "Silver Broaches each of which passes for a Shilling and are as current among the Indians as Money," while "the younger sort" of both sexes used "Bobs and Trinkets in their Ears and Noses, Bracelets on their Arms and Rings on their Fingers."[29]

A further distinction within the Indian fashion arose between the costumes of sachems and warriors. Johnson's account for presents he distributed during King George's War gives detailed portraits of the well-dressed sachem and the well-dressed warrior.[30] For example, on May 11, 1747, ten Senecas appeared at Johnson's home with news about Indian affairs. To nine of them Johnson gave a shirt, paint, and knives. To the tenth, whom he identified as "the Capt[ain]," he also gave paint and knives, along with "A Shirt very fine with Ruffles & ribon" and "A fine lac'd Hatt . . . with a Cockade."[31] The same account shows that Johnson distributed shirts, blankets, stockings, laps, ribbons, paint, combs, scissors, razors, and looking glasses to warriors, along with weapons and provisions. Sachems received many of these goods, but their presents always included a ruffled shirt, laced hat, silver medal, or fine coat. Presents for warriors—paint, razors, combs, ribbons, mirrors—emphasized bodily decoration for battle. Presents for sachems featured clothing—fine shirts, hats, and coats—appropriate for diplomacy (images 3 and 4).

Judging from contemporary reports, Indians attending treaty conferences with Europeans observed this fashion distinction between sachems and warriors. Visitors in the Mohawk Valley recognized a visual difference between "the common sort" of Indians, who generally wore clothing limited to "a Shirt or Shift with a Blanket or Coat," and their leaders, who were more likely to "imitate the English Mode" and appear in hats, coats, and ruffled shirts.[32] Europeans viewed Indian costume in the same way that they looked at their own—as an indication of the wearer's place within a hierarchical social order.

Dressing for Success

3. Guerrier Iroquois. Hand-colored etching
by J. Laroque. From Jacques Grasset de Saint-
Sauvier, *Encyclopedie des voyages* . . . , vol. 2,
Amerique. Paris, 1796. Ref. no. c-003163.
Library and Archives Canada.

4. Grand Chef de Guerriers Iroquoise.
Hand-colored etching by J. Laroque. From
Jacques Grasset de Saint-Sauvier, *Encyclopedie
des voyages* . . . , vol. 2, Amerique. Paris,
1796. Ref. no. c-003161. Library and
Archives Canada.

Coming from a culture that regulated colors and fabrics worn by different classes, Europeans interpreted the Indian fashion as a similar means of establishing social distinctions. A sachem who appeared at a public treaty meeting wearing a ruffled shift, fine coat, and laced hat became the visual counterpart of the colonial gentlemen across the council fire. Even such novices to Indian affairs as Dr. Hamilton could readily distinguish sachems from "a multitude of the plebs of their own complexion" by analyzing their dress.[33]

Indians attached their own meaning to the European clothing they wore. Ethnohistorians and anthropologists have argued that Indians invested presents they received from Europeans with ideological value that often outweighed their utilitarian value. Beads and cloth of a certain color or shape, for example, represented physical or emotional well-being and gave spiritual wealth to their possessor. Presents received at a treaty council symbolized friendship between the giver and recipient, and Indians perceived them as material evidence of peace and goodwill.[34] The context in which Indians acquired European clothing thus shaped the way they used it: they might invest clothing presented to them at a treaty conference with a ceremonial significance that would merit saving and wearing it again on similar occasions. Such ideological value helps explain why Indian men were more likely than Indian women to dress in a distinctive fashion when among Europeans. Johnson's accounts reveal that he distributed clothing to sachems and warriors personally—often in one-to-one encounters—when going to war, honoring the dead, or entertaining friends. When he gave clothing to Indian women and children, he distributed it in much greater quantities and for more utilitarian reasons: on May 24, 1747, for example, he entered a debit in his accounts of £49.17.0 for "Cloathing for their [Indian warriors'] Women and Children being naked."[35] Under such circumstances, men were more likely than women or children to attach ideological value to their presents; warriors and sachems more often received clothing as a result of diplomatic ceremony than of simple need.[36]

Europeans and Indians recognized the peculiar type of costume known as the Indian fashion, but for entirely different reasons. Europeans distributed clothing in ways that allowed them to construct a visual sense of social difference and hierarchy among Indians. Indians incorporated this clothing into their dress for the decorative, ideological, and utilitarian value they attached to it. This blending of European goods with Indian custom enabled each side to interpret the clothing from its own perspective yet still use it as an agent of cultural exchange and mediation. The Indian fashion became part of the middle ground between Europeans and Indians in the Mohawk Valley. Because this fashion relied on the acquisition and distribution of material goods, individuals involved in European-Indian trade and diplomacy could manipulate it to their advantage. Johnson's and Hendrick's attention to self-presentation thus contributed to their power. Realizing that an impressive outfit, a well-orchestrated entrance, or a ceremonial presentation of a gift could speak volumes, Johnson and Hendrick used the nonverbal language of appearance to negotiate cultural borders.

Hendrick's life blended European and Indian experiences on the Mohawk Valley's middle ground. Born a Mahican sometime around 1680, he was adopted by the Mohawks as a child and converted to Christianity as a young man. The various names he used throughout his life attest to his cultural mobility. At an Albany conference in 1701, Hendrick signed his mark to the proceedings, and the colonial secretary penned "Teoniahigarawe alias Hendrik" alongside it.[37] When he visited the court of Queen Anne nine years later, Englishmen rendered his Indian name as "Tee Yee Neen Ho Ga Row" and attached to it the title, "Emperour of the Six Nations."[38] British records also identify him as King Hendrick and Hendrick Peters. Pennsylvania Indian interpreter Conrad Weiser knew him as "Henery Dyionoagon."[39] Each of these names reveals a different facet of Hendrick's reputation. "Tee Yee Neen Ho Ga Row" and "Dyionoagon" obviously had Indian origins. "Hendrick

Dressing for Success

Peters," a name he most likely acquired at the time of his baptism, reflected his interaction with the local Dutch. "King Hendrick" carried the authority of an ambassador to royal courts and colonial governments.[40]

Englishmen often called Hendrick "king" or "emperour," but his interests and concerns were rooted in a much smaller world than such a title would indicate. He was one of the headmen of Canajoharie, the "upper castle" of Mohawks, located about sixty miles west of Albany. As a representative of Canajoharie at treaty conferences, he conducted land sales, presented grievances against trade and land frauds, and negotiated terms of war, alliance, and peace with European neighbors. Although his reputation reached throughout the northern colonies and across the Atlantic, Hendrick's perspective on European-Indian relations remained local, and his constituency rarely stretched beyond the perimeter of his village.[41]

Hendrick had a reputation for pride and stubborn independence that often frustrated colonial officials. European contemporaries called him a "politician," a term that implied opportunism, intrigue, and deceit in the eighteenth century, as it often does today. Johnson referred to him as "the Politician Hendrick." Peter Wraxall, Johnson's secretary, noted "the great Hendricks Political Talents." Thomas Pownall called Hendrick "a bold artfull intriguing fellow [who] has learnt no small share of European politics." Weiser, who grew up in Mohawk country, expressed a similar sentiment. He lamented that the Indians had become "apostates as to their Old Natural Principle of Honesty" and in the same sentence vented his distaste for "that Proud and Impudent Henery Dyionoagon." Even Dr. Hamilton, the touring physician from Annapolis, knew enough of Hendrick's reputation to call him "a bold, intrepid fellow."[42]

Hendrick's appearance blended European and Indian identities in a way that created a special category of Indian: the intercultural diplomat who learned European politics but remained independent of European control. Consider the earliest portrait of Hendrick, painted in 1710 when he and three other Indians visited Queen Anne's court. Two leading New Yorkers, Peter Schuyler and Francis Nicholson, sponsored this trip in an effort to win royal support for an expedition against Canada. Styling their Native ambassadors "the Four Indian Kings," they introduced Hendrick as Tee Yee Neen Ho Ga Row, "the Emperour of the Six Nations." So that the Indians would make an appearance befitting their titles, Schuyler and Nicholson provided them with new clothing, including scarlet mantles trimmed in gold. At court, the Indians made a speech, most likely spoken by Hendrick, and the queen responded with presents including cottons, woolens, necklaces, combs, scissors, mirrors, tobacco boxes, and a sword and pair of pistols for each king. She also commissioned John Verelst to paint their full-length likenesses.[43]

Comparison of two of these portraits (images 5 and 6) reveals Hendrick's emerging role as an intercultural diplomat. Both Indians appear in standard poses, wearing scarlet mantles. Each stands before a wooded background that includes an animal denoting his clanship (wolf, bear, or turtle). Several important differences set Hendrick, or Tee Yee Neen Ho Ga Row, apart from the others. Each king holds a weapon—gun, club, or bow—except Hendrick, who displays a wampum belt, a tool of diplomacy. Hendrick is the only king wearing the genteel costume of breeches and buckled shoes; the others wear hunting shirts draped over bare legs and moccasined feet. The portraits indicate that Hendrick's power is derived from his political skills rather than his martial talents.[44] These paintings were reproduced as prints and widely circulated in England and the colonies, making Hendrick's visage one of the most common images of an Indian in the British empire.[45]

The elements of an Indian diplomat's appearance are confirmed in the portrait done when Hendrick returned to London in 1740 (image 2). In this work Hendrick is the well-dressed sachem described in Johnson's accounts, wearing a laced hat, fine coat, and

5. Tee Yee Neen Ho Ga Row, Emperour of the Six Nations. Engraving by J. Simon after John Verelst, 1710. The John Carter Brown Library at Brown University.

6. Sa Ga Yeath Qua Pieth Tow, King of the Maquas. Engraving by
J. Simon after John Verelst, 1710. The John Carter Brown Library
at Brown University.

ruffled shirt. The influence of Native custom on the Indian fashion is apparent in the tattooing on Hendrick's face. The wampum belt so prominently displayed in the 1710 portrait has been reduced to a single string held at the waist, and he now flourishes an impressive tomahawk in his right hand. While this portrait is more militant than the previous one, the most important element remains consistent: Hendrick's fine court dress.

Hendrick's costume added to his prestige and influence among Indians as well. Much of his power as a sachem rested on his ability to funnel goods from his European counterparts to his fellow villagers. In this capacity, the people of Canajoharie could not have asked for a more productive emissary. From 1701, when his name first appears in English records, until his death in 1755, Hendrick regularly attended treaty conferences and received presents from colonial and royal officials. His diplomacy played an important role in his village's livelihood. By the 1730s, Canajoharie faced a precarious existence: the fur trade had bypassed the village in the late 1720s with the construction of Oswego. At about the same time, the Albany magistrates who administered New York's Indian affairs turned their attention from the Mohawks to the Canadian Indians who carried furs south from Montreal.[46] Missionaries in the region reported that Canajoharie's population declined as families "have gone over to the french Interest & settled in their Territories."[47] In this context of shrinking population and eroding economic independence, Hendrick's diplomacy helped sustain the village.

Hendrick's influence peaked between 1744 and 1755, precisely at the time when Canajoharie—because of a decreasing land base, warfare, and disrupted trade—was losing other means of support. In his own brand of shuttle diplomacy, Hendrick traveled beyond the Mohawk Valley to attend European-Indian councils in Montreal, Boston, New York City, and Philadelphia. These missions enabled him to tap into the flow of goods in the British-Atlantic economy and divert a larger share of them to his village. Before European audiences, he followed the Indian fashion. Costume enabled Hendrick to gain further access to European presents, which, when redistributed at Canajoharie, increased his standing among the villagers.[48] Dress, in short, helped preserve Hendrick's reputation abroad and at home, among Indians and Europeans.

Europeans who observed Hendrick's activities in the 1740s and 1750s often accused him of greed and extortion. Pownall, reporting on New York Indian affairs in 1753, believed Hendrick made himself rich through presents, taking "at different times above six hundred dollars of [New York governor] Mr. Clinton."[49] In 1745, New York Indian interpreter Arent Stevens warned that Hendrick would not do business without "a promise of a handsom present" and advised his superiors always to provide the Mohawk sachem with more "than you gave him hopes of."[50] Weiser, conducting diplomacy in the Mohawk Valley in 1750, claimed that Hendrick offered assistance if Weiser would make him "a handsome Present."[51] The New York Assembly, aware of Hendrick's reputation for avarice, recommended that Governor Clinton privately present him with twenty Spanish dollars before ending an Indian conference in 1753.[52]

Hendrick, it seems, had become almost too European. When Weiser and Pownall complained of his familiarity with "European politics," they lamented the loss of honesty they associated with Indians they met in public councils. William Smith, the eighteenth-century New York historian, referred to sachems as blanket-clad republicans gathered in outdoor assemblies, like "the ancient orators of Greece and Rome."[53] Hendrick's willingness, and that of other sachems, to dress in genteel finery called to mind instead images associated with European courtiers. Such sachems might say one thing and mean another; they might deceive to further private ambition. These Indians wore clothing that reflected power rather than humility, intrigue rather than honesty. The Indian diplomat enjoyed greater mobility because his costume helped him move beyond his village into colonial council chambers and royal courts. Hendrick, like any other participant in the eighteenth-century consumer revolution, adapted himself to a changing world by taking part in it, and the goods he acquired expanded rather than limited his choices in presenting himself to others.

Hendrick's wide-ranging influence in the 1740s and 1750s represented a moment in European-Indian affairs in the Mohawk Valley when British goods had penetrated the region, but colonists and soldiers did not yet control it. During this time of mediation, the well-dressed sachem emerged as a model of Indian leadership. His dress incorporated European elements but did not symbolize submission to European authority. Once this period of accommodation passed, however, so too did this image of intercultural diplomacy.

The transition is evident in portraits of Hendrick published after his death. In them, he has lost his genteel costume and donned clothing and accoutrements that European artists more commonly attributed to Indians. A print published in London in 1756 presents him as one of the blanket-clad sachems William Smith likened to the orators of antiquity (image 7). The transformation is complete in an 1847 lithograph entitled "Soi-En-Ga-Rah-Ta, or King Hendrick" (image 8). Here the facial scarring and tattoos visible in the 1740 portrait (image 2) have been grafted onto a much younger Indian warrior draped in an animal robe and bareheaded except for a scalplock decorated with feathers. Gone are the wampum, scarlet mantle, breeches, buckled shoes, cocked hat, ruffled shirt, and fine coat that Hendrick wore or carried in portraits completed during his lifetime. Gone, in short, is Hendrick the well-dressed intercultural diplomat, replaced by a nineteenth-century artist's stereotypical depiction of the nearly naked, noble savage.[54]

Hendrick's cooperation with William Johnson in European-Indian diplomacy began during King George's War (1744–48). In 1746, Governor George Clinton appointed Johnson New York's Indian agent. By distributing presents and supplies, Johnson sponsored Mohawk raids on French colonists and their Indian allies. In his expense account between December 1746 and November 1747

Hendrick the Sachem, or Chief of the Mohawks.

Etched from an Original Drawing.

Publish'd according to the Act March 31 1756. by T.Jefferys at Charing Cross.

7. Hendrick the Sachem, or Chief of the
Mohawks. Etching published by T. Jeffrys,
1756. Negative #7722. Collection of the
New-York Historical Society.

he identified by name more than thirty Indians with whom he conducted this business. Hendrick's name appears in thirteen entries, eight more than any other. He received from Johnson a pair of boots, a laced coat, medicine, cash, and an unspecified "private present" as well as provisions, transportation, and entertainments for his friends, warriors, and dependents.[55]

After the war ended, Johnson and Hendrick continued their diplomatic partnership. In this Irish trader, Hendrick found a supplier of goods for his village to replace the Albany Dutch, who now curried the favor of Canadian Indians. Johnson's mercantile business and political reputation profited from the relationship. As a merchant supplying the western fur trade at Oswego, he needed to preserve friendly relations with his Indian neighbors, and his success in this regard made him a favorite of Clinton and other royal officials. Indian diplomacy also provided Johnson with constant demand for his goods. The presents he distributed among Indians came from his own stock, and he charged the expense to the colonial treasury.

By the early 1750s, Johnson and Hendrick had become indispensable to New York's Indian relations. Johnson provided the Mohawks with goods, and they refused to treat with any New York official except him. His influence was obvious at a treaty conference convened in 1751. Johnson, who had recently resigned as the colony's Indian agent because the assembly refused to pay his expenses, declined the governor's invitation to the meeting. In Albany, Hendrick told Clinton "one half of Collo. Johnson belonged to his Excellency [Clinton], and the other to them [the Mohawks]." He then asked permission to send a messenger to Johnson, who attended after receiving the Indians' request.[56] At another conference three years later, Johnson and Hendrick reversed these roles. This time the Mohawks failed to show for an Albany conference called to address their grievances. They finally arrived after the governor prevailed on Johnson to secure their attendance.[57] In December 1754, Pennsylvania's colonial secretary Richard Peters

8. Soi-En-Ga-Rah-ta, or King Hendrick. The image
came from an 1847 edition of Henry R. Schoolcraft's
*Notes on the Iroquois: Contributions to American History,
Antiquities, and General Ethnology*. Special Collections
Research Center, Syracuse University Library.

enlisted Johnson's help in convincing the Mohawks to confirm a land deed in Philadelphia. Hendrick was reluctant to go at first, but he agreed after Johnson promised to "join, & back him here among the Six Nations."[58] Cooperation between Hendrick and Johnson enabled both to extend their reputations and cement their hold over Covenant Chain proceedings.

Through his involvement with Indian trade and diplomacy Johnson became interested in the Indians' material culture. Like many eighteenth-century gentlemen, he collected and displayed within his home "curiosities," objects he valued for beauty, craftsmanship, or rarity. These included wampum, bows and arrows, calumets, and Indian clothing. Other gentleman-collectors requested Johnson's assistance in procuring such items of Indian dress as beaver coats, moccasins, and belts.[59] A Continental army officer visiting Johnson Hall in 1776 noted many such artifacts, including "Trappings of Indian Finery" and "good old King Hendrick's Picture."[60]

Johnson's curiosities attested to his acquaintance with and influence among the Indians. Colden believed Johnson owed this influence to his "compliance with their humours in his dress & conversation." Johnson's secretary, Wraxall, noted that the Indians looked on his boss "as their Cheif, their Patron & their Brother." Johnson himself wrote of his relationship with the Indians, "I am no Stranger to their Customs & Manners."[61] Red Head, an Onondaga sachem, thanked Johnson at a 1753 conference for speaking to the Indians "in our own way, which is more Intelligable to us, because more conformable to the Customs and Manners of our Fore Fathers."[62]

Johnson spoke to the Indians in their own way in actions and appearances as well as words. He made a constant effort to transact his business in the Indians' cultural context. No colonial agent was more successful in presenting himself in a pleasing and impressive manner. This ability extended far beyond Johnson's willingness to don Indian dress and war paint: he cultivated the art of self-presentation in various forms adapted to Covenant Chain treaty making.

In staging entrances, conducting negotiations, and distributing presents, Johnson used material goods to create appearances that advanced his reputation among Indians and Europeans.

Johnson's success as an Indian agent began with his work as a merchant. Johnson, the primary supplier of manufactured goods between Albany and Oswego, commanded considerable business and dominated the Mohawk Valley trade.[63] Two lists of presents he distributed among the Indians illustrate the types of goods that flowed along this route.[64] They fall into six broad categories. The first is weapons and ammunition—rifles, pistols, hatchets, knives, swords, powder, shot, and flints—to assist the Indians in hunting and warfare. Second, the Indians received tools and wares for everyday tasks: kettles, frying pans, scissors, needles, awls, pen knives, fire tongs. Toys and novelties such as jew's harps, hawks bells, looking glasses, liquor, tobacco, pipes, tea, and sugar make up a third category. In times of war and famine, Johnson provided a fourth category: grants of food, including cows, corn, bread, and peas. Fifth, he made occasional cash grants for influential sachems. Clothing, the sixth category, is the most diverse, comprising the manufactured items that shaped the Indian fashion, from such staple products as blankets and strouds to such finery as laced hats, ribbons, buttons, and beads.

Table 2 offers a closer look at some goods Johnson purchased for a treaty conference at his home in June 1755. All of the categories described above are represented except food, which Johnson distributed along with numerous other incidental gifts once the meeting convened.[65] As the table indicates, clothing made up by far the largest part of the purchase. It accounted for fifteen kinds of items and approximately 66.5 percent of the total value of the presents.

The sheer amount of goods supplied by Johnson could be misleading: quantity was not the only factor that contributed to his success. Indeed, any agent with resources from a colonial or royal treasury could dump goods in Indian laps. Critics of Albany's Commissioners of Indian Affairs often complained of just that: colonial officials saddled visiting Indians with wagon loads of goods, caring little for how the goods were presented or how the Indians got them home. Local merchants then traded rum to the Indians for their presents as they left the city, only to sell the goods back to them at "a dear rate" later.[66] Such conduct on the part of colonial officials indicated either stubborn ignorance or callous disregard for the ceremonial nature of gift giving.

Johnson, by contrast, exhibited a keen appreciation for the cultural dynamics of this practice. An account he kept during King George's War illustrates how he went about distributing presents. In table 3, all the presents of clothing Johnson made between December 1746 and November 1747 are classified by recipient. Warriors received items necessary to outfit war parties: paint, shirts, ribbon, gimps, caps, laps, hides, and snowshoes. Sachems received finery associated with the Indian fashion: laced hats, fine coats, ruffled shirts, and silver medals. Johnson gave strouds, hose, shirts, and other necessaries to the women and children of Indian men who went to war. Lastly, he clothed the dead by presenting black burial strouds to their relatives.

Women and children received most of the clothing Johnson distributed: they accounted for almost 69 percent of his total expenditure on clothing during this period. Outfitting warriors and sachems accounted for 16.3 percent and 12.5 percent respectively and outfitting the dead only 2.6 percent. Johnson distributed presents to warriors and sachems in small quantities, usually valued at no more than £1 or £2 at a time, when they visited his home to share news or hold councils. The presents he gave to women and children involved much larger donations. Of the twenty-four entries for presents of this type, fourteen were for disbursements valued at £10 or more, and two top £100. By comparison, only three entries for warriors' presents and two for sachems' presents top £10. Presents made for outfitting the dead seem to have involved the most personal contact between Johnson and the recipient. Of five

TABLE 2. Goods distributed by William Johnson at a treaty conference, June 1755

Item	Quantity	Value
Weapons and Ammunition:		
Long Knives, Sheathed	10 dozen	£ 6.0.0
Large Pistols	10 dozen	5.0.0
Gun Flints	3,000	5.5.0
Holland Gun Powder	9 kegs	8.0.0
Lead in Small Bars	2,000 lb.	45.0.0
Subtotal:		69.5.0
Tools and Wares:		
Brass Kettles	400	60.0.0
Frying Pans	50	12.10.0
Razors	10 dozen	7.10.0
Awl Blades	4 gross	2.0.0
Cups: 1 Gill	1 dozen	
½ Gill	2 dozen	8.10.0
Brass Wire	20 lb.	4.10.0
Subtotal:		95.0.0
Toys and Novelties:		
Looking Glasses	8 dozen	12.0.0
Jew's Harps	24 dozen	3.0.0
Fine Wrought Pens	30 dozen	12.0.0
Hawks Bells	38 dozen	4.15.0
Buckling Combs	20 dozen	5.0.0
Pipes	1 case	
Tobacco	1,000 lb.	21.12.4
Subtotal:		58.7.4
Cash:		
Private Grants to Sachems		107.4.0
Subtotal:		107.4.0
Clothing and Bodily Decoration:		
Strouds	16 pieces	144.0.0
Blankets	8 pieces	72.0.0
Penniston	3 pieces	39.17.4
Garlix	6 pieces	40.0.0
Calico	8 pieces	26.0.0

Item	Quantity	Value
Callamancoe	16 pieces	24.0.0
French Blankets	40	32.0.0
French Blankets, second size	40	20.0.0
French Blankets, third size	40	16.0.0
Flowered Serge	4 pieces	20.0.0
Gartering	20 rolls	7.0.0
Gimps	40 pieces	12.0.0
Vermillion	40 lb.	28.0.0
Worsted Clocked Hose	8 dozen	11.4.0
Worsted Clocked Hose, small	10 dozen	9.10.0
Private Presents—Stroud, Shirt, and Lap to Each Sachem	97	155.4.0
Subtotal:		656.18.4
Total:		£986.11.8

Source: *Johnson Papers*, 2:570–71.

entries, none exceeded £10, and in two of them Johnson mentions the living recipient by name.[67]

Johnson selected his gifts according to the intended recipient, and he often presented these goods in person. In this sense, he owed his influence to his role as a distributor of Indian goods rather than as a mere supplier of them. Indians treated presents as tangible symbols of reciprocity and friendship; to them, peace and alliance could not be purchased by large, one-time donations of goods. Rather, they needed to be continually renewed and strengthened by the periodic exchange of presents. As Johnson explained it, in addition to large presents made at treaty conferences, the Indians "expect to be indulged with constant little Presents, this from the Nature of the Indians cannot be avoided & must be complied with."[68]

A large proportion of the goods Johnson distributed fell into the category of "constant little Presents."[69] The expense was staggering. By his own account, Johnson spent £7,177 on Indian presents during King George's War. Between March 1755 and October 1756, early in the Seven Years' War, he expended a total of £17,446.[70]

TABLE 3. Clothing distributed by William Johnson as Indian presents, December 1746–November 1747

	Number of Account Entries	Value	Number of Entries Greater Than £10	Percent of Total Expense
Clothing for Warriors (shirts, paint, ribbon, caps, laps, snowshoes, hides)	25	£ 149.8.7	3	16.3
Clothing for Sachems (laced hats, fine coats, ruffled shirts, silver medals)	15	114.11.0	2	12.5
Clothing for Families (blankets, strouds, hose, caps, laps, shirts, deerskins)	24	629.5.2	14	68.6
Clothing for the Dead (black burial strouds)	5	24.8.0	0	2.6
Total:	69	£917.12.9	19	100.0

Source: *Johnson Papers*, 9:15–31.

His liberality caused friction with the New York assembly, which refused to reimburse him fully for outlays during King George's War. Johnson blasted the assembly for failing to help "defray from time to time the expences I am dayly obliged to be at in treating with all sorts of Indians—The well ordering of whom is of much more importance to the Welfare of His Ma[jes]tys Government than the whole act of governing the unruly Inhabitants [of New York]." On the eve of renewed Anglo-French hostilities in 1754, Johnson predicted disaster for New York because of the assembly's parsimony, noting that it had appropriated only "the miserable pittance of £170 [New] York Curr[en]cy P[er] Annum" for Indian presents.[71]

Johnson knew that the practice of gift giving required more than deep pockets. His greatest asset as an Indian agent was his penchant for ceremonial presentations of both himself and the goods he distributed. He had a flair for the theatrical that suited the pageantry of treaty making, as evidenced in his taste for spectacular entrances. His arrival at Albany in 1746 dressed as a Mohawk war captain is one example. Two years later, he staged another grand entrance, this time at Onondaga, the seat of the Iroquois confederacy. Johnson arrived at this treaty conference with a party of Indian and European attendants. On entering Onondaga, he found "all the Sachims & Warriours . . . stood in order with rested arms and fired a Volley, after which my Party returned the Compliment." That evening, he provided two feasts, one for the village's sachems and one for "the Warriours & dancers who I hope will be merry which is my greatest pleasure to make & see them so."[72]

In such instances, Johnson imitated, not Albany's Indian commissioners, but French Indian agents, whom he praised for always putting on a good show. Unlike the Albany Dutch, Johnson explained to Clinton in 1749, the French "observe a quite different conduct, much to their own advantage. . . . They never employ a Trader to negotiate any matters with the Indians but a Kings officer, who in whatever Rank or capacity is attended by a Retinue of Soldiers accordingly to denote his consequence[.] If he be but a Lieutenant or Ensign it is sufficient to command Respect from the Savages, who tho' somewhat warlike are actuated by their Fears at *a small appearance of Power*."[73] Johnson cultivated this small appearance of power in his Indian negotiations not only through his dress but also through warriors and sachems who accompanied him and served as visual testimony of his influence. Such a retinue could not be secured or maintained without the liberal distribution of personal presents detailed in Johnson's accounts.

Johnson paid attention to the ceremonial nature of gift giving and particularly honored the Indians' condolence rituals. When a treaty conference began, Europeans and Indians usually exchanged condolence speeches to honor each side's recent dead. The Indians also expected and customarily received a present of black burial strouds. When colonial agents omitted these presents, Indians might delay negotiations or express anger that the proper ceremony had not been observed.[74] Johnson regularly complained that the Albany magistrates ignored this custom in treating with the Indians. "This ceremony is also attended with a great deal of form," he explained to Clinton in 1749. "It was always neglected in the late [Albany Indian] Commiss[ione]rs time, which gave the French an opportunity of doing it." To Weiser, Johnson wrote that the condolence ceremony was "always expected by the five Nations to be performed by Us, and [is] what th[e]y look much upon." As the evidence in table 3 indicates, Johnson also made private condolence presents to Indians when requested.[75]

In distributing goods, Johnson never lost the opportunity to enhance his appearance as the Indians' friend and benefactor. At a conference in June 1755, Indians from several nations approached Johnson with three young men they claimed worthy to be sachems and asked him to "distinguish them with the usual cloathing." Johnson readily complied. His accounts show an entry from the same day for "3 Ruffled Shirts for 3 young Sachems."[76] Through such presentations, Johnson moved beyond merely supplying the

Dressing for Success

Indians with goods to inserting himself into their rituals and identities. The Indians' consumer revolution redefined how a sachem was supposed to dress, and Johnson, through the manipulation of material goods, made himself a pivotal figure in those changing definitions.

Just as Hendrick appreciated the importance his European contemporaries attached to clothing, so Johnson understood the Indians' interpretation of presents. When Europeans bestowed presents, they believed the goods symbolized the recipients' submission to and dependence on a crown or colonial government. The Indians, on their part, perceived these presents as evidence of mutual regard between treaty participants. By making "constant little Presents" and observing ceremonial detail, Johnson recognized the important role goods played in the Indians' view of the Covenant Chain. The Indians acknowledged his incorporation of their values by accepting him into their councils and naming him "Warraghiyagey," doer of great business.[77]

Between 1744 and 1755, Hendrick and Johnson became the two most influential figures in the Covenant Chain. Their participation in treaty conferences was essential for preserving peace between New Yorkers and Indians. Each one, however, continued to operate independently of the other and for different reasons. Johnson pursued political influence and royal favor. Hendrick's perspective remained local, as he employed his diplomatic skills to acquire presents and restore Canajoharie's prominence in New York's Indian relations.[78] Both men made masterly use of the material culture of the other, manipulating goods associated with the Indian fashion to extend and preserve their influence on the Mohawk frontier.

Close examination of the careers of Johnson and Hendrick suggests the great potential of material culture methods to enlighten us about European-Indian relations. The Indian trade was not simply a matter of economics, of European supply versus Indian demand. Participants attached meaning to these goods beyond the utilitarian value of a new gun, a shirt, or a knife. The goods that passed between Europeans and Indians, like the rituals involved in their exchange, created a language of speech, deportment, and appearance that crossed cultural barriers. Today, Iroquois nations in western New York continue to receive bolts of cloth from the United States according to eighteenth-century treaty obligations. The federal government has offered to convert these grants into monetary payments, but the Iroquois have declined, explaining that the cloth's value as a symbol of their territorial and political sovereignty cannot be rendered in a cash equivalent.[79] Johnson's and Hendrick's use of clothing illustrated the ideological element in the material culture of European-Indian relations, which allowed both sides to express themselves in ways not typically recorded in treaty minutes.

Notes

Timothy J. Shannon wishes to thank T. H. Breen, Frank Ray, John Shedd, Don Wright, and the anonymous readers at the *William and Mary Quarterly* for their comments on drafts of this article. Research was partially funded by a Faculty Research Grant from SUNY, Cortland.

1. On the early life of William Johnson, see Milton W. Hamilton, *Sir William Johnson: Colonial American, 1715–1763* (Port Washington NY, 1976), 3–14, and James Thomas Flexner, *Lord of the Mohawks: A Biography of Sir William Johnson*, rev. ed. (Boston, 1979; orig. pub. 1959), 13–27. On Hendrick's early life see Hamilton, "Theyanoguin," in George Brown, ed., *Dictionary of Canadian Biography*, vol. 3, *1741 to 1770* (Toronto, 1974), 622–23. The best introductions to the Covenant Chain alliance are Francis Jennings, *The Ambiguous Iroquois Empire: The Covenant Chain Confederation of Indian Tribes with the English Colonies from Its Beginnings to the Lancaster Treaty of 1744* (New York, 1984), and Daniel K. Richter and James H. Merrell, eds., *Beyond the Covenant Chain: The Iroquois and Their Neighbors in Indian North America, 1600–1800* (Syracuse NY, 1987). William Johnson's and Hendrick's careers in the 1740s and 1750s are examined in Jennings, *Empire of Fortune: Crowns, Colonies, and Tribes in the Seven Years War in America* (New York, 1988), 71–108, and Richard Aquila, *The Iroquois Restoration: Iroquois Diplomacy on the Colonial Frontier, 1701–1754* (Detroit, 1983), 85–112. I would also like to thank Dan Murphy of Hanover College for allowing me to read his unpublished paper on Johnson's and Hendrick's

diplomatic partnership. For a recent study of the Iroquois confederacy during the seventeenth and early eighteenth centuries see Richter, *The Ordeal of the Longhouse: The Peoples of the Iroquois League in the Era of European Colonization* (Chapel Hill, 1992).

2. In a letter to his father, Johnson complained about his appearance in this portrait. He wrote, "The Drapery I would have altered . . . the greatest fault in it is, the narrow hanging Shoulders, w[hic]h I beg you may get altered as Mine are verry broad and square." These comments are indicative of the careful attention he paid to dress and appearance whenever presenting himself to an audience. See Johnson to Christopher Johnson, Oct. 31, 1754, in *The Papers of Sir William Johnson*, 14 vols., ed. James Sullivan, Alexander C. Flick, Milton W. Hamilton, and Albert B. Corey (Albany, 1921–62), 1:931. On the costume of an eighteenth-century English gentleman, see James Laver, *The Concise History of Costume and Fashion* (New York, 1969), 134–38.

3. [New York], *A Treaty between His Excellency . . . George Clinton . . . and the Six . . . Nations* (New York, 1746), 8. Alice Mapelsden Keys attributed the authorship of this pamphlet to Colden in *Cadwallader Colden: A Representative Eighteenth Century Official* (New York, 1906), 155–57.

4. This anonymous portrait, in all likelihood completed during Hendrick's last trip to London in 1740, was published as a print after his death in 1755. His clothes match a description Anne Grant made of clothing worn by Hendrick's son when she encountered him in 1760; Grant, *Memoirs of an American Lady, with Sketches of Manners and Scenes in America as They Existed Previous to the Revolution* (1808), 2 vols. (New York, 1901), 1:62, 2:57–58. Also see R. W. G. Vail, "Portraits of 'The Four Indian Kings of Canada': A Bibliographical Footnote," in *To Doctor R.: Essays Here Collected and Published in Honor of the Seventieth Birthday of Dr. A. S. W. Rosenbach, July 22, 1946*, comp. Percy E. Lawler et al. (Philadelphia, 1946), 218–26.

5. Carl Bridenbaugh, ed., *Gentleman's Progress: The Itinerarium of Dr. Alexander Hamilton, 1744* (Chapel Hill, 1948), 112.

6. Grant McCracken, *Culture and Consumption: New Approaches to the Symbolic Character of Consumer Goods and Activities* (Bloomington IN, 1988), 57–58.

7. See Fred Davis, *Fashion, Culture, and Identity* (Chicago, 1992), Joanne Finkelstein, *The Fashioned Self* (Philadelphia, 1991), and Alison Lurie, *The Language of Clothes* (New York, 1981).

8. See Neil McKendrick, "The Commercialization of Fashion," in McKendrick, John Brewer, and J. H. Plumb, eds., *The Birth of a Consumer Society: The Commercialization of Eighteenth-Century England* (Bloomington IN, 1982), 34–99, and McCracken, *Culture and Consumption*, 16–22.

9. The literature on the eighteenth-century consumer revolution in the British-Atlantic empire has been growing in recent years. See especially Richard L. Bushman, *The Refinement of America: Persons, Houses, Cities* (New York, 1992), Carole Shammas, *The Pre-industrial Consumer in England and America* (Oxford, 1990), and T. H. Breen, "'Baubles of Britain': The American and Consumer Revolutions of the Eighteenth Century," *Past and Present*, no. 119 (1988): 73–104, and "An Empire of Goods: The Anglicization of Colonial America, 1690–1776," *Journal of British Studies* 25 (1986): 467–99.

10. James Axtell looked at the consumer revolution from the Indians' perspective in "The First Consumer Revolution," in *Beyond 1492: Encounters in Colonial America* (Oxford, 1992), 125–51. For the Indians' adaptive response to European goods, see Richter, *Ordeal of the Longhouse*, 75–104, and James H. Merrell, *The Indians' New World: Catawbas and Their Neighbors from European Contact through the Era of Removal* (Chapel Hill, 1989), 32–34. On the Indians' role as consumers, see Arthur J. Ray, "Indians as Consumers in the Eighteenth Century," in Carol M. Judd and Ray, eds., *Old Trails and New Directions: Papers of the Third North American Fur Trade Conference* (Toronto, 1980), 255–71. For analysis of the ideological meanings that Indians invested in European trade goods, see Christopher L. Miller and George R. Hamell, "A New Perspective on Indian-White Contact: Cultural Symbols and Colonial Trade," *Journal of American History* 73 (1986): 311–28.

11. A classic study of the role of presents in eighteenth-century European-Indian diplomacy is Wilbur R. Jacobs, *Diplomacy and Indian Gifts: Anglo-French Rivalry along the Ohio and Northwest Frontiers, 1748–1763* (Stanford CA, 1950). For more recent discussions of the cultural context of gift giving, see Richard White, *The Middle Ground: Indians, Empires, and Republics in the Great Lakes Region, 1650–1815* (Cambridge, 1991), 94–119, Richter, *Ordeal of the Longhouse*, 47–48, and Merrell, *Indians' New World*, 149–50.

12. White, *Middle Ground*, 50–93.

13. Jonathan Prude has noted that in the commercial culture of eighteenth-century America contemporaries worried that people would use new consumer goods to create "masks" for themselves—purposely deceptive appearances that enabled them to project status or attributes they did not possess. See Prude, "To Look Upon the 'Lower Sort': Runaway Ads and the Appearance of Unfree Laborers in America, 1750–1800," *Journal of American History* 78 (1991): 127. A similar theme was apparent in the colonists' concern over impressions they left on British army officers who witnessed colonial consumption of British goods during the Seven Years' War. See Breen, "Narrative of Commercial Life: Consumption, Ideology, and Community on the

Eve of the American Revolution," *William and Mary Quarterly*, 3d ser., 50 (1993): 471–501.

14. For descriptions of the eighteenth-century Mohawk Valley, see William Smith, *The History of the Late Province of New-York* . . . , 2 vols., in New-York Historical Society, *Collections*, 4–5 (1829–30), 1:264–66, and T[homas] Pownall, *A Topographical Description of the Dominions of the United States of America* . . . (1776), ed. Lois Mulkearn (Pittsburgh, 1949), 33–38. For a good introduction to this region during the colonial era, see Thomas E. Burke, Jr., *Mohawk Frontier: The Dutch Community of Schenectady, New York, 1661–1710* (Ithaca, 1991).

15. An excellent brief description of the Mohawk Valley trade may be found in Lewis Evans, *An Analysis of a General Map of the Middle British Colonies in America* . . . (Philadelphia, 1755), 20, reprinted in Lawrence Henry Gipson, *Lewis Evans* (Philadelphia, 1939), 141–76.

16. See Johnson to Peter Warren, May 10, 1739; Johnson to Capt. Ross, May 30, 1749; Samuel and William Baker to Johnson, Jan. 22, 1749/50; and Johnson to the Bakers, Sept. 12, 1751, *Johnson Papers*, 1:4–7, 229–30, 259–60, 346–47.

17. Johnson to Samuel and William Baker, Dec. 31, 1748, ibid., 198.

18. Johnson to Capt. Ross, May 30, 1749, and Johnson to Samuel and William Baker, Feb. 19, 1749/50, ibid., 229–30, 264–65.

19. On Johnson Hall, see Hamilton, *William Johnson*, 311–19. On the symbolic import of the Georgian mansion to eighteenth-century notions of gentility, see Bushman, *Refinement of America*, 3–25.

20. See Adolph B. Benson, ed., *Peter Kalm's Travels in North America: The English Translation of 1770*, 2 vols. (New York, 1937), 1:343. On the insular quality of colonial Albany, see Patricia U. Bonomi, *A Factious People: Politics and Society in Colonial New York* (New York, 1971), 39–48, and Stefan Bielinski, "The People of Colonial Albany, 1650–1800: The Profile of a Community," in William Pencak and Conrad Edick Wright, eds., *Authority and Resistance in Early New York* (New York, 1988), 1–26.

21. Benson, ed., *Peter Kalm's Travels in North America*, 1:190–91. On Johnson's use of tea and related items in Indian presents, see *Johnson Papers*, 2:576, 587, 618.

22. Archaeological evidence from the site of the Indians' chapel at Fort Hunter includes teapots, teacups, and saucers, indicating that "the tea ceremony was a ritual adopted by members of the eighteenth-century community at this site"; Kevin Moody and Charles L. Fisher, "Archaeological Evidence of the Colonial Occupation at Schoharie Crossing State Historic Site, Montgomery County, New York," *The Bulletin: Journal of the New York State Archaeological Association*, no. 99 (1989): 8.

23. For descriptions of the "Indian Fashion" by Mohawk Valley visitors, see Mark E. Lender and James Kirby Martin, eds., *Citizen Soldier: The Revolutionary War Journal of Joseph Bloomfield* (Newark NJ, 1982), 91; Richard Smith, *A Tour of Four Great Rivers: The Hudson, the Mohawk, the Susquehanna, and the Delaware in 1769*, ed. Francis W. Halsey (Fleischmanns NY, 1989; orig. pub. 1906), 149–50; Grant, *Memoirs of an American Lady*, 2:58; and "Journal of Tench Tilghman," in Samuel A. Harrison, ed., *Memoir of Lieut. Col. Tench Tilghman, Secretary and Aid to Washington . . .* (Albany, 1876), 87.

24. For the Indians' use of European cloth, see Axtell, *The European and the Indian: Essays in the Ethnohistory of Colonial North America* (New York, 1981), 57–59, 254–55, and Richter, *Ordeal of the Longhouse*, 79–84.

25. See *Johnson Papers*, 2:898–900.

26. Ibid.

27. Benson, ed., *Peter Kalm's Travels in North America*, 2:560, 520–21.

28. See Johnson's account for presents distributed during King George's War, in *Johnson Papers*, 9:15–31.

29. See Richard Smith, *Tour of Four Great Rivers*, 134–35, 149–50.

30. See *Johnson Papers*, 9:15–31. This account covers Johnson's expenditures as New York's Indian agent from Dec. 13, 1746, to Nov. 7, 1747.

31. Ibid., 23.

32. Richard Smith, *Tour of Four Great Rivers*, 149–50.

33. Bridenbaugh, ed., *Gentleman's Progress*, 112.

34. See Millet and Harmell, "New Perspective on Indian-White Contact," 316–18, White, *Middle Ground*, 99–112, and George R. Hamell, "Strawberries, Floating Islands, and Rabbit Captains: Mythical Realities and European Contact in the Northeast during the Sixteenth and Seventeenth Centuries," *Journal of Canadian Studies/Revue d'études canadiennes* 21, no. 4 (1987): 79–90.

35. See *Johnson Papers*, 9:24. Johnson's accounts from King George's War indicate that he often granted presents to Indian women and children to provide for their subsistence while the men were away fighting. See ibid., 15–31.

36. One notable exception to this trend is Johnson's practice of presenting gifts to Indian women whose sons or husbands died in battle. Such presents included black burial strouds for the deceased as well as food and clothing for the family. See ibid., 24, 28.

37. Deed from the Five Nations to the King of their Beaver Hunting Ground, July 19, 1701, in E. B. O'Callaghan, ed., *Documents Relative to the Colonial History of the State of New-York*, 15 vols. (Albany, 1853–87), 4:911 (hereafter cited as *NYCol. Docs.*).

38. See Richmond P. Bond, *Queen Anne's American Kings* (Oxford, 1952).

Dressing for Success

39. Weiser to Richard Peters, Mar. 15, 1754, in *The Susquehannah Company Papers*, vol. 1, ed. Julian P. Boyd (Ithaca, 1962; orig. pub. 1930), 66.

40. For a full listing of Hendrick's aliases, see Brown, ed., *Dictionary of Canadian Biography*, 3:622. Of these names, I use "Hendrick" for two reasons: it is most commonly used in the documents that are my source, and it appears to have been that one most widely recognized by his neighbors in the Mohawk Valley.

41. Hendrick's representation of Canajoharie's interests in European-Indian councils is well documented in the treaty records of this period. In particular, see the proceedings from treaty councils held in 1745, 1746, 1748, 1751, 1753, 1754, and 1755 in O'Callaghan, ed., *NYCol. Docs.*, 6:289–305, 317–26, 441–52, 717–26, 781–88, 853–92, 964–89.

42. Johnson to Richard Peters, Dec. 9, 1754, *Minutes of the Provincial Council of Pennsylvania*, vol. 6 (Harrisburg PA, 1851), 269; Wraxall, "Some Thoughts upon the British Indian Interest in North America . . . ," in O'Callaghan, ed., *NYCol. Docs.*, 7:22; Weiser to Richard Peters, Mar. 15, 1754, in Boyd, ed., *Susquehannah Papers*, 1:66; Pownall, "[Notes on] Indian Affairs" (1753–54), Loudoun Papers–Americana, LO, 460:8–9, Huntington Library, San Marino CA; Bridenbaugh, ed., *Gentleman's Progress*, 112.

43. For the four Indian kings' trip, see Bond, *Queen Anne's American Kings*, and John G. Garratt with the assistance of Bruce Robertson, *The Four Indian Kings* (Ottawa, 1985). The kings' speech to Queen Anne is reproduced in Bond, *Queen Anne's American Kings*, 94–95.

44. See Robertson, "The Portraits: An Iconographical Study," in Garratt and Robertson, *Four Indian Kings*, 143–44.

45. Nicholson brought back several sets of the portraits on the four Indian kings' return to New York. In 1712, a Society for the Propagation of the Gospel in Foreign Parts missionary brought over many more for distribution to each of the Five Nations and the colonial governments of New York, New Jersey, Massachusetts, New Hampshire, Rhode Island, Pennsylvania, Maryland, and Virginia; ibid., 10–14.

46. On the changing nature of New York's fur trade and Indian relations, see Thomas Elliot Norton, *The Fur Trade in Colonial New York, 1686–1776* (Madison WI, 1974), 43–197.

47. See John Ogilvie to Philip Bearcroft, July 27, 1750, in Records of the Society for the Propagation of the Gospel in Foreign Parts, Letterbooks (microfilm) (London, 1964), series B, 18:102–3.

48. Richter, *Ordeal of the Longhouse*, 21–22, discusses the redistributive economics involved in village leadership.

49. Pownall, "Notes on Indian Affairs," 9.

50. Arent Stevens, Oct. 5, 1745, in Francis Jennings et al., eds., *Iroquois Indians: A Documentary History of the Diplomacy of the Six Nations and Their League* (microfilm) (Woodbridge CT, 1985), reel 12.

51. Entry for Aug. 27, 1750, "A Journal of the Proceedings of Conrad Weiser in his Journey to Onondago," *Minutes of the Provincial Council of Pennsylvania* (Harrisburg PA, 1851), 5:471.

52. June 15, 1753, New York Council Minutes, 23:78, New York State Archives, Albany.

53. William Smith, *History of New York*, 1:54.

54. For further information on these portraits, see Vail, "Portraits of 'The Four Indian Kings of Canada,'" 223–25, and Garratt and Robertson, *Four Indian Kings*, 148–49.

55. *Johnson Papers*, 9:15–31. Other Indians named multiple times in this account include Hendrick's brother Abraham (4 times), his son Young Hendrick (2 times), and Mohawks David (5 times), Brant (4 times), Nickus (3 times), and Seth (3 times).

56. Ibid., 1:341–42.

57. See New York Council Minutes, June 26, 1754, 23:191; [William Livingston and William Smith, Jr.], *A Review of Military Operations in North-America* (New York, 1757), 76; and John Penn and Richard Peters to James Hamilton, [Aug. 5, 1754], *Pennsylvania Archives*, 4th ser., vol. 2, *Papers of the Governors, 1747–1759* (Philadelphia, 1900), 699.

58. Johnson to Peters, Dec. 9, 1754, *Johnson Papers*, 9:150.

59. Wanda Burch provided an excellent description of Johnson's collection in "Sir William Johnson's Cabinet of Curiosities," *New York History* 71 (1990): 261–82.

60. Lender and Martin, *Citizen Soldier*, 49.

61. Colden, "The present state of the Indian affairs with the British & French Colonies in North America," Aug. 8, 1751, in Cadwallader Colden Papers, N.-Y. Hist. Soc., *Colls.*, 53 (1920), 272; Wraxall, *An Abridgment of the Indian Affairs Contained in Four Folio Volumes, Transacted in the Colony of New York, from the Year 1678 to the Year 1751*, ed. Charles Howard McIlwain (Cambridge MA, 1915), 248n1; Johnson to William Shirley, Dec. 17, 1754, *Johnson Papers*, 1:433.

62. Minutes of Johnson's Conference at Onondaga, Sept. 8–10, 1753, in New York Council Minutes, 23:114.

63. Colden referred to Johnson as "the most considerable trader with the Western Indians & sends more goods to Oswego than any other person does," in "Present State of the Indian Affairs," 273.

64. For these two lists, see Johnson's account, Mar. 1755 to Oct. 1756, and a list of goods requested for the Northern Indian Department, in *Johnson Papers*, 2:566–646, 898–900.

65. For a list of these items, which Johnson distributed between June 21 and July 5, see ibid., 575–79.

66. See the complaints levied against the Albany Indian Commissioners by New York councilor Archibald Kennedy, in *The Importance of Gaining and Preserving the Friendship of the Indians to the British Interest, Considered* (New York, 1751), 23. See also Thomas Pownall to Lord Halifax[?], July 23, 1754, in Beverly McAnear, ed., "Personal Accounts of the Albany Congress of 1754," *Mississippi Valley Historical Review* 39 (1953): 743. New York governors attending Albany treaty conferences often issued proclamations that forbade trading with the Indians for their presents, but as Pownall observed, local merchants ignored such prohibitions. For one such proclamation, issued by Gov. James DeLancey on July 5, 1754, see New York Colonial Manuscripts, 103 vols., New York State Archives, Albany, 78:146.

67. See *Johnson Papers*, 9:15–31.

68. Johnson to William Shirley, May 16, 1755, ibid., 1:505.

69. See, for example, the detailed listing of items that Johnson distributed between Mar. 1755 and Oct. 1756, ibid., 2:566–646.

70. Ibid., 1:343, 2:646.

71. See Johnson to George Clinton, Nov. 22, 1749, in O'Callaghan, ed., *NYCol. Docs.*, 6:541, and Johnson to Clinton, Mar. 12, 1754, *Johnson Papers*, 9:126–27.

72. Journal entry, Apr. 24, 1748, *Johnson Papers*, 1:155, 157.

73. Johnson to Clinton, Nov. 22, 1749, in O'Callaghan, ed., *NYCol. Docs.*, 6:540–41 (emphasis added). Johnson expressed a similar sentiment to William Shirley, Dec. 17, 1754, *Johnson Papers*, 1:429–34.

74. For a typical example of a condolence exchange, see the minutes to a council held in Albany, July 3, 1751, *Johnson Papers*, 1:340–42. At a treaty conference in Carlisle, Pennsylvania, in 1753, the Indians refused to begin negotiations until the proper condolence presents arrived. See *A Treaty Held with the Ohio Indians at Carlisle in October, 1753* (Philadelphia, 1753), 3. Also of note is Hendrick's angry speech to Pennsylvania governor Robert Hunter Morris, Jan. 17, 1754/5, in which he complained that after King George's War, "No Presents were given—No Notice of Peace—No Satisfaction for Blood spilled," a reference to the New York government's failure to acknowledge properly the Mohawks' losses. See *Minutes of the Provincial Council of Pennsylvania*, 6:283.

75. Johnson to Clinton, May 26, 1749, in O'Callaghan, ed., *NYCol. Docs.*, 6:512–13; Johnson to Weiser, Apr. 2, 1751, *Johnson Papers*, 1:326.

76. For the exchange between Johnson and the Indians, see O'Callaghan, ed., *NYCol. Docs.*, 6:977. For the account entry, see *Johnson Papers*, 2:577.

77. On Johnson's Indian name and acceptance among the Indians, see Hamilton, *William Johnson*, 45, and Wraxall, *Abridgment of Indian Affairs*, 248n1.

78. See Timothy J. Shannon, "The Crossroads of Empire: The Albany Congress of 1754 and the British-Atlantic Community" (PhD diss., Northwestern University, 1993), 94–125, 274–328.

79. See Francis X. Clines, "Peace Prevails in an Offering of Simple Cloth," *New York Times*, Sept. 25, 1994, p. 39.

18. The Flow of European Trade Goods into the Western Great Lakes Region, 1715–1760

DEAN L. ANDERSON

Since the pioneering work of Francis Parkman and Frederick Jackson Turner in the late nineteenth century, the North American fur trade has been conceptualized primarily as a Euro-American institution. For the most part, historians have characterized the fur trade as the initial, pathbreaking incursion of Euro-American influence into the interior of northeastern North America. Thus, scholarly treatment of the trade has been mainly concerned with the exploits of Euro-American traders and with the role of the trade as the vanguard of Euro-American settlement (Turner 1970) and as the extension of the European economic system into North America (Innis 1970). In this view of the fur trade, Indian peoples have been portrayed as minor characters who played a limited part in the conduct of the trade. Consequently, relatively little attention has been paid to understanding Indian participation in the trade.

Over the past twenty years, however, a different perspective has emerged on the role of Native peoples in the fur trade. A number of studies have disputed the conventional wisdom that Indian peoples were merely passive pawns in the trade who were caught up and swept along in a tide of Euro-American enterprise (Francis and Morantz 1983; Krech 1984; Lohse 1988; Ray 1974; Yerbury 1986). To the contrary, it has been demonstrated that Native peoples were active, and indeed aggressive, participants in the fur trade. No less than their Euro-American counterparts, Indian peoples sought to shape the trade according to their cultural values (B. White 1984, 1986) and to use the trade to serve their best interests. Such studies have emphasized that the fur trade was not organized, controlled, and carried out by Euro-Americans who imposed the trade upon Native peoples. Rather, the trade arose through a process of cultural compromise in which Euro-Americans accommodated Native values and customs at least as much, and perhaps more, than Indian peoples accommodated Euro-American ideas (R. White 1991).

It has become increasingly clear that the fur trade was a cultural partnership and that there is a great deal to be learned about the involvement of Indian peoples in the trade. Toward this end, one of the major trends in current fur trade research is the effort to specifically investigate both the way Native peoples contributed to shaping the trade as well as the way they adapted to new conditions produced by the trade (Krech 1984: x).

Indian Peoples and European Trade Goods

The fur trade exchange relationship was a complex one which presented Indian peoples with new social, political, and economic circumstances and opportunities (Peterson and Anfinson 1984). However, the most tangible consequence of the fur trade for Native peoples was the introduction of European manufactured goods. The flow of trade goods into Indian societies was an important part of the impact of the trade upon Native peoples. The adoption of European goods altered Native material culture which, in turn, influenced change in other aspects of Native life.

How did Indian peoples respond to the introduction of European materials? Contrary to the popular perception that Indian peoples were smitten by the irresistible appeal of obviously superior European goods, it has been shown that Native peoples critically evaluated European products and appropriated those that met their needs and interests. Indian peoples were not passive recipients of European goods but aggressive, discriminating consumers (Ray 1980; Krech 1984).

In the active pursuit of European technology, then, what types of goods did Indian peoples seek to obtain and what patterns in Indian acquisition of trade goods can be identified? These may seem like

---

The Flow of European Goods

simple questions and it may also seem that they are questions that are already well understood, since there is considerable discussion in the fur trade literature of the types of trade goods acquired by Indian peoples. It is the premise of this study, however, that the flow of European goods into Indian societies is not well understood. While there is a great deal of comment in the literature on the goods traded to Indians, there have been few systematic, quantitative studies of the flow of goods into Indian societies.

This article examines the flow of European goods into the western Great Lakes region (map 4) during the period from 1715 to 1760. It may be noted that there are several studies which discuss the acquisition of trade goods by Indian peoples during the pre-1760 period in areas to the north of the western Great Lakes region (Ray 1974, 1980; Ray and Freeman 1978; Morantz 1980). In that area, the Hudson's Bay Company was the principal supplier of goods and the vast records of the HBC have served as a valuable source of data on Indian trading habits. By comparison, the flow of goods through the French trade system into the western Great Lakes region during the period prior to 1760 is less well known.

The Montreal Merchants' Records
This paper uses data taken from an extensive collection of documents known as the Montreal Merchants' Records (hereafter referred to as the MMR). The MMR are composed of portions of the business records of several different Montreal merchants. As part of their business, the merchants sold trade goods and supplies to fur traders preparing to travel to posts in the interior. The MMR record the shipment of trade goods to diverse geographic locations during much of the eighteenth century. The documents are, however, an especially important body of data regarding the French-period trade in the western Great Lakes area. Temporally, the documents mainly record the shipment of goods during the period from 1715 to 1760. Further, most of the shipments of goods recorded were to posts in the western Great Lakes region. Importantly, the fact

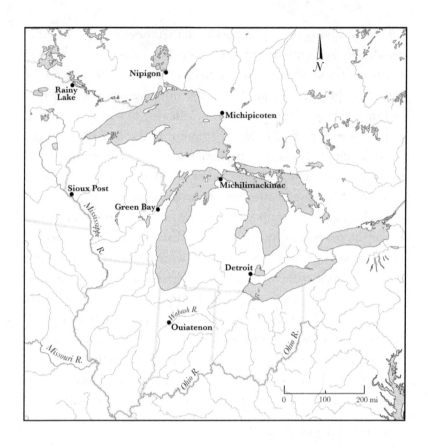

MAP 4. French-period outposts in the western Great Lakes region for which Montreal Merchants' Records data were compiled.

that the documents record the shipment of goods to a number of different posts provides a broad, regional view of the flow of trade goods into the western country.

The merchants' account books contain detailed invoices which list trade goods to be shipped to the posts. In this respect, the MMR are different from Hudson's Bay Company post records that have been used to examine Indian acquisition of trade goods. Hudson's Bay Company post records record the sale of goods by European traders to Indian customers. The MMR, in contrast, record the sale of goods by European merchants to European traders. Although the MMR do not explicitly record the purchase of goods by Indian peoples, it is argued that the MMR still provide a valid, if not precise, record of the goods which Native peoples obtained. It is suggested that although the MMR are not specifically a record of the goods for which Native peoples traded, Indian demand for European goods shaped the contents of the inventories of goods purchased by traders. If we accept that the fur trade was a sophisticated exchange relationship in which both Indian and European participants were knowledgeable about their trading partners, it follows that European traders purchased goods according to their understanding of Indian interests in trade goods. Consequently, it is argued here that the general patterns in trader purchasing of types of goods and quantities of goods recorded in the MMR are a valid reflection of general patterns in Indian trading. This is not to suggest that European traders were always completely accurate in their anticipation of what Indian peoples would purchase. Certainly European traders could not anticipate every change in the needs and desires of their Indian customers. Thus, while the inventories of goods purchased by European traders are not an absolute representation of what Indians ultimately obtained, it is suggested that those inventories are an essentially accurate representation of Indian acquisition of trade goods.

The Fur Trade Invoices

The fur trade invoices in the MMR contain a detailed record of the materials that fur traders purchased from the merchants. The invoices are usually similar in form and include a variety of information. At the head of the invoice, the date of the sale is recorded. Next, a brief statement appears which identifies the purchaser and which usually indicates the post to which the goods were to be taken. The main body of the invoice follows, consisting of an itemized listing of the goods, supplies, and services sold to the trader. While the invoice entries are rather concise, they often describe the items purchased on the basis of type, size, color, material, or place of manufacture. Commonly, the descriptive terms distinguish between items of different price, such as different sizes and styles of knives or different sizes of capotes. Each entry records the quantity of the item purchased and the unit of measure in which it was sold, such as 10 axes, 5 pounds of beads, or 50 ells of cloth. In addition, each invoice entry includes the unit price for the item and the total cost for the quantity purchased. In some invoices, profit margin is added to the itemized charges. All of the price information in the account books is recorded in the French Canadian monetary system of the period, consisting of livres, sols, and deniers (20 sols equal 1 livre, 12 deniers equal 1 sol).

The Outfits

The fur trade invoices in the MMR are scattered throughout the account books and are interspersed among postings for the sale of merchandise to local Montreal citizens. Identifying and organizing those invoices that specifically recorded trade goods presented a problem because of the variability in the invoices. Some fur trade invoices are extremely long and are easily recognizable in the pages of the account books. In these cases, trade goods and supplies were purchased by a trader in one large transaction, resulting in a single invoice that might continue for several pages. In some instances, though, a trader made more than one purchase, perhaps over a

The Flow of European Goods

period of several days, resulting in two or more invoices. Sometimes a posting for the purchase of just a few items would follow a main invoice, suggesting the addition of goods that were forgotten or added as an afterthought.

Because of the variability in the invoices in the account books, the concept of an "outfit" is used in this study to organize the invoices. As the term is used here, an outfit consists of the trade goods and supplies shipped to a specific location by a trader or partnership of traders within a calendar year, whether the goods are listed in one invoice or in several. In this way, a number of invoices could be consolidated, including those for materials purchased by the trader's engagés. This means that a single small invoice was designated as an outfit if it was the only one posted for a specific trader and a specific location during a calendar year. In so doing, the presence of trade goods in a single invoice was the prerequisite for identifying it as an outfit; a lone invoice that was made up entirely of supplies or personal items was not considered an outfit. It is important to point out that the identification of an assemblage of goods as an outfit carries no implications about the size of that group of goods. An outfit may be represented by the purchase of a few items or by the purchase of several thousand livres worth of goods.

The Posts

A total of eighty-three outfits shipped to the western Great Lakes region before 1760 were identified in the MMR account books. Thirteen of these outfits were omitted because they lacked certain information, such as prices for goods or the specific destination of the outfit. This left a total of seventy outfits from which data were taken. These outfits represent the shipment of goods to eight different trading posts. The posts, and the number of outfits recorded for each of them, are listed in table 4. The locations of the eight posts are shown in map 4. The outfits enumerated for each post in table 4 were shipped over the forty-five-year span from 1715 to 1760. Since the total number of outfits for each post is considerably less

TABLE 4. Number of outfits for each post, 1715–1760

Post	Number of Outfits
Detroit	15
Michilimackinac	14
Green Bay	13
Ouiatenon	10
Sioux Post	8
Rainy Lake	6
Nipigon	3
Michipicoten	1

than forty-five, it is apparent that outfits were not recorded every year for any of the posts. This is because the trader clientele of the merchants fluctuated from year to year. Each year, the merchants did business with different traders who were operating at different posts. Consequently, there is not a continuous, year-by-year record of outfits for any of the posts. Rather, outfits for any given post occur with varying frequency and regularity in the account books.

Isolating the Trade Goods

The first step in the analysis of the invoice data was to separate the trade goods from the supplies. Although the outfits purchased by the traders were generally composed mainly of goods intended for trade to Indians, they also included a variety of non-trade items. Frequently, various kinds of supplies and equipment for the trip into the interior and for the stay at the post were part of the outfit. For example, canoe gear and the materials needed to repair canoes were commonly listed in the invoices. These included poles to lie in the bottom of the canoe to support cargo, sponge to bail the canoe, and bark, gum, and spruce root to make repairs. On some occasions, even the canoes were purchased through the merchant. Camping gear for the trip was also invoiced, such as bark to construct temporary huts, an axe, a large cooking kettle, and sometimes tents. Provisions such as pork, flour, peas, and biscuit, along with wine and brandy, were also purchased by the trader.

The Flow of European Goods

Occasionally items were listed that were purchased by the trader to be given to the engagés. These were usually articles of clothing or pieces of cloth but sometimes combs, knives, or even guns were purchased for the engagés. In a few of the invoices, some of the non-trade-good materials were specifically identified. Canoe gear and equipment for the trip were listed under the heading "Furnished for the canoes" (Moniere, M849, 8:358, 409). Provisions were identified as "Food and drink for the engages" (Moniere, M849, 8:237, 294). And items purchased for the engagés were listed as "For the men" or were listed under the names of specific individuals (Moniere, M849, 8:112–13, 183). In many of the invoices, however, such non-trade items were not explicitly identified.

In addition, a number of items appear in the invoices that may or may not have been intended for trade to Indians. Examples of these include playing cards, drinking glasses, soap, and shoes. Many of these types of items were probably intended for use by Europeans, but at least some of them may have been trade items.

In isolating the trade goods, the invoices were analyzed and each entry in the invoices was designated as either a trade item (for trade to Indians) or as a supply item (for use by Europeans). To make the designations, three criteria were used: (1) archaeological and documentary evidence, (2) the location of the entry in the invoice, and (3) the quantity of the item recorded in the entry. All three criteria do not necessarily apply to each entry, but usually a combination of at least two of the criteria played a part in making a designation.

1. Archaeological and Documentary Evidence
If an item listed in the invoices has been reported to occur on French-period Indian sites, this was considered evidence for designating the item as a trade good. Mainly, evidence used for this purpose came from archaeological sites in the western Great Lakes region including the Lasanen site (Cleland 1971), the Gros Cap Cemetery site (Nern and Cleland 1974), the Bell site (Wittry 1963), the Fletcher site

(Mainfort 1979), the Rock Island site (Mason 1986), the Marquette Mission site (Branstner 1984, 1985, 1986, 1987), the Marina site (Salzer and Birmingham 1981), and the Zimmerman site (Brown 1975) as shown in map 5. However, other sites were consulted as well, including the Guebert site (Good 1972) in southern Illinois and the Burr's Hill site (Gibson 1980) in Rhode Island. Similarly, if an item listed in the invoices appeared on French-period trade lists in documentary sources, this was also taken as evidence for designating the item as a trade good. In addition to lists of goods specifically for the western Great Lakes region (e.g., WHC 1904), lists for Hudson's Bay Company posts (Ray and Freeman 1978; Heidenreich and Ray 1976) and lists of goods for the Illinois country (Pease and Werner 1934) were also examined.

2. Location of an Entry in the Invoice

The position of an entry in the invoice was often a factor in designating an item as a trade good or as a supply item. If the entry appeared in a list of goods whose purpose was specifically identified, such as those mentioned earlier, the designation was obvious. But there was also a tendency in the invoices, whether the specific purpose of some goods was identified or not, to group supplies and personal items together. The common pattern was for trade goods to be listed first in the invoice and for non-trade materials to follow. Thus, if an entry appeared in the latter part of an invoice surrounded by materials that were apparently supplies, it suggested that the entry in question was also a supply item. By the same token, an entry appearing at the beginning of an invoice was more likely a trade good. The listing of goods by bales and by crates was virtually always done at the very beginning of the invoice. The contents of the bales and crates were heavily dominated by trade goods. If an entry was listed as part of the goods packed in a bale or in a crate, it suggested that the entry was a trade good. The inclusion of an item in a bale or crate was not, however, indisputable evidence that it was a trade good. For example, a bale shipped to Green Bay

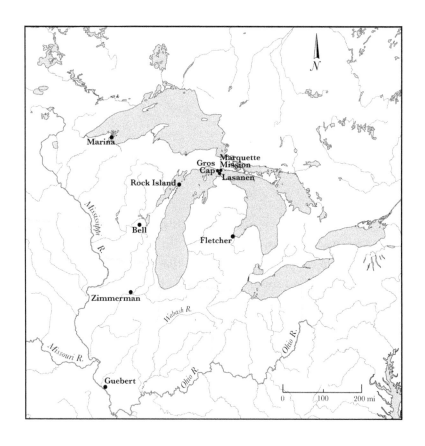

Map 5. French-period Native sites
consulted for trade good data.

TABLE 5. Number of types of goods for each post, 1715–1760

Post	Types of Goods
Green Bay	66
Rainy Lake	66
Michilimackinac	59
Ouiatenon	57
Detroit	56
Sioux Post	54
Nipigon	46
Michipicoten	38

in 1725 contained such probable trade goods as: 42 tomahawks, 300 gunflints, 144 awls, and 9 pounds of glass beads. However, the same bale also contained several items that were probably supplies, namely, one-half-pound of sulphur, one half-pound of alum, two sticks of sealing wax, and 200 flooring nails. Consequently, the presence of an item in a bale or crate was not taken as a definitive indication of its status as a trade good.

3. Quantity of an Item

In some cases, the quantity of an item was also a clue in identifying it as a trade good. As a very general rule, trade goods tended to be purchased in large quantities. Again, this was not a hard and fast guideline. Vermilion, for example, a trade good that was included in most outfits, was often purchased in quantities of one pound or less. The purchase of large amounts of an item, however, especially if it occurred in a number of different outfits, suggests that the item was intended for trade.

Once the trade goods in the invoices had been designated, an inventory of the types of goods shipped to each post during the 1715–60 period was compiled. Table 5 indicates the number of types of goods in the inventories for each post. The inventories of goods shipped to the posts provide a view of the flow of goods into the western Great Lakes region. Because of the number of types of goods involved, however, it is cumbersome to try and make sense of the flow of goods on the basis of individual types. Instead, an effort

The Flow of European Goods

was made to clarify Indian interests in trade goods by looking at the flow of goods in terms of activities or purposes represented. Toward this end, the types of goods in the inventories were organized into functional categories.

Functional Categories

The first step in defining functional categories of trade goods was to combine the individual inventories for the eight posts into a single, composite inventory. Then, the duplication of types of goods from different posts was deleted. This produced a comprehensive inventory of the types of goods shipped to the eight posts. This composite inventory consisted of eighty-six types of trade goods. This inventory was then used in defining functional categories. In this way, functional categories could be identified on a regional basis rather than on the basis of individual posts.

In organizing the inventory of types of goods into functional categories, it was assumed that, in use by Indian peoples, the primary functions of trade goods were those intended by the European manufacturers of the goods. Categories were identified with the objective of creating a valid representation of the functional diversity in the inventory. This resulted in the definition of the following thirteen categories: Clothing, Hunting, Cooking and Eating, Alcohol Use, Tobacco Use, Weapons, Woodworking, Adornment, Grooming, Digging/Cultivation, Fishing, Maintenance, and Amusements. Table 6 indicates the way the types of goods were grouped in arriving at the identification of these categories.

Comparison of the Posts

Patterns in the flow of goods into the western Great Lakes region may be sought by comparing the representation of the categories of goods at each of the eight posts. To do this, the individual inventories of goods for each of the posts were organized into the functional categories. Table 7 lists the categories of goods represented at each post. Two questions about the representation of categories at the eight posts were posed. The first question was, are

TABLE 6. Types of goods by functional category

Adornment
azure
bead
bell
black lead
brooch
finger ring
glass bead
hawk bell
necklace
runtee
verdigris
vermilion
12

Clothing
awl
blanket
breeches
buckle
button
cap
capote
cloth
dress
dress suit
garter
gartering
glove
gown
handkerchief
hat
laces
legging
mantelet
mitten
needle
pin
scarf
scissors
shawl

Clothing (*continued*)
shoe
shirt
sleeve
stocking
thimble
thread
trim
tuque
yarn
34

Cooking and Eating
firesteel
fork
kettle
knife
ladle
spoon
6

Grooming
brush
comb
hair puller
mirror
4

Hunting
dart
gun
gunflint
gunpowder
gun sheath
gun worm
ice chisel
musket ball
powder horn
shot
wire
11

Weapons
bayonet
dagger
pistol
3

Woodworking
adze
ax
2

Amusements
fan
jew's harp
2

Digging and Cultivation
hoe
pickaxe
2

Alcohol Use
brandy
wine
2

Fishing
fishhook
fishing line
net
3

Maintenance
file
rasp
2

Tobacco Use
pipe
tobacco
2

there substantial differences between the posts in terms of which categories are represented at each one? Table 7 indicates that nine of the thirteen categories are represented at all eight posts. Those nine categories are Clothing, Hunting, Cooking and Eating, Tobacco Use, Adornment, Alcohol Use, Grooming, Woodworking, and Digging/Cultivation. At six of the eight posts, at least one category is not represented. There are, however, no more than three unrepresented categories at any post, and that situation occurs only at Michipicoten, for which only one outfit was recorded. In each case, the unrepresented categories are the Fishing, Maintenance, Amusements, or Weapons categories. The Fishing category is absent at Nipigon, Michipicoten, Detroit, and Michilimackinac. The Maintenance category is absent at Ouiatenon, Michipicoten, and Michilimackinac. The Amusements category is absent at Sioux Post, Nipigon, and Michipicoten. The Weapons category is absent only at Detroit.

The second question posed was, how did the relative emphasis upon different categories of trade goods vary at each of the posts? Addressing this question required that the categories could be measured in some manner. One possibility was to measure the categories in terms of the quantities of goods sold since that information is recorded in the invoice entries. Quantity, however, is not a basis for measurement that is well-suited to making comparisons among types of goods or among functional categories. This is because quantity was measured in numerous different types of units among the trade goods. Many types of goods were measured by count, but others were measured in units of weight, volume, or area. Further, some types of goods were measured in units that are difficult to interpret, such as bundles or masses. This diversity of units of measure makes quantity an unsuitable basis for comparison.

The invoices do, however, record a variable that is common to all types of goods and which is recorded in the same unit of measure. This variable is the cost—or trader expenditure—for the goods. Trader expenditure provides a consistent basis for comparison

TABLE 7. Functional categories in ranked order by percentage of expenditure

Detroit

1. Clothing	75.58
2. Hunting	11.91
3. Alcohol Use	4.83
4. Cooking and Eating	4.28
5. Adornment	1.73
6. Grooming	.54
7. Tobacco Use	.50
8. Woodworking	.46
9. Digging and Cultivation	.09
10. Maintenance	.07
11. Amusements	.02
12. Weapons	—
13. Fishing	—

Sioux Post

1. Clothing	43.87
2. Hunting	25.23
3. Cooking and Eating	11.73
4. Woodworking	5.17
5. Adornment	4.69
6. Alcohol Use	4.34
7. Weapons	1.65
8. Tobacco Use	1.62
9. Grooming	.98
10. Digging and Cultivation	.55
11. Fishing	.07
12. Maintenance	.04
13. Amusements	—

Rainy Lake

1. Clothing	55.28
2. Hunting	15.46
3. Adornment	7.06
4. Alcohol Use	6.92
5. Cooking and Eating	5.08
6. Woodworking	4.38
7. Tobacco Use	3.96
8. Grooming	.95
9. Weapons	.44
10. Fishing	.19

11. Digging and Cultivation	.16
12. Maintenance	.12
13. Amusements	.02

Green Bay

1. Clothing	65.08
2. Hunting	18.09
3. Cooking and Eating	4.59
4. Alcohol Use	4.37
5. Adornment	2.95
6. Woodworking	2.39
7. Tobacco Use	1.61
8. Grooming	.87
9. Weapons	.19
10. Digging and Cultivation	.07
11. Maintenance	.06
12. Fishing	.03
13. Amusements	.01

Michipicoten

1. Clothing	59.82
2. Hunting	10.86
3. Alcohol Use	9.02
4. Cooking and Eating	8.29
5. Woodworking	5.91
6. Tobacco Use	3.00
7. Adornment	1.75
8. Weapons	.57
9. Digging and Cultivation	.51
10. Grooming	.31
11. Fishing	—
12. Maintenance	—
13. Amusements	—

Michilimackinac

1. Clothing	72.04
2. Hunting	12.40
3. Adornment	4.57
4. Cooking and Eating	3.40
5. Alcohol Use	3.07
6. Tobacco Use	2.05

7. Woodworking	1.32		11. Weapons	.02
8. Grooming	.95		12. Fishing	.01
9. Digging and Cultivation	.16		13. Maintenance	—
10. Weapons	.03			
11. Amusements	.01		**Nipigon**	
12. Fishing	—		1. Clothing	65.89
13. Maintenance	—		2. Hunting	13.34
			3. Cooking and Eating	9.28
Ouiatenon			4. Alcohol Use	3.56
1. Clothing	55.04		5. Woodworking	3.17
2. Hunting	20.28		6. Tobacco Use	1.64
3. Cooking and Eating	7.22		7. Adornment	1.53
4. Alcohol Use	6.95		8. Grooming	1.22
5. Adornment	5.62		9. Digging and Cultivation	.24
6. Woodworking	2.25		10. Maintenance	.08
7. Grooming	1.24		11. Weapons	.03
8. Tobacco Use	1.20		12. Fishing	—
9. Digging and Cultivation	.10		13. Amusements	—
10. Amusements	.08			

between the functional categories represented by the inventory of goods at each post. Using the cost information in the invoice entries, trader expenditure can be computed for each type of trade good at each post. Then, trader expenditure for all types of goods within a category can be summed to arrive at total trader expenditure for the category. Expenditure for each category at a given post, then, can be expressed as a percentage of total trader expenditure for all goods for that particular post.

In table 7, the functional categories represented at each post are arranged in ranked order according to the percentage they comprise of total trader expenditure for all goods for the post. Examination of the lists in table 7 indicates that there is considerable consistency among the posts in the ranked order of categories. The Clothing category is ranked number one and the Hunting category is ranked number two at every post. At the bottom end of the rankings, the Maintenance, Fishing, and Amusements categories are three of the last four categories at every post. The remaining eight categories occur in positions three through twelve in the ranked listings, but

TABLE 8. Rank positions in which each category occurs

Category	Rank Positions												
Clothing	1												
Hunting		2											
Cooking and Eating			3	4	5								
Alcohol Use			3	4	5	6							
Adornment			3		5		7						
Woodworking				4	5	6	7	8					
Tobacco Use						6	7	8					
Grooming						6	7	8	9	10			
Weapons							7	8	9	10	11	12	
Digging and Cultivation									9	10	11		
Maintenance										10	11	12	13
Fishing										10	11	12	13
Amusements										10	11		13

they do not occur randomly across those positions. Each of the eight categories tends to occur in certain positions and thus to display patterned relationships with the other categories. Table 8 illustrates this by indicating all of the positions in the rankings in which each of the thirteen categories occur.

To gain a summary picture of the flow of goods into the region, trader expenditure for the categories of goods can be determined for the combined inventory of goods for all eight posts. Trader expenditure for each category of goods may be expressed as a percentage of the total expenditure for all goods. Table 9 presents the functional categories of goods in ranked order according to the percentage of expenditure they represent for the combined inventory of goods.

Conclusions

This analysis of the MMR invoice data allows a number of observations to be made about patterns in Indian trading for European goods in the western Great Lakes region during the latter part of the French period. The MMR data suggest the range of functional types of European goods for which Indian peoples traded during this period. The data also suggest that there were marked patterns

Category	% of Expenditure
1. Clothing	62.85
2. Hunting	17.00
3. Cooking and Eating	5.65
4. Alcohol Use	4.84
5. Adornment	3.73
6. Woodworking	2.71
7. Tobacco Use	1.84
8. Grooming	.75
9. Weapons	.32
10. Digging and Cultivation	.15
11. Maintenance	.06
12. Fishing	.05
13. Amusements	.01

in the relative emphasis that Native peoples placed upon different functional categories of goods. In addition, the pattern of relative emphasis on trade for different categories of goods was very consistent across the region.

The most striking aspect of the analysis is the indication of a very strong emphasis in the trade upon clothing—both finished clothing and the materials to make clothing. The Clothing category accounts for more than 50 percent of trader expenditure at every post except the Sioux Post, and it accounts for over 60 percent of expenditure for all goods shipped to all eight posts. This is an important observation in light of the common perception that the trade hinged upon firearms and metal implements like kettles and axes. Certainly those goods were important components of the trade. But it is also clear that there was a strong demand for clothing. This demand, in concert with the fact that it was a commodity that would have required virtually constant replenishment, made clothing perhaps the cornerstone commodity of the trade. This pattern has also been demonstrated for British-period trade in the western Great Lakes region (B. White 1987: 170–71).

This importance of cloth and clothing has implications for

understanding the part that Native women played in the fur trade. Access to ready-made clothing, bolt cloth, and blankets, along with iron awls, pins, needles, and thread probably reduced the amount of time and labor that women had to invest in the production of clothing. The prominence of clothing and clothing-related materials in the trade suggests that women made considerable input into decisions about the types of goods to be obtained in trade. Further, the savings in time and labor could have been reinvested in the production of clothing in the form of time spent adorning articles of attire with beadwork. Or it could have been invested in endeavors associated with the fur trade, such as the processing of pelts or the production of other trade commodities such as garden produce. If the trade in clothing and textiles reduced the domestic labor requirements for women and allowed them to become more involved in activities related to the trade, it may have had an important impact on women's roles in historical-period Indian societies.

The data also suggest an emphasis on the Hunting category, which ranks second at each post. This reflects an emphasis upon the trade for firearms and the materials necessary for their use. Of course, the prominence of the Hunting category is a result of the decision to categorize firearms as primarily hunting tools rather than as weapons. This is a difficult determination to make, but it was assumed that firearms were probably used more routinely for hunting and were used more sporadically as weapons; thus they were assigned to the Hunting category. With the inclusion of firearms in the Hunting category, it appears that the European technology that was adopted by Indian peoples for subsistence pursuits was mainly materials used in hunting activities. In addition to the firearms complex, these materials included darts (apparently iron projectile points), ice chisels, and wire. Subsistence-related implements are also represented in the Digging/Cultivation category and in the Fishing category. But both of these are relatively minor categories, suggesting that there was not a significant use of European goods in these activities. For some posts, such as Michipicoten, Nipigon, and Rainy Lake, the lack of trade for cultivation implements is not surprising, since these posts were in climatic zones where agriculture was impractical. The data suggest, however, that Native peoples in the western Great Lakes area were not inclined to trade for cultivating tools even in those areas where agriculture was an important part of the subsistence base. A similar situation obtains with regard to the Fishing category. At posts like Ouiatenon or the Sioux Post, one might not expect there to have been a brisk trade in fishing implements. But at the other posts, it would be reasonable to expect an emphasis upon trade for fishing gear given the importance of fishing in the subsistence economy of the western Great Lakes region (Cleland 1982). The fact that the MMR data indicate that neither cultivating implements nor fishing gear were important trade items suggests that Native peoples perceived their traditional technology as perfectly sufficient for their needs and that European versions of those implements did not confer a sufficient advantage to make them a priority in trading.

In addition to the Digging/Cultivation and the Fishing categories, the Maintenance and Amusements categories are also among the lowest-ranked categories. The weak Amusements category indicates that Native peoples had little interest in trading for novelties or trinkets. The poorly represented Maintenance category indicates that Indian peoples were not equipped to repair and resharpen the European goods they acquired in trade. In fact, it could be argued that files and rasps, which comprise the Maintenance category, were not offered as trade items. In analyzing the invoices, files and rasps were designated as trade goods because files appear on lists of goods traded by the Hudson's Bay Company (Ray and Freeman 1978: 92, 130–31; Heidenreich and Ray 1976: 77). However, files and rasps are not common in the MMR invoices and when they do appear, it is not in great numbers, nor does their position in the invoices tend to suggest strongly whether they are trade goods or supplies. But perhaps of more significance is the fact that archaeological evidence for files at French-period Indian sites in the western country is extremely rare. No files or file fragments are reported from the Guebert site (Good 1972), the Lasanen site (Cleland 1971), or the Bell site (Wittry 1963). One file fragment has been recovered from French-period deposits at the Marquette Mission site (Branstner: personal communication). Four triangular file fragments were reported from the Fletcher site, the dating of which spans the end of the French period and the beginning of the British period (Mainfort 1979). A single file fragment is also reported from Rock Island (Mason 1986), but it is unclear whether it was associated with French-period deposits or with later deposits. On the other hand, thirty-seven files were reported by Stone (1974: 298) from excavations at Michilimackinac. He suggests that the specimens date to the period from 1740–80 and that they were primarily of French use. The archaeological evidence, then, suggests that files were transported to posts during the French period but that they were primarily for European use and were not commonly traded to Indians. In fact, keeping files out of Indians' hands may have been a part of French trading strategy, since it would curtail the opportunity to repair and resharpen implements and thus would promote the replacement of worn and damaged goods.

The Alcohol Use category is, on one hand, among the higher ranking categories, but it is perhaps not as highly ranked as might be expected. The representation of this category in the MMR invoices is difficult to evaluate. It may be that this is a valid picture of the trade in alcohol relative to other important goods such as clothing, firearms, and kettles. The use of alcohol in the trade in the western Great Lakes region had probably not reached its peak by the late French period. On the other hand, if substantial quantities of alcohol were shipped to the western country through channels that pre-empted the recording of it in documents like the merchants' accounting records, the MMR may underrepresent the trade in alcohol.

The MMR data also present an interesting perspective on the materials included in the Adornment category. The trade in articles of adornment has commanded a great deal of attention. Glass beads, in particular, are commonly thought of as the currency of the trade and have been referred to as "the denominator of the trade" (Woodward 1970: 15). This view has resulted in part from archaeological research which has demonstrated that large quantities of glass beads were traded and that other adornment items are common in archaeological deposits as well (e.g., Fitting 1976). The MMR data do not refute the importance of glass beads and other materials in the Adornment category, but they do place the trade in adornment articles in perspective relative to the trade for other types of goods.

In summary, this analysis of data taken from the MMR invoices offers insight into the adoption of European trade goods by Indian peoples in the western Great Lakes region during the last several decades of the French period. Organizing the trade-good data into functional categories allowed the acquisition of goods to be examined in terms of the purposes for which goods were used rather than in terms of individual types of goods. The data suggest that there were definite patterns in the flow of goods into Native societies and that these patterns were quite consistent across the western Great Lakes region. It is clear that Indian peoples traded for a functionally varied group of European goods, but it is also apparent that there was considerable variation in the emphasis placed upon different categories of goods. Most conspicuous in this regard is the indication of a strong demand for clothing and the materials with which to make clothing. While this does not negate the importance of metal implements in the trade, it does temper the perspective that, for Native peoples, the fur trade was an increasingly imperative quest for European metal goods.

References

Branstner, Susan M. 1984. *1983 Archaeological Investigations at the Marquette Mission Site.* Planning Report submitted to the St. Ignace Downtown Development Authority by The Museum, Michigan State University, East Lansing.

————. 1985. *1984 Archaeological Investigations at the Marquette Mission Site.* Planning Report submitted to the St. Ignace Downtown Development Authority by The Museum, Michigan State University, East Lansing.

————. 1986. *1985 Archaeological Investigations at the Marquette Mission Site.* Planning Report submitted to the St. Ignace Downtown Development Authority by The Museum, Michigan State University, East Lansing.

————. 1987. *1986 Archaeological Investigations at the Marquette Mission Site.* Planning Report submitted to the St. Ignace Downtown Development Authority by The Museum, Michigan State University, East Lansing.

Brown, Margaret Kimball. 1975. "The Zimmerman Site: Further Excavations at the Grand Village of Kaskaskia." *Reports of Investigations,* no. 32. Springfield: Illinois State Museum.

Cleland, Charles E., ed. 1971. "The Lasanen Site: An Historic Burial Locality in Mackinac County, Michigan." *Anthropological Series* 1 (1): 1–147. Publications of The Museum, Michigan State University, East Lansing.

————. 1982. "The Inland Shore Fishery of the Northern Great Lakes: Its Development and Importance in Prehistory." *American Antiquity* 47 (4): 761–84.

Fitting, James E. 1976. "Patterns of Acculturation at the Straits of Mackinac." In *Cultural Change and Continuity,* edited by Charles E. Cleland. New York: Academic Press.

Francis, Daniel, and Toby Morantz. 1983. *Partners in Furs: A History of the Fur Trade in Eastern James Bay 1600–1870.* Kingston and Montreal: McGill-Queen's University Press.

Gibson, Susan G. 1980. "Burr's Hill: A 17th Century Wampanoag Burial Ground in Warren, Rhode Island." In *Studies in Anthropology and Material Culture,* vol. 2. Haffenreffer Museum of Anthropology, Brown University, Providence RI.

Good, Mary Elizabeth. 1972. "Guebert Site: An 18th Century Historic Kaskaskia Indian Village in Randolph County, Illinois." In *Memoir,* no. 2. St. Louis: Central States Archaeological Societies, Inc.

Heidenreich, Conrad E., and Arthur J. Ray. 1976. *The Early Fur Trades.* Toronto: McClelland and Stewart Ltd.

Innis, Harold A. [1930] 1970. *The Fur Trade in Canada.* Rev. ed. Toronto and Buffalo: University of Toronto Press.

Krech, Shepard III, ed. 1984. *The Subarctic Fur Trade: Native Social and Economic Adaptations.* Vancouver: University of British Columbia Press.

Lohse, E. S. 1988. "Trade Goods." In *Handbook of North American Indians: History of Indian-White Relations,* vol. 4, edited by Wilcomb Washburn, 396–403. Washington DC: Smithsonian Institution.

Mainfort, Robert C., Jr. 1979. "Indian Social Dynamics in the Period of European Contact: Fletcher Site Cemetery, Bay County, Michigan." *Anthropological Series* 1 (4): 269–418. Publications of The Museum, Michigan State University, East Lansing.

Mason, Ronald J. 1986. "Rock Island: Historical Indian Archaeology in the Northern Lake Michigan Basin." *MCJA Special Paper No. 6.* Kent OH: Kent State University Press.

Moniere, Alexis. 1712–68. *Account Books of Eighteenth Century Merchants of Montreal 1712–1806.* Michigan State University Library Microfilm no. 19014 (microfilm of originals housed at the Antiquarian and Numismatic Society of Montreal).

Morantz, Toby. 1980. "The Fur Trade and the Cree of James Bay." In *Old Trails and New Directions: Papers of the Third North American Fur Trade Conference,* edited by Carol Judd and Arthur Ray, 39–58. Toronto: University of Toronto Press.

Nern, Craig F., and Charles E. Cleland. 1974. "The Gros Cap Cemetery Site, St. Ignace, Michigan: A Reconsideration of the Greenlees Collection." In *Michigan Archaeologist* 20 (1): 1–58.

Parkman, Francis. [1865–92] 1983. *France and England in North America.* 2 vols. New York: The Literary Classics.

Pease, Theodore, and Raymond Werner. 1934. "The French Foundations 1680–1693." French series, vol. 1. In *Collections of the Illinois State Historical Library,* vol. 23. Springfield: Illinois State Historical Library.

Peterson, Jacqueline, and John Anfinson. 1984. "The Indian and the Fur Trade: A Review of Recent Literature." In *Scholars and the Indian Experience,* edited by W. R. Swagerty. Bloomington: Indiana University Press.

Ray, Arthur J. 1974. *Indians in the Fur Trade: Their Role as Trappers, Hunters, and Middlemen in the Lands Southwest of Hudson Bay 1660–1870.* Toronto: University of Toronto Press.

———. 1980. "Indians as Consumers in the Eighteenth Century." In *Old Trails and New Directions: Papers of the Third North American Fur Trade Conference,* edited by Carol Judd and Arthur Ray, 255–71. Toronto: University of Toronto Press.

Ray, Arthur J., and Donald Freeman. 1978. *"Give Us Good Measure": An Economic Analysis of Relations between the Indians and the Hudson's Bay Company before 1763.* Toronto: University of Toronto Press.

Salzer, Robert J., and Robert A. Birmingham. 1981. *Archaeological Salvage Excavations at the Marina Site (47 As 24) Madeline Island, Wisconsin.* Report submitted to Interagency Archaeological Services, National Park Service, Denver.

Stone, Lyle M. 1974. "Fort Michilimackinac 1715–1781: An Archaeological Perspective on the Revolutionary Frontier." *Anthropological Series* 2:1–367. Publications of The Museum, Michigan State University, East Lansing.

Turner, Frederick J. [1891] 1970. *The Character and Influence of the Indian Trade in Wisconsin.* New York: Burt Franklin.

WHC. 1904. *Collections of the State Historical Society of Wisconsin,* 16:400–407. Madison: State Historical Society of Wisconsin.

White, Bruce. 1984. "'Give Us a Little Milk': The Social and Cultural Significance of Gift Giving in the Lake Superior Fur Trade." In *Rendezvous: Selected Papers of the Fourth North American Fur Trade Conference, 1981,* 185–97, edited by Thomas C. Buckley. St. Paul: Minnesota Historical Society.

———. 1986. "A Skilled Game of Exchange: Ojibway Fur Trade Protocol." *Minnesota History* 50 (6): 229–40.

———. 1987. "Montreal Canoes and Their Cargoes." In *Le Castor Fait Tout: Selected Papers of the Fifth North American Fur Trade Conference,* edited by Bruce Trigger, Toby Morantz, and Louise Dechêne, 164–92. Montreal: Lake St. Louis Historical Society.

White, Richard. 1991. *The Middle Ground: Indians, Empires, and Republics in the Great Lakes Region, 1650–1815.* Cambridge: Cambridge University Press.

Wittry, Warren L. 1963. "The Bell Site, Wn9: An Early Historic Fox Village." *Wisconsin Archaeologist* 44 (1): 1–57.

Woodward, Arthur. 1970. *The Denominators of the Fur Trade: An Anthology of Writings on the Material Culture of the Fur Trade.* Pasadena CA: Socio-Technical Publications.

Yerbury, J. C. 1986. *The Subarctic Indians and the Fur Trade 1680–1860.* Vancouver: University of British Columbia Press.

19. The Matchcoat

Gail DeBuse Potter

The term "matchcoat" is derived from an Algonquian word meaning a cloak or a petticoat (Hodge: 819). It was a garment worn
by Indians throughout the East. Its prehistoric form was that of a
cloak or mantle usually made of furs sewn together with the fur
side in, against the wearer. In 1705 Virginia governor Robert Beverley described their use: "seldom any but the Elder people wore
the Winter Cloaks, (which they call Match-coats,) till they got a
supply of European goods; and now most have them of one sort
or other." About the same time, John Lawson wrote that men and
women alike wore matchcoats and also used them for bedding
(Swanton: 460–61).

Matchcoats were sometimes cut from bolts of cloth called match-
cloth or matchcoating woven for that purpose. Often as not, they
were made from duffel cloth or stroud. Colors mentioned include
red or blue in both these types of cloth, and white or striped duffel
as well. Sometimes matchcoats were listed by points, indicating they
were made from blankets. Usually they were decorated with metal
lace, frequently called tinsel in colonial records, or a worsted wool
binding tape known in the eighteenth century as caddis.

The significant difference between a matchcoat and a blanket
is that the matchcoat apparently had lapels and a collar of contrasting color. One of the few sources that describes this is the
following statement made at the July 18, 1716, meeting of the
Carolina Indian Trade Commissioners: "Resolved that the twenty-
one Indian Burdeners, that brought down the Bever, be paid for
that service and for carrying the Goods which we are to send by

9. Oil painting of Cherokee chief
Stalking Turkey (Cunne Shote) by
Francis Parsons, 1762. #0176.1015.
From the collection of the Gilcrease
Museum, Tulsa, Oklahoma.

them to our Factor at the Cherikees, each, one Yard and a Half of Blew Duffields for Match-coats, and a quarter Yard Strouds, for Flaps" (McDowell: 82).

The best illustration of the "flaps" or lapels and a collar of a matchcoat is the portrait of Stalking Turkey on the cover. A suggested reconstruction of an eighteenth-century matchcoat in image 9. It is based on the duffel cloth being the standard sixty-three inches wide by fifty-four inches long for the body and the stroud being the standard fifty-four inches wide by nine inches long for the lapels and collar. Note that Stalking Turkey's matchcoat had a tasseled cord to fasten it at the throat.

While the matchcoat was an Indian garment, whites also wore them. A curator at the Smithsonian told me during the U.S. Bicentennial that George Washington wore one during his 1754 expedition against the French.

References

Hodge, Frederick Webb, ed. *Handbook of Indians North of Mexico.* BAE Bulletin 30, part 1, p. 819. Washington DC: Smithsonian Institution.

McDowell, William L., Jr., ed. *Journals of the Commissioners of the Indian Trade, September 20, 1710–August 29, 1718.* Columbia: South Carolina Department of Archives and History, 1955.

Swanton, John R. *The Indians of the Eastern United States.* BAE Bulletin 137. Washington DC: Smithsonian Institution.

20. Chiefs Coats Supplied by the American Fur Company

ALLEN CHRONISTER

"Chiefs Coats" were fabric outer garments usually cut and orna-
mented in a military or semi-military style and worn by Indian
men. They were fixtures of Indian–Euro American relations in
North America for over two hundred years, both as gifts to Indian
men to seal trade and governmental relationships, and as items of
commerce (J. Hanson; Brown; Provo: 92, 102, 119; Thwaites: 276;
Viola: 117–18). The high point in the popularity of Chiefs Coats,
at least in terms of the numbers produced and distributed, seems
to have been reached in the American West in the first half of the
nineteenth century where the American Fur Company was heavily
involved in manufacturing and supplying them to its customers.

In 1823 Indian Agent Benjamin O'Fallon purchased Chiefs Coats
from the Company to use as presents to Indian men (AFC, Ledger J,
26). The 1836 annuities for the Oto and Missouri tribes, purchased
from the AFC, included ten blue cloth Chiefs Coats with lace (AFC,
Ledger z, 2). In September 1833, Prince Maximillian witnessed the
Company's "dressing" of the Piegan chiefs at Ft. McKenzie in red
uniforms, calico shirts, and red felt hats with red plumes (Thomas
and Ronnefeldt: 117). Rudolph Kurz noted a similar ceremonial
dressing of the chiefs of a group of Saulteaux from the Red River
who visited Ft. Clark on the Missouri in 1851 (Kurz: 85). The records of the American Fur Company posts on the Missouri contain
references to quantities of Chiefs Coats (Schuler: 89–90).

The Company manufactured the coats both in St. Louis and at
its larger posts in the field. Fort Union, for example, had its own
tailor shop, and the fort's inventory in 1851 included 8 blue and 7

scarlet "Chiefs Coats not made" (Contributions: 209). This seems to indicate that the garments had been started but not finished. In St. Louis the Company regularly employed local seamstresses to construct clothing, including Chiefs Coats. It had 67 Chiefs Coats made between June 30 and August 12, 1836 (AFC, Ledger z, 53), and between March and October of 1833 it paid Mrs. Marly at the rate of $.75 each for making 331 Chiefs Coats (AFC, Ledger u, 417).

Despite the quantity of Chiefs Coats made for the western trade in the nineteenth century, extremely few have survived. This may be due to several factors. The coats began to go out of style after the Civil War, when mass distributions of surplus military and civilian garments of all types were made as part of treaty negotiations (Hanson: 108; Murray). There is evidence that they were often worn for many years, probably until they literally fell apart, especially by men who had received them as gifts in recognition of their status (Viola: 120). Many were probably buried with their owners (Brown).

Whatever the reasons may be for the present rarity of Chiefs Coats, the result is that their appearance is subject to some conjecture. However, there is evidence from which many of the details of the Chiefs Coats supplied by the AFC can be reconstructed. Chiefs Coats fortunately appear in numerous drawings by Indian men during the first half of the nineteenth century, and the appearance of each of these coats is very similar. There is a very early buffalo robe painted with battle scenes which is unattributed, but which probably dates from the late eighteenth or early nineteenth century (Horse Capture et al.: 67, 103). One of the prominent figures on that robe is a man wearing a large flaring war bonnet and a long red coat open-front with dark colored cuffs and front facings. If this painting was done around 1800, it indicates that the coats later supplied by the AFC could have been based upon an established style.

Another robe and a hide shirt probably slightly later than the robe, and both painted with battle scenes, were collected prior to 1837. A central figure on the shirt wears a long red coat with dark facings down the front, and a figure on the robe (which is attributed to the famous Mandan chief Mato Tope) wears a long red coat with contrasting color (possibly green) cuffs and facings (Mauer: 145, 148). A third robe, unattributed but collected prior to 1866 and probably made before 1850, also contains a figure wearing a similar long red coat (Mauer: 151).

The Mandan artist Sih-Chida painted a self-portrait in 1833 wearing a long red coat with a blue stand-up collar and blue cuffs. The collar and cuffs had a light colored trim, possibly lace, and the coat body may have been made from saved list cloth (Thomas and Ronnefeldt: 224). The Jesuit artist/missionary Nicholas Pointe collected several Indian drawings around 1846–47, probably in the Upper Missouri River area. Two of these show Indian men wearing long red open-front coats with dark cuffs, stand-up collars, and dark and light striped facings (Peterson: 112–13).

Chiefs Coats also appear in pre-1850 depictions of Indian men by Euro-American artists. George Catlin's 1832 portrait of The Dog, a Sioux man, shows him wearing a very similar red coat with dark and light facings. The Dog's coat was further decorated with beaded shoulder and arm strips, and with fringe of either hide or hair, it is unclear (Hassrick: 159). In 1851 Kurz sketched a Hidatsa man wearing similar coat decorated with shoulder strips which appear to be quilled (Kurz: Plate 15). The Kurz coat is viewed from the rear, showing details not evident in the other drawings, including the "riding slit" and the buttons and tabs at the waist level. The length, open front, stand-up collar, and contrasting color collar, cuffs, and facings are consistent in these coats.

The owners of most of these coats probably had ready access to one of the American Fur Company trading posts. Surviving AFC records are helpful in reconstructing the appearance of Chiefs Coats because they contain detailed information on the materials that were used. Several entries are illuminating. In September 1823, the Company supplied 41 ¼ yards of saved-list blue cloth; 5 ⅝ yards of scarlet list cloth; 2 ¾ yards of lace;[1] 7 ½ dozen yellow and the same quantity of white metal coat buttons;[2] 15 skeins of blue silk[3] and 75 pairs of hooks and eyes, all of which went into making fifteen Chiefs Coats. J. Conklin was paid $7.62 for the sewing (AFC, Ledger K, 43). Chiefs Coats were sold to Indian Agent Benjamin O'Fallon at about the same time for $12.00 each (AFC, Ledger J, 26).

Using this list of materials and the pictorial representations noted above, we can suggest a reconstruction of the coats. The body was made from about 2.7 yards of white-selvege blue wool cloth. Since the red cloth works out to a little less than half a yard per coat, it was probably used only as trim on the facings, collar, and cuffs. The coats seem to have had either white or yellow buttons, about a dozen per coat. These buttons were probably not functional—which would hold down the construction costs—since there were five sets of hooks and eyes included for each coat. The sewing was done with the blue silk thread. There is nothing in this list of materials that is inconsistent with the coats in the historical drawings noted above.

The 1823 list, and other evidence, indicates that there may also have been grades of coats. The list contains 2 ¾ yards of lace, which was rather expensive at $4.50 and which was not enough to divide among fifteen coats and have more than a few inches for each one. Therefore, it is possible that the lace was used on only one coat which was more elaborately decorated than the rest. Sih-Chida's coat was clearly decorated with light-colored narrow trim on the collar and cuffs, which could have been silver lace. In addition, the dark and light panels on the facings of several of the coats noted above could have been created with light-colored lace.

Another entry in the AFC records in 1827 contains the materials that went into a single coat: 3 ½ yards of blue cloth; ¾ yard green cloth; 1 dozen gilt buttons; ½ yard unbleached cotton; and 3 ¼ yards of lace (AFC, Ledger M, 230). This one coat was clearly considerably more elaborate than the coats made from the 1823 list in that it included gilt buttons,[4] lots of lace, and possibly some lining. The fact that some Chiefs Coats were more elaborate than others is reflected in other AFC records. The Company carried both "Chiefs Coats" and "Common" or "Indian" coats (NPS; AFC, Ledger z, 53). At Fort Hall the tailor's shop recorded making both "Chiefs Coats" and "Indian Coats" (Wyeth, Ledger 2, 107). The coats made from the 1823 AFC list were probably "Common" or "Indian" coats, while the more elaborate 1827 coat was probably a top of the line "Chiefs Coat."

The "Chiefs Coat" or "Indian Coat" supplied by the AFC was therefore probably a knee length red or blue wool cloth coat open in front and probably slit almost to the waist in back. It had a stand-up collar, cuffs and front facings made from a contrasting color fabric. Plain brass or pewter buttons were probably sewn to the cuffs, front facings and possibly the collar, and it closed with hooks and eyes. Higher grade coats were further decorated with military-style lace on the collar, cuffs and facings, and the buttons were likely to be gilt.

Notes

1. The term "lace" in this context almost certainly refers to heavy decorative braid using metallic thread and not to the light, delicate material presently associated with that term. A probable Chiefs Coat excavated in South Dakota was decorated with lace woven from a combination of thin flat metal strips, fine wire and cotton (Wedel: 146–48). Such lace was frequently used on military uniforms and could be made with gold, silver, silk or wool (worsted) (Steffen: 90, 94, 102).

2. The yellow buttons were probably plain flat brass buttons with a wire loop on the back while the white were probably some type of cast pewter (Wedel: 146–48; Miller: 71–72).

3. Silk sewing thread was commonly put up in skeins (C. Hanson).

4. Before 1840, higher grade buttons were commonly gilt with gold over another base metal (Miller: 71; Wedel: 146–48).

References

American Fur Company. Fur Trade Ledgers 1802–71. 74 vols. Microfilm. St. Louis: Missouri Historical Society.

Brown, Margaret. "An Eighteenth Century Trade Coat." *Plains Anthropologist* 16 (May 1971): 52.

Contributions to the Historical Society of Montana. Vol. 10. Boston: J. S. Connor & Co., 1966.

Hanson, Charles. "Thread in the Fur Trade." *Museum of the Fur Trade Quarterly* 25 (Summer 1989): 2.

Hanson, James A. "Laced Coats and Leather Jackets: The Great Plains Intercultural Clothing Exchange." In Ubelaker, Douglas, and Viola Herman, *Plains Indian Studies*, Smithsonian Contributions to Anthropology no. 30. Washington DC: Smithsonian Institution Press, 1982.

Hassrick, Royal. *The George Catlin Book of Indians.* New York: Promontory Press, 1988.

Horse Capture, George P., Anne Vitart, and W. Richard West. *Robes of Splendor: Native North American Painted Buffalo Hides.* New York: The New Press, 1993.

Kurz, Rudolph F. *Journal of Rudolph Freiderich Kurz.* Lincoln: University of Nebraska Press, 1970.

Mauer, Evan. *Visions of the People: A Pictorial History of Plains Indian Life.* Minneapolis: Minneapolis Institute of the Arts, 1992.

Miller, Carl. *The Excavation and Investigation of Fort Lookout Trading Post.* Bureau of American Ethnology Bulletin 176. Washington DC: Government Printing Office, 1960.

Murray, Robert. "Treaty Presents at Ft. Laramie 1867–68." *Museum of the Fur Trade Quarterly* 13 (Fall 1977): 3.

Peterson, Jacqueline. *Sacred Encounters.* Norman: University of Oklahoma Press, 1993.

Provo, Daniel. *Ft. Esperance in 1793–1795: A Northwest Company Provisioning Post.* Lincoln NE: J & L Reprint Co., 1984.

Steffen, Randy. *The Horse Soldier 1776–1943.* Vol. 1. Norman: University of Oklahoma Press, 1977.

Thomas, David, and Ronnefeldt, Karin. *People of the First Man.* New York: E. P. Dutton & Co., 1976.

Thwaites, Ruben G. *The Original Journals of the Lewis & Clark Expedition 1804–1806.* Vol. 6, pt. 2. New York: Dodd & Mead Co., 1905.

Viola, Herman. *Diplomats in Buckskins.* Washington DC: Smithsonian Institution, 1981.

Wedel, Waldo. *Archaeological Materials from the Vicinity of Mobridge, South Dakota.* Bureau of American Ethnology Bulletin 157. Washington DC: Government Printing Office, 1955.

Wyeth, Andrew. Columbia River Fishing and Trading Company, Fort Hall Accounts 1834–39. Microfilm. Oregon Historical Society.

21. The Myth of the Silk Hat and the End of the Rendezvous

James A. Hanson

If the general public thinks it knows anything about the fur trade, it is that beaver skins were used to make hats. When the silk hat was invented, it revolutionized men's fashion overnight. Beaver pelts became worthless, the rendezvous collapsed, trappers were thrown out of work, and the fur companies shifted to trading for other commodities such as buffalo robes. This concept, built upon faulty assumptions of cause and effect, is a myth and cannot be supported when the chronology of events is examined.

The Silk Hat Theory

George Frederick Ruxton, the English military officer who toured the West and then wrote the first mountain man novel, penned this explanation in 1847 for the beaver's decline:

> Beaver has so depreciated in value within the last few years that trapping has been almost abandoned—the price paid for the skin of this valuable animal having fallen from six and eight dollars per pound to one dollar, which hardly pays the expenses of traps, animals, and equipment for the hunt, and is certainly no adequate remuneration . . . The cause of the great decrease in the value of the beaver is . . . more than all, in the use of silk in the manufacture of hats, which has in great measure superceded that of beaver.[1]

Anthropologist Lewis H. Morgan undoubtedly read Ruxton and reached the same conclusion. His remarkable treatise on the beaver was published in 1868. Morgan wrote: "After the substitution of silk for fur in the manufacture of hats, the value of beaver peltry greatly declined . . ."[2]

The great fur trade historian Hiram Chittenden wholeheartedly accepted the Ruxton-Morgan view of a connection between the rise of the silk hat and the decline of the beaver. Chittenden, however, implied a connection between the silk hat and the end of the rendezvous which Ruxton and Morgan had not. He bolstered his assumption with a line from a letter written from Paris in 1832 by American Fur Company president John Jacob Astor to his colleagues in St. Louis: "I very much fear beaver will not sell very soon unless very fine. It appears that they make hats of silk instead of beaver."[3]

Leroy Hafen, another outstanding fur trade historian, embraced Chittenden's theory and gave it full expression: "The introduction of the silk hat in the style centers of the world, in the early 1830s, soon reduced the demand for beaver pelts used in the production of the high-topped beaver headgear. So beaver pelts declined."[4] He even took the silk hat a step further by making it a principal reason for Astor's departure from the fur trade: "Astor, age seventy, wanted to retire. He had noted the introduction of the silk hat in style centers of the world and was conscious of the effect this would have on the sale of beaver hats and the price of beaver pelts."[5]

Other historians added to this interpretation. John Sunder stated: "By the mid-1830s the mountain trade had passed its prime. Men preferred silk hats to beaver hats . . ."[6] Robert Glass Cleland provided the full-blown version of the silk hat's impact when he emphatically stated: "So between 1830 and 1835 . . . fashion joined forces with the merchants and decreed that men's hats should be made of silk instead of fur. That decision closed the chapter of the Western fur trade and concluded the era of the mountain man."[7] Mari Sandoz, whose popular but unreliable books are erroneously accorded status as good history, wrote with characteristic hyperbole:

Some had heard of the elegant French duke, who, it was said, had lost his beaver hat in China and, unable to have it replaced, had a similar one made of silk. The first sight of the hat on his return to Paris sent the fops into cries of envy. Immediately they began to discard their beavers and ordered hats of silk. The usual great train of little imitators, the sheep of fashion, followed. The fad reached London, Montreal, New York and Canton. No more beavers.[8]

These scenarios all depend upon the silk hat coming into vogue in the 1830s. On the Continent, at least, silk hats were common before the end of the eighteenth century. After Britain won Canada, London controlled the world beaver supply except for what Spain brought out through New Orleans. With the coming of the French Revolution and then Napoleon, trade virtually ceased between France, her client states, and Great Britain. In 1793 the price of beaver in London plummeted from $5 to $2 a pound.[9]

The French still needed hats, and here is a more reliable version of the legend that Sandoz garbled: "About the time that the American [French] Revolution was getting underway, a Frenchman named Betta, living in Canton, China, ordered a Chinese hatter to make him a top hat of silk, using one of his old beavers as a model. He carried the new headpiece back to Paris where it became all the rage."[10] Astor saw hats being made of silk in Paris in 1832 and mistakenly assumed that this was something new. In any event, if silk hats were such a fashion craze in the early 1830s, why did the rendezvous system survive until 1840?

The Nutria Theory

Ruxton had also mentioned another cause for the collapse of the price of beaver. He stated that demand for beaver was also diminished by "the substitute which has been found for it in the skins of the fur seal and nutria [and] the improved preparation of other skins of little value, such as the hare and rabbit . . ."[11]

Charles Hanson had noticed records of large importations of South American coypu skins, commonly known by the Spanish name, nutria, in the 1830s. He realized that the fur of this large aquatic rodent was used to make felt hats. He believed that the hundreds of thousands of cheap skins imported each year must have devastated the price of beaver. To support this theory, Hanson cited two 1836 letters from American Fur Company president Ramsay Crooks to Pratte, Chouteau & Company in St. Louis. The first, sent February 19, 1836, stated: "The Upper Missouri Beaver has come fully up to my expectations . . . Nutria can now be had at about half the price it brought a year since, and the Silk Hat gives up such a vigorous competition, that Beaver cannot possibly rise in value." The second letter, sent July 6, stated: "Nutria has diminished the consumption of Beaver so much, that we fear a decline in the price of [beaver] must be submitted to."[12]

T. Lindsay Baker endorsed the importance of the nutria in explaining the declining demand for beaver. "The fur companies discovered that they could buy nutria skins in South America far cheaper than they could secure beaver pelts from the Rocky Mountains and within a dozen years [by 1833] the nutria displaced the beaver for almost all hat manufacture. The final death blow for beaver felt came a few years later with the introduction of the silk hat . . ."[13]

In fact, nutria was a commodity regularly listed on the New York exchange along with beaver before the first rendezvous was ever held.[14] Nutria generally did not compete with beaver. Rather, it was often used as a substitute for muskrat fur in less expensive felt hats. Two 1835 letters from Crooks illustrate the interrelation of beaver, muskrat, and nutria. "Beaver will probably maintain last year's value . . . If Muskrats get no worse it is all we can count on. There are too many . . . to hope for any rise . . ." and "The Hudson's Bay Company have enough [muskrats] to supply all the Hatters, both in Europe and America . . . Rats must come down in price unless the trade drops in their present substitutes [nutria]." Ramsay Crooks wrote in 1840: "We continue selling a few muskrats at our previous rates and hope to clear a good many more this spring unless . . . large importations of nutria destroy the demand for hatting purposes." And in 1836, at the same time Crooks was lamenting the nutria's deleterious effects on the price of beaver, his London agent was reporting that the demand for beaver was rising dramatically![15]

The theories about the silk hat and nutria fur replacing beaver have some basis in truth, but those changes occurred *after* the rendezvous ended. R. MacFarlane, a chief factor of the Hudson's Bay Company, stated it concisely: "The introduction of nutria and silk in the manufacture of hats in the early forties struck a deadly blow at the value of the beaver . . . from which it has not yet quite recovered."[16] One contemporary Canadian author places the changeover in the 1850s:

> The fur trade itself, at least in beaver hats, had declined precipitately almost from the instant Prince Albert, Queen Victoria's consort, had appeared at a public function in 1854 wearing a topper not of beaver felt but of silk. A trend toward the much less expensive substitute swept European society . . . Although there was . . . strong demand for specialty pelts from North America, London's fur industry was turning towards other, less expensive sources, and to nutria.[17]

The Disappointed Capitalist Theory

In the 1970s, several western historians tried to fit the mountain man into the social, political, and economic framework of Jeffersonian and Jacksonian Democracy. One historian referred to the beaver trapper as an "expectant capitalist." At least two historians saw the end of the beaver trade in terms of market forces beyond the trapper's control.

Robert Murray rejected both the silk hat and the substitute fur explanations for the trapper's demise. He simply stated: "The 'mountain man' required too high returns for his furs to meet the market."[18] William Goetzmann was similarly dismissive of other theories:

> It was certainly true that the mountain man had made his impact on . . . fashion, but the beaver hat was by no means the only impact. Furs continued to be used for coats, for trim, for gloves . . . Nor does the

idea that the beavers were all trapped out of the mountains make perfect sense either. Less than a thousand men could never have accomplished this in the face of ever-hostile Indians.

Goetzmann instead blamed the Panic of 1837 and the resulting decline of the fur market, which "placed the widely scattered individual entrepreneur-trapper at the mercy of the marketplace. As the price of furs dropped, the risk of trapping was not worth the mountain man's time."[19]

The Price of Beaver

All three of these theories—silk hat, nutria, and economic conditions—are predicated on the assumption that the price of beaver declined dramatically in the late 1830s. The price of fur has always been a speculative gamble, but there is no evidence of a price collapse for beaver in the five years before or following the last rendezvous. In fact, beaver seems to have increased slightly in the long term despite dramatic short-term price fluctuations associated with any commodity market. Here are some actual price quotations.

In December 1824, six months before the first rendezvous was held, the New York wholesale price of beaver was fixed at $4 to $4.50 a pound for northern pelts and $1 to $3.25 for southern and western skins. Following an 1834 downturn in fur sales, by January 1835 the New York beaver market had, "contrary to all expectations . . . materially improved." Santa Fe beaver brought $3.25 and Rocky Mountain beaver were $4.25 a pound.[20]

In 1841, the year following the last rendezvous, the Hudson's Bay Company reckoned the retail value of a prime 1 ½ pound beaver skin at $7.68.[21] The 1841 sales were well attended; Canadian beaver sold 5 percent higher. American beaver was $4.20 to $5.40 a pound, up 5 to 8 percent over last year. Santa Fe beaver was in demand and selling well, around $3.75, in France and the U.S. The market was overstocked, however, and the wholesalers were buying their own stocks to insure high prices. This practice generated excited and "hostile comments . . . in the sale rooms from some of our leading Hat manufacturers." In November, the London sales agent for the American Fur Company reported he had sold 3,000 beaver at "satisfactory" prices—from $4.50 to $5 per pound.[22]

These figures indicate that after the rendezvous ended, beaver prices were just as high or higher than they were before it began and during its heyday. The silk hat and the nutria had undoubtedly flattened the market at times, but if they, or a collapsing market, had ruined the beaver trade, why were London hatters still buying beaver pelts and paying inflated prices for them?

The wholesale prices actually quoted in the markets at the time belie the astonishing beaver prices mentioned in the literature. Ruxton said skins brought $6 to $8 per pound at the rendezvous, and Morgan repeated it. Philips wrote that in 1838 beaver was $5 a pound. Cleland stated that around 1832 the rendezvous price was $4 to $6 a pound, but that by 1840 it was down to $1 or $2 a pound. Wishart's estimate is that in the 1820s beaver was $3 a pound, but rose to as much as $6 in the early 1830s.[23]

These "mountain prices," like gold rush prices, are interesting but meaningless. Rendezvous markups were as much as 2000 percent over cost. Stewart noted at the 1837 rendezvous that men received $4 to $5 for beaver, but paid $4 a pint for whiskey, $2 a pound for sugar, and $20 for a blanket. In 1841 trappers received $10 for a beaver, but paid $2 a pound for tobacco, $1.50 to $2.50 a pound for powder and lead, and $30 to $60 for a rifle.[24]

Despite claims of high prices and profits, the fur traders relied on volume. Between 1834 and 1840, New Mexican merchants paid $3 for beaver. Delivered to St. Louis, the skins brought $3.25, which in turn sold in New York for $3.75. Morgan saw that beaver brought $1.25 a pound at Fort Benton in 1862. Chouteau accounts reveal the company collected 2,024 beaver skins weighing 3,003 pounds and sold them for $1.65 per pound. Salaries, transportation, insurance, and depreciation had to come from a gross profit of a mere 40 cents per pound.[25]

The Myth of the Silk Hat

Post-1840 Trapping Campaigns

In 1843 Fremont wrote that the mountain men had "almost disappeared." In 1844 James Clyman stated that there were less than thirty beaver hunters left. But as historian Paul Phillips observed, "The trapping complement of the Far West was indeed reduced, but not to so great an extent as this. Trappers were hard to find because they no longer operated from the same centers or in the same way."[26] In fact, the mountain man had not priced himself out of business, there was still a demand for his product, and he continued to trap beaver.

When the American Fur Company ended its rendezvous system in 1840, the Hudson's Bay Company returned to using trapping brigades in the Northwest and California and continued them until 1843. The Colorado Rockies became the most important American trapping area in the 1840s. Mountain man Bill Hamilton mentioned trapping there in 1842. "Our party now started to get ready for the fall trapping season, which opened in the mountains on the 15th of September."[27]

The trappers also cast covetous glances to the north, but an 1843 visitor wrote: "The whites trap only in the Crow and Black Feet Country, when in sufficient strength to disregard them, considering a camp of about eighty men strong enough to travel through either nation."[28] Jim Bridger had heard that beaver were plentiful in Blackfeet country and in the fall of 1843 he led a brigade of about 30 men to trap the Milk River. The campaign was "particularly unsuccessful" but he announced plans for another hunt on the Milk in the spring of 1844 and then "to make an expedition into the California, which . . . is rich with Beaver. I shall take from 30 to 40 men for that purpose to trap it thoroughly."[29]

In 1845 Sioux trader David Adams realized his business was bankrupt. In a desperate and apparently unsuccessful effort to recoup his losses, he organized a beaver trapping expedition into the Laramie Range of the Wyoming Rockies. That same year, nearby Fort Laramie took in 2,000 pounds of beaver.[30] When historian

Francis Parkman visited there in 1846, he met several trappers actively pursuing their vocations. When two of them, Saraphin and Rouleau, left for a hunt, they entrusted seven beaver skins to Antoine Reynal. "Well," confided Reynal, "if they are killed, I shall have the beaver. They'll fetch me fifty dollars at the fort, anyhow."[31] Of course Reynal meant $50 in trade, but in 1846, beaver was about as high as it had ever been.

The Declining Harvest

Half a continent had been trapped out by the time the first rendezvous was held, and some prime western fur regions were soon in precarious shape. For example, in 1835 Fort Clark on the Upper Missouri took in 1,100 pounds of beaver. In 1836 only 360 pounds were produced.[32] That year HBC trader David Ross wrote: "The beaver are utterly gone, finished, annihilated; which closes that chapter, and the profits of the Athabaska forever and ever more."[33] Traders on ships bound for China found it almost impossible to obtain furs on the West Coast. An 1840 Congressional report offered this assessment: "It appears that the [fur] business is declining in every part of the continent, but particularly in the territories drained by the Columbia, in consequence of the disappearance of the animals yielding the furs and skins. On the Columbia . . . every part is yearly ransacked by traders and trappers . . ."[34]

The same situation was occurring in the region served by the annual rendezvous. The rendezvous functioned as the collection point in the Central Rockies for the beaver being trapped there by both whites and Indians. According to an 1843 observer, "The country having been trapped so much on account of there being no danger among these Indians, the beaver have now become very scarce."[35]

The Northern Rockies were not a hospitable trapping ground for American mountain men. Canadian trappers virtually ruled the Snake and Columbia River basins of the Oregon country. Their furs didn't go to market via the rendezvous, leaving instead on ships bound for England or China. The Northern Rockies were also home to the Crows, who robbed unwelcome interlopers, and the Blackfeet, who killed them.[36] The Southern Rockies and California were, until 1847, Mexican territory. Mountain men such as James O. Pattie and Milton Sublette had unpleasant experiences with Mexican bureaucrats, which may have reduced the region's appeal for some. The furs taken there went south to Mexico or to St. Louis via the Santa Fe Trail, rarely to the annual rendezvous.

Thus the American trappers concentrated in the Central Rockies, scouring the countryside until the few beaver left were extremely shy. The catch declined alarmingly. Mountain man Doc Newell attended the 1837 rendezvous and wrote: "times is getting hard all over this part of the Country beever Scarce and low all peltries are on the decline."[37] Pierre Chouteau Jr. commented that the 1837 returns from the rendezvous "were low, but . . . this was of little consequence because the demand for beaver was also low." The total American Fur Company Rocky Mountain harvest that year was only 53 packs, or about 3,200 beaver.[38]

The 1838 return was even worse. The American Fur Company had 125 trappers, traders, and workers employed in the mountains, and they produced "a little over 2000 Beaver and otter skins." An HBC man smugly remarked: "Their trade cannot certainly support such expensive machinery."[39]

St. Louis doctor F. A. Wislizenus noted the diminishing supply at the 1839 rendezvous: "Formerly single trappers on such occasions have . . . wasted a thousand dollars. But the days of their glory seem to be past, for constant hunting has very much reduced the number of beavers. The diminution in the beaver catch made itself noticeable at this year's rendezvous in the quieter behavior of the trappers." Chouteau's forty-man party "made a poor collection of furs."[40]

Joe Meek also recognized the situation: "The decline of the business of hunting furs began to be quite obvious . . . The fact was becoming obvious that the beaver was being rapidly exterminated."[41] His friend Doc Newell commented tersely on the 1840 rendezvous: "Times was certainly hard no beaver and everything dull."[42] Although the 1840 rendezvous was well attended, the fur harvest was abysmal for the third straight year. The American Fur Company decided to end what had become an expensive, "costly, nerve-shattering, and, at times, even humiliating event."[43] The simple reason for the collapse of the rendezvous is that there was not enough beaver to make it worthwhile.

Alternative Markets

One additional factor that weakened the rendezvous by reducing the number of pelts going to it was the rapid construction of trading posts, each of which siphoned off a portion of the Indian and mountain man trade. Leroy Hafen observed that "while the end of the rendezvous in 1840 meant transfer of traffic to the trading post, this change occurred only in the central Rockies region. In other areas the trading fort had been the hub of the traffic from the very beginning."[44]

Fort Union (1829), Fort Clark (1831), Fort Pierre (1832), and Fort McKenzie (1832) on the Missouri; and Fort Cass (1832) and Fort Van Buren (1835) flanked the northeast side of the beaver range. To the southeast, on the upper Arkansas, stood Bent's Fort (1833), while Fort Vasquez (1835), Fort Lupton (1837), Fort Jackson (1837), and Fort St. Vrain (1837) had been erected on the South Platte. Forts Uinta, Uncompahgre, and Davy Crockett, all built in 1837, dominated the southwest. Fort Laramie (1834) on the North Platte to the east and Fort Hall (1834) on the Snake to the west, along with eight HBC posts in Oregon territory, completed the ring around the rendezvous' trade area. A trapper could obtain his supplies at any one of these posts. By the late 1830s there was little reason other than camaraderie to attend the rendezvous.

When Did the Rendezvous Really End?

Most historians agree that the last rendezvous was held in 1840.[45] That is the last year the American Fur Company organized the affair, but there is some good evidence to contradict that date.

Antoine Robidoux organized the "Robidoux Rendezvous" at Fort Uinta "which attracted trappers from all sides as the northern rendezvous deteriorated." Fort Uinta operated until about 1846, but when this spin-off rendezvous occurred is not known.[46]

In 1841 beaver trappers gathered at what was then termed a "rendezvous" on the Green River. The Bidwell-Bartleson party, the first train of emigrants headed for Oregon, stopped to trade for three days in late July with about sixty mountain men and an unknown number of Indians. The trappers were described as "half breeds, French and Dutch, and all sorts of people collected together in the mountains, and were a wicked, swearing company of men."[47]

Bill Hamilton left a lively account of a trapper gathering in 1842 which sounds exactly like an old-fashioned rendezvous:

> Several traders had come from the States with supplies, and there was quite a rivalry among them for our furs. Bovey [Beauvais] & Company were the most liberal buyers, and we sold them the entire lot. Besides the trappers there were at the rendezvous many Indians . . . who came to exchange their pelts. . . . It was just such a crowd as would delight the student were he studying the characteristic of the mountaineer and the Indian. The days were given to horse-racing, foot-racing, shooting matches; and in the evening were heard the music of voice and drum and the sound of dancing. There was an abundance of reading matter for those inclined in that direction.[48]

Finally, we have the record of a curious rendezvous conducted on the Sweetwater in 1843. Sir William Drummond Stewart hired Bill Sublette to lead a large party of sportsmen, hunters, and old trappers from St. Louis to the Rockies. "While marching on the Sweet Water we sent an express to Bridger's Fort on Blacks Fork . . . to request the Snake Indians to come over and see us. . . . Two days later about a dozen trappers with their families (all having Indian wives) . . . came over to see us."[49]

TABLE 10. Importations of beaver pelts to England

Year	U.S. and Other Sources	Hudson's Bay Company
1820} *includes*	56,000	15,683
1821} *North West Co.*	58,300	20,565
1822} *returns under U.S.* . . .	65,652	59,847
1823	10,016	46,202
1824	2,616	76,060
1825	9,677	766,600
1826	5,923	61,400
1827	4,906	51,125
1828	12,581	57,200
1829	9,388	65,614
1830	7,332	25,718
1831	12,002	87,000
1832	5,753	70,100
1833	17,871	32,203
1834	13,641	98,288
1835	3,318	78,908
1836	4,460	51,788
1837	17,065	82,927
1838	10,559	61,868
1839	9,024	56,288
1840	975	55,431
1841	6,587	50,900
1842	5,638	40,305
1843	12,022	39,086
1844	7,361	38,252
1845	2,433	41,111
1846	4,181	65,189
1847 (lowest importation recorded)	2,692	26,892
1848	709	40,845
1849	416	32,502
1850	1,829	49,517
1851	800	62,131
1852	850	52,430
1853	3,211	60,691
1854	3,204	62,914
1855	6,681	72,425
1856	12,256	76,825
1857	10,087	86,414
1858	12,050	94,053
1859	18,120	106,797
1860 (new high import total)	28,040	107,745

Source: Henry Poland, *Fur-Bearing Animals in Nature and in Commerce* (London: Gurney & Jackson, 1892), xxiv–xxx.

Note: This schedule of beaver imports into England does not show beaver consumed in America, or those shipped to continental Europe or China. It does, however, show that through the rendezvous period the United States supplied about 12 percent of the beaver used in England. In 1840, the year of the final rendezvous, the American portion fell to less than 2 percent of the total. In support of Ruxton's comments, the total English importation of beaver in 1847 fell below 30,000, a record low. The year 1860 marked a new high in British beaver consumption.

Notes

1. Leroy R. Hafen, *Ruxton of the Rockies* (Norman: University of Oklahoma Press, 1950), 225.

2. Lewis H. Morgan, *The American Beaver* (New York: Dover Publications, 1986), 228.

3. Hiram Martin Chittenden, *The American Fur Trade of the Far West*, 2 vols. (New York: The Press of the Pioneers, 1935), 1:385.

4. Leroy R. Hafen, *The Mountain Men and the Fur Trade of the Far West*, 10 vols. (Glendale CA: Arthur H. Clark Co., 1965–72), 1:174.

5. Ibid., 1:137.

6. John E. Sunder, *The Fur Trade on the Upper Missouri, 1840–1865* (Norman: University of Oklahoma Press, 1965), 11.

7. Robert Gass Cleland, *This Reckless Breed of Men* (New York: Alfred A. Knopf, 1950), 344.

8. Mari Sandoz, *The Beaver Men* (New York: Hastings House, 1964), 309.

9. Robert Murray, "Some Interpretive Notes on the Fur Trade in Its Declining Years," *Museum of the Fur Trade Quarterly* 3 (Summer 1967): 6.

10. Ruth Edwards Kilgour, *A Pageant of Hats, Ancient and Modern* (New York: Robert M. McBride Co., 1958), 64.

11. Hafen, *Ruxton*, 225.

12. Charles E. Hanson, Jr., "The Nutria and the Beaver Hat," *Museum of the Fur Trade Quarterly* 12 (Fall 1976): 8.

13. T. Lindsay Baker, "Beaver to Buffalo Robes: Transition in the Fur Trade," *Museum of the Fur Trade Quarterly* 23 (Spring 1987): 5.

14. *New York Price-Current*, Dec. 28, 1824, 4.

15. Ramsay Crooks to J. B. Beaubien, Jan. 23, Entry 29; Crooks to Henry Sibley, Feb. 20, 1835, Letterbook, 1:202; Crooks to C. M. Lampson, Mar. 30, 1830, LB, 16:58–60; and Lampson to Crooks, June 29, 1836. American Fur Company Papers, New York Historical Society.

16. R. McFarlane, "Notes on Mammals Collected and Observed in the Northern Mackenzie River District . . . ," *Proceedings of the United States National Museum* (Washington: GPO, 1905), 744.

James A. Hanson

17. Peter Newman, *Caesars of the Wilderness*, vol. 2 of *The Company of Adventurers* (New York: Viking, 1987), 344.

18. Murray, "Interpretive Notes," 8.

19. William H. Goetzmann, "The Mountain Men," *American West* 15 (July–August 1978): 17. His remark of a thousand trappers being unable to "trap out" 250,000 beavers in sixteen years seems naïve when we know a thousand buffalo hunters killed six million buffalo in a decade.

20. Crooks to Pratte, Chouteau & Co., Jan. 31, 1835, AFC Papers.

21. The Engages, "The Hudson's Bay Company in the 1840s," *Museum of the Fur Trade Quarterly* 28 (Winter 1992): 4.

22. Lampson to Crooks, Jan. 22, 1841, and Nov. 27, 1841, Letter Received, 11816, AFC Papers.

23. Cleland, *Reckless Breed of Men*, 345; David J. Wishart, *The Fur Trade of the American West, 1807–1840* (Lincoln: University of Nebraska Press, 1979), 167.

24. Hafen, *Mountain Men*, 1:158; Doyce E. Nunis, ed., *The Bidwell-Bartleson Party: 1841 California Emigrant Adventure* (Santa Cruz: Western Tanager Press, 1991), 37, 244.

25. David J. Weber, *The Taos Trappers: The Fur Trade in the Far Southwest, 1540–1846* (Norman: University of Oklahoma Press, 1971), 219; Morgan, *American Beaver*, 228; Hanson, "The Nutria," 3.

26. Paul C. Phillips, *The Fur Trade*, 2 vols. (Norman: University of Oklahoma Press, 1961), 2:526.

27. Wishart, *The Fur Trade*, 166; Leroy R. Hafen, "Fort Davy Crockett, Its Fur Men and Visitors," *Colorado Magazine* 29 (January 1952): 31–32.

28. John E. Sunder, ed., "Report of a Journey to the Rocky Mountains," *Bulletin of the Missouri Historical Society* 11 (October 1954): 49–50.

29. J. Cecil Alter, *Jim Bridger* (Norman: University of Oklahoma Press, 1962), 209–10.

30. Charles E. Hanson, Jr., ed., *The David Adams Journals* (Chadron: Museum of the Fur Trade, 1994), 97; Hafen, *Mountain Men*, 1:175.

31. Francis Parkman, *The Oregon Trail* (New York: Dodd, Mead & Co., 1964), 208.

32. Baker, "Beaver to Buffalo Robes," 5.

33. "Fur Traders' Letters," *The Beaver* (September 1938): 54.

34. Robert Greenhow, "Memoir, Historical and Political, on the Northwest Coast of America," published as "A View of the Oregon Territory in 1840," *Museum of the Fur Trade Quarterly* 31 (Fall 1995): 9.

35. Sunder, "Report," 49.

434 *The Myth of the Silk Hat*

36. Ibid.

37. Hafen, *Mountain Men,* 1:160.

38. Wishart, *The Fur Trade,* 165.

39. Ibid.

40. Hafen, *Mountain Men,* 1:163; Sunder, *The Fur Trade,* 12.

41. Wishart, *The Fur Trade,* 165.

42. Hafen, *Mountain Men,* 1:164.

43. Sunder, *The Fur Trade,* 10.

44. Hafen, *Mountain Men,* 1:168.

45. Phillips, *The Fur Trade,* 2:526, stated the last rendezvous was held in 1839.

46. Ibid., 2:534–35.

47. Nunis, *Bidwell-Bartleson,* 244.

48. Hafen, "Fort Davy Crockett," 31–32.

49. Sunder, "Report," 49.

PART 5

Gender, Kinship, and Community

Introduction

Women's involvement in the trade has primarily emerged from scholarship focused on the exchange process in the Great Lakes basin and in present-day Canada, collectively referred to as the *pays d'en haut*. These regions developed a trade often mediated by Indian women who married fur traders and who positioned themselves as cultural mediators between European and Indian worlds. Most of these women left no personal records and information about them often comes from obscure sources, such as baptismal and marital registers. In "Women, Kin, and Catholicism: New Perspectives on the Fur Trade," we see how female conversion to Catholicism allows us to locate these otherwise silent voices. These women relied on Catholicism to create an ever-expanding kinship network. They served repeatedly as godmothers, so that by the end of the eighteenth century they were members of interrelated networks of kin that successfully controlled the trade at a large number of forts and trading posts. Frequently, these women established themselves as independent traders, and they influenced commodity production, when their households became suppliers of the trade.[1]

Marriage was a planned extension of familial kin networks, and offspring generally identified themselves by their kin networks, rather than by evoking specific ethnic or racial labels. Many of these women and their offspring acquired a distinctive metis identity, although this occurred primarily in Canada's *pays d'en haut*. In "'The Custom of the Country': An Examination of Fur Trade Marriage Practices" Sylvia Van Kirk analyzes how informal practices of marriage, marriage *à la façon du pays*, became a social building block of fur trade society.[2] In "Woman as Centre and Symbol in the Emergence of Metis Communities" Jennifer Brown suggests that many Indian communities were characterized by matriorganizations, in which new husbands, particularly fur traders, took up residence among their wife's relations. "Women's traditional productive capacities, in preparing furs, netting snowshoes, foraging, securing small game, and so forth, often came to be fully utilized and much valued in both the HBC and Montreal trades."[3] Brown's work offers a socially viable alternative to the standard patrilineal interpretation of Indian communities. Brown's work is noteworthy because she suggests that the circumstances that led to the evolution of a Métis society in Canada may have emerged from this continuum of matrifocality. Brown's analysis suggests that the sudden and rapid expansion of the metis population in the late eighteenth and early nineteenth centuries may have been due to women's roles in promoting the fur trade.

Jacki Peterson also focuses on the evolution of mixed-ancestry communities, her work shifts our focus south to Green Bay, Wisconsin. Peterson contends that a sizeable metis population evolved in the towns and villages of the western Great Lakes and that they were the predecessors of the Red River Métis community that evolved in Canada. Like her contemporaries, Van Kirk and Brown, Peterson also stresses the role that women played in the evolution of the Great Lakes fur trade. Those traders and upwardly mobile clerks in the fur trade who sought marital alliances with influential tribal families helped create these distinctive metis communities in the Great Lakes, but they were short-lived. The cessation of Indian land claims pressured many metis to move west, into the Plains and the Canadian North West, where trade remained profitable.[4]

With Helen Hornbeck Tanner's "The Glaize in 1792: A Composite Indian Community" we move south from Green Bay to one of the region's most well traversed eighteenth-century pathways, the Glaize, near present-day Defiance, Ohio. This was a multicultural frontier where multiple Indian towns had regrouped: three Shawnee, two

Delaware, one Miami, as well as a European trading town. Tanner provides remarkable insight into how long-standing ties developed between diverse populations in the Great Lakes fur trade. About two thousand people lived here in 1790, and its outlying dwellings, gardens, pastures, and cornfields were brutally destroyed by Anthony Wayne in 1792. Almost fifty miles of highly productive cornfields were stripped and torched. What was remarkable about the Glaize was the distinctive ways in which these people drew together into a functioning community, without evolving into a metis community. Thus, Tanner's article offers evidence for a variety of models of community formation, each distinguished by a kin network that radiated throughout the multiple trading posts.[5]

While many historians consider the fur trade a male-defined domain, this section of the book takes an opposite approach, drawing attention to the role that women played in the trade. Men were the primary participants, but rather than view them through a type of "frontier" perspective, as rough, hardy men who lived as Indians, Carolyn Podruchny analyzes their activities at Montreal's Beaver Club, where retired fur traders gathered for monthly club meetings. In "Festivities, Fortitude, and Fraternalism: Fur Trade Masculinity and the Beaver Club, 1785–1827" Podruchny explores masculine values, what roles the fur trade played in the lives of these men, and the values that they claimed for their distinctive lifestyles. Podruchny uncovers a masculine space, where men venerated "risk-taking, the spirit of adventure, and a taste for the exotic."[6]

Notes

1. Susan Sleeper-Smith, "Women, Kin, and Catholicism: New Perspectives on the Fur Trade," *Ethnohistory* 47, no. 2 (Spring 2000): 424–52.

2. Sylvia Van Kirk, "'The Custom of the Country': An Examination of Fur Trade Marriage Practices," in *Essays on Western History*, ed. Lewis H. Thomas, 47–80 (Edmonton: University of Alberta Press, 1976).

3. Jennifer S. Brown, "Woman as Centre and Symbol in the Emergence of Metis Communities," *The Canadian Journal of Native Studies* 3, no. 1 (1983): 40–41.

4. Jacqueline Peterson, "Prelude to Red River: A Social Portrait of the Great Lakes Métis," *Ethnohistory* 25, no. 1 (Winter 1978): 41–67.

5. Helen Hornbeck Tanner, "The Glaize in 1792: A Composite Indian Community," *Ethnohistory* 25, no. 1 (Winter 1978): 15–39.

6. Carolyn Podruchny, "Festivities, Fortitude, and Fraternalism: Fur Trade Masculinity and the Beaver Club, 1785–1827," in *New Faces of the Fur Trade: Selected Papers of the Seventh North American Fur Trade Conference, Halifax, Nova Scotia, 1995*, ed. Jo-Anne Fiske, Susan Sleeper-Smith, and William Wicken, 12–29 (East Lansing: Michigan State University Press, 1998).

22. Women, Kin, and Catholicism

New Perspectives on the Fur Trade

Susan Sleeper-Smith

Scholars who have studied the fur trade of the western Great Lakes offer conflicting interpretations of its impact on Native American societies. Those who view the trade as synonymous with the intrusion of market forces, particularly the pursuit of profit, generally link both indigenous decline and the depletion of animal populations with the trade. Other scholars contend that the fur trade had overarching political and diplomatic ramifications, however, and that profit making was often subordinated to maintain the Algonquian-French alliance.[1] Most recently, Richard White has envisioned the fur trade as integral to an ever evolving arena of cultural negotiation, which he labeled the "middle ground." For White "the creation of the middle ground involved a process of mutual invention" created by "people who shared neither their values nor their assumptions about the appropriate way of accomplishing tasks" and "which grew according to the need of people to find a means, other than force, to gain the cooperation or consent of foreigners."[2]

This article focuses on four native women, married to French fur traders, whose lives offer insight into the process of sociological and cultural adaptation that occurred as Indian villages of the western Great Lakes became increasingly involved in the trade. This essay suggests that the conception of White's *Middle Ground* is a viable way in which to describe interaction between Indian and Euro-Americans and that it should be expanded to emphasize the prominent role that native women played as cultural mediators. The Indian women who married fur traders were "negotiators of change."[3] They lived in a region where the exchange process occurred primarily at wintering grounds or in villages, and, because trade had social as well as economic ramifications, intermarriage played an integral role in the trade's evolution. Traders who married these women thus had an advantage over their rivals. Marriage, either in the "manner of the country" or performed by missionary priests, assured traders inclusion as members of indigenous communities and facilitated access to furs.[4]

A fur trader's presence enhanced the importance of the community where he lived and simultaneously enhanced his wife's authority and prestige among her people. Native women did not marry out; rather, they incorporated their French husbands into a society structured by native custom and tradition.[5] Although access to trade goods enhanced the power and influence of these native women, they did not simply reinvent themselves as French. Although early Jesuit records, particularly marital and baptismal registers, provide the opportunity to study such women's lives, unfortunately they also effectively mask indigenous identity. Many women were simply identified by their baptismal names or by the surname of their husbands.

The Native women who are the focus of this article can be identified in Jesuit records by both their Indian and Christian names. Because we are aware of their native ancestry, we can consequently see how they were involved in the creation of Catholic kin networks. These women repeatedly served as godmothers to numerous children of mixed ancestry. Over time this Catholic kin network became increasingly more complex, as large numbers of such children and godchildren entered the fur trade. Baptism and marriage provided the means through which this diverse and fictive kin network could be continually expanded. Marital and baptismal records suggest that these networks, created by Catholicism, facilitated access to peltry while simultaneously allowing these women to negotiate for themselves positions of prominence and power. Also, many of the traders who married into these networks became prominent fur-trade figures. Therefore, by the mid-eighteenth century an identifiable

Catholic kin network had evolved that was compatible with and often parallel to that of indigenous society.

Female members—especially of the Barthe, Bourassa, Chaboyer, Chevalier, La Framboise, and Langlade families—appear frequently in baptismal registers of the western Great Lakes. These women were godmothers to each other's children and grandchildren, and their surnames span generations. The godparenting roles modeled by mothers were emulated by daughters and granddaughters.

The contention that Catholicism had important social ramifications that enhanced female autonomy contradicts the view that Catholicism instituted a male patriarchal order, which increasingly subordinated native women to men. This later perspective, espoused in Carol Devens's *Countering Colonization* and Karen Anderson's *Chain Her by One Foot*, views Christianity as the means through which indigenous female autonomy was subverted.[6] These conclusions do not appear uniformly applicable to all Native communities in the western Great Lakes. Instead, this article suggests that Catholicism could also serve as a pathway to social prominence.[7] The Jesuits generally recruited catechizers or instructors among native women. These female converts were often the most visible proof of Jesuit success. It would have been foolhardy for these priests to foster female subjection to the authority of men whom the Jesuits frequently despised. Indeed, most missionary priests viewed the fur-trade husbands of these converts as licentious drunkards who undermined Christian ideals; the Jesuits even vigorously supported a seventeenth-century royal policy that banished traders from the western Great Lakes. The Jesuits also frequently dismissed the elders of native communities, many of whom scorned Christianity. Therefore, it would have been problematic for the Jesuits to support the establishment of a male patriarchal order that subjected their pious female converts to the authority of male fur traders and unconverted headmen.

Just as the profit-making dimensions of the fur trade were mediated by the Algonquian-French political alliance, the repressive patriarchal order was mediated by the Jesuits' reliance on native women. During the eighteenth century these women were also the beneficiaries of the dramatic decline in the number of Jesuit priests. Not only did missionary fervor wane, but in the last quarter of the century the Jesuits were temporarily disbanded. In the absence of priests, many female converts fashioned a type of "frontier Catholicism" in which they assumed the role of lay practitioners.

Amid the dynamics of this changing social landscape, Indian women who married fur traders relied on the interface between two worlds to position themselves as mediators between cultural groups, to assume leadership roles in religious training, to influence commodity production, and eventually, at least in a few cases, to establish themselves as independent traders. Through it all these women retained their Indian identity, as evidenced by their language, names, and tribal affiliations. More important, they relied on their Catholicism to maintain relative autonomy in relation to their husbands. The complicated dynamics of such behaviors are evidenced by four women, whose lives spanned the seventeenth and eighteenth centuries. Two of the women were Illini: Marie Rouensa-8cate8a[8] and Marie Madeleine Réaume L'archevêque Chevalier.[9] Each used Catholicism to resist and reshape indigenous societal constraints. Rouensa lived during the early years of the fur trade, when Catholicism was shaped by Jesuit missionaries. Réaume lived later in the eighteenth century, when priests were few in number, lay practitioners became increasingly important, and "frontier" or "folk" Catholicism emerged.[10] Over time, the syncretic nature of Catholicism facilitated the creation of an ever-expanding kin network that extended the parameters of women's worlds from those of their immediate family and community to fur-trade posts throughout the Great Lakes and Mississippi River valley.

These women used the fictive ties created by godparenting to create an ever-expanding kinship network, and by the end of the eighteenth century these networks had evolved as strategic alliances that enabled some Native women to successfully establish themselves as independent fur traders. This was the case for Magdelaine Marcot La Framboise and Thérèse Marcot Lasaliere Schindler, who were raised in Odawa communities and were incorporated from birth into the Catholic kin networks of fur-trade society.[11] They negotiated the hazardous world of the late eighteenth- and early nineteenth-century fur trade when Frenchmen were displaced, first by the English and later by American traders. Both La Framboise and Schindler prospered because their centrality in indigenous kin networks gave them access to a stable supply of furs. These women retained their independence because they were at the locus of Catholic kin networks that were rooted in indigenous communities and that structured Great Lakes fur-trade society.[12]

These women, who have appeared tangentially in the fur-trade literature, have been depicted either as historical outliers or as women who did not challenge traditional spheres of male authority.[13] White used Rouensa to exemplify the cultural inventions of an evolving middle ground, when compromise, rather than force, convinced Rouensa to marry the fur trader Michel Accault. After her marriage, Rouensa disappeared from the "middle ground."[14] Marriage was not her gateway to invisibility, however. Marriage, coupled with her Catholicism, afforded access to power and prestige, which is apparent when examining the whole of Rouensa's life.[15]

Her centrality as a historical actor resulted from the economic and social adaptations that Indian communities experienced as they became increasingly involved in the western Great Lakes fur trade. Rouensa's village, located just south of Lake Michigan, became involved in the fur trade in the late 1670s, when Robert La Salle established a French presence in Illinois Country. Her father was an important headman among the Kaskaskia, one of the seven nations of the Iliniwek Confederacy.[16] In 1790 he arranged for Rouensa to marry a fur trader who had ventured west with La Salle in 1679.

Among the Kaskaskia, women were free to reject such arranged marriages. But in the 1690s, when the Fur Trade Wars engulfed the

Great Lakes, access to trade goods and alliances with the French were considered important strategies that countered Iroquois hostilities. Rouensa would have experienced tremendous community pressure to accede to her father's request and to the wishes of her village. Had she acquiesced to such pressure, her behavior would have escaped historical attention. But Rouensa refused to marry, and she turned to the Jesuit Father Jacques Gravier for support.

Rouensa was one of Gravier's more prominent female converts among the Kaskaskia, of whom the Jesuits converted more women than men. Their efforts reinforced the Illini matrifocal households, which linked women in communal living arrangements and encouraged female conversions.[17] A 1712 Jesuit letter described how this process occurred among the Illinois: "We call those instructors, who in other missions are called catechists, because it is not in the Church, but in the wigwams that they instruct the catechumens and the proselytes."[18]

Gravier's enthusiastic search for converts encouraged these young women to speak out, and he (perhaps inadvertently) provided the tools for social empowerment to them.[19] In turn, female proselytes used Christianity to challenge the traditional wisdom of the tribal elders. Many young women became known for "mock[ing] the superstitions of their nation."[20]

> Although this nation is much given to debauchery, especially the men, the Reverend Fathers of the Jesuits, who talk their language with perfect ease manage . . . to impose some check on this by instructing a number of girls in Christianity, who often profit by their teaching, and mock at the superstitions of their nation, which often greatly incenses the old men and daily exposes these Fathers to ill treatment, and even to being killed.[21]

Given this scenario, it is not surprising that the Jesuits could "find hardly a single young man upon whom we can rely for the exercises of religion."[22]

Christian conversion enabled Rouensa to position herself as a teacher among her people. She expanded the culturally innovative dimensions of the middle ground when she translated Gravier's Christian message into her Kaskaskia language. Because she was an effective mediator of that message, Gravier loaned Rouensa books with pictures that supplemented her Christian storytelling and privileged her among the Kaskaskia: "Not only did she explain them at home . . . speaking of nothing but the pictures or the catechism,—but she also explained the pictures on the whole of the Old Testament to the old and young men whom her father assembled in his dwelling."[23]

Gravier further reinforced such behaviors of young female proselytes when he shared with them stories of female saints. Virtue and mystical experiences produced European celibates, and strong similarities in indigenous behavior encouraged the Kaskaskia converts to dedicate their lives to the church. Illini women who traditionally elected to remain single usually entered warrior society. Christian conversion created an alternative option, and, facing the threat of an undesirable marriage, Rouensa "resolved to consecrate her virginity to God." Catholic conversion encouraged her to resist a proposed marriage, even though it was arranged by her parents. Her professed devotion to virginity, to the love of Christ, intensified when her parents chose for her husband Michel Accault, a fifty-year-old grizzled veteran of the fur trade. Rouensa called on Gravier to defend her decision to remain a celibate Catholic woman:[24] "She had resolved never to marry, in order that she might belong wholly to Jesus Christ. She answered her father and her mother, when they brought her to me in company with the frenchman whom they wished to have for a son-in-law, that she did not wish to marry; that she had already given all her heart to God."[25]

Gravier supported his young convert's decision. To have abandoned her would have resulted in the inevitable loss of his female congregation. Gravier was ridiculed by the fort commandant, and Rouensa's father banned his people from attending mass. Few attended, and although Gravier proposed prayer as the solution for the impasse, Rouensa proposed a more practical solution. She consented to marry the disreputable French trader if her parents agreed to become Christian converts. They readily assented to her demands.

In this manner Rouensa used Catholicism to reshape an otherwise potentially dismal outcome.[26] A marriage "in the manner of the country" would have given her minimal control over a husband who was "famous in this Illinois Country for all his debaucheries."[27] Now she could demand Christian reformation of Accault's character. As the priest's able assistant, Rouensa helped define what was expected of a Christian husband, and she relied on both her parents and her community to apply the necessary social pressures. Her parent's conversion was soon followed by the baptism of an additional two hundred people, and Gravier, obviously pleased with Rouensa's solution, counted more than three-fourths of the Kaskaskias present during catechism.[28]

Catholic marriages were sanctioned by Illini headmen, and consequently Christian strictures about the sanctity of marriage were incorporated into enforceable communal norms. Rouensa's father publicly proclaimed that "the black gowns were the witnesses of true marriage; and that to them alone God had given orders to pray for all who wished to be marry, and they would be truly married."[29] Although marriage "in the manner of the country" often acquired long-range stability, marriage partners like Accault, better known for their wayward ways than their faithful behavior, were problematic husbands. Not surprisingly, after his marriage Accault publicly proclaimed himself a reformed man. Surrounded by Christian Indians, he atoned for his sins. The sincerity of Accault's confession may be questioned, but Rouensa's matrifocal household, as well as her larger community, relied on Christian strictures about the sanctity of marriage to establish the invisible but effective links that ensured a reliable supply of well-priced trade goods.

French fur traders were eager to marry native women with extensive kin networks, particularly socially prominent women like

Women, Kin, and Catholicism

Rouensa. The exchange of trade goods for peltry occurred on a face-to-face basis, along a kinship continuum. Kin networks controlled access to furs and marriage ensured Euro-American men inclusion as kin. When French traders married Illini women, they joined their wives' households. This gave women, who controlled productive resources, increased access to trade goods. Trade goods reinforced ritual gift-giving and enhanced both the power and prestige of matrifocal households and individual women.

Households, like that of Rouensa, remained rooted within indigenous society and proved highly resistant to any efforts to impose patriarchal authority. Gravier was justifiably reluctant to accord Accault authority over his wife, for she was both an effective Catholic proselytizer and a more rigorous and faithful Christian than her husband. In this instance Catholicism proved to be a socially innovative mechanism that enhanced female authority. Simultaneously, access to trade goods reinforced the continued viability of Rouensa's matrifocal household, when it came under the stress of recurrent relocations. For Rouensa, her household, and her community, Accault was a desirable spouse, but only because this amorous adventurer was transformed into a reliable presence. Rouensa effected Accault's transformation, with the enthusiastic assistance of Gravier.

Such households not only frustrated attempts to impose hierarchical notions of European authority on Native women, they also fostered the expansion of the western fur trade. Native women became active participants in the trade because they controlled access to productive resources, particularly agricultural produce. European fur traders in the western Great Lakes were dependent on the indigenous food supply. Trade permits allowed each recipient only two canoes for the upper country, and men who married into these indigenous households were able to devote the limited cargo space of transport canoes almost entirely to trade goods. That was because the matrifocal households to which they were connected produced an agricultural surplus sufficient to feed not only their immediate family but also to feed the more transient fur trade population.

In Native American society agriculture was considered women's work, and in Illinois Country matrifocal households produced rich grain and vegetable harvests. Most historians have assumed that crops like wheat were not grown by native people because they required extensive milling, but in Illinois Country wheat was harvested by both Indians and Jesuits. In Father Gabriel Marest's Iliniwek village on the Kaskaskia, two leagues from the Mississippi,[30] the Jesuits had their own mill, while the Illini operated two mills.[31]

During Rouensa's life the Kaskaskia migrated south to settle on the Mississippi's rich alluvial lands near St. Louis. Rouensa was left a widow after seven years of marriage to Accault, after which she married another Frenchman, Michel Philippe. He arrived in Illinois Country as an obscure voyageur, or canoeman, who probably earned less than a thousand livres a year.[32] For the next twenty years the Kaskaskia baptismal records detail the evolution of their increasingly large family. Rouensa gave birth to six more children, and by her death in 1725 she had amassed an estate that was sufficient to probate and inventory. The estate was divided between her second husband and her children from both marriages.

Before her death, Rouensa dictated her will to Father Baptiste Le Boullenger, and it was written down by a notary. The will was then read to her twice, in her Illini language. Her request that the document be written in her native tongue indicated that Rouensa's household and children were probably conversant in her language, rather than in her husband's French tongue. Each of her children, upon maturity or marriage, received 2,861 livres from an estate valued at 45,000 livres. Her property included several agricultural tracts of land. Two substantial houses, each thirty-six by twenty feet with stone fireplaces, were located within the Kaskaskia village. There were two barns filled with hay to feed the livestock: oxen, thirteen cows, three horses, thirty-one pigs, and forty-eight chickens. There were ox and horse carts and plows to cultivate the fields. Rouensa owned four African slaves (two couples, both married) as well as an Indian slave.[33] The female slaves probably planted and harvested the oats, wheat, and maize. The male slaves were more likely to work in the fur trade, but they were also woodcutters, for there were nine tons of wood, cut and debarked. The barns also contained wheat and oats. The wheat, valued at 3,300 livres, had been sheaved but not yet ground at the nearby mill. Nineteen to twenty arpents of maize or Indian corn remained to be harvested.[34]

The community of Kaskaskia itself underwent a complex evolution as a result of these relationships. It was a mature settlement, which historians have often erroneously identified as founded by the French. The fur traders intermarried among the indigenous people. Although numerous French names appear in marital and baptismal registers, Native women baptized by missionary priests assumed Christian names. During the first twenty years following European contact, there were few French women. As a consequence, of the twenty-one baptisms recorded by the Jesuits, only one was the child of a French woman.[35] There was a ready market in supplying fur traders as well as in shipping agricultural produce and furs north to Montreal and, in some instances, south to New Orleans. The establishment of Kaskaskia in close proximity to Cahokia created a new center of farming activity in the American Bottoms. Rouensa's household profited from the fur trade.[36]

Over time, communities like Kaskaskia evolved as a blending of indigenous and French cultures, but for the first generation they were more Illini than French.[37] Agriculture, for instance, remained the province of women. The continuity of these matrifocal households encouraged French husbands to become traders rather than farmers. But fields mounded in Indian fashion or cultivated by the small French *en bardeau* plows led travelers to condemn French men as lazy, simply because native women's agricultural work was invisible to these Euro-American outsiders. These women also resisted the women's work associated with French households. Among the probated wills and inventories of the river community residents, there were none of the traditional tools associated with French home industry—spinning wheels, looms, or even knitting needles.[38] In these communities it appears that indigenous gender roles gave women the management and allocation of resources. Even in the Illinois lead mines in the Fox-Wisconsin riverway region, women engaged in mining and seem to have influenced mining techniques and access to the mines.[39]

The fur trade and Catholicism enhanced not only the authority of women, but it also accorded them new avenues to social prominence. Women became Christian instructors. They also rang the chapel bells that summoned Catholic Indians to services in the morning and evening.[40] One of the most important figures at the River L'Abbe Mission, the French colonial church for the Cahokia Indians on Monks Mound, may have been the Illini woman who was buried with the chapel bell.[41] It was Rouensa who achieved one of the highest honors, however, for she was buried inside the Kaskaskia mission church.

Illini Catholicism was a shared female experience that was initially facilitated by Jesuit missionaries who consciously shaped Catholicism to be compatible with Indian beliefs and practices. Catholicism was then taught to Indian women by other female converts and was probably transformed even further by the verbal transmission process. By the mid-eighteenth century when Jesuit priests declined in number and when the order was suppressed in 1773, these Catholic women thus emerged as Catholicism's primary proselytizers. It was therefore not surprising that Catholicism then appealed to larger numbers of Native people.[42]

Catholicism acquired increased centrality in the fur trade because of its social ramifications. During the eighteenth century, female converts used their "frontier" Catholicism to construct kin networks, both real as well as fictive. Native women married to fur traders served as godmothers to each other's children, and during the eighteenth century these women constructed kinship ties with distant and dispersed communities throughout the western

Women, Kin, and Catholicism

Great Lakes region. In the interface of two disparate worlds, these women relied on long-established kinship behaviors to re-create the familiar within a Christian context. Catholicism did not entail the dissolution of indigenous culture.

Distinctive métis communities eventually evolved from these Catholic kin networks as mixed-ancestry women married Frenchmen or mixed-ancestry fur traders. Métis communities existed at important fur-trade posts, like Michilimackinac and Green Bay, but at smaller fur-trade communities the lives of these women continued to be shaped by the indigenous communities in which they lived. The power of habit structured their lives, just as it organized Indian society and enabled traditional economies to meet the demands of an emerging transatlantic market economy.[43]

Catholic kin networks were indispensable to the fur trade because they linked the larger fur-trade posts (the centers of exchange) with the smaller fur-trade posts (the sources of supply). How that kinship system operated is apparent in the life of another Illini woman, Marie Madeleine Réaume, the daughter of Simphorose Ouaouagoukoue and Jean Baptiste Réaume.[44] She was born early in the eighteenth century, shortly before Rouensa's death. Although both were Illini women and Catholic converts, their lives differed dramatically. Unlike Rouensa, Réaume had neither social prominence nor was her conversion of particular significance to any of the Jesuit fathers. She did not possess sufficient wealth to leave legacies for her children. In every respect she was a less conspicuous historical figure, and consequently she left no written records or will for the perusal of curious historians. But Réaume's life was illustrative of the prominent role women played in the evolution of fur-trade communities. Her life bridged two disparate worlds and illustrated how kin networks linked indigenous and French societies. Exchange remained embedded in social relationships, kinship mediated that process, and Catholic kin networks linked the distant fur-trade outposts of an expanding fur-trade society. For native people, however, trade remained a process of collective

exchange, while for Europeans exchange was an increasingly individualistic transaction within an emerging transatlantic market
economy.[45]

Réaume, like the other women discussed in this article, was
married "in the eyes of the church." Her husband was Augustin
L'archevêque, a licensed trader in the Illinois Country.[46] During
the course of their sixteen-year marriage, Réaume gave birth to six
children and remained relatively anonymous until her husband's
death.[47] Her name then started to appear in the fort's reimbursement records. Now identified as the Widow L'archevêque, she was
reimbursed by the St. Joseph commandant for "one fat pig, a heifer,
an ox, four pairs of snowshoes, a bark canoe, and another fat pig."
Other invoices indicate that the widow also supplied sacks with
wheat, oats, and corn.[48] It is clear that Réaume's household produced
both a marketable agricultural surplus as well as specific goods for
the trade.[49] Her agricultural holdings paralleled those of Rouensa,
although they were far less significant. Réaume had "ten houses,
good lands, orchards, gardens, cattle, furniture, [and] utensils."[50]
Such women, and the agriculturally oriented communities in which
they lived, were common throughout the Great Lakes. As far north
as Michilimackinac, other Indian communities served as agricultural
suppliers of the trade. At Waganagisi (L'Arbe Croche or Crooked
Tree) the Odawa "raised large surpluses of corn and vegetables,
produced fish, and later maple sugar, and manufactured canoes,
snowshoes, and clothing essential to the Great Lakes fur trade."[51]

These communities experienced seasonal population shifts, but
they acquired an increasingly larger core of permanent residents.
Réaume, for instance, lived at Fort St. Joseph for almost seventy
years; because of this longevity, she gradually established under the
umbrella of Catholicism fictive and real kin networks that linked
her household with similar fur-trade communities throughout the
Great Lakes.[52]

Réaume's first attempt to expand her familial and fictive kin
network to other prominent fur-trade families took place after

her husband's death.[53] She had kin connections in the Illinois Country, but it was Michilimackinac that was emerging as the most important entrepôt of the eighteenth-century fur trade. In the summer of 1748, the thirty-eight-year-old widow traveled north to Michilimackinac. This was a journey of more than three hundred miles, which she made in a birch-bark canoe with her three-year-old son and her two eldest daughters, seventeen-year-old Marie Catherine and fifteen-year-old Marie Joseph Esther. Réaume relied on baptism and marriage to incorporate her family into the more prominent Catholic kin network of Michilimackinac. Members of the Bourassa and the Langlade families served as godparents to Réaume's son and as witnesses at the weddings of her daughters.[54] The ceremonies and celebrations completed, Réaume returned to St. Joseph. Both daughters and their fur-trader husbands returned to St. Joseph and became part of Réaume's household.[55]

After the marriage of Réaume's daughters, increasingly complex behavioral strategies enveloped this entire household and included not just the children but also Réaume herself. Three years after the 1848 trip to Michilimackinac, Réaume, then forty-one years old, gave birth to a son. The child's father was a prominent Michilimackinac trader, Louis Therèse Chevalier, whom Réaume later married at the St. Joseph mission.[56] Chevalier was thirty-nine.[57] Although Chevalier had married among the Odawa, he nevertheless married this forty-two-year-old widow and relocated to the southeastern shore of Lake Michigan.

The apparent marital strategy of Réaume was to join her prosperous agricultural household to Michilimackinac, which was the most important trading outpost in the western Great Lakes. For Chevalier marriage extended his already extensive kin network and provided him with an entrée into the prosperous St. Joseph trade. Following Chevalier's marriage to Réaume, the Chevaliers garnered a substantial portion of the St. Joseph trade. Chevalier's father had traded there in 1718, but he subsequently did not receive a permit for the area. His eldest sister and her husband had lived in the community for more than twenty years, but reimbursement invoices signed by the post commandant were for Louis Deshêtres's work as a blacksmith. The Chevaliers were Michilimackinac traders who were long denied entrée into the St. Joseph trade. The other men in the Chevalier family had all married native women on the western shore of Lake Michigan. In fact, Chevalier himself had married, in the manner of the country, an Odawa woman before his Christian marriage to Réaume, through whom he planned to enter the St. Joseph trade.[58]

The Chevalier kin network was gradually integrated into the St. Joseph community. One of Réaume's daughters married Chevalier's younger brother, Louis Pascal Chevalier.[59] Another daughter married her stepfather's Montreal trading partner, Charles Lhullic dit Chevalier. The groom was a recent forty-five-year-old widower; the bride, Angelique L'archevêque, was twenty-one.[60] Réaume's youngest daughter, seventeen-year-old Anne, also married a fur trader, and they initially remained part of the St. Joseph community.[61]

Marriage integrated these two distant families, and in time the offspring migrated to other fur-trade communities. Mobility strengthened kinship ties not only with Michilimackinac but also to the south, creating a network that became increasingly important to the entire St. Joseph River valley when the British took control of the western Great Lakes. During the 1850s Réaume's two eldest daughters, their husbands, and their children moved to Fort Pimiteoui, now Peoria, and eventually to Cahokia.[62] Réaume's fourth daughter, Marie Amable, and her husband also eventually joined their L'archevêque kin at Cahokia.

Geographically distant kin links were also greatly reinforced by the godparenting roles that siblings played to each others' children. For example, Réaume's daughters were frequent godparents to their nieces and nephews.[63] After they no longer lived in the Fort St. Joseph community, they returned annually when missionary priests arrived from distant posts. Louis Chevalier's siblings also became godparents to the L'archevêque grandchildren, and Réaume's daughters were godmothers of the Chevalier grandchildren.

During the mid-eighteenth century an important demographic shift took place when Fort St. Joseph reverted to a predominantly indigenous settlement, and an increased number of Potawatomis became Catholic converts. By 1755 there was no longer a resident priest. In addition, many of the French families who had earlier lived at St. Joseph had now moved to Detroit.[64] Consequently, Réaume became the community's most important lay practitioner.[65] She employed Catholicism as a socially integrative tool that incorporated increased numbers of native people. *Panis*, or Native slaves, and Indian women were baptized at the St. Joseph mission church. Réaume, for instance, was the godmother to Marie Jeanne, a thirteen-year-old slave, as well as to Thérèse, a forty-year-old Potawatomi woman.[66] One Miami couple, Pierre Mekbibkas8nga and his wife, had their "indian style marriage" sacramentally sanctioned by a visiting priest.[67] The incorporation of their four adult daughters through baptism revealed even more strongly the influence of the L'archevêque-Chevalier family. One daughter selected Louis Chevalier as her godfather; two other daughters chose Réaume as their godmother.[68]

The French departure did not signal the demise of St. Joseph as a fur-trade community. Instead, the number of furs harvested increased dramatically. More engagements or contracts for hiring canoemen were issued in this decade than in any previous period and fur exports increased.[69]

By 1755, Réaume and Louis Chevalier were linked through trade and intermarriage to the Potawatomi villages of the St. Joseph River valley. Their son, Louison, probably married among the Potawatomi. In this smaller fur-trade community, on the banks of the St. Joseph River, Réaume and Chevalier remained part of an indigenous kin system.

Kinship facilitated fur-trade exchange and had political, as well as social and economic, dimensions. French authority over the North American interior rested on the hegemony of these kin networks.

The French traders living among native people were central to New France's highly effective communications network that linked distant western outposts. French traders relayed messages, solicited warriors, and mediated potentially disruptive disputes. Following the French and Indian War, when the British displaced the French, these kin networks frustrated the transfer of power. The garrisoning of former French forts proved an explosive event, when fur traders failed to assume their traditional role as mediators. Instead, in the uprising of 1763, they remained passive observers as the forts at Le Boeuf, Michilimackinac, Miami, Ouiatenon, Presqu'Isle, St. Joseph, Sandusky, and Verango fell to Native American forces.[70]

England lacked a sufficient presence to govern through force, and when the English ignored or attempted to displace French traders and their native wives, this threatened to destabilize a highly complex, kin-related world of the upper Great Lakes region. Although Chevalier was described by the British as "so connected with the Potawatomis that he can do anything with them,"[71] his influence was actually attributable to his wife. Réaume had lived at Fort St. Joseph for more than fifty years and had incorporated Chevalier into her kin network.[72] Communities like St. Joseph were the locus of Catholic kin networks, and women like Réaume were the demographic links in a world defined by kinship. Her behavior followed the pattern of godparenting common in the western Great Lakes. She was the godmother to the children of her children, her slaves and their offspring, fellow Native American converts, and even to the children of unconverted native women. Eventually, Réaume's kinship network extended south to Saint Louis, Cahokia, and Kaskaskia; north to Michilimackinac; and west to Green Bay. Both her mother and first husband were people of the Illinois Country. Her uncle Simon Réaume was considered the most important trader at Fort Ouiatenon until his death in the 1730s.[73] Her father eventually established himself as a Green Bay trader, and her younger sister, Suzanne, was raised in that community. Réaume's oldest daughter was the godmother to Suzanne's son.[74] Réaume's marriage to

Chevalier was the impetus for incorporation of the Chevalier kin at Michilimackinac into the Fort St. Joseph community. Chevalier's Montreal trading partner[75] and his younger brother (Louis Pascal Chevalier) both married Réaume's daughters.[76]

Kinship facilitated the exchange process and had important social ramifications as well. The kinship ties that linked traders through female kin networks at St. Joseph mediated fur-trade exchange in the western Great Lakes. Jesuit baptismal registers reveal a great deal about the nature of kinship and describe a complex social system wherein one was less an individual and more a member of a larger kinship group.[77] The kin networks that evolved from intermarriage between fur traders and Native American women were rooted in and paralleled, extended, and further complicated those of Native American society. The more visible dimensions of these interrelationships were personified by the Catholic kin networks of women like Réaume.

English commandants who ignored women such as Réaume and their French fur-trader husbands thwarted effective governance in the western Great Lakes. Those Francophobic English commandants who advocated removal of French fur traders failed to appreciate that many mixed-ancestry offspring were now indistinguishable from the Indian people among whom they lived. In 1780, when Patrick Sinclair, the Michilimackinac commandant responsible for the St. Joseph post, ordered the forcible removal of the forty-eight French people resident at St. Joseph, including Réaume and Chevalier, he learned a bitter lesson about the folly of ignoring these kinship ties.[78] Shortly after their arrival, the English fur traders sent to Fort St. Joseph were attacked by Réaume's Illinois kin network. This force was composed of her immediate family, her son-in-law, and thirty of his friends. Although this first raid was unsuccessful, it was followed by a larger, more effective force from Cahokia, Kaskaskia, and St. Louis, with Madeleine's son, thirty-year-old Louison Chevalier, as the guide and interpreter. The Potawatomi reckoned the number to be "one hundred white people and eighty Indians," while other estimates placed the number at sixty-five white men and a large Native American contingent.[79] Young Louison Chevalier ensured the attack's success because he divided the British goods among the St. Joseph Potawatomi. The attack proved devastatingly effective, and the invaders were gone when the British arrived the next day.[80]

The St. Joseph invasion is often described as a minor skirmish of the Revolutionary War, but such descriptions fail to appreciate the extent to which such events reflected fur trade rather than military rivalries. This 1781 incident prevented the establishment of British traders in the St. Joseph River valley and secured the economic interests of the L'archevêque-Chevalier kin network.

Kinship facilitated the exchange process, and by the beginning of the nineteenth century, access to the best peltry in the western Great Lakes was increasingly controlled by these complex kin networks. When the American Fur Company entered the Great Lakes trade, company managers relied on this established kinship network and chose to supply two Odawa women, rather than their male competitors. They were Thérèse and Magdelaine Marcot, who were born into the St. Joseph kin network. They were part of an intermediate link that joined that river valley to the Odawa community fifty miles farther north, in the Grand River valley. Direct access to trade goods encouraged their emergence as independent traders.

Thérèse and Magdelaine were the children of an Odawa woman known as Thimotée and a French trader named Jean Baptiste Marcot. Marcot was a St. Joseph trader and, along with the Chevaliers, his family had been forcibly removed in 1781.[81] Thimotée returned with the children to her Odawa community in the Grand River valley, while her husband relocated to present-day Wisconsin.[82] He was killed in 1783, when Thérèse and Magdelaine were young children of three and four. They were raised as Odawa, since their mother was the daughter of Chief Kewinaquot (Returning Cloud).[83] Both children were baptized at Michilimackinac, and their godparents were members of generationally prominent fur-trade families, part of the Chevalier, Barthe, and La Framboise kin networks. Thérèse and

Magdelaine, despite being Catholic and the daughters of a French father, were identified as Odawa by the missionary priest.[84]

At first, the lives of both Thérèse and Magdelaine were remarkably similar to that of Marie Rouensa and Marie Madeleine Réaume L'archevêque Chevalier. Like their predecessors, Thérèse and Magdelaine were raised in indigenous society and married French fur traders. They married young, at fourteen, and their husbands paid the bride-price required by the Odawa. Magdelaine remained in the Grand River valley with her husband, Joseph La Framboise, and he traded among her people; Thérèse moved with her fur-trader husband, Pierre Lasaliere, to the St. Joseph River valley.[85] After several years Lasaliere and Thérèse separated, and he moved to the west side of Lake Michigan to join the Wisconsin trade.[86] Like her mother, Thérèse returned to raise her daughter in her Odawa village in the Grand River valley. Then in 1799 she took her nine-year-old daughter to Michilimackinac to be baptized.[87] Once again, the Michilimackinac priest identified both Thérèse and her child as Odawa, not French. After her husband's departure, Thérèse remained an attractive marital prospect because of her dual-kinship heritage. Her second husband was an Anglo fur trader, George Schindler, who started trading among the Odawa in 1800.[88]

Early in the nineteenth century the lives of the two sisters changed dramatically. In 1804 their country marriages were consecrated by a missionary priest at Michilimackinac. Well-known Catholic fur-trade families witnessed the event, including their old friends the Chevaliers from St. Joseph. Joseph La Framboise had lived with Magdelaine for ten years and they had two children.[89] After Thérèse's marriage to Schindler, Thérèse moved to his house on the island. Now legal kin, the La Framboise and Schindler families also formed a business partnership. They planned to obtain trade goods from Claude La Framboise, Joseph's brother in Montreal, but unfortunately the business alliance never fully materialized.[90] In 1806, several years after the Michilimackinac celebration of his marriage, Joseph was killed by an irate Indian.[91] Magdelaine buried her husband and continued on her journey to the Odawa wintering ground with her infant son Joseph, two African American slaves, Angelique and Louison, and twelve voyageurs.[92]

After her husband's death, Magdelaine, then in her twenties, emerged as an independent trader. She chose not to remarry, unlike Marie Rouensa and Marie Madeleine Réaume. Magdelaine's centrality in the Catholic kin networks of fur-trade society, her social prominence as a young Odawa woman, and her experience in the fur trade coincided with trader John Jacob Astor's eager search for an entrée into the Great Lakes trade. Kinship worked to Magdelaine's advantage and encouraged her independence. For the next fifteen years, until she retired from the trade in 1822, she traveled annually between the Grand River valley and Michilimackinac to exchange peltry for trade goods. She lived among her Odawa kin in the Grand River valley, and each year wintered with them. Magdelaine established herself as Madame La Framboise, obtained trading licenses, first from the British and then, after the War of 1812, from the Americans. She hired voyageurs to accompany her, secured trade goods on credit, and returned each June to Michilimackinac to sell her furs and resupply her outfit.

Several years after Joseph La Framboise's death, a stroke left George Schindler an invalid.[93] Thérèse, like Magdelaine, became an independent fur trader, but traded at L'Arbe Croche, the Odawa community closest to Michilimackinac. Thérèse's operations rapidly expanded. She often served as Magdelaine's supply source for the Grand River valley trade, but she also supplied a large number of French fur traders, men drawn from her kin network.[94] She sold goods to traders from the Barthe, Chevalier, and La Framboise families, all members of her fictive kin network. Men from her Catholic kin network appeared regularly on the pages of her fur-trade journals. Thérèse increasingly acquired prominence as a supplier, while her sister Magdelaine remained an active, independent trader.[95]

Women, Kin, and Catholicism

In 1816, when the American Fur Trade Company acquired greater control of the Great Lakes trade, it incorporated both women. By 1818 their supplies came from the American Fur Trade Company.[96] Magdelaine may have earned as much as five thousand to ten thousand pounds a year, while the average fur trader probably earned no more than a thousand pounds a year. The Grand River territory shipped about one hundred packs of furs a year to Michilimackinac. In 1800 furs were valued at twenty pounds per pack, and Magdelaine secured the majority of furs exported from the Grand River valley. She eventually retired from the fur trade and moved next door to her sister on Michilimackinac.[97]

These women negotiated for themselves positions of prominence in an era when the fur trade proved to be a precarious male venture. Many independent male traders were eliminated when John Jacob Astor and the American Fur Company gained control of the Great Lakes trade. The furs Thérèse Schindler and Madame La Framboise had first sold to Ramsay Crooks, Astor's representative in the Great Lakes, established their standing credit with Astor's newly formed American Fur Company.[98]

Marie Rouensa, Marie Magdelaine Réaume L'archevêque Chevalier, Magdelaine Marcot La Framboise, and Thérèse Marcot Lasaliere Schindler were part of a world where identity was defined not by nationality but by kinship. Kin networks, like those of the St. Joseph community, characterized every fur-trade community in the western Great Lakes. The fictive and familial relationships created by the umbrella of frontier Catholicism further strengthened and expanded an already complex indigenous kinship system.[99] The Catholic kin network, in which these women played so prominent a role, served a socially integrative function, which enhanced the role and importance of these women.

In 1680 and 1711, Rouensa and Réaume were born into a demographically chaotic and socially unstable world. The Fur Trade Wars pitted Iroquois against the Algonquian-speaking people. The

Jesuits contributed to that social disruption when they condemned fur traders as licentious and dismissed shamans as "jugglers." Indian women emerged as the cultural mediators of this eighteenth-century landscape. The Jesuit presence offered native women an opportunity to interface between two disparate worlds, and as Catholic converts these women constructed an ever-expanding world of real and fictive kin under the umbrella of Western religion. They raised children conversant with European and indigenous cultures, drew a livelihood for themselves and their households from the emerging market economy, and facilitated the evolution of the fur trade in the western Great Lakes. Fur-trade exchange was clearly much more than the simple economic transaction of a marketplace economy; instead, it was defined by kinship and friendship. The fur trade remained collective on one side and individualistic on the other, and this world of individual and collective exchange was bridged by Native women. These women's lives mirrored the complex interactions of indigenous societies and demonstrated how traditional economies met the demands of an emerging transatlantic economy.

Great Lakes people defined themselves by their relatives, while Anglo outsiders identified them as French or Native American. During the nineteenth century a distinctive métis society developed from the intermarriages within kin networks, especially those involving the more prominent fur-trade families, such as the Barthes, Chevaliers, Bourasses, Langlades, and La Framboises, who resided in the larger fur-trade communities like Detroit, Michilimackinac, Green Bay, and St. Louis.[100] At Fort St. Joseph, the forcible removal of the French traders and their families abruptly terminated a society evolving in that direction. Social boundaries remained ill-defined and children of Native American mothers and fur-trade fathers identified themselves as French or Canadian, but many preferred their indigenous identity. Réaume's son Louison, for example, was referred to by the British as Indian. Chevalier's son, Amable, by his first wife, became an important Odawa headman.[101] The Great

Lakes kin network, with its diversity and multiplicity of names and identities, can never be fully untangled. It led to anonymity but simultaneously determined one's social position.

Change for these women was always defined by the extensive kin networks that controlled and mediated the exchange process of the fur trade. Three of these women were the daughters of fur traders, and many of their daughters married fur traders. Marriage served as a planned extension of familiar kin networks, further extended through the fictive kinship of Catholic ritual. Therefore, as offspring moved to other fur-trade communities, mobility became the warp on which the fabric of the fur trade was woven.

Native women married to fur traders played a pivotal role in brokering social change. These multilingual translators fostered the spread of Christianity among Great Lakes people, just as they mediated the face-to-face exchange of goods for peltry. These women suggest alternative perspectives from which we might revise prevailing views about the fur trade and Catholicism. Native women were "negotiators of change," and Rouensa, Réaume, Schindler, and La Framboise were indicative of how that occurred and how women were active participants and emerged as central actors in the colonial era of the western Great Lakes.

Notes

I would like to thank Kerry Trask, Nancy Shoemaker, and Jeani O'Brien-Kehoe for their insightful comments, assistance, and encouragement. I am also grateful to people who commented on earlier versions of this paper: Helen Hornbeck Tanner, Alfred Young, and participants at the Newberry Library Seminar in Early American History; to my History Department colleagues David Bailey, Lisa Fine, and Maureen Flanagan, and to those who participated in our Department Seminar; to members of the NEH American Indian Ethnohistory Seminar organized by Gary Anderson at the University of Oklahoma, especially Jacki Rand, Lee Anne Howe, Bob Craig, and Eldon Lawrence; to R. David Edmunds, who encouraged my initial research in ethnohistory in 1995 and have remained faithful mentors; to Daniel Richter, who has repeatedly and insightfully commented on my work at conferences. In addition, the participation of Lucy Eldersveld Murphy and Alice Nash as copresenters on OAH and ethnohistory panels have proved invaluable. This article has also benefited from the suggestions and comments of the anonymous reviewers for *Ethnohistory*.

To readers familiar with French spelling and phonetics, the spelling of some names in this article may appear nonstandard (e.g., "Angelique" rather than *Angélique*). Occasionally, they vary among different holders of the same name. These are not typographical errors; on the contrary, I have sought to reproduce faithfully the spellings as given in the *St. Joseph Baptismal Register* and other primary sources in the interest of facilitating further research into these families. Where possible, the *Dictionary of Canadian Biography* (University of Toronto Press) has been used to standardize spelling.

1. Harold Innis, in *The Fur Trade in Canada* (Toronto, 1970), views the North American fur trade as an extension of a European economic system. The effect of trade as not simply economic but also destructive of indigenous cultures is described by Lewis O. Saum in *The Fur Trader and the Indian* (Seattle, 1965), and the literature that supports similar perspectives is discussed at length by Donald F. Bibeau in "Fur Trade Literature from a Tribal Point of View: A Critique," in *Rendezvous: Selected Papers of the Fourth North American Fur Trade Conference, 1981*, ed. Thomas C. Buckley (Saint Paul MN), 83–91. The idea that the fur trade was exemplative of how a common ground of understanding was established between two cultures "without sacrificing their unique characteristics and without annihilating one another" was described by Carolyn Gilman in *Where Two Worlds Meet: The Great Lakes Fur Trade* (Saint Paul MN, 1982), 1–4. Most recently, Richard White, in *The Middle Ground: Indians, Empires, and Republics in the Great Lakes Region, 1650–1815* (New York, 1991), asserts that the trade was a cultural compromise in which Europeans accommodated to the customs of native people. The idea that native people were assertive and early participants in the trade has been explored by Bruce J. Bourque and Ruth Holmes Whitehead in "Tarrentines and the Introduction of European Trade Goods in the Gulf of Maine," *Ethnohistory* 32 (1985): 327–41.

2. The western Great Lakes was referred to by the French as the *pays d'en haut* and initially included all of the "lands bordering the rivers flowing into the northern Great Lakes and the lands south of the lakes to the Ohio." See White, *Middle Ground*, x–xi, 50, 52. For an explanation of the "middle ground," see chapter 2, pp. 50–93.

3. Clara Sue Kidwell, "Indian Women as Cultural Negotiators," *Ethnohistory* 39 (Spring 1992): 97–107. The term *negotiators of change* is borrowed from Nancy Shoemaker's *Negotiators of Change: Historical Perspectives on Native American Women* (New York, 1995).

4. "Marriage 'after the custom of the country' was an indigenous marriage rite which evolved to meet the needs of fur trade society. . . . Although denounced by the Jesuit priests as immoral, the traders had taken their Indian wives according to traditional native marriage rites and distinct family units had developed." Sylvia Van Kirk, *Many Tender Ties: Women in Fur-trade Society, 1670–1870* (Norman OK, 1983), 28. These marriages combined both Indian and European marriage customs; the unions, although not always permanent, were neither casual nor promiscuous. For a further explanation of how marriage *à la façon du pays* became institutionalized as integral to the Great Lakes fur trade, see especially Jacqueline Peterson's "Prelude to Red River: A Social Portrait of the Great Lakes Métis," *Ethnohistory* 25 (1978): 48, 41–67, in which she shows how "the force of tribal custom . . . French peasant practices and the *coutume de Paris*" encouraged intermarriage. See also Jennifer S. H. Brown, *Strangers in Blood: Fur Trade Company Families in Indian Country* (Norman OK, 1980), 62–63; also Jacqueline Peterson and Jennifer S. H. Brown, eds., *The New Peoples: Being and Becoming Métis in North America* (Fort Garry MB, 1985), especially Peterson's "Many Roads to Red River: Métis Genesis in the Great Lakes Region, 1680–1815," 37–73. See also Sylvia Van Kirk's "The Custom of the Country: An Examination of Fur Trade Marriage Practices," and John E. Foster's "The Origin of the Mixed Bloods in the Canadian West," in *Essays on Western History*, ed. Lewis H. Thomas (Edmonton AB, 1976), 49–68, 71–80.

5. Sylvia Van Kirk, "Toward a Feminist Perspective in Native History," in *Papers of the Eighteenth Algonquian Conference*, ed. José Mailhot (Ottawa, 1987), 386.

6. For a discussion of missionization among Native American women that relies on an assimilationist model, see Karen Anderson, *Chain Her by One Foot: The Subjugation of Women in Seventeenth-Century New France* (New York, 1991); Carol Devens, *Countering Colonization: Native American Women and Great Lakes Women, 1630–1900* (Berkeley CA, 1992); Eleanor Burke Leacock, "Montaignais Women and the Jesuit Program for Colonization," in *Myths of Male Dominance: Collected Articles on Women Cross-Culturally*, ed. Eleanor Burke Leacock (New York, 1981), 43–62.

7. For the parallel circumstance of Catholic women among the Iroquois, see Nancy Shoemaker, "Kateri Tekawitha," in *Negotiators of Change*, ed. Nancy Shoemaker (New York, 1995), 49–71; and Natalie Zemon Davis, "Iroquois Women, European Women," in *Women, "Race," and Writing in the Early Modern Period*, ed. Margo Hendricks and Patricia Parker (New York, 1994), 243–61.

8. The number eight appears throughout the St. Joseph Baptismal Register and indicates the phonetic equivalent for parts of Native American languages that were not spelled in French. *8* was a digraph or shorthand for *ou*.

9. Before their conversion to Catholicism, the Illini were polygamous, and this has been attributed to the high ratio of women to men. Early observers reported that women outnumbered men four to one and for this reason men espoused the younger sisters of their first wives. Village dwellings consisted of substantial oblong cabins that housed from six to twelve families. Consequently, village houses brought substantial numbers of women together. These women also exercised control over productive resources and men turned over the food of the hunt to them. Women owned all household possessions, while a man's property consisted only of his weapons and clothes. Clarence Walworth Alvord, *The Illinois Country, 1673–1818* (Chicago, 1920), 41–46.

10. The term *frontier Catholicism* suggests that lay Catholics were instrumental in the spread of Catholicism in the western Great Lakes. This was a result of the scarcity of priests, a situation worsened in 1762 by the secularization of the Jesuits. The role lay people played in the transmission of dogma is unclear. The term *baptized conditionally* appears frequently in baptismal registers and indicates that a child had previously received lay baptism when a priest was unavailable.

11. The Odawa were semisedentary and moved their villages only when the soil was no longer fertile or when enemies threatened attack. Women remained resident in the village while hunting parties were an all-male activity. Although divorce was uncommon, when it did occur the children remained with the women. Children belonged to the women, and for this reason it appears that descent was traced through women. James E. Fitting and Charles E. Cleland, "Late Prehistoric Settlement Patterns in the Upper Great Lakes," *Ethnohistory* 16 (1969): 295–96; W. Vernon Kinietz, *The Indians of the Western Great Lakes* (Ann Arbor MI, 1990), 270–74.

12. All four women—Marie Rouensa-8cate8a, Marie Madeleine Réaume L'archevêque Chevalier, Magdelaine Marcot La Framboise, and Thérèse Marcot Lasaliere Schindler—were Catholic, hence the presence of Christian names.

13. Carl J. Ekberg with Anton J. Pregaldin, "Marie Rouensa-8cate8a and the Foundations of French Illinois," *Illinois Historical Journal* 84 (Fall 1991): 146–60; John E. McDowell, "Therese Schindler of Mackinac: Upward Mobility in the Great Lakes Fur Trade," *Wisconsin Magazine of History* 61 (Winter 1977–78): 126–27; David A. Armour, "Magdelaine Marcot La Framboise," *Dictionary of Canadian Biography* (Toronto, 1991), 7:582–83; McDowell, "Madame La Framboise," *Michigan History* 56 (Winter 1972): 271–86; Keith R. Widder, "Magdelaine La Framboise, Fur Trader and Educator," *Historical Women of Michigan: A Sesquicentennial Celebration*, ed. Rosalie Riegle Troester (Lansing MI, 1987), 1–13. *Dictionary of Canadian Biography*, hereafter as DCB.

14. White, *Middle Ground*, 70–75.

15. See Louise Tilly, "Gender, Women's History, and Social History," *Social Science History* 13 (1989): 339–480 (esp. 447), which suggests that women's history became more analytical and addresses issues central to the historical agenda.

16. The Algonquian-speaking Illinois included several groups: the Cahokia, Chipussea, Coircoentanon, Kaskaskia, Michigamea, Moingwena, Peoria, and Taponero. The French referred to the area as the "Illinois Country," which included the present state of Illinois, plus eastern Missouri and eastern Iowa. Emily J. Blasingham, "The Depopulation of the Illinois Indians," *Ethnohistory* 3 (1956): 193. The term *Iliniwik* comes from *ilini* or man, *iw* is *ek*, the plural termination and was changed by the French to *ois*. Alvord, *Illinois Country*, 31.

17. In a matrifocal household the woman is the focus of the relationship but not the head of the household. Women evolved as the center of economic and decision-making coalitions with their children, despite the presence of a husband-father. Raymond Smith, "The Matrifocal Family," in *The Character of Kinship*, ed. Jack Goody (New York, 1973), 124–25.

18. From Father Gabriel Marest, Missionary of the Society of Jesus, to Father Germon of the same Society, 9 November 1712, *Lettres édifiantes* (Toulouse, 1810), 6:207.

19. Raymond E. Hausner, in "The *Berdache* and the Illinois Indian Tribe during the Last Half of the Seventeenth Century," *Ethnohistory* 37 (1990): 54, has suggested that the status of Illinois women was limited by sororal polygony and that brothers played an important role in the selection of a husband. The conversion to Catholicism would have clearly ended the practice of polygony as well as the marital influence exercised by men.

20. DeGannes, "Memoir of DeGannes Concerning the Illinois Country," in *The French Foundations, 1680–1692*, ed. Theodore Calvin Pease and Raymond C. Werner, *Collections of the Illinois State Historical Library* (Springfield IL, 1934), 23:361.

21. Mary Borgias Palm, *The Jesuit Missions of the Illinois Country, 1673–1763* (Cleveland, 1933), 25; DeGannes, "Memoir Concerning Illinois," 38–40.

22. Reuben Gold Thwaites, ed., *The Jesuit Relations and Allied Documents, Travels and Explorations of the Jesuit Missions in New France, 1610–1791* (Cleveland, 1896–1901), 65:67, hereafter *JR*.

23. *JR*, 64:229.

24. *JR*, 64:205, 195–205.

25. *JR*, 64:195.

26. Rouensa married Accault within the church. Gravier described the

circumstances of the wedding and baptized their first son, Peter Accault, on 20 March 1695 at Pimiteoui. For the baptism, see "Kaskaskia Church Records," *Transactions of the Illinois Historical Society*, vol. 2 (Springfield IL, 1904), 394; Marthe F. Beauregard, *La population des forts français d'Amérique* (Montreal, 1982), 2:108.

27. *JR*, 64:213.

28. *JR*, 64:233; Palm, *Jesuit Missions*, 26.

29. *JR*, 64:209.

30. Palm, *Jesuit Missions*, 42.

31. Pierre Margry, ed., *Découvertes et établissements des Français dans l'ouest et dans le sud de l'Amérique septentrionale, 1614–1698* (Paris, 1879–88), 5:375–586; Father Gabriel Marest to Father Germon, *JR*, 66:218–95; also in Father Watrin's summary of his work among the Kaskaskia, *JR*, 70:218–95.

32. Brown and Laurie C. Dean, *The Village of Chartres in Colonial Illinois, 1720–1765* (New Orleans LA, 1977), 871; Ekberg, "Marie Rouensa," 156.

33. For a description of African American slavery in Illinois Country, see Carl J. Ekberg, "Black Slavery in Illinois, 1720–1765," *Western Illinois Regional Studies* 12 (1989): 5–9. For Native American slavery in the Great Lakes, see Russell M. Magnaghi, "Red Slavery in the Great Lakes Country during the French and British Regimes," *Old Northwest* 12 (Summer 1996): 201–17.

34. An arpent is a French unit equal to about 0.84 acres or, when used as a linear measurement, equal to 192 English feet. Winstanley Briggs, "Le Pays des Illinois," *William and Mary Quarterly* 47 (1990): 38.

35. Palm, *Jesuit Missions*, 42; Beauregard, *La population*, 2:107–81.

36. Daniel H. Usner, in *Indians, Settlers, and Slaves in a Frontier Exchange Economy* (Chapel Hill NC, 1992), 7, indicates that the Illinois Country was under the political administration of New Orleans but was economically more integrated with the Great Lakes.

37. Palm, *Jesuit Missions*, 42–43, 80.

38. Susan C. Boyle, "Did She Generally Decide? Women in Ste. Genevieve, 1750–1805," *William and Mary Quarterly* 44 (1987): 783–84.

39. Lucy Eldersveld Murphy, "Autonomy and the Economic Roles of Indian Women of the Fox-Wisconsin River Region, 1763–1832," in Shoemaker, *Negotiators of Change*, 72–89; see esp. 81–82.

40. Gilbert J. Garraghan, "New Light on Old Cahokia," *Illinois Catholic Historical Review* 2: 99–146.

41. John A. Walthall and Elizabeth D. Benchley, *The River L'Abbe Mission: A French Colonial Church for the Cahokia Illini on Monks Mound*, Studies in Illinois Archaeology, no. 2 (Springfield IL, 1987), 71–73.

42. Thomas Hughes, *History of the Society of Jesus in North America* (London, 1917), 2:418–19.

43. See chapter 3, "Structures, Habitus, Practices," in Pierre Bourdieu, *The Logic of Practice* (Stanford CA, 1980), 52–65.

44. Marie Madeleine Réaume's father was the trader, Jean Baptiste Réaume. The first official reference to Jean Baptiste Réaume was in 1720, when the New France governor, Vaudreuil, sent him to the reestablished Fort St. Joseph post with two canoes loaded with gifts for the Miami. In 1717 her father served as the post interpreter and later moved onto Green Bay. Marie Madeleine Réaume first appears in the St. Joseph Register when she was listed as a godmother, in March 1729, and was identified as the daughter of Simphorose Ouaouagoukoue and the post's interpreter, Sieur Jean Baptiste Réaume. "St. Joseph Baptismal Register," *Mississippi Valley Historical Review* 13 (June 1926–March 1927): 212 (hereafter MVHR).

45. For an explanation of exchange in indigenous societies, see Marcel Mauss, *The Gift: The Form and Reason of Exchange in Archaic Societies* (New York, 1990).

46. Variant spellings for *L'archevêque* include *Larchesveque* and *Larche*. Certificate, Montreal, signed de Villiers, 18 July 1745; *ANCol*, C11A, 117:325. In 1741 Augustin L'archevêque contracted to hire canoemen to accompany him to Illinois Country. For engagements or contracts hiring canoemen at St. Joseph from 1722–45, see *Rapport de l'Archiviste de la Province de Québec*, 1929–30, 233–465, hereafter RAPQ.

47. The daughters lived to maturity, but the son probably did not reach adulthood. The first daughter, Marie Catherine, was born the day after her mother and father were married. She was baptized on 13 January 1731. Her godfather was the past commandant, Nicholas Coulon de Villiers, and her godmother was Marie Catherine, of the Illinois nation, "St. Joseph Baptismal Register," ed. Rev. George Paré and M. M. Quaife, MVHR 13: 213. The second daughter, Marie Esther (referred to as Marie Joseph Esther), was born sometime in 1733 and baptized one year later at Michilimackinac on 1 January 1734, "The Mackinac Register," *Collections of the State Historical Society of Wisconsin*, 19:4, hereafter WHC. The third daughter, Marie Anne, was twenty-one months and eight days old at the time of her baptism at St. Joseph in April of 1740. Her godfather was Nicolas Coulon de Villiers, the post commandant, and her older sister, Marie Joseph Esther. "St. Joseph Register," 218. The fourth daughter, Marie Amable, was baptized at St. Joseph on 27 July 1740 by the post commandant, Nicolas Coulon de Villiers, and subsequently by Father Lamorine on 29 June 1741. The godparents were Claude Caron and Charlotte

Robert, the wife of the post interpreter. "St. Joseph Register," 219. The fifth daughter was Angelique (Agathe), baptized in March 1744. Her godfather was Monsieur de Lespiné de Villiers, a cadet in the troops of the colony's marine detachment. Her godmother was her oldest sister, Marie Catherine. "St. Joseph Register," 221.

48. Joseph Peyser, *Fort St. Joseph Manuscripts: Chronological Inventory and Translations* (Niles MI, 1978), 121, 104.

49. The seventeenth-century Jesuits attested to the lushness of the Saint Joseph River valley and to the profusion of wild grapes that grew along riverbanks. The dune area around southern Lake Michigan also produced large quantities of huckleberries, wild currants, gooseberries, and blackberries. Plum, crab apple, and cherry trees grew along the river bottoms. Brown, *Aboriginal Cultural Adaptations*, 60; JR, 55:195.

50. "Petition of Louis Chevallier," reprinted from the Haldimand Papers, Canadian Archives, Ottawa, *Michigan Pioneer and Historical Society: Collections and Researches* (hereafter MPHC) 13 (1889): 61.

51. James M. McClurken, "Augustin Hamlin, Jr.: Ottawa Identity and the Politics of Persistence," in *Being and Becoming Indian*, ed. James A. Clifton (Chicago, 1989), 85.

52. These communities had a settled agricultural appearance. There were agricultural fields, log cabins, framed houses, and fruit orchards. The usual markers of European society, houses and cabins, were also indicative of Native American society. At Réaume's St. Joseph village, a French carpenter had even built a house for a Potawatomi headman. A jail was even constructed by the blacksmith Antoine Deshêtres. It was made of stone and measured eight feet by ten feet. Certificate, St. Joseph, signed Piquoteé de Belestre, 13 May 1750. *ANCol*, C11A, 96:313. The post interpreter Pierre Deneau dit Detailly submitted a certificate to receive a thousand livres for building a house for a medal chief. Certificate, St. Joseph, 30 April 1760, Archives Nationales, vol. 7, 345: 99. Ottawa: National Archives of Canada.

53. In Sainte Genevieve, Illinois Country, French widows were more active in the local economy and were more likely to file legal grievances than either single or married women. Boyle, "Did She Generally Decide?" 788–89.

54. Augustin L'archevêque was baptized on 7 July 1748. He probably never reached adulthood. His godfather was Augustin Langland and his godmother was Marie Catherine Lerige Bourassa. "Mackinac Baptisms," WHC, 19:24–5; Marie Catherine married Jean Baptiste Jutras (Joutras), and the wedding took place at St. Ignace on 7 July 1748. He was a trader from Trois Rivières. Witnesses included Legardeur de St. Pierre Verchere, Bourassa, Langlade, and

Charles Langlade. "Mackinac Register," *WHC*, 18:475. The wedding of Marie Joseph Esther and Jacques Bariso de La Marche took place at Saint Ignace on 2 August 1748. Some witness signatures were illegible, but both those of Langlade and Bourassa remain legible, "Mackinac Register," *WHC*, 18:476. The bridegroom was probably related to the Montreal merchant with whom Réaume's father had traded. In 1729 Jean Baptiste Réaume owed Charles Nolan LaMarque 4,000 livres in furs. *RAPQ*, 1929–30, 244–408. Joseph Esther was twice widowed and at the age of forty-six, on 8 June 1779, she married Thomas M. Brady. He became the Indian agent at Cahokia. She had children and grandchildren living in Cahokia until well into the 1800s. Webster and Krause, *Fort Saint Joseph*, 115.

55. Catherine married Jean Baptiste Jutras (Joutras). Her youngest daughter, Esther, married Jacques Bariso de La Marche, who was probably related to the Montreal merchant with whom Réaume's father had traded. He was the son of a Montreal merchant, which would have guaranteed the St. Joseph community an adequate and annual supply of trade goods.

56. The Chevaliers were a large French family. There were seventeen children. Jean Baptiste Chevalier and his wife, Marie Françoise Alavoine, probably moved from Montreal to Michilimackinac in 1718. Baptismal registers at Michilimackinac and St. Joseph provide information about fifteen of the seventeen children born to Chevalier and Alavoine: five, possibly six, children were born at Montreal; eleven were baptized at St. Ignace. The four children born in Montreal included Charlotte (1712), Marie Anne (Chabouillez) Catherine (1714), Michel Jean Baptiste and Marie Josephe (1718). The eleven children baptized at the St. Ignace Mission included Constance (1719), Louis Thérèse (1720), Marguerite Josephe (1723), Marie Magdaleine (1724), Anne Charlotte Veronique (1726), Charles (1727), Joseph Maurice (1728), Louis Pascal (1730), Anne Thérèse Esther (1732), Angelique (1733), and Luc (1735). John M. Gram, "The Chevalier Family and the Demography of the Upper Great Lakes" (unpublished paper, Mackinac Island State Park Commission, Lansing MI, 1995).

57. Their marriage coincided with the baptism of their son, Louis, who was born in October 1751 and was baptized by his uncle, Louis Pascal Chevalier. In April 1752 he was baptized by the priest, Father DuJaunay. His godfather was his oldest stepsister's husband, Joutras, and his godmother was another stepsister, Madeleine Chevalier. "St. Joseph Baptismal Register," *MVHR*: 223.

58. Gram, "The Chevalier Family," 20.

59. Marie Magdelaine L'archevêque appears to have been one of Madeleine's daughters, but this cannot be confirmed by the baptismal registers.

Louis Pascal was baptized at Michilimackinac on 22 July 1730. He died before 1 January 1779. Louis Pascal and his wife had four children baptized at St. Joseph between 1758 and 1773. "St. Joseph Baptismal Register," *MVHR* 12: 223n38; *WHC*, 8:490; *WHC*, 19:3; Webster and Krause, *Fort Saint Joseph*, 120–21.

60. The Chevaliers were partners, but they were not related. Charles Lhullic Chevalier's trading partner now became his step-father-in-law. Charles and Angelique were married at St. Joseph, where three of their children were later baptized. Chevalier died in 1773; he was about sixty-four. His death was the last entry in the St. Joseph Baptismal Register. Webster and Krause, *Fort Saint Joseph*, 115–17; Idle, "Post of the St. Joseph," 253–54n104; "St. Joseph Baptismal Register," *MVHR* 12: 230.

61. The register does not mention the marriage of Anne L'archevêque and Augustin Gibault. When she served as godmother to the daughter of her sister Marie Joseph in 1756, she was identified as Anne L'archeveque. By 1758 she was identified as Gibault's wife. "St. Joseph Baptismal Register," *MVHR* 12: 228, 230.

62. Marie Amable married Jean Baptiste François Lonval. Lonval's ties were to the fur-trade community at Trois Rivières. The Lonvals settled in Cahokia, where they appear on the 1787 Cahokia census. Webster and Krause, *Fort Saint Joseph*, 117–18; "St. Joseph Baptismal Register," *MVHR* 12: 231, 233–34.

63. Both Joseph Esther's and Marie Amable's children were baptized at the Fort Saint Joseph Mission. Four of Esther's children were baptized there. In 1753 her sister Catherine was the godmother to her sixteen-month-old son, Louis, and to her three-year-old son, Etienne Joseph. Esther's sister Anne was the godmother to her three-year-old daughter, Marie Joseph. In 1756, Esther's sister Magdeleine was the godmother to her five-month-old daughter, Angelique. "St. Joseph Baptismal Register," 225, 225–26, 228. In 1761, Amable's two-month-old daughter was baptized at St. Joseph, "St. Joseph Baptismal Register," *MVHR* 12: 233–34.

64. The prolonged absence of priests at frontier missions led lay Catholics and even non-Catholics to perform baptisms. Priests were only intermittently assigned to the St. Joseph Mission, but they did serve continuously from 1750 to 1761. During other times the post was reliant on the missionary priests assigned to the Illinois Country; generally these priests resided at either Cahokia or Kaskaskia. Growth of the frontier Catholic church was hampered in 1762, when the French government decreed secularization of the Jesuits. The Supreme Council of New Orleans put the decree into effect on 3 July 1763. Father Meurin was allowed to remain in the Illinois Country at Sainte Genevieve on the Spanish side of the river. Priests from other orders were at

the Saint Joseph mission in 1761, 1768, and 1773. A new missionary priest, Father Gibault, was assigned to the Illinois Country in 1773. "St. Joseph Register," 204–5; George Paré, *The Catholic Church in Detroit, 1701–1888* (Detroit, 1951), 78–103. For an account of the banishment, see *JR*.

65. The term *baptized conditionally* appears frequently in baptismal registers and indicates that a child had previously received lay baptism when a priest was unavailable. For an explanation of the term *baptized conditionally*, see p. 7, n. 25, of "The Mackinac Register, 1696–1821: Register of Baptisms of the Mission of St. Ignace de Michilimackinak," *WHC*, vol. 19.

66. "St. Joseph Baptismal Register," *MVHR* 12: 218, 238.

67. His godfather was Mr. Marin de La Perrière and his godmother was Madeleine de Villiers, de La Perrière's wife. Her godfather was Louis Metivier, a master carpenter, and the godmother was Marie Fafard, Metivier's wife. Five years later Marie, Pierre's wife, died. "St. Joseph Baptismal Register," *MVHR* 12: 221–23.

68. On 22 April 1752, one of Pierre's daughters, 8abak8ik8e, was baptized. She was about thirty-five years old and took the name Marie as her Christian name. Louis Chevalier signed as the godfather. On 1 May 1752, three more of Pierre's children, all women, were baptized; one was twenty-six or twenty-seven, the second was twenty-five, and the third was fifteen or sixteen. The eldest, a widow and identified as Temagas8kia, took the name Marguerite. Her godmother was Marguerite of the Saki nation. Both other daughters elected Marie Madeleine Réaume Chevalier as their godmother. The middle daughter, age twenty-five, was identified as being married to Pi8assin, who was listed as still unconverted. The third daughter took the name Suzanne. "St. Joseph Baptismal Register," *MVHR* 13: 222–23.

69. Idle, "Post of the Saint Joseph River," 182; *RAPQ*, 1929–30, 233–465.

70. Howard Peckham, *Pontiac and the Indian Uprising* (Detroit, 1994); Ian K. Steele, *Warpath: Invasions of North America* (New York, 1994), 237–42; Charles E. Cleland, *Rites of Conquest: The History and Culture of Michigan's Native Americans* (Ann Arbor MI, 1994), 134–43; White, *Middle Ground*, 269–314; Gregory Evans Dowd, "The French King Wakes up in Detroit: Pontiac's War in Rumor and History," *Ethnohistory* 37 (1990): 254–78; Gregory Evans Dowd, *A Spirited Resistance: The North American Indian Struggle for Unity, 1745–1815* (Baltimore MD, 1992).

71. "To General Gage from Lt. Campbell, April 10, 1766," Gage Papers #308, Ayers Manuscript Collections, Newberry Library, Chicago, Illinois; "To General Haldiman from A. S. DePeyster, August 15, 1778," *MPHC* 9: 368.

72. British traders who attempted to break the exclusionary St. Joseph

trade barrier met a dire fate. In 1773 four English traders were murdered near St. Joseph by the Potawatomi. Chevalier was suspected, but the British were reluctant to remove him. Gérard Malchelosse, "St. Joseph River Post," *French Canadian and Acadian Genealogical Review*, nos. 3–4 (1970): 189.

73. Joseph L. Peyser, "The Fate of the Fox Survivors: A Dark Chapter in the History of the French in the Upper Country, 1726–1737," *Wisconsin Magazine of History* 73 (Winter 1989–90): 110; R. David Edmunds and Joseph L. Peyser, *The Fox Wars: The Mesquakie Challenge to New France* (Norman OK, 1993), 144.

74. "The Mackinac Register," WHC, 19:25.

75. The Chevaliers were partners, but they were not related.

76. Louis Pascal was baptized at Michilimackinac on 22 July 1730. He died before 22 July 1740. Pascal and his wife had four children baptized at the mission church between 1758 and 1773. "St. Joseph Register," 223; WHC, 8:490, 19:3.

77. Three baptismal and one wedding register are part of this research: "The St. Joseph Baptismal Register," MVHR 8: 202–39; "The Mackinac Register," WHC, 19:1–161; "The Mackinac Register, 1725–1821: Register of Marriages in the Parish of Michilimackinac," WHC, 18:469–513; "Kaskaskia Church Records," *Transactions Illinois State Historical Society*, 395–413.

78. Memorial of Louis Joseph Ainsse, 5 August 1780, MPHC 13: 58–59, 10: 415. The pretense for removal was Governor General Haldimand's order that the traders whose loyalty was questionable be prevented from living among the Indians. Haldimand to DePeyster, 6 May 1799, MPHC 9: 357–58; Keith R. Widder, "Effects of the American Revolution on Fur Trade Society at Michilimackinac," in *The Fur Trade Revisited: Selected Papers of the Sixth North American Fur Trade Conference, Mackinac Island, Michigan, 1991*, ed. Jennifer S. H. Brown, W. J. Eccles, and Donald Heldman (East Lansing MI, 1994), 307.

79. "Indian Council held at Detroit 11th March, with the Pottewatimies from St. Josephs, Terre Coupe, and Coeur de Cerf," MPHC 10: 453–54.

80. The attack from Cahokia was led by Thomas Brady and Jean Baptiste Hamelin. Brady had married Réaume's widowed daughter, Marie Joseph, and Hamelin kin were frequent godparents for St. Joseph children. Descriptions of the attack on and destruction of Fort St. Joseph include Joseph Peyser, ed., *Letters from New France: The Upper Country, 1686–1783* (Chicago, 1992), 219–21; A. P. Nasatir, "The Anglo-Spanish Frontier in the Illinois Country during the American Revolution, 1779–1783," *Illinois State Historical Society Journal* 21 (1928): 291–358; Ralph Ballard, *Old Fort St. Joseph* (Berrien Springs MI, 1973), 46–48; Gérard Malchelosse, "The St. Joseph River," *French Canadian and Acadian Genealogical Review*, nos. 3–4 (1970): 204–6; Rufus Blanchard, *The Discovery*

and Conquest of the Northwest (Chicago, 1880), 165–66; B. A. Hinsdale, *The Old Northwest* (New York, 1888), 173–74; Charles Moore, *Northwest under Three Flags* (New York, 1900), 257–60; John Francis McDermott, *Old Cahokia: A Narrative and Documents Illustrating the First Century of Its History* (St. Louis MO, 1949), 31–32, 200; Clarence W. Alvord, "The Conquest of St. Joseph Michigan, by the Spaniards in 1781," *Michigan History* 14 (1930): 398–414.

81. Thimotée is also called Marie Neskesh by the Jesuits. Thérèse was ten and Magdelaine was six when they were baptized on 1 August 1786, "Mackinac Register," WHC, 19:86.

82. "Census of the Post of St. Joseph," MPHC 10: 406–7.

83. In 1783, Marcot was killed by Indians at the portage between the Fox and Wisconsin Rivers. His widow returned to her native Odawa village to raise her children among her people. Magdelaine was the youngest of seven children. McDowell, "Therese Schindler."

84. Baptisms of Native American women occurred most frequently during the summer months, and multiple baptisms took place in a day.

85. "Marguerite—Magdelaine Marcot (La Framboise)," DCB, 582; Milo M. Quaife, *Lake Michigan* (Indianapolis, 1944), 201–6.

86. WHC, 19:86, 117, 118; 11:164–65.

87. "Mackinac Register," WHC, 19:117–18.

88. Quaife, *Lake Michigan*, 115.

89. "Mackinac Register," WHC, 18:507–8.

90. George Schindler to Solomon Sibley, 9 July, 22 August 1807, and Claude La Framboise to John Kinzie, 11 June 1807, Solomon Sibley Papers, Burton Historical Section, Detroit Public Library; McDowell, "Therese Schindler," 131.

91. Claude La Framboise to John Kinzie, 11 June 1807, Solomon Sibley Papers, Burton Historical Collection, Detroit Public Library.

92. Elizabeth Thérèse Baird, "Reminiscences of Early Days on Mackinac Island," WHC, 14:38–39.

93. Baird, "Reminiscences of Early Days on Mackinac Island," 22; Elizabeth Thérèse Baird, "Reminiscences of Life in Territorial Wisconsin," in WHC, 15:213.

94. "Account Book of Mackinac Merchant," Michigan Manuscripts, c, in Archives Division, State Historical Society of Wisconsin; *Michigan Pioneer and Historical Collections*, 37:143; McDowell, "Therese Schindler," 135–36.

95. Baird, "Reminiscences of Mackinac," WHC, 14:22; Baird, "Reminiscences of Life in Territorial Wisconsin," in WHC, 15:213; "Account Book of a Mackinac Merchant," Michigan Manuscripts, c, in Archives Division, State

Historical Society of Wisconsin; MPHC 27: 143; McDowell, "Therese Schindler," 128, 135–136.

96. Ida Amanda Johnson, *The Michigan Fur Trade* (Grand Rapids MI, 1971), 130–31; DCB, 7:582.

97. Gordon Charles Davidson, *The North West Company* (Berkeley CA, 1918), 72; McDowell, "Madame La Framboise," 278.

98. John Denis Haeger, *John Jacob Astor: Business and Finance in the Early Republic* (Detroit, 1991), 149–52.

99. When increased numbers of mixed-ancestry offspring migrated to larger fur trade communities, such as Michilimackinac, Green Bay, and St. Louis, they increasingly intermarried among themselves. These intermarriages resulted in the emergence of a distinctive métis community. As the number of mixed hereditary offspring continued to increase, these young women of mixed marriages appeared with increasing frequency as the spouses of French fur traders, but these favored marital choices had kin networks rooted in indigenous society. Kinship networks ensured access to peltry and insured viability as a fur trader. Women with extensive kinship networks remained the most desirable marriage partners. It was for this reason that Marie Madeleine, at age forty, was a desirable fur-trade widow.

100. For a description of the St. Louis community, see especially Tanis C. Thorne, *The Many Hands of My Relations* (Columbia MO, 1996).

101. DePeyser to Gen. Haldimand, 15 August 1778, MPHC 9: 368; DePeyser to Sinclair, 12 March 1780, MPHC 9: 581; WHC, 9:93, 95; Mr. Claus to Secretary Foster, 22 May 1815, MPHC: 115.

23. "The Custom of the Country"

An Examination of Fur Trade Marriage Practices

SYLVIA VAN KIRK

Although extensive work has been done on the economic and political aspects of the fur trade in western Canada, historians in the past have neglected the important social side of this far-flung enterprise. From the interaction between two very different cultures—European and Indian—grew an early Western society which was a blend of Indian, British, and French attitudes and traditions. Little appreciated has been the extent to which this society developed its own mores and customs in response to the particular needs of the environment which gave it birth. This paper will attempt to trace the evolution of a fundamental institution in fur trade society—marriage *à la façon du pays*.[1] It was according to this rite that hundreds of fur traders formed unions with Indian and, later, mixed-blood women.

If the concept of marriage *à la façon du pays* is not actually articulated in the early annals of the Hudson's Bay Company, it is because of the official policy formulated by the remote London Committee which prohibited any social contact between its servants and the Indians. Almost as soon as posts were established on the Bay, the men showed a tendency to form relationships with Indian women, but to the Committee this seemed a reprehensible practice which could only result in the debauching of its servants, the wasting of provisions, and illicit trade. The London Committee admonished its governor on the Bay in 1683:

> We are very sensibly [*sic*] that the Indian Women resorting to our
> Factories are very prejudiciall to the Companies affaires . . . It is

therefore our possitive order that you lay your strict Commands on every Chiefe of each Factory upon forfiture of Wages not to Suffer any woman to come within any of our Factories . . .[2]

Although similar remonstrances were to be sent out many times in future, the Committee's regulation remained only loosely or, at best, sporadically enforced. However sensible the official policy may appear in theory, in practice it proved largely unworkable because it failed to make allowances for the realities of fur trade life.

Sex was, of course, a motivating factor in the development of intimate ties between white men and Indian women. No white women were permitted to accompany their men to Hudson Bay, a situation which precluded the possibility of connubial comforts in the conventional European sense.[3] It is apparent, however, that many Englishmen found Indian females not unattractive representatives of their sex. According to James Isham, Cree maidens were most enticing:

. . . very frisky when Young & . . . well shap'd . . . their Eyes Large and Grey yet Lively and Sparkling very Bewitchen . . .[4]

It was certainly within the context of their own moral code for the Indians to sanction liaisons between their women and the Company's men. As Richard White, a witness at the parliamentary enquiry of 1749, put it: "The Indians were a sensible people, and agreed their Women should be made use of . . ."[5] Both the Cree and the Chipewyan practiced the custom, common among primitive people, of offering their wives or daughters to strangers as a token of friendship and hospitality.[6] To an Englishman, it appeared that an Indian took a wife with scant ceremony and a rather shocking disregard for the precepts of chastity and fidelity.[7] However, the Indian was not without his own standards. When found guilty of a clandestine amour, a wife could expect violent punishment or even death, but a husband deemed it perfectly proper to lend his wife to another man for anywhere from a night to several years,

"The Custom of the Country"

after which she was welcomed back together with any children born in the interim.[8]

If the sexual mores of the Indians encouraged the growth of intimate relations, the development of a body of "Home" Indians around each post meant that frequent contact was unavoidable. Traders on the Bay, who soon appreciated the essential role to be played by the women in making moccasins and netting snowshoes, defended the necessity of admitting women to the factories:

> . . . we cannot do without Snowshoes & other Necessarys for our Men who are always abroad & requires a Constant Supply of Shoes for the winter otherwise we can Kill no partridges nor, be able to provide our Selves with fireing.[9]

In spite of the Committee's ruling, the governors or chief factors themselves took the lead in forming unions with Indian women. Such alliances, they realized, helped to cement trade ties. Among the Cree, a daughter was esteemed because, once married, her husband was obliged to contribute to the maintenance of her parent's household.[10] To have a fur trader for a son-in-law would thus be seen to promise unlimited security and prestige. Although the specific identity of most of the Indian women kept by the early HBC factors remains unknown, it appears that they were usually the daughters or wives of leading "Home" Indians. During his governorship of Albany in the 1760s, Humphrey Marten formed a union with Pawpitch, a daughter of the "Captain of the Goose Hunters."[11] Several decades earlier, another factor, Joseph Adams, had had a child by a Cree woman described as being of "ye blood Royal."[12]

Among the Cree, as in most Indian tribes, polygamy was an economic necessity, and a man's prestige was enhanced by the number of wives he could support. Significantly, a number of HBC factors appear to have adopted the practice which, however contrary to European morality, would have found favor in Indian eyes. James Isham, described as the "Idol of the Indians" during his rule at York Factory in the 1740s and '50s, maintained more than one Indian lady.[13] Similarly, Robert Pilgrim kept two Indian women with their children in his apartments at Fort Prince of Wales in the 1740s.[14] One of his successors, Moses Norton, who assumed command of Churchill in 1762, was reputedly a most notorious polygamist. If the very unsavory character-sketch written by his arch-enemy Samuel Hearne is to be believed, Norton kept a selection of five or six of the finest Indian girls to satisfy his passions, being quite ready to poison anyone who dared refuse him their wives or daughters.[15]

By the mid-eighteenth century, it had become an established practice for a Company governor to take an Indian "wife." Andrew Graham, who himself fathered at least two children during his time on the Bay, affirmed that "the Factor keeps a bedfellow within the Fort at all times."[16] The term "wife" is not inappropriate when one considers that from the Indian point of view these unions would have been seen as marriages. Furthermore, the appearance of such phrases as "father-in-law" and "son-in-law" in the post journals indicates that the English themselves were beginning to acknowledge a marital relationship.[17] Children were a strong factor in cementing ties between mother and father, and the resulting domesticity must have done much to alleviate the loneliness of life on the barren shores of Hudson Bay. Humphrey Marten's intense concern for the Indian girl Pawpitch, for example, was revealed when she fell ill of a fever. He must have been watching over when she died for he records her death, an unusual step in itself, as occurring at precisely ten minutes to three on the morning of January 24, 1771. The father worried about the fate of his "poor Child" now motherless. He feared to entrust the little boy to his in-laws, as would have been customary, because Pawpitch's father was now old and already burdened with a large family.[18]

The extent to which the Committee's policy was applied to the lower ranks of the service varied with the capability and inclination of each individual governor, most of whom had exempted themselves from the ruling. The situation at York Factory in the mid-eighteenth century is illustrative. James Isham, one of the Company's most

"The Custom of the Country"

successful governors during the early period, readily permitted his men to have the company of Indian women outside the fort at the goose hunters' tents or on short journeys where they were especially useful. Some women were allowed to reside with servants inside the factory as well since Isham undoubtedly observed that such liaisons had a conciliating effect upon the men. His successor Ferdinand Jacobs, however, roundly denounced such license when he took over in 1761, declaring that "the worst Brothel House in London is Not So Common a Stew as the men's House in this Factory." He refused to admit Indian women to men they regarded as husbands, a move so unpopular that several servants feigned sickness and refused to work.[19] This vacillation in enforcing the rules led to a good deal of resentment on the part of both the men and the Indians.[20]

Although its prohibition regarding Indian women was frequently ignored, the official policy of the Hudson's Bay Company during its first century did work to prevent the widespread development of marriage relationships between its servants and Indian women. As a general rule, only a chief factor was permitted to keep a woman permanently within the factory. "At proper times," a factor might allow an officer to entertain an Indian lady in his apartment provided she did not stay there overnight, but ordinary servants were usually limited to chance encounters and took to sneaking over the walls at night.[21] Even these restrictions were to break down when the Company began to move inland to confront a powerful Canadian rival which actively encouraged the formation of intimate ties with the Indians.

The men of the Montreal-based North West Company, inheritors of the framework and traditions of the French colonial fur trade after the conquest of 1763, readily adopted the attitudes of their predecessors with regard to Indian women. The coureur de bois had realized that his adaptation to and understanding of Indian society on which his success depended could be greatly facilitated by an Indian mate. Besides helping to secure trade ties and familiarizing the trader with the customs and language of her tribe, the Indian woman performed a myriad of domestic tasks essential to wilderness survival.

The North West Company, therefore, gave its sanction to unions between its employees and Indian women, and it was among the Nor'Westers that marriage *à la façon du pays* first developed into a recognized and widespread custom. All ranks, bourgeois, clerk, and engagé, were allowed to take a woman, and the Company accepted the responsibility for the maintenance of Indian wives and families.[22] It irked more than one HBC officer to observe the high style in which his Canadian counterpart traveled. The bourgeois always had "his girl" who was carried in and out of his canoe and shared the luxury of his tent and feather bed; furthermore, if a clerk "chuses to keep a girl which most of them does the Master finds her in Apparel so that they need not spend one farthing of their Wages."[23] The only restriction placed on an engagé taking an Indian wife was that he had to obtain the consent of his bourgeois to his proposed match.[24]

It is important to emphasize the extent to which "the custom of the country" derived from Indian marriage rites. The active involvement of the Indians in securing unions between their women and the Nor'Westers is much in evidence. According to one observer, many among the Cree kept one or more of their daughters specifically to offer as wives "for the white People."[25] Simple as the Indian notions of matrimony appeared to the Nor'Westers,[26] a trader could not take a wife without giving credence to the customs of her people. Of fundamental importance was the consent of the girl's parents. In the words of an old voyageur:

> On ne se joue pas d'une femme sauvage comme on veut. . . . Il y aurait du danger d'avoir la tête cassée, si l'on prend la fille dans ce pays, sans le consentement des parents. C'est le père et la mère qui donnent les femmes, et s'ils sont morts, ce sont les plus proches parents.[27]

To obtain the consent of the parents, the Nor'Wester was required to make a suitable present. This bride price could vary considerably, but it usually took more than a few trifles to gain the hand of an Indian maiden. At Fort Alexandria in 1801, Payet, one of Daniel Harmon's interpreters, gave the parents of his Cree bride rum and dry goods to the value of two hundred dollars.[28] According to the younger Henry, the common medium of exchange was a horse for a wife.[29] On the Pacific coast, the marriages of several Nor'Westers to the daughters of the powerful Chinook chief Concomely involved more elaborate ceremony with a mutual exchange of gifts. In July 1813, for instance, a rich dowry of pelts accompanied the bride of proprietor Duncan McDougall, but it took McDougall until the following April to discharge his part of the bargain:

> Mr. D. McDougall this afternoon completed the payment for his wife ... he gave 5 new guns, and 5 blankets, 2 ½ feet wide, which makes 15 guns and 15 blankets, besides a great deal of other property, as the total cost of this precious lady.[30]

Before being consigned to her new husband, it became common for an Indian woman to go through a "ritual," performed by the other women of the fort, designed to render her more acceptable to a white man. She was scoured of grease and paint and exchanged her leather garments for those of a more civilized style. At the Nor'Wester posts, wives were clothed, usually at the expense of the Company, in "Canadian fashion" which consisted of a shirt, short gown, petticoat, and leggings.[31] The trader then conducted his bride to his quarters and, without further ado, the couple was considered man and wife. The women assumed their husbands' last names, and the engagés respectfully addressed the wives of the bourgeois as "Madame."[32]

Initially marriage à la façon du pays, in accordance with Indian custom, was not viewed as a binding contract.[33] Should the relationship prove unhappy, both parties were free to separate and seek a more congenial union. Even a moralist such as Daniel Harmon, as he became more familiar with the ways of the fur trade, conceded that this attitude had merit:

> for I cannot conceive it to be right for a Man & Woman to cohabit when they cannot agree, but to live in discontent, if not downright hatered [*sic*] to each other, as many do.[34]

In contrast to Indian practice, however, the Nor'Westers appear to have taken a definite stand against polygamy both for moral and economic reasons. The Indian was understandably slow to comprehend white man's morality since in his view "all great men should have a plurality of wives." Such was the argument used by Alexander Henry the younger's father-in-law, himself the husband of three sisters, when he pressed the trader to take his second daughter.[35] The reluctance evinced by Henry in taking his first Indian wife and his adamant refusal of a second typifies the attitude of many bourgeois, and polygamy was never part of "the custom of the country" as practiced by the Nor'Westers.[36] While HBC officers, in their isolation on the Bay, appear to have been susceptible to polygamy, the economic implications of such a practice when moving into the interior served to reaffirm the desirability of monogamy. By 1780, according to Philip Turnor, English officers stationed inland from York Factory found themselves besieged with offers of wives:

> the Masters of most of your Honors Inland settlements . . . would Labour under many difficulties was they not to keep a Woman as above half the Indians that came to the House would offer the master their Wife the refusal of which would give great offense to both the man and his Wife; though he was to make the Indian a present for his offer the Woman would think her self slighted and if the Master was to accept the offer he would be expected to Cloath her and by keeping a Woman it makes one short ready answer (that he has a Woman of his own and she would be offended) and very few Indians make that offer when they know the Master keeps a Woman. . . .[37]

"The Custom of the Country"

Thus marriage *à la façon du pays* was essentially an adaptation and not an adoption of Indian marriage rites. In particular, the Indian attitude that marriage did not constitute a union for life was corrupted to suit the needs of the transient fur trader. The men of both companies never intended to remain permanently in the Indian Country, but the growth of family ties during their sojourn placed many traders in an agonizing dilemma when it came time to retire. After the unhappy experience of one of its officers, the Hudson's Bay Company actively discouraged any attempt on the part of its servants to remove their families from Rupert's Land. In 1750 Robert Pilgrim had taken his Indian wife Thu a Higon and their infant son to England. Unfortunately, Pilgrim died within a few months of his arrival, having stipulated in his will that, while the child was to remain in England with his brother, Thu a Higon was to be properly looked after until she could be sent back to Churchill.[38] An irritated London Committee, fearing that dependents brought to Britain might easily become a burden on the Company, sent Thu a Higon back to Hudson Bay accompanied by a strict order forbidding all ship's captains to allow any Native man, woman, or child to be brought to Great Britain without its express written consent.[39]

Whether Thu a Higon could have overcome the almost insuperable problems of adjustment she would have had to face in England is doubtful. This consideration helps to explain the action of most early bourgeois. Many of the Nor'Westers were men of education who, having won sizeable fortunes, intended to retire to enjoy the fruits of civilization in eastern Canada or Britain. An Indian family had little place in such a design; the wife especially would have to cope with an alien way of life where too often she might meet with "impertinent insult" and "unmerited obloquy."[40] While many of the early wintering partners sent their children east to be educated, most forsook the Indian mothers of these children and felt at liberty to marry white women upon retirement.[41]

Yet until the founding of the Red River settlement in the early

1800s, even the most devoted father could not have remained in Rupert's Land with his family after his contract had expired.[42] It distressed more than one HBC officer to witness the suffering caused by the breakup of families owing to "the want of an Asylum in this part of the Country to which a Parent might retire with a prospect of supporting his Family and which would prevent the Miseries of a Separation and check the Increase of a Burden on the Factories."[43] Before the creation of the colony, it had of necessity become customary to leave one's Indian family behind. Although the unions between HBC men and Indian women had shown an increasing tendency to last for the duration of the husband's stay on the Bay, the usual and accepted course had always been for an Indian wife and her offspring to return to her own relations in the event of his death or departure. An Indian husband, whether old or new, readily adopted "the Englishman's children," an act which reflected the strong kinship ties and great love of children characteristic of Indian society.[44]

While the London Committee had tacitly had to accept that it could do little to prevent its men from having Native families, it refused to assume any official responsibility for their maintenance. This accounts for the fact that the Indian families of HBC men were absorbed back into the "Home Guard" bands, but it was also a spur to conscientious fathers to make some provision for their families. Many of the officers' and servants' wills which have survived from the late eighteenth and early nineteenth centuries clearly reveal the growth of definite family ties and a marked concern for the welfare of Native dependents. The action of John Favell, an early inland officer in the Albany district, is typical. Upon his death in 1784, Favell left an annuity for his Indian wife Tittimeg and their four children, earnestly requesting "the Honorable Company" to implement this part of his will so that his family would receive an annual supply of goods from the Company's warehouse.[45]

Similarly, an Indian woman who had formed a union with a Nor'Wester could expect to be taken back into her tribe. According

"The Custom of the Country"

to the elder Henry, Cree women who had been kept by the men received a ready welcome along with their progeny:

> One of the chiefs assured me, that the children borne by their women to Europeans were bolder warriors, and better hunters, than themselves. . . . The women, so selected, consider themselves as honoured.[46]

However, there was less impetus for a family of a Nor'Wester to return to live with the Indians. The Company itself accepted the responsibility for at least feeding the families of its servants who had died or left the country, and some traders did provide their wives with a small annuity to purchase cloth and other goods from the company stores.[47] Furthermore, the Nor'Westers were not insensible to the problems which could arise from divorcing an Indian wife and her children from the life of a fur trade post to which they were accustomed. A concomitant of marriage *à la façon du pays*, therefore, was the growth of another custom, known as "turning off," whereby a trader leaving the country endeavored to place his spouse under the protection of another. Ross Cox declared that many a voyageur for "a handsome sum" would be happy to take over "*la Dame d'un Bourgeois.*"[48] On his wedding day in 1806, Daniel Harmon was obviously expressing a contemporary attitude when he confided to his journal that he intended to keep his wife

> as long as I remain in this uncivilized part of the world, but when I return to my native land shall endeavour to place her into the hands of some good honest Man, with whom she can pass the remainder of her days in this Country much more agreeably, than it would be possible for her to do, were she to be taken down into the civilized world, where she would be a stranger to the People, their manners, customs, & Language.[49]

Although Harmon, like others, may be accused of wanting to enjoy the best of both worlds, there was a good deal of truth in the generally held view that this was the kinder course of action.

Since the late eighteenth century, the men of both companies had, in fact, been espousing the daughters of their predecessors, an action which emphasizes the extent to which miscegenation had taken place. Owing to the restriction of marital unions in the Hudson's Bay Company, most of the marriageable mixed-blood girls were initially daughters of former officers.[50] Of Matthew Cocking's daughters, for example, the eldest, Ke-the-cow-e-com-e-coof, became the country wife of Thomas Staynor, governor at Churchill in the 1790s, while another, Agathas, married William Hemmings Cook who took charge of York Factory in the early 1800s.[51] As the British moved inland, the pattern of intermarriage spread among the servants. Although Neskisho, the wife of Orkney servant James Spence, is referred to as "Indian" like many other daughters of HBC men, she was actually a daughter of the early inlander Isaac Batt.[52]

The daughters of the French-Canadian engagés, on the other hand, constituted the largest group of eligible females for the Nor'Westers. Many of the bourgeois wed the daughters of voyageurs or freemen in unions which cut across both class and racial lines. Ross Cox tells the story of one doughty old voyageur, Louis La Liberté, who felt he could address himself with familiarity to one of the Company's proprietors because he was father-in-law to three wintering partners.[53] Like Indian girls, the daughters of the men of both companies were given in marriage when very young. To cite a famous instance, Daniel Harmon took his metis bride Elizabeth Duval when she was only fourteen years old.[54]

By the early 1800s, the replacement of the Indian wife by one of mixed-blood had become a widespread phenomenon in fur trade society. As the mixed-blood population grew, it naturally evolved that wives should be drawn increasingly from its ranks. In the first place, a fur trader's daughter possessed the ideal qualifications to become a fur trader's wife. A very child of the fur trade, she knew no other way of life. From her Indian mother, the mixed-blood girl learned those Native skills so valuable to the trade such as making moccasins, netting snowshoes, and preparing pemmican. Her familiarity with Indian language and customs enabled her to act as an interpreter,[55] and on more than one occasion, her timely intervention reputedly saved the life of a white husband.[56] The mixed-blood wife was thus in a position to adequately perform the functions which had made the Indian woman such a useful helpmate but, unlike the Indian woman, there was little danger of her becoming a source of friction between Indian and white. In fact, by the turn of the century, partly because of the violence and drunkenness occasioned by the trade war, Indian-white relations had seriously deteriorated. In well-established areas, marriage alliances were no longer so important, and many Indians deeply resented the flagrant way in which the Nor'Westers in particular now abused their women.[57]

Secondly, the white man generally evinced a decided personal preference for a mixed-blood wife whose lighter skin and sharper features more closely approximated his concept of beauty. Many, according to Alexander Ross, were captivating with "their delicacy of form," "their nimble movements," and "the penetrating expression of their bright black eyes." The officers especially considered the greater potential of a mixed-blood girl for adapting to "civilized ways" as increasingly desirable. "With their natural acuteness and singular talent for imitation," Rose declared, they could acquire considerable grace and polish.[58]

Furthermore, the fur traders had a collective responsibility for the fate of their daughters. They were not Indian; even those raised among the "Home Guard" were taught that their paternity gave them a definite superiority.[59] But they were not white; fathers were actively discouraged from sending their daughters to the civilized world to be educated.[60] Being women, however, the only way in which mixed-blood girls could remain an integral part of fur trade society was through marriage, either to new men coming in or at least to fur traders' sons. This consideration can be seen in the ruling introduced by the North West Company in 1806 which prohibited men of all ranks from taking any more pure-blooded Indian women as wives. Although primarily instigated to reduce the enormous cost of maintaining the growing families of its servants, the resolution can also be seen as encouraging Nor'Westers to marry "the Daughter of a white man" in an effort to ensure them husbands.[61]

Significantly, as mixed-blood wives became the rule, the "custom of the country" increasingly evolved towards white concepts of marriage. There is much evidence to suggest that the men of both companies came to view a union contracted *à la façon du pays* as a union for life. A respected HBC officer, J. E. Harriott, explained that "the custom of the country" involved a solemn agreement between the father of the girl and the man who was taking her to wife. When Harriott espoused Elizabeth, a daughter of Chief Trader J. P. Pruden, he "made a solemn promise to her father to live with her and treat her as my wife as long as we both lived. I kept this promise until her death." He further declared that he considered his union as binding as if celebrated by an archbishop:

> It was not customary for an European to take one wife and discard her, and then take another. The marriage according to the custom [of the country] was considered a marriage for life . . . I know of hundreds of people living and dying with the woman they took in that way without any other formalities.[62]

Although it was more difficult for the lower ranks to maintain permanent unions, the engagés, in general, recognized the permanency of the marriage bond. According to one old voyageur, Pierre Marois, whose marriage *à la façon du pays* lasted over twenty years, "nous regardons cette union comme union de mari et femme . . . et union aussi sacrée."[63]

Within fur trade society, "the custom of the country" was undoubtedly regarded as a bona fide marriage rite. As one clerk declared, "I never knew or heard of a man and woman living together in the North-West without being married."[64] Although the actual ceremony remained simple, the union was accorded public recognition through festivities similar to those found at European weddings. It became customary to celebrate a fur trade marriage with a dram to all hands and a dance which might see the fun-loving engagés jigging till morning.[65] When the young clerk Robert Miles took Betsey Sinclair as "a Femme du Pays" at York Factory in the fall of 1822, a friend recorded, "we had a Dance & supper on the occasion, when no one but the happy Swain was allowed to go sober to bed."[66] Whereas initially a trader had been required to make a substantial present to his Indian in-laws for his bride, it was now not unusual for a fur trader to provide his own daughter with a handsome dowry.[67]

Numerous examples of the development of lasting and devoted relationships between white men and their mixed-blood wives could be cited. HBC officer George Gladman, for instance, emphasized that he considered Mary Moore to be his "lawful wife."[68] Like many of his contemporaries, he made generous provision for her in his will, specifically entreating his sons to see that their mother was well cared for in her old age.[69] Significantly, growing numbers, especially among the Nor'Westers, now took their wives and families with them when they retired to the East. A most famous example is that of Daniel Harmon who took his wife back to his home in New England in 1819. Although the deeply religious Harmon could never deny the sanctity of a church marriage, he, like others before him, had come to realize that something much deeper than mere ceremony bound him to his wife:

> Having lived with this woman as my wife, though we were never formally contracted to each other, during life, and having children by her, I consider that I am under a moral obligation not to dissolve the connexion, if she is willing to continue it. The union which has been formed between us, in the providence of God, has . . . been cemented by a long and mutual performance of kind offices. . . . How could I spend my days in the civilized world, and leave my beloved children in the wilderness? The thought has in it the bitterness of

death. How could I tear them from a mother's love, and leave her to mourn over their absence, to the day of her death?. . . . On the whole, I consider the course which I design to pursue, as the only one which religion and humanity would justify.[70]

Once outside fur trade society, though some maintained it was unnecessary,[71] most submitted to a church ceremony if only to conform to "civilized" convention. Such action was seen, however, as merely "un bénédiction" and not an admission that no marriage had existed before. J. E. Harriott maintained that he would have gone through "the civilized form of solemnizing marriage . . . to please people and to conform to the custom of society. I would not consider myself more strongly bound to that woman than before."[72]

Within fur trade society, however, one was expected to conform to its own social norm with regard to marriage, that of "the custom of the country." While no laws existed to enforce morality in the Indian Country, it is evident that the society itself exerted considerable pressure on a newcomer to adopt a code of behavior which had gained its own legitimacy through long usage. One can observe this social conditioning working on Nor'Westers such as Daniel Harmon, Alexander Henry the younger, and George Nelson. Arriving fresh from a society which recognized only the legitimacy of church marriage, these young men were initially shocked by "the custom of the country" which seemed only a form of concubinage. They therefore began by refusing all the offers of wives made to them, but eventually an increased understanding of the ways of the fur trade, coupled with the loneliness and the attractiveness of the girls themselves, led them to follow in the footsteps of their predecessors and take a wife *à la façon du pays*.[73] As James Douglas very perceptively observed, only through such adaptation could one become reconciled to fur trade life:

There is indeed no living with comfort in this country until a person has forgot the great world and has his tastes and character formed on the current standard of the stage. . . . To any other being . . .

the vapid monotony of an inland trading post would be perfectly unsufferable, while habit makes it familiar to us, softened as it is by the many tender ties, which find a way to the heart.[74]

Even though the desirability of a lasting union had become widely acknowledged, the security of a Native wife ultimately depended upon individual conscience. Because "the custom of the country" had evolved from two very different sets of attitudes towards marriage, it was inevitable that irregularities should persist. "Turning off" remained a problem, it being not uncommon for a mixed-blood woman to have two or three husbands in her lifetime.[75] After the amalgamation of the two companies in 1821, the Hudson's Bay Company took definite steps to regulate country marriages by introducing marriage contracts which were signed by both parties in the presence of witnesses. In 1824 the Council of the Northern Department further resolved:

> That no Officer or Servant in the company's service be hereafter allowed to take a woman without binding himself down to such reasonable provision for the maintenance of the woman and children as on a fair and equitable principle may be considered necessary not only during their residence in the country but after their departure hence. . . .[76]

Since marriage *à la façon du pays* contained all the elements of "civilized" marriage except the blessing of the church, it might be supposed that the arrival of missionaries in Rupert's Land would have been welcomed. In fact, the intolerant and unsympathetic attitude of particularly the Protestant missionaries toward "the custom of the country" provoked a good deal of hostility. The Reverend John West, the first Anglican chaplain of the Hudson's Bay Company who arrived at Red River in 1820, refused to acknowledge that marital relationships already existed. In his view, all couples were merely "living in sin" and too often a man might "turn off" his woman after having enjoyed the morning of her days.[77] While abuses undeniably existed, West in seizing upon the exception rather than the rule encountered much resentment. To many an old trader, the pronouncement of a clergyman could add no more legality or sanctity to a country union which had existed for decades. Although West, who firmly believed that "the institution of marriage and the security of property were the fundamental laws of society," performed a total of sixty-five marriages before his departure in 1823, it is clear that he had had to force his view in many cases.[78] Resistance seems to have come from some of the most prominent settlers in Red River such as James Bird and Thomas Thomas, retired HBC chief factors, who continued to live with their Indian wives *à la façon du pays*. West, being especially concerned that such men set an example to the rest of the community, was much gratified when both couples agreed to take the vows of the Church of England on March 30, 1821.[79]

West's successors, David Jones and William Cockran, continued to rail against the immoral habits of the fur traders. Jones's dogmatic stance was hardly conciliating. It had been West's custom to baptize traders' wives immediately before the marriage ceremony, but Jones was adamant that it would be a sacrilege to pronounce "our excellent Liturgy" over persons entirely ignorant of its meaning. When several traders maintained that there would be little point in having a church marriage since their wives would still be regarded as "heathens" unless baptized, Jones declared they were merely looking for an excuse to continue "living in sin."[80]

By the end of the 1820s, however, Cockran, the assistant chaplain, was optimistic about the changing attitude in Red River:

> It is encouraging to view the growing attention of the people to divine ordinance. Many that could not be prevailed upon formerly to marry their women have now seen the sin of despising the ordinance, and have felt truly sorry for the contempt and neglect of it.[81]

Equally gratifying to the missionaries was the spread of the church rite along the route between the colony and York Factory. On his way out to England in 1828, Jones was rejoiced "to unite two officers of high standing to their partners" at Oxford House. These proved to be Chief Factor Colin Robertson and his half-breed wife Theresa Chalifoux, and Clerk James Robertson and Margaret, a daughter of Chief Factor Alexander Stewart and his half-breed wife Susan Spence.[82]

In the post-1821 period, the Red River colony became the hub of fur trade society since increasing numbers retired there with their families, and schools were established for the children of the men in the field. Thus, the doctrines of the missionaries gained widespread acceptance. In 1835 Parson Jones jubilantly observed that it had become customary for traders passing through Red River to seek religious sanction for their unions: "This laudable practice is now becoming General, in fact the revolution in these respects during the past 10 years had been immense."[83]

Indeed, the mid-1830s mark a definite change in attitude toward "the custom of the country" in the environs of the settlement. Chief Trader Archibald McDonald emphasized that the acceptance of the church rite was now the only proper course for an honorable gentleman:

> All my colleagues are now about following the example, & it is my full conviction few of them can do no better—the great mistake is in flattering themselves with a different notion too long—nothing is gained by procrastination, but much is lost by it.[84]

After attending the annual meeting of Council, McDonald himself had had his union with his half-breed wife Jane Klyne blessed by the church in a well-attended ceremony at the parsonage in Red River on June 9, 1835. Yet he could not resist pointing out the humor in the solemn pronouncements of the clergy as he and his beloved Jane had lived in a most exemplary fashion since he had wed her *à la façon du pays* ten years before:

> [we] were joined in Holy wedlock & of course declared at full liberty to live together as man & wife & to increase & multiply as to

them might seem fit—and I hope the validity of *this* ceremony is not to be questioned though it has not the further advantage of a Newspaper Confirmation.[85]

Even old die-hards eventually gave in. Although William Hemmings Cook had retired to Red River with his wife Mary [Agathas] and family in 1815, it took till 1838 before he could be persuaded to tie the solemn knot. As one of the guests at his wedding feast sarcastically observed, old Cook had "stood manfully forth . . . bringing his 35 years courtship to an early close."[86]

Just at the time when Red River was becoming firmly reconciled to the European form of marriage, a bitter feud over this issue erupted at Fort Vancouver, the headquarters of the Columbia district. The desirability of a mission to the Columbia had been suggested as early as 1824, but Governor Simpson, in enumerating the qualities of such a missionary should possess, issued a prophetic warning:

> . . . he ought to understand in the outset that nearly all the Gentlemen & Servants have Families altho' Marriage ceremonies are unknown in the Country and that it would be all in vain to attempt breaking through this uncivilized custom.[87]

Simpson appears to have forgotten his own advice, however, when selecting the Company's first Pacific Coast chaplain because, in spite of his name, the Reverend Herbert Beaver could not have been a more unfortunate choice. According to Beaver, Fort Vancouver, upon his arrival in the fall of 1836 with his English wife Jane, presented a "deplorable scene of vice and ignorance."[88] He refused to give any credence to "the custom of the country," styling the traders' wives as concubines and chastising the men for indulging in fornication.[89] This most insulting and inappropriate assessment of the well-regulated domestic situation at the fort provoked much hostility.

No one resented Beaver's slanders on his wife's character more than the fiery-tempered ruler of Fort Vancouver, Chief Factor John

McLoughlin. Around 1811, while a young Nor'Wester in the Rainy Lake area, McLoughlin had wed Margeurite Wadin McKay *à la façon du pays*. Four children were born to the couple, and when McLoughlin assumed charge of the Columbia district in 1824, Margeurite and the youngest children made the long journey overland with him.[90] McLoughlin treated his wife with respect and devotion, and the remarks of contemporaries indicate that she played her role as first lady of Fort Vancouver well. According to Chief Trader James Douglas, Madame McLoughlin was respected by all for "her numerous charities and many excellent qualities of heart."[91] Narcissa Whitman, the wife of one of the first American missionaries to reach the post, is unlikely to have been guilty of bias in describing Margeurite as "one of the kindest women in the world."[92]

But to Beaver, good Mrs. McLoughlin was only a "kept Mistress" who could not be allowed to associate with respectable married females such as Mrs. Beaver.[93] He demanded that McLoughlin set an example by entering into a legal union with Margeurite. This, McLoughlin, who had Catholic predilections, absolutely refused to do. However, in order to silence once and for all any charge of illegality against his union, he had James Douglas, acting in his capacity of Justice of the Peace, perform a civil ceremony.[94] When Beaver and his wife, therefore, continued to heap invective upon Mrs. McLoughlin, her husband's anger reached such a pitch that on one occasion he could not refrain from giving the parson a sound drubbing with his own cane.[95]

Beaver also encountered stiff opposition when he attempted to prevent the "country marriage" of the clerk A. C. Anderson to a daughter of Chief Trader James Birnie. Anderson, at this time stationed in New Caledonia, had commissioned Chief Factor Peter Skene Ogden to conduct the girl north with the annual brigade. Beaver refused to baptize the girl prior to her departure and wrote a scathing letter to Anderson denouncing the contemplated union as "immoral and disgraceful"; he threatened to deny Anderson the church's blessing forever if he persisted in willfully denying God's ordinance.[96] Ogden paid no heed to Beaver's rantings, declared that he would have the girl baptized by the American missionaries en route or do it himself and, as a Justice of the Peace, ultimately presided over Anderson's marriage.[97] Anderson himself wrote a spirited letter to Beaver giving a sophisticated defense of his action. In the first place, he claimed, legal authorities acknowledged that marriage was essentially a civil contract, the religious ceremony being merely a social convention. Scottish law, he pointed out, did not require church rites for marriages to be considered legal.[98] Furthermore, laudable as Beaver's presence at Fort Vancouver might be, he was of little use to Anderson hundreds of miles away. Even Church authorities had previously recognized that

> marriages contracted in these wild and secluded regions in positions where the intervention of a person duly ordained may not be immediately available are valid and irreproachable.[99]

While few officers actually denied the desirability of a church marriage when a clergyman was present, Beaver's insufferable attitude alienated even the most devout. Such was the case of James Douglas who had wed Amelia, a daughter of Chief Factor William Connolly and his Cree wife, according to "the custom of the country" at Fort St. James in 1828. Douglas was anxious to have his marriage recognized by the church, however, and on February 28, 1837, Beaver performed the Church of England rite for the first, and almost last, time.[100] Even though she was now regularly married, Beaver still regarded the kind and gracious Mrs. Douglas as "little calculated to improve the manners of society."[101] Douglas, who was extremely sensitive to such unjust slanders, stoutly defended the honor of the ladies of the country when he assumed temporary command of Fort Vancouver in 1838. To Beaver's accusation that the Factor's house was "a common receptacle for every mistress of an office in the service, who may take a fancy to visit the Fort," Douglas retorted that only the *wives* of officers visited the fort when their husbands were on brigade business:

"The Custom of the Country"

> I neither have nor would suffer any person, of whatever rank, to
> introduce loose women into this Fort, an attempt which, to the
> honor of every gentlemen here, was never made.[102]

Beaver and his wife created such friction that all were gratified
when he was relieved of his post and the haughty pair departed in
the fall of 1838.

The dismal failure of Beaver was in sharp contrast to the suc-
cess of the Pacific Mission established by the Catholic missionaries
F. N. Blanchet and Modeste Demers who traveled overland to the
Columbia in 1838. Although the majority of the populace at Fort
Vancouver were Catholic, the priests' conciliatory attitude toward
"the custom of the country" also contributed to their welcome.
The Protestant missionaries in Red River had denounced their
Catholic counterparts for refusing to marry persons of different
religious persuasions "as though it were better for them to live in
fornication, than that they should violate the rigid statutes of the
Papal see."[103] Blanchet and Demers, however, had received special
dispensation, and the records show that a considerable number of
the marriages they performed in their progress across the country were between Protestant and Catholic. Although the Catholic
Church did not recognize the sanctity of a "country marriage," the
priests did acknowledge the existence of a marital bond by considering that every cohabiting couple was living in a state of "natural
marriage." The only children stigmatized with illegitimacy were
those whose parents could not be identified. Furthermore, the
general tenor of the Catholic rite was that the parties were "renewing and ratifying their mutual consent of marriage" and formally
recognizing the legitimacy of their children.[104] On November 19,
1842, to the priests' undoubted satisfaction, McLoughlin, who had
just turned Catholic, had his union with Margeurite "his legitimate
wife," blessed by the church:

> ... wishing to renew their consent of marriage in order to discharge
> the grave bonds on receiving the sacrament of marriage, we priests

. . . have received the renewal of their consent of marriage and have given them the nuptial benediction . . . [105]

The coming of the missionaries to Rupert's Land with their insistence on the prerogative of the church in the sphere of marriage made it inevitable that "the custom of the country" would become a thing of the past. Even the "civil" contracts enacted by the Hudson's Bay Company contained the proviso that the marriage would receive the sanction of the church at the first possible opportunity.[106] The slow spread of missionary activity to more remote areas, however, meant that for many this opportunity never actually arose. As a result, official civil powers were granted to the chief officers of the Company; in 1845 the Council of the Northern Department resolved that, in the absence of a clergyman, chief factors only could solemnize marriages, but no person could take a wife at any establishment without the sanction of the gentleman in charge of the district.[107]

If the missionaries introduced "civilized" conventions into Rupert's Land, it was not without painful repercussions for fur trade society. "The custom of the country" had been regarded as a bona fide marriage rite, entailing all the obligations toward wife and children that marriage implies. Around the time of the union of the two companies, however, a significant change in the behavior of newly arrived men toward Native women can be observed. The stand of the church, it can be argued, worked to block the traditional conditioning process by which a newcomer had adapted to fur trade custom. The Native woman was now often reduced to the status of mistress or even prostitute—someone with whom to gratify one's passions but never actually marry.

Unfortunately, the classic practitioner of this new attitude was the governor himself, George Simpson, a man who had only wintered one year in Rupert's Land before assuming control of the Northern Department. Simpson showed little sympathy for the marital concerns of his associates partly because he did not recognize "the custom of the country." His lack of understanding is shown in his initial liaison with Betsey Sinclair, a daughter of the late Chief Factor William Sinclair and his Native wife Nahovway. While Betsey was acknowledged as "Mrs. Simpson" by his contemporaries, the Governor treated her as a casual mistress and felt little compunction in getting rid of her when he tired of her charms.[108] Simpson, in fact, gained a notorious reputation for his womanizing,[109] and his behavior is not typical of officers who had had long experience in the fur trade.

He further shattered the norms of fur trade society by bringing a British wife out to Red River in 1830, even before he had severed his connection with Margaret Taylor whom all had come to regard as his "country wife."[110] Although none dared openly criticize the governor for this action, widespread shock was expressed when a former Nor'Wester John George McTavish followed suit and renounced Nancy McKenzie, his "country wife" of long standing. His unfeeling violation of fur trade custom provoked one old comrade, John Stuart, to declare their friendship at an end:

> . . . what could be your aim in discarding her whom you clasped to your bosom in virgin purity and had for 17 Years with you, She was the Wife of your choice and has born you seven Children, now Stigmatized with ognominy . . . if with a view to domestick happiness you have thus acted, I fear the Aim has been Missed and that remorse will be your portion for life. . . .[111]

That white women might become the wives of fur traders had been a possibility ever since the founding of the Red River settlement. But, because her numbers were so few, the white woman tended to be put on a pedestal, to be regarded as a "lovely tender exotic."[112] The presence of white women helped to reinforce the attitudes and customs of the society their men had previously left behind, which made Native women appear less desirable as marriage partners. As the clerk James Hargrave observed in 1830, "this influx of white faces has cast a still deeper shade over the faces of our Brunettes in the eyes of many."[113] Hargrave himself, however, was not immune to "the fascinations of dark-eyed beauty,"[114] but studiously avoided any permanent attachment, ultimately bringing a Scottish bride Letitia Mactavish out to York Factory in 1840.

Significantly, the church gave support to this trend. William Cockran, who actively discouraged young officers from marrying mixed-blood girls, upheld Chief Factor Duncan Finlayson as worthy of emulation since he, though almost alone, had managed to evade "the snare which has ruined many of our countrymen."[115] So great was the Rev. Beaver's concern to prevent his wife from being tainted by association with "loose females" that he actually proposed that all who had not been married by a clergyman should be barred from Fort Vancouver. They might, however, be maintained outside the walls where the men could visit them on the sly to at least conform with the "outward decorum" which men in civilized societies observed in relation to their mistresses.[116] Such a plan which would have completely subverted the existing state of morality provoked an angry rebuttal from Chief Trader Douglas. A *wife* according to "the custom of the country" bore no resemblance to a prostitute in European society:

> The woman who is not sensible of violating [any] law, who lives chastely with her husband of her choice, in a state approved by friends and sanctioned by immemorial custom, which she believes strictly honorable, forms a perfect contrast to the degraded creature who has sacrificed the great principle which from infancy she is taught to revere as the ground work of female virtue; who lives a disgrace to friends and an outcast from society.[117]

Native women were particularly victimized by the introduction of the Victorian double standard. While men might indulge their pleasure without obligation, women were now expected to abide by rigid European standards of propriety. It was grossly unfair to blame Native women for perpetuating immorality, even though they were influenced by Indian sexual mores which were much more lenient compared to those of white society.[118] Beaver, for example, proposed to punish the women directly for the sinful state of affairs at Fort Vancouver by denying them rations and medical attention to bring them to a sense of their shame.[119] A major concern of the boarding school established in Red River in the 1820s for the daughters of officers was to estrange them from their Indian heritage and inculcate proper notions of feminine virtue, particularly chastity.[120] After the stern disciplinarian John MacCallum took over the school, the children were even forbidden any contact with their mothers if they had not had a church marriage. One tragic victim of this situation was the poor Indian wife of a trader Kenneth McKenzie who had gone off to join the American Fur Company. She never saw her two daughters who had been placed in the school, except when they, at risk of severe punishment, would sneak out to visit their mother. Wives who could claim "benefit of clergy" were taught to look upon those who could not as most debased creatures. But Letitia Hargrave, though not always charitable in her remarks about Native women, protested against such hypocrisy:

> This may be all very right, but it is fearfully cruel for the poor unfortunate mothers who did not know that there was any distinction & it is only within the last few years that anyone was so married. Of course had all the fathers refused, every one woman in the country wd have been no better than those that are represented to their own children as discreditable.[121]

Although "the custom of the country" had fallen into disrepute in fur trade society by the mid-nineteenth century, the purpose of this paper has been to show that it was in itself an honorable and recognized marriage rite. In spite of increasing pressure to conform to the norms of white society, there were a few notable traders who insisted upon living with their wives *à la façon du pays* as they had always done.

The romantic story of how the young Nor'Wester John Rowand

was rescued after a serious fall from his horse by the Native girl who became his wife has become legend.[122] Rowand took Lisette Umphreville for his country wife sometime around 1811, and their relationship through the years as Rowand rose to become the most prominent officer on the Saskatchewan appears to have been a devoted one. Significantly, while the Catholic priests baptized four of his daughters and solemnized the marriage of one on their visit to Fort Edmonton in 1838,[123] Rowand did not feel that his "natural marriage" needed further benediction. Perhaps there is no greater testimony to the bond that existed between them than Rowand's simple lament when he learned that Lisette had died while he was returning to Fort Edmonton with the brigades in the summer of 1849: "my old friend the Mother of all my children was no more."[124] According to tradition, Chief Factor Peter Skene Ogden continually refused the church's sanction for his union with his remarkable Indian wife, known as "Princess Julia." "If many years of public recognition of the relation and of his children did not constitute sufficient proof," he declared, "no formal words of priest or magistrate could help the matter."[125]

This argument was to be used to uphold the validity of marriage *à la façon du pays* in the famous Connolly case of the late 1860s in which the judges of Lower Canada displayed a degree of tolerance and humanity in sharp contrast to the pious denunciations of the clergy.[126] In 1803 William Connolly, a newly appointed clerk in the North West Company, had contracted an alliance with Suzanne Pas-de-Nom, the fifteen-year-old daughter of a Cree chief, partly to secure his influence with this band in the Athabasca country. For the next twenty-eight years, the couple had lived together as man and wife and at least six children were born to them. According to one HBC officer:

> I often saw Suzanne at his house at different posts and he intro-
> duced her to me as Mrs. Connolly. She passed and was universally
> acknowledged as his wife at the different posts where I met her . . .

"The Custom of the Country"

her children by William Connolly were always acknowledged in public as the lawful issue of their marriage.[127]

Connolly had, in fact, earned a reputation as one who stoutly maintained that it would be "a most unnatural proceeding" to desert the mother of one's children,[128] and he took Suzanne and his family east with him in 1831. The family was first settled in Saint Eustache where two of Connolly's daughters were baptized and Suzanne was introduced to the community as Mrs. Connolly. Shortly after the Connollys moved to Montreal, however, Connolly inexplicably repudiated his Indian wife and married his cousin Julia Woolrich in a Catholic ceremony on May 16, 1832. Nevertheless, Connolly, now stationed at Tadoussac, continued to support Suzanne in Montreal until 1840 when he arranged for her to return to a convent in Red River where she remained until her death in 1862. Connolly himself had died in 1848, but his second wife, who had always known of the existence of Suzanne and even cared for some of the children, continued to make annual payments for the Indian woman's support. Then in 1867, Connolly's eldest son by Suzanne instituted a suit against Julia Woolrich as Connolly's executrix, claiming that the marriage of his mother and father had been legal and that, therefore, by law Suzanne had been entitled to one-half of his father's estate. Upon her death, this inheritance would have passed to her children, and John Connolly maintained that, as a legitimate heir, he was entitled to one-sixth of the estate.

The question as to whether a valid marriage had existed between Connolly and his Indian wife was thus the central issue of the case. On the basis of the testimony of numerous witnesses who had lived in Rupert's Land and an extensive examination of the development of marriage law, Chief Justice Monk ruled that their union constituted a valid marriage: firstly, because Suzanne had been married according to the custom and usages of her own people and secondly, because the consent of both parties which was the essential element of civilized marriage had been proved by twenty-eight years of repute, public acknowledgement, and cohabitation as man and wife.[129] Connolly had further given his name to Suzanne and shown considerable concern for the care and education of his offspring.

In a moving vindication of "the custom of the country," the Chief Justice summed up:

> It is beyond all question, all controversy, that in the North West among the Crees, among the other Indian tribes or nations, among the Europeans at all stations, posts, and settlements of the Hudson's Bay, this union, contracted under such circumstances, persisted in for such a long period of years, characterized by inviolable fidelity and devotion on both sides, and made more sacred by the birth and education of a numerous family, would have been regarded as a valid marriage in the North West, was legal there; and can this Court, after he brought his wife and family to Canada, after having recognized her here as such, presented her as such to the persons he and she associated with, declare the marriage illegal, null and void? Can I pronounce this connection, formed and continued under such circumstances, concubinage, and brand his offspring as bastard. . . . I think not. There would be no law, no justice, no sense, no morality in such a judgment.[130]

Notes

This chapter was read by Ms. Van Kirk at the annual meeting of the Canadian Historical Association, University of Toronto, 1974.

1. Variations of this phrase, which means "after the fashion of the country," are also found such as *en facon du nord* and "after the fashion of the North West."

2. E. E. Rich, ed., *Copy-Book of Letters Outward, 1680–1687*, vol. 11 (Toronto: Champlain Society, 1948), 40–41.

3. In the 1680s, a governor at Albany had been allowed to bring out his wife and her companion. They proved such a nuisance, however, that the London Committee soon withdrew this privilege and ordered all captains to make sure that no women were aboard its ships when they departed from Gravesend.

4. E. E. Rich, ed., *James Isham's Observations and Notes, 1743–1749*, vol. 12 (London: Hudson's Bay Record Society, 1949), 79.

5. Hudson's Bay Company Archives, *Report from the Committee, appointed to inquire into the State and Condition of the Countries Adjoining to Hudson's Bay and of the Trade carried on there, 24 April 1749*, 219.

6. Samuel Hearne, *A Journey to the Northern Ocean, 1769, 1779, 1771, 1772*, ed. Richard Glover (Toronto, 1958), 82; W. Kaye Lamb, ed., *The Journals and Letters of Sir Alexander Mackenzie* (Cambridge, England, 1970), 134.

7. Rich, *Isham's Observations*, 101: "When a Young Man has a mind for a Wife, they do not make Long tedious Ceremony's nor yet use much formalities"; Glyndwr Williams, ed., *Andrew Graham's Observations on Hudson's Bay, 1767–1791*, vol. 18 (London: HBRS, 1969), 153: "I cannot with propriety rank fornication and adultery (though very frequent amongst them) among their vices as they think no harm in either."

8. Rich, *Isham's Observations*, 95; Hearne, *Journey to Northern Ocean*, 83–84; Williams, *Graham's Observations*, 57–58. It was usually the failure of the white man to respect Indian mores, even though they were much more lenient than his own, which led to hostility.

9. HBCA, Churchill Journal, November 27, 1750, B.42/a/36, f. 23. For a summation of the important economic role played by native women in the fur trade, see Sylvia Van Kirk, "Women and the Fur Trade," *The Beaver* (Winter 1972): 4.

10. J. B. Tyrell, ed., *Documents Relating to the Early History of Hudson's Bay*, vol. 28 (Toronto: Champlain Society, 1931), 229–30. See also Joseph Robson, *An Account of Six Years Residence in Hudson's Bay from 1733 to 1736, and 1744 to 1747* (London, 1752), 52.

11. HBCA, Albany Journal, January 24, 1771, B.3/a/63, f. 18d.

12. HBCA, Moose Journal, March 4, 1744, B.135/a/14, f. 32.

13. *Parliamentary Report, 1749*, 224; Rich, *Isham's Observations*, 322, 325.

14. HBCA, London Committee to R. Pilgrim, May 6, 1747, A.6/7, f. 110d.

15. Hearne, *Journey to Northern Ocean*, 39–40.

16. Williams, *Graham's Observations*, 248.

17. HBCA, T. Mitchell to G. Spence, February 3, 1745, B.3/b/2, f. 12; Moose Journal, May 16, 1742, B.135/a/11, f. 64.

18. Albany Journal, January 18–24, 1771, B.3/a/63, fos. 18–18d. Marten eventually succeeded in sending his son to England, having implored the London Committee to make an exception to the ruling passed in 1751 that no person of Indian or part-Indian extraction be allowed passage to Britain.

19. HBCA, York Journal, September 22–24, 1762, B.239/a/50, f. 5–5d.

20. Numerous examples could be cited. Part of Samuel Hearne's hatred for Moses Norton undoubtedly stemmed from the fact that Norton went to

great lengths to prevent any of his subordinates from having any dealings with Indian women (Hearne, *Journey to Northern Ocean*, 39–40). A servant at Moose Fort in the 1740s, Augustin Frost, became very refractory when the tyrannical James Duffield cut him off from his Indian family (Moose Journal, May 16–18, 1742, B.135/a/11, fos. 64–66). Indian resentment at being barred from Henley House while their women were kept there by the master resulted in an attack on the post in 1755 (George Rushworth to London Committee, September 8, 1755, A.11/2, fos. 173–74).

21. Williams, *Graham's Observations*, 248; HBCA, Churchill Journal, November 2–4, 1751, B.42/a/38, fos. 13–15.

22. W. S. Wallace, ed., *Documents Relating to the North West Company*, vol. 20 (Toronto: Champlain Society, 1934), 211.

23. J. B. Tyrell, ed., *Journals of Samuel Hearne and Philip Turnor, 1774–1792*, vol. 21 (Toronto: Champlain Society, 1934), 252–53.

24. "Connolly vs. Woolrich, Superior Court, 9 July 1867," *Lower Canada Jurist* 21: 228; hereafter cited as "Connolly Case, 1867."

25. Toronto Public Library, George Nelson Papers, Journal 1810–11, pp. 41–42. This phenomenon is also seen among the Chinooks, Frederick Merk, ed., *Fur Trade and Empire: George Simpson's Journal, 1824–25* (Cambridge MA, 1931), 99.

26. L. R. Masson, ed., *Les Bourgeois de la Comapagnie du Nord-Ouest* (New York, 1960 [reprint]), 251–52; Richard Glover, ed., *David Thompson's Narrative, 1784–1812*, vol. 40 (Toronto: Champlain Society, 1962), 82, 255; Lamb, *Journals of Mackenzie*, 151–52.

27. "Johnstone et al. vs. Connolly, Appeal Court, 7 Sept. 1869," *La Revue Legale* 1: 280–81; hereafter cited as "Connolly Appeal Case, 1869."

28. W. Kaye Lamb, ed., *Sixteen Years in the Indian Country: The Journal of Daniel Williams Harmon, 1800–1816* (Toronto, 1957), 53.

29. Elliot Coues, ed., *New Light on the Early History of the Greater Northwest; The Manuscript Journals of Alexander Henry and of David Thompson, 1799–1814* (Minneapolis MN, 1965 [reprint]), 1:228.

30. Ibid., 2:901.

31. Ross Cox, *The Columbia River*, ed. Edgar Stewart and Jane Stewart (Norman OK, 1957), 209–11; Lamb, *Harmon's Journal*, 28–29.

32. "Connolly Appeal Case, 1869," 280–82: "Une homme engage repectait la femme d'un bourgeois comme si elle eute ete la premiere femme dans ce pays."

33. Glover, *Thompson's Narrative*, 82.

34. Lamb, *Harmon's Journal*, 53.

"The Custom of the Country"

35. Coues, *New Light on the Greater Northwest*, 1:211.

36. "Connolly Case, 1867," 239: "I never heard of any of the men keeping two women at a time, it was not customary. A man could only have one wife at time."

37. Tyrell, *Journals of Hearne and Turnor*, 275.

38. Public Record Office, England, Will of Robert Pilgrim, November 23, 1750, Prob. 11/784, f. 396.

39. Sailing Orders, May 16, 1751, A.6/8, f. 54d. See also Williams, *Graham's Observations*, 145.

40. Cox, *Columbia River*, 224.

41. Numerous examples of bourgeois who followed this course of action could be cited, i.e. Roderick Mackenzie of Terrebonne, Patrick Small, William McGillivray, Charles Chaboillez, and Nicholas Montour. For an account of the feting of the retired Nor'Wester by eastern society, see Cox, *Columbia River*, 361–62.

42. The exception to this general statement would be the action of old NWC engagés who became "freemen" rather than leave their Indian families. They, however, had little prospect of returning to a comfortable life in eastern Canada and were the only group prepared to live a semi-nomadic life akin to that of the Indians. In the early 1800s, the North West Company had developed a plan for a settlement at Rainy Lake for superannuated engagés and their families, but this came to naught owing to the bitter trade struggle (Lamb, *Harmon's Journal*, 5–6).

43. Thomas Thomas to George Gladman, March 3, 1813, B.3/b/49a, f. 10d.

44. HBCA, *Andrew Graham's Observations, 1771*, E.2/7, f. 5d; Williams, *Graham's Observations*, 145.

45. PRO, England, Will of John Favell, February 19, 1784, Prob. 11/1795, f. 551. The London Committee, which had received similar requests before, readily complied with Favell's wish. In fact, the administration of annuities for native families was to become a regular duty of the Company secretary in London. Many other examples could be cited of HBC men who left detailed instructions in their wills for the care of their native families, i.e. William Bolland, Robert Goodwin, Matthew Cocking, and James Spence.

46. Alexander Henry, *Travels and Adventures in Canada and the Indian Territories, 1760–1776*, (Edmonton, 1969 [reprint]), 248.

47. The continuing support given to the families of NWC servants, plus the growth of a body of "freemen," helps to account for the fact that the mixed-blood progeny of the Nor'Westers were early identifiable as group distinct

---

from the Indians. It took much longer for the mixed-blood offspring of HBC men to become a recognizable group because they were absorbed directly into Indian society. In the eighteenth century, no distinction was made between "half-breed" and "Indian," and it appears that many of the "Home" Indians around HBC posts were actually first or second generation mixed-bloods. This phenomenon has been elaborated by anthropologist Jennifer Brown in an unpublished manuscript entitled, "'Halfbreeds': The Entrenchment of a Racial Category in the Canadian Northwest Fur Trade" (University of Chicago, 1973).

48. Cox, *Columbia River*, 361; "Connolly Appeal Case, 1869," 289: "L'habitude de quitter les femmes est tres-commune dans les pays sauvages, et j'ai meme connu des personnes qui donnaient de l'argent a d'autres pour prendre ces femmes comme leurs propres personnes, et aussi les charger le leur soutien et de leur famille."

49. Lamb, *Harmon's Journal*, 98.

50. Graham's Observations, 1771, E.2/7, f. 27.

51. PRO, England, Will of Matthew Cocking, January 27, 1797, Prob. 11/1322, f. 256; HBCA, W. H. Cook to R. Miles, May 25, 1825, B.239/c/1, f. 201.

52. HBCA, Will of James Spence, November 6, 1795, A.36/12.

53. Cox, *Columbia River*, 306. This is an important aspect of the pattern of intermarriage which developed among the Nor'Westers; a long list of officers who married metis women could be cited, such as Peter and John Warren Dease, Colin Robertson, Francis Heron, William McIntosh, and Thomas McMurray.

54. Lamb, *Harmon's Journal*, 98. See also John Franklin, *Narrative of a Journey to the Shores of the Polar Sea, 1819–22* (London, 1824), 86: "The girls at the forts, particularly the daughters of the Canandians, are given in marriage very young; they are very frequently wives at 12 years of age, and mothers at 14."

55. E. E. Rich, ed., *Simpson's Athabaska Journal and Report, 1821–22*, vol. 1 (London: HBRS, 1938), 245: "Simpson was anxious to secure a match between one of his clerks and the daughter of an old voyageur Cayenne Grogne because she spoke French, Cree, and Mountainy [Chipewyan] fluently."

56. Charles Wilkes, *Narrative of the United States Exploring Expedition, 1838–1842*, 5 vols. (Philadelphia, 1845), 4:396–97.

57. By the late eighteenth century, the Nor'Westers on Lake Athabasca appear to have built up a nefarious traffic in Chipewyan women. When finally in 1800, a delegation of Chipewyan begged the bourgeois James Mackenzie that no more women should be traded "on any account," they received the curt reply that "it was not their business to prescribe rules to us." (Masson, *Les*

Bourgeois, 2:387–88). See also Tyrell, *Journals of Hearne and Turnor*, 446, 449.

58. Alexander Ross, *The Fur Hunters of the Far West*, ed. Kenneth Spaulding (Norman OK, 1956), 191.

59. Williams, *Graham's Observations*, 145.

60. HBCA, A. Graham to London Committee, August 26, 1772, A.11/115, f. 144d; London Committee to J. Hodgson, May 25, 1803, A.6/16, fos. 159d–60.

61. Wallace, *nwc Documents*, 211. A change in attitude can also be noted on the part of HBC officers, partly because of the coming of settlement: "As the Colony is at length set on foot and there is a prospect of Civilization diffusing itself among Us in a few years I would not advise you for the sake of the rising Generation to consent to either Officers or Men contracting Matrimonial Connections unless with the daughters of Englishmen" (W. H. Cook to J. Swain, December 17, 1811, B.232/a/82, fos. 9d–10).

62. "Connolly Appeal Case, 1869," 286–87.

63. Ibid., 284–85. Marois' testimony was corroborated by another engagé, Amable Dupras, p. 282.

64. Ibid., 284.

65. George Nelson, Journal 1808, Fort Dauphine: "we were obliged to leave off and prepare for a dance . . . in honour to Mr. Seraphim's wedding—Mr. McDonald played the violin for us"; Coues, *New Light on the Greater Northwest*, 1:571: "My neighbour [HBC at Fort Vermillion] gave a dance in honor of the wedding of his eldest daughter to one of his men."

66. HBCA, George Barnston to James Hargrave, February 1, 1823, B.235/c/1, fos. 3d–4.

67. HBCA, G. Simpson to J. G. McTavish, January 7, 1824, B.239/c/1, f. 134.

68. HBCA, Eastmain Register, 1806–1826, B.59/z/1.

69. PRO, England, Will of George Gladman, March 25, 1820, Prob. 11, 1663, f. 585.

70. Lamb, *Harmon's Journal*, 194–95. Other Nor'Westers who took their mixed-blood wives to eastern Canada in the early 1800s were David Thompson, John "Le Pretre" Macdonell, and John "Le Borgne" MacDonald. According to Ross Cox, those with means of coming to Canada with their families "purchase estates, on which they live in a kind of half-Indian, half-civilized manner, constantly smoking their calumet and railing at the fashionable frivolities of the great world" (361).

71. "Connolly Appeal Case, 1869," 287.

72. Ibid., 285–87.

73. Lamb, *Harmon's Journal*, 62–63, 93–99; Coues, *New Light on the Greater Northwest*, 1:58, 162, 211; George Nelson, Journal 1803–04, p. 51 and Reminiscences, Part 5, pp. 206–207.

74. G. P. de T. Glazebrook, ed., *The Hargrave Correspondence, 1821–1843*, vol. 24 (Toronto: Champlain Society, 1938), 381.

75. Ross Cox tells the story of Francoise Boucher, the daughter of a Canadian, who was married at fourteen to an interpreter. After he died, she was taken by a bourgeois in the Athabasca country, but when he left the district, she was handed on to his successor with whom she remained permanently (363–64). Although in a minority, one witness at the Connolly appeal case declared: "It was very common to change women in the Indian country. The French Canadians, in the North-West Company's employ and the English, did it too" (287).

76. E. E. Rich, ed., *Minutes of Council of the Northern Department of Rupert's Land, 1821–31*, vol. 3 (London: HBRS, 1940), 94–95.

77. John West, *The Substance of a Journal during a residence at the Red River Colony, 1820–23* (London, 1827), 51–52.

78. West, *Red River Journal*, 26: ". . . having frequently enforced the moral and social obligation of marriage . . ."

79. HBCA, Red River Register, E.4/1b, f. 195d; Nicholas Garry, *Diary of . . .*, ser. 2, vol. 6 (Ottawa: Transactions of the Royal Society of Canada, 1900), 137: "Mr. West has done much good in persuading these Gentlemen to marry."

80. Church Missionary Society Archives, England, David Jones to Rev. Pratt, July 24, 1824, CC1/039.

81. CMSA, William Cockran, Journal, March 3, 1829, CC1/018, vol. 3.

82. CMSA, Jones, Journal, August 25, 1828, CC1/039, f. 35; CC1/018, Marriage Register.

83. CMSA, Jones, Journal, June 9, 1835, CC1/039.

84. BC Provincial Archives, Arch. McDonald to Edward Ermatinger, April 1, 1836, MB40, M142A.

85. Ibid., my emphasis.

86. BCA, Thomas Simpson to Donald Ross, February 20, 1836, AE R73, si5.

87. Merk, *Fur Trade and Empire*, 108

88. Thomas E. Jessett, ed., *Reports and Letters of Herbert Beaver, 1836–38* (Portland OR, 1959), 2.

89. Ibid., 86.

90. For details of McLoughlin's family life, see T. C. Elliott, "Margeurite Wadin McKay McLoughlin," *Oregon Historical Quarterly* 36 (1935): 338–47.

91. Jessett, *Beaver's Reports and Letters*, 141.

92. C. M. Drury, *First White Women Over the Rockies* . . . , 3 vols. (Glendale CA, 1963), 1:111.

93. Jessett, *Beaver's Reports and Letters*, 58.

94. Ibid., 77. Marriage by a Justice of the Peace had, in fact, been made legal by a law of 1836 in Canada and England (xxi, 46, 116).

95. Jessett, *Beaver's Reports and Letters*, 93.

96. Ibid., 48–50.

97. Ibid., 50–51.

98. HBCA, A. C. Anderson to H. Beaver, 1838, B.223/b/20, fos. 62–66d. It is significant that in Scotland it was possible for a legal marriage to be contracted without the sanction of either civil or religious authority. See F. P. Walton, *Scottish Marriages, Regular and Irregular* (Edinburgh, 1893). The fact that most of the fur traders were of Scottish origin may, therefore, help to explain their acceptance of "the custom of the country."

99. B.223/b/20, fos. 62–66d; HBCA, Company Secretary to Rev. W. Hamilton of Orkney, March 17, 1823, A.5/7, fos. 78d–79: It was the opinion of "one of the Highest Dignitaries of the Church of England" that "the Custom of living together in Hudson's Bay be to all intents and purposes a valid marriage."

100. Marion B. Smith, "The Lady Nobody Knows," *British Columbia: A Centennial Anthology* (Vancouver, 1958), 473–75; "Cathedral of the Pioneers," *The Beaver* (December 1940): 12.

101. Jessett, *Beaver's Reports and Letters*, 35.

102. Ibid., 120, 143–45.

103. West, *Red River Journal*, 75–76; CMSA, CC1/039, Jones, Journal, September 13, 1824, f. 11.

104. For numerous examples, see. M. L. W. Warner and H. D. Munnick, eds., *Catholic Church Records of the Pacific Northwest* (St. Paul OR, 1972).

105. Ibid., Vancouver, 11:5, 6, 7.

106. HBCA, Marriage contract between Magnus Harper and Peggy La Pierre, Oxford House, August 18, 1830, B.156/z/1, f. 96. As has been seen, those with commissions as JPs were allowed to perform marriages in accordance with the law of Lower Canada that "a civil contract of marriage, executed before competent witnesses and in the presence of a J.P., shall be perfectly valid in all respects, if no clergyman within 10 French leagues" (B.223/b/20, fos. 62–66d).

107. HBCA, Minutes of Council, June 7, 1845, B.239/k/2, f. 183d.

108. Van Kirk, "Women and the Fur Trade," 11.

109. "Connolly Appeal Case, 1869," 288.

110. For a more detailed account of the story of Simpson and McTavish and their country wives, see Van Kirk, "Women and the Fur Trade," 11–18.

---

111. HBCA, J. Stuart to J. G. McTavish, August 16, 1830, E.24/4.

112. Glazebrook, *Hargrave Correspondence*, 311.

113. Public Archives of Canada, James Hargrave to Charles Ross, December 1, 1830, MG19, A21(1), vol. 21.

115. PAC, Thomas Simpson to J. Hargrave, January 27, 1839, MG19 A21(1), vol. 7, p. 1574; J. Hargrave to Cuthbert Grant, November 30, 1828, vol. 21.

115. PAC, Wm. Cockran to J. Hargrave, August 8, 1835, MG19 A21(1), vol. 5, p. 1078. According to Hargrave, while there were still some young gentlemen who married daughters of officers for money or perhaps "Kinder Motives," "a different tone of feeling on these matters had gradually come around" (Hargrave to Letitia Mctavish, July 24, 1838, MG19 A21(1), vol. 21).

116. Jessett, *Beaver's Reports and Letters*, 57.

117. Ibid., 147–48.

118. Cox, *Columbia River*, 359.

119. Jessett, *Beaver's Reports and Letters*, 141.

120. CMSA, Wm. Cockran to London Secretary, July 30, 1827, CC1/018, vol. 1; G. Simpson to D. Jones, July 14, 1832, CC1/039.

121. Margaret A. Mcleod, ed., *The Letters of Letitia Hargrave*, vol. 28 (Toronto: Champlain Society, 1947), 177–78.

122. W. S. Wallace, "Lefroy's Journey to the North-West," sec. 11, vol. 32 (Ottawa: TRSC, 1938), 93.

123. Catholic Church Records, Vanc., vol. 1, 8th and 9th pages.

124. HBCA, John Rowand to George Simpson, September 14, 1849, D.5/25, f. 82d.

125. "Indian Women Rise to Social Eminence," December 14, 1913, Spokane, Wash. (newspaper clipping courtesy of Mrs. Jean Cole, Peterborough, Ontario). See also Archie Binns, *Peter Skene Ogden: Fur Trader* (Portland OR, 1967), 355.

126. The following account has been constructed from the testimony given in the original case of 1867 and the appeal case of 1869. See *Lower Canada Jurist* 21: 197–265 and *La Revue Legale* 1: 253–400.

127. "Connolly Case, 1867," 231.

128. HBCA, G. Simpson to J. G. McTavish, December 2, 1832, B.135/c/2, f.96.

129. "Connolly Case, 1867," 230, 248.

130. Ibid., 257. The decision was appealed by the associates of Julia Woolrich who had died in the interim before 1869. Four of the five appeal judges upheld the original decision. Plans were then made for an appeal to the Privy Council, but the parties ultimately settled out of court.

24. Woman as Centre and Symbol in the Emergence of Metis Communities

JENNIFER S. H. BROWN

Biologically, *métissage* in North America can be described in a unitary way, as the meeting and mingling of Indian and white racial groups. Socially and culturally, it has had a complex history over many generations—one that continues into the present, as people of this dual descent decide which of their many ancestral roots they wish to tap in defining a contemporary identity. This history-in-process has always been multifaceted and has become more complicated with the passage of time, as much recent research is demonstrating (for samplings of work in this field, see the papers in Peterson and Brown, *The New Peoples.*)

By the early nineteenth century, biracial families in the fur trade context of northern North America numbered in the thousands. Their progeny were moving in varied cultural and ethnic directions—Indian, white, Metis. We still have much to learn about the dynamics of the diverse courses that they followed in their lives as individuals and as familial and community members. This paper suggests that women's studies provides one important perspective, among several, that is especially useful in tracing these processes. The study of women's roles, social, economic, and symbolic, in the critical years before the mid-nineteenth-century ascendancy of white settlers, missions, and rampant officialdom, requires further attention and will repay us in broadened insights and understanding of the human backgrounds, contexts, and consequences of métissage.

One initiative for this discussion comes from a recent paper by Charles A. Bishop and Shepard Krech III, entitled "Matriorganization:

the Basis of Aboriginal Subarctic Social Organization." Bishop and Krech argue that early postcontact subarctic Indian groups were typically matrilocal, i.e., a new husband took up residence, at least temporarily, with his wife's relations. They also call attention to evidence for early matrilineality among the Montagnais and Cree, as well as among some western Athapaskan groups (1980:35–36). During the nineteenth to twentieth centuries, disruptions of resource availabilities and subsistence patterns led to replacement of matriorganizational emphases by the modern "flexible and fluid bilocal-bilateral organization" documented by ethnographers of this century (1980:36). But if subarctic Indian societies were indeed characterized by matriorganization through their earlier histories and until ca. 1800 to 1900 (depending on location), it seems that we should inquire whether Native women in emergent metis groups looked for and found ways to maintain this organizational bias in their own families and social lives. To what extent did women form the consistent nuclei of such groups? To what extent did biracial families later trace ancestry through women; or at least back to a female apical ancestor who represented in herself the meeting of races that founded a new lineage? Jacqueline Peterson has been concerned with such questions in the Great Lakes–Red River area (1981, 1982), and we might usefully ask them of data from many other localities. Some continuities with aboriginal matriorganization (on which we also need more data) may emerge from such questioning.

Another starting point for this discussion is the work of Sylvia Van Kirk (1980) on the socioeconomic role of women in the fur trade. It is clear that Indian women's traditional productive capacities, in preparing furs, netting snowshoes, foraging, securing small game, etc., often came to be fully utilized and much valued in both the HBC and Montreal fur trades. In the post setting, Indian wives of traders often transmitted these skills to daughters of mixed descent. The maintaining, in this way, of women's traditional productivity was little respected or understood by the white women and other

Woman as Centre and Symbol

newcomers who began to penetrate the northwest from the 1820s on. But again it raises questions for metis history: did the persistence of such economic roles afford women a special place among the new peoples or help to maintain a sense of their continuity with the aboriginal past? The sources may fail us on this point, but any metis statement contrasting the productivity of these women and the practical value of their heritage with the relative frailty and oft-idolized economic uselessness of their "fairer sisterhood" would be very interesting evidence on this question.

A third incentive for writing this paper comes from pursuing the implications of what I have called the patrifocality that character-ized some upper-level fur trade families in the late eighteenth to early nineteenth centuries (Brown 1980:218). Numbers of com-pany officers made more or less large and lasting commitments of resources and affection to their Native families, although not required by law or church to honor their marriages "according to the custom of the country." By this period, however, these families tended to be large, ranging from six to a dozen or more surviving children (Brown 1976). Officer fathers who maintained these bonds often did so selectively, choosing or being obliged financially to favor certain children to education and a "civilized" upbringing. A sampling of these fathers, consisting of Nor'Westers who had Na-tive children baptized in Montreal's St. Gabriel Street Presbyterian Church between 1796 to 1821 (Brown 1982), indicates that sons were selected over daughters for such attentions by a margin of about two to one. The other side of this picture is that daughters of these families were more likely by a two-to-one margin to remain in the Indian country, marrying there and contributing to the very rapid growth of biracial population in the northwest at that time. As daughters of officers, they were unlikely to revert to the Indian communities of their maternal heritage. They often continued to bear European surnames that were well remembered and re-spected. They might marry relatively well in fur trade terms, as did the daughters of Patrick Small and William Connolly, or they might marry lower-ranked employees of French descent. Perhaps it seemed that their high-ranked fathers ultimately abandoned them, and perhaps they did. Yet if a father had been on the scene long enough to begin investing in certain of his sons, he probably conveyed to the daughters, too, a sense of their distinctiveness and non-Indianness.

Some such daughters eventually lived out their lives among the white fur trade elite, although perhaps leaving children who joined metis groups. Others may be more immediately identified with métissage (sociocultural) in the northwest. Louise Frobisher, daughter of Joseph Frobisher, was by the time of the late nineteenth-century half-breed scrip commissions, the founder and perhaps matriarch of a numerous, three-generation descent group. As I suggested in discussing matriorganization, it would be interesting to investigate systematically how many metis families by the late nineteenth century looked back to an apical woman ancestor who, like Louise Frobisher, combined femaleness and a European father's surname. The obverse of patrifocality—white fathers pulling sons more than daughters into the orbits of their own lives and "civilization"—might in the northwest be matrifocality, daughters remaining, more often than not, with their mothers in the Indian country, and having that familial tie as a continuing core of their lives. Nineteenth-century HBC records can shed some light on comparative figures regarding daughters and sons, since district officers became required early in that century to enumerate their fur trade post populations. In the Ile à la Crosse district in 1823, besides numerous intact fur trade families, there were listed fifteen daughters and ten sons who had been left behind by retired, transferred, or deceased traders and were evidently with their mothers or with other families.[1] This sample by itself is too small to generalize from. But in combination with the St. Gabriel church records, and numerous other indications about the ratios of female to male offspring remaining in the orbit of the fur trade in the northwest, it is suggestive of a broader pattern.

One might carry this discussion a step farther, with respect particularly to residence patterns. Michael Asch has called attention to a pattern that he calls unilocality among the Slavey Indians—that is, a tendency for the siblings of one sex only (sisters or brothers) to remain with their parental groups upon marriage (1980:48). There may be use in looking for unilocal residence patterns in at least a proportion of fur trade and early metis families. We might watch for tendencies of two or more sisters to maintain "matrilocal" residence with their descendants in the Indian country, while their brothers gravitated to the father, and into the male-linked kin groups that characterized in particular the fur trade–oriented society of Montreal. Some such brothers, of course, eventually themselves returned to the fur trade country, as did Cuthbert Grant whom William McGillivray described in 1818 as "principal chief of the half-breed tribe" (Anonymous 1819:142). In his case, a sister's residency and relations in the northwest no doubt provided a base for him to renew his contacts there after an extended absence, and the same may have been true for other Native sons returning in this way.

The development and roles of semi-autonomous female-headed family units need further attention in looking at metis emergence. There are a few signs that by the early 1800s, Native women with a background of ties to fur traders could be found living with their offspring, relatively independently, in the orbit of one or another of the posts. The journals of Nor'Wester George Nelson in the Lake Winnipeg area around 1810, for example, refer to at least two such instances. In this northern region where metis groups were just becoming visible as such, the offspring of such female-headed units would have contributed to metis emergence, being themselves neither Indian nor trading post residents.

A further line of inquiry relates to women's symbolic roles in the formulation of concepts of metis descent and identity, in contradis-tinction to the patrilineal European identities that were not readily available to this new people. Parliamentary and court testimonies bearing on the Hudson's Bay/North West Company conflicts over

Red River Settlement between 1812 and 1819 show that the issues of just who these people were and of their problematic legitimacy were discussed in public at that time. These officially published texts probably reflected broader currents of discussion among both whites and metis, as problems of metis identity and legal status began to draw general attention. Three such texts are of particular interest in their content and in their contrasts and similarities.

First, we have the pronouncements of the Hon. William B. Coltman, commissioner hearing witnesses on the Red River troubles and testifying in court at York (Toronto) in October 1818. Being an outsider to the fur trade country, he took a simpler view of its Natives than some. The half-breeds, he said, were all "the progeny of Indian women, living with their mothers," although they varied "in character, information, and manners," some having been educated in Montreal or England. Overall, they ranged along a continuum: "they may be considered as filling every link, from the character of pure Indians to that of cultivated men" (Anonymous 1819:177). As for those half-breeds involved in the Seven Oaks massacre, they should be punished in accord with their place on this continuum. An example should be made of those Canadians and half-breeds who had had a civilized education and religious instruction, whereas the crimes of those who had never been out of the Indian country were palliated by "their half savage state," and by their being accustomed to "the general system of revenge recognized among the Indians" (Anonymous 1819:193).

Fur trader witness Pierre Pambrun, in contrast, gave emphasis to metis distinctiveness and to the metis consciousness thereof, although raising the specter of their illegitimacy. "The Bois-brules," he said, "are the bastard children either of French or English fathers, by Indian women; . . . some of them I know have been sent to Lower Canada, and received their education at Montreal and Quebec. I do not think they consider themselves as white man, or that they are so considered by white men, nor do they consider themselves as only on a footing with the Indians" (Anonymous 1819:112).

Significantly, William McGillivray, North West Company partner and leader, and himself the father of a half-Cree family, went the farthest of the three in his analysis both of metis identity and of the legitimacy question. Writing to Coltman on 14 March 1818, he observed that many of these half-breeds were more or less linked to the North West Company "from the ties of consanguinity and interest . . . yet they one and all look upon themselves as members of an independent tribe of natives, entitled to a property in the soil, to a flag of their own, and to protection from the British Government." He went on to enlarge upon the "independent tribe" concept, after spelling out his view of the legitimacy question:

> It is absurd to consider them legally in any other light than as Indians; the British law admits of no filiation of illegitimate children but that of the mother; and as these persons cannot in law claim any advantage by paternal right, it follows, that they ought not to be subjected to any disadvantages which might be supposed to arise from the fortuitous circumstances of their parentage. . . .
>
> That the half-breeds under the denominations of *bois brules* and metifs have formed a separate and distinct tribe of Indians for a considerable time back, has been proved to you by various depositions (Anonymous 1819:140).

McGillivray, then, was unequivocal about metis identity and separateness. But his legitimacy argument is also very interesting. The denial of paternal filiation meant, under British law, the affirmation of maternal right. McGillivray did not specify what this might entail. But in British legal practice, the maternal filiation of illegitimates would have comprised the right to use the mother's surname and to inherit from her as a blood relative. We might surmise that, by extension, McGillivray had in mind upholding metis rights to Indian tribal status and to land and other inheritances, through such maternal filiation. Although he did not spell it out, he urged the point indirectly: "the fortuitous circumstances of their parentage" should not subject them "to any disadvantages."

Of course, as a Nor'Wester, McGillivray spoke with an element of self-interest; the new nation was politically useful to his company. Yet he also spoke truth: metis identity and solidarity were indeed taking form. And his argument on legitimacy was expressed in accord with commonly held Canadian and North West Company views regarding marriages "according to the custom of the country" as unions without legal standing (for amplification of this point, see Brown 1980:90–96); he simply extended that argument logically in the direction of explicitly asserting mother right or maternal filiation as a positive claim.

Although McGillivray's statement is the most detailed, he, Coltman, and Pambrun were all in accord in calling attention to the maternal element as formative in metis emergence. One could respond that they were simply saying the obvious; we all have mothers. But the reiteration of this theme in these writings suggests its centrality in early thinking about the metis.

It is also of interest that Louis Riel, who would not have known the texts cited above, returned to this theme in his own thought, focusing on the symbolism of motherhood in at least two different ways. There was first his well-known recommendation that the metis attend to their maternal as well as their paternal descent: "It is true that our Indian origin is humble, but it is indeed just that we honour our mothers as well as our fathers" (Tremaudan 1982:200). In a second and different vein was his statement to the court during his 1885 trial, on his homeland as mother: "The North-West is also my mother, it is my mother country . . . and I am sure that my mother country will not kill me . . . because a mother is always a mother, and even if I have my faults if she can see I am true she will be full of love for me" (Morton 1974:312).

The data and examples gathered here are of varied origins and substance. But it seemed useful in this forum to present some preliminary ideas and evidence about possible avenues for thought and research on the numerous topics relating to women in metis history. A full range of subjects concerning the social, economic, cultural, and symbolic roles of women are available for investigation, and can be pursued in the context of a variety of social science and humanistic disciplines.

I would like to conclude by suggesting one specific research strategy that could serve to make our knowledge of women in metis communities more precise. It would help to refine available data on this topic in generational terms. We often tend to collapse fairly broad time spans and to telescope generations in looking at developments over a century or more, when it would be useful to distinguish these phases of familial and domestic cycles more clearly as the microcosms from which metis communities grew. The alliances of white traders and Indian women in fur trade post contexts were qualitatively different from second-generation alliances involving the first women of biracial descent, and second-generation from third-generation ones. More detailed family histories with time depths of three, four, and five generations could bring out important and subtle comparisons and paths of change, as the experiences of these Native families accumulated, and as persons outside them in turn responded and reacted to them, helping to confer on them a new ethnicity. More broadly, such studies would also contribute to better knowledge of metis demographic profiles. The rapid expansion of metis families between the late eighteenth and mid-nineteenth centuries is a major phenomenon whose implications, social, economic, and political, remain to be fully worked out. Its analysis, along with that of many other issues in metis history, must begin with the family—the dynamics of relationships between women and men, parents and children, and their close kin and contemporaries. It is all too easy to learn more about the men than the women; but new kinds of systematic study can redress the balance, contributing richer perspectives not only on individuals and families, but on metis social history in its broadest sense.

Notes

1. Hudson's Bay Company Archives, 1823, District Report on Ile à la Crosse, by George Keith. B.89/e/1. Winnipeg: Provincial Archives of Manitoba.

References

Anonymous. 1819. *Papers Relating to the Red River Settlement.* Includes Report of the Proceedings Connected with the Disputes between the Earl of Selkirk and the North-West Company at the Assizes Held at York, in Upper Canada, October 1818. London: House of Commons.

Asch, Michael I. 1980. Steps toward the Analysis of Athapaskan Social Organization. *Arctic Anthropology* 17 (2): 46–51.

Bishop, Charles A., and Shepard Krech III. 1980. Matriorganization: The Basis of Aboriginal Subarctic Social Organization. *Arctic Anthropology* 17 (2): 34–45.

Brown, Jennifer S. H. 1976. A Demographic Transition in the Fur Trade Country: Family Sizes and Fertility of Company Officers and Country Wives, ca. 1750–1850. *Western Canadian Journal of Anthropology* 6 (3): 61–71.

———. 1980. *Strangers in Blood: Fur Trade Company Families in Indian Country.* Vancouver: University of British Columbia Press.

———. 1982. Children of the Early Fur Trades. In *Childhood and Family in Canadian History,* ed. Joy Parr, 44–68. Toronto: McClelland and Stewart.

Morton, Desmond, ed. 1974. *The Queen v. Louis Riel.* Toronto: University of Toronto Press.

Nelson, George. 1808–11. Unpublished Journals. George Nelson Papers. Metropolitan Library of Toronto.

Peterson, Jacqueline. 1981. The Matrons of Michilimackinac: A Female Metis Lineage. Paper presented at the American Society for Ethnohistory, Colorado Springs.

———. 1982. Honoring Our Mothers: Intergenerational Female Metis Networks and the Transmission of Metis Culture in the Great Lakes Region. Conference on the History of Women, College of St. Catherine, St. Paul MN.

———, and Jennifer S. H. Brown, eds. *The New Peoples: Being and Becoming Metis in North America.* Papers from the Newberry Library Conference on the Metis, Chicago, 1981.

Van Kirk, Sylvia. 1980. *"Many Tender Ties": Women in Fur-Trade Society, 1670–1870.* Winnipeg: Watson and Dwyer.

25. Prelude to Red River

A Social Portrait of the Great Lakes Métis

JACQUELINE PETERSON

During a single autumn week in 1824, the ancient fur-trading community of LaBaye, or Green Bay, Michigan Territory, lost its dignity. In hindsight, the event seems insignificant, even comical. Arriving from "civilization," a zealous circuit court judge—the Honorable James Duane Doty—called into special session the first grand jury that French-speaking Green Bay had ever encountered. At Doty's instigation, the muddled jurors indicted thirty-six of the town's principal male inhabitants for fornication and two for adultery. The majority pleaded guilty and to escape the fine stood before a justice of the peace to legitimize their connubial unions. Among those publicly embarrassed were Charles and Jean Baptiste Grignon, scions of one of Green Bay's most illustrious families (Doty 1824).

At least eight householders refused to admit their immorality, however. Two carried their indignation into extended litigation, holding

> that they were legally married, had lived a great many years with their wives, and had large families of children—that their marriages had been solemnized according to the customs of the Indians. (Childs 1859:166–67)

John Lawe, LaBaye's most prominent citizen of British extraction, acknowledged his guilt, but in defiance of the American court never married his wife to Doty's satisfaction, even though he and Therese Rankin lived contentedly together until her death in 1842 (Lawe 1754–1800). Perhaps Lawe felt confident enough to ridicule American pretensions. Yet Doty's gesture was a harbinger, full of more than puritanical pique. Lawe's mortified descendants would refer to their grandmother as "Lawe's consort" (Grignon 1820–55).

In fact, John Lawe was prescient. A year before Doty's arrival within the newly created Brown County, the Green Bay trader had been settling his tangled accounts with the American Fur Company on Mackinac Island. The once lively emporium seemed as dreary as "any Sunday." The human wreckage of the American political and economic ascendancy in the Great Lakes region shook Lawe to the bone. He mourned to the part-Ojibway wife of his close friend Robert Hamilton of Queenstown, Ontario:

> The old times is no more that pleasant reign is over & never to return any more. I am afraid and amcertain [*sic*] in this country. . . . (Lawe 1911:277–78, 308–10, 351–53)

What Lawe saw passing was a unique lifeway—an occupational subculture and regional community which had, for more than a century, enjoyed a sympathetic relationship with the Native inhabitants of the Great Lakes. Choosing to accommodate rather than to confront, the old residents of LaBaye and elsewhere challenge the historical assumption that mediation was impossible, that the cultures of Indian and Euro-American societies were irreconcilable, and that the wholesale destruction of the former was inevitable. Clearly, deleterious effects resulted wherever the intent of the European invaders was economic exploitation of Amerindian peoples. The Great Lakes mediators we are about to describe were no exception. However, their adaptive lifeway serves to illustrate that roles and responses alternative to those adopted by the vast majority of Anglo-Americans were at least feasible, if not permanently viable.

John Lawe was a member of the ruling class and a spokesman for the LaBaye community; but, as a relative newcomer and a Briton, he was never a full-fledged member of the subculture. Born to a Jewish mother and a Yorkshire father who had served as a fleet commander in the English navy, Lawe was apprenticed in his early teens to a fur trader uncle at Montreal, Jacob Franks. Like other Montreal pedlars in competition with the Hudson's Bay Company, Franks cast a roving eye on the rich fur fields to the south and west of Lake Superior. By the early 1790s he had established a base at Mackinac and in 1797 he sent his nephew to Green Bay as clerk for the Wisconsin traffic (Lawe 1754–1800).

Although British and American fur traders had erratically wintered at LaBaye from 1761 forward, Lawe and Franks were the first permanent English-speaking residents. They were not alone, however. Taking up lands on the east bank of the Fox River, they settled among some two dozen households, or a base population fluctuating seasonally from fifty to one hundred persons. A number of these inhabitants, notably, the prolific Grignons, the Langlades, LaRoses, Carons and Jourdains, could trace their ancestry at the Bay to the 1730s and 1740s. All were French-speaking, Catholics without a priest, who had bound their fortunes to the Indian trade. All had extensive kin ties with their neighbors, the Menomini and Ottawa (Grignon 1904:241–42).

Franks maintained homes at both Mackinac and Green Bay until the War of 1812 when his pro-British activities drove Americans to pillage his island residence. Fearing continued harassment, he retired to Montreal, selling his lucrative trade and landed improvements to his nephew Lawe at the Bay. In the bargain, Lawe also inherited Franks' former part-Ottawa wife, Therese LaRose, and several mixed-blood children (Lawe 1754–1800).

Franks' offspring swelled an already burgeoning household. Around 1807, Lawe had stolen the wife of his commercial rival, Charles Grignon. Sophia Therese Rankin, or Ne-kick-o-qua, was the daughter of a British trader and granddaughter of Ashawabemy, an Ottawa from the environs of Mackinac who had settled among the French-speaking families at the Bay during the latter third of the eighteenth century. Although joining himself to a prominent Menomini line, the Francophile Ashawabemy built a bark cabin with a central fireplace and married off his semi-enculturated daughters and granddaughters to traders and voyageurs, granting each a portion of his lands along the west bank of the Fox River (Reaume 1809; Grignon, Lawe, and Porlier 1712–1855, "Miscellaneous legal documents," 29).

When Therese Rankin moved in with Lawe, she had already borne two daughters by Grignon, whom she apparently left behind. At war's end, however, Lawe's patriarchal compound included four new children, Therese LaRose's family, and numerous Canadian engagés and Indian retainers (Lawe 1754–1800; Baird 1882:319–23). The community about them had likewise grown to about ninety households, most of whom had supported the British and now faced the threat of American reprisal.

LaBaye was not an exceptional instance of community formation far beyond the line of supposed "White" settlement. Deep within what John Quincy Adams called a howling wilderness, by the last third of the eighteenth century some two dozen towns and villages followed the arc of the Upper Lakes and interrupted the banks of rivers which wove themselves into Lakes Superior, Huron, and Michigan and into the great Mississippi drainage basin.[1]

The fur trading center at Michilimackinac boasted forty houses in 1749 and twice that number in 1797, exclusive of the settlement at St. Ignace on the north shore of the straits which had been established in the 1690s (de Lotbiniere 1749; Sheldon 1856:327). Vincennes on the lower Wabash contained forty male inhabitants, their families, and slaves by 1746; and, Fort St. Joseph in southwestern Michigan listed forty–fifty families three years later (Barnhart and Riker 1971:95–96; Moore 1959:26; Quaife and Pare 1926–27:201–39). Detroit, the rising star on the Great Lakes horizon had eighty to one hundred houses in 1767, and by 1780 Prairie du Chien was also a considerable town (Portheous 1767; Carver 1976:66).

By the 1790s, trading hamlets housing from a single extended family to several hundred persons had been established at Peoria, Cahokia, Chicago, Fort Wayne, Ouiatenon, Parc aux Vaches, Riviere Raisin, Sault Ste. Marie, Petit Kaukalin, Portage, La Pointe, and elsewhere. Perceived but dimly by the seaboard world, and largely ignored between 1763–1816, the inhabitants of these towns, like those of LaBaye, were, as it happens, people of primarily mixed race—Métis.

The lack of historical notice previously given these folk of the Great Lakes region is curious. Sources are fairly abundant, although they have been used primarily by local historians. Unconsciously, perhaps, American colonial historians in the wake of Francis Parkman, Reuben Gold Thwaites, and Louise Phelps Kellogg have relegated the inland region so long under the aegis of French and British administrators to their northern counterparts across the border. If this is so, it is unfortunate, since Canadian scholars have shown little interest in Canadian settlements placed under American jurisdiction after the American Revolution.

It may be that there is more to American neglect. Most American historians, like their colonial forebears, have shown a remarkable myopia with regard to racial mixture within the continental United States. An Anglo-Saxon smugness pervades the literature of colonial expansion and exploitation in the Western Hemisphere. Sexual exploitation, at least, was peculiarly the folly of Spanish, Portuguese, and French invaders, although a recent Canadian historian would argue that the French were as unwilling as the English to "embrace" the Indian (Jaenen 1976:161–62, 165). There were Anglo-American exceptions to be sure: misanthropic mountain men, White captives, pernicious squaw men, misguided amalgamationists, but they were rare (Billington 1976:6, 11; Nash 1974:87–108; Washburn 1975:73). So rare, that in Turner's crucible, it was the "immigrants [who] were fused . . . into a mixed race" (Turner 1920:22–23).

Such thinking flies in the face of evidence mounting from the 1820s that mixed-bloods were a sizeable and influential body within tribal society, coerced and pandered to by treaty commissioners. Moreover, it ignores the horde of non-tribal Métis—coming seemingly from nowhere—who bellowed in the bitter aftermath of removal for tardy recognition, annuities, and allotment (Clifton

1977:281–82, 315–16, 363–69; Lyon 1838–40). Finally, it suggests that dispassionate historical investigation has been seriously hampered by an unconscious acceptance of the stereotypical "half-breed," that unhappy accident of nature which Lewis Cass termed an "anomaly," and James McKenzie a "spurious breed" (Cass 1830; James McKenzie in Saum 1965:206).

It is no coincidence that many of the labels describing the off-spring of interracial unions articulate an implicit wish to blot out or sterilize the human consequences of miscegenation. Thus, like the derogation *mulatto*, which stems from mule, and *griffe*, the monstrous winged child of black and Indian parents, "half-breed," "breed," and "mixed-blood" hint broadly at cultural and biological impotence.

The term employed here, "Métis," possesses no greater scientific validity. Blood does not mix. On the other hand, it lacks the opprobrious connotations of its English language counterparts. Moreover, it was to become the primary self-identifier of these descendants of Indian-European marriages who in 1869–70 under Louis Riel proclaimed themselves "the new Nation," now numbering in Canada some 750,000 persons, including non-status Indians. Within the context of this study, Métis designates less a racial category than an incipient ethnic group, entry into which could be acquired through marriage and self-designation, as well as birth (New Nation 1976:15; Brasser 1975; Kohl 1860:260–61).

Until recently, the Métis phenomenon has been tied to the western Canadian plains, where it has received considerable scholarly attention following M. Giraud's monumental study of *Le Métis Canadien* (1945). Lately, three dissertations have appeared concerned with the demographic and cultural aspects of métisization in western Canada (Brown 1976; Kirk 1975; Foster 1973). While there is no question that Louís Riel's proclamation signaled the political maturation of the Manitoba Métis, it did not mark the beginnings of a distinctive Métis culture. Instead, Riel's Rebellion was the culmination of nearly two centuries of ethnic formation rooted along the St. Lawrence and in the Upper Great Lakes and transplanted, of necessity, in the northern Red River valley.

Two separate problems attend the conclusion that Great Lakes Métis were a significant historical population antecedent to or concurrent with their cultural kinsmen at Red River. One is the relatively simple proof that widespread intermarriage was occurring, even increasing, into the first decades of the nineteenth century. The second more nettlesome proposition is that certain patterns of intermarriage produced or accompanied the spread of Métis identity and culture.

Intermarriage went hand-in-glove with the trade in skins and furs from the first decades of discovery. This was as true in Virginia as it was in Acadia, although the rapid transition to an agricultural economy in the south diminished the usefulness of interracial unions. In the north, climate, governmental policy, easy river access and a population top-heavy with mercenary adventurers and mariners favored the perpetuation of the Indian trade long after farming proved feasible. Intermarriage in New France was so frequent between 1607 and 1675 that "there were few Acadian families with no Indian blood in their veins" (Bailey 1969:112–13). Along the St. Lawrence, where the "terrible dispersion" of habitants and seigneurs inhibited governmental meddling, Indianization or "Canadianization" proceeded apace. Ironically, the French crown did meddle, briefly after 1665, by encouraging and rewarding biracial marriage. Catastrophic results ensued. "Those with whom we mingle," the Marquis de Denonville complained in 1685, "do not become French, our people become Indian" (Cass 1826; Harris 1968:163, 179–80).

By 1680, fully eight hundred or one-fifth of French Canada's male population between twenty and sixty years had fled the colony for the fur fields of the interior. Their prodigal behavior encouraged the disposition of the colony's young men to "live like savages," to "go about naked and tricked out like Indians." But repeated ordinances aimed at these disorderly coureurs de bois failed to halt the population drain (Henripen 1954:20; Harris 1968:115; Morrison 1955:258).

Increasingly, however, French Canadian society bifurcated itself. After 1695, peace with the Iroquois promoted along the River of Canada the resuscitation of agriculture, urban concentration, and French culture. Moreover, the proportion of French women to men had risen from 36.8 percent in 1665 to 47.4 percent by the turn of the seventeenth century. Thereafter, intermarriage in eastern Quebec apparently dwindled, leading latter-day scholars to conclude that Quebec's Métis children, however numerous, had merged with their native mothers' tribal bands (Henripen 1954:19; Harris 1968:164, 114–15; Jaenen 1976:162; Bailey 1969:112–13).

Peace also pulled down the barricades to the northwest dragging the locus of the fur trade and its mobile, semi-Indianized personnel away from Montreal towards the Upper Lakes. There, beginning in the 1690s, missionary, governmental, and travelers' accounts proclaim in an intensifying chorus that the new trade centers were producing all the irregularities of their eastern predecessors. Particularly lawless was the hump-backed island at the straits of Lakes Huron and Michigan, Michilimackinac—birthplace of the Central Algonkian culture hero, Nanabohza, and strategic center of the Great Lakes World (Carheil 1959).

As early as the 1630s, voyageurs and missionaries were haunting the straits. By 1695, commandant La Mothe Cadillac boasted of the emporium of the west as "one of the largest in all Canada." Sixty bark-covered dwellings housing traders, Native consorts, and the first generation of mixed-blood offspring straggled along the northern shore. Five years later, 104 outlaw traders and voyageurs illegally resided there, despised by the Jesuit missionary Carheil for their apostasy and lewd commerce with Native women (WHC 1898:19; Sheldon 1856:173–74; Scanlan 1937:21).

Carheil's bitter refusal to recognize or sanctify marriages between heathens and apostates, drunkards, and bigamists was commonplace among conscience-stricken missionaries. The rebuke was no inhibitor, however, neither at Michilimackinac nor at less conspicuous trading villages. Just as seventeenth- and eighteenth-century Quebec couples surreptitiously married themselves "*a la gomine*" to circumvent legal and ecclesiastical restrictions, most interethnic marriages in the Great Lakes region would be contracted *à la façon du pays*—that is verbally, and in the absence of notary or priest (Henripen 1954:101).

The institutionalization of "country" marriages between English-Canadian Hudson's Bay employees and their Native and mixed-blood spouses has been well documented recently (Van Kirk 1972, 1976, 1975). To the south of the present international border, marriage customs developed in a similar fashion, although, until monopoly companies successfully controlled the region, less frequent turnover among voyageurs and residence in agricultural communities appear to have created greater opportunities for stability. Métis village life, which seems not to have had a parallel in the north, provided niches for unproductive persons at both the lower and upper ends of the age spectrum. Even in the absence of formal clergy and magistrates, group pressure in town served to minimize sexual excesses, among Anglo-Canadians as well as French-Canadians. Life in the winter trading camps was another matter, entirely. It was here that young Métis males and "White" newcomers to the trade had their first, and usually ephemeral, encounters with Native women.

Age and experience contributed to stability as well. Most of the Green Bay men indicted in 1824 had in fact been responsible husbands for many years. Although a loosely appointed justice, Charles Reame, had been officiating at elite marriage ceremonies since about 1800 and several prominent traders had escorted their broods and wives to Mackinac for tardy baptism and marital confirmation, no one at the Bay questioned the legitimacy of marriages contracted by verbal agreement (*WHC* 1876:178; Grignon, Lawe, and Porlier 1712–1855, "Certificates of Marriages, Baptisms and Divorces"). In contrast to Englishmen long accustomed to church and civil requirements surrounding lawful marriage, third- and fourth-generation Great Lakes Métis looked to the force of tribal custom and to French peasant practices and the *coutume de Paris* for assurance. The practical sense of an early modern French proverb may still have held true at Green Bay in 1824: *Boire, manger, coucher ensemble C'est marriage, ce me semble* (Hunt 1970:64).

If country marriage satisfied the need for legitimacy and stability in the interior, its ubiquitousness stymies accurate enumeration of the Métis population. At best, lists of voyageurs licensed to trade in the Great Lakes offer only a suggestive gauge. In 1777, for example, 2,431 voyageurs were officially licensed. Despite turnover, Grace Nute has estimated that twice that number were actually working the interior after the limited French licensing system gave way to British expansion (Nute 1931:7). There were two groups of voyageurs. First were the licensed Montreal greenhorns, or *mangeurs de lard,* who if they weathered the first critical year customarily took a Native or Métis spouse and in worn old age retired to Green Bay, Prairie du Chien, or a sister community. But second, and of increasing importance, were the growing numbers of homegrown voyageurs—Métis from the back settlements who signed on at home or at Mackinac rather than Montreal (American Fur Company 1892). Countless others, calling themselves *gens de libre* or "freemen" plied the trade on their own hook or in tandem with a local independent trader, ranging from Sault Ste. Marie to Red River after the American Revolution (Keating 1825, 1:48; Johnston 1828; Johnston 1869:524).

If total numbers are unobtainable, relative percentages can be ventured, at least for two towns. Bearing in mind that the Michilimackinac register grossly underenumerated vital events, its birth and marriage entries nonetheless indicate that Métis were a significant portion of the population up to 1820 (Mackinac Register 1908:469–513; 1910:1–149). Tax rolls for the 1820s provide corroborative evidence (Dousman 1806–24). Likewise, at Green Bay, reconstitution of three generations from 1765 to 1829 illuminates a growing pool of indigenous and prolific Métis families (tables 11 and 12).

Prior to 1795, twenty-two of twenty-seven, or 81 percent of all

TABLE 11. Michilimackinac marriages, 1698–1818

Type	Number	Percent
Marriages: 1698–1765 N = 62		
Between Canadians	20	32.3
Canadians and Indians	17	27.4
Canadians and Métis*	13	21.0
Between Métis	1	1.6
Métis and Indians	3	4.8
Between Indians	1	1.6
Uncertain ethnicity	7	11.3
Marriages: 1765–1818 N = 43		
Between Euro-Americans**	8	18.60
Euro-Americans and Indians	6	13.95
Euro-Americans and Métis	22	51.16
Between Métis	2	4.65
Between Métis and Indians	2	4.65
Between Indians	0	0.00
Between Blacks	1	2.33
Uncertain ethnicity	2	4.65

Source: Based upon "The Mackinac Register" transcribed and reprinted in *Collections of the State Historical Society of Wisconsin* 18:469–513, 19:1–149.
*Persons of at least one-eighth Indian ancestry.
**Canadians and/or Americans.

male householders had married known Indian or Métis women, although only three males were themselves Métis. Fourteen years later, as second generation Métis began to establish families of their own, the number of new Métis householders had risen to a minimum of forty, or 42 percent, or a maximum of sixty, or 63 percent. Including known wives, 87 percent of the eighty-four households in 1816 (population approximately 533) were Métis. The Métis percentage of total households declined in 1829 to 60 percent due to the gradual influx of Americans engaged in non-trading occupations. Many of the Americans were single or childless, however. If we count only those couples with known offspring (104 of 142

TABLE 12. Michilimackinac births

1698–1765 N = 351		
Ethnicity	Number	Percent
Métis	136	38.75
Euro-Americans	78	22.22
Indian	115	32.76
Black	4	1.14
Uncertain ethnicity	18	5.13
1765–1797 N = 131		
Ethnicity	Number	Percent
Métis	94	71.76
Euro-Americans	8	6.11
Indian	13	9.92
Black	2	1.53
Uncertain ethnicity	14	10.69

households), 78 percent of Green Bay's fertile families were Métis on the eve of Green Bay's Americanization. And they were prolific, nearly as prolific as the legendary French-Canadian families of seventeenth-century Quebec (table 13).[2]

As the 1830 Michigan Territory census shows (table 14), both Mackinac and Green Bay groaned under the weight of single adult males. Sex imbalance was endemic to the Métis trading communities, but the 1830 figures are misleading because, at Green Bay, the majority was single male American speculators and adventurers who had arrived the same year. At Mackinac, where the census was taken in August, the male surplus reflected the summer ingress of "vacationing" voyageurs—there to carouse, exchange their peltry, and re-ingage for the coming winter season. Their wives and children remained at home, to farm and fish, at a tribal village or one of the inland Métis communities spawned by the Indian trade (Harlan and Case 1961; Hubbard 1818).

The living arrangements, material culture and occupations of Métis set them apart from both their Indian kin and neighbors and

TABLE 13. Green Bay, 1750–1829

	Household heads	Est. pop.*	Métis heads	Métis hh's**	Percent
1740–1796	27	171	4	22	81.48
1796–1816	84	533	22	72	86.90
1816–1820	142	897	40–60	85	59.86

Based on reconstitution of families of household heads who appeared as residents in at least two different years.
* Household heads multiplied by a factor of 6.35, the average family size in 1830 according to the Federal Census of Michigan Territory for Brown County.
** Includes all households where one or both parents were more than one-eighth Indian.

from European society to the east. The establishment of permanent villages and towns, geographically separate and visually distinct from adjacent band villages, was a critical hallmark of Métis development (Corps n.d.). However, like other peasant and tribal communities practicing a subsistence-barter economy, Métis villages were never large. The maximum size appears to have been something less than one thousand, even for commercial emporia like Mackinac and Detroit. Further growth was inhibited by occupational dependence upon the fur trade rather than farming. Adequate grain, sugar, and animal and fish protein required assistance from local bands and tribal kin. Because each town could sustain only as many traders and voyageurs as the regional fur-bearing and tribal populations could bear, overconcentration and depletion of game reserves propelled the periodic search for new Natives allies and satellite town sites to the north and west.

The physical layout of Métis villages was vaguely reminiscent of earlier French string settlements fronting the St. Lawrence, settlements which themselves had been adaptations to a fur trading economy rather than replications of European agricultural village patterns. Lacking a core, rectangular grid structure, and in many cases verifiable land titles, Métis towns rambled along the shoreline of inland rivers and lakes, seemingly without design.

The apparent disorder and backwardness of these settlements shocked outside observers (Carver 1976:75; Keating 1825, 1:75–76).

TABLE 14. Based on the 1830 census of Michigan Territory

Mackinac
Michilimackinac County

Total males	Total males less mission	Total females	Total females less mission	Total pop.	Pop. less mission school
568	511	305	249	873	779

Households	Single male households	Av. # per family	Av. # per family less singles	GFR	EFR (age 15–49)
252	152	3.10	7.79	1109.76	1277.11

Green Bay
Brown County

Total males	Total males less fort	Total females	Total females less fort	Total pop.	Total less fort
931	513	410	363	1341	876

Households	Single male households	Av. # per family	Av. less single households	GFR	EFR (women 15–49)
138	21	6.35	7.3	772.7	970.6

William Keating dismissed the small, upright log (*pieux en terre*), bark-covered cabins with their high-peaked roofs and mud and thatch fireplaces as mere "rude huts" (Keating 1825:165–66; Lockwood 1855:119; McKenney 1827:276–77; Fonda 1868:232). Such houses leaned into the primary highway, the water road, where they often tumbled after years of decay. Behind them, narrow, picketed gardens trailed off into the timber, protecting tiny patches of peas, potatoes, and garlic from the unfettered meanderings of horses, hogs, and horned cattle. Agriculture, such as it was, was confined to a modest-sized common field. At Green Bay, only two square miles had been set aside (*American State Papers* 1860:97).

Travelers with a humorous bent could poke fun at the crude Métis farms and the medieval implements and conveyances, but early nineteenth-century Americans, in general, were contemptuous of these suspiciously Indian-like folk who had lost their sense of private property and its full exploitation. Métis themselves had developed a remarkable self-derisive humor. They referred ironically to their clearings as "deserts," even making a verb out of it, "deserter"—i.e., "to desolate the forest, or introduce cultivation" (Kohl 1860:304, 304n).

Like Métis architecture, which blended Algonkian construction techniques and materials with Norman design and comfort, the clothing, cuisine, amusements, transportation, medical practices, language, beliefs, and customs of Great Lakes Métis borrowed and adapted as freely from Native culture as they did from European cultural tradition. Jonathan Carver noted at Detroit, in 1766, that

> it is not uncommon to see a Frenchman with Indian shoes and stockings, without breeches, wearing a strip of woolen cloth to cover what decency requires him to conceal. Yet at the same time he wears a fine ruffled shirt, a laced waistcoat with a fine handkerchief on his head. (Carver 1976:66)

According to Carver, the "French" at Detroit had "laid by many of their savage customs" following the arrival of the English, but sixty years later Métis fashion was still distinctive. Métis voyageurs were visually identifiable as much by their blue pantaloons, capot, and fiddle, as by their leggings, red finger-woven sash, moccasins, hair feathers, and tattoos (Baird 1898:63; 1882:322–23; Keating 1825, 1:76; McKenney 1827:350).

Métis festivals and the foods which accompanied them were equally syncretic. Women at Green Bay, Mackinac, and other northern villages celebrated Lent and courting time at the sugar bush in Central Algonkian cabins near their Native kin. There, young couples tossed French crepes sweetened with maple sugar, a condiment as essential as garlic in the Métis preparation of fish and game. At home, wizened old voyageurs, long retired to their gardens, carefully nurtured cuttings from Quebec pear, plum, and apricot trees from which brandies and wines were distilled for the traders' tables. The aged and poor rarely shared in the groaning feasts of pastry and *pate d'ours* ("bears' paws"). They were fortunate if they could acquire sufficient tobacco and tea (Baird 1898:21; McKenney 1827:263; Ellis 1876:219–22).

J. G. Kohl succinctly summarized Métis cultural hybridization in 1860:

> ... the Canadian half-breeds often swagger with two genealogies—a European commencing with a "lieutenant du roi," and an Indian, from some celebrated chief. I met one half-breed, a man tolerably well off, who had engraved both his French coat of arms and his Indian totem (an otter) on his seal-ring. (Kohl 1860:297)

Such artful amalgamation of two lineages and two culture complexes did not render Métis marginal people torn between two identities. Rather, some Great Lakes Métis prior to 1830 drew a line between themselves and their *sauvage* clients, with whom they were intimate, just as others would distinguish between themselves and "Whites." While self-denominators are rare in the literature (some Métis residents of Green Bay referred to themselves as French "creole," i.e., native born), one can infer from the labels attached to outsiders, whether "Indians" or "Whites," that Métis community members considered themselves distinct. One of Kohl's informants suggested that the term "White" was reserved for Americans (Vieau 1882:234; Kohl 1860:261).

The word *Métis* appears infrequently, even in the French correspondence, but its synonyms—*chicot, bois brulé, gens de libre,* and even *Canadese* or *Canadian,* were gaining currency by the end of the War of 1812. It is significant, however, that these designations pointed to either occupational or mobility patterns characteristic of Métis, rather than to race. Robert Dickson simply referred to Green Bay Métis as "the people," an interesting borrowing of Indian terminology in its own right (Keating 1825, 1:45; Dickson 1888:293, 297).[3]

One of the primary reasons that Great Lakes Métis were able to construct a separate identity was their monopolization of the middle occupational rungs of the fur trading system. Unlike their seventeenth-century forerunners, the coureurs de bois, the progenitors of the Great Lakes Métis generally did not transform themselves into White Indian hunters and give themselves up to Indian society. Instead, the first Canadians to migrate into the Great Lakes region after 1695 fatefully walked into a vacuum occasioned by the Iroquois blockade of the Montreal trade routes and the temporary dislocation and devastation of the Huron and Ottawa middlemen. Aggressively seizing a position of influence at Michilimackinac, Sault Ste. Marie, Green Bay, Prairie du Chien, and elsewhere, they and their Métis children carved out a broker relationship between Central Algonkian and Siouan bands to the northwest and European society to the east, functioning primarily as traders, voyageurs, and clerks who journeyed to and lived among their Native clients.

The occupational culture complex which developed around the Métis brokers was partially shared in the Lake Superior region by the Ojibway, who also vied for middlemen status. Certain elements of Métis material culture derived in fact from the trade-oriented, Ojibway-inspired pan-Indianism of the eighteenth century (Quimby

1966:129–30). However, the core denominator of Métis identity was not participation in the fur trading network per se, but the Métis' intermediary stance between Indian and European societies. Thus, while tied to the "occupation," Métis magnified their symbolic role by serving as portage and ferry tenders, mail carriers, guides, interpreters, negotiators, barge and oarmen, officers and spies in the Indian service, as well as tribal business agents and employees of missions and Indian agencies. In each case, they functioned not only as human carriers linking Indians and Europeans, but as buffers behind which the ethnic boundaries of antagonistic cultures remained relatively secure (Keating 1825:104–5, 323–26; Brisbois 1882:284; Kohl 1860:66; Clifton 1976).

While the widespread employment of Native hunters in the fur trade has often been cited as cause for the delayed and less direct or directed cultural annihilation of the northern Great Lakes and western Canadian tribes, it may be useful to consider the role of mixed-bloods in shielding traditional Indian leaders, their families, and way of life from Euro-American contamination, and in prolonging the period during which Native peoples could choose to spurn European languages, education, religion, and values. It was after all the mixed-blood component of the Great Lakes tribes which first turned to farming and filled the missions and schoolhouses of government-sponsored philanthropists (McCoy 1827; Warren 1885:386; Paquette 1892:406; WHC 1898:406n). Their apparent willingness to become "civilized" pacified well-intentioned Whites, at least for a time, took the pressure off more traditional tribal members.[4]

During the eighteenth and early nineteenth centuries, assumption of the favored broker role necessitated a perpetual cycle of intermarriage, even when miscegenation had so enlarged the Métis population as to facilitate Métis endogamy. Canadians and their Métis offspring did not take Native spouses for lack of accessible European women, but rather out of shrewd choice. Not only were Indian women preferable—as cooks, guides, herbal physicians, house builders and transporters, farmers, and stoic companions during long and hazardous migrations—but Canadian seigneurs and peasants alike drew the same meaning and security from kinship alliance that the Indians did (Van Kirk 1977; McKenney 1827:319; Peterson 1977). Long before European traders employed intermarriage as a diplomatic device to ensure social cooperation, Indians were consolidating commercial and military alliances through intertribal marriage. Thus, whatever the ultimate conundrum Métis offspring presented for tribal society, band leaders encouraged and often demanded intermarriage, as well as bride price and bride services (Campau n.d.; Armstrong 1892:100).

At the lower end of the occupational hierarchy, marriages of the peripatetic voyageurs and engagés were relatively unstable, but not unstructured. Marriage was "limited as to time, and was contracted for life, or for six or twelve months." If cohabitation persisted without contractual renewal, the voyageur was called to account by public opinion or, at Green Bay at least, by a local justice for "contumacy or neglect" (Biddle 1854:58–60). Successive engagements generally resulted in enduring marriage, the voyageur retiring with his wife and children into a Métis village. His children would retrace the cycle. Sons often married Native women. His daughters, whose youth had likely been spent in Indian encampments under the tutelage of Native women, normally wed other Métis men of the trade, although if attractive and canny they might attract an incoming Euro-American trader (Shaw 1855:226).

Traders and upwardly mobile clerks, on the other hand, determinedly sought marital alliance with influential tribal families. Despite considerable divorce, especially among British and American traders, and an easy conscience about sexual rites of passage for adolescent males, marriages of the elite with high-born Native or Métis women generally held fast. Not until British and American monopoly companies engrossed the trade after 1800 and American troops exempt from community law had arrived, did prostitution and unlicensed cohabitation bedevil the stability of the Great Lakes trading community (Curot 1911:418; *WHC*, 8:320–21; Armstrong 1892:128–29, 132–33). Similarly, by the turn of the eighteenth century, Central Algonkian and Siouan bands were being forced to confront the ticklish problem of clan affiliation for countless abandoned Métis children. It is suggestive, however, that whereas the Ojibway were compelled to create totemic clans for children of British and American fathers—appropriately the "Lion" and "Eagle" clans—no such clan name has been discovered for children of French-Canadian fathers of this period (Quimby 1960:151).

The Grignon family at LaBaye and the LaFramboise family of Mackinac were typical of the several dozen leading Métis families in the Great Lakes region. Charles Grignon and his six trader brothers sired the last generation of identifiable Métis at Green Bay, just as the LaFramboise cousins were the last at the island community and at Chicago. Their patriarchal compounds, composed of extended kin, servants, employees and engagés, and Native retainers, were finely crafted educational cells—designed to spin off a new generation of Métis mediators. Ironically, however, the children, born between 1800 and 1820, found themselves stripped at maturity of inheritance. The anguish of the children's readjustment to American values and a rigidifying system of racial classification can only be inferred from subsequent life patterns. But a brief look at the patriarchal ancestors may clarify the uniqueness of the world that had suddenly been lost.

In 1728, Charles Grignon's great-grandfather, Sieur Augustin Mouet de Langlade, acquired a license to trade at Michilimackinac through the only family connections a second-generation Canadian officer of the marine could wrangle for his youngest son. Although only twenty-five, the ambitious Langlade married the widow Villeneuve and took in her six children, one a teenager. It was a fortuitous choice, if not romantic. Domitille Villeneuve (her baptismal name) was the sister of the local Ottawa band chief, La Fourche, and daughter of chief Kewanoquat. The lifelong alliance, coupled with Langlade's kin affiliation with the commandant of the garrison at the straits, ensured his success as a trader among the Ottawa south to Grand River and with the Menomini at Green Bay (*WHC* 1876:125, 179–85).

Langlade's dual connections also allowed him to pass on to his only child—Charles Langlade—both an established Ottawa trade, and a commission in the French army, albeit the Indian service. Charles Langlade's brilliant career as Indian military leader, strategist, and agent stretching over nearly forty years and three empires is well known. Less attention has been given to his functional marginality. The product of two cultures and education systems, Langlade moved comfortably between Indian and European societies. When not wintering with the hunting band, he was tutored by Jesuit missionaries at the straits. His grace and intelligence impressed both French and British military leaders, although they rightfully suspected his allegiance.

Similarly, Langlade held the admiration and respect of his Ottawa kin, who named him Akewangeketawso—military conqueror. As early as age ten, he was carried into battle against the Chickasaws under the protective arm of his maternal uncle—La Fourche. The Ottawa thought Langlade possessed a powerful *manito*, and had he desired, he might have risen to prominence within the tribe.

Langlade chose not to identify his interests with either power. Rather, like his military compatriots, Claude Gauthier (a Métis nephew), J. B. Cadotte, and Louis Chevalier, all early Michilimackinac traders and voyageurs, he preferred an intermediary stance. Langlade and the others were the elite nuclei around which stable Métis communities were formed at Green Bay, Prairie du Chien, La Pointe, and St. Joseph.[5]

As suggested previously, intermarriage was vital to the expansion and hegemony of the Métis population. However, we do not mean only marriage into the local band; absorption of incoming Euro-Americans was equally important to Métis solidarity and influence. Thus three patterns, seemingly contradictory, emerged which are typified by Langlade and his descendants. First, European or Métis initiation into the trade was often accompanied by a short-term "country" marriage with a Native woman. After the trader had secured the trust of her band, however, he might seek a permanent marital alliance with a prominent Métis or a French creole woman of a Great Lakes trading family. The second wife ordinarily assumed responsibility for the education and rearing of her husband's other children, as well as her own. Similarly, Métis sons were more likely, at least for the first marriage, to wed Native women, rather than Métis in order to reinforce kin ties and to propagate sons with easy access to the local bands. Conversely, Métis daughters generally married other Métis or, if members of the elite, incoming Euro-Americans, thus integrating potentially disruptive and competitive strangers. The result was a growing core population of Métis at the fur trade settlements.

Charles Langlade predictably married first an Ottawa woman of La Fourche's band. However, his fame after the destruction of Pickawillany and Braddock's defeat secured him both a perpetual superintendency of the Indians of Green Bay and the hand of a French creole daughter of a Detroit trader. Langlade moved permanently to Green Bay after 1763, having traded there with his father and kin from the 1740s. He carried with him an aging mother and father, his wife and two small daughters, his nephew Gauthier, and his part-Ottawa son Charles and daughter Agathe.

The children received a proper education. Charles Jr., after schooling in Montreal, joined his father in the trade, and later became a British Indian interpreter. The daughters, tutored at home, married traders and a voyageur from Michilimackinac. The youngest, Domitille, inherited the family compound and trade at Green Bay and with her husband, Pierre Grignon, launched the third generation of influence.

By the time Charles Langlade and Claude Gauthier died, just after the turn of the century, their related dynasties were well entrenched at Green Bay, Michilimackinac, and Prairie du Chien. Their Métis children and grandchildren all functioned successfully as traders, traders' wives, interpreters, and militia and Indian service officers. Moreover, their grandsons were already renewing the cycle—seeking wider affiliations whose by-product inevitably would swell the Métis ranks.

Of Domitille Grignon's eight sons (including one male survivor of her husband's first marriage to a Winnebago woman) four are known to have made strategic matches. Pierrishe married into the Winnebago Dekaury; Louis took the daughter of an Ojibway chief; Charles wed, first Therese Rankin (later wife of John Lawe), granddaughter of a Menomini chief, and Augustin, a relative of Menomini Chief Oshkosh. Amable's first wife was Ojibway; his second, the daughter of a Red River Métis trader.

Simultaneously, at Michilimackinac, to cite a single example, the LaFramboise clan had formed kinship alliances with the Potawatomi, Sioux, and Ottawa. Neither the Grignon nor LaFramboise lineages were unique. Every Métis community had several such lineages, all of which by 1820 had so entangled themselves through marital and commercial alliances that Métis identity had become regionalized rather than place-specific (figure 1). The expansive engine of the fur trade, coupled with the French Métis system of wintering out with the tribe, made such a development certain. In the 1850s, when the trade had shifted to the northwest, J. G. Kohl happened upon a Métis whose self-description might easily have been uttered by the men of the trade a generation earlier:

> Ou je reste? je ne peux pas te le dire. Je suis Voyageur—je suis Chicot, Monsieur. Je reste partout. Mon grand-père était Voyageur: il est mort en voyage. Mon pêre était Voyageur: il est mort en voyage. Je mourrai aussi en voyage, et un autre Chicot prendra ma place. Such is our course of life. (Kohl 1860:260)

The denouement in the Great Lakes region came rushing in on the heels of American Fur Company absorption and destruction of the independent traders. Intense competition between American and British trading companies had stripped much of the Great Lakes of

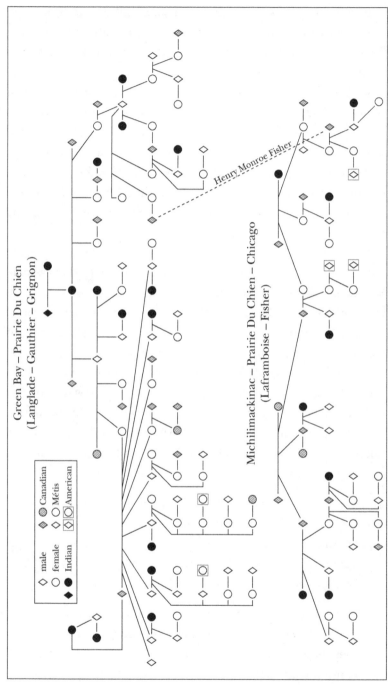

Green Bay – Prairie Du Chien
(Langlade – Gauthier – Grignon)

Michilimackinac – Prairie Du Chien – Chicago
(Laframboise – Fisher)

Henry Monroe Fisher

male ◇
female ○
Indian ●◆

Canadian ◈
Métis ◇○
American ◇○

FIG. 1. Great Lakes Métis

furs by the early 1830s. Thereafter, Indian cessions and removals and American land speculation and settlement conspired to disenfranchise the Métis middlemen. American farmers and businessmen did not need a broker class or a buffer between themselves and a broken Indian population herded onto sad reserves.

Some Métis had sensed the end and had migrated northwest to Minnesota and to Red River. Others sat on their haunches. As early as 1800, the Grignons and their extended kin were wintering as far west as the headwaters of the Mississippi River and Pembina in search of better peltry. However, they like John Lawe spurned Robert Dickson's and Lord Selkirk's suggestions in 1816–1819 that the Green Bay Métis community emigrate with the Menomimi to Red River (Dickson 1911:105–6; Selkirk 1911:109–13). Now in middle age, they would only painfully dislodge themselves, if at all. John Lawe never left, although his attempt to compete with Yankee businessmen left him nearly destitute.

The children had fewer means at their disposal, and frail defenses against American prejudice. Most of those who remained slipped into impoverished anonymity. A few married Americans and turned awkwardly to farming. The majority, however, fled to the sanctuary of Native kin, or pulled up stakes and migrated to former trading stations and new town sites close to a reservation or band village where their mediational and transportation skills could be employed for a few decades more (Keesing n.d.; Grignon 1820–55; Vieau 1882:226–33; Vieau 1900:465–67; Porlier 1900:439–47).

By the 1840s, Green Bay's Métis population had in effect disappeared. Curiosity seekers would have to travel to Bay Settlement, to DePere, to Kaukauna, to Butte des Morts, to Wisconsin Rapids, to Portage, to Prairie du Chien, to the upper Mississippi and the lakes of Minnesota to find the odd bark cabins and picket fences, the French voices in Indian clothing, the remnants of peaceful coexistence and accommodation. Ultimately, they would have to travel to Red River, where many of the Grignons' counterparts from the Bay, Mackinac, and Sault Ste. Marie had already sequestered themselves among the "freemen" and Métis voyageurs of the combined Northwest and Hudson's Bay Companies (Keating 1825, 1:39; Nute 1942:14–16; Grignon 1820–55; Chaput 1975:14–17). What separate identity remained, rightfully belongs to the Canadian prairies where it continues to nourish itself.

Notes

This paper won the student competition at the 25th annual meeting, American Society for Ethnohistory, Chicago, Illinois, October, 1977.

1. A complete listing of sources used in the dissertation upon which this paper is based would fill many pages. Documentary evidence detailing the growth and patterning of the Great Lakes Métis is rich, although fragmentary. Prior to 1830, few usable censuses were taken, and only the spotty Michilimackinac register is extant, northwest of Detroit. However, partial life and family histories have been reconstructed through linkage of missionary reports; parish records; lists of treaty claimants; correspondence and employee rosters of major trading companies; contemporary narratives; travelers' accounts; captivity narratives; family papers, histories and genealogies; muster rolls; poll tax lists; and Indian Agency and War Department records. A clear indication from comparison of reconstituted families at Green Bay, Michilimackinac, and Chicago is that these communities were part of the same fabric, possessing the same culture, and tied together by an intricate kinship web. Data for the Langlade-Grignon lineage, for example, were gathered from the *Collections of the State Historical Society of Wisconsin*, 30 volumes (Madison WI, 1854–1931); Michigan *Historical Collections*, 40 volumes (Lansing MI, 1877–1929); the Porlier, Lawe, and Grignon Papers, the Green Bay and Prairie du Chien Papers, the Charles Grignon Papers, the Henry S. Baird Papers, and the James D. Doty Papers, part of the Wisconsin Manuscripts collection at the Wisconsin State Historical Society, Madison, Wisconsin; the Lyman S. Draper Notes in the same archive; the Lucius Lyon Papers in the Clements Library, Ann Arbor, Michigan; the Charles C. Trowbridge Collection, Burton Historical Collection, Detroit Public Library; the John Lawe Collection and miscellaneous smaller files at the Chicago Historical Society; Letters Received from the Green Bay Agency, National Archives Microfilm Publications, Record Group M 234, rolls 314–15; the *American State Papers*, as well as numerous published travelers' accounts.

2. Green Bay's stable population was reconstituted by collecting data on household heads found in land claim records, highway assessment rolls, militia rolls, lists of grand and petit jurors, "Judge" Charles Reaume's memoranda

book, the Mackinac and Detroit registers, travelers accounts, family papers, and voyageur and trader contracts. Nearly as many male heads were excluded as included in the post 1800 tabulations in fidelity to the requirement that all resident heads be located at least twice, in two separate years. Given the lack of a vital register for early Green Bay, and the propensity of all records to ignore the poor and illiterate, the population base should probably be viewed as a minimum. See Jacques Henripen (1954:57–89) for the remarkable fecundity of seventeenth- and eighteenth-century French Canadian women.

3. The Métis synonym, "chicot," is interesting. J. G. Kohl translated it as "half-burnt stump," and assumed that like its companion, "bois brule," it referred to the dark facial coloring of Métis, a definition he may have acquired from Alexander Ross. "Chicot" was in use along the St. Lawrence as early as the seventeenth century, however. A term coined in the New World with no apparent French language stem (possibly of Algonkian origin?) "chicot" was used to describe New France's erstwhile coureurs de bois and rovers. Such men had the habit of taking a *roture*, but instead of cultivating the land and settling down, stripping the timber, selling it, and then abandoning the denuded plot for another further downriver. This early definition suggests that the occupational mobility, disregard for intensive agriculture, and occasional resort to wood gathering as a supplementary income of early nineteenth-century Métis may have been the basis for the later application of "chicot" and "bois-brule" to mixed-bloods, rather than skin color.

Both "chicot" and "bois brule" express a relationship between man and the environment, specifically one in which White men and their offspring were engaged in the spoliation of native lands and life ways. Whether one regards the Métis as wood burners or as charred remains, the irony is that if Métis had "half" completed the process, full destruction of the original habitat by American expansionists buried the Métis and his clearing, or "desert" in its wake (see Harris 1968:144).

4. Despite the fact that traders' sons, or mixed-bloods are today often despised as pariahs by their own tribal kin from whom they take their identity, it seems probable that they are still being used as cultural buffers—pushed forward to assume contact positions with Whites, e.g., as tribal chairmen, contract administrators, lobbyists, liaisons, etc. Literally behind the backs of such frequently untrustworthy mediators, traditional tribal ways persist, making the best of a painful and difficult situation.

5. For the Langlade-Grignon family, see WHC, 7:104–29, 179–85, passim. For the Cadottes at La Pointe, see William Whipple Warren (1885), and for Gauthier, WHC, 11:100n; WHC, 18:490–95, 507.

References

American Fur Company. 1892. Roster of Employees of the American Fur Company for the Years 1818 and 1819. *Collections of the State Historical Society of Wisconsin* 12:154–69.

American State Papers. 1860. Documents of the Congress of the United States in Relation to the Public Lands from the First Session of the Twentieth to the Second Session of the Twentieth Congress enclusive, vol. 5. Washington DC: Gale & Seaton.

Armstrong, Benjamin G. 1892. *Early Life among the Indians, Reminiscences*. Ashland WI.

Bailey, Alfred Goldsworthy. 1937, 1969. *The Conflict of European and Eastern Algonkian Cultures, 1504–1700*. Toronto: University of Toronto Press.

Baird, Elizabeth Therese. 1882. Indian Customs and Early Recollections. *Collections of the State Historical Society of Wisconsin* 9:303–26.

———. 1898. Reminiscence of Early Days on Mackinac Island. *Collections of the State Historical Society of Wisconsin* 14:17–64.

———. 1900. Reminiscence of Life in Territorial Wisconsin, 1824–42. *Collections of the State Historical Society of Wisconsin* 15:205–63.

Barnhart, John D., and Dorothy Riker. 1971. *Indiana to 1816: The Colonial Period*. Indianapolis: Indiana Historical Society.

Barth, Frederik, ed. 1969. *Ethnic Groups and Boundaries: The Social Organization of Cultural Difference*. Boston: Little Brown & Co.

Biddle, James W. 1854. Recollections, Green Bay, 1815–16. *Collections of the State Historical Society of Wisconsin*, vol. 1, appendix no. 4.

Billington, Ray Allen. 1967. *Westward Expansion: A History of the American Frontier*, 3rd ed. New York: The Macmillan Company.

Brasser, T. J. 1975. Metis Artisans. In *The Beaver* (Autumn): 52–57.

Brisbois, B. W. 1882. Traditions and Recollections of Prairie du Chien. *Collections of the State Historical Society of Wisconsin* 9:282–302.

Brown, Jennifer. 1976. Company Men and Native Families: Fur Trade Social and Domestic Relations in Canada's Old Northwest. PhD dissertation, University of Chicago.

Campau, Andrew. n.d. Interview. Charles Adam Weissert Collection, box 1, Bentley Historical Library, University of Michigan, Ann Arbor MI.

Carheil. 1959. Letter of Jesuit Carheil to M. Louis Hector de Callieres, August 30, 1702. In Reuben Gold Thwaites, ed., *The Jesuit Relations and Allied Documents, Travels and Explorations of the Jesuit Missionaries in New France 1610–1791* 65:193–95. New York: Pageant Book Company.

Carver, Jonathan. 1976. John Parker, ed., *The Journals of Jonathan Carver and*

Related Documents 1766–1770. Minneapolis-St. Paul: Minnesota Historical Society Press.

Cass, Lewis. 1826. His translation of Denonville in "Indian Treaties and Laws and Regulations." War Department, 1826, Lewis Cass Papers, vol. 2, Clements Library, Ann Arbor MI.

———. 1830. Excerpt from the *North American Review*. Lewis Cass Papers, Clements Library, Ann Arbor MI.

Chaput, Donald. 1975. The "Misses Nolin." In *The Beaver* (Winter): 14–17.

Childs, Col. Ebenezer. 1859. Recollections of Wisconsin since 1820. *Collections of the State Historical Society of Wisconsin* 4:153–95.

Clifton, James R. 1976. Captain Billy Caldwell: A Reconstruction of an Abused Identity. Paper read at the American Historical Association, Washington DC.

———. 1977. *The Prairie People: Continuity and Change in Potowatomi Indian Culture, 1665–1965*. Lawrence KS: The Regents Press.

Corps, David. n.d. Reminiscences. Emerson R. Smith Papers, Bentley Historical Library, University of Michigan, Ann Arbor MI.

Curot, Michael. 1911. A Wisconsin Fur Trader's Journal, 1803–04. *Collections of the State Historical Society of Wisconsin* 20:396–471.

de Lotbiniere, Michael Chartier. 1749. Attributed to, Relation tres abrege de Mon Voiage de Michilimackinac. Original in the New York Historical Society Library. Photostat in Public Archives of Canada, Ottawa, Ontario, MG 18, K3, vol. 3.

Dickson, Robert. 1888. Letters of February 6 and March 4, 1814, to John Lawe. *Collections of the State Historical Society of Wisconsin* 11:293, 297.

———. 1911. Robert Dickson to John Lawe, April 23, 1819. CSHSW 20:105–6.

Doty, James D. 1824. Trials and Decisions. James D. Doty Papers, box 3, Wis Mss DD, State Historical Society of Wisconsin, Madison WI.

Dousman, Michael. 1806–24. Poll tax and voting rolls and personal property rank at Michilimackinac in the 1820s. Michael Dousman Papers, folder 1, Burton Historical Collection, Detroit Public Library, Detroit MI.

Ellis, General Albert G. 1876. Fifty-four Years Recollections of Men and Events in Wisconsin. *Collections of the Wisconsin State Historical Society* 7:210–68.

Fonda, John H. 1868. Early Reminiscences of Wisconsin. *Collections of the State Historical Society of Wisconsin* 5:205–84.

Foster, John Elgin. 1973. The Country-born in the Red River Settlement: 1820–1850. Unpublished PhD dissertation, Department of History, University of Alberta, Edmonton AB.

Giraud, Marcel. 1945. *Le Metis Canadien.* Paris: Institut d'Ethnologie.

Grignon, Augustin. 1904. Seventy-two Years Recollections of Wisconsin. *Collections of the State Historical Society of Wisconsin* 3:195–295.

Grignon, Charles A. 1820–55. Unbound letters, box 1. Charles A. Grignon Papers, box 1, Wis Mss PF, State Historical Society of Wisconsin, Madison WI.

Grignon, Lawe, and Porlier. 1712–1855. Bound letters and documents. Especially vol. 55, "Certificates of Marriages, Baptisms and Divorce" and vol. 61, "Miscellaneous legal documents." In Grignon, Lawe, and Porlier Papers, Wis Mss B, State Historical Society of Wisconsin, Madison WI.

Harlan, Elizabeth Taft, and Elizabeth Case, eds. 1961. *1830 Federal Census—Territory of Michigan.* Detroit MI.

Harris, Richard Coleman. 1968. *The Seigneurial System in Early Canada: A Geographical Study.* Madison WI: University of Wisconsin Press.

Henripen, Jacques. 1954. *La Population Canadienne au Debut de XVIIIe Siecle: Nuptialite, Fecondite, Mortalite infantile.* Paris: Presses Universitaires de France.

Hubbard, Gurdon S. 1818. Gurdon S. Hubbard to Abby Hubbard, August 24, 1818. Gurdon S. Hubbard Papers, Chicago Historical Society, Chicago IL.

Hunt, David. 1970. *Parents and Children in History: The Psychology of Family Life in Early Modern France.* New York: Harper Torchbooks.

Jaenen, Cornelius. 1976. *Friend and Foe: Aspects of French-AmerIndian Cultural Contact in the Sixteenth and Seventeenth Centuries.* Toronto: McClelland and Stewart, Ltd.

Johnston, George. 1828. Report. RG 44, Executive Office 1810–1910, box 232, f. 4 "Indians," State Archives of Michigan, Lansing, Michigan, manuscript 22 pp., October 1, 1828.

Johnston, John. 1860. Letter to Colonel Trimble, January 24, 1822, St. Mary's Falls. In Henry Rowe Schoolcraft, *Archives of Aboriginal Knowledge* 2:524. Philadelphia: Lippincott and Company.

Keating, William S. 1825. *Narrative of an Expedition to the Source of St. Peter's River, Lake Winnepeek, Lake of the Woods etc. Performed in the Year 1823,* 2 vols. London: Geo. B. Whittaker.

Keesing, Felix. n.d. Leaders of the Menomini Tribe. Typescript in United States Manuscripts, Wisconsin State Historical Society, Madison WI.

Kohl, J. G. 1860. Kitchi-Gami, *Wanderings Round Lake Superior.* London: Chapman and Hall. Reprinted in Minneapolis: Ross and Haines, 1956.

Lawe, John. 1754–1800. Information Folder. John Lawe Papers, box 1, Chicago Historical Society, Chicago IL.

———. 1911. Letters of August 26, 1822, September 5, 1823, and September

12, 1824. *Collections of the State Historical Society of Wisconsin* 20:277–78, 308–10, 351–52.

Lockwood, James H. 1855. Early Times and Events in Wisconsin. *Collections of the State Historical Society of Wisconsin*, vol. 2, appendix no. 6.

Lyon, Lucius. 1838–40. "Mixed Blood Claims." Lucius Lyon Papers, Clements Library, Ann Arbor MI.

Mackinac Register. 1908. *Collections of the State Historical Society of Wisconsin* 28:469–513.

———. 1910. *Collections of the State Historical Society of Wisconsin* 29:1–149.

McCoy, Isaac. 1827. Newspaper account of Indian students at McCoy's school, March 27, 1827. Isaac McCoy Papers, manuscript division Kansas State Historical Society, Topeka KS. See also Correspondence, 1823–1838, for considerable correspondence regarding education of mixed-blood pupils (above on roll 5).

McKenney, Thomas L. 1827. *Sketches of a Tour to the Lakes, of the Character and Customs of the Chippeway Indians, and of Incidents Connected with the Treaty of Fond du Lac.* Baltimore MD: Fielding Lucas, Jun'r.

Moore, Powell A. 1959. *The Calumet Region: Indiana's Last Frontier.* Indianapolis: Indiana Historical Bureau.

Morrison, Samuel Eliot, ed. 1955. *The Parkman Reader: From the Works of Francis Parkman.* Boston: Little Brown.

Nash, Gary. 1974. *Red, White and Black: The Peoples of Early America.* Englewood Cliffs NJ: Prentice-Hall.

New Nation. 1976. *The New Nation: A Monthly Native Newspaper of Manitoba.* Vols. 7 and 8. Winnipeg.

Nute, Grace. 1931. *The Voyageur.* New York and London: D. Appleton & Company.

———. 1942. *Documents Relating to the Northwest Missions, 1815–1827.* St. Paul: Minnesota Historical Society.

Paquette, Moses. 1892. Narrative. *Collections of the State Historical Society of Wisconsin* 12:399–433.

Pare, Rev. George, and Mil M. Quaife. 1926–1927. The St. Joseph Baptismal Register. *Mississippi Valley Historical Review* 13:201–39.

Peterson, Jacqueline. 1977. "Beauty and the Beast: An Inquiry into the Intimate Relations of Great Lakes Indian Women and EuroCanadian Men." Conference on the History of Women, St. Paul MI, October 21–23.

Portheous, John. 1767. Letter John Portheous, August 16, 1767, from Michilimackinac. John Portheous Papers, 1761–1771, Burton Historical Collection, Detroit Public Library, Detroit MI.

Quimby, George. 1960 *Indians in the Upper Great Lakes Region*. Chicago: University of Chicago Press.

———. 1966. *Indian Culture and European Trade Goods*. Madison WI: University of Wisconsin Press.

Reaume, Judge Charles. 1809. Contract between Ashwabemy and Gabriel St. Dumond. Judge Charles Reaume Papers, Memoranda book, Wis Mss AS, State Historical Society of Wisconsin, Madison WI.

Ross, Alexander. 1856. *The Red River Settlement, Its Rise, Progress and Present State*. London: Smith, Elder & Company.

Saum, Lewis. 1965. *The Fur Trader and the Indian*. Seattle: University of Washington Press.

Scanlan, Peter L. 1911. Lord Selkirk to Robert Dickson, May 21, 1819. *Collections of the State Historical Society of Wisconsin* 20:109–13.

———. 1937. *Prairie du Chien: French, British, American*. Menasha WI: George Banta.

Shaw, Col. John. 1855. Personal Narrative. *Collections of the State Historical Society of Wisconsin*, vol. 2, appendix no. 7.

Sheldon, E. M. 1856. *The Early History of Michigan: From the First Settlement to 1815*. New York: A. S. Barnes; Detroit: Kerr, Morley & Co.

Turner, Frederick Jackson. 1920, 1947. *The Frontier in American History*. New York: Henry Holt & Company.

Van Kirk, Sylvia. 1972. Women and the Fur Trade. In *The Beaver* (Winter): 4–21.

———. 1975. The Role of Women in the Fur Trade Society of the Canadian West, 1700–1850. Unpublished PhD thesis, University of London.

———. 1977. "Women in Between": Indian Women in Fur Trade Society in Western Canada. Paper read at the Canadian Historical Association, Fredericton, New Brunswick.

Vieau, Andrew J., Sr. 1882. Narrative. *Collections of the State Historical Society of Wisconsin* 9:218–33.

Vieau, Peter J. 1900. Narrative. *Collections of the State Historical Society of Wisconsin* 15:458–69.

Warren, William Whipple. 1885. History of the Ojibway. *Collections of the Minnesota Historical Society* 5:21–394.

Washburn, Wilcomb. 1975. *The Indian in America*. New York: Harper Colophon Books.

26. The Glaize in 1792

A Composite Indian Community

Helen Hornbeck Tanner

Introduction

The Glaize, an old buffalo wallow on the Maumee River at the mouth of the Auglaize (present-day Defiance, Ohio, fifty miles southwest of Toledo) is the geographical focus for this description of a multicultural frontier society in 1792. The appearance, surroundings, and activities of this late eighteenth-century community can be at least partially reconstructed from contemporary literature. At this particular place, the year 1792 has a special significance because in the fall of 1792, The Glaize became the headquarters for the militant Indian confederacy protesting American advance northwest of the Ohio River. The distinctive place name, assigned by the French, referred to the clay banks most conspicuous on the southwest side of the confluence of the two streams (Sabrevois 1902:375). The north-flowing river entering the Maumee at that point became known as the river "at the *glaize*" or Auglaize River.[1]

The vicinity of The Glaize was already well-known to hunters and traders as a rich hunting ground by the middle of the eighteenth century (Le Porc Epic 1940:168), but was not used as a place for longer residence until about the period of the American Revolution when Ottawa lived at the river juncture (Hamilton 1951:113). Traffic up and down the Maumee and Auglaize rivers increased as intertribal war parties gathered at The Glaize for attacks on settlers in southern Ohio and Kentucky. The principal war path for Indians from Detroit and the upper Great Lakes led up the Maumee River from Lake Erie, crossing to the west bank of the Auglaize River right at The Glaize, and continued southward along the courses of the Auglaize and Miami rivers to the Ohio River near modern Cincinnati.

The complete pattern of Indian towns gathered around The Glaize in 1792 was a recent development, a regrouping formed in response to American expeditions launched from Cincinnati in 1790, and from both Vincennes and Cincinnati in 1791 (McKee 1895:366; Mesquakenoe 1923:228). The military objective of these expeditions had been the population of Shawnee, Delaware, and Miami then living at "The Miami Towns" on the headwaters of the Maumee River, present-day Fort Wayne. In 1790, the seven "Miami Towns" comprised two Miami, two Shawnee, and three Delaware villages, along with Fort Miami whose inhabitants were principally French and British traders (Butterfield 1890:246; Hay 1915:255; Harmar 1790). General Josiah Harmar's expedition in October, 1790 burned three hundred houses and twenty-thousand bushels of corn at the temporarily abandoned villages. After he withdrew, an intertribal Indian force attacked and killed about two hundred of his troops (Harmar to Knox 1832:104; Horsman 1964:60–63). The Indians rebuilt their homes, but soon began to transfer to safer locations. The nucleus for the new town formation down river at The Glaize was Captain Johnny's Shawnee town in existence near the mouth of the Auglaize River probably since 1789 (Hay 1915; Tanner 1956:7; Voegelin 1794b:417–19). As it developed by 1792, the total community at The Glaize encompassed seven main towns all within ten miles of the river mouth: three Shawnee, two Delaware, one Miami, and a European trading town, as well as outlying dwellings, gardens, pastures, and cornfields (Aupaumut 1827:97–98). Combined population for these towns is estimated at about two thousand persons.

Children and adults of European heritage, as well as warriors and families from eastern and southern Indian tribes, formed an integral part of this Ohio frontier society. One noticeable population component was the White captives, some adopted in childhood and raised as members of Indian families, and other more recent arrivals, mainly White but a few Black, taken in the periodic raids on river boats and pioneer settlements along the Ohio River. Among the residents of the trading town were French settlers, and British traders who had Indian wives and families. The interesting diversity of this composite community coupled with the pervading sense of common interest, is revealed by a closer examination of life in the individual towns. The description will begin with the Shawnee towns, since they represented the dominant population element.

The Indian Towns

Shawnee military headquarters on the Maumee River in 1792 was the town of the Shawnee leader Blue Jacket, located a mile below The Glaize on the north bank of the river.[2] The town was composed of perhaps thirty or forty bark cabins housing a population estimated very roughly at three hundred people. Vegetable gardens and pasture lands for horses and cattle lay behind the town, while the extensive acreage of unfenced cornfields were across the river separated from potentially marauding livestock (Spencer 1968:79, 96).

Blue Jacket himself was an impressive figure, dignified in appearance. His wife was half-French, daughter of a Shawnee woman and Colonel Duperon Baby, prominent Detroit resident and former Indian agent (Draper 1863).[3] A young visitor at Blue Jacket's home on an important social occasion in July of 1792 wrote the following description of this Shawnee leader and his family:

> His person, about six feet high was finely proportioned, stout, and muscular; his eyes large, bright, and piercing; his forehead high and broad; his nose aquiline; his mouth rather wide, and his countenance open and intelligent, expressive of firmness and decision. . . . He was dressed in a scarlet frock coat, richly laced with gold and confined around his waist with a part-colored sash, and in red leggings and moccasins ornamented in the highest style of Indian fashion. On his shoulders he wore a pair of gold epaulets, and on his arms broad silver bracelets; while from his neck hung a massive silver gorget and a large medallion of His Majesty, George III.

Around his lodge were hugh rifles, war clubs, bows and arrows, and other implements of war; while the skins of deer, bear, panther, and otter, the spoils of the chase, furnished pouches for tobacco, or mats for seats and beds. His wife was a remarkably fine looking woman; his daughters, much fairer than the generality of Indian women, were quite handsome; and his two sons, about eighteen and twenty years old, educated by the British, were very intelligent. (Spencer 1968:89–92)

Blue Jacket maintained a broad range of contacts among the regional French inhabitants, the British governmental administration, and occasionally even American agents sent from Vincennes or Cincinnati. In the complex affairs of the Northwest Indian Confederacy formed in 1786, Blue Jacket often served as representative to the British officials in Detroit and Montreal, speaking in behalf of the Delaware and Miami as well as the Shawnee (Blue Jacket 1895:135). In 1790, when his home was near the Miami towns at the head of the Maumee, he had provided lodging for Isaac Freeman, messenger from John Cleves Symmes, promoter of the American settlement at Cincinnati (Symmes 1926:104). The same spring he had entertained at his residence the American emissary, Antoine Gamelin, sent from Fort Knox, the military post at Vincennes (Gamelin 1882:157).

A second Shawnee village, Snake's Town, was situated about eight miles down the Maumee River from Blue Jacket (Voegelin 1974:200). A noted warrior, but less striking than his neighboring tribal leader, The Great Snake was described in 1788 as an "elderly, robust and rather corpulent" individual, whose wife remained a "pretty, well-looking woman" of stately carriage (Ridout 1890:366–67). Four years later, The Snake seemed to be "a plain, grave chief of sage appearance" (Spencer 1968:92). Snake's Town occupied the most easterly position of the group of Indian towns around The Glaize.

The third and oldest Shawnee town in the area lay on the east bank of the Auglaize more than a mile south of the Maumee River. The intervening land between the village and the mouth of the Auglaize River comprised part of a vast tract of Indian cornfields extending several miles along the south bank of the Maumee River (Spencer 1968:85, 96). This central town site is associated with Captain Johnny, in 1791 identified as "chief of the River Glaize" (Anonymous 1895:223). In the immediate vicinity were small settlements of Nanticokes, originally from the Potomac Bay region, and Chicamaugua, Cherokee warriors from Tennessee. The Cherokee's long connection with the Shawnee in Ohio is indicated by their frequent participation in intertribal councils and war parties north of the Ohio River, beginning in 1750 (Trent 1911:294, 297). Living within the Shawnee towns were families of Mohawk, Cayuga, and Seneca who were sometimes classified together as "Mingoes of the Glaize." The term *Mingo*, of Algonquian language origin, was commonly used during the eighteenth century to identify independent splinter groups of Six Nations Iroquois living in Ohio and western Pennsylvania (Hodge 1911, 1:867–68). A separate Delaware group also formed part of the Auglaize Indian community, and may have been located adjacent to Captain Johnny's town.

Across the Auglaize from the third Shawnee town, occasional dwellings spread southward about four miles along the west bank of the river. The south end of this Indian metropolitan district, about eight miles upriver on the Auglaize, was marked by a prominent Delaware village headed by Buckongahelas, principal warrior, and Big Cat, civil leader. A small village of Conoys, another eastern refugee group from Potomac Bay, formed part of the Delaware community (Aupaumut 1827:97–99). Big Cat himself lived in a bark-roofed log cabin lacking a floor, but possessing a fine door of hewed puncheons and a fireplace with a chimney constructed in the French fashion of reeds and clay. The principle interior furnishings were the beds made by supports of forked sticks driven into the earth with cross pieces inserted in holes in the log walls. On these frames were laid large slips of bark covered over with skins.

Big Cat acquired a second dwelling, a fine military marker, as part of his booty from St. Clair's defeat on November 4, 1791. This engagement, which took place at the later site of Fort Recovery, has been recognized as the most humiliating defeat ever suffered by the American army, with the loss of 630 lives out of a force of 1,400 (St. Clair 1812:69, 71; Horsman 1964:68–69).[4]

Big Cat's family in 1792 included an adopted son, John Brickell, a Pennsylvania lad captured by a Delaware warrior in May of 1791. Throughout his later life, Brickell retained a feeling of warmth and admiration for this exceptionally kindly Indian leader. Recounting his four years' experience living with Big Cat, Brickell observed:

> The Delawares are the best people to train up children I ever was with. They never whip, and scarce ever scold them. I was once struck one stroke, and but once while a member of the family, and then but just touched. They are remarkably quiet in the domestic circle. A dozen may be in one cabin, of all ages, and often scarcely noise enough to prevent the hearing of a pin fall on a hard place. Their leisure hours are, in a great measure, spent in training up their children to observe what they believe to be right. They often point out bad examples to them and say, "See that bad man; he is despised by everybody. He is older than you; if you do as he does, everybody will despise you by the time you are as old as he is." They often point good as worthy of imitation, such as brave and honest men. I know I am influenced to good, even at this day (1842) more from what I learned among them, than what I learned among my own color . . . (Brickell 1842:47–48)

The final town to be covered in this description of a pan-Indian settlement complex is Little Turtle's Miami village located that year on the north bank of the Maumee River near the Tiffin River about five miles west of Blue Jacket's Town (Spencer 1968:111). His customary residence was Eel River town twenty miles northwest of the Miami Towns (Hodge 1907:771). In 1792, Little Turtle, son of a Miami chief and a Mahican woman, was recognized as leading

The Glaize in 1792

warrior of the Northwest Indian Confederacy, his reputation based in large measure on his role in the stunning victory of the Indian forces over St. Clair's army in 1791. Similar in composition to the neighboring Indian towns, this Miami village also had a representation from the pioneer White settlements. Little Turtle's own family is a good example. The military hero of the Miamis took as his second wife a White captive, Polly Ford, previously married to a Frenchman living at Vincennes (Graves 1937).

His adopted son, later his son-in-law, was William Wells, member of a prominent Kentucky family, captured in 1784 at the age of thirteen. Although he had fought in 1791 with the Indian contingent, in 1792, Wells was employed by the American army staff at Vincennes to carry pacifically phrased messages to the "hostile tribes" on the Maumee River (Putnam 1791a, 1791b, 1903:371–74). Consequently, he often passed back and forth from Little Turtle's town at The Glaize within British territory to the American occupied town on the lower Wabash River (Spencer 1968:114).

The Mohawk Woman's Cabin

On the north bank of the Maumee between the towns of Little Turtle and Blue Jacket, stood a solitary cabin of considerable importance in local society. This lone dwelling belonged to Coo-coo-chee, an independent and influential Mohawk woman frequently consulted by Indian leaders because of her highly valued spiritual power and knowledge of herbal medicine. Before the outbreak of the American Revolution, Coo-coo-chee and her husband, with three sons and a daughter, left their homeland on the Richelieu River in the St. Lawrence Valley near Montreal and came to live with the Shawnee in Ohio. The husband and father of this Mohawk family, a distinguished leader of the Bear clan, was mortally wounded in hand-to-hand combat with an American soldier during Harmar's 1790 attack on the Miami towns at present Fort Wayne. Since his death, Coo-coo-chee had moved out of Blue Jacket's town, selecting as a site for her widow's cabin a sloping hillside opposite the mouth of the Auglaize River. Behind the cabin, she cultivated a large vegetable garden and five acres of corn. Her food resources also included a maple grove for spring sugar-making located a few miles away near a creek on the south side of the Maumee (Spencer 1968:77–78, 125).

In 1792, the four children no longer lived with the Mohawk woman. Two grown sons, Black Loon and White Loon, were leading warriors in Blue Jacket's town, while the third brother had his home on the Auglaize River about five or six miles upstream (Spencer 1968:74). The daughter was the wife of George Ironside, a British merchant living in the trading village established on the point of land on the west side of the Auglaize River entrance, directly across the Maumee River from her bark cabin.

Yet Coo-coo-chee did not lead a solitary existence. Her household in which Shawnee served as the common language, included two grandchildren, a thirteen-year-old girl and a younger boy, as well as the "faithful dog" ever-present in an Indian family. The boy, whom his grandmother called "Simon" was rumored to be a son of Simon Girty, British partisan leader of many Indian expeditions and probably the man most hated by frontier Americans of that period. For seven months beginning in July 1792, the Mohawk woman also had charge of an eleven-year-old boy, Oliver Spencer, captured by a Shawnee and her son, White Loon. The Shawnee warrior had come across the boy on the Ohio River returning to his new home in Columbia from a Fourth of July celebration in Cincinnati (Spencer 1968:41–47, 82, 120).

Spencer's captivity narrative provides an illuminating inside view of Coo-coo-chee's establishment and the events in which she participated, the details contributing to a general understanding of the contemporary Indian society. Her cabin in its construction was typical of homes in the surrounding villages, but somewhat above average in size (fourteen by twenty-five feet) and more elaborate in its furnishings. As Spencer described the building:

The Glaize in 1792

. . . Its frame was constructed of small poles, of which some, planted upright in the ground, served as posts and studs, supporting the ridge poles and eave bearers, while others firmly tied to these by thongs of hickory bark formed girders, braces, laths and rafters. This frame was covered with large pieces of elm bark seven or eight feet long and three or four feet wide; which being pressed flat and well dried to prevent their curling, fastened to the poles by thongs of bark, formed the weather boarding and roof of the cabin. At its western end was a narrow doorway about six feet high, closed when necessary by a single piece of bark placed beside it, and fastened by a brace, set either within or on the outside as occasion required. (Spencer 1968:83)

Spencer also noted that neither locks nor bolts were used in Indian villages:

. . . a log placed against its door affords ample protection to its contents and abundant evidence of the right of possession in its owner; a right seldom violated even by the most worthless among them. The same respect is paid, even in the wilderness, to property known or believed to belong to Indians of the same tribe, or to those of other tribes at peace with them. (Spencer 1968:68–69)

The unusual feature of Coo-coo-chee's home was its two-room interior, for Indian cabins seldom had more than a single living space. The main room of her cabin had on the outside walls a low frame covered with bark and deerskins, serving as seats and bedsteads. Fires for cooking and warmth were laid in the center of the room, directly under the opening in the roof for smoke, while from the ridgepole was suspended a wooden trammel used to support a cooking kettle. The inner room, separated by a bark partition, was her private religious sanctuary, though the area also served as a pantry for food storage and spare bedroom. The addition to Coo-coo-chee's home had been built by William Moore, a fellow townsman of young Spencer from Columbia, captured earlier in

1792 by her sons, White Loon and Black Loon. Moore became a great favorite of the Mohawk woman and was often at her home that summer (Spencer 1968:97–98, 101).

Coo-coo-chee's personal possessions included all the implements and containers that were considered basic necessities in frontier living, and probably differed little from the household articles used in American pioneer homes at the same time. As Oliver Spencer observed:

> Her household furniture consisted of a large brass kettle for wash-
> ing and sugar making; a deep, close-covered copper hominy kettle;
> a few knives, tin cups, pewter and horn spoons, sieves, wooden
> bowls, and baskets of various sizes; a hominy block, and four beds
> and bedding comprising each a few deerskins and two blankets . . .
> (Spencer 1968:86–87)

The Mohawk woman resembled other older women of the Shaw-nee village in which she had been living for many years. She wore a long calico shirt fastened in front with a silver brooch, a skirt of blue cloth with white edging belted at the waist with a striped sash, matching blue cloth leggings, and deerskin moccasins. Younger belles of the town fancied more elaborate attire displaying their own handiwork, such as beaded designs and quillwork on moccasins, and more beading and ribbon borders around the bottom of skirts. Young women were also extremely fond of silver jewelry, covering skirt bodices with rows of silver buttons and brooches, lining their arms with bracelets one to four inches wide, and attaching tinkling silver bells to leggings. Yet they were seldom as ostentatious as the warriors who suspended as many as five sets of heavy ornaments from the rims of their ears (Spencer 1968:87–88). The importance of silver jewelry is illustrated by the fact that General Rufus Putnam, sent from Philadelphia in 1792 to make a peace treaty with the Northwest Indians, took along with him twenty sets of silver jewelry and additional ear and nose ornaments. The jewelry was intended to serve as presents at the treaty signing (Knox 1903:265).

During the course of the spring and summer of 1792, Coo-coo-chee presided over two important Indian ceremonies at her home, the annual Feast of the Dead and the Green Corn Festival. In observance of the Feast of the Dead, her husband's bones were reverently removed from their original burial site and placed in a grave a few rods from her cabin, in view of the warrior's path crossing the Maumee River. The Mohawk leader was buried in a sitting posture facing westward; and by his side were placed all the items necessary for a successful warrior and hunter, his rifle, tomahawk, knife, blanket, and moccasins. Friends attending the ceremony dropped additional gifts into the open grave. When the reburial was completed, a four-foot post was placed at the head of the grave. This marker, painted bright red, had near the top a rudely carved image of a face, below which was recorded the number of scalps he had taken in battle. On important occasions thereafter, as many as nineteen scalps attached to a long, slender pole, swayed in the wind over his gravesite (Spencer 1968:80–82).

The next important ceremony at Coo-coo-chee's cabin, the Green Corn Festival, took place in mid-August. The Shawnee were among the more northern groups to share this harvest tradition, annually observed by agriculturally skilled Indian people from East Texas to Florida. At Coo-coo-chee's home in 1792, the festival was an all-day celebration with somber, sportive, joyous, and dangerously rowdy phases. Her guests included her three sons and their wives, her daughter and George Ironside, William Moore, and a number of other Shawnee families. The program opened with the ritual of passing a pipe several times around the circle of participants seated on the grass. Next, a venerable leader delivered a solemn speech first extolling the bountiful gifts provided for Indian people by the Great Spirit, then denouncing the murderous oppression of the encroaching "pale faces." At the conclusion of his oration, the speaker exhorted the warriors to drive the Americans from the land, or at least force them back to the other side of the Ohio River. This rousing finale drew the listeners to their feet with whoops of approval for the commencement of the sports contests (Spencer 1968:102–4).

In preparation for this next section of the festivities, William Moore had built a viewing stand behind Coo-coo-chee's cabin. This structure consisted of a raised platform with a rear wall and roof to shield the older guests from the sun as they watched the athletic events. Footraces where first on the schedule, followed by a series of wrestling matches and a special test of warrior strength in retaining a grip on a slippery length of greased leather thong. Moore was permitted to join in the wrestling competition and managed to throw one of the principal Shawnee contestants. This imprudent victory he managed to explain as a lucky accident rather than superior skill, for he knew that it was scarcely safe to demean the physical prowess of his captors (Spencer 1968:105, 111).

At mid-day, everyone joined in the feast provided by Coo-coo-chee. The menu consisted of boiled jerky, fish, stewed squirrels, venison, squashes, roast pumpkins, and corn in several forms. Tender ears of corn on the cob were prepared, along with a mixture of cut corn and beans called succotash, regular corn bread, and a special pounded corn batter poured into a corn-leaf mold and baked in ashes. All the food was served in wooden bowls, and eaten with wooden, horn, or tin spoons. Most of the guests carried their own knives to cut the meat (Spencer 1968:106–7).

Following a short interval of after-dinner smoking, a small keg of rum was brought out and passed around. At this point, the men turned all their knives and tomahawks over to Coo-coo-chee for safekeeping before continuing with the sports. Among the Shawnee, this safeguard was observed before indulging in any "frolic." Later in the afternoon, the recreation turned to social dancing led by an experienced singer who also beat a small drum, adjusting the tempo to suit each number. Men and women formed separate dance circles, rotating in opposite directions.

By nightfall, when the Green Corn Festival reached the final stage of an intoxicated revel, George Ironside, William Moore, and young Oliver Spencer had all left the scene. Unfortunately, White Loon challenged a fellow warrior to a final wrestling match and was badly burned when he was thrown into the fire, a circumstance that brought the day's activities to a hasty close (Spencer 1968:112–13).

The Traders' Town

When George Ironside and Coo-coo-chee's daughter retired from the Green Corn celebration, they crossed the Maumee to their home in the British and French trading village at the point of land most precisely defining the *grand glaize*. The high ground southwest of the juncture of the Maumee and Auglaize rivers had long been a seasonal trading site, but the local population increased markedly early in 1792 when the last European inhabitants of Fort Miami at "The Miami Towns" followed their Indian clientele downriver to new sites at The Glaize (McKee 1895:366; Vigo 1792). Here they settled in a clearing two hundred yards wide and a quarter of a mile long, bordered on the west and south by tall oak trees and hazel underbrush. At the north end of the clearing, half a dozen buildings had been erected for traders and for the British Indian agency. Further upstream on the Auglaize River lived several more French and English families as well as an American couple who had been taken prisoner at St. Clair's defeat in November, 1791. The Americans were working to repay their ransom fee, the woman by washing and sewing, and the man by serving as oarsman on the boats plying between The Glaize and the British supply base at The Rapids, sixty miles farther downriver on the Maumee (Spencer 1968:95–96). This small trading settlement adjacent to six sizeable Indian towns probably numbered no more than fifty individuals.

The traders living on The Point in 1792 were all men prominent in the history of the Old Northwest. George Ironside, the most wealthy and influential of the small group, had attended King's College, Aberdeen, before coming to North America and entering the Indian trade (Quaife 1928:332n77). His establishment, most northerly in the row of traders, was a three-room hewed log cabin with a loft, used as a dwelling, store, and warehouse. Next to him lived the French baker named Perault, who supplied bread for the entire European settlement, and occasionally to Indians (Spencer 1968:95).

The other side of the bakery stood the building belonging to John Kinzie, a silversmith and trader whose father had been a British surgeon during the Seven Years' War. John Kinzie was born in Quebec in 1763 shortly before his father's death. After his mother remarried and took him to New York, he ran away to Quebec where he became a silversmith's apprentice. He subsequently moved to Detroit and began making jewelry for Indians in the Maumee River valley. The mother of his two children was a Shawnee captive taken from her father's home in West Virginia in 1774, when she was ten years old, and ransomed in Detroit in 1784 (Andreas 1884:100–102).

Between George Ironside's establishment and the banks of the Auglaize River, a small stockade enclosed two buildings belonging to men who had been living and trading with the Shawnee for almost thirty years by 1792. One building served as a supply depot intermittently used by Alexander McKee, British Indian agent in Detroit, and his assistant, Matthew Elliott (Horsman 1964:59). The second building was occupied by the trader James Girty, who shared his home for considerable periods of time during the summer and fall of 1792 with his older brother, Simon Girty. These men to varying degrees had been integrated into Indian society through family and trading connections, yet they also had played significant roles in American and British diplomacy and warfare in the Ohio valley. A sketch of their interwoven personal histories indicates their long connection with the Shawnee and allied tribes, and their place in the composite community at The Glaize in 1792.

The Indian life of the Girtys—Simon, James, and a younger brother, George—began in the summer of 1756 when their ages were thirteen, eleven, and nine. With the rest of their family they were captured by a Delaware-Shawnee war party on the Pennsylvania frontier, but were repatriated in 1759. For three years, Simon lived with the Seneca, James with the Shawnee, and George with the Delaware. The social experience and knowledge of Indian language gained during the period of captivity actually determined the subsequent course of their lives. The trio first became official interpreters for the British Indian agency at Pittsburgh (Butterfield 1890:8, 13–15).

Before the outbreak of the American Revolution, James Girty along with the deputy Indian agent at Pittsburgh, Alexander Mc-Kee, and Matthew Elliott were all traders in the Shawnee villages clustered around Chillicothe, Ohio, on the Scioto River and its tributaries. Elliott, an Irishman who had come to Pennsylvania in 1761, entered the Shawnee trade after serving in Colonel Henry Bouquet's expedition against the Delaware towns on the Muskingum River near present Coshocton, Ohio, in 1764 (Cruikshank 1923:157n.). In Dunmore's War, 1774, the first military action directed against the Shawnee in Ohio, Simon Girty scouted for Lord Dunmore; while Matthew Elliott carried the peace message to Dunmore from the Shawnee (Gibson 1842, 1:18).

The political sympathies of the Indian agency staff at Pittsburgh were open to question throughout the early years of the American Revolution. The year 1778 was a watershed year marking the divide between the American and British associations of the McKee, Elliott, and Girty factions. Early in 1778, all three Girtys were involved in American projects organized in Pittsburgh. Their changing personal loyalties became evident on the night of March 28, however, when McKee, Elliott, and Simon Girty precipitously left American-occupied Pittsburgh, picked up James Girty in the Ohio Shawnee country, and enlisted in the British Indian service at Detroit. For the balance of the Revolutionary War, and throughout the battles of mutual retaliation between Kentuckians and the Northwest Indian Confederacy beginning in 1786, all these men were active partisans in Indian warfare, although McKee as top officer was seldom involved in actual combat (Butterfield 1890:47–51, 75 et ff).

Living within the stockaded section of the trading town at The Glaize with a Shawnee wife, James Girty in 1792 evinced a wariness of strangers and overt hostility toward captured Americans (Spencer 1968:132). His brother, Simon, joined him at intervals while performing the duties of mobile trouble-shooter for the British Indian service. By this time, Simon Girty at the age of fifty-three had become an awesome veteran of Ohio frontier warfare, his sunken grey eyes shaded by heavy brows meeting above a flat nose, and a forbidding facial expression. Dressed in Indian attire but without the usual silver ornaments and decorations worn by tribal leaders, he customarily wore a silk handkerchief knotted about his shaggy head and pulled low over one eyebrow to conceal an ugly scar. Simon had received a serious tomahawk wound not from an enemy, but from an ally, the Mohawk leader Joseph Brant, about whom he had made allegedly disparaging remarks following a joint expedition across southeastern Ohio in 1781 (Spencer 1968:92). Socially as well as spatially, James Girty existed on the periphery of the predominantly British-French trading town at The Glaize. He had little in common with the French inhabitants whose homes were further from The Point; his ties were much closer to his Shawnee relatives and associates.

Very little detailed information about the social life of the trading community at The Glaize in 1792 has survived, but a vivid account of the manners and customs of the same group at Fort Miami (modern Fort Wayne) has been preserved in the journal entries of a Detroit visitor who lived in the town from late December, 1789 until April of 1790 (Hay 1915:208–61). Fort Miami, an old French settlement, had a closely knit population of about a dozen families, some of whom had been there thirty to fifty years by 1790. Social leader of the community, Madame Adahmer, wife of one of the older French traders, ran a household largely dependent upon the labor of a "ponnie wench," a term identifying a Pawnee or any other western Indian captured by eastern tribes and sold into slavery. The ladies of the traders' town served tea and coffee at afternoon gatherings, supplying ample quantities of port, madeira, and sometimes grog at dinners and evening parties. Menus were European in character, including such items as roast turkey, corned pork, loin of veal, cucumber pickles, and cheese (Hay 1915:220, 225, 227–29).

Card playing, singing, and dancing were the regular pastimes in the predominantly French atmosphere. Frequently music was provided by two violinists, John Kinzie the silversmith and a trader named LaChambre, and by the Detroit visitor who brought along his flute. The same trio played for morning mass and vespers on Christmas Day. On Sundays, the settlers were called to prayers held at the home of an elderly inhabitant, by three small boys who circulated through the village ringing cow bells (Hay 1915:221, 224–25, 255).

A gallant young man at Fort Miami began the New Year by kissing all the ladies and in the following weeks joined the impromptu serenades further honoring the female contingent in the small town. On the evenings preceding special saints' days, everyone joined in presenting a bouquet to the person bearing the name of that particular saint, then carrying the bouquet from house to house, stopping each time for a round of dancing. When the creeks and marshes froze, ice skating became a popular outdoor activity (Hay 1915:239, 242).

British traders promoted a full day's celebration of Her Majesty's Birthday on January 18, 1790. In the morning, the sergeant of the small contingent of Canadian volunteers was persuaded to fire off three volleys, a noise that brought The Snake and other Shawnee leaders into town to inquire the cause of the disturbance. The grand ball held that evening, opening with a formal minuet, marked the third consecutive night of dancing in Miamitown. In honor of this patriotic occasion, two of the leading French traders appeared in "very fine fur caps on their heads adorned with a great quantity of black ostrich feathers," also sporting "amazingly large cockades" of white tinsel ribbon (Hay 1915:240–41). Small hats with large feathers were in vogue among the Indians at that time, but the cockades were a European embellishment (Ridout 1890:358). At the ball, singing following dancing, and one trader's wife toward the end of the evening contributed a lively ballad with undeniably double-entendre verses. On the holiday calendar for Fort Miami, Mardi Gras and St. Patrick's Day also called for special observance (Hay 1915:250, 258).

Early in 1790, the most prominent traders, including John Kinzie and George Ironside, formed a fraternal organization called "The Friars of St. Andrews" with rules written in English and translated into French. It is interesting to note that although they were trading in the area at the time, James Girty with the Shawnee and George Girty with the Delaware, neither became a member of this exclusive club. On the other hand, the list of members did include the acting Miami chief, J. B. Richardville, son of a deceased Quebec trader and an enterprising Miami woman known as Maria Louisa, who was busy at her trading post that winter improving the substantial family fortune (Hay 1915:223, 246–47).

Day-to-day activities in the neighboring Miami, Shawnee, and Delaware towns were always of interest to residents of Fort Miami. The casual comments in the 1790 journal reveal the deferent but sympathetic personal relations that had developed between the tribal leaders, traders, and settlers. For example, Blue Jacket, The Snake, and other Indians were commonly entertained by the traders at breakfast time. Indian families frequently sent gifts of turkey or venison, receiving in return tobacco and rum or brandy. George Ironside accompanied James Girty back to the Shawnee camp to help collect furs. Later, George Girty brought his Delaware wife and her sister from their hunting lodge for a recreational trip to town. Blue Jacket in company with the French trader Antoine Lascelle, whose more distinguished relatives were members of The Friars of St. Andrew, arrived from a brief excursion to the Ouiatenon village lower on the Wabash, present Lafayette, Indiana (Hay 1915:229, 235–36, 244, 250).

More unusual, perhaps, as an example of intercultural relations is the billeting of Indian warriors at the homes of the European residents of Fort Miami. When LeGris, the Miami chief, returned from a military expedition, he divided his war party according to the accommodations available at each French or British household, assigning as many as six Indians to a single home. In March of 1790, when the Shawnee had decided to build an additional town for families scattered by the recent period of hostilities, they convoked a town meeting of the European traders and settlers to announce their intentions, requesting presents of vermillion and tobacco. After the assembled Fort Miami residents had signified their unanimous assent, the leading Indian handed to the leading trader the string of wampum signifying this decision. Such incidents point out the way in which Europeans became involved in the life of their Indian neighbors on the frontier (Hay 1915:221, 222, 255, 257).

The convivial spirit of Fort Miami and the easy association of the settlers and traders with Indian people in the adjoining towns, demonstrated so clearly in the 1790 journal, were social qualities undoubtedly carried along to their new location in 1792. At The Glaize, even the pattern of town sites virtually duplicated the previous formation at the headwaters of the Maumee (Voegelin 1974:159–61; Tanner and Hast 1976:21). In addition to their personal ties, the trading group also maintained strong economic links to the Indian community through the fur trade. At this time, traders operating out of Detroit, backed by firms in Montreal, were struggling to preserve British control over an Indian hunting territory southwest of Lake Erie valued at thirty thousand pounds annually. Although this sum represented only about 20 percent of the income from the Mackinac hinterland, it was still far from negligible in an era of generally declining fur trade returns (Henry et al. 1895:163).

While life on the local scene at The Glaize followed a traditional round of economic and ceremonial events, in the broader sphere of Indian affairs, the region became prominent as the headquarters for the intertribal front line of hostilities along the Ohio River. The geographical location of The Glaize, equidistant from the nearest British and American forts, points up the intermediate frontier position of the confederate towns in the Maumee River valley in 1792. Detroit, about 110 miles northeast of The Glaize by water routes, functioned as a rear supply base for the Northwest Indian Confederacy centered at the juncture of the Maumee and Auglaize rivers. Directly to the south, about 110 miles of open country intervened between the clustered Indian towns and the nearest American outpost, Fort Jefferson. Seventy miles further, the principal American base, Fort Washington at present-day Cincinnati, had been constructed as recently as 1790.

The military strength of the Northwest Indian Confederacy attained impressive concentration by 1792. A thousand warriors and their families gathered at The Glaize in May for a spring council with Matthew Elliott, deputy Indian agent for the British government (Western Indian Nations 1923:157). Allied with the community at the mouth of the Auglaize River were Ottawa, Wyandot, and Delaware located near McKee's supply base at the rapids of the Maumee River. The Ottawa village at Roche de Bout had been established by Pontiac's followers in 1764, but Snipe's Wyandot town and Capt. Pipe's Delaware and Munsee followers had moved from the Upper Sandusky River in 1791 concurrent with the movement of villages from the Miami Towns to The Glaize (Peckham 1947:250; Knox 1960:23). Many well-known tribal leaders, particularly of the Shawnee, were not in evidence at the Maumee in 1792 because they were living in secret camps or patrolling the Ohio River banks. For example, Tecumseh, by 1812 a reknowned pan-Indian leader, made his first notable appearance as a warrior in 1792 during an engagement with Kentuckians on the lower course of the Little Miami River (Draper n.d., 5 BB:83, 101; 9 BB:47).

On the other hand, the Indians assembled at The Glaize represented only a part of the total tribal manpower. In 1791, a number of Shawnee and Delaware had emigrated from the Miami Towns to Missouri, occupying land near Cape Girardeau granted by the Spanish governor of Upper Louisiana (Vigo 1792; Trudeau 1909:51).

Other Shawnee were living with the Creeks and a few of the most militant were with the "outcast Cherokee" in Tennessee, at Running Water Town, present-day Chattanooga, Tennessee (Draper n.d., 1 YY 14; Finnelson 1832:390; Leonard 1832:308). The dispersed Delaware included two communities in the Chippewa country on the Thames River, Canada (Tanner and Hast 1976:21). Most of the Miami remained within the area of present day Indiana.

In assessing the overall capability of the allied Indians, the role of the British in Detroit was a critical factor. The British Indian agency, scarcely distinguishable from the trading interests, provided the arms and ammunition vital to continuation of the Indian protest against American encroachment. Moreover, in the spring of 1792, Agent Alexander McKee distributed five hundred bushels of seed corn to families at The Glaize who had exhausted their reserves in order to feed allies during the previous two years of strenuous but successful warfare (McKee 1895a:366).

The question of peace or continued war was debated at length among the leaders of the Confederacy as well as among their potential military allies as soon as invitations to a general meeting were sent out early in the year. The future course of the Northwest Confederacy became a matter of concern to Indian people from Quebec to Missouri, and in the Cherokee and Creek country of the South. In addition, British, American, and Spanish administrations sought to influence the outcome of deliberations by sending messages or emissaries to the confederated Indians in 1792. The intensity and complexity of diplomatic affairs increased during the summer as runners came and went from all four directions, delegations arrived, and news and rumor circulated through the villages and camps. Activity reached a climax at the grand council held at The Glaize from September 30 to October 9, an occasion requiring considerable linguistic skill and management of intertribal protocol (Aupaumut 1827:76–125; McKee 1895b:483–98).

Preparations for the general Indian council were well under way by May of 1792, even in the distant St. Lawrence River valley, upper New York, and the city of Philadelphia. By 1793, the Iroquois tribes comprising the Six Nations, the Mohawk, Oneida, Onondaga, Cayuga, Seneca, and Tuscarora, were living on both sides of the Great Lakes in territory now divided between the United States and Canada. The Seven Nations of Canada included Catholic groups organized by French missionaries in the vicinity of Montreal: Hurons of Lorette, Caughnawaga Mohawk, St. Regis Mohawk, St. Francis Abenaki, Lake of the Two Mountains or Oka Mohawk, Oka Algonkin, and Oka Nipissing.

In the spring of 1791, three eastern Indian leaders, representing the Seven Nations of Lower Canada, the Six Nations Iroquois, and the Stockbridge (Mahigan), conferred with American Secretary of War Henry Knox before their parties left for the Maumee River meeting ground. Most pro-American of the three was Col. Louis, Indian-Negro chief of the Caughnawaga Mohawks and a man of influence among the Seven Nations of Canada, who had received his military title after serving as an American spy during the Revolutionary War. Joseph Brant, representing a pro-British faction among the Six Nations, cautiously sent a messenger to the Maumee to secure approval for going alone to Philadelphia, an action at variance with the Confederacy's agreed procedure to talk with Americans only in authorized group delegations. The third man, Capt. Hendrick Aupaumut of the Mahigan Indians, ultimately undertook the difficult task of bearing the peace message of the United States to the hostile tribes' central headquarters (Knox 1903:59n, 257–67; Aupaumut 1827:113).

In performing this service, Capt. Hendrick conscientiously carried on a two-hundred-year-old responsibility of the Mahigan people for taking news of the White people on the Atlantic coast to the western Indians. From Oneida, he fetched his own bag of peace containing ancient wampum, and took along written messages as well as messages in the form of specially prepared belts and strings of wampum. On his way from Philadelphia, he conferred with the Six Nations at Buffalo Creek, New York, the Delaware on the Thames River, and Capt. Pipe at the Maumee Rapids. Before settling with a fellow Mahican living at Big Cat's Delaware town, he bought bread and salt at the traders' town at The Glaize. The news he brought received varying reactions: indifference to the wars among European nations, audible enthusiasm for the report that slaves were killing their masters in the Caribbean, and long pondering over the import of the "peace" message from the United States (Aupaumut 1827:76, 79, 89, 98).

Capt. Pipe had advised Capt. Hendrick to circulate the peace message through the Delaware, Wyandot, and Chippewa, accumulating a block of support before the message was formally presented to the Shawnee. Hendrick was never able to carry out his instructions from Knox, to arrange for a delegation from the tribes assembled at The Glaize to meet General Rufus Putnam at Fort Jefferson. After receiving a series of excuses, Hendrick realized that since a war party had killed haymakers at Fort Jefferson, the ground was "bloody" and no peace meeting could take place there. Ultimately, the reports that General Wayne was organizing a new army at Pittsburgh, and Fort Jefferson was being reinforced, and additional posts erected became knowledge more persuasive than the beautiful four foot wampum belt with the fifteen squares representing the fifteen United States displayed by Capt. Hendrick (Aupaumut 1827:95, 121, 126–30). The Mahigan visitor frankly criticized the obviously superior position of the Shawnee war leaders whom he observed sitting in front of civil leaders at councils, contrary to traditionally accepted seating arrangements (Aupaumut 1827:118).

In the meantime, delegations arrived and set up their camps. Among the earliest were Shawnee and Delaware from the Spanish side of the Mississippi River (Johnson 1895:422). The Seven Nations of Lower Canada arrived at The Glaize, complained of the primitive facilities to which they were not accustomed, and soon departed leaving behind a few representatives. Most of the Chippewa and Ottawa, weary of waiting and anxious about the arrival of fall storms, left for the upper lakes before the council officially commenced.

The large sixty-five member Six Nations delegation crossed Lake Erie on the same vessel bringing William Johnson, British Indian Interpreter, and members of the British army staff from Niagara (W. Johnson 1895:468–70; Aupaumut 1827:114). Neither these men nor Alexander McKee attended the sessions, for the council at The Glaize was a pan-Indian conclave. Delegates from west of Lake Michigan were the last to arrive. Early in the year, Blue Jacket had toured the western nations and brought back a calumet presented at the council. In response to his messages and counter-propaganda from Col. Hamtramck at Vincennes, eleven western nations had held a preliminary conference in June at the confluence of the Kankakee and Desplaines rivers, predictably resulting in divided opinions (McKee 1895b:485; Hamtramck 1792).

After a series of private conferences among the various factions represented, the Grand Council at The Glaize finally opened on September 30, 1792. Indians who participated in the meeting represented the following tribes: Shawnee, Wyandot, Delaware, Munsee, Miami, Conoy, Nanticoke, Mahigan, Ottawa, Chippewa, Potawatomi, Cherokee, Creek, Sauk, Fox, Ouiatenon, Six Nations, and the Seven Nations of Lower Canada. All these Indian people knew absolutely that the Ohio River had been set as the permanent boundary between Indian and White settlements by the Treaty of Fort Stanwix in 1768 with the British, and had been agreed to by American authorities in Pittsburgh at the beginning of the American Revolution. Yet the problem of illegal American settlements in the Indian country, the basis for eighteen years of hostilities, remained unresolved. On October 7, the council decided to demand recognition of the border stipulated in the 1768 treaty, i.e., the Ohio River, "a fine natural boundary" in the opinion of a Six Nations speaker. Joseph Brant, detained in New York by illness, did not arrive at The Glaize until after this decision had been made. Brant himself favored a compromise line along the Muskingum River that would cede to Americans an area of Ohio from which it would be difficult to evict settlers (McKee 1895b:482, 496; Aupaumut 1827:117; W. Johnson 1895:470).

The outcome of the decision made by the Grand Council in 1792 is part of the standard history of the Northwest Territory. The Indian towns at The Glaize became General Anthony Wayne's military target. Though the buildings were razed in August of 1794, the residents were warned by an American deserter, and escaped down the Maumee River to regroup near the rapids. At the traders' town, Wayne established his military headquarters, Fort Defiance. The ripe corn along the south bank of the Maumee, visible from the high ground at that site, was the beginning of the impressive fifty miles of cornfields that Wayne boasted of destroying. Final defeat of the Northwest Indian Confederacy came at the Battle of Fallen Timbers, August 20, 1794, not far from McKee's post and a hastily constructed British fort at the foot of the Maumee rapids (Wayne 1960:351–55). This event usually marks the end of a chapter in northwestern frontier history, except to add that the Indian tribes agreed to give up the southern two-thirds of Ohio at the Treaty of Greenville in 1795. On the other hand, the Indian community from the region of The Glaize did not come to an end with the destruction of the townsite on the Maumee River. After relying on the British for food distribution for two years, most of the tribal groups filtered back to familiar territory in Ohio and Indiana.

But there is a more important epilogue to this brief account of the life and death of the multicultural society at The Glaize. The Europeans who formed an unobtrusive part of the local community advanced to more spectacular careers. From this milieu emerged the men with a dual cultural heritage who became the principal intermediaries in Indian-White relations, particularly treaty negotiations, in Canada and the United States for more than a quarter of a century. A glance at the subsequent life of the traders and Indian agents at The Glaize indicates that they, as well as their Indian associates, readjusted their lives following the double loss represented by the Greenville treaty with the Indians and the concessions made by the British in the Jay Treaty of 1794. Although the British army had to give up Detroit in 1796, the British Indian department continued the direction of Indian affairs on both sides of the American-Canadian border well into the nineteenth century from their new base at Fort Malden at Amherstberg on the east bank of the Detroit River. Furthermore, several members of a second generation carried on as intermediaries in Indian relations.

Alexander McKee was succeeded as British Indian agent by his Shawnee son Thomas, who unfortunately became an alcoholic. Old Matthew Elliott, at nearly seventy years of age, then had to undertake responsibility for managing Indian military support of the British during the War of 1812 (Horsman 1964:177 et ff). His clerk and storekeeper, George Ironside, next served as British Indian agent until 1831 and was succeeded by his son George Ironside, Jr., who in all probability was the grandson of the Mohawk woman, Coo-coo-chee, although George himself thought his mother was Shawnee. Young George became involved in Wyandot affairs, and Reserve problems at Manatoulin Island. A second son, Robert Ironside, at times served as physician to the Indians in Ontario (G. Ironside, Sr. 1831; G. Ironside, Jr. 1831; and R. Ironside 1845).

On the American side of the border, William Wells became Indian Agent at Fort Wayne at the request of the Miami, though they knew he had served with General Wayne. He died at the Chicago massacre in 1812, sacrificing his life in trying to evacuate the residents and the Fort Dearborn garrison. Indian assailants, who admired his personal courage and bravery, paid him the tribute of eating his heart (Quaife 1913:224–28).

John Kinzie, in later years more trader than silversmith, apparently also gave up violin playing. The aftermath of the Battle of Fallen Timbers dislocated his personal life more than the lives of other men who transacted business at The Glaize. The father of his Indian captive wife came from Virginia and took back from Detroit all Kinzie's family. Kinzie later married a woman widowed by the Battle of Fallen Timbers, who had been a captive among the Seneca as a child. He took up trading among the Potawatomi and in 1804 moved to a more advanced frontier location at Chicago.

Treated as a neutral, he and his family survived the Fort Dearborn massacre. The children of his first family came from Virginia to become part of the new pioneer community on the southwest side of Lake Michigan. The oldest child of his second family, John H. Kinzie, served as Indian agent at Fort Winnebago at the portage between the Fox and Wisconsin rivers. By 1830, his network of relatives was involved in Indian affairs as traders and government agents from Mackinac Island to Peoria, Illinois (Quaife 1913:246, 269, 280, 347, 361–64).

Billy Caldwell, who became prominent in Potawatomi affairs at Chicago in 1829, also stems from the tight-knit circle of people concerned with developments at The Glaize and along the Maumee River. In 1792, at age twelve, Billy had recently transferred from his Mohawk mother's home near Niagara to the Amherstberg residence of his father, Captain William Caldwell of the British Rangers. His father had been a trading partner of Matthew Elliott at Cuyahoga in 1785, and in 1794 brought belated military support to the Indian contingent at the Battle of Fallen Timbers. His stepmother, Susan Baby, was a half-sister of Blue Jacket's wife, both being daughters of Col. Duperon Baby (Quaife 1928, 1:292n11). The old Shawnee leader, Blue Jacket, established his post-war town on the American side of the Detroit River near Brownstown, the Wyandot village at present-day Gibraltar, Michigan. His daughters married into the local French population (Quaife 1928, 1:561). In 1843, Blue Jacket's descendants and other Shawnee were still in the Detroit area living on the Wyandot reservation established in 1818 at Flat Rock on the Huron River.

Conclusion

This local-history vignette has been created for multiple purposes: (1) to call attention to the diverse cultural components of a complex eighteenth-century community and demonstrate the long-standing ties that developed between Indian people and Europeans in a frontier setting; (2) to indicate the geographic range of the communications network radiating from a single Indian nerve center; (3) to reconstruct the events of a critical year; and finally, (4) to point out that the community at The Glaize—active in 1792 and struck off the map in 1794—left a recognizable legacy in the history of Indian-White relations on the Great Lakes Frontier.

Notes

1. The author wishes to thank Gordon Day for information on the Seven Nations of Canada, Jacqueline Peterson for notes on the Caldwell and Baby families, and James A. Clifton for information on George Ironside and Billy Caldwell. Research was supported by a grant from the Research Tools Program of the National Endowment for the Humanities.

2. In the eighteenth century, the Maumee River was usually called *Miami-of-the-Lakes* to distinguish it from the Great Miami and Little Miami rivers flowing into the Ohio River near Cincinnati. The transition to Maumee began with the French *Au Miami* for "at the Miami," abbreviated to *Au Mi*, and phonemically into English as *Omee*. This term was used in American correspondence beginning about 1790 (Harmar 1790). Americans also called the river the *Tawa*, an abbreviation of *Ottawa*. The name *Maumee* as a development from *Au Mi* and *Omee* took place in the early nineteenth century.

3. The erroneous notion that Blue Jacket was actually a White captive named Marmaduke Van Swearingen has received wide acceptance since the 1967 publication of Allen W. Eckert's novel *The Frontiersman*. The identity is based on a family tradition originating in Kansas in 1877. After a thorough examination of available evidence, it is apparent that one crucial inconsistency is the matter of age. Blue Jacket was a recognized chief of the Mequachake division of the Shawnee in 1772, while Marmaduke was reportedly but a youth at the time of his capture tentatively dated at 1778.

4. Indians publicized this victory by painting the trees near their homeward encampment: ". . . the general colour was red and all the small samplings were stripped and painted with hieroglyphicks quite to their top branches. You know, sir, this is their general custom after signal victories . . ." (Winthrop Sargent to Arthur St. Clair, Feb. 8, 1792). Winthrop Sargent Papers, Massachusetts Historical Society, Transcript in Ohio Valley-Great Lakes Ethnohistorical Archives, Indiana University.

References

American State Papers. 1832. Indian Affairs, 2 vols. Vol. 1. Washington: Gale and Seaton.

Andreas, A. T. 1884–86. *History of Chicago,* 3 vols. Chicago: A. T. Andreas.

Anonymous. 1895. Journal, Detroit, 1st of May 1791. In *Collections and Researches Made by the Michigan Pioneer and Historical Society* 24:220–23.

Aupaumut, Hendrick. 1827. A Narrative of an Embassy to the Western Indians from the Original Manuscript of Hendrick Aupaumut. B. H. Coates, ed., *Memoirs, Historical Society of Pennsylvania* 2:1:63–131.

Blue Jacket. 1895. Information of Blue Jacket, Blue Jacket's Speech and Answer No. 1, 1790. In *Collections and Researches Made by the Michigan Pioneer and Historical Society* 29:135–38.

Brickell, John. 1842. John Brickell's Narrative. *American Pioneer,* 2 vols. 1:43–46. Cincinnati: R. Clarke and Company.

Butterfield, Consul W. 1890. *History of the Girty's.* Cincinnati: R. Clarke and Company.

Cruikshank, Ernest A. 1923. *The Correspondence of Lieut. Governor John Graves Simcoe,* 5 vols. Vol. 1, 1789–1793. Toronto: Ontario Historical Society.

Draper, Lyman. 1863. Interview with Nanette Caldwell. Draper mss. s17, 176, Wisconsin Historical Society.

———. n.d. ms. 1 YY 14, 9 BB:47, and 5 BB:83–101, Wisconsin Historical Society. Transcripts in Ohio Valley Great Lakes-Ethnohistorical Archives, Indiana University.

Finnelson, Richard. 1832. Information of Richard Finnelson, enclosed in Blount to Knox, Sept. 26, 1972. *American State Papers,* Indian Affairs 1:287–90. Washington: Gale and Seaton.

Gamelin, Antonine. 1882. Journal of Antoine Gamelin. In W. H. Smith, *The St. Clair Papers* 2:155–60. Cincinnati: R. Clarke and Company.

Graves, William J. 1937. William Wells' Genealogy. Manuscript. Collections: Wells, William, 1770–1812, Chicago Historical Society.

Hamilton, Henry. 1951. The Journal of Henry Hamilton, 1778–1779. *Henry Hamilton and George Rogers Clark in the American Revolution,* ed. John D. Barnhart, 101–205. Crawfordsville IN: R. E. Banta.

Hamtramck, John Francis. 1792. Hamtramck to St. Clair, June 17, 1792. Manuscript. Copy in Wayne Papers, vol. 20, Historical Society of Pennsylvania. Transcript in Ohio Valley-Great Lakes Ethnohistorical Archives, Indiana University.

Harmar, Josiah. 1790. Report of Harmar to Knox, Nov. 23, 1790. Manuscript. Harmar Papers, 11:16–28, Letter 8, Clements Library, University of Michigan.

———. 1832. Harmar to Knox, Nov. 4, 1790. *American State Papers,* Indian Affairs 1. Washington: Gale and Seaton.

Hay, Henry. 1915. Journal of Henry Hay: A Narrative of Life on the Old Frontier. Milo M. Quaife, ed., Wisconsin Historical Society *Proceedings* 1914:208–61.

Henry, Alexander et al. 1895. Memorial and Petition of the Merchants of Montreal Trading to the Indian or Upper Country, December 28, 1790. *Collections and Researches made by the Michigan Pioneer and Historical Society* 24:162–64.

Hodge, Frederick W. 1907–10. *Handbook of American Indians North of Mexico*, 2 vols. Bureau of American Ethnology Bulletin 30. Washington: Smithsonian Institution.

Horsman, Reginald. 1964. *Matthew Elliott, British Indian Agent.* Detroit: Wayne State University Press.

Ironside, George, Jr. 1831. Letter to Jas. Given, June 6, 1831. Manuscript. Record Group 10, Indian Affairs v. 569, Public Archives of Canada, Ottawa.

Ironside, George, Sr. 1831. Letter to Mudge, April 11, 1831. Manuscript. Record Group 10, Indian Affairs v. 569, Public Archives of Canada, Ottawa.

Ironside, Robert. 1845. Memorial of Robert Ironside, MD, Dec. 26, 1845. Manuscript. Record Group 10, Indian Affairs v. 122:5722, Public Archives of Canada, Ottawa.

Johnson, John. 1895. Journal of William Johnson's proceedings from Niagara to the Westward. *Collections and Researches Made by the Michigan Pioneer and Historical Society* 24:468–72.

Knox, Henry. 1903. Instructions to Brigadier General Rufus Putnam, May 22, 1792. Rowena Buell, comp., *The Memoirs of Rufus Putnam*, 257–67. Boston & New York: Houghton Mifflin and Company.

———. 1960. Knox to Wayne, June 22, 1792. In Richard C. Knopf, ed., *Anthony Wayne: A Name in Arms.* Pittsburgh: University of Pittsburgh Press.

Leonard, James. 1832. Information of James Leonard to James Seagrove, July 24, 1792. *American State Papers*, Indian Affairs 1:307–8. Washington: Gale and Seaton.

Le Porc Epic. 1940. Report of Le Porc Epic, March 15, 1750. Theodore C. Pease and Ernestine Jenison, eds., *Illinois on the Eve of the Seven Years' War. Collections of the Illinois State Historical Library* 29:166–68. Springfield: Illinois State Historical Library.

McKee, Alexander. 1895a. Alexander McKee to John Johnson, Jan. 28, 1792. *Collections and Researches Made by the Michigan Pioneer and Historical Society* 24.

———. 1895b. Proceedings of a General Council of Indian Nations. *Collections and Researches Made by the Michigan Pioneer and Historical Society* 24:483–98.

Messquakenoe. 1923. Speech of Messquakenoe at the Indian Council at the Glaize, 1792. In Ernest A. Cruikshank, ed., *The Correspondence of Lieut. Governor John Graves Simcoe*, 5 vols. Vol. 1, 1789–1793:228. Toronto: Ontario Historical Society.

Peckham, Howard H. 1947. *Pontiac and the Indian Uprising.* Princeton: Princeton University Press.

Putnam, Rufus. 1792a. Letter of Rufus Putnam, July 14, 1792. Manuscript. Copy in Wayne Papers, Reel 6, Historical Society of Pennsylvania. Transcript in Ohio Valley-Great Lakes Ethnohistorical Archives, Indiana University.

———. 1792b. Putnam to Wells, Sept. 7, 1792. Manuscript. Putnam Papers, vol. 3, no. 52, Marietta College Library. Transcript in Ohio Valley-Great Lakes Ethnohistorical Archives, Indiana University.

———. 1903. Putnam to Knox, Dec. 20, 1792. Rowena Buell, comp., *The Memoirs of Rufus Putnam.* Boston & New York: Houghton, Mifflin and Company.

Quaife, Milo M. 1913. *Chicago and the Old Northwest, 1673–1835.* Chicago: University of Chicago Press.

———. 1928. *The John Askin Papers,* 2 vols. Vol. 1. Detroit: Detroit Library Commission.

Ridout, Thomas. 1890. Narrative of the Captivity among the Shawanese Indians, in 1788, of Thomas Ridout, Afterwards Surveyor-General of Upper Canada. In *Ten Years of Upper Canada in Peace and War, 1805–1815,* appendix: 339–71. Toronto: William Briggs.

Sabrevois de Blury, Jacques. 1902. Memoir on the Savages of Canada as Far as the Mississippi River, Describing Their Customs and Trade. *Collections of the State Historical Society of Wisconsin* 16:363–76.

Spencer, Oliver M. 1968. *The Indian Captivity of O. M. Spencer.* Milo M. Quaife, ed. New York: The Citadel Press.

St. Clair, Arthur. 1812. *A Narrative of the Manner in Which the Campaign against the Indians in the Year One Thousand Seven Hundred and Ninety-One Was Conducted* . . . Philadelphia: Jane Aitken.

Symmes, John Cleves. 1926. Symmes to Jonathan Dayton, July 17, 1789. In Beverly Bond, ed., *The Correspondence of John Cleves Symmes.* New York: MacMillan.

Tanner, Helen, and Adele Hast. 1976. Southern Indian Villages, 1760–1794, and Indian Villages, Ohio, Pennsylvania, New York, 1760–1794. In Lester Cappon, ed., *Atlas of Early American History.* Princeton: Princeton University Press.

Tanner, John. 1956. *A Narrative of the Captivity and Adventures of John Tanner,* ed. Edwin James; Introduction and notes by Milo M. Quaife. Minneapolis: Ross and Haines.

Trent, William. 1911. Trent's Journal. In Charles A. Hanna, *The Wilderness Trail*, 2 vols. 2:291–98. New York & London: G. P. Putnam's Sons.

Treudeau, Zenon. 1909. Trudeau to Louis Lorimer, May 1, 1793. In Louis Houck, ed., *The Spanish Regime in Missouri*, 2 vols. Chicago: R. R. Donnelly and Sons Company.

Vigo, Francois. 1792. Vigo to Sargent, April 12, 1792. Manuscript. Winthrop Sargent Papers, Massachusetts Historical Society. Transcript in Ohio Valley-Great Lakes Ethnohistorical Archives, Indiana University.

Voegelin, Erminie W. 1974a. *Indians of Northwest Ohio*. New York: Garland Publishing Inc.

———. 1974b. *Indians of Ohio and Indiana Prior to 1795*, 2 vols. New York: Garland Publishing Inc.

Wayne, Anthony. 1960. Wayne to Knox, August 28, 1794. In Richard C. Knopf, ed., *Anthony Wayne: A Name in Arms*. Pittsburgh: University of Pittsburgh Press, 351–55.

Wentworth, John. 1881. *Fort Dearborn*, appendix. Chicago: The Fergus Publishing Company.

Western Indian Nations. 1923–31. Speech of the Western Indian Nations to Captain Matthew Elliott, May 16, 1792. In Ernest A. Cruikshank, ed., *The Correspondence of Lieut. Governor John Graves Simcoe*, 5 vols. Vol. 1, 1789–1793:157. Toronto: Ontario Historical Society.

27. Festivities, Fortitude, and Fraternalism

Fur Trade Masculinity and the Beaver Club, 1785–1827

Carolyn Podruchny

In 1785, wealthy fur trade merchants in Montreal founded the Beaver Club, an elite dining club restricted to men who had wintered in the North American interior, often referred to as "Indian Country." Although the Beaver Club existed alongside other dining and entertainment clubs in Montreal, it was unique in its membership, raison d'être, and rituals. The club was initiated to provide a forum for retired merchants in which to reminisce about the risky and adventurous days of fur trading, and a forum for young fur traders to enter Montreal's bourgeois society.[1] The initial membership of nineteen expanded to a peak of fifty-five, as the club met regularly until 1804. Following a three-year suspension, dinners were then resumed. It probably began to decline after the merger between the North West Company and Hudson's Bay Company in 1821, when the business center of the fur trade moved from Montreal to Hudson Bay. Evidence shows that members continued to meet until 1824, when the club ended. Efforts to resurrect the club in 1827 were unsuccessful.

The Beaver Club is a well-known institution of the Montreal fur trade. Many scholars have glorified the exclusive fraternity and the extravagant style of the dinners, and idealized the strength of the men who wintered in "Indian Country." Although mention of the Beaver Club is widespread, details are few, and its treatment is uncritical, romantic, celebratory, and lacking in historical context.[2] This chapter explores the social meaning of the Beaver Club for its members and for wider Montreal society. The club should be seen as a variant of men's club typical of the North Atlantic world in the late eighteenth and early nineteenth century.

Fraternal association provided a forum for men to establish business connections, share ideas, and construct and cement a common culture of shared values and social ideals. One of the most important of these ideals was the respectable man. Club rules and rituals defined the substance and boundaries of respectable behavior. The Beaver Club was distinct from many fraternal associations because it embodied a fascination with the "wild" and "savage." Men who had braved the unknown, encountering what they thought were strange, exotic, and potentially menacing Natives, and surviving the rigors and dangers of travel by canoe, came together in Montreal to remember and honor their rugged adventures in the North American interior. In some ways fur trade merchants appropriated the "rugged" and "wild." Although they did not actually share the physical experiences of their laborers or the Natives with whom they traded, they pretended to have done so in their reminiscences. At the same time members forged a bourgeois civility, which excluded women and the working class. In the privacy of the club, the fur traders could enjoy acting in a rough manner while upholding their respectable reputations to the outside world. In some ways the divergent ideals of respectability and rowdiness reflected a transition from an earlier fur trade society dominated by rough and ready traders whose claims to status and power came solely from their success in the trade, to a later society dominated by a professional, mostly English and Anglican, elite, who brought urban middle-class ideals to their management of the fur trade.

I. Bourgeois Men's Clubs

Montreal was a mercantile city that relied on the fur trade and international import-exports for its economic survival until 1821. It served as the financial heart for a large part of the fur trade in North America. After 1770 its local economy became more vigorous, with a growing population and diversification of economic interests.[3] Although Montreal and Quebec City constituted the major urban centers of the Canadian colonies, their populations in the mid-eighteenth century reached only five thousand, less than half the size of New York, Philadelphia, and Boston, the largest cities in the Thirteen Colonies.[4] Montreal's middle class, which included businessmen, liberal professionals, and colonial officials, were the beneficiaries of the post-Conquest economic growth. Within this group the merchant bourgeoisie increased in number, diversity, and power. Fur trade merchants' prestige and influence were especially strong. This group of more than one hundred men made fast fortunes in the fur trade, bought property, gained political power, and became a part of the governing class of the colony. Partners in Montreal fur trade firms were commonly referred to as bourgeois. The dozen or so large companies began to pool resources in the early 1770s and eventually merged into the North West Company in 1784.[5]

As Montreal flourished, clubs became important institutions for urban sociability. Increasing affluence and leisure time among merchants led to the growth and popularity of clubs that provided organized forums for social entertainment, fellowship, and business networking. Similar patterns existed in eighteenth-century England, where voluntary organizations fostered a new sense of social order in towns, promoted urban advancement, were committed to intellectual innovation and social improvement, transmitted new ideas, and contributed to public vitality. Clubs played significant social and cultural roles in the transition from a preindustrial order to a modernizing industrial society by promoting social division based on class and wealth rather than rank and status, and by stressing harmony and order within the middle class.[6] In eighteenth-century America, fraternities, such as the Freemasons, accompanied the growth of market relations and towns. Clubs forged patronage relationships, which formed the primary means of survival and advancement in the eighteenth-century business world. Merchants relied heavily upon the reputation and ties of trust provided by clubs.[7] In Montreal, sodalities, such as the Beaver Club, helped to cement the bonds between members of the bourgeois class, provided vehicles for business and social bonding, and instilled values that helped shape their attitudes and behavior.

The Beaver Club dinners were part of a large continuum of vigorous socializing among fur traders and Montreal's bourgeoisie. Men and women entertained regularly, and one of the most popular activities was dining. In December 1797, Colonel George Landmann had not been in Montreal for more than twenty-four hours before receiving invitations to dine for the next ten days from army officers, government officials, and merchants. His descriptions of feasting and hard drinking extended to parties held by fur traders before spring fur brigades set out.[8] Montreal businessman and fur trader Joseph Frobisher's dining diary from 1806 to 1810 illustrates his participation in the broad circuit of dining and parties among Montreal's social elite. Even though Frobisher was not in the best health, he frequently dined out or entertained in his home every night of the week.[9] Although men and women frequently dined together, fraternization among men was formalized in clubs and associations, such as the Beaver Club. Other men's dining clubs that formed part of the pattern of socializing among Montreal's bourgeoisie included the Brothers in Law Club, which, like the Beaver Club, allowed members of the same occupation to meet in a convivial setting. This exclusive group of Montreal lawyers met several times a year to dine, between 1827 and 1833.[10] Others included the Bachelor's Club, the Montreal Hunt Club, and the exclusive Montreal Fire Club, to which many Beaver Club members belonged.[11]

Several Beaver Club members and many of their guests became members of the Masonic order, one of the most prestigious and well-connected fraternal associations in the North Atlantic world. Although it drew men from many backgrounds, its character was bourgeois, and like the Beaver Club, it helped its membership forge a bourgeois identity. Sir John Johnson, an Indian department official and member of the legislative council of Lower Canada, was a regular guest at Beaver Club dinners. He was appointed the

Masonic Provincial Grand Master for Canada in 1788. His father, Sir William Johnson, a prominent merchant and superintendent of Indian affairs for northern British North America, founded one of the first Masonic lodges in New York in 1766. Beaver Club member William McGillivray became Provincial Grand Master of the District of Montreal. His younger brother, Simon McGillivray, also a Beaver Club member, became a Freemason in 1807 and was appointed provincial grand master of Upper Canada in 1822.[12] Many lodges were founded at fur trade and military posts in the late eighteenth century, such as Michilimackinac, Niagara, Cataraqui, and Mackinaw. As well, colonial military regiments, whose officers regularly attended Beaver Club dinners, were closely tied to early Masonic lodges.[13] The last meeting of the Beaver Club was held at the Masonic Hall Hotel.[14] These ties with Freemasonry aided the fur traders in business and politics. Fur trade scholar Heather Devine has found that the rapid success of Scottish Nor'Westers as merchants was due to their entry into Sir William Johnson's political, social, and economic networks. Through patronage, Johnson established close ties with some Scottish émigrés, particularly Simon McTavish.[15] These ties seemed to persist into the nineteenth century in Montreal, as Sir John Johnson was a regular guest at the Beaver Club.

The club was comprised mainly of men who either worked for or were sympathetic to the North West Company. Members included the most powerful men in the fur trade business, such as Charles-Jean-Baptiste Chaboillez, Maurice Blondeau, Benjamin Frobisher, Joseph Frobisher, Thomas Frobisher, James McGill, John McGill, William McGillivray, Duncan McGillivray, and Roderick McKenzie, as well as some of the most famous explorers of the North American interior, such as Alexander Henry the younger, Alexander MacKenzie, and Simon Fraser.[16] Some members were less socially prominent, and a few had dubious backgrounds, such as interpreter and trader Joseph-Louis Ainsse, who was accused of plundering at Michilimackinac, who betrayed a commandant, and who embezzled from the Indian Department. American trader Peter Pond, described as violent and unprincipled, was suspected of being involved in the murders of at least three fur traders.[17] However, in the context of the Beaver Club, these social differences were often flattened, and suspect backgrounds were ignored in the interests of maintaining a respectable appearance. Fur traders who worked in rival companies, such as the XY Company, were not welcome, even if they had been members previously. For example, Alexander MacKenzie was elected to the club in 1795, disappeared from its records while he was a partner of the XY Company, but was reelected in 1808, four years after the XY Company's dissolution. At the same meeting former XY partner A. N. McLeod was also elected. Another XY Company partner, John Gregory, was initially elected in 1791, but does not reappear in the club minutes until 1809.[18] Some well-known fur traders, such as David Thompson and Daniel Williams Harmon, never became members, probably because they spent most of their lives in the northwest.[19]

Beaver Club folklore extolled the political and economic power of its members. Member James Hughes recalled the club as the "acme of social attainment and the pinnacle of commercial success in Lower Canada," proudly reported distinguished visitors to the club, and hinted that the fur traders controlled affairs of state.[20] Guests included militia officers, government officials, businessmen, and professionals, such as judges, lawyers, and doctors, as well as distinguished visitors to Montreal, including John Jacob Astor, Washington Irving, and Thomas Moore. The political and economic networks formed between fur trade businessmen, colonial officials, Indian Department administrators, and military officers were encouraged by their regular socializing. Members and guests were often connected through family as well as through business. For example, the frequent guest Alexander Auldjo was a leader among Montreal businessmen, supporter of the English Party, and member of the Scotch Presbyterian Church. David David, a fur trader, businessman, and militia officer who became a Beaver Club member in 1817, was appointed director of the Bank of Montreal in 1818.

Another frequent visitor was John Forsyth, a successful merchant actively involved in improving Montreal's financial infrastructure, a militia officer, and a member of the legislative council.[21]

Meetings were held in the off-season of the trade once a fortnight from the first week in December until the second week in April. Beginning at four in the afternoon, dinners often lasted until four in the morning.[22] Dinners were held in various Montreal hotels and taverns, such as City Tavern, Richard Dillion's Montreal Hotel, Palmer's Hummums, and Tesseyman's, as was common for private parties, business and political meetings, and gatherings of male friends in the eighteenth century.[23] The passing around of a calumet, or peace pipe, marked the beginning of the club's formal rituals, continuing with a speech, or "harangue," made by the evening's president, and formal toasts.[24] Dinner fare included country food, such as braised venison, bread sauce, "Chevreuil des Guides" (stew), venison sausages, wild rice, quail, and partridge "du Vieux Trappeur," served in crested glass and silverware.[25] After dinner, the club became more informal, as men began to drink more heavily, sing voyageur songs, and reminisce about the good old fur trading days. Festivities continued until the early morning, with men dancing on the tables, reenacting canoeing adventures, and breaking numerous bottles and glasses. The approbation of rough and rowdy behavior, at odds with the urbane civility of other Montreal dining clubs, especially those where women were included, allowed fur traders a private space in which to embrace rugged masculine ideals.

II. Gender, Class, and Fraternalism

The Beaver Club was instrumental in developing the gender and class identities of its members. It brought bourgeois men together in an insulated setting and promoted representations of idealized masculinity. Gender formation and class formation were closely associated in the late eighteenth- and early nineteenth-century North Atlantic world. Some scholars, such as British middle-class historians Leonore Davidoff and Catherine Hall, argue that class and gender always operate together, and that class always takes a gendered form.[26] As bourgeois men came together in business and fraternal orders, they began to limit the boundaries of their collective identity. The increasing marginalization of women from the world of public commerce after the Conquest extended to their exclusion from fraternal associations, which were often seen as extensions of men's business interests. Bourgeois men also sought to distinguish themselves from other classes. They generally considered the lower orders as their social and economic inferiors and, despite their aspirations to gentry, they often called the higher orders their moral inferiors.[27] Through fraternal associations, the bourgeois were able to consolidate their class and forge bourgeois harmony.

Women were excluded from most fraternal associations for various reasons. One of the key components to middle-class constructions of femininity and masculinity was the division between the public sphere, the realm of rational activity, market forces, and production, and the private sphere, the realm of morality, emotion, and reproduction. Although men and women moved in both these spheres, men appropriated the former, while women dominated the latter.[28] The subsequent marginalization of women in the public sphere contributed to the exclusion of women from club meetings, as fraternal associations were frequently associated with men's trade and business. Like many other men's clubs, Beaver Club meetings were held in taverns, where few middle-class women ventured. Hall argues that taverns were increasingly defined as inappropriate settings for women who wished to maintain their gentility, as temperance movements became an important component of the evangelical project to raise the moral tone of society.[29] Other scholars suggest that the absence of women was important to the process of forging masculinity. Mark Carnes's study of fraternal associations in Victorian America argues that their rituals provided solace and psychological guidance, away from women, for a young man's passage from the maternal affection of childhood to manhood.[30]

In the all-male atmosphere men could practice distinctive social behaviors, such as smoking, swearing, gambling, and drinking, with little interruption. In her work on American mariners, Margaret Creighton asserts that these masculine activities were not meant to make the men more appealing to women; rather, they made them more acceptable to other men.[31] Men were subject to gender expectations generated by both sexes. Away from women, men could focus on themselves, cultivate their own desires and identities, and escape the pressures of women's expectations. In the Beaver Club, fur traders were able to revere their lives in the North American interior, where, away from their Euro-American wives and mothers, they pursued their aspirations for rugged adventure.

Fur trade laborers, such as voyageurs, interpreters, and guides, were almost never included in Beaver Club festivities. The social organization of the Montreal fur trade firmly divided partners from low-ranked workers.[32] In the mid-eighteenth century, some men were able to rise from the rank of worker to manager, but by the time of the emergence of the North West Company in the 1780s, the hierarchy was firmly in place. Older fur traders counseled young clerks to be obedient and polite to superiors, to be self-important when out in the field, and to hold themselves apart from their laborers to command respect and submission.[33] However, bourgeois attitudes to lower orders could be complex and contradictory, especially for fur traders who had lived and worked alongside their labor force in an isolated and dangerous setting. Many fur trade bourgeois admired voyageurs for their strength and skill, and established relationships with them built on trust and interdependence. At the same time most fur trade bourgeois considered voyageurs to be thoughtless, irrational, and rude.[34] Club rituals imitating voyageurs helped the bourgeois to distance themselves from their workers. The romanticization of voyageurs' activities cast them as exotic curiosities. At the same time, bourgeois men appropriated voyageurs' experiences in the fur trade. They reminisced about paddling canoes and running through rapids, even though this was the work of the voyageurs.

The bourgeois did not risk their lives in rapids and portages, carry back-breaking packs, paddle at outrageous speeds, nor survive on minimal food, as did the voyageurs. Rather, they directed crews, managed accounts, distributed food, and had better rations than their voyageurs. Both the distancing from and the imitation of voyageurs reflected a code of ethics that applauded rugged behavior of the bourgeois in the right settings.

Most eighteenth- and nineteenth-century bourgeois admired upper orders, and cherished noble values such as courage, loyalty, prowess in combat, and gallantry in love.[35] This admiration was not unproblematic, as the bourgeois found aristocratic behavior often at odds with many of their notions of respectability and honor. None-theless, members of higher social orders were not excluded from the Beaver Club. The desire to achieve the status of a gentleman inspired in the fur trade bourgeois a fascination for nobility and aristocracy. Although many Anglophone merchants were hostile to the old seigneurial order, they were nonetheless influenced by it. Military service, purchasing noble titles, and acquiring property were common ways that the bourgeoisie could associate themselves with nobility and aspire to gentry.[36] Fur trade bourgeois usually procured their own crest and motto, which were important signi-fiers of membership in the gentry.

Aristocratic association was a common theme in club folklore. Members honored nobility, such as the Duke of Kent, Lord Selkirk, and Lord Dalhousie, the governor-general of Canada, by inviting them to club dinners.[37] For example, at an 1894 auction Brian Hughes was delighted to buy his grandfather's snuffbox bearing the inscription: "The Earl of Dalhousie to James Hughes, Esq., in remembrance of the Beaver Club, May 24, 1824."[38] Club members also tried to imitate nobles through lavish spending and material ac-coutrements. Hughes relates his grandfather's memories of members richly adorned with their medals, ruffles, gold lace, gold-clasped garters, and silver-buckled shoes. Members often displayed their wealth through hospitality to their peers and to visitors.[39] When

Festivities, Fortitude, and Fraternalism

traveling through Montreal in the early nineteenth century, John Lambert describes how the "Nor'Westers" lavish displays of hospitality inspired both jealous resentment and "interested deference" in nonmembers.[40]

Status anxiety may have been behind the merchants' desire to cultivate a strong noble demeanor. One British visitor in 1820, Edward Talbot, cautioned his readers about the vanity and lack of refinement of the newly rich merchants in Montreal, originally servants or mechanics "of low origin and scanty acquirements" who made fortunes in the fur trade. Talbot was appalled by the aristocratic pretensions of this group, but grudgingly admitted that some members of the North West Company belonged to the highest class in Montreal society.[41]

Despite their affinity for the aristocracy, bourgeois values also reflected the struggles of a vigorous urban elite to establish independent claims to power and status. Davidoff and Hall assert that the British middle-class challenge to aristocratic hegemony was based on their claim to moral superiority.[42] Robert Nye has found that the French bourgeois were preoccupied with moral discipline, inner values, and control of reproduction and sex to carefully regulate inheritance strategies.[43] Many similarities can be found with the fur trade bourgeois, who earned their position through hard work, careful planning, and merit. One of the club's medals was inscribed with the motto "Industry and Perseverance," which emphasized the efforts of men rather than their birthright.[44] Loyalty and commitment were also important ideals to club fraternity, as members were expected to attend the meetings if in town, and were forbidden from hosting parties or accepting other invitations on club days.[45] Like other bourgeois, the fur traders were encouraged to marry within their social group. For example, John Forsyth married the daughter of prominent Quebec merchant Charles Grant; Joseph Frobisher married the daughter of Jean-Baptiste Jobert and niece of Charles-Jean-Baptiste Chaboillez, founding members of the Beaver Club; Simon McTavish married the daughter of Chaboillez; and William

McGillivray married the daughter of Beaver Club member Sir John McDonald of Garth.[46] However, many of the North West Company bourgeois married Native or mixed-blood women, especially after spending many years in the interior. These marriages were often strategies for building trading alliances and surviving in the bush.[47] Some, such as McGillivray, abandoned their country wives when they left the interior to become merchants in Montreal.[48]

In the Beaver Club gender and class divisions came into sharp relief, as membership was explicitly restricted to bourgeois men. However, the club was less selective of ethnicity and religion. Of the nineteen initial Beaver Club members, eight were French Canadian, six were Scottish, three were English, and two were American.[49] Although Scots came to dominate the Montreal fur trade and the Beaver Club, a French Canadian presence persisted.[50] The inclusion of a variety of ethnicities and religious affiliations reflected the composition of people involved in the Montreal business and fur trade world. The fraternal rituals of the club helped to smooth over tension arising from ethnic and religious difference. Hall suggests that clubs and voluntary associations in late eighteenth- and early nineteenth-century Britain gave their members a sense of collective identity, which helped unite men of different religious backgrounds, trades, and classes.[51] The same was probably true of the Beaver Club, which helped smooth ethnic and religious differences between its members.

The club was characterized by an odd tension between its efforts to promote harmony and a collective bourgeois identity, and its hierarchical nature. The ideal of egalitarianism was manifested in the club's organizational structure. Each member had an equal vote in electing new members, deciding on fines for those who had broken club rules, and in other club affairs. Also, members took turns rotating as president, vice president, and cork of the club, enforcing general equality without challenging the structure of hierarchy.[52] The privacy of the club probably contributed to the spirit of egalitarianism. Members felt the privilege of belonging,

Festivities, Fortitude, and Fraternalism

being set apart from the rest of society, and sharing in secrets from the outside world.[53]

Exclusivity expressed in numerical limits helped to maintain social hierarchy. Initially the Beaver Club began with nineteen men, but was expanded to forty with eight honorary members by 1807, to fifty and ten honorary members in 1815, and by 1816 the limit was fifty-five members and ten honorary members.[54] Only men who received a unanimous vote and met the club requirements could join. Bourgeois respectability required wealth and leisure, as the men were expected to dedicate time and money to the club. Members had to purchase a gold medal recording the date of their first winter spent in the interior. They were fined for breaking club rules, such as failing to attend a dinner if they were in Montreal, not wearing their medals to the dinners, and forgetting to notify the secretary of guests they intended to bring to dinner.[55] Members were required to pay for their dinners even if they did not attend club meetings, and were only excused from the fee if they were ill.[56] Social pressure to drink large amounts of alcohol at the meetings was high, and men had to pay for their drinks.[57]

The club also served to distinguish fur traders from other bourgeoisie. The condition that men had to winter in the interior to join the club verified the candidate's strength and fortitude. Members were differentiated from guests by their medals, which served as a common marker to identify the members as a group. Private dinners that excluded guests were held at the beginning of every year to plan the year's events.[58] Only members had voting privileges, and each was provided with a printed book of the club's mandate, the rules and regulations, and membership list.[59]

The club's five formal toasts reflected the tension between the ideals of an emerging urban bourgeoisie, and those of an older rough and ready fur trade society. The first toast, "the mother of all the saints," paid respect to the church, while toasts to the king and the fur trade honored the state and commerce. The rules and regulations did not indicate allegiance to any specific church, and members ranged from Roman Catholics to Presbyterians to Anglicans. The toast to "the mother of all the saints," probably the Virgin Mary, may have been a convenient way to acknowledge the importance of religion without restricting devotion to a single church. At the same time, the toast may have paid homage to an earlier fur trade world dominated by Roman Catholicism. In the toast to "voyageurs, wives, and children," the fur traders venerated themselves and the institution of the family. It is unclear whether the toast to "voyageurs, wives, and children" referred to the fur traders themselves and their families, or to those the fur traders considered their dependents, that is, their workers, wives, and children. Finally, the last toast, to absent members, could be seen as a tribute to fraternity and brotherly love. By acknowledging these values through ritual toasts, fur traders reinforced bourgeois standards of virtue among themselves and taught them to young clerks, as the club served to initiate young fur traders and bring those who had spent years in the North American interior back into respectable society.[60] Formal toasting was a way to draw the group together to participate in a unified activity, sharing similar sentiments about religion, occupation, and masculinity that were different from that of the larger society. Perhaps the jovial and convivial atmosphere allowed these men to reassert older values while recognizing their contradiction within a changing world.

Two Beaver Club members, Simon Fraser and John McDonald of Garth, wrote a memorandum in 1859, near the end of their lives, which captured the spirit of fur traders' masculine ideals:

> We are the last of the old N[orth]. W[est]. Partners. We have known one another for many years. Which of the two survives the other we know not. We are both aged, we have lived in mutual esteem and fellowship, we have done our duty in the stations allotted us without fear, or reproach. We have braved many dangers, we have run many risks. We cannot accuse one another of any thing mean & dirty through life, nor done any disagreeable actions, nor wrong

Festivities, Fortitude, and Fraternalism

to others. We have been feared, loved & respected by natives. We have kept our men under subordination. We have thus lived long lives. We have both crossed this continent, we have explored many new points, we have met many new Tribes, we have run our Race, & as this is probably the last time we meet on earth, we part as we have lived in sincere friendship & mutual good will.[61]

III. The Gentleman and the Wild Man

The fur trade bourgeois differed from other North Atlantic bourgeoisie in their masculine ideals and in their struggles to attain respectable status. As merchants, the fur traders often worked independently of social hierarchies and were open to a wide variety of cultures.[62] Merchants have been described as adventurers, gamblers who took risks for which they expected a high return.[63] The fur trade brought them into the midst of the wild, where they experienced first hand the wonders of exotic people and places. Fur traders struggled to manage their fascination with the wild and savage while operating within an urban context of respectability. They cultivated respectability and patriotism in order to secure business contacts, and also were subject to the exigencies of their class. Yet, the rough skills learned by the fur traders in their perilous adventures were a source of pride, and they helped to create a distinction between "refined" women and "rough" men in an urban context.

The traders thus constructed their own particular type of masculinity, combining bourgeois ideals of respectability with their rugged and wondrous fur trade experiences. These two impulses were not dichotomous nor necessarily in conflict, as strength was important to respectability and honor. The Beaver Club became a safe and private forum for honoring coarse and rude behavior, such as excessive drinking and carousing, not acceptable for bourgeois men in public settings. At the same time, gentility was represented in the club's stately settings, formal rituals, and illustrious assembly. Visitors, such as Landmann, commented on the wild feasting and hard drinking that went on during club dinners, and yet gratefully recalled the "greatest civilities" received from club members.[64] While the club helped fur traders to reconcile their desires to be both rough and gentle, however, it also served to emphasize boundaries between civilized bourgeois society on the one hand, and on the other the rough bush society of voyageurs, country wives, and Natives.

Some of the most interesting aspects of the Beaver Club were the formal and informal ceremonies of the meetings. The solemn rituals instilled meaning in the club's ideals, while the revelry provided a place and time in which to cement fraternal bonds. Rituals and ceremonial occasions can be seen as sites of struggles between competing representations, serving as markers for collective identity.[65] The dominant impulse in the rituals was a romanticization of the fur trade, which emphasized its importance in the men's lives, but also eased anxiety about the lack of fit between fur trade life and urban bourgeois society.

The tension between the fur traders' desire to be refined and to be rash found expression in the structure of club meetings. The dinners began formally, following specified rituals, but then developed into wild and reckless parties. The fixed scheduling of club dinners contributed to the formal atmosphere. Formality was also expressed in codes of dress. At club functions members were obliged to wear their medals on blue ribbons or on black ribbons to honor a member's death.[66] The dinner itself reflected a tension between the savage and the civil. Country food, such as wild rice and venison, was served in crested glass and silverware in stately settings.[67] After the formal rituals of club dinners, informal socializing and frolicking could begin. A defined social space was an important part of the fraternal process because it was a time to solidify bonds and express brotherly love and harmony. Conversations must have often turned to business, with deals discussed and strategies developed.[68] However, the time for play at the dinners was also a time to turn tables, reverse meanings, and poke at the social order expressed in the

Festivities, Fortitude, and Fraternalism

rituals and rules of the club. Frequent amusements were the singing of voyageur songs, such as *La claire Fontaine* and *En roulant ma boule*.[69] James Hughes's stories include an account of the men arranging themselves on the floor, then imitating the vigorous paddling of a canoe and mounting wine kegs to "shoot the rapids" from the table to the floor.[70] Rules ensured that every member could drink as he pleased after the toasts had gone around, firmly dividing the formal ritual from informal play.[71] In winter 1797 Landmann described in detail a wild club party: initially all men consumed a bottle of wine during the dinner, but after the married men retired, leaving the bachelors to "drink to their health," the party really began in "right earnest and true highland style," which involved war whoops, singing, heavy drinking, breaking plates and glasses, and dancing on the tables. Landmann estimated about 120 bottles of wine had been consumed at the dinner by about twenty men.[72]

In the eighteenth century, consumption of alcohol was considered a gratifying and convivial activity and accompanied almost every social occasion. In the Beaver Club it contributed to the building of trust and friendships.[73] Lambert felt that the wild abandon of the fur traders' spending and celebrating was well deserved considering the rigors and risks of fur trading.[74] Perhaps many of the members considered the wild revelry a necessary release from the tension and discomfort of their experiences in the bush. Hughes also recounted that retired fur traders tried to recreate the "untrammeled license" that they enjoyed in the wilderness.[75] Club dinners provided a safe social space for licensed wildness and drinking closely associated with release. Holding one's liquor was a source of pride. At one party Landmann admired Alexander Mackenzie and William McGillivray for being the only two men remaining in their seats when everyone else had passed out.[76] Excessive drinking could have been a demonstration of wealth. Lambert hints that the North West Company bourgeois aroused the jealousy and resentment of Montreal society for their lavish spending and incredible hospitality, which was meant to display wealth.[77]

However, disapproval of excessive drunkenness in public, and especially alcoholism, led the bourgeois to confine heavy drinking and wild abandon to an appropriate context. In a letter to John Askin, Alexander Henry inquired if he enjoyed his visit to the Beaver Club, where he no doubt joined in the merriment of drink, and a few paragraphs later criticized a late colleague for excessive drinking.[78] In the late eighteenth century public drunkenness and swearing were increasingly condemned.[79] Serious drinking was recognized as a social ill, and associated with poverty, misery, disease, and death.[80] Beaver Club members may have been especially cautious to define a framed time and place for their wild abandon.

Some rituals especially captured the tension in fur traders' attitudes toward their bush experiences. Passing the calumet,[81] common to many Native cultures, often marked the beginning of conferences or treaties, and paid tribute to spirits.[82] Although the fur traders probably appreciated the solemn and sacred nature of the calumet, a greater appeal must have lain in the exotic aspects of adopting Native traditions. Traveler John Palmer noted that Indian manners, customs, and language, especially war whoops, were closely imitated at club dinners.[83] The attitude of the fur traders toward Natives was complex and often contradictory. Fur traders lived with Natives, often married them, depended on them for survival, and traded with them. Respect and common understanding existed in the relationship. Yet, to the fur traders, Natives were a savage people, both appealing and dangerous. The tradition of bourgeois traders marrying Native women created a particular anxiety for the bourgeois to distance themselves from Native influences in a respectable urban environment. Fur traders were fascinated with the savage, and the safe and constricted atmosphere of the club allowed them a place and time to explore and revel in savagery, while maintaining a respectable distance. Ritualizing Native customs may have provided a way for the bourgeois to both dissociate from and honor them. Also, exotic rituals instilled romance in fraternal orders, and spoke to the desire for spiritualism. Passing the peace

Festivities, Fortitude, and Fraternalism

pipe around must have underscored the values of brotherly love and fraternity, as club rules refer to the calumet as the "usual emblem of Peace."[84]

A significant aspect of fraternal bonding was reminiscing about fur trade experiences, an activity that was so highly valued it was part of the mandate published in the members' club rules.[85] In retelling his own adventures, each member asserted claims to valor and strength, while also renewing links of friendship and camaraderie.[86] Reminiscing allowed members to recast their fur trade memories by highlighting acceptable aspects of that life, such as the manly honor of completing difficult journeys, while silencing other memories, such as abandoned country wives and families. Yet at the same time, retelling their experiences may have allowed many to mourn their country families and friends, and their lost youth. Reminiscing was an essential method in teaching and revering the masculine values of strength, courage, fortitude, and perseverance gained in fur trade experience. A poem presented to the club by John Johnston on 19 November 1814 described the pleasure of meeting together with the wanderers of Canada's wide domain, "to recount the toils and perils past." While urging members to participate in the War of 1812 to protect the fur trade, the poem complimented traders for their force, skill, and "manly heart," and lauded their brave suffering in difficult situations.[87] Military service was valued because it provided evidence of a man's courage and honor. Fur traders reminded each other to protect their honor, to avoid imposition, and to always defend themselves when attacked. Not only was strength in action highly valued, but also strength in rhetoric. One clerk congratulated another for his force and elegance with words and manly roughness with his argument in his letters.[88] The motto of the club, "fortitude in distress," clearly indicated the primacy of the masculine ideals of ruggedness, might, and courage. The mandate of the club proudly asserted that all initial members had been fur traders from an early age, referring to them as "voyageurs."[89] Members even considered changing the name to the "Voyageur Club."[90]

There was no clear definition of the term *voyageur*. It was used for all hardy travelers, and yet often the term referred only to French Canadian fur trade laborers. Regardless of the bourgeois' use of language, their attitudes toward fur trade workers were no less ambiguous than their attitudes toward Natives. The Beaver Club toast to "voyageurs, wives and children" may have been another example of the bourgeois trying to mimic their workers by calling themselves voyageurs. By singing voyageurs' songs, and by reenacting canoeing, fur traders could identify with voyageur toughness and rugged risk-taking masculinity, while they distanced themselves from their men in the everyday world. At the same time, the bourgeois appropriated the voyageurs' experiences and culture, as they revered the activities and adventures of their workers, in which the bourgeois did not participate.

IV. Conclusions

Fur traders were different from other elite men in Montreal. Their experience in the fur trade was foreign to respectable urban society but was not easily forgotten by its participants. Their rough ways formed in bush society were both a source of anxiety and a source of pride. The Beaver Club provided them with a forum in which to make sense of their past experiences, cast them in a positive light, and assert their particular brand of the ideal man. At the same time, the Beaver Club was primarily a respectable men's dining club, where Montreal's bourgeois society met to forge business alliances, exchange information, share ideas, and cement social ties. Although the club allowed members to indulge in idealization of the savage and an older rough and ready fur trade world, the respectable man remained the dominant ideal.

At club meetings, secluded from women, the lower orders, and Native people, Montreal's bourgeois men could focus on themselves, cultivate their own desires and identities, and affirm their values. Men could honor strength, courage, and perseverance, all acceptable aspects of bourgeois masculinity, but they could also venerate risk taking, the spirit of adventure, and a taste for the exotic, qualities that bordered on the rough and uncouth. The privacy of the club allowed the traders to indulge in rough behavior, while protecting their respectable reputations. These masculine ideals also brought the distinction between rough men and refined women into greater relief. The secluded fraternal setting, where men shared their memories and emotions, could not be confused with the domestic sphere, which was the domain of women.

Notes

1. I use the term *bourgeois* in this chapter sometimes to refer to the emerging middle class. However, in the Montreal fur trade merchants and managers were referred to as "bourgeois." Although most of the fur trade bourgeois were part of Montreal's bourgeoisie, the terms have distinct meanings.

2. For examples, see Lynn Hetherington, "Canada's First Social Club," *The University Magazine* 9 (April 1910): 296–305, esp. 297, and Robert Watson, "The First Beaver Club," *The Beaver* Outfit 262, no. 3 (December 1931): 334–37, esp. 335. Many works on fur trade and Montreal history cite frequently George Bryce, *The Remarkable History of the Hudson's Bay Company including that of the French Traders of the North-West, xy, and Astor Fur Companies* (Toronto: William Briggs, 1900) and *Mackenzie, Selkirk, Simpson: The Makers of Canada* (Toronto: Morang & Co., Ltd., 1910); Clifford P. Wilson, "The Beaver Club," *The Beaver* Outfit 266, no. 4 (March 1936): 19–24, 64; Donald Creighton, *The Empire of the St. Lawrence* (Toronto: MacMillan Co., 1956), 27; Marjorie Wilkins Campbell, *The North West Company* (New York: St. Martin's Press, 1957) and *McGillivray: Lord of the Northwest* (Toronto and Vancouver: Clarke, Irwin & Co. Ltd., 1962). An exception is provided by Lawrence J. Burpee, who does not cite his evidence, but discusses primary and secondary sources within the text. Lawrence J. Burpee, "The Beaver Club," *Canadian Historical Association Annual Report* (1924): 73–91. Another exception is Jennifer Brown, whose brief mention of the Beaver Club describes its role of easing the transition of fur traders back into community life after long absences in the interior. Jennifer S. H. Brown, *Strangers in Blood: Fur Trade Company Families in Indian Country* (Vancouver: University of British Columbia Press, 1980), 44.

3. Louise Dechêne, "La Coissance de Montréal au XVIII^c Siècle," *Revue d'histoire de l'Amérique française* 27, no. 2 (septembre 1973): 163–79, esp. 167; Jean-Paul Bernard, Paul-andré Linteau, and Jean-Claude Robert, "La Structure professionnelle de Montréal en 1825," *Revue d'histoire de l'Amérique française*

30, no. 3 (decembre 1976): 383–415, esp. 390–91. Fernand Ouellet argues that the Montreal fur trade began to decline as early as 1803, but admits that "even in decline, the famous fur trade would continue to exert a considerable influence on certain elements of society." Fernand Ouellet, *Economic and Social History of Quebec, 1760–1860* (Ottawa: Institute of Canadian Studies, Carleton University, 1980), 181–82, 186.

4. David T. Ruddel, *Québec City, 1765–1832* (Ottawa: Canadian Museum of Civilization, 1987), 23.

5. Fernand Ouellet, *Lower Canada 1791–1840, Social Change and Nationalism*, trans. Patricia Claxton (Toronto: McClelland and Stewart, 1980), 38–39, 63, and *Economy, Class, and Nation in Quebec: Interpretive Essays*, ed. and trans. Jacques A. Barbier (Toronto: Copp, Clark, Pitman, 1991), 79–80; and Brown, *Strangers in Blood*, 35–36. See also Creighton, who describes the political program of the Montreal merchants in *Empire of the St. Lawrence*, 23, 35–55.

6. Peter Clark, "Sociability and Urbanity: Clubs and Societies in the Eighteenth Century City," The Eighth H. J. Dyos Memorial Lecture (Leicester: University of Leicester, Victoria Studies Centre, 1986), 17–19, 23.

7. Steven Conrad Bullock, "The Ancient and Honorable Society: Freemasonry in America, 1730–1830" (PhD diss., Brown University, 1986), 5, 78, 84.

8. George Landmann, *Adventures and Recollections of Colonel Landmann, Late of the Corps of Royal Engineers* (London: Colburn and Co., 1852), 232–33, 295–96. Ottawa, National Archives of Canada, Masson Collection, Miscellaneous Papers, MG19 C1, vol. 44, microfilm reel #C-15639, "Notes By Roderick McKenzie on books read by him . . . ," Part One, n.d. pages 11–19; Charles Bert Reed also describes the parties at Fort William in *Masters of the Wilderness* (Chicago: University of Chicago Press, 1914), 70–71. Reed's article on the Beaver Club is almost entirely a quotation of Brian Hughes describing the stories he was told by his grandfather, James Hughes, who was a Beaver Club member. Burpee is skeptical about much of the information provided by Hughes because many of the particulars are inconsistent with other historical sources. Burpee, "The Beaver Club," 89–90.

9. Ottawa, National Archives of Canada, McTavish, Frobisher & Company Collection, MG19 A5, vol. 4, Journal of Joseph Frobisher, 1806–10.

10. Montreal, McCord Museum of Canadian History Archives, M21413, Brothers in Law Society of Montreal Minute Book, 1827–33.

11. The Bachelor's Club was listed frequently in the Journal of Joseph Frobisher and mentioned in a letter from James Caldwell, Montreal, to Simon McTavish, New York Coffee House in London, 5 December 1792. Montreal, McGill Rare Books, MS 431/1, Simon McTavish Correspondence, 1792–1800.

The Montreal Hunt Club was formed in 1826, with Beaver Club member John Forsyth as its first president. Marcel Caya, ed., *Guide to Archival Resources at McGill University* (Montreal: McGill University Archives, 1985), 3:294. Many Beaver Club members belonged to the Montreal Fire Club, which operated between 1786 and 1814, with a membership limit of fourteen. It was formed to provide mutual assistance in case of fire, as well as convivial association. Montreal, McGill Rare Books, MS 437, Montreal Fire Club Minute Book, 1786–1814. Some of the clubs seemed to be class based, and not exclusive to men. In the late 1790s, Isaac Weld describes a club of Montreal's "principal inhabitants," both men and women, which met once a week or fortnight to dine. Isaac Weld, Jr., *Travels Through the States of North America, and the Provinces of Upper and Lower Canada, During the Years 1795, 1796, and 1797*, 4th ed., 2 vols. (London: John Stockdale, 1807), 1:315.

12. A. J. B. Milborne, *Freemasonry in the Province of Quebec, 1759–1959* (Knowlton QC: P.D.D.G.M. G.L.Q., 1960), 40, 67–68; J. Lawrence Runnalls, "Simon McGillivray 1783–1840," *The Papers of the Canadian Masonic Research Association* (Hamilton: 44th Meeting of the Association of the Heritage Lodge, no. 73, A.F. & A.M., G.R.C., 1966), 3:1487–89.

13. John E. Taylor, "Freemasonry in Old Canada and the War of 1812–15," *The Papers of the Canadian Masonic Research Association* (Toronto: 23d Meeting of the Association, A.F. & A.M., G.R.C., 1958), 2:783, 787; A. J. B. Milborne, "The Murals in the Memorial Hall, Montreal Masonic Memorial Temple," *The Papers of the Canadian Masonic Research Association* (Montreal: 8th Meeting of the Association, A.F. & A.M., G.R.C., 1953), 1:255–57.

14. Montreal, McCord Museum of Canadian History Archives, M14449, Beaver Club Minute Book, 1807–27, Original, 3 February 1827, 120. Photostats and typescripts can also be obtained at McGill Rare Books and the National Archives of Canada.

15. Heather Devine, "Roots in the Mohawk Valley: Sir William Johnson's Legacy in the North West Company," in *The Fur Trade Revisited: Selected Papers of the Sixth North American Fur Trade Conference, Mackinac Island, Michigan, 1991*, ed. Jennifer S. H. Brown, W. J. Eccles, and Donald P. Heldman (East Lansing: Michigan State University Press, 1994), 217–42, esp. 228–30. Also see Brown, *Strangers in Blood*, 36–38.

16. It is difficult to determine whether Simon McTavish, general director of the North West Company, was a member of the Beaver Club. His name does not appear in the Minute Book, but he is listed as a member since 1792 in the 1819 issue of the *Rules and Regulations of the Beaver Club: Instituted in 1785* (Montreal: W. Gray, 1819), McCord Museum of Canadian History Archives,

M144450, 10 (the name "De Rocheblave" is written on the front cover). Some scholars assert that fur traders disliked McTavish so much that they never invited him to join, or that "the Marquis" himself refused to meet his colleagues on an equal footing in the club. Burpee, "The Beaver Club," 74–75.

17. David A. Armour, "Ainsse (Ainse, Hains, Hins), Joseph-Louis (Louis-Joseph)," in *Dictionary of Canadian Biography* (hereafter DCB) (Toronto: University of Toronto Press, 1983), 5:7–9; Barry M. Gough, "Pond, Peter," in DCB, 5:681–86.

18. Beaver Club Minute Book, 4, 26, 47.

19. This is suggested by Burpee, "The Beaver Club," 75.

20. Reed, *Masters of the Wilderness*, 75, 77, 79, 80.

21. Gerald J. J. Tulchinsky, "Auldjo, Alexander," in DCB, 6:18–20; Elinor Kyte Senior, "David, David," in DCB, 6:179–81; Gerald J. J. Tulchinsky, "Forsyth, John," in DCB, 7:309–11; Bruce G. Wilson, *The Enterprises of Robert Hamilton: A Study of Wealth and Influence in Early Upper Canada, 1776–1812* (Ottawa: Carleton University Press, 1983), 12–13.

22. Reed, *Masters of the Wilderness*, 69.

23. Thomas Brennan, *Public Drinking and Popular Culture in Eighteenth-Century Paris* (Princeton NJ: Princeton University Press, 1988), 8; Kym Rice, *Early American Taverns: For the Entertainment of Friends and Strangers* (Chicago: Regnery Gateway, 1983), 88.

24. *Rules and Regulations*, 3; Beaver Club Minute Book, 2.

25. For an example of a Beaver Club menu, see Jehane Benoît, "Wintering Dishes," *Canadian Collector* 20, no. 3 (May/June 1985): 25–27. For mention of Beaver Club glass and silverware, see Watson, "The First Beaver Club," 337.

26. Leonore Davidoff and Catherine Hall, *Family Fortunes: Men and Women of the English Middle Class, 1780–1850* (Chicago: University of Chicago Press, 1987), 13, 30.

27. Ibid., 18–23. Also see Robert A. Nye, *Masculinity and Male Codes of Honor in Modern France* (New York: Oxford University Press, 1993), 8, 31–33.

28. Davidoff and Hall, *Family Fortunes*, 13, 25, 29.

29. Catherine Hall, *White, Male and Middle Class: Explorations in Feminism and History* (New York: Routledge, 1992), 158.

30. Mark C. Carnes, *Secret Ritual and Manhood in Victorian America* (New Haven CT and London: Yale University Press, 1989), 14.

31. Margaret S. Creighton, "American Mariners and the Rites of Manhood, 1830–1870," in *Jack Tar in History: Essays in the History of Maritime Life and Labour*, ed. Colin Howell and Richard J. Twomey (Fredericton NB: Acadiensis Press, 1991), 132–63, esp. 147.

32. Brown, *Strangers in Blood*, 35, 47–48.

33. Toronto, Archives of Ontario, George Gordon Papers, MU 1146, G. Moffatt, Fort William, to George Gordon, Monontagué, 25 July 1809.

34. For example, see W. Kaye Lamb, ed., *Sixteen Years in Indian Country: The Journal of Daniel Williams Harmon, 1800–1816* (Toronto: MacMillam Company of Canada Ltd., 1957), 197–98.

35. Davidoff and Hall, *Family Fortunes*, 18; Nye, *Masculinity and Male Codes of Honor*, 32.

36. Ouellet, *Economy, Class, and Nation*, 62, 80, 94–95, 109.

37. Campbell, *The Northwest Company*, 130, 140; "Incidents, Deaths, &c." *Canadian Magazine* 2, no. 11 (14 May 1824): 473.

38. Reed, *Masters of the Wilderness*, 57–58.

39. Ibid., 68, 75.

40. John Lambert, *Travels through Canada, and the United States of North America, in the Years 1806, 1807, & 1808. To Which are Added, Biographical Notices and Anecdotes of Some of the Leading Characters in the United States*, 2d ed., 2 vols. (1813; London: C. Cradock and W. Joy, 1814), 295–96, 524.

41. Edward Allen Talbot, *Five Years' Residence in the Canadas: Including a Tour through Part of the United States of America in the Year 1823*, 2 vols. (London: Longman, Hurst, Rees, Orme, Brown and Green, 1824), 2:282–84. John Duncan also criticizes the Montreal bourgeoisie for their deficiency in enterprise and public spirit. John M. Duncan, *Travels through Part of the United States and Canada in 1818 and 1819*, 2 vols. (Glasgow: Wardlaw and Cunninghame, 1823), 2:156–57.

42. Davidoff and Hall, *Family Fortunes*, 18–20, 30.

43. Nye, *Masculinity and Male Codes of Honor*, 32–34.

44. Hetherington, "Canada's First Social Club," 298.

45. Beaver Club Minute Book, 2; *Rules and Regulations*, 5.

46. Tulchinsky, "Forsyth," 311; Fernand Ouellet, "Frobisher, Joseph," in *DCB*, 5:331–34, esp. 333 and "McTavish, Simon," in *DCB*, 5:560–67, esp. 566; Campbell, *McGillivray*, 111.

47. Brown, *Strangers in Blood*, 81–110; Van Kirk, *"Many Tender Ties": Women in Fur Trade Society in Western Canada, 1670–1870* (Winnipeg MB: Watson and Dwyer Publishing, Ltd., 1980), 28–52.

48. Campbell, *McGillivray*, 68; Brown, *Strangers in Blood*, 90; Van Kirk, *Many Tender Ties*, 50.

49. Beaver Club Minute Book, 3.

50. For example, F. A. Larocque and J. M. Lamothe were elected in 1815 and Dominique Ducharme attended the last meeting in 1827. Beaver Club Minute Book, 94, 112, 121.

51. Hall, *White, Male and Middle Class*, 157.

52. Beaver Club Minute Book, 1–2; *Rules and Regulations*, 5–6.

53. Bullock found the same with the Freemasons. Although the organization kept its work and rituals secret, they participated visibly in public life and believed they were working toward a public, rather than a private, good, and they demanded public honor. Bullock, "The Ancient and Honorable Society," 4–5.

54. Beaver Club Minute Book, 1, 90, 113; *Rules and Regulations*, 5.

55. *Rules and Regulations*, 3–6. Hetherington discusses three surviving medals at the Chateau de Ramezay in Montreal and at the Library of the Parliament Buildings in Ottawa, as well as some privately owned plates and snuff boxes. Hetherington, "Canada's First Social Club," 298. Watson mentions that cups and silver plates bearing the mark of the Beaver Club were put up at auctions throughout the country. Watson, "The First Beaver Club," 337. Also, a picture of a gold brooch of a beaver, said to be worn by wives of Beaver Club members, appears in "The HBC Packet," *The Beaver* Outfit 264, no. 3 (December 1933): 5–6.

56. For an example of a member charged for a dinner he did not attend, see Beaver Club Minute Book, 21 January 1809, 32. For an example of a member excused from dinner fees because of illness, see Beaver Club Minute Book, 53, 82.

57. See the accounts listed at the end of every dinner in the Minute Book.

58. For example, see the first meeting of the years 1815–16 and 1816–17, Beaver Club Minute Book, 97–98, 113.

59. *Rules and Regulations*, 4.

60. Ibid., 3.

61. Montreal, McCord Museum of Canadian History Archives, M18638, Memorandum recording the meeting of Simon Fraser and John McDonald of Garth, the last two surviving partners of the North West Company, 1 August 1858, Original. Published in W. Kaye Lamb, ed., *The Letters and Journals of Simon Fraser, 1806–1808* (Toronto: MacMillan Company of Canada, 1960), 271.

62. Brown, *Strangers in Blood*, 2–3.

63. Wilson, *The Enterprises of Robert Hamilton*, 12, 20–21.

64. Landmann, *Adventures and Recollections*, 233–34.

65. Nye, *Masculinity and Male Codes of Honor*, 10–11.

66. Beaver Club Minute Book, 1–2; *Rules and Regulations*, 5.

67. Benoît, "Wintering Dishes," 25–27; Watson, "The First Beaver Club," 337.

68. Reed, *Masters of the Wilderness*, 68.

69. *Rules and Regulations*, 3; Reed, *Masters of the Wilderness*, 68.

70. Reed, *Masters of the Wilderness*, 68.

71. Beaver Club Minute Book, 1; *Rules and Regulations*, 6.

72. Landmann, *Adventures and Recollections*, 234, 238.

73. Rice, *Early American Taverns*, 98. Bullock found that for Masons convivial drinking and conversation were very important for specific expressions of brotherly love and fraternity (Bullock, "The Ancient and Honorable Society," 62).

74. Lambert, *Travels through Canada*, 295.

75. Reed, *Masters of the Wilderness*, 65.

76. Landmann, *Adventures and Recollections*, 296; Rice, *Early American Taverns*, 98.

77. Lambert, *Travels through Canada*, 295–96, 524. Clark found that in eighteenth-century English clubs conspicuous consumption and excess were an essential ingredient of club sociability (Clark, "Sociability and Urbanity," 20).

78. Alexander Henry, Montreal, to John Askin, Strathbane, 9 May 1815, *The John Askin Papers*, vol. 2, *1796–1820*, ed. Milo M. Quaife (Detroit: Detroit Library Commission, 1928–31), 781–83.

79. Clark, "Sociability and Urbanity," 21.

80. Rice, *Early American Taverns*, 101.

81. *Rules and Regulations*, 3.

82. Basil Johnston, *Ojibwa Ceremonies* (Toronto: McClelland and Stewart, 1982), 33, 160.

83. John Palmer, *Journal of Travels in the United States of America and in Lower Canada, Performed in the Year 1817; Containing Particulars Relating to the Prices of Land and Provisions, Remarks on the Country and the People, Interesting Anecdotes, and an Account of the Commerce, Trade, and Present State of Washington, New York, Philadelphia, Boston, Baltimore, Albany, Cincinnati, Pittsburg, Lexington, Quebec, Montreal, &c.* (London: Sherwood, Neely, and Jones, 1818), 216–17.

84. Other bourgeois fraternities also imitated Native culture, the most obvious being the Improved Order of the Red Men, established in the United States in 1834. Carnes describes in detail the order's rituals and language, inspired by Native culture, such as sachems invoking the "Great Spirit of the Universe" and pale-face warriors fearlessly facing death. Unfortunately Carnes's only explanation for why Native culture was chosen as a model for the fraternity is that the men who were transforming America into an urban, industrial society desired to recreate a primitive past. Mark C. Carnes, "Middle-Class Men and

the Solace of Fraternal Ritual," in *Meetings for Manhood: Construction of Masculinity in Victorian America*, ed. Mark C. Carnes and Clyde Griffen (Chicago: University of Chicago Press, 1990), 37–52, esp. 39–45.

85. *Rules and Regulations*, 3.

86. Reed, *Masters of the Wilderness*, 69.

87. Beaver Club Minute Book, 83.

88. Frederick Goedike, Aguiwang, to George Gordon, Michipicoten, 29 October 1811, George Gordon Papers.

89. *Rules and Regulations*, 1.

90. Beaver Club Minute Book, 28 September 1807, 6–7.

Index

Page numbers in italics refer to illustrations.

Abenaki, 23–24, 52, 97, 221–22, 582
abortion, 261
Acadia, xxiii, xxiv, 105, 219, 220
Accault, Michel, 269, 270, 449–52
Achiganaga, 276, 278, 280–81
Adahmer, Madame, 576
Adams, David, 427
Adams, Joseph, 483
adoptees, 116, 117
adultery, 259, 260, 511n7, 529
advertising, 173
agriculture, xvii, l, lii, 535; Armouchiquois, 34; in Canada, 88–113; cultivating tools for, 405; and destruction of cornfields, 441, 562, 585; French, 223; Illini, 451–53, 456, 474n52; Iroquois, 185, 199; métis, 543; Odawa, 456
Ainsse, Joseph-Louis, 597
Alaska Commercial Company, 171, 172
Albany, xxx, xxxi, xliii, 217, 226, 227, 236, 349. See also Fort Albany
alcohol, 224–25, 226, 229, 232; Beaver Club and, 605, 607–8, 609–10; Freemasons and, 619n73; as gift, 348, 578; Iroquois and, 186; Montreal Merchants' Records and, 406; murder and, 274; Ojibwa and, 125–27. See also brandy; rum
Algonquian Indians, 29, 84, 137, 216; abandoned métis children and, 548; anarchism of, 253–54; French and, 246–304, 443; of Lake Nipissing, 94, 95, 96; sexual mores of, 258–73, 511n7; view of, on murderers and redemption, 291. See also Abenaki; Conoy; Cree; Illini; Menomini; Miami (people); Micmac; Muskwakiwuk; Odawa; Ojibwa; Potawatomi; Shawnee
Algonquian women, 258, 259, 260, 261–62,

443–80, 511n7. See also Illini women; Odawa women; Ojibwa women
American Fur Company (AFC), 162–67, 169, 172, 175, 177n2, 317; beaver and, 412, 423, 426, 429; Chiefs Coats and, 414–18; independent traders and, 551; Marcot sisters and, 462, 465; rendezvous system of, 427, 430
American Revolution, 462, 575
Amherst, Jeffrey, 235
Amikwas, 280
Amsterdam, xvii, xxvi
Anadabijou, 29, 30
Anderson, A. C., 501–2
Anderson, Karen: *Chain Her by One Foot*, 445
Anglo-Americans, 231–32, 234, 236, 529–32, 533
Anglo-Indian War (1763–65). See Pontiac's War
animal-Indian relations, 75, 77, 118–19, 125, 141. See also clan animals
Anishinabeg. See Mississauga; Odawa; Ojibwa
Anishinabeg historiography, 45–63
Anne of Great Britain. See Queen Anne
antelope, 161
Aramepinchieue, 269–73, 290, 304n80, 446, 447–53
archaeology, lviiin64, 405–6
Archer, Gabriel, 30
architecture, li, 474n52, 543
arctic trade, 3
arctic travel, 139
aristocracy. See upper class
Arkansas (people). See Quapaw
Armand, Louis. See Lahontan, Baron de
armbands, xliii
Armouchiquois, 30, 32, 34, 38
arrows, 34

Asch, Michael, 523
Ashwabemy, 531
asking, 135n29, 152. *See also* begging
Assikinack, Francis, 47, 48, 51
Assiniboine, 50, 71, 95
Astor, John Jacob, 166, 421, 422, 464, 465, 598
Athapaskan Indians, 84, 137, 520
athletic contests, 572, 573
Atlantic islands, xx, xxiv
Auglaize River, 561–62
Auldjo, Alexander, 598
Aulneau, Father, 95
Aupaumut, Hendrick, 582–83
axes, 39

Baby, Duperon, 563, 587
Baby, Susan, 587
Bailey, Alfred, 40, 97
Baker, T. Lindsay, 423
Bannor, Samuel, 323
baptism, xlviii, 265, 268, 444, 450, 453, 459, 479n84. *See also* lay baptism
Barthe family, 445, 462, 464
Basque language, 31
Basque-style boats. *See* shallops
Batt, Isaac, 492
Battle of Fallen Timbers, 585, 586
Battle of the Wabash. *See* St. Clair's Defeat
beads, xix, 33, 34, 85, 130, 152, 347, 351; Montreal Merchants' Records and, 396, 407; spiritual wealth and, 355
bears, 20–21, 118–19
bearskins, 161, 163, 175
Beauharnois, marquis de, 225, 228, 237
beaver, xvii, xxiii, xxxvi, 164, 167–68, 317; arctic, xxviii; dams of, 12–14; decline of, 175, 420–35; as dominant fur, 165–67; eating of, 13; export of, 163, 166, 172, 180n33; Father LeClercq on, 11–14, 16n10; as gift, 250, 252; of Great Lakes, 84; hunting of, 11–14, 189; in Native cosmology, xxxvii, 8–9; price of, 166, 167, 420, 422, 425–26; and seventeenth-century market glut, 215; silk hats and, 420–22; spearing of, 17; U.S. economy and, 172
Beaver, Herbert, 500–503, 506, 507
Beaver Club, 441, 593–620
Beaver Wars. *See* Fur Trade Wars
begging, 84, 103, 152, 154
Bellenger, Etienne, 26, 36

berdaches, 258
Bering Sea, 176
Berryer, Nicolas-René, 235
Besabes, 32, 36–37
Beverley, Robert, 411
Biard, Pierre, 37, 38, 97
Bibeau, Donald, 5
Big Cat, 565–66
bilingualism, liv
biracial people. *See* métis; mixed-ancestry people
Bird, James, 498
Bird, Thomas, 334–35
Birnie, James, 501
Bishop, Charles A., 69, 70, 72, 77, 519–20
Blackbird, Andrew J., 47, 48, 49, 52
Blackfeet, 427, 429
Black Loon, 568, 570
Black-Rogers, Mary, 84
blacksmiths, 326, 336
Blanchet, F. N., 503
blankets, xxxix, xli, 316, 323, 571
blessings, 141, 148
blood revenge. *See* revenge
Bloomfield, Joseph, 195, 200
Blue Jacket, 563–64, 578, 584, 587, 588n3
boarding schools, 507
body paint, 351
Boisbriant, Sieur de, 292
Bois-Brûlé, 524, 525
"bois brule" (label), 555n3
Boucher, Françoise, 516n75
Bouquet, Henry, 234–35, 575
Bourassa family, 445, 457
"bourgeois" (word), 613n1
bourgeoisie, 593–620
Bourgmont, Etienne de Véniard, 307–8
Braddock, Edward, 232, 550
Bradstreet, John, 181
Brady, Thomas, 478n80
brandy, 224, 234
Brant, Joseph, 199, 576, 582, 584
Brant, Molly, 199
brassware, 22, 39, 322
breast feeding, 115, 126–27
Brereton, John, 22, 23, 29
bribery, 114
Brickell, John, 566
bride price, 487, 547
Bridger, Jim, 427

Britain. *See* Great Britain

Broken Arm. *See* Kesconeek

Broken Tooth. *See* Katawaubetai

Brothers in Law Club, 596

Brown, Jennifer, 440

Buckongahelas, 565

buffalo, 71, 90, 161, 173

buffalo robes, 3, 161, 165, 415

Bungi. *See* Plains Ojibwa

burials, 294n9, 571

burial strouds, 369, 374, 380n36

Butler, Thomas, 195

buttons, xli, 334, 351, 417, 418

Cabahis, 36–37

Cabot, John, xxi, xxiv, 24

Cabot, Sebastian, 24

Cacagous, 32

Cadillac, Sieur de, xlviii, 249–53, 282, 307; Detroit killings of 1706 and, 285–89, 302n69; intermarriage and, 267, 269; Michilimackinac and, 536; on sexual freedom of Algonquian girls, 262

Cadot, Michael, 136

Cadotte, J. B., 549

Cahokia, xlviii, xlix, 223, 290, 453

Caldwell, Billy, 587

calumet, 120, 277, 290–91, 320, 584, 599, 610–11

Canada, xvi, 78, 88–113, 215–45

Canadian Shield, xxiii, xxxiv, 101

Canaghquayeson, 181

Canajoharie, 344, 349, 357, 361, 375

cannibalism, 139, 155n3

canoes, li, liii; beaver hunting and, 17; and cargo, xlvi, 232, 451; equipment for, 392, 393; and Father Allouez, 7–8; flotillas of, xxviii, xxix; food supply and, 90, 451; in Great Lakes, xlix; and Marie Madeleine Réaume, 457; moose hunting and, 11; of Odawa, 456; provisioning of, 94, 100; single-piece, 35; vulnerability of, 223

Cape Breton, xxiv, 27, 221

capitalism, 183, 184, 200, 202, 424–25. *See also* cash economy

capital punishment, 260, 278, 279, 280, 286, 287

captives, 562, 566, 567, 568–70, 573, 574–76

Carheil, Father, 263, 267, 536

Caribbean area, xvii, xx

caribou, 143

Carnes, Mark, 600, 619n84

Carnor, Robert, 323

Caron family, 531

Carteret, George, xxxii, xxxiii

Cartier, Jacques, 27

Carver, Jonathan, 543

Casco Bay, 23–24

cash economy, 191, 194, 197

Catholicism, 272–73, 439, 445, 451, 606. *See also* lay Catholicism

Catholic kin networks, liii, lv, 444–47, 454, 457–67

Catlin, George, 416

Cayuga, 565

celebrations, 577–78. *See also* festivals

celibacy, 258, 266, 449

Chaboillez, Charles-Jean-Baptiste, 603

Chain Her by One Foot (Anderson), 445

chalcedony, 36

Champlain, Samuel de, xxvii, 28, 29, 34, 36, 92, 96, 97, 99

chaplains, Anglican, 497–99, 500–503

Charles I, xxxii

chastity, 261, 266, 507

Chaurette, Simon, 136

Chequamegon Bay, xlix, 100

Cherokee, lvi, 581, 584

chert, 36

Chevalier, Amable, 466

Chevalier, Louison, 459, 461, 462, 466

Chevalier, Louis Pascal, 458, 461

Chevalier, Louis Thérèse, 457, 459, 461, 477n68, 549

Chevalier family, 445, 457–62, 463, 464, 475nn56–57, 476n60

Chevelier, Marie Madeleine Réaume. *See* L'archeveque, Marie Madeleine Réaume

Chicago, 532

Chicago massacre (1812). *See* Fort Dearborn massacre

Chickamauga Cherokee, 565

Chickasaw, 291, 549

"chicot" (word), 555n3

Chiefs Coats, 316–17, 414–19

child-rearing, 566

children, 21, 126–27, 188, 470n11, 507

China, 171

Chipewyan, 482

Chipewyan women, 514n57

Chippewa. *See* Ojibwa

Chittenden, Hiram, 421
Choiseul, duc de, 235–36
Chouart, Médard. *See* Groseilliers, Sieur des
Chouteau, Pierre, Jr., 166, 429
Chouteau companies, 163, 164, 165, 172, 426
Christianity, 251, 256–57, 265, 284, 356, 450
Churchill, E. A., 27–28
church workers, 194
civil marriage, 517n106
clan animals, 358, 548
class stratification, 197–99, 254, 352, 355, 599–607
Clayton, James, 84
Cleland, Robert Glass, 421
Clinton, George, 362, 363, 365
cloth, xxxix–xl, xli, xlii, xliv, xlv, 97, 224, 316; English, 335, 336; flawed, 332; French, 335, 336; Iroquois and, 186, 376; Montreal Merchants' Records and, 403–4. *See also* woolens
clothing, li, 34, 85, 224, 316; as gift, 121, 128, 130, 154, 157n19, 347–48, 352, 355, 368–72; Iroquois and, 187, 200, 347–48, 350–52, 355; Montreal Merchants' Records and, 398, 401, 403–4, 407; as sign of friendship, 120; social difference and, 356. *See also* coats; hats
clothing styles, xliv, 23, 85–86, 200, 316–18, *319*; métis, 543–44; Mohawk, 350–52, 356, 570; Shawnee, 563; of traders, 577–78
Clyman, James, 427
C. M. Lampson and Company. *See* Lampson and Company
coats, 340n33. *See also* Chiefs Coats; matchcoats
Cockran, William, 498, 506
cod industry, xxi, xxii, 23
cohabitation, 547
Colbert, Jean, xxv, xxvi
Colden, Cadwallader, 344, 367
colonialism, 5, 77, 78
colonists, 97, 349, 575
colonization, xxii
Coltman, William B., 524, 526
combs, 332, 334, 351, 393
Company of New France, 96
Company of One Hundred Associates, 215
competition, 144–45, 147–48
Connolly, William, 502, 508–9, 521
Conoy, 565, 584
consumer choice, 345

consumer demand, xvii–xviii, 320–43, 347, 386, 389
contracts. *See* legal contracts
Coo-coo-chee, 567–73, 586
Cook, William Hemmings, 492, 500
copper, xliv, 23, 39
Copway, George, 47, 48, 49, 51, 54, 61n19
corn, 94–103, 453, 563, 565, 568; and Coo-coo-chee, 572; as currency, 196; destruction of, 441, 562, 585; seed, 581. *See also* Green Corn Festival
costume, 348. *See also* clothing styles
Council of the Northern Department, 504
Countering Colonization (Devens), 445
coureurs de bois, xxx, xxxi, xxxvii, xlvii, l, 255, 269; intermarriage and, xxx, 266–69, 485; sexual relations and, 264, 265, 266
Covenant Chain, 344, 347, 367, 375
Cox, Ross, 492, 515n70, 516n75
coypu. *See* nutria
Cree, 50, 71, 94, 95, 97; bride price and, 487; daughters of, 486; matrilineality and, 520; respect and, 141; sexual mores of, 482, 483; and trade at Chequamegon, 100; William Connolly and, 508
Creek, 203n4, 581, 584
Cree language, 230
Creighton, Margaret, 601
Croghan, George, 199
Crooks, Ramsay, 166, 423, 465
Crow, 427, 429
Cuoc, Elizabeth. *See* Tichenet, Madame
culture change, 66–71, 246–304

Dablon, Father, 100
d'Aigremont, François Clairambault, 243n69, 254
Dakota (people), lv, 255; alliance of, with Saulteurs, 276; Chiefs Coats and, 416; French and, 223, 274; La Framboise family and, 551; peacemaking and, 119–20, 122; warfare of, with Aninishinabeg, 49, 50, 52, 54, 62n37. *See also* Bois-Brûlé
Dalhousie, Lord, 602
d'Argenteuil, Sieur, 303n72
d'Arnouville, Jean-Baptiste de Machault, 232
daughters of chiefs, 132, 269–73, 462, 487, 508, 551
daughters of traders, 492–94, 501, 502, 505, 507, 520, 521, 522, 547, 548
David, David, 598

Davidoff, Leonore, 600, 603
death penalty. *See* capital punishment
de Buade, Louis. *See* Frontenac, comte de
Dechene, Louis, 295n19
de Contrecoeur, Capitaine, 243n74
deerskins, xxxiv, xliii, 161, 163, 164
defective goods. *See* flawed goods
de Fleury, André-Hercule, 229
de la Barre, Nouvel à M., 300n60
de la Boische, Charles. *See* Beauharnois, marquis de
de la Gallissoniére, Roland-Michel Barrin, 230
de la Malgue, Paul Marin, 232
de La Mothe, Antoine Laumet. *See* Cadillac, Sieur de
de La Tour, Sieur, 178
Delaware (people), 231–32, 234, 581; Blue Jacket and, 564; captives of, 566, 574–75; Northwest Indian Confederacy and, 580, 583, 584; U.S. wars against, 562
de Lévis, François, 235
Deliette, Pierre, 260, 261
de Menneville, Ange. *See* Duquesne, marquis
Demers, Modeste, 503
de Monts, Sieur, xxvii, 92
Deneau dit Detailly, Pierre, l
Denonville, Marquis de, 535
Detroit, xlv, xlviii–xlix; agriculture and, 99, 223; American Fur Company in, 175; Cadillac's plan for, 267; fees for trade in, 220; founding of, 219, 282–83; and killings of 1706, 281–90, 302n66; number of houses in, 532
Devens, Carol: *Countering Colonization*, 445
Devine, Heather, 597
Devon, xxi
diaries, traders', 137
Dickson, Robert, 545, 553
diplomacy, 121–22, 125–27, 248–49, 252–53, 362–63. *See also* Covenant Chain
disease, 37–38, 40, 155n5
divorce, 262, 470n11, 547
dodem. See totem
dogs, 17–19, 21
Doty, James Duane, 529–30
Douglas, James, 496–97, 501, 502, 506
dowry, 487, 495
Dreuillettes, Gabriel, xxix
dried fish, 94
Drummond Island, 126

Duchesneau, Jacques, lv
Duffield, James, 150, 512n20
Dulhut, Daniel Greysolon, 276–81, 300n60
Dunmore's War, 575
Duquesne, marquis, 231, 232, 233, 243n69, 292
duties. *See* taxes
Duval, Elizabeth, 492
dwellings, li–lii, 470n9, 531, 536; Delaware, 565–66; destruction of, 562; furniture in, 570; métis, 543; Mohawk, 568–59; Shawnee, 563

eating habits, 18, 95, 133n2, 586. *See also* fasting; feasts and feasting; food; tea drinking
Eccles, William, 86, 106
Edict of Nantes, xxix
Eid, Leroy V., 57
elk, 161
Elliott, Matthew, 574, 575, 580, 587
embargoes, 162
England, xxvii, xxxvi, xxxix, xliv; Anishinabeg and, 50, 51, 52; beaver import and, 180n33, 428–29, 432; Blue Jacket and, 564; Chevalier kin network and, 460; copying of French goods by, xxxix, 323, 326, 334–35, 336, 338n7; Detroit and, 581, 585; dismissal of Acadia and Newfoundland by, xxiii; fishing trade and, xxi–xxii; Fort Malden and, 586; Fort St. Joseph and, 461–62; France and, 217–19; Great Lakes and, xlix, 579; Hudson Bay and, xxxi, xxxiii–xxxiv; Iroquois and, 186, 191, 192–93, 199, 344; Native legal rights and, 72; Native visitors to, 358; New Amsterdam and, xxxii; New England coastal exploration and, 22, 24; Ojibwa and, 123; quality of goods of, xxxviii–xli, 224, 315, 320–43; raccoon import and, 170; taking of Quebec from France by, xxiv; and War of 1812, 586; wars against Indians by, 568, 575; white fur and, xxvi. *See also* Great Britain
environment, 555n3
epidemics, 37–38, 40, 50, 140, 144, 155n5, 276
Eschkebugecoshe, 123
Etchemin, 29–30, 31, 33, 35, 37–38, 40
Etienne-François. *See* Choiseul, duc de
etiquette, Ojibwa, 131–32
Eurocentrism, 45–46
Ewing, George, 167, 169
Ewing, William, 167, 169

execution, 260, 278, 279, 280, 281
explorers, xxiv–xxv, 22, 24, 26–27
exports, xxiv–xxv, 161–63, 164–65, 172, 189, 428–29; balance of, with imports, 173–74; of fur seal, 171; of raccoon, 168, 170, 176; statistics of, 432. *See also* reexportation
extended family, 115–16

Fagnundes, João Alvares, 24, 27
Fallen Timbers. *See* Battle of Fallen Timbers
family, 115–17, 133n3, 489–96, 521, 548–52, 606. *See also* extended family
family trees, 552
farming. *See* agriculture
fasting, 118, 130
Favell, John, 490, 513n45
feasts and feasting, 572, 596
Fernandez, Simão, 26
festivals, 544, 571
Fidler, Peter, 158n23
files (tools), 405–6
Finlayson, Duncan, 506
firearms, xxvii, 68, 71, 224, *360*; defective, 144, 326–28, 338n15, 339n17; English, xxxviii, 323, 325; as gifts, 121, 130, 358, 368, 393; Iroquois and, 186, 187
fishing, xvii, xxi, xxv, 23, 27–28, 39, 143, 201. *See also* cod industry
Flat Mouth. *See* Eschkebugecoshe
flawed goods, xxxix–xl, 323, 333–34
flints, xl, 332, 333, 396
Fond du Lac, 126
food, 95; beaver as, 13; at Beaver Club dinners, 599, 608; begging for, 84; deprivation, 140; dogs as, 18; at Fort Miami, 577; gifts of, 129, 349, 368; at Green Corn Festival, 572; imported, 98, 104; trade of, for furs, 97, 104; wild, 104, 201, 474n49
food supplies, li, 34–35, 90, 103, 451
Forbes, John, 234
Ford, Polly, 567
Forest, Sieur de la, 267
fornication, 529
Forsyth, John, 599, 603
Fort Albany, xxv, xliv, 335
Fort Alexander, 487
Fort Beauharnois, xlix
Fort Churchill, 329, 334, 484, 492
Fort Clark, 428
Fort Dearborn massacre, 586, 587
Fort Defiance, 585

Fort Duquesne, 232
Fort Edmonton, 508
Fort Hall, 418
Fort Hunter, 379n22
Fort Jefferson, 580, 583
Fort Knox, 564
Fort Laramie, 427
Fort Malden, 586
Fort McKenzie, 414
Fort Miami, xlix, 562, 573, 576–79
Fort Michilimackinac, 52
Fort Necessity, 232
Fort Niagara, xliii, xliv, 125, 189, 225, 232–33, 235, 584
Fort Nipigon, xlix
Fort Orange, xx, xxxvi
Fort Oswego, xliii, xliv, xlvi, xlix, 181, 189, 192, 228, 229, 349, 361
Fort Ouiatenon, 460
Fort Pimitoui, 265, 273, 458
Fort Prince of Wales, 484
Fort Recovery, 566
Fort Stanwix, 193
Fort St. Francois, xlix
Fort St. James, 502
Fort St. Joseph, xlix, li, lii, liii, 456–63, 466, 478n80, 532
Fort St. Joseph Mission, 476nn63–64
Fort St. Louis, xlix, 254–55, 258, 265, 270, 273, 298n36
Fort Uinta, 431
Fort Union, 414
Fort Vancouver, 500–503, 506, 507
Fort Washington, 580
Fort Wayne IN, xlix, 562
Fort Winnebago, 587
fox, 163
Fox (people). *See* Muskwakiwuk
France, xxxi; Algonquian Indians and, 246–304, 443; and beaver importation, xxv–xxvi; and biracial marriage, 535; Cape Breton and, xxiv; and colonial trade, xxv, xxvi, xxvii, xxix, xxxii, xlvi; and copying of goods, xxxviii, 323, 326, 334–36; and cost of maintaining posts, 229; Dakota people and, 223, 274; England and, 217–19; and fishing trade, xxi–xxii; Great Lakes and, xlvii, 92; Gulf of Maine and, 27, 37; Hudson Bay and, xxxiii, xxxiv; Huron and, 95; imperial ambitions of, 86, 215–45; Iroquois and, 186,

217–19, 227, 231, 536; in Native cosmology, xxxvii; Native legal rights and, 73; Native visitors to, 32, 36; northern plains and, xxxvi; Ojibwa and, 123; provisioning problems of, 91, 97; and quality of goods, xxxviii–xxxix, 224; Sourisquois and, 31–32; Spain and, 219; and subarctic trade, 334–36. *See also* New France

Franklin, John, 139, 155n4

Franks, Jacob, 531

Fraser, Simon, 597, 606–7

fraternal organizations, 600, 619n84

Freeman, Isaac, 564

Freemasons, 595, 596–97, 618n53, 619n73

"freemen," 513n42, 513n47, 538, 554

freezing to death, 139, 155n2

Fremont, John, 427

French-Algonquian relations, 246–304; and Anishinabeg, 50, 51, 52, 53, 55, 56; and Detroit killings of 1706, 282–90; and murder, 274, 276–82; and sexual relations, 258–64

"Frenchified" Indians, 334, 340n30

French-Indian intermarriage, xlvii, liii–lvi, 267–73, 450–53, 481–518; chiefs' daughters and, 132; kin networks and, xlvi, lii, liii–liv, 4–5, 457, 458, 461–63; suppression of, 268–69

French women, 247, 258

Friars of St. Andrew, 578

Frobisher, Benjamin, 597

Frobisher, Joseph, 522, 596, 597, 603

Frobisher, Louise, 522

Frobisher, Thomas, 597

Frontenac, comte de, lixn40, 225

Frost, Augustin, 512n20

fruit orchards, 474n52, 544

fur processing, 171, 173, 174

furriers, 173, 174

"furs" (word), 160

fur seal, 160, 165, 170–72, 176

Fur Trade Wars, xxvii, xxviii–xxix, 465

Galbraith, J. S., 88

Gamelin, Antoine, 564

gang rape, 260

gardens, 92, 543, 563, 568

Gaspesians, 10–16, 38

Gauthier, Claude, 549, 550

gender, 53–54, 351–52, 599–601

gender imbalance, 540

gender relations, 212n57, 260

gender roles, 261–62, 452, 453–54, 483, 519, 520

gens de libre. See "freemen"

George II, 345

German settlers, 189–90, 192, 196, 349

Germany, xxiv, 168, 174

Geyer, George, 325, 326

Gibault, Pierre, liv

Gibson, James R., 108, 109n3

gift giving, xlvi, 317, 451; at Fort Miami, 578; Hendrick as recipient of, 362; Iroquois and, 185, 186, 188, 194, 347, 355; murder reparation and, 275; Ojibwa and, 114–59; of William Johnson, 351–52, 365, 368–75, 380nn35–36

gift refusal, 250, 252

Gilbert, Humphrey, 26

Gilfallen, Joseph A., 151

Gillis, John, lviin16

gin, 224

ginseng, 192, 349

Giraud, Marcel, 534

Girty, George, 574–75, 578

Girty, James, 574–76, 578

Girty, Simon, 574–76

Gladman, George, 495

The Glaize, 561–92

gloves, 333

godparents and godparenting, liii, liv, 444–46, 454, 458–60, 462

Goetzmann, William, 424–25

gold, xxi

Gomez, Estévan, 24

Gosnold, Bartholomew, 22, 30

Graham, Andrew, 484

Grand Banks, 27

grand jury sessions, 529

Grant, Charles, 603

Grant, Cuthbert, 523

Gravé du Pont, Francois, 29

Gravier, Jacques, 265, 270–73, 448–51

Great Britain, 161–63, 168, 170, 171, 174, 180n33, 189, 217, 225. *See also* England

Great Carrying Place, 192

Great Lakes, xxix, xxxiv, xlvii, xlix, 3, 175–76; beaver population in, 84; Catholic kin networks and, li; hunting camps and, xl–xli, xlvi; Native historiography and, 45–64; raccoon and, 168, 169. *See also* western Great Lakes region

The Great Snake, 564, 578
Green Bay, xxix, xlv, xlix, 460; agriculture and, 99; intermarriage and, liii–liv, 529–33; Keweenaw murders and, 276; métis and, 538–41, 548, 553; population statistics of, 541, 542
Green Corn Festival, 571–73
Gregory, John, 598
"griffe" (word), 534
Grignon, Charles, 529, 531, 532
Grignon, Domitille, liv, 550, 551
Grignon, Jean-Baptiste, 529
Grignon, Pierre, 550
Grignon family, 531, 548, 552
Groseilliers, Sieur des, xxix–xxx, xxxviii, 321–22
grouse. See partridge
Gulf of Maine, 22–44
Gulf of Mexico, xxxi
Gulf of St. Lawrence, xxi, 22, 25, 27, 38, 41
gunpowder, xxxviii, 98; flawed, xl, 315, 332; as gift, 121, 130, 131; as trade item, 103, 104
guns. See firearms
gunsmiths, 326, 327, 336

Hafen, Leroy, 421, 430
Haldimand, Frederick, 478n78
"half-breed" (term), 534
Hall, Catherine, 600, 603
Hamelin, Jean Baptiste, 478n80
Hamilton, Alexander, 345, 355, 357
Hamilton, Bill, 427, 431
Hamilton, Robert, 530
Hamtramck, Jean François, 584
handkerchiefs, xliii
Hanson, Charles, 422–23
hare, xxxvii, 8–9, 422
Hargrave, James, 505–6, 518n115
Hargrave, Letitia, 506, 507
Harmar, Josiah, 562, 567
Harmon, Daniel, 487–88, 491, 495–96, 598
harpoons, 19, 20
Harriott, J. E., 494, 496
Harris, R. Cole, 106
hatchets, 322, 323, 324, 325, 333, 337n6
hats, xv, xvii, xxv–xxvi, 317, 420–22, 423, 577–78
Hearne, Samuel, liv, 484, 511n20
Heidenreich, Conrad, 93
Hendrick, 190, 344, 347–48, 356–67, 375–76, 383n74; portraits of, 345, 346, 358, 359, 360, 364, 366, 377n4

Henry, Alexander, 100, 118, 122–23, 125, 130–31, 491
Henry, Alexander ("the younger"), 487, 488, 496, 597, 610
herbalists, 567
Hickerson, Harold, 203n4
Hidatsa, 99, 416
hides, 160–61
Hilger, Inez, 119
historiography, 65–79. See also Anishinabeg historiography
Hitchcock, Robert, xxii
Hoffman, B. G., 42
Holland, xvii, xxiv, xxvi, xxix, xxxii, xl, xlvi
homosexuality, 258
Hopocan. See Captain Pipe
horticulture, 91, 185. See also fruit orchards; gardens
Hotreouati, 216
household furnishings, 570
houses. See dwellings
Hudson, Henry, xxiv, 33
Hudson Bay, xxix, xxxi, 9, 222
Hudson River, xlvi
Hudson's Bay Company (HBC), xix, xxxvi, xxxvii, 3, 108, 223; and American Fur Company, 497, 554; corn supply and, 103; establishment of, xxxii; France and, 222; and Galbraith study, 88; imitation brandy of, 224; and London Committee, 481–82, 490; marriage "in the manner of the country" and, 481–98, 504, 508, 510–18; monopoly of, 106; Native demands and, 315; and quality of goods, 320–43; records of, 387, 389; return policy of, xli–xlii; steady decline of, 236; trapping brigades and, 427
Hughes, Brian, 614n8
Hughes, James, 598, 609, 614n8
humility, 151
humor, 146, 151, 152, 159n38, 543
hunger, 84, 118, 148, 151
Hunt, George T., 66–70, 72, 73, 78
hunting, 17, 20, 21, 71, 98, 99, 142–43, 191. See also overhunting
hunting camps, xlii
"hunting women," 261–63, 264–65, 268
Huron, xxvii, xlviii, 50, 51; agriculture and, 92, 93–94, 95, 96, 98, 101; collapse of, 99, 215, 216; at Flat Rock, 587; George Ironside Jr. and, 586; Northwest Indian Confederacy and, 580, 582, 583, 584

Huron-Petun, 249–52, 265, 277–78, 280, 282, 283, 287–89
hypochondria, 155n5

ice chisels, xxxviii, xli, 323, 324, 330, 404
Ickoue ne Kioussa. *See* "hunting women"
Illini, xlviii, xlix, liii, 216; Christianity and, 265–66, 269–73, 454–55; Iroquois and, 276; sexual mores of, 260, 261, 262, 271; subgroups of, 471n16. *See also* Cahokia; Kaskaskia; Peoria (people)
Illini women, 265–66, 268–73, 296n24, 446–61, 470n9
Illinois River, 216
imitation goods, xxxix
imperialism, 215–45
imported furs, 97, 173
imports: balance of, with exports, 173–74; from England, 345–46; to England, 161–63, 168, 170, 171, 180n33, 189, 225, 428–29, 432
Improved Order of the Red Men, 619n84
Indiana, xlix
Indian aesthetics. *See* Native aesthetics
Indian-animal relations. *See* animal-Indian relations
Indian cosmology. *See* Native cosmology
Indian culture. *See* Native culture
Indian labor. *See* Native labor
Indian land cessions. *See* Native land cessions
Indian legal rights. *See* Native legal rights
Indians. *See* Native people
Indian women. *See* Native women
inequality, social. *See* class stratification
Ingram, David, 24, 26
inheritance, 525, 548, 603
Innis, Harold, 27, 89–90, 93, 106
intermarriage, 120, 531, 547. *See also* French-Indian intermarriage
interpreters and translators, liv, 449, 467, 493, 575
intertribal war parties, 561, 562, 583
Iowa (people), 62n37
Ipswich MA, 38
Ironside, George, 568, 571, 572–73, 574, 578, 586
Ironside, George, Jr., 586
Ironside, Robert, 586
ironware, xxii, xli, xlii, xlv, 94, 97, 187, 324–25, 329
Iroquois, xxvii, xxix, xxxvi; agriculture of,

185, 199; Anishinabeg and, 51, 54, 57; and blockade of trade routes, 545; economy and, 85, 181–214; fashion of, 353, 354; fear of, 281; French and, 186, 217–19, 227, 231, 536; George T. Hunt on, 69–70; historiography of, 78; housewares and, xliv–xlv; Huron-Petun and, 249, 252; imperialistic drive of, 216, 276; Madame Montour as representative of, lvi; as "Mingoes," 565; Northwest Indian Confederacy and, 582, 584; Odawa and, 100, 249, 279; six nations of, 203n4; U.S. treaty obligations to, 376. *See also* Cayuga; Mohawk (people); Oneida; Onondaga; Seneca (people)
Iroquois women, 182, 194–95
Irving, Washington, 598
Isham, James, xl, 315, 320, 329, 333, 334, 482–85

Jacobs, Ferdinand, 485
Jaenen, Cornelius J., 70, 72–74, 77
James II, 217
Jay Treaty, 72, 585
The Jesuit Relations, 3, 15n7, 97
Jesuits, xlviii, liii, lviin32, 37–38, 215, 219–20, 225, 416, 466; Algonquian sexual mores and, 258–73; Charles Langlade and, 549; decline of, 454; Huron-Petun and, 249–50, 251, 252; legitimate standing of, 256; Native women and, 260–73, 446, 448–51; secularization of, 470n10, 476n64
jewelry, xliii, 118, 197, 200, 201, 351, 353, 358, 563, 570
Jobert, Jean-Baptiste, 603
Johnson, Guy, 199–200
Johnson, John, 596–97
Johnson, William, 124–25, 344, 347–52, 355–58, 368–84, 584; dress of, 344; Freemasonry and, 597; gift giving of, 351–52, 365, 368–75, 380nn35–36; Hendrick and, 363, 365; Iroquois and, 181, 188, 193–94, 195, 196, 199, 227, 375; Iroquois name of, 375; portraits of, 344, 377n2
Johnston, John, 611
Johnston, William, 117, 120
Jones, David, 498–99
Jones, Peter, 47, 48, 49, 51
Jones, R. L., 109n3
Jourdain family, 531
Joutel, Henri, 262
Jutras, Jean Baptiste, 474nn54–55

Kahgegagahbowh. *See* Copway, George

Kahkewaquonaby. *See* Jones, Peter

Kalm, Peter, 350

Kaministiquia, xlvii

Kankakee River, 85, 168

Kaskaskia, xxix, xlviii, xlix, 223, 447–53; as converts to Christianity, 265, 269–73, 448–49, 454; murder of French soldier and, 290–92; polygamy and, 264; resettlement of, on Mississippi, 273

Kataolauibois, 302n69, 303n72

Katawaubetai, 126

Kaye, Barry, 108

Keeshkemun, 136

Kegg, Maude, 152

Kekionga, liv

Kennebec River, 30

Kesconeek, 129, 130

Ke-the-cow-e-com-e-coof, 492

kettles, xxxviii, xli, 33, 34, 315, 320, 325, 332, 334, 336

Keweenaw murders (1682 or 1683), 276–81

Khionontateronon, 50

kidney beans, 95

King Charles. *See* Charles I

King George II. *See* George II

King George's War, 187–88, 192, 230, 371, 373, 383n74

King Hendrick. *See* Hendrick

King James II. *See* James II

Kinouge, 286, 302n69

kinship and kin networks, xlvi, lii, liii, lv, 4, 450–51; chiefs and, 132; Iroquois and, 186; La Framboise family and, 551; metaphorical, 125, 131–32; Ojibwa and, 115–16, 121. *See also* Catholic kin networks

Kinzie, John, 574, 577, 578, 586–87

Kinzie, John H., 587

Kiraoueria, 290–92, 304n81

Kischkouch, 302n66

Kiskakon Odawa, 264, 265

Klyne, Jane, 499

knives, xliv; burial of, with owner, 571; English, xli, 323, 325, 335; flawed, 329, 333; French, xxxviii, 33, 322, 335; as gifts, 34, 393

Knox, Henry, 582, 583

Kohl, Johann Georg, 115, 544, 545, 551, 555n3

Koutaoileone. *See* Kataolauibois

Krech, Shepard, III, 519–20

Kurz, Rudolph, 414, 416

La Barre, Jean-François Le Febvre de, 216–17

LaBaye. *See* Green Bay

labor supply, 106

labor value, 85, 195, 201

Labrador, 36

Lac du Flambeau, 136

La Chenette. *See* Tichenet, Madame

Lafitau, Father, 260

La Fourche, 548, 549, 550

La Framboise, Claude, 463

La Framboise, Joseph, 463, 464

La Framboise, Magdelaine Marcot, 447, 462–65

La Framboise family, 445, 462, 548, 551, 552

Lahontan, Baron de, 259, 261, 262

Lake Huron, 7

Lake Michigan, xxix

Lake Nipigon, 9, 129

Lake Nipissing, 94, 95

Lake of the Woods, 102–3, 130

Lake Pepin, xlix

Lake Superior, xxxvii, 8, 50, 100

Lake Superior region, 114–59

La Liberté, Louis, 492

Lambert, John, 603

Lampson and Company, 171, 177n3

land: cession of, 221; commoditization of, 183, 190; expropriation of, 184, 189, 232; ownership of, 198

Landes, Ruth, 117

Landmann, George, 596, 607–8, 609

Langlade, Augustin Mouet de, 548–49

Langlade, Charles, 549–50

Langlade, Charles, Jr., 550

Langlade family, 445, 457, 531, 552

language learning, liii

La Pointe, xlix, 47, 119, 532

L'Arbe Croche, li, 456, 464

L'archeveque, Angelique, 458

L'archeveque, Augustin, liii, 456

L'archeveque, Marie Madeleine Réaume, liii–liv, lv, 455–61, 477n68

La Rochelle, xvii, xxvi, 225

LaRose, Therese, 531, 532

Lasaliere, Pierre, 463

La Salle, Robert de, xxxi–xxxii, lixn40, 216, 256, 447

Lascelle, Antoine, 578

La Vérendrye, Pierre Gaultier de Varennes de, 95, 340n30
Lawe, John, 529–32, 553
Lawson, John, 411
Lawson, Murray G., 203n4
lawsuits, 508–10, 518n130, 529
lay baptism, 470n10, 476n64, 477n65
lay Catholicism, 446, 454, 470n10
"lazy" (word), 145, 153
League of the Iroquois (Morgan), 78
Le Blanc, Jean. *See* Otontagan
Le Boullenger, Baptiste, 452
Le Brochet, 278–79, 280
Leech Lake, 117, 123–24
legal contracts, 114, 242n66. *See also* marriage contracts
legal rights, Native. *See* Native legal rights
Leipzig, 173
Le Pesant, 282, 283, 285–89, 302n69, 303n72
liquor. *See* alcohol
Lisbon, 331
literacy, 46, 247
Little Turtle, 566–67
Long, John, 129, 130
longhouses, 186
Lonval, Jean Baptiste François, 476n62
looking glasses, 351, 352, 358, 368
Lord Dunmore's War. *See* Dunmore's War
Louis XIV, 216–19, 221, 223
Louisbourg, 221, 235
Louisiana, xlix, 219
loyalty, 122, 199
lying, 146–47, 154
lynx, 21

MacCallum, John, 507
MacFarlane, R., 424
Mack, J. Martin, 192
Mackawdebenessy. *See* Blackbird, Andrew J.
MacKenzie, Alexander, 597, 598, 609
Mackenzie, James, 514n57
Mackinac Island, 99, 530, 536
MacLeitch, Gail, 85
Mactavish, Letitia. *See* Hargrave, Letitia
Madeline Island, xlix
Mahican, 356, 566, 582–83, 584
Mailhot, José, 149, 151
maize. *See* corn
Malecite Indians, 98–99, 221
Malhiot, 136
malnutrition, 139, 140

Ma-mong-e-sa-da, 121
Mandan, 95, 99, 416
"manido" (word), 149
manidos. *See* manitous
Manitoba, 102, 104
Manitoulin Island, 56, 586
manitous, 247, 248, 255, 549
mansions, 349–50
manufactured goods, xli, li, liii; British, xxxviii–xli, 224, 322–30, 332–36, 338n7, 345; French, xxxviii–xxxix, 224, 322; Iroquois, 182, 194–95
maple sugar, li, 6n5, 456
Marcot, Jean Baptiste, 462, 479n83
Marcot, Magdelaine. *See* La Framboise, Magdelaine Marcot
Marcot, Thérèse. *See* Schindler, Thérèse Marcot Lasaliere
Marest, Gabriel, 452
Marois, Pierre, 494
marriage: Algonquian, 260, 267; "in the eyes of the church," 456, 498, 499, 503–4; "in the manner of the country," lviiin32, lxin68, 4–5, 267, 450, 458, 463, 469n4, 481–518, 521, 526, 537–38, 550; métis, 550; at Michilimackinac, 539; in Scotland, 517n98; statistics for, 539; of voyageurs and engagés, 547. *See also* civil marriage
marriage contracts, 497
marten, xliii, 34, 144, 163
Marten, Humphrey, 483, 484
Martin, Calvin, 69, 75–76, 77
Marx, Karl, 135
Mascouten, 50, 51, 276
masculinity, 600–601, 607
matchcoats, 316, 345, 411, *412*, 413
material culture, 67, 68–71, 127, 224, 345, 375
matrifocal households, 448, 471n17
matriorganization, 520, 522
Maumee River, xlix, liii, 561, 562, 588n2
Maurepas, comte de, 225, 226
Mauss, Marcel, lxn65
Mawman and Company, 331–32
McCliesh, Thomas, 330, 332, 334
McDonald, Archibald, 499–500
McDonald, John, 604, 606–7
McDougall, Duncan, 487
McGill, James, 597
McGill, John, 597

McGillivray, Duncan, 225, 597
McGillivray, Simon, 597
McGillivray, William, 523, 525, 526, 597, 603–4, 609
McKay, Marguerite Wadin, 501
McKee, Alexander, 574, 575, 581, 586
McKee, Thomas, 586
McKenney, Thomas L., 120, 126
McKenzie, Kenneth, 507
McKenzie, Nancy, 505
McKenzie, Roderick, 597
McLeod, A. N., 598
McLoughlin, John, 500–501, 503
McTavish, John George, 505
McTavish, Simon, 597, 603, 615n16
McVicar, Robert, 146
medicinal plants, 119, 192
medicine, Native. See Native medicine
Meek, Joe, 429
Membre, Father, 254
Menomini, liv, 276, 278, 531, 549, 553
Merasilla, 302n66
Messamouet, 31–32, 34, 35, 36, 38
métis, 273, 307, 439–40, 455, 466, 480n99, 519–28; Alexander Henry on, 491; Alexander Ross on, 493; endogamy of, 546–47; as "independent tribe," 525; labeling of, 544–45, 555n3; as "new Nation," 534; roles of, 546; self-identity of, 544–45; villages of, 541, 543
Meurin, Father, 476n64
Mexico, 429
Miami (people), xlviii, lii, liv, 51, 216, 459, 581; Blue Jacket and, 564; Detroit killings of 1706 and, 282, 283, 287–89; at European households, 579; at The Glaize, 566–67; Northwest Indian Confederacy and, 584; portraits of, 318; sexual mores of, 260, 261; U.S. wars against, 562; women chiefs of, 296n24
Michabous, 8
Michilimackinac, xxviii, xlvii, xlviii, xlix, liv, 8, 457; Andrew Blackbird and, 47; birth statistics of, 540; corn and, 100; and fees for trade, 220; Marcot sisters and, 465; métis and, 536–37, 538–40; number of houses at, 532; 1763 attack on, 124. See also Fort Michilimackinac; Mackinac Island
Micmac, 22–44, 69, 96, 97, 99, 221
Micmac language, 15nn4–5, 15n7

middle class. See bourgeoisie
The Middle Ground (White), 86, 305
"middle ground" theory, 246–311, 348, 356, 443
Miles, Robert, 495
milk, 83–84, 125–27, 131
Milk River, 427
mills, 452, 453
Minavanana, 122
mines, lead, 454
"Mingo" (name), 565
mink, 163, 170
Minnesota, 62n37, 101, 102, 151, 553
mirrors. See looking glasses
Miscouaky, 302n69
missionaries, 215, 497–504
Mission Iroquois of Sault St. Louis, 226
Mississauga, 45, 47, 101
Mississippi River, xxxi–xxxii, liii
Missouri Indians, 308, 414
Missouri River, 173, 308
mixed-ancestry people, lii–liv, lv, 307, 440, 513n47, 587; boarding schools and, 507; as daughters of traders, 492–94, 502, 505, 507; as historians, 47–64; as "idlers" and "libertines," 269; Ojibwa and, 117; as wives of traders, 492–94, 499, 502, 515n70. See also métis
moccasins, li, 85, 182, 194–95, 483, 493, 570, 571
Mohawk (people), 39, 344; captives of, 569–70; class stratification and, 197–98; clothing styles of, 350–52, 356; economy and, 181, 185–86, 196, 197–98; gift giving and, 347–48; King George's War and, 187–88; land ownership and, 189, 190, 191; Northwest Indian Confederacy and, 582; Pontiac's War and, 194; raids of, on French colonists, 363; in Shawnee towns, 565; tea drinking and, 350
Mohawk Valley, 347–52, 363
Mohican. See Mahican
Montagnais, 29, 33, 40, 96, 520
Montcalm, marquis de, 235
Montour, Madame. See Tichenet, Madame
Montreal, xx, xxvii–xxxi, 217, 225; Fort St. Joseph and, 475nn54–56; founding of, xxvii; French dependence on, xxxii, xxxiii; French surrender at, 235; New York trade and, 226, 340n35

Montreal Fire Club, 596, 615n11
Montreal Hunt Club, 596, 615n11
Montreal Merchants' Records (MMR),
 387–407
Moodie, D. W., 83
Moore, Mary, 495
Moore, Thomas, 598
Moore, William, 569–70, 571, 572
moose, 10–11, 14nn1–2, 26, 31, 34, 161
Moose Factory, 146–47, 150, 340n33
Morgan, Lewis, 420, 426; *League of the Iroquois*,
 78
Morison, Samuel Eliot, 23, 24
Morris, Robert Hunter, 383n74
Morton, W. L., 89–90, 104, 107
"mountain men," 173, 424–25, 428–29, 533
"mulatto" (word), 534
Munsee, 580
murder, 232, 273–82, 290–93, 478n72, 598
Murray, Robert, 424
musk oxen, 155n4
muskrat, 163, 164, 165, 167, 170, 423
Muskwakiwuk, 50, 51, 276, 291, 304n80, 584

Nanabohza, 536
Nanticoke, 565, 584
Narva, xvii
Natchez, 254
Native aesthetics, 315–18
Native cosmology, xxxvii, 8–9
Native culture, 610–11, 619n84
Native labor, 181, 182
Native land cessions, 169
Native legal rights, 72–73
Native medicine, 10–11, 119, 567
Native people: and environment, 140–41; as
 slaves, 453, 459, 576; travel of, to Europe,
 32, 36, 358, 511n18
Native war parties. *See* intertribal war parties
Native women, 439–42; clothing trade and,
 404; dog suckling of, 17; historiography
 and, 53–54; as interpreters and translators,
 liv, 449, 467; marriage of, to Frenchmen,
 xxx, xlvii, xlviii, lii, liii, 4–5, 267–68, 443,
 450–53, 457, 462, 463; relations of, with
 outsiders, lvi; stereotyping of, 75; as suppliers of manufactured goods, li, 194–95; tea
 drinking and, 350
Ne-kick-o-qua. *See* Rankin, Sophia Therese
Nelson, George, 159n38, 496, 523
Neskesh, Marie. *See* Thimotée

Neskisho, 492
Netherlands. *See* Holland
New Amsterdam, xxxii
New Brunswick, 98–99
Newell, Doc, 429
Newfoundland, xxii–xxiii, 27, 28, 39, 221
New France, xxxi, xxxvi, xlii; agriculture of,
 88, 96, 97, 105–6, 215–45; Anishinabeg
 and, 51; communications in, 460; fall of,
 188
New Orleans, xlviii, xlix, liv, 166, 175
Niagara. *See* Fort Niagara
Nichols, John, 149, 151
Nicollet, Joseph N., 127
Nixon, John, 323–26
North Dakota, 99
Northern Ojibwa, 69, 70, 101–2
North Sea (Canada). *See* Hudson Bay
North West Company, 103; Beaver Club and,
 595, 597–98, 603, 604; family and, 521;
 "freemen" and, 513n42, 513n47; and Hud-
 son's Bay Company, 497; marriage "in the
 manner of the country" and, 485–96, 508,
 514n53, 515n70, 526; métis and, 523–26;
 and settlement for retired employees,
 513n42; traffic in Chipewyan women and,
 514n57
Northwest Indian Confederacy, 575, 580–85
Northwest Passage, lviin16, 24
Norton, Moses, 484, 511n20
Norumbega (mythical city), 26
Nouvel, Father, 274, 281
Nova Scotia, 26, 34
nutria, 422–24
Nye, Robert, 603

Odawa, xxvii–xxviii, li, 45, 470n11; adoptees
 of, 116; agriculture and, li, 99–100, 101;
 Detroit killings of 1706 and, 283–89,
 302n66, 302n69, 303n72; French and, 249,
 252, 283–89; The Glaize and, 561; of Green
 Bay, 531; historiography and, 46; Keweenaw
 murders and, 277–80; La Framboise family
 and, 551; Langlade family and, 549, 550;
 Northwest Indian Confederacy and, 580,
 583, 584; scaffold burials of, 294n9. *See also*
 Kiskakon Odawa; Sable Odawa
Odawa women, 462–65
O'Fallon, Benjamin, 414, 417
offerings, 118–19
Ogden, Peter Skene, 501–2, 508

Ohio River valley, xlii, 189, 216
Ojibwa, xlviii; agriculture and, 100–103; asking for food by, 84, 103; Dakota and, 119–20, 122, 276; gift giving and, 114–59; historiography and, 45–64; humor of, 146, 151, 152; Keweenaw murders and, 277–78; métis and, 545; Northwest Indian Confederacy and, 583, 584; power and, 115, 141, 149; relations of, with Europeans, 121–32; respect and, 141. *See also* Northern Ojibwa; Plains Ojibwa; Saulteaux
Ojibwa language, 134n9, 148
Ojibwa women, 318, *319*
Okeemakeequid, 120
Onaske, 286, 302n69, 303n72
Oneida, 181, 185–86, 189, 190, 191, 192, 194, 196
Onemechin, 31–37
Onondaga, 216, 367
Ontario, 57, 72, 100–101
oral tradition, 46, 53, 57
orchards. *See* fruit orchards
Osage (people), liv, 169
Oshkosh, lv, 551
Oswego. *See* Fort Oswego
Oto, 414
Otontagan, 285, 286, 302n69, 303n72
Ottawa (people). *See* Odawa
Ottawa River, xxviii, 40
otter, 163
Ouaouagoukoue, Simphorose, liii, 455
Ouellet, Fernand, 614n3
Ouiatenon. *See* Fort Ouiatenon
Ouigamont, 32
Ouigoudi, 31
Ouisaketchak, 8
overhunting, xxxvii, 189

paid labor. *See* wage labor
Palmer, John, 610
Pambrun, Pierre, 524, 526
pandemics, 38
pan-Indianism, 545
pan-Indian settlements, 561–92
Panoniac, 32
parchment beaver, xxvi
parent and child as metaphor, 127–28, 130, 135n18
Parkman, Francis, 49, 428, 533
partridge, 21
Pas-de-Nom, Suzanne, 508–9

paternalism, 121–22
patriarchy, 284–85
patrifocality, 521, 522
Pattie, James O., 429
Pawpitch, 483, 484
pays d'en haut, 306, 439, 468n2
peace pipe. *See* calumet
Pearce, Roy Harvey, 67
Pecan, liv
Peezhikee, 119
pemmican, 91, 104, 493
Penobscot (people). *See* Armouchiquois
Penobscot Bay, 24, 26, 27, 33
Penobscot River, 29, 30, 39
Peoria (people), xlviii, xlix, 273
Peoria IL, 458
Perillaut, 290, 292
Perrot, Nicholas, 71, 95, 260, 262
Peshewa. *See* Richardville, Jean Baptiste
Peters, Hendrick. *See* Hendrick
Peters, Richard, 365, 367
Peterson, Jacqueline, 520
Petun. *See* Khionontateronon
Phélypeaux, Jean-Fréderic. *See* Maurepas, comte de
Philippe, Michel, 452
Phipps, William, xxiv
Pickering, Timothy, 198
Piegan, 414
Pilgrim, Robert, 484, 489
Pimitoui. *See* Fort Pimitoui
pine marten. *See* marten
pipe, 119, 123, 125, 571. *See also* calumet
piracy, xxi, 28
"pity" (word), 117, 130, 148–50, 154
Placentia, 30
Plains Ojibwa, 101–2
Pocahontas, lvi
Podruchny, Carolyn, 441
Pointe, Nicholas, 416
Poland, 168
Poland, Henry, 162, 170
polygamy, 259, 264, 470n9, 483, 484, 488
polygony, sororal, 471n19
Pond, Peter, 597–98
Pontchartrain, Louis Phélypeaux de, 215, 283
Pontiac, 580
Pontiac's War, 50, 188, 194
"poor" (word), 152, 158n23
Popham, Francis, 37

portages, xxviii, xlvii, xlix, liv, 232–33

portaging business, 192, 194

portraits, 381n45, 416; of Hendrick, *345, 346,
358, 359, 360,* 363, *364, 366,* 377n4; of William Johnson, 344, 377n2

Port Royal, xxiv, 32, 37

Portugal, xvii, xxi, xxii, 331

Post, Frederick, 234

Potawatomi, xlviii, li, lv, 7, 276, 281, 461–62;
Billy Caldwell and, 587; as converts to
Christianity, 459; John Kinzie and, 586;
Louis Chevalier and, 460; Northwest Indian
Confederacy and, 584; portraits of, 318

powder horns, xli, 322, 333

Pownall, Thomas, 357, 362

Prairie du Chien, 120, 123, 532

presents. *See* gift giving

prices, 37; of beaver, 166, 167, 420, 422,
425–26; of mink, 170; of muskrat, 167; of
raccoon, 169; of skunk, 170

Prince Albert, 424

Prince Maximilian, 414

Prince Rupert, xxxiii

Pring, Martin, 22, 29

privateers, xx, 28

prostitution, 547

"prostitution" (word), 263

Providence Island, xxiv

provisions and provisioning, 88, 91, 104,
392–93. *See also* food supplies

Prude, Jonathan, 378n13

Pruden, J. P., 494

prunes, 97

Putnam, Rufus, 570, 583

quality of goods, 320–43

Quapaw, 311

Quebec, xxiii, xxiv, xxvii, 92, 96, 235, 283,
284, 285

Queen Anne, 358

Quetico-Superior Underwater Research
Project, lviiin64

Quiatanon, xlix, li

Quinn, David, 23, 24, 28

rabbit, 422

raccoon, xliii, 85, 160, 161, 164, 175, 318; as
dominant fur, 165, 167–70; export of, 163,
167, 176, 178n14; Ohio River valley and,
178n15

racialization, liv

Radisson, Pierre, xxix–xxx, xxxviii, lviiin30,
55, 321–23

Rainy Lake, 103, 151, 513n42

Ramezay, Claude de, xlviii

Rankin, Sophia Therese, 529, 531, 532, 551

ransoms, 304n80, 573, 574

rattlesnakes, 125

Ray, Arthur J., 70, 71

Reame, Charles, 537

Réaume, Jean Baptiste, 455, 473

Réaume, Marie Madeleine. *See* L'archeveque,
Marie Madeleine Réaume

Réaume, Simon, 460

reburials, 571

Red Head, 367

Red Lake Ojibwa, 102, 103

Red River Colony, 90–91, 105–7, 489–90,
497–500, 505, 507, 524, 553

Red River valley, 89, 535

reexportation, xxiv, 168, 171

Reid, John Phillip, 299n48

reindeer, 139

rendezvous system, 420, 421, 425, 426,
428–31

revenge, 275, 277–80, 285, 290, 291, 292,
299n48

Revolutionary War. *See* American Revolution

Reynal, Antoine, 428

Richardville, Jean Baptiste, liv, 578

Richardville, Joseph, liv

Riel, Louis, 516, 534

River L'Abbe Mission, 454

Roanoke, lviiin16

Robertson, Colin, 158n24, 499

Robertson, James, 499

Robidoux, Antoine, 431

Rocky Mountain Fur Company, 172

Rogers, E. S., 138, 154

Roman Catholicism. *See* Catholicism

Rompiechoue, Marie, 290, 304n80

Rosier, James, 28

Ross, Alexander, 555n3

Ross, David, 428

Rouensa, 269–73

Rouensa, Marie. *See* Aramepinchieue

Rouillé, Antoine-Louis, 226, 231

Rousseas, Jacques, lvi

Rowand, John, 507–8

rum, 85, 125–27, 129–30, 187, 188, 224,
229, 572

Rupert, Prince. *See* Prince Rupert
Rupert's Land, xliii, 89, 489
Russia, xxvi, 109n3, 168, 170, 171
Russian-American Company, 108
Ruxton, George Frederick, 420

Sable Odawa, 280, 282, 283, 287, 288
sachems and sachemship, 198, 200, 355, 361,
    374–75
Saco, 31, 32, 34
Saguenay River, xxiii, 29, 40
Sahlins, Marshall, lxn65, 126, 246
Salisbury, Neal, 23–24
Sandoz, Mari, 421–22
Saskatechewan, 101
Sauk, 281, 584
Saulteaux, 276, 277, 278, 281, 414
Sault Ste. Marie, xlix, 8, 56, 57, 71
Saum, Lewis O., 68–69, 70–71, 74–75
"*sauvages*" (word), 247, 255
Schindler, George, 463, 464
Schindler, Thérèse Marcot Lasaliere, 447,
    462–65
Schmalz, Peter S., 57
Schoolcraft, Henry, 102, 123–24
Scotland, 517n98
Scottish émigrés, 597, 604
scurvy, 223
seal. *See* fur seal
sea otter, 172
Secoudon, 31, 34, 38
Selkirk, Lord, 553, 602
Seneca (people), 228, 233, 565, 586
Sepúlveda, Juan Ginés de, 74
Sergeant, Henry, 325
settlers, 189, 190–91, 194, 196, 217, 221, 349,
    350, 584
Seven Nations of Canada, 582–84
Seven Oaks massacre, 524
Seven Years' War, xxxi, xl, liii, 50–52, 181,
    188–96, 236
sex traffic, 514n57
sexual freedom, 260, 261–62
sexual mores, 258–73, 482–83, 506–7, 511n7,
    537, 547
shallops, 23, 30–40
Shawnee, 231–32, 234, 580–81; captives of,
    568, 574–75; at Detroit, 586; Fort Miami
    and, 579; at The Glaize, 562–65, 571–72;
    Northwest Indian Confederacy and, 580,
    583, 584; U.S. wars against, 562

shipwrecks, xxxii
Shirley, William, 181, 193
Sichangu. *See* Bois-Brûlé
Siebert, Frank, 23, 33
Sih-Chida, 416
silversmiths, 574
Simpson, George, 146, 504–5
Simpson, Thomas, 500
Sinclair, Betsey, 495, 505
Sinclair, Patrick, 461
Sinclair, William, 505
Sioux. *See* Dakota (people)
sisters, 462–65
Six Nations. *See* Iroquois
skunk, 170
slaves, 194, 275, 277, 350, 452–53, 464, 583
slave trade, xvii
Slavey Indians, 523
Small, Patrick, 521
small game, 21, 440, 520
smallpox, 37, 50
Smith, John, 37
Smith, Richard, 194, 195, 199, 201
Smith, William, 362, 363
smiths. *See* blacksmiths; gunsmiths;
    silversmiths
smuggling, 226, 340n34
The Snake. *See* The Great Snake
Snow, Dean, 23
snowshoes, li, 10, 369, 440, 456, 483, 493, 520
sons of traders, 459, 461, 522, 547
Souriquois, 30–38, 40
Spain, xvii, xviii, xxi, xxiv, 72, 74, 219
Spanish Armada, xxiv
Spence, George, 327
Spence, James, 492
Spence, Susan, 499
Spencer, Oliver, 569, 572
sports contests. *See* athletic contests
squash, 95, 102
squirrel, 21
Stalking Turkey, 412, 413
starvation, 97, 130
"starving" (word), 84, 137–59
Staynor, Thomas, 492
St. Clair's Defeat, 566, 567, 573
St. Cosme, Father, 267
stereotyping and stereotypes, xviii, xix, 74–75,
    86, 336, 534
Stevens, Arent, 362

Stewart, Alexander, 499
Stewart, William Drummond, 431
St. John River, 29, 31, 39
St. Joseph River, liii
St. Lawrence Bay, xxii, xxiii
St. Lawrence River, xxvii, xxxiii, liii, 26, 29, 88, 541
St. Lawrence valley, 217
St. Louis, 165, 173, 175, 180n34
St. Lusson, Simon François Daumont de, 56, 71
St. Maurice River, 40
stone tools, 35–36, 68
stroud, xlii, 187, 335, 340n34, 411, 413. *See also* burial strouds
Stuart, John, 505
subarctic trade, 3, 137–59, 329–30, 336
Sublette, Bill, 431
Sublette, Milton, 429
subsidies, 169
subsistence, 5, 94, 185, 201
sugar bush, 544
Sunder, John E., 175, 421
supplies and supplying. *See* provisions and provisioning
Sutherland, James, 157n15
Sweden, xxvi
Symmes, John Cleves, 564

Tadoussac, xxii, xxiv, xxvii, 29, 30, 34, 40, 509
Talbot, Edward, 603
Tanner, John, 116
tariff revenue, 172
Tarrentines, 32–33, 38, 40, 41. *See also* Armouchiquois; Etchemin; Souriquois
tattoos, 351, 361, 363
Taucumwa, lii
taxes, xxiii, xxv, xxvi, xxx, 172
Taylor, Margaret, 505
tea drinking, 350, 79n22
Tecumseh, 580
Tee Yee Neen Ho Ga Row. *See* Hendrick
"terentyns." *See* Tarrentines
theft, 274
Thevet, André, 26
Thimotée, 462, 479n81
Thomas, David Hurst, 66
Thomas, Thomas, 498
Thompson, David, 598
Three Rivers. *See* Trois Riviéres
Thu a Higon, 489

Tichenet, Madame, 307–8
Tinnawabeno, 144
Tippecanoe Archives, 318
Tittimeg, 490
tobacco, xlii, 34, 121; Brazilian, 315, 320, 330–31, 339n23; ceremonial use of, 118–19; English, 330; French, 97; as gift, 130; Portugal and, 331–32; as trade item, 92, 94, 95, 97
tobacco pipe. *See* pipe
tomahawks, 345, 361, *366*, 396, 571, 576
Tonti, Henri de, 216, 267, 270, 298n36
torture, 300n56
totem, 116, 548
trading posts, 4, 73, 189, 192, 216, 223, 391–92, 397–406, 430
translators and interpreters. *See* interpreters and translators
transportation, 105, 232
trapping, 14, 85, 143
treaties and treaty meetings, 72; at Albany, 344; at Fond du Lac, 126; gift giving and, 355, 570; Hendrick and, 357, 361; Indian debt payment and, 169; pelagic sealing of, 172; at Prairie du Chien, 120, 123; wampum and, 121; William Johnson and, 373, 375
Treaty of Easton, 234–35
Treaty of Fort Stanwix, 191, 197, 584
Treaty of Greenville, liv, 585
Treaty of Utrecht, 222
Trigger, B., 34, 40, 93, 96
trinkets, 405
Trois Riviéres, 96, 106, 474n54, 476n62
Tshusick, 318, *319*
Turner, Frederick Jackson, 66, 68, 69, 71–72, 73, 89
Turnor, Philip, 488
twine, xli, 333

Umphreville, Lisette, 508
unilocality, 523
United States, 172, 174, 562, 566, 567
upper class, 602–3

Van Kirk, Sylvia, 439–40, 520
Van Swearingen, Marmaduke, 588n3
Vaudreuil, Philippe de Rigaud de, xxxix, 225, 228, 233–34, 269, 283–89, 303n72, 473n44
Vente, Sieur de la, 268
verdigris, 351
Verelst, John, 358

vermilion, xxxviii, 85, 187, 323, 351, 579
Verrazzano, Giovanni da, xxiv, 23, 26
Villeneuve, Domitille, 548
Villiers, Nicholas Coulon de, 473n47
violence, 274, 306
Virginia, xxiv
Virgin Mary cult, 266
vision quests, 118
Vitoria, Francisco de, 72
"voyageur" (word), 612
voyageurs, xxxvii, li, 220, 464; Beaver Club
    and, 601–2, 609, 611, 612; contracts of,
    242n66; Indians and, 223–24, 276, 452;
    licensing of, 538; métis as, 544; at Michili-
    mackinac, 536, 540

Wabasha I, 121
Waganagisi. See L'Arbe Croche
wage labor, 181, 182, 192, 194, 195, 210n43
Wagner, Roy, 246
Walker, John, 26, 36
Walpole, Robert, 229
wampum, xliii, 118, 125, 213n63, 579, 582;
    as currency, 196, 197; definition of, 121;
    Detroit killings of 1706 and, 288; Keweenaw
    murders and, 280–81; in portraits of Hen-
    drick, 345, 346, 359, 361
Ward, Nancy, lvi
War of 1812, 531, 586, 611
War of the Austrian Succession. See King
    George's War
War of the Spanish Succession, 218
Warren, Peter, 349
Warren, William Whipple, 47–53, 120–21
wars, xxiv, 49–53, 98. See also specific wars
Washington, George, 232, 316, 413
Waymouth, George, 28
Wayne, Anthony, 441, 583, 585, 586
weasel, 160, 362
Weiser, Conrad, 356
Weld, Isaac, 615n11
Wells, William, 567, 586

Wendat. See Huron
Wentzel, Willard Ferdinand, 137–38
Wermuth, Thomas S., 214n76
Wessel, Thomas, 92–93, 98
West, John, 497–98
western Great Lakes region, 385–410
whaling industry, xviii, 182
wheat, 452, 453
White, Bruce, 83, 148
White, Richard, 348, 443, 447, 482; The Middle
    Ground, 86, 305
White Loon, 568, 570, 573
Whitman, Narcissa, 501
wild rice, 101, 104, 129, 131
William of Orange, 217
wills, 452, 453, 513n45. See also inheritance
Winnebago, 50, 551
Winnipeg, 107
Winter, George, 318
Wisconsin, 72, 101
Wizlizenus, F. A., 429
wolf, 163
women: as chiefs, 296n24; as converts to
    Christianity, 265, 266, 439, 445, 454, 455,
    466; marginalization of, 600; as miners, 454;
    as shamans, 296n24; violence against, 260,
    266. See also Algonquian women; Chipewyan
    women; French women; Illini women;
    Iroquois women; Native women; Odawa
    women; Ojibwa women
woolens, 229, 335, 347, 351, 358
Woolrich, Julia, 509, 518n130
wordplay, 146
Wraxall, Peter, 357, 367
Wyandot. See Huron
Wyoming, 427

xy Company, 598

York Factory, 330, 332, 335, 340n30, 484–85,
    492